Windows XP
Concepts & Examples

Carolyn Z. Gillay
Saddleback College

Franklin, Beedle & Associates, Inc.
8536 SW St. Helens Drive, Suite D
Wilsonville, Oregon 97070
503-682-7668
www.fbeedle.com

President and Publisher	Jim Leisy (jimleisy@fbeedle.com)
Production	Stephanie Welch
	Tom Sumner
	Bran Bond
Proofreader	Bran Bond
Cover	Ian Shadburne
Marketing	Christine Collier
Order Processing	Krista Brown

Printed in the U.S.A.

Gillay, Carolyn Z.
    Windows XP: concepts & examples / Carolyn Z. Gillay.
      p. cm.
    Includes index.
    ISBN 1-887902-81-3
    1. Microsoft Windows (Computer file) 2. Operating systems (Computers) I. Title.

QA76.73.O63 G56 2002
005.4'4769--dc21

2002027120

CONTENTS

Chapter 3 ◉ Viewing Files and Folders in My Computer ◉ 115

Chapter 4 ◉ Windows Applications—Outlook Express,
Notepad, WordPad, and Paint ◉ 165

Chapter 5 ⊛ Exploring Files and Folders ⊛ 237

Chapter 6 ⊛ Using My Computer/Windows Explorer ⊛ 291

Chapter 7 ⊛ Managing Files ⊛ 341

Chapter 8 ◦ Organizing and Managing Your Disk ◦ 397

Chapter 9 ◦ Fonts and Printers ◦ 439

Chapter 10 ◦ Customizing Your System ◦ 477

Chapter 11 ◦ File and Disk Maintenance ◦ 537

Chapter 12 ◦ Connectivity ◦ 583

PREFACE

This book provides an overview of the hardware, software, and operating system concepts used with personal computer systems. Windows XP Professional is the vehicle used to teach the operating system concepts. Therefore the book can be used in a course that focuses exclusively on Windows XP Professional or as the Windows XP Professional supplement in a multi-platform operating systems course, a networking course, or a programming course. It can be used for self-study, as well.

For Beginning and Experienced Computer Users

Students come to this material with varying levels of knowledge and experience. In an effort to lessen the disparities, the book includes an appendix that covers hardware and terminology used in the computing world. Although it is intended for novices, it is useful reading for everyone since it covers the latest technologies.

To reiterate, no prior knowledge or experience with computers, software, operating systems, or Windows XP Professional is assumed.

Focuses on Real-World Skills and Conceptual Mastery

The approach is unique: Windows XP Professional is presented as it will actually be used in the working world rather than with the usual "point-and-click-driven" method. After working carefully through the material in this book, students should know the how and why of this operating system's features. Further, students are encouraged to understand that the primary function of Windows XP Professional, as of any operating system, is the management of the entire computer system (hardware, software, and files).

An Integrated Presentation of Concepts and Skills

Each section of the book is presented in a careful step-by-step approach. Numerous screens show the expected results of each step. This not only minimizes the need for assistance in a lab environment, but also eases the difficulties of those working on their own computers at home or work. Interspersed between the steps are the reasons for and the results of each action taken. At the end of each chapter, Application Assignments provide opportunities to apply knowledge independently and to enhance mastery of the subject area through critical thinking.

A Student Activities disk is bundled with the book. This disk, labeled XPRODATA, contains the files that are needed to successfully complete the step-by-step activities embedded in each chapter. This directory with its accompanying files needs to be installed on either a server or local computer. The student only views or copies files from this directory, so there is no requirement to write to the hard disk.

A computer system is required for problem-solving exercises using WindowsXP Professional and applications within Windows XP Professional beginning with Chapter 1. Most chapters include three sets of Application Assignments. The first set requires a computer. The second set contains brief essay questions that encourage further thought about the material. The last set is a scenario that presents an open-ended activity. It requires students to analyze a problem and create a solution. These three types of assignments reinforce critical thinking skills.

A Note to Instructors

Having taught different operating systems MS/DOS through Windows XP Professional) for over 18 years, I have had an opportunity to teach a wide range of beginning students. Through trial and error I have gained a knowledge of how to present the skills and concepts in an easily digested manner. The docucentric paradigm on which Windows XP Professional is based is difficult for beginners to comprehend. It is best to begin at the rudimentary level. Students need to understand what different programs do so they know which program to select. In addition, a grasp of the hierarchical file system is important. The first time a document needs to be located or saved, Windows XP Professional or the application program will ask for its name and where it should be found or saved. To properly respond, one must have mastered the approach used to organize files and data in Windows XP Professional. This is a skill that is needed not only for beginning users but also for intermediate and advanced users. Too often, productive use of Windows XP Professional is a totally ignored topic.

The ability to work with several programs at the same time is one of the great strengths of Windows XP Professional. Most users do not take full advantage of its multitasking ability because they do not understand it. By doing exercises that incorporate multitasking, students will gain an understanding of how it works and how they can use it effectively. When appropriate, Windows XP Professional's bundled applications and shareware applications will be used to enhance the learning experience.

Two major forms of computer connectivity are covered in this book: networking and the Internet. I have found there is a gap in too many students' knowledge of basic networking concepts. So they are taught how to set up a peer-to-peer network (it may not be possible to implement this at your school) and how to share files, folders, and devices. Networking techniques, such as mapping drives, are also covered.

It may be desirable to bring aspects of the Internet into a Windows XP Professional course, so various options for connecting to the Internet are explored. Simple activities using Microsoft Internet Explorer are included. Students learn how to effectively use and customize Internet Explorer. A brief introduction to TCP/IP concepts is included because when using the Internet, many students find protocols and IP addresses baffling. This overview gives them an understanding of some of these important terms so that they better understand basic Internet functions.

Furthermore, a knowledge of email and newsgroups are critical in today's Internet-driven world, so a portion of this book is devoted to concepts and activities in those areas. Email is introduced fairly early so that if instructors can use email to contact students if they wish to do so.

It is paramount that students learn how to keep their hard disks in good working order to optimize their performance, so disk maintenance programs included with Windows XP Professional (like Disk Defragmenter and System Restore) are covered. In addition, the command line interface is included in an appendix so students can gain an understanding of when and how to use the DOS window for troubleshooting and to use TCP/IP utilities such as Ping.

One of the hardest aspects of teaching a Windows XP Professional class is developing assignments that provide consistent grading standards in addition to teaching the requisite critical thinking skills. Assignments should also not overload instructors. Where I teach, enrollments typically have been over 350 students per semester. Managing the assignment overhead generated by so many students was a real headache and interfered with my teaching time. To remedy this situation, I began to employ Scantron testing and, when appropriate, print-outs that exhibit mastery of the subject. I have used this technique over the past several years and have found it most successful in meeting teaching objectives. Plus, the rapid feedback that it offers is appreciated by my students. So I have made it possible to use this option with the assignments included in this book.

The essay questions and scenarios must be provided in an essay format. Notepad and WordPad are introduced early to discourage hand-written essays. Where hands-on assignments are not possible, such as in the section on joining MSN, students still have an opportunity to answer brief essay questions that promote deeper understanding.

Windows XP Professional Settings

Windows XP Professional is very customizable. Because of this, students' screens could look different from those in the book. To ensure that their screens look like the book's, instructions are given within the applications to alter the screen to match the text displays.

Instructor Materials

Instructor Materials are available to teachers who adopt this book for use in a course. These include teaching suggestions for each chapter, as well as the answers for every question and application exercise; a midterm and a final; a sample syllabus; additional chapter tests; and PowerPoint presentations, which provide an overview of each chapter. This material is provided digitally to enable customization to the unique requirements of each instructor's course.

Acknowledgments

A project of this scope is difficult to complete successfully without the contribution of many individuals. Special thanks go to:

* Bette Peat, whose eagle eyes are invaluable for finding anything I left out, for always offering great suggestions as well as alerting me to any particular problems that labs may encounter.
* Steven Tuttle for sharing his extensive Internet knowledge.
* Kathryn Maurdeff for providing questions, answers, and PowerPoint presentations.
* All the authors of the shareware included with this book.
* My students at Saddleback College, who always want to know more and who make all of this worthwhile.
* My colleagues in the Computer Information Management Department at Saddleback College.

* The California Business Education Association and the National Business Education Association for providing forums for professional growth as well as inviting me to make presentations sharing my teaching experiences.

* All the sung and unsung heroes at Franklin, Beedle & Associates, especially Jim Leisy, a publisher with grace and class. Thanks, too, to Stephanie Welch, Tom Sumner, Ian Shadburne, Christine Collier, and Krista Brown. Check out the Franklin, Beedle & Associates Web site at www.fbeedle.com.

* And, as always, Frank Panezich, my incomparable partner in all things and in all ways.

Anyone who wants to offer suggestions or improvements or just share ideas can reach me at czg@bookbiz.com.

CHAPTER 1

Exploring
Windows XP Professional

In this chapter, you will be introduced to the primary features of Windows XP Professional. You will learn how to use the desktop and the taskbar, and you will familiarize yourself with menus and their uses. You will learn about windows, the different techniques to manipulate them, and the proper terminology and concepts behind the basic features of Windows XP Professional, such as objects and properties. You will also learn how to prepare a disk and how to exit Windows XP Professional properly.

1

Learning Objectives

1. Explain the purpose and function of the desktop.
2. Explain the purpose and function of the objects found on the desktop.
3. Explain the purpose and function of pointing devices.
4. List and differentiate among the types of pointing devices.
5. Identify the items found on the Start menu.
6. Explain the purpose and function of menus and submenus.
7. Compare and contrast dialog boxes and message boxes.
8. Explain the purpose and function of sizing and moving windows.
9. Explain the difference between minimizing and sizing a window.
10. Explain the purpose and function of a property sheet.
11. Explain the purpose and function of an object.
12. Describe the difference between a parent and a child window.
13. Define the term docucentric.
14. Explain the purpose and function of multitasking and multithreading.
15. Compare and contrast foreground and background windows.
16. Compare and contrast cascading and tiling windows.
17. Explain the purpose and function of formatting a disk.

Student Outcomes

1. Start and exit Windows.
2. Open the Start menu and use the submenus.
3. Identify by name and function the basic components of the desktop.
4. Move and resize a window.
5. Change the location and size of the taskbar.
6. Access and use the taskbar property sheet.
7. Open and close child and parent windows.
8. Move between foreground and background windows.
9. Use the taskbar to tile and cascade windows.
10. Format a disk.

1.1 • Installing or Upgrading to Windows XP Professional

Software is always being improved. Almost all the software you buy will, at some later time, be updated. In order to stay current with the latest changes in software, you purchase upgrades. An upgrade is the newest version of software that replaces old software. You may install or upgrade a program. To *install* a program is to copy new files to your hard drive. These files are not yet on the hard drive. To *upgrade* is to copy over existing files with the new versions of the files.

In order for a computer to work, it must have an operating system installed. In fact, when you buy a new computer, it typically comes with an operating system already installed. The necessary files have already been copied to the hard disk. You do not have to do anything to get ready to use the computer. An operating system is also software, so you may also upgrade an operating system. However, there are some special considerations in upgrading to Windows XP. First, Windows XP comes in two primary varieties—Windows XP Home and Windows XP Professional. Both versions look and act in similar ways with the major differences being that Windows XP Professional provides corporate network support, backup and more security with Windows. There will also be multiple server versions of XP which will be called Microsoft .NET Servers. These products are aimed at the corporate marketplace. In order to upgrade to Windows XP Professional, you must have installed on your system Windows 98, OSR2, Second Edition, Windows Millennium Edition, Windows NT 4.0 or Windows 2000 Professional. Thus, if you own a personal computer that had an older operating system on it, such as Windows 95, you could not upgrade. Second, if you have an older computer, you may not have the correct hardware that will support Windows XP. But if you have the correct hardware and version of windows, you could upgrade to the latest version—Windows XP Professional. Windows XP Professional will come on a CD-ROM. Usually an operating system upgrade is a special process that you do only when a new version of the operating system is released. The new operating system files are copied from the CD to the hard drive. The upgrade replaces old files with new files. Once you install the new operating system to the hard drive, you have completed the upgrade process. This text assumes the installation of Windows XP Professional.

1.2 ● Activating Windows

If you performed an upgrade or installation of Windows XP, at that time you were asked to key in a 25 character product key that was located on your Windows XP compact disc. Part of the setup routine is gathering the unique serial numbers that are on various hardware components within your system. Once Windows XP is installed, there is a further step you must take. Microsoft *requires* you to activate your copy of Windows. If you do not activate Windows within 30 days of use, you will not be able to log onto your computer. By using this activation scheme, Microsoft is trying to prevent the casual piracy of software. Thus, you cannot "lend" your copy of Windows to anyone else nor install it on more than one computer you own. Each computer you own must have its own copy of Windows XP.

When you purchase Windows XP, you are purchasing a license which allows you to install the Windows XP operating system on a single computer. If you try to use the same installation CD on a different computer, you will be unable to activate the operating system because the hardware serial numbers will be different. Although the setup program will ask you to activate the operating system at time of installation, it is wise to wait a few weeks to be sure that all of your hardware and software is working with Windows XP. Activation is done either by using the Internet or by phone. When you click the activation icon on the taskbar, it presents you with the following wizard. See Figure 1.1.

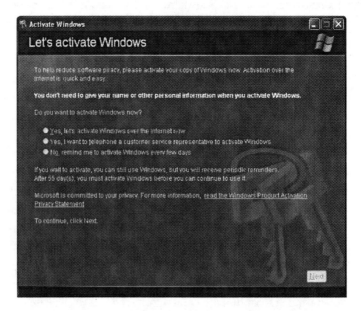

Figure 1.1 ◦ Windows XP Activation Wizard Screen

If you choose to activate over the Internet, the process happens automatically. If you choose to activate via phone, you see the following screen. See Figure 1.2.

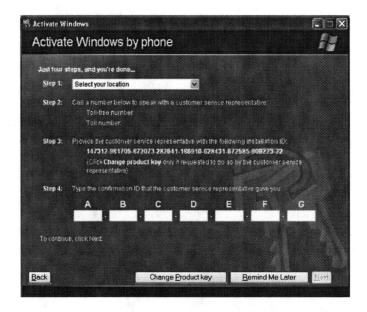

Figure 1.2 ◦ Windows XP Telephone Activation Screen

You will be given a toll free number to call. When you call the number, you will be given the 25 digit code over the phone. There are some facts that you should be aware of regarding activation.

If you purchase a new computer with Windows XP is preinstalled, the activation process may have been completed and you will not need to activate Windows XP.

You are allowed to reinstall Windows XP an unlimited number of times on the same computer. If you reinstall with the same system, Windows performs a check against the serial numbers of your hardware. If they match, then the activation is automatic and you need not activate again. However, if you add, replace or upgrade more than 10 new hardware components, such as new hard drive, CD-ROM drive, more memory and so on, within 120 days, the activation process will assume that you have installed the operating system on a new computer and will require you to reactivate your system either via the Internet or a phone call. However, to be safe and avoid this problem, try not to install, upgrade or replace more than three hardware components within 120 days.

If you are a business or educational institution that has purchased a volume license, you will not be required to activate the operating system.

1.3 ● The Desktop

To use your computer, you must place the operating system files in memory or boot the system. ***Booting the system*** means that the operating system files are copied from the hard disk to memory. For you, this is the process that occurs when you turn on or power up the computer. Once you have powered up the computer, the Windows workplace, called the desktop, appears on the monitor screen.

When you want to work, you usually sit at a desk that contains objects, the tools you need to use. If you needed to do your taxes, for example, you would place the income tax form on your desk as well as the instructions on how to fill out the form. You would also have tools, such as a calculator, to help you with your task. In Windows XP Professional you also have a desk, but you must boot the system to see it. Your desk is called the ***desktop***, which is your primary work area. (See Figure 1.3.) Like your desk, it is a convenient location to place objects such as your tools, your program files, your document files, and your devices. It can also provide access to a network, if you are on a network.

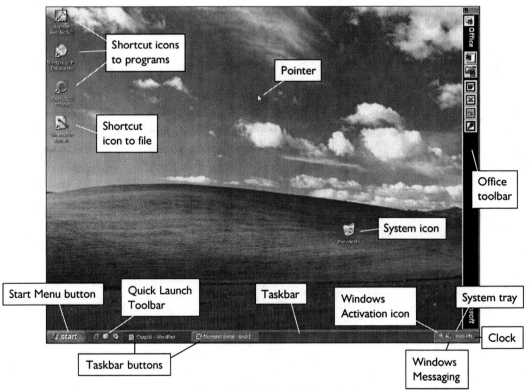

Figure 1.3 ● The Desktop

When Windows XP is installed, it presents a clean desktop with nothing on it but the Start button, Taskbar, and system tray. Usually the Recycle Bin icon will also appear. However, computer manufacturers may present a different desktop with more items on it. But even though the desktop varies depending on what objects have been placed on it, certain items are always present:

Taskbar and Start menu button

The focal point of Windows XP Professional is the taskbar. The *taskbar* is a graphic toolbar used to select, via the mouse, one of a number of software programs that you have opened. Typically located at the bottom of the screen, the taskbar contains the ***Start button***. Clicking this button displays a ***menu*** that allows you to launch programs, open documents, alter the look of the desktop, and search for files on your system or for information on the Internet. Also, it gives you access to Help if you are unsure of what to do. Lastly, it is the location of the commands for shutting down the computer or for logging on as a different user.

System tray

The *system tray* is on the right side of the taskbar where Windows XP Professional provides information about the status of your system. Any program can place information or notification of events in the system tray, also called the ***status area***. For instance, if you were connected to the Internet via a modem, an icon of a modem would appear in the status area whenever the connection is active. Windows XP Professional also places information in the status area. In Figure 1.3, the Clock and Activation icons appear in the system tray. The digital clock indicates what time it is. The activation icon tells you how many days you have remaining before you activate Windows XP.

As you begin using Windows, other items commonly appear on the desktop. These include the following items.

Toolbar

In Windows XP Professional, a toolbar appears as a row, column, or block of related buttons or icons. When a button or icon is clicked with the mouse, a certain function of Windows is activated, such as launching a program or opening a document. The Quick Launch toolbar is an example of a common toolbar that is located on the taskbar. It provides icons for launching Internet Explorer (a Web browser), Show Desktop, and Windows Media Player. Show Desktop will make all open windows icons. Windows Media Player is a center for playing and organizing multimedia on your computer and on the Internet. Media Player provides multimedia options. You may use Media Player to listen to radio stations, play and copy CDs, look for movies that are available on the Internet, and create customized lists of all media on your computer.

Taskbar button	When you open a program, a document, or a folder, a labeled button is placed on the taskbar. There will be a button on the taskbar to represent each open program or folder. You can use the *taskbar buttons* to move between open windows. By clicking the desired button on the taskbar, you easily switch to a different task. All open windows are represented on the taskbar. The active window is identified by its button being in a three-dimensional highlighted view.
Icon	An *icon* is a pictorial representation of an object. An icon may represent a program, a document, or a folder that holds programs or documents. Shortcut icons provide convenient access to objects that are stored elsewhere. Icons can appear on the desktop and in windows; they can also open windows. The primary place you work and interact with data is in a window.
Pointer	The *pointer* is the visual representation of your location on the screen.

1.4 ◦ Windows

The Windows XP Professional operating system got its name from its use of specially delineated areas of the screen called windows. A *window* is a defined work area (a rectangular frame) on the screen that is moveable and sizable; in it, information is displayed with which you, the user, can interact. All windows-based programs run in windows. Some programs use windows that are split vertically or horizontally. The resulting window divisions are called *panes*. Figure 1.4 shows a window divided vertically into panes.

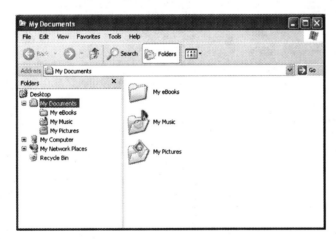

Figure 1.4 ◦ A Window Divided into Panes

Windows come in two varieties—program windows and document windows. A program window contains a program or houses folders or objects. A program window can be moved freely around the desktop and can be minimized to a task button or maximized to fill the entire screen. Figure 1.5 shows some examples of program windows.

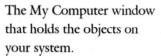

The My Computer window that holds the objects on your system.

A program window that holds the game Solitaire.

A window that shows the printer objects on your system.

Figure 1.5 ◦ Program Windows

A **document** is a self-contained piece of work created with an application program and, if saved on disk, given a unique file name by which it can be retrieved. Thus, a document window is an on-screen window (enclosed work area) in which the user can create, view, or work on a document. **Document windows** are windows that belong to program windows and are always contained within a program window. A document window can be minimized, maximized, moved, or sized but must always remain within the confines of the program window. Many Windows-based programs allow the user to have more than one document open at one time. Each document is in a separate document window. Figure 1.6 is an example of a program window (Word) with two document windows open.

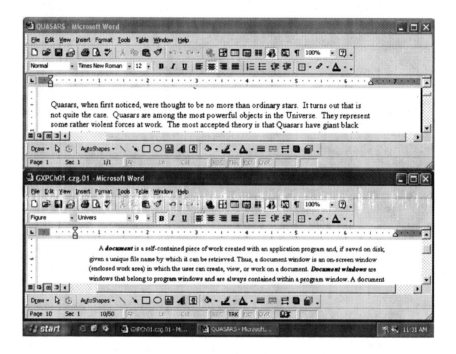

Figure 1.6 ◦ A Program Window with Two Document Windows

1.5 ◉ Pointing Devices

A graphical user interface allows you to select and manipulate objects on the screen. In Windows XP Professional, an arrow, called the ***mouse pointer*** or ***cursor***, tells you where you are on the screen. You manipulate the pointer by moving the pointing device. The most common pointing device is the mouse. As you move the mouse on a flat surface, it responds by moving the arrow on the screen. When you position the arrow over an object, you are ***pointing*** to it.

When you position the arrow over an object and click the left mouse button, you are selecting or activating that object. ***Clicking*** is the process of pressing and then immediately releasing the left mouse button once. ***Double-clicking*** means quickly pressing and releasing the left mouse button twice. When you double-click an object, you are usually about to act upon it. The left mouse button is called the ***primary mouse button***. Pressing the right mouse button, the secondary mouse button, is called ***right-clicking***. Thus, an instruction to click means press and release the left mouse button. Remember, *click* refers to the left mouse button; *right-click* refers to the right mouse button.

When you select an object and then press and hold the left mouse button, you are preparing to drag the object across the screen. Dragging is the process of moving an object. When you release the mouse button, you place the object in another location. This process is called ***drag and drop***. ***Dragging*** means holding the left mouse button while you drag. ***Right-dragging*** means holding the right mouse button while you drag.

This textbook will refer to a mouse, but the same instructions may be followed for a trackball or integrated pointer. In addition, when the textbook refers to placing the mouse pointer on an object, it will use the term mouse, though technically it is a cursor.

The shape of a pointer changes. When it is an arrow, you can move it around the screen. When it changes to an hourglass shape, it is telling you to wait while Windows XP Professional completes a task. If you are working with text, the shape of the pointer becomes an I-beam. If the pointer changes its shape to a circle with a slash through it, the standard international symbol for No, Windows XP Professional cannot do what you asked.

1.6 ◉ Activity ◉ Starting Windows XP Professional

Note 1: If you are on a network, you may have special procedures. Check with your network administrator for the procedures in your lab environment.

Note 2: In Windows XP Professional, when you are done working, you do not turn off your computer. You must follow the proper shut-down procedure, which you will learn.

1   Locate the on/off switch for the monitor and turn it on.

2   There should not be disks in any drive. Turn on the computer by locating the power switch. The type of switch and its location will vary from computer to computer. Sometimes the switch is a lever; sometimes it is a button. It may be located on the front, side, or back of the computer.

WHAT'S **HAPPENING?** You have booted Windows. If you have a computer system that was set up with more than one user (a home network), you will see the Welcome Screen in Figure 1.7. You would simply click your name and enter a password, if required, by your system.

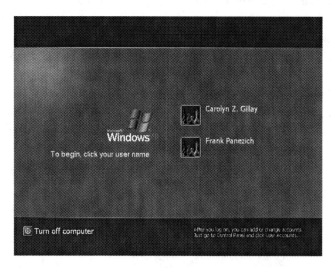

*Figure 1.7 * Windows Welcome Screen with Multiple Users*

WHAT'S **HAPPENING?** If you are on a network, you may see a screen that requires you to press **Ctrl** + **Alt** + **Delete**. Once you press those keys, you will be presented with a Log On to Windows dialog box that requires you to enter your user name and password. If you are in a school or work environment, you will need to ask your network administrator for your user name and password.

Windows XP Professional is very customizable. Because of this, your screens could look different from those in the book. You may have more or less icons or items on your desktop.

1.7 ● Activity ● Using the Start Menu

I   Click the **Start** button on the taskbar.

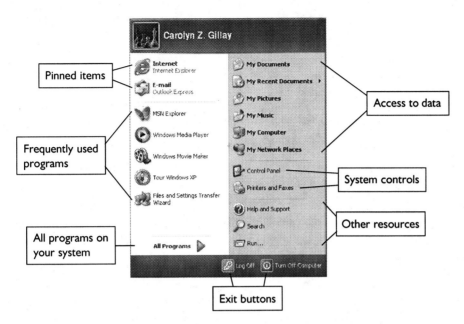

WHAT'S HAPPENING? You have opened a menu that presents a list of items from which you may choose. The Start menu lists the major functions on your system as well as the ways to access your data. These choices include:

Pinned Items   Items that are pinned to the menu are those items that will always appear on this menu. You may add items here. By default, Internet Explorer (a way to browse the web) and Outlook Express (the email program that comes with Windows) are placed here.

Frequently Used Programs   Windows monitors which program you use most often. As you use a program, it will be added to the list at the top. Each time an item is added, the bottom most item (least frequently used programs) drops off the list. You can decide how many items you wish to appear on this menu but you cannot add items, nor can you change the order of the list.

All Programs   Takes you to other menus that list the all the application programs on your system.

Access to data   Windows displays different locations for your data. Microsoft sets up folders (My Documents, My Recent Documents, My Pictures, and My Music) that are containers for the kinds of data indicated by the title of the folder. The My Computer folder is a list of all the drives on your local system and My Network Places allows you access to data on remote systems.

System Controls   The Control Panel takes you to a window that has different programs that allows you to alter the appearance and behavior of your Windows XP Professional environment and the Printers and Faxes allows you access to your printers and fax machine.

Other resources include:

Search   Takes you to a menu where you can search for files, folders, computers, networks, and items on the Internet.

Help   Takes you to a help program that can show you how to accomplish tasks.

Run   Allows you to use a command line interface to execute programs. The interface is character-based; you key in names of programs or files rather than click icons.

Exit Buttons   Allows you to turn off your computer or log off as one user and let another user log on without turning off the computer.

Windows XP Professional uses cascading menus. A *cascading menu* is a menu that opens another menu, called a *submenu*. In a cascading menu structure, the first in a series is a *parent menu* to the menu that follows. Each subsequent *child menu* becomes a parent to the next menu. Thus, a cascading menu is also referred to as a *hierarchical menu;* each time you make a choice, another menu opens. Since not all menus are cascading menus, a right-pointing triangular arrow appears to the right of any menu that can be cascaded. You can easily identify a cascading menu by the triangular arrow on its right as shown below:

As you move the mouse pointer, you can tell which item is selected on a menu because it is highlighted, like ![All Programs]. The purpose of highlighting is to identify a selected item. *Highlighting* alters the appearance of a selection usually by displaying the selected item in a different color.

2   Move the mouse pointer to **All Programs** on the Start menu.

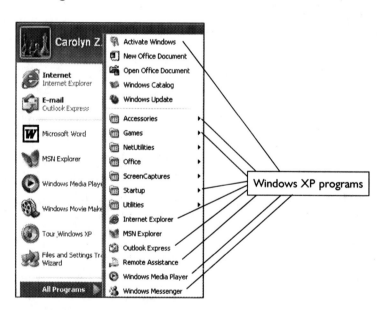

WHAT'S **HAPPENING?** To point is to place the mouse pointer on a specified item. Since All Programs has a triangular arrow, another menu opens. One of the nice features of Windows XP Professional is that you do not have to press the mouse button when selecting cascading menus. You simply point to the next menu. What is on your All Programs menu will vary depending on what software you have installed on your computer. There are certain items placed on this menu by Windows XP. The other items are those programs that were user installed.

3   Point to **Accessories**.

WHAT'S **HAPPENING?** Again, the highlighting told you that you selected Accessories. When you pointed the mouse to Accessories, the next menu opened. All of these programs are part of Windows XP.

4   On the All Programs menu, slide the pointer down to **Games**.

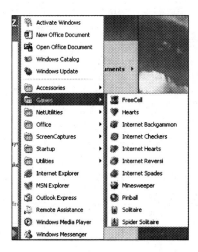

WHAT'S **HAPPENING?** The Games menu displays a list of games that come with Windows XP Professional. Since not one of the choices on the Games menu has a triangular arrow, there are no more menus. The games that are prefaced by Internet are those games you can play on the Internet with other players. However, at this point, you want to play a game that does not require access to the Internet.

5   Click **FreeCell**.

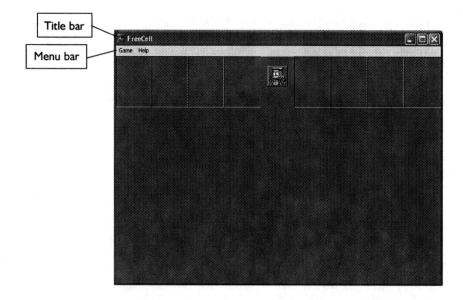

WHAT'S HAPPENING? FreeCell is an application program. When you clicked it, you loaded the program files into memory. When a program is in memory, it may be used. You can now play a card game called FreeCell. Playing this game will allow you to become familiar with your mouse as well as introduce you to some of the common elements of an application program.

Every application program has a *title bar* with its name in it. In addition, an application program will usually have a *menu bar*. The FreeCell menu bar has two menu choices: Game and Help. If you press the [Alt] key, the choices will then have an underlined letter: [Game] [Help]. Then, Game has the letter G underlined, and Help has the letter H underlined. Whenever you see an underlined letter on a menu bar, you may open, or *drop down*, the menu by pressing the underlined letter. If there is no underlined letter, you can press [Alt] and the first letter of the menu item. You may also select the menu by clicking it. Most people prefer clicking the mouse.

6   Click Game.

WHAT'S HAPPENING? You have several choices on the menu. If an item appears dimmed, it is unavailable. For instance, Undo is dimmed. You have not yet done anything, so there is nothing to undo. If you had used the [Alt] key and a letter to open a menu, then all these menu choices would also have an underlined letter as indicated in Figure 1.8.

Figure 1.8 ⊛ Using the [Alt] Key and a Letter to Open a Menu

WHAT'S HAPPENING? ⊳ Pressing the underlined letter in that case would select that choice. Also, many choices have a keystroke, or a combination of keystrokes, next to the menu choice. Rather than clicking the mouse, you may use the keyboard commands. You are going to select a specific game to play. You could press the **F3** key on the keyboard, but you are going to use the mouse.

7 Click **Select Game**.

WHAT'S HAPPENING? ⊳ A dialog box appears. A *dialog box* either presents information to you or requests information from you. Most dialog boxes have a default choice. This dialog box default choice is the number of a specific game. If you do not key in other information, the game number in the box will be selected. If you do not want to use the default selection, you may override it by keying in the number of the game you wish to play.

8 Key in the following: **5500** [Enter]

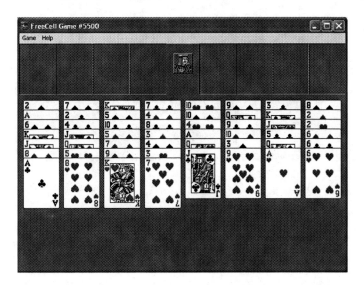

WHAT'S HAPPENING? ⊳ Now you may play the game. The object of the game is to place all the cards in the four empty right-hand squares above the cards. The cards should be separated by suit and stacked in order of rank, beginning with the ace, then the two, and so on. You may temporarily place cards in the left-hand empty squares as you move the cards around. On the playing field, you must place the red and black cards in alternate order.

9   Click the ace of clubs.

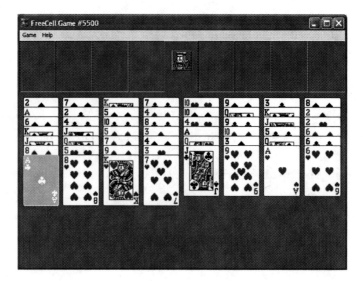

WHAT'S **HAPPENING?** You can tell that you have selected the ace of clubs because it is high-lighted.

10   Click the empty square farthest to the right.

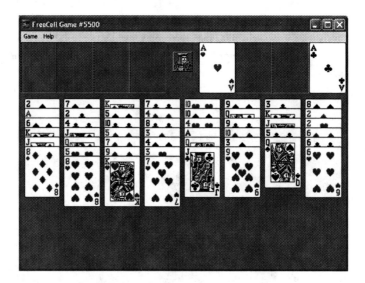

WHAT'S **HAPPENING?** You moved the ace of clubs to the top. At the same time, the ace of hearts also moved.

11   Click the queen of spades and then the king of hearts.

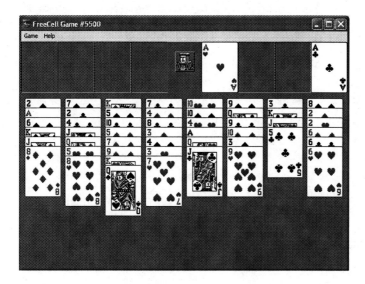

WHAT'S **HAPPENING?** You put the queen of spades on top of the king of hearts. If you wanted more information on how to play this game, you would select Help on the menu bar. At this point, you are going to close the program and return to the desktop.

12 Click **Game**. Click **Exit**.

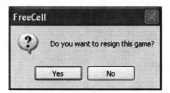

WHAT'S **HAPPENING?** You are presented with a message box. A *message box* is a box that informs you of a condition. It interrupts your current task to alert you to a problem with your system, to inform you of an error you have made, to request a confirmation of a command that could have serious consequences, or to explain why the command you have chosen will not work. These message boxes usually display a graphical symbol to alert you to the problem.

Question:

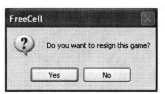

Information:

Warning:

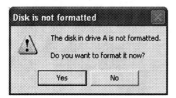

Critical error:

Message boxes most often ask you to confirm, cancel, or retry an action after you have corrected the problem. Both message boxes and dialog boxes provide command buttons to accomplish these tasks.

A *command button* is an example of a *control* because it controls what happens. In this case, you have two choices—Yes, which acknowledges that you do wish to carry out your command of Exit FreeCell, and No, which cancels your command to quit the game. Command buttons also have default values. If you look carefully at the Yes command button, you will see two signs that it is the default button—its border is darker than the border of the No button and a shaded rectangle surrounds the Yes. With a mouse, you choose a button by clicking it. With the keyboard, you may use the Tab key to move between the buttons. You can carry out the selected action (the default) by pressing Enter.

13   Click **Yes**.

WHAT'S **HAPPENING?** You have closed FreeCell and returned to the desktop.

14   Click the **Start** button.

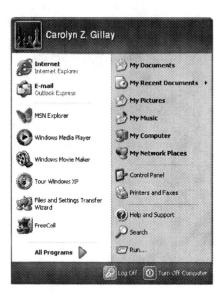

WHAT'S **HAPPENING?** Notice how FreeCell is now at the bottom of the Frequently Used Programs menu. If you have many items on the menu, FreeCell may not appear. As you continue to use programs, the menu items will change.

1.8 ● Activity ● Exploring the Desktop

1   Hold the pointer over the **Start** button until you see the following ToolTip.

WHAT'S **HAPPENING?** Whenever the mouse pointer pauses over a button on a toolbar or on the taskbar, a ToolTip appears. A *ToolTip* is either a brief description of a button's function or its name.

2   Right-click the **Start** button.

WHAT'S HAPPENING? You have opened a shortcut menu. A *shortcut menu* provides an efficient way for you to perform an operation on an object. It shows you the most frequently used commands for an object. The object in this case is the Start button. The options on your Start menu may be different from the example shown, depending on the software installed on your computer. Shortcut menus, sometimes called *pop-up menus* or *context menus*, are displayed at the location of the pointer. They eliminate the need to move the pointer to the menu bar and then select from the menu. Usually, these menus open with a right-click on the object. Sometimes other programs, when you install them, add items to the shortcut menu.

3 Click the desktop to close the shortcut menu.

4 Hold the pointer over the time.

WHAT'S HAPPENING? In this instance, the ToolTip is a display of the current day and date. ToolTips reveal information about selected objects. To use ToolTips, hold the mouse pointer over an object for a few seconds.

5 Right-click the time on the taskbar.

WHAT'S HAPPENING? You have opened another shortcut menu. The object in this case is the clock. You have choices such as to adjust the date and time.

6 Left-click the mouse to close this menu. Click the sound icon. (*Note:* If you do not have a sound card, this option will not be available. If you have a sound card but do not have this icon, click **Start**. Click **Control Panel**. Click **Sounds, Speech, and Audio Devices**. Click **Adjust the System Volume**. Click **Place volume icon in the taskbar**. Click **OK**. Close the Sounds, Speech, and Audio Devices window.

WHAT'S HAPPENING? Here is another example of a control. Controls are graphic objects that represent the operations or properties of other objects. This one is a slider control. A *slider* lets you adjust or set values when there is a range of values. You set or adjust the control by moving the slider with the mouse. In this case, the action is changing the volume level from high to low.

Another control in this dialog box is the check box. A *check box* is a toggle switch. A *toggle switch* is either on or off, much like a light switch. You click in the check box to turn the feature off or on. When there is a check mark in the box, the feature is set (enabled or on). When the box is empty, as this one is, the feature is not set (disabled or off). Your choice here is to have no sound (a check mark in the Mute check box) or to have sound (the Mute check box is empty).

7   Click the check box.

WHAT'S **HAPPENING?** You have turned off the sound.

8   Click outside the Volume box to close it.

WHAT'S **HAPPENING?** On the taskbar, in the status area, the international symbol for No (a circle with a bar through it) shows that the sound is off.

9   Click the sound icon, and then click the **Mute** check box to set the volume. Click the desktop to close the dialog box.

10 Right-click the sound icon.

WHAT'S **HAPPENING?** You have opened another shortcut menu. The object in this case is the volume. You have two choices. You may open the Volume Control dialog box or the Audio property sheet.

11 Click outside of the shortcut menu to close it.

12 Click the Start button. Click **My Computer**. Click **View**. Click **Tiles**.

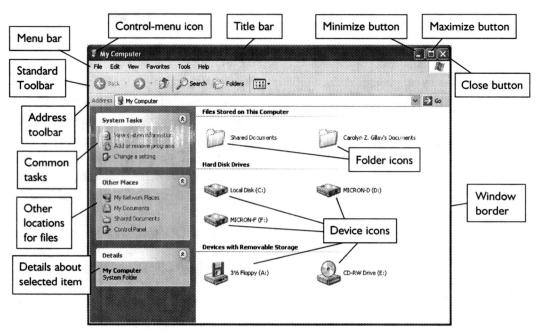

WHAT'S HAPPENING? Your view may have already been in Tiles view, so clicking View and clicking Tiles made no change in the window. You have opened a window with objects in it. If you look at the taskbar, you will see that My Computer appears as a button. The button is highlighted, indicating that it is active. The title bar of the My Computer window is also highlighted, indicating that it is the active window. The My Computer window allows you to access your storage devices, such as disk drives and folders that contain objects that control your system. How your window is arranged depends on your settings. If your display is different and you want to match the text, click View. Point to Arrange Icons by and be sure Show in Groups has a check mark. The My Computer window has the following items:

Control-menu icon	When clicked, it will drop down a menu for controlling the window using the keyboard or the mouse. In some instances, if you right-click the Control-menu icon, it will open another menu for locating files and creating shortcuts.
Title bar	The name of the window.
Minimize button	When clicked, the *Minimize button* will keep the window open but minimize it. The window will still appear on the taskbar as a button.
Maximize button	When clicked, the *Maximize button* makes the window fill the entire screen.
Close button	When clicked, the *Close button* will close the window and the application. Since the application will be closed, it will no longer have a button on the taskbar. You may also double-click the Control-menu icon to close a window.
Device icons	*Device icons* represent the devices on your system. Each icon shows what type of device it represents, such as a floppy disk drive, a hard drive, or a CD-ROM drive. The devices are separated into those that cannot be removed such as your hard drive and those that have removable media such as a floppy disk drive.
Folder icons	*Folder icons* represent folders that contain other objects such as your data files.
Window border	The *window border* identifies the boundaries of the window.
Address toolbar	Allows you to key in a Web page address (URL) without first opening the Internet Explorer browser or to key in a drive or directory location. If you do not have an address toolbar, click View. Point to Toolbars. Click Address Bar.
Standard Toolbar	Toolbars contain buttons, usually with icons (small images) to identify each button. Each button performs some function. The Standard toolbar contains all the buttons required to move around in My Computer. The first three buttons are Back, Forward, and Up. You use Forward and Back to move between locations you have visited. The Up button takes you up one level in the directory structure. The Search and Folders buttons control the view in the left pane of the window. Search allows you to search for files and folders and Folder lets you look at your files and folders in a hierarchical manner. The last icon, the Views, provides different looks to the right pane.

Menu bar	Contains available menus for this window. Clicking on a menu choice will open a menu with more choices.
Common Tasks	Each time you open a different folder, My Computer lists the tasks it thinks you would most like to do at this time. Since you are in the "main" window, the list is of system tasks such as adding or removing programs.
Other locations	Provides a list of other drives and directories where you can locate your files. Also provides access to Control Panel. This is a special folder that contains objects that lets you control your system.
Details	Each time you select an object, details about that object will appear in this section.

13   Click the Up Arrow, [⌃], in System Tasks, Other Places, and Details.

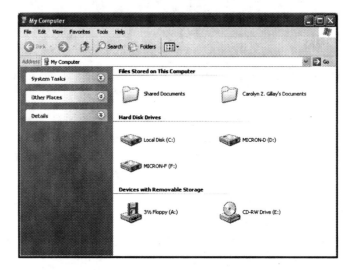

WHAT'S **HAPPENING?** You have now collapsed the menus. Notice that the arrow is now a down pointing arrow.

14   Click the Down Arrow, [⌄], in System Tasks, Other Places, and Details.

WHAT'S **HAPPENING?** You have expanded the menu selections.

15   Click the Minimize button on the My Computer window.

WHAT'S HAPPENING? You have minimized the window. It is now a button on the taskbar. My Computer is open but not active.

16 Click the **My Computer** button on the taskbar.

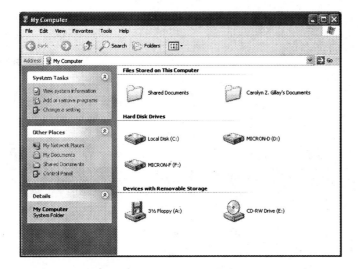

WHAT'S HAPPENING? You have restored the window to its previous size. It is now open and active. When you click the button on the taskbar, the application toggles between being a button on the taskbar and an open and active window.

17 Click the Maximize button on the My Computer title bar.

WHAT'S HAPPENING? The window now fills the entire screen. Look at the buttons on the right side at the top of the window. You have a new button, the **_Restore button_**, ⬚, instead of the Maximize button.

18 Click the Restore button.

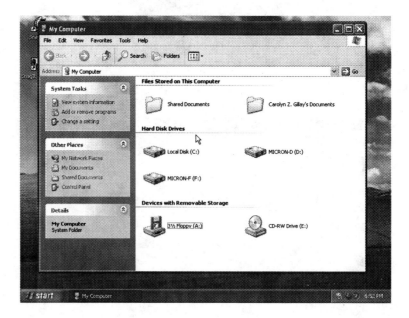

WHAT'S **HAPPENING?** You have restored the window to its previous size. Once again, if you clicked the button on the taskbar, you would toggle between an open window and a button on the taskbar. If you did not restore the window, the next time you opened the window, it would be maximized.

19 Click the Control-menu icon on the My Computer title bar.

WHAT'S **HAPPENING?** You have dropped down the *Control menu*. You can minimize, maximize, move, or size the window by clicking a selection, pressing the down arrow to move to a selection and pressing **Enter**. If you open the Control menu icon of an active program window by pressing the **Alt** + **Space Bar** keys, a letter is underlined in each command. When you press that letter, you activate that command. To open the Control menu for an active document window, you may press the **Alt** + **Hyphen** keys. Again, pressing the underlined letter will activate that command. When you do so, you will have used keyboard shortcuts to manipulate the window. Restore is dimmed because the window is already in its restored position. The Control menu is available in all program and document windows. It provides a set of window management commands common to all programs.

20 Click outside the menu to close it. Click the Close button on the My Computer title bar.

WHAT'S **HAPPENING?** You have closed My Computer and have returned to the desktop. You could have also closed the window by double-clicking the Control-menu icon, by selecting the Control menu and choosing Close, or by pressing the **Alt** + **F4** keys.

1.9 ● Moving and Sizing Windows

In addition to minimizing, maximizing, and closing a window, you can move a window to other locations on the screen. You may also change the size of a window. Moving windows allows you to arrange your desktop just as you would a desk by moving items such as a phone or an address book. Sizing a window differs from minimizing or maximizing a window. Minimizing a window shrinks it so it appears only as a button on the taskbar, but is still open. Maximizing a window makes it fill the screen. Sizing a window means changing its size and shape. If you wanted to have two or more windows visible on the screen, you could adjust, or size, both windows.

1.10 ● Activity ● Sizing and Moving Windows

1   Click **Start**. Click My Computer.

2   Place the mouse on the title bar of the window. Hold down the left mouse button and drag the mouse downward.

WHAT'S **HAPPENING?** As you see, you moved the window. To move any window, you use the title bar as a handle and grab it with the mouse. You cannot move the window by placing the mouse anywhere else within the window.

3   Move the window back to its original location.

4   Place the mouse on the window's left border. The pointer should change to a double-headed arrow.

5   Click and hold the left mouse button down on the border and move the pointer to the left. The window should expand to the left. When you have expanded it about an inch, release the left mouse button.

WHAT'S HAPPENING? The window is now larger. Once you have adjusted the size of the window, this new size becomes the default restore size.

6 Place the mouse on the window's left border. The pointer should change to a double-headed arrow.

7 Click and hold the left mouse button on the border and move the pointer to the right. The window should contract to the right. When you have contracted about an inch, release the left mouse button.

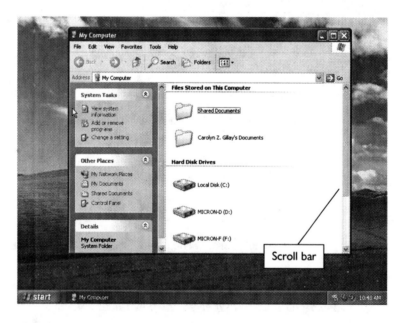

WHAT'S HAPPENING? You have returned the My Computer window to its original size, which is now its default restore size. When you see a scroll bar, it indicates that you are not seeing everything in the window and must scroll through the window in order to see the rest of the items.

Another way to size a window is to place the pointer on any corner of the window, which allows you to move two sides at the same time.

8 Place the mouse pointer on the upper-left hand corner of the window. Hold the left mouse button and push the window's borders inward and downward.

WHAT'S HAPPENING? You have made the window smaller by adjusting two sides at the same time

9 Place the mouse pointer on window corner to return the window to its previous size.

10 Close the My Computer window.

1.11 ● Manipulating the Taskbar with a Property Sheet

The Taskbar in Windows XP is how you access every thing on your computer system. Since Windows XP in a default installation places no icons or programs on your desktop, you must use the Start button, located on the taskbar to perform any tasks. As you have seen, open programs place a button on the taskbar so you may access your open programs. You may add toolbars to the Taskbar to easily access often used programs or documents. The Taskbar is a floating taskbar.

A *floating* taskbar or button bar can have its size or location altered. Not all taskbars or button bars float, but the Windows XP Professional taskbar does. You may also manipulate the taskbar in other ways. You may hide it, have it always on top, have it display the time, or change the size of the icons. To manipulate the taskbar settings, you use a property sheet.

A property sheet is a kind of dialog box. A dialog box is a window in which you provide information to a program. A *property sheet* is just a more complex dialog box. Almost every object in Windows XP Professional (folders, files, the desktop, the taskbar, disk drives, modems, and so on) has properties associated with it that can be viewed or altered. The settings in an object's property sheet affect how the object looks and, sometimes, how it works. A property sheet allows you to look at or change information about an object. A property sheet can be accessed easily by right-clicking an object and then clicking Properties on the shortcut menu.

When you open a property sheet, there may be multiple sheets. Each sheet has its name on a tab, much like the tabs on file folders. To access a sheet of interest, click its tab.

1.12 ● Activity ● Working with the Taskbar

I   Right-click the taskbar.

WHAT'S HAPPENING? You have opened a right-click menu also called a shortcut menu. A shortcut menu lists commands that pertain only to that screen region or selection. In this example, the Lock the Taskbar is on. You know this because there is a checkmark by Lock the Taskbar. To turn off any checked item, you click it. Again, it is a toggle—click to turn on and click to turn off. When the taskbar is locked, it is locked into its current position and cannot be moved. It also locks any the size and position of any displayed toolbars.

2   Click Lock the taskbar to clear it.

3   Place the mouse on the taskbar in an empty location. Click and hold the left mouse button and begin to drag the taskbar to the right. When the taskbar is at the right side of the screen, release the left mouse button.

WHAT'S HAPPENING? The taskbar changed locations. You may drag, or float, the taskbar to the top, left, or bottom of the screen provided the Lock the Taskbar is disabled. You may also change the taskbar width.

4 Place the pointer on the outside edge of the taskbar. When it becomes a double-headed arrow, drag to the left. When the taskbar is about two inches wide, release the left mouse button.

WHAT'S **HAPPENING?** The taskbar is much wider. You can make it narrower by moving its border in the opposite direction.

5 Place the pointer on the outside edge of the taskbar. When it becomes a double-headed arrow, drag to the right until the taskbar returns to its previous size.

6 Place the pointer on an empty location on the taskbar and hold the left mouse button. Drag the taskbar to the bottom of the screen.

WHAT'S **HAPPENING?** The taskbar returned to its default position and size.

7 Right-click the taskbar.

WHAT'S HAPPENING? Since the taskbar is an object, it has properties.

8   Click Properties.

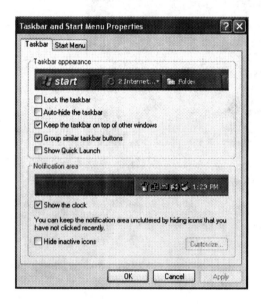

WHAT'S HAPPENING? You are looking at Taskbar and Start Menu Properties, which contains settings that control the taskbar and the Start Menu. An object could have more than one series of settings to view or change. If it did, it would have multiple property sheets. Each sheet would have a labeled tab. You click the tab of the sheet you wish to use. Taskbar and Start Menu Properties has two choices one for the Taskbar and one for the Start Menu.

9   Click the tab for Start Menu.

WHAT'S HAPPENING? By clicking the tab, you brought the Start Menu property sheet to the front. There are two option button displayed, Start Menu and Classic Start menu. *Option buttons* gives you a choice between mutually exclusive choices. In other words, you can either have the new Start menu OR use the Classic Start menu. You cannot use both choices. The Classic Start menu can be used for those users who prefer the Windows 2000 Professional (or Windows Me) look and feel.

10   Click Classic Start menu. Click OK.

WHAT'S **HAPPENING?** This ability to switch the look and feel of the desktop was provided so that those users who had learned Windows 98/Windows ME or Windows 2000 would not have to relearn the interface. The "look" of a desktop is cosmetic. Once you have learned what an operating system is, what its features and functions are, changes in the interface will not faze you. You can find what it is albeit in a different location or with a different icon.

When you use the Classic Start menu, your desktop looks somewhat different. In addition the My Documents, My Computer, My Network Places and Internet Explorer icons are placed on the desktop. The Start menu also looks different.

11 Click **Start.**

WHAT'S **HAPPENING?** The Start menu also has a different look and feel. However, certain principles are the same. A right arrow indicates that submenus will appear when you point to the arrow. You will also find that sometimes the location of programs or selections will vary. However, since you are using Windows XP, for the remainder of the text, you will be using the new interface.

12 Click outside the menu to close it. Right-click the taskbar. Click **Properties**.

13 Click the Start Menu tab. Click **Start Menu**. Click **Customize**.

WHAT'S **HAPPENING?** Here the Customize Start Menu property sheet has two tabs—General and Advanced. As you can see, you can customize the look of the Start menu. Each of these options will change what is displayed on your system.

14 Click **Small Icons**. In the Programs section, click **Clear List**. Click **OK**. Click **OK**.

15 Click the Start button.

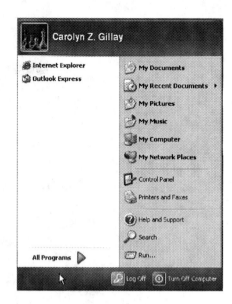

WHAT'S **HAPPENING?** You cleared the Start menu. Now no programs are listed. However, the next time you open a program, it will appear on this menu. The icons look the same size—the Small Icons refers to the Program icons.

16 Point to **All Programs**. Point to **Games**. Click **Solitaire**. Click **Game**. Click **Deal**. Close Solitaire.

17 Click the Start button.

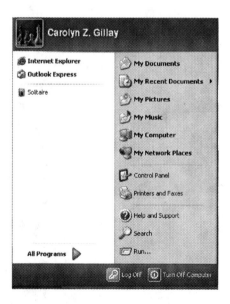

WHAT'S **HAPPENING?** Now Solitaire appears as a small icon.

18 Right-click the taskbar. Click **Properties**. Click the Start Menu tab. Click **Customize**. Click **Large Icons**. Click **OK**. Click the **Taskbar** tab.

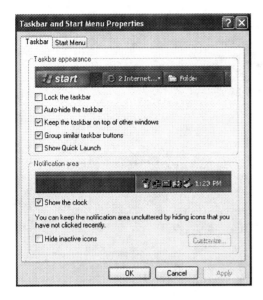

WHAT'S **HAPPENING?** In this example, certain check boxes contain checks, indicating that they are the set, or enabled, choices. In the Taskbar appearance area, Keep the taskbar on top of other windows and Group similar taskbar buttons are enabled. Lock the taskbar, Auto-hide the taskbar and Show QuickLaunch have no check mark; they are disabled. In the Notification area, Show the clock is enabled (set) whereas Hide Inactive icons is not enabled (not set). (*Note:* Your settings could be different.) If you would like a description of a property sheet feature, it is readily available.

19 Click the question mark icon on the Taskbar and Start Menu Properties title bar. A question mark attaches itself to the cursor, ⒂?. Drag the cursor to Group similar taskbar icons and click.

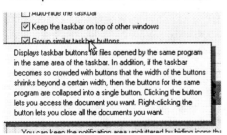

WHAT'S **HAPPENING?** A pop-up description appears, telling you the function of the Group similar taskbar icons feature. Whenever you see a question mark icon on the title bar of any window, you may click it and drag it to any item in question. The question mark on the title bar is known as the What's This? command.

20 Click outside of the description to close it. Click **OK**.

21 Click the Start button.

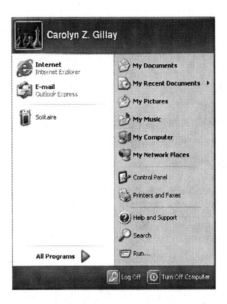

WHAT'S **HAPPENING?** The program icon, Solitaire, is now the large icon size. icons are smaller in the Start menu. You may also access property sheets by right-clicking an object, in this case, right-clicking the taskbar.

22 Click outside the Start menu to close it. Right-click the Start button.

WHAT'S **HAPPENING?** You have quickly opened the shortcut menu that relates to the taskbar and start menu.

23 Click **Properties**.

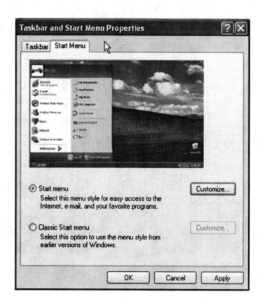

WHAT'S HAPPENING? You have again opened the Taskbar and Start Menu Properties sheet. Here you may alter the characteristics of the Taskbar or the Start menu.

24 Click **OK**.

WHAT'S HAPPENING? You have returned to the desktop.

1.13 • Objects

In Windows XP Professional, nearly every item is considered an *object*. In general, objects can be opened and have properties. Properties can have values. For an example of the object-property-value relationship, think of a person. A person is an object. All objects of the same type (people) have the same properties. Some properties of a person object are name, height, and eye color. The value of an object's properties can differ. One person's name property value could be John Jones; another person's name property value could be Olivia Wu. A newborn person has a name property but no value has been assigned to it.

In Windows XP Professional, an object can be a program item icon that represents an executable program file. An executable program is a tool that allows you to accomplish some task. FreeCell is an example. When you selected it from the menu, it opened and became a game you could play. An object can be a document icon that represents a data file created with an application program. When you select it, you launch the program that created the data file as well as open the document. An object may be a device such as a disk drive. Its properties include its size and how much data is on it. These vary from disk to disk. All disks will have a size, but that size can vary. An object can be a folder that holds program icons, document icons, files, or other folders that hold more objects or folders.

In Windows XP Professional, objects have properties, settings, and parameters. Each object usually has a property sheet, a collection of information about the object's properties. Usually, properties can be changed or adjusted. Properties of an object affect what the object does or what you can do to the object. For instance, the desktop is an object. It has properties such as its background color. You can alter the values or the colors of the desktop—the object.

An object can be manipulated in various ways, depending on what the object is. Object behavior is supposed to be consistent. Once you know how to deal with a specific object, you know how to deal with all similar objects because they will behave the same way. A folder is an object that can be opened. It can contain other objects such as folders, files, or devices. The folder itself has properties with values such as location. You can manipulate the folder by moving it, copying it, or deleting it. All folder objects can be manipulated in the same way. Remember though, what you can do with an object depends on what the object is.

1.14 • Activity • My Computer as an Object

1   Click **Start**. Click My Computer.

2   Click **Tools** on the menu bar. Click **Folder Options**.

WHAT'S HAPPENING? The default option for Browse Folders is to Open each folder in the same window. This means that when you open one window, the window that was open closes. To see the hierarchical nature and relationship among windows, you are going to change this option to Open each folder in its own window.

3   Click the empty circle (option button) by Open each folder in its own window to set it. Click **Apply**. Click **OK**.

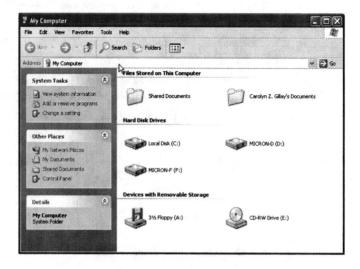

WHAT'S HAPPENING? Your display will be different depending on how your system was set up and how many devices and how many users you have. If you have scroll bars, you can size the window so you can see all the objects or else you can scroll through the list. You have returned to the My Computer window. This is called a ***parent window*** because it is the origin of the objects within it. A parent window may have one or more ***child windows***, but a child window can have only one parent. This relationship is called a hierarchy because there is a dependency relationship between the objects. As shown above, the My Computer parent window has seven objects, or children. Five of the objects are devices—the drives on this system. There is one floppy drive (Drive A), one CD-RW drive (Drive E), and three hard drives (Drive C, D and F)

Two of the objects are folders (Shared Documents and Carolyn Z. Gillay's Documents). Folders contain other files and folders. Every system should have a Shared Documents folder icon. Each user then has his or her own folder for their documents. If another user logs on, you will see his or her folder for their individual documents. See Figure 1.9.

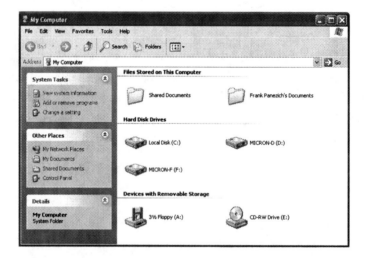

Figure 1.9 ＊ Different User Logged On

If there is more than one user on the system, you will see more folders for each person. See Figure 1.10. Again, what is displayed is dependent on how your system was set up. My Computer gives you access to your files and folders on all the devices that are available to you on your system.

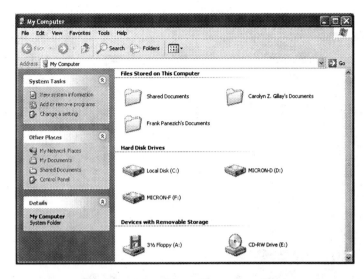

Figure 1.10 ∘ More Than One User

4   Place the XPPRODATA disk that came with the text in Drive A. Double-click the Drive A icon. If the Drive A window is full screen, click the Restore button.

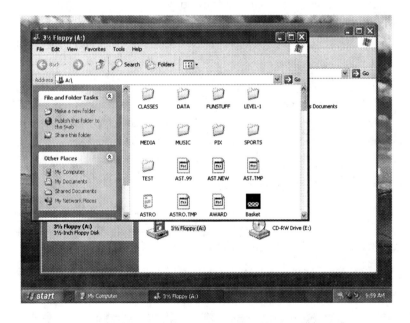

WHAT'S **HAPPENING?** ⟩ You have opened the Drive A window. This window is a child window of the My Computer window. The Drive A window is subservient to the My Computer window and therefore beneath it in the hierarchical structure. This child window contains files and folders and therefore has objects and children. It has only one parent, My Computer. The Drive A window is the active window. If you look at the taskbar, you see a button for both open windows with the Drive A window highlighted indicating it is the active window.

5   Press the ⌷Backspace⌷ key.

WHAT'S **HAPPENING?** When you press the Backspace key, you make the parent window of a child window active without closing the child window. In this case, My Computer, the parent of the Drive A window, became the active window. The Drive A window may be hidden behind the My Computer window. If you do not see the Drive A window, you may drag the My Computer window to a different location. Also the taskbar button indicates which is the active window.

6   Click the Drive A window to make it active. If you cannot see it, click the Drive A button on the taskbar. Both My Computer, the parent, and Drive A, the child, are open windows. You can close each window individually, but there is a shortcut to close both windows at the same time.

7   Hold down the Shift key and click the Close button on the Drive A window.

WHAT'S **HAPPENING?** You closed both the child window, Drive A, and the parent window, My Computer, in one action. When you hold the Shift key and click the Close button, you close the child window and any and all parent windows above it in the hierarchy.

8   Click **Start**. Click **My Computer**. Double-click the Drive A icon. Click **View**. Click **Icons**. Click **Tools**. Click **Folder Options**. Click the **View** tab. Click **Restore Defaults**.

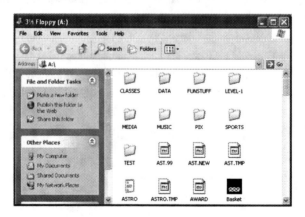

WHAT'S **HAPPENING?** You are looking at what is on the disk in Drive A. What is on the disk are folders which are recognizable by the file folder icons such as . File folders are containers that can hold files as well as other folders. The other icons in the window represent document files. A *file* is a named program or a named document created with a program and stored on a disk. In this example, folder and document files are represented. If Windows XP Professional does not know which program created a document, it displays a generic document icon—an icon that looks like a piece of paper with a dog-eared corner, . If Windows XP Professional knows what program created a document, it will display an icon representing that program such as or . What icons appear can vary, depending on your video card as well as what programs you have installed. Windows XP Professional will always remember the last size and arrangement of the display for each window you have opened. Thus, the look of each window will vary, depending on the last action you took before you closed the window.

9   Size the Drive A window so it is approximately the size of the textbook example following step 4. Click **View** on the menu bar.

WHAT'S **HAPPENING?** You have dropped down the menu and can see all the different ways to manipulate the window. In this case, Status Bar does not have a check mark

in front of it, indicating that the status bar is disabled. Yours may be on. There is also a dot by Icons indicating its enabled status. The dot means that this feature is on. The dot is an option button. Remember, an option button indicates that only one item in the section can be selected. Options are mutually exclusive choices; it is either one or another. If Icons is not enabled, set it by clicking it.

10   Point to **Arrange Icons by**.

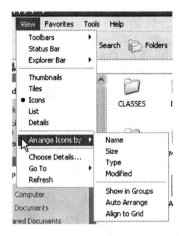

WHAT'S **HAPPENING?** Arrange Icons by has a triangular arrow, so it has a cascading or submenu. You can arrange your icons by Name, Size, Type, or Modified The default choice is by Name. In this example, Auto Arrange has no check mark and therefore is not enabled. Auto Arrange means that, when you open a window, the icons will automatically be fitted into the window in the most efficient way. Show in Groups will group the icons by the category you choose and Align to Grid will "snap" each icon to an invisible grid.

11   Click **Name**. Click **View**. Click **Status Bar** to enable or set it.

Note: Depending on your resolution, you may need to size your windows to see all of them. In a lower screen resolution, each open window may fill the screen.

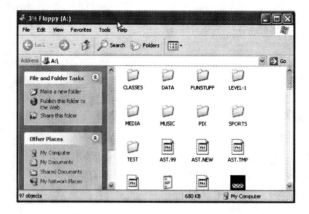

WHAT'S HAPPENING? The title of this child window is 3½ Floppy (A:). The Status Bar tells at the bottom of the window tells you that there are 97 objects in it; that they take 680 KB and that the parent window is My Computer. The taskbar tells you which windows are open. Look at the taskbar.

The taskbar shows that the open windows are My Computer and 3½ Floppy (A:). The 3½ Floppy (A:) button is highlighted and indented, indicating that it is the *active window*, the one in which you are currently working. There may be many open windows, but only one window may be active at a time. Folder and document icons are in the Drive A window. The folders are children of the Drive A parent.

12   Double-click the **Level-1** folder.

WHAT'S HAPPENING? In this window, the Status bar is not on. You must set options for each window. Look at the taskbar. You will see that My Computer, the Drive A window, and Level-1 are all open, but Level-1 is the active window. Level-1 contains a child, the folder called Level-2. It also contains a document called Hello.

13   Double-click the **Level-2** folder.

WHAT'S **HAPPENING?** Look at the taskbar. You will see that My Computer, the Drive A window, Level-1, and Level-2 are all open, but Level-2 is the active window. Level-2 contains a child, the folder called Level-3. It also contains a document called Hello.

14 Double-click the **Level-3** folder.

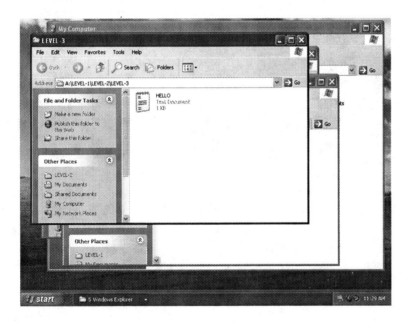

WHAT'S **HAPPENING?** Look at the taskbar. Depending on your screen resolution, you may see that now the open windows are indicated by a single button—5 Windows Explorer. Because the Taskbar and Start Menu properties had Group similar taskbar buttons enabled, the open windows are grouped. The 5 indicates how many are open. To see the specifics, you may click the down arrow button. The Level-3 window is the active window. Level-3 contains no folders but does contain a document called Hello.

15 Click the down arrow on the Windows Explorer Taskbar button, if available.

WHAT'S HAPPENING? You may choose any of the items on the menu.

16   Click the Close button on the Level-3 window.

17   On the taskbar, click the **3½ Floppy (A:)** button to make it the active window. If necessary, open the Windows Explorer button and click **3½ Floppy (A:)** to make it active.

18   Hold the **Shift** key down and click the Close button on the 3½ Floppy (A:) title bar.

WHAT'S HAPPENING? The hierarchy of parent to child windows is My Computer, then 3½ Floppy (A:), then Level-1, and then Level-2. Since you made 3½ Floppy (A:) the active window and then held the **Shift** key, when you clicked the Close button, you closed the 3½ Floppy (A:) window and its parent My Computer. Since you closed in the middle of the hierarchy, you did not close the Level-2 or Level-1 windows.

19   Click the Level-2 window to make it active. Double-click **Hello**.

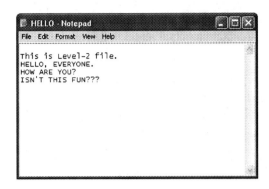

WHAT'S HAPPENING? You have opened a program called Notepad so that you may look at the document called Hello. The document's name is actually Hello.txt, but the .txt is not displayed in this setting. Notepad is in an *application window;* it is a program that performs a task. As its name indicates, it acts like a pad of paper for creating and viewing short documents. The document in question is a data file called Hello.

Windows XP Professional employs a docucentric approach. *Docucentric* means that what is most important is the data, not the program that generated the data. However, there is a catch to this approach; you cannot open a document without also opening the program that created the document.

On the title bar is the Control-menu icon, which is represented by the icon for the Notepad program, followed by the name of the document (Hello), followed by the name of the application program that created the document (Notepad). Applications that were not written for Windows XP Professional and are not docucentric will have first the name of the program (Notepad), then the name of the document (Hello).

If you look at the taskbar, you will see buttons for all of the open windows.

20 Click the Level-2 button on the taskbar to make it the active window. In the Level-2 window, hold down the `Shift`

key and click the Close button on the title bar.

WHAT'S HAPPENING? You closed all the child and parent windows. However, you did not close the application program Notepad and its open document Hello. Notepad is still open. You must close application programs separately. When you open a folder window, you are seeing what files and folders you have. When you open a program, you are planning to do work.

21 Click the Close button for Notepad.

22 Click **Start**. Click **My Computer**. Click **Tools**. Click **Folder Options**. Be sure the General tab is on top. Click **Restore Defaults**.

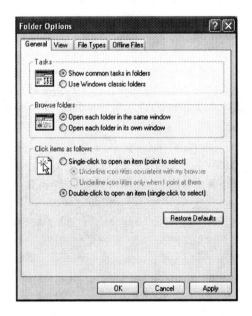

WHAT'S HAPPENING? You have restored the defaults so that Open each folder in the same window is selected.

23 Click **OK**. Close the My Computer window.

24 Remove the XPRODATA disk from Drive A.

WHAT'S HAPPENING? You have returned to the desktop.

1.15 ● Working with Application Programs

Windows XP Professional allows *multitasking*, which means that it can run more than one program at a time. Multitasking is a useful and important feature. You will find yourself using it often. To see how multitasking works, imagine you are writing a friend a letter using the application program Microsoft Word for Windows. You want to mention who won the Academy Award for Best Actor of 1988 to your friend, but you do not remember the actor's name. A word-processing program, such as Word, does not have answers to such questions, but another program you own, called Bookshelf, does. Bookshelf is a reference tool that includes a dictionary, almanac, thesaurus, atlas, and other common reference works. While Word is open, you access the almanac and find your answer—Dustin Hoffman won for *Rain Man*. When you appear to use two programs at the same time, you are multitasking.

In reality, you are moving from one task to another or from one process to another sequentially, rather than simultaneously. A *process* is a program or a part of a program that is a coherent sequence of steps. Windows XP Professional concentrates on different tasks or processes. It lets you key information into Word and open the almanac. It also performs some operating system tasks, such as accessing a disk or drawing the screen. Windows XP Professional switches from one task to another very rapidly, giving you the impression that you are doing many things simultaneously. Although there are computers that have more than one processor, and hence allow processes or programs to run at the same time, this is not true in the personal computer (PC) world. In the PC world, a computer usually has only one processor (the central processing unit, or CPU) and can do only one task at a time. Windows XP Professional, as the operating system, manages time allocation so that the CPU can process each task. Imagine filming a busy intersection—cars go and stop to allow other cars to go through the intersection. If you ran the film, you would see that each car stops and starts; but, if you ran the film at a high speed, it would look as if the cars never stopped moving.

To speed up processing, Windows XP Professional also allows *multithreading*. A *thread* is a small part of a program with a very narrow focus. Within an application program, tasks are divided into smaller tasks called threads. For instance, in a spreadsheet program, one thread could be used for recalculation, another for printing, and another for keyboard input. Within the program, all these threads could be working and running concurrently without interfering with each other. This would be an example of a multithreaded application. The purpose of multithreaded applications is to help you work faster. Not only must applications be written specifically to support multithreading, but the operating system must also support multithreading. Windows XP Professional does. In fact, Windows XP Professional itself is a multithreaded operating system. As applications are written or updated for Windows XP Professional, they will more than likely use multithreading.

In the multitasking Windows XP Professional environment, you may have many applications open and running, but there is only one active application. Considered the *foreground application* or active window, the active application has its title bar highlighted and is stacked above all other open applications. If all the open application windows are minimized, the active application is represented on the taskbar by the button that is in contrasting colors. You may only work in the active, open window. Objects such as My Computer, not just applications, also appear in windows.

1.16 ● Activity ● Moving Between Foreground and Background Windows

1   Click **Start**. Point at **All Programs**. Point at **Games**. Click **FreeCell**.

2   Click **Start**. Point at **All Programs**. Point at **Games**. Click **Solitaire**.

3   Click **Start**. Point at **All Programs**. Point at **Accessories**. Click **Calculator**.

4   Click **Start**. Point at **All Programs**. Point at **Accessories**. Click **Notepad**.

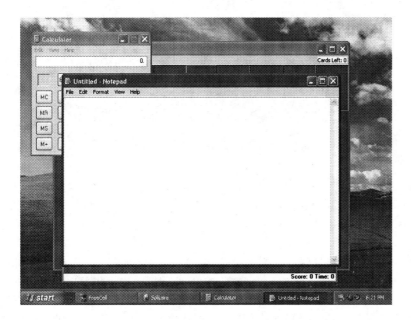

WHAT'S **HAPPENING?** ⟩ You have opened four programs. Notepad, the last one you opened, is on top. It is the active and *foreground window*. Look at the taskbar. All the open windows are listed on the taskbar but only Notepad has its button highlighted. You can move among the open windows making each one active in turn.

5   Click the **Solitaire** window. If you cannot see it, click the **Solitaire** button on the taskbar.

WHAT'S **HAPPENING?** ⟩ By clicking on a window or a taskbar button you make that window active.

6   Click the Calculator button on the taskbar.

WHAT'S **HAPPENING?** Calculator is now the active window. The taskbar can become very crowded. In fact, sometimes you will not be able to read entire names. Remember, if you hold the pointer over a button, the full name of the window will appear. In addition, since Group similar taskbar button is set, if the taskbar becomes crowded, Windows will place all those applications in a button that can be opened. Since Notepad is a program, the document name (Untitled) and the program name (Notepad) become visible. Not all applications programs create documents. For instance, Solitaire and FreeCell are games. They have no document windows. Calculator is a tool and it also has no documents. A button can also represent a window such as My Computer, which holds files and folders.

6   Hold down the **Alt** key and tap the **Esc** key until you have cycled through all the application windows. End when Notepad is the active application.

WHAT'S **HAPPENING?** Look at the taskbar. As you cycled through the open applications, the buttons depressed indicated the active application. If a window is minimized, only the button on the taskbar will be highlighted. This technique for switching between open applications is a slow method because it requires drawing the entire screen. A faster technique is to use the **Alt** + **Tab** key combination.

7   Hold the **Alt** key and tap the **Tab** key so you cycle through all the open applications.

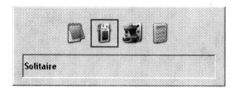

WHAT'S **HAPPENING?** When you use the **Alt** + **Tab** key combination, you also cycle through the open windows. However, rather than drawing the window of an application, the **Alt** + **Tab** key combination displays the icon and the name of the application. It also shows you all the open application icons with a box around the current selection.

8   Right-click the Solitaire button on the taskbar.

WHAT'S HAPPENING? You opened the Control menu, from which you may manipulate the window by moving, sizing, minimizing, maximizing, or closing it. Restore is dimmed because Solitaire is already an open window.

9 Click **Close** on the menu.

10 Close all the open application windows.

WHAT'S HAPPENING? You have returned to the desktop.

1.17 ● Manipulating the Display

When you have many applications open, you may display them in several ways. You saw how to make each active in turn, but what if you wanted to see all of them at once? In Windows XP Professional, you may display all of the open windows in either a cascaded or a tiled fashion. *Cascaded* means that the open windows will be layered, one on top of the other, with all of the title bars visible. *Tiled* means that the screen will be divided so that each open window has a portion of the screen. If a window is minimized, it will not be included in the tiled or cascaded display.

1.18 ● Activity ● Using the Taskbar to Manipulate Windows

1 Click **Start**. Point at **All Programs**. Point at **Games**. Click **FreeCell**.

2 Click Start. Point at **All Programs**. Point at **Accessories**. Click **Notepad**.

3 Right-click the taskbar in an empty spot.

WHAT'S HAPPENING? You have opened the shortcut menu for the open objects on your screen.

4 Click **Tile Windows Horizontally**.

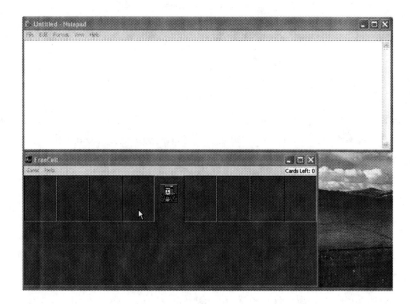

WHAT'S **HAPPENING?** When you tiled horizontally, you divided the screen between the two open windows. The active window has the title bar highlighted. If no title bar is highlighted, no window is active.

5   Click **FreeCell**. Click **Notepad**. Click **FreeCell**. Click **Notepad**.

WHAT'S **HAPPENING?** As you click each window, it becomes active.

6   Right-click the taskbar in an empty spot. Click Undo Tile.

WHAT'S **HAPPENING?** You have undone the tiling. You may not be able to see the FreeCell window, but, if you look at the taskbar, you will see that FreeCell has a button.

7   Right-click the taskbar in an empty spot. Click **Tile Windows Vertically**.

WHAT'S **HAPPENING?** You have tiled the windows side-by-side.

8   Click **Notepad**. Click **FreeCell**. Click **Notepad**.

WHAT'S **HAPPENING?** As you click each window, it becomes active.

9 Right-click the taskbar in an empty spot. Click **Undo Tile.**

WHAT'S **HAPPENING?** You have undone your tiling.

10 Right-click the taskbar in an empty spot. Click **Cascade Windows.**

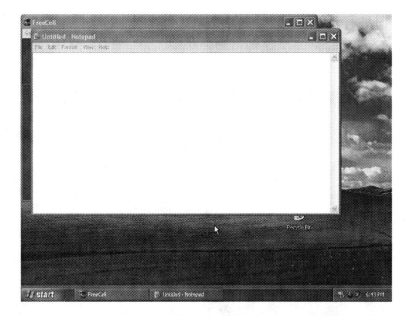

WHAT'S **HAPPENING?** You have cascaded the open windows, layering them one upon another with all the title bars visible.

11 Click FreeCell. Click Notepad.

WHAT'S **HAPPENING?** As you click each window, it becomes active. If you cannot see a window, you can click the button on the taskbar.

12 Right-click the taskbar in an empty spot. Click **Undo Cascade.**

13 Right-click the taskbar in an empty spot. Click **Show the Desktop.**

WHAT'S **HAPPENING?** Now all the windows are minimized and appear as buttons on the Taskbar. If you look at the taskbar, you can see buttons for all the open windows. If you are not sure which windows are open, choosing Show the Desktop will minimize all the open applications to buttons on the Taskbar.

14 Right-click the taskbar in an empty spot.

WHAT'S **HAPPENING?** You now have a new choice, Undo Minimize All.

15 Click Undo Minimize All.

WHAT'S **HAPPENING?** Your windows are restored.

16 Right-click the taskbar in an empty spot. Click **Show the Desktop.**

17 Click **Start.** Click **My Documents.**

18 Click **Start.** Click **My Computer.**

19 Right-click the taskbar in an empty spot. Click **Undo Minimize All.**

20 Right-click the taskbar in an empty spot. Click **Tile Windows Horizontally.**

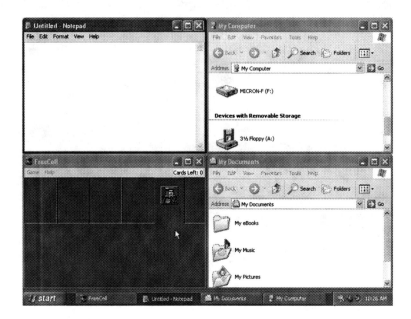

WHAT'S **HAPPENING?** Now you have two application windows open (Notepad and FreeCell) and two object windows open (My Computer and My Documents). Your windows are equally divided on the desktop. Notice that an application window and an object window behave in the same way.

21 Right-click the taskbar in an empty spot. Click **Tile Windows Vertically.**

WHAT'S **HAPPENING?** The screen display did not change. When you tile, you divide the desktop among the open windows. You see the difference between vertical and horizontal tiling only when there are fewer windows open. You can make any window active by clicking it.

22 Click the Close button on the My Documents window.

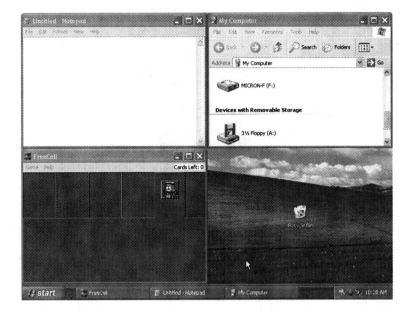

WHAT'S **HAPPENING?** You closed the My Documents window. Now your screen has three windows open.

23 Right-click on the taskbar on an empty spot. Click **Tile Windows Horizontally**.

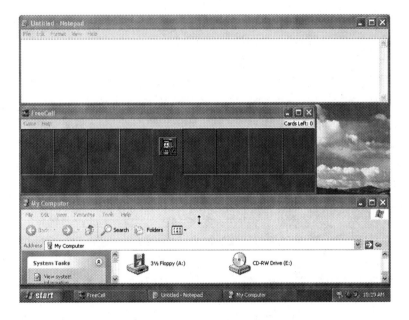

WHAT'S **HAPPENING?** Now the three windows divide the screen horizontally.

24 Right-click the taskbar in an empty spot. Click **Tile Windows Vertically**.

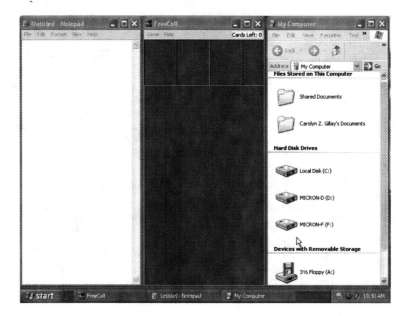

WHAT'S HAPPENING? Now the windows are arranged side-by-side.

25   Right-click the taskbar in an empty spot. Click **Undo Tile**.

26   Right-click the taskbar in an empty spot. Click **Cascade Windows**.

27   Close all the open windows.

WHAT'S HAPPENING? You have closed all the windows and returned to the desktop. There are no Control-menu choices such as Close All Windows or Close All Applications. Each window must be closed independently. You undid the tiling and then cascaded the windows. Had you not done that, each window would have remembered its vertical shape; the next time you opened the window, it would be in a narrow, vertical window.

1.19 ● Formatting a Disk

Before placing files and folders on a floppy disk, you must prepare the disk for use. This process is called *formatting* a disk. Today, when people purchase floppy disks, they tend to purchase preformatted disks that are ready to use. Nonetheless, if you wish to erase all information from a disk or if you purchase unformatted disks, you must format them.

1.20 ● Activity ● Formatting a Disk

1   Remove the XPRODATA disk from Drive A. Do not use the XPRODATA disk that came with this textbook. Get a blank disk or a disk with information you no longer need. Place a label on the disk and write MYDATADISK, your name, and today's date on it. It is wise to place a date on a disk so that you know when you created it.

2   Place the disk in Drive A.

3   Click **Start**. Click **My Computer**. Right-click the Drive A icon.

WHAT'S HAPPENING? You have opened a right-click menu for the disk in Drive A. One of the choices is Format. Several choices have three dots following them. The three dots are called an ellipsis. When ever you click a menu choice with an ellipsis, you will open a dialog box. A dialog box contains certain command buttons and other options through which you can carry out a command or a task. Property sheets display information (properties) about the selected object. But when properties of an object can be edited, they also can contain command buttons and options just like dialog boxes. Both property sheets and dialog boxes can have tabbed pages that will group similar sets of options or properties. Essentially, a dialog box is a kind of property sheet.

4   Click Format.

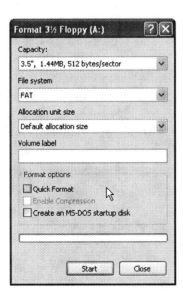

WHAT'S HAPPENING? You have opened a Format dialog box. In this example, Drive A contains a 3½-inch floppy disk. You can see the capacity of the disk. You also have some choices. In Format options, you can choose Quick Format . This choice can be used only on a previously formatted disk. You also have an option to create an MS-DOS startup disk. This is an emergency boot disk. Enable Compression is not available since only disks that use the NTFS file system can be compressed. Floppy disks are always formatted as FAT disks.

5   Click the Start button.

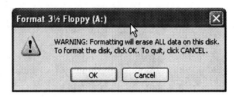

WHAT'S HAPPENING? You receive a warning that you will delete any data on this disk.

6   Click OK.

WHAT'S HAPPENING? If you look at the bottom of the dialog box, you see a progress indicator. A *progress indicator* reports to you the progress of a task. When the disk is formatted, you will see the following report:

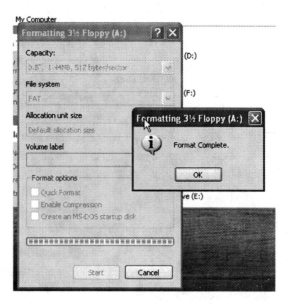

You see a dialog box that tells you that the task is complete. In addition, you can see that your progress indicator is complete. This disk is now formatted. It is ready to receive files and folders.

7   Click **OK**. Click **Close**.

8   Close the My Computer window.

9   Remove the MYDATADISK disk from Drive A.

1.21 • Exiting Windows

To leave Windows XP Professional, do not simply turn off the computer's power. You must complete a shut-down process. This process allows Windows XP Professional to close files and write the information it needs to disk so that, when you use your computer again, you will be returned to the desktop as you left it. Windows XP Professional also has general housekeeping tasks it must perform before shutting down completely. When you select Turn Off the computer, this shuts down Windows correctly and you then can turn off the computer power. Many newer computer systems will shut down the power automatically. You may or may not need to turn off the monitor separately. In addition, you may choose to log off. When you log off from the computer, you close your user account but the computer remains on for easy access the next time you wish to log on. If you have multiple user accounts, another user can log on. When multiple users share a computer, logging off and logging on to the computer in order to switch users can become tiresome. There is a feature that can be turned on called Fast User Switching that if you are not on a domain, you may quickly switch between users without actually logging off. For instance, if you are working on your computer and need to do something, and your child wishes to play a game, you can leave your programs running, and allow your child to log on to play a game. When you switch back, your programs are still running as you left them.

1.22 ● Activity ● Exiting Windows XP Professional

1   Click **Start**.

WHAT'S **HAPPENING?** The bottom two choices, as shown here, are Log Off and Turn Off Computer. Logging off does not turn off the computer. It shuts down any open programs and allows another user to key in her or his user name and password without having to go through a power cycle (turning the computer off and then back on).

2   Click **Log Off**.

WHAT'S **HAPPENING?** This computer system has Fast User Switching enabled as you have two choices, Switch User and Log Off. If you click Switch User, you would a screen like Figure 1.11.

Figure 1.11 ● Fast User Switching

WHAT'S **HAPPENING?** In this example, there is only one user account. In this account, two programs are running. If there was another user, you could switch users and leave the Carolyn Z. Gillay account open with two programs running.

3   Click **Cancel**.

4   Click **Start**. Click **Turn Off Computer**.

WHAT'S **HAPPENING?** You have three choices, Stand By, Turn Off and Restart. You may have also have another choice, Hibernation. When your computer is hibernating, every thing that is memory is saved to your hard disk and your computer is turned off. When you turn the computer back on, all your programs and documents that were open are restored to the state when you turned off the computer. You must have a computer that supports this option. Standby is a state whereby your computer is on but uses less power. Information in memory is not stored on your hard disk. If you lose power, you will lose what is in memory. Restart reboots your computer. Every thing in memory is lost. The normal choice here is Turn Off. This turns off the computer. You want to shut down or turn off the computer.

5   Click Turn Off.

WHAT'S **HAPPENING?** If your computer does not shut off automatically, you may see a message that states that is safe to turn off your computer. When you see that screen, it is okay to turn off your computer. On a computer that automatically shuts down, the screen will simply go blank, and your computer is turned off.

6   If necessary, turn off the power. Turn off the monitor.

Chapter Summary

This chapter introduced the basic features of Windows XP Professional. You learned about the work area, called the desktop. You learned what a window is. You acquainted yourself with the taskbar, the primary tool for seeing which windows are open. You learned how to manipulate the floating taskbar and move among windows using the taskbar buttons. You were presented with the features of pointing devices. Knowing the meaning and usage of mouse-related terms such as click, double-click, drag, right-click, and right-drag is important for working effectively in Windows XP Professional.

Menus are an important feature of Windows XP Professional. One of the most important is the Start menu that, as its name implies, gets you started. You identified and used cascading menus. You familiarized yourself with the keyboard and mouse by making selections from menus. By pressing the **Alt** key and an underlined letter, you selected a menu item. When you used the mouse, you clicked your menu choices. Since everything in Windows XP Professional appears in a window, you focused on techniques to manipulate windows. These techniques include moving, sizing, minimizing, maximizing, and restoring. Sizing a window is adjusting the borders of a window, whereas minimize, maximize, and restore refer to making a window a button on the taskbar, filling the entire screen with a window, or restoring a window to its default size.

You were introduced to the concept of objects, which can be opened and have properties. Properties of an object are accessed through its property sheets, collections of information about the object. Property sheets allow you to view or alter properties of an object and are most often accessed by right-clicking the object and choosing Properties from the shortcut menu.

You learned about parent and child windows and the hierarchical nature of windows. You learned how to manipulate your windows by tiling and cascading them. You were introduced to application windows. You learned how to open and close windows and use shortcuts.

You used the Format command to prepare a disk for use, because all disks must be formatted before you place information on them. And you learned the proper process to exit Windows XP Professional.

Key Terms

active window	file	pop-up menu
application window	floating	primary mouse button
booting the system	folder icon	process
cascaded	foreground application	progress indicator
cascading menu	foreground window	property sheet
check box	formatting	Restore button
child menu	hierarchical menu	right-clicking
child window	highlighting	right-dragging
clicking	icon	shortcut menu
Close button	install	slider
command button	Maximize button	Start button
context menu	menu	status area
control	menu bar	submenu
Control menu	message box	system tray
cursor	Minimize button	taskbar
desktop	mouse pointer	taskbar button
device icon	multitasking	thread
dialog box	multithreading	tiled
docucentric	object	title bar
document	option button	toggle switch
document window	pane	ToolTip
double-clicking	parent menu	upgrade
drag and drop	parent window	window
dragging	pointer	window border
drop down	pointing	

Discussion Questions

1. What does it mean to boot the system?
2. What is activation? Why must you activate Windows?
3. Explain the purpose and function of the desktop.
4. Explain the purpose and function of the taskbar, the Start button, icons, taskbar buttons, and the system tray area.
5. What is a window? How is it used?
6. What is the purpose and function of pointing devices?
7. What is a cascading menu? How can you determine if a menu is a cascading menu?
8. What is the purpose and function of a dialog box?
9. What is the function of a command button?
10. What is a ToolTip?
11. What is a control? Give two examples of a control.

12. Explain the purpose and function of moving a window and of sizing a window.
13. What is the difference between minimizing and sizing a window?
14. Explain the purpose and function of property sheets.
15. Name one way a property sheet can be accessed.
16. How can you display the taskbar property sheet on the screen?
17. Compare and contrast a parent window and a child window.
18. Compare and contrast multitasking and multithreading.
19. Compare and contrast foreground and background windows.
20. Open windows can be displayed either tiled or cascaded. Explain.
21. Compare and contrast tiled and cascaded windows.
22. When multiple windows are open, how can you identify the active window?
23. How can you quickly close parent and child windows?
24. Why is it necessary to format a disk?
25. Why is it important to go through a shut-down process, rather than just turn off the computer?

True/False Questions

For each question, circle the letter T if the statement is true or the letter F if the statement is false.

T   F   1. Tiled windows divide the space on the desktop equally.
T   F   2. The My Computer folder contains only devices and no folders.
T   F   3. To select a cascading menu, you must click the mouse button.
T   F   4. Sizing a window turns it into an icon on the Taskbar.
T   F   5. The My Documents window is a child window to the My Computer window.

Completion Questions

Write the correct answer in each blank space.

6. A pictorial representation of an object is known as a(n) _____.
7. To select an object, you must click the _____ mouse button.
8. To allow you to look at or change information about an object, Windows XP Professional uses a type of dialog box called a(n) _____.
9. For determining what windows are open, buttons are placed on the _____.
10. Windows XP Professional's approach of treating the user's data as more important than the applications is called a(n) _____ approach.

Multiple Choice Questions

Circle the letter for the correct answer to each question.

11. Booting the system is the process of
    a. copying system files from a CD-ROM to the hard drive.
    b. copying system files from the hard drive into memory.
    c. placing a data disk in Drive A.
    d. attaching the CPU to the other computer components.

12. The current day and date can be displayed by
    a. choosing Show Day/Date from the Start menu.
    b. double-clicking on the time icon.
    c. holding the mouse over the time icon.
    d. right-clicking on an empty area of the taskbar.
13. You may access the taskbar's property sheet by
    a. choosing Start, then choose Properties of the Taskbar.
    b. right-clicking on an empty area of the taskbar.
    c. right-clicking on an empty area of the taskbar and choosing Properties.
    d. both a and b
14. Menu items which are unavailable
    a. have no alternative keystrokes.
    b. appear dimmed.
    c. are not shown on the menu.
    d. have no underlined letter.
15. The My Computer icon represents
    a. a diagnostic program that describes your system.
    b. a document that lists the current settings for your system.
    c. a utility program that allows you to make changes to the desktop.
    d. a window that can be opened that contains the devices on your system as well as other folders such as the My Documents folder.

Application Assignments

Problem Set I—At the Computer

Note: For Problem Set I to work correctly, open My Computer. Click Tools. Click Folder Options. On the General tab, click Restore Defaults. Click Apply. Click the View tab. Click Restore Defaults. Click Apply. Click OK.

Problem A

❋ Click the Start button.

    1. You have opened a
      a. menu.
      b. dialog box.

❋ Open FreeCell.

    2. To open FreeCell, you used
      a. cascading menus.
      b. only a dialog box.

❋ Choose game number 555.

    3. The only ace among the fully exposed cards is the
      a. ace of clubs.
      b. ace of diamonds.
      c. ace of hearts.
      d. ace of spades.

❋ Play FreeCell if you wish. When you are finished, you must exit or close the program. Before you close FreeCell, begin a new game, but do not finish it.

4. Which button must you click to close FreeCell?
    a. ▪
    b. ▫
    c. ✖

5. When you close FreeCell, you are
    a. immediately returned to the desktop.
    b. first presented with a message box.

Problem B

* Click Start. Click My Computer. Maximize it.

6. The title bar contains the word(s)
    a. My Computer.
    b. File.

7. The menu bar contains the word(s)
    a. My Computer.
    b. File.

* Click the Control-menu icon in the upper-left corner of the My Computer window.

8. Which of the following commands are unavailable for use?
    a. Restore
    b. Minimize
    c. Maximize

9. You knew a command was unavailable in the menu you opened above because it
    a. was dimmed.
    b. was highlighted in red.
    c. did not appear on the menu.

* Minimize My Computer.

10. My Computer
    a. is closed.
    b. is open.

* Right-click the My Computer button on the taskbar. You have opened a shortcut menu—the Control menu. Different choices are on this menu.

11. You may close My Computer using the menu you opened by clicking **Close** or pressing
    a. Ctrl + F4
    b. Shift + F4
    c. Alt + F4

* Click Restore on the Control menu, click the Restore button on the My Computer title bar, then click the Close button on the My Computer title bar.

Problem C

* Open My Computer. Move the My Computer window to the lower-right corner of the desktop.

12. You moved the My Computer window by placing the mouse on the
    a. My Computer title bar and double-clicking it.
    b. My Computer title bar and dragging it.

* Expand the My Computer window by about an inch.

13. By expanding the My Computer window, you are
    a. maximizing it.
    b. minimizing it.
    c. moving it.
    d. sizing it.

14. When you expanded the My Computer window, the pointer changed shape. It became
    a. double-headed arrow.
    b. single-headed arrow.

❋ Return the My Computer window to its original size. Move it back to its original position. Close the My Computer window.

Problem D

❋ Open the property sheet for the taskbar. Click the Taskbar tab. Click the question mark icon, then click the Start button in the property sheet example.

15. The following description appears:

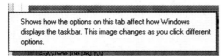

    a. true
    b. false

16. A property sheet is a type of
    a. menu.
    b. cascading menu.
    c. dialog box.

❋ Close the property sheet.

Problem E

❋ Place the XPRODATA disk that came with this textbook into Drive A. Open My Computer. Double-click the Drive A icon.

17. Arrange the icons by modified in the Drive A window. Which folder is first?
    a. CLASSES
    b. FUNSTUFF
    c. Y.FIL
    d. AST.99

18. Arrange the icons by size in the Drive A window. Which file is first?
    a. CLASSES
    b. FUNSTUFF
    c. Y.FIL
    d. AST.99

❋ Arrange the icons by name. Open the Media folder by double-clicking it.

19. Does the Media folder have any child folders?
    a. yes
    b. no

20. The parent of the Media folder is
    a. My Computer.
    b. 3½ Floppy (A:).

* Open Notepad.

* Cascade all the windows.

21. Which window is on top?
    a. Notepad
    b. Media
    c. My Computer
    d. 3½ Floppy (A:)

* Undo the cascading. Close all open windows.

Problem F

* Exit Windows XP Professional properly.

22. The fastest way to exit Windows XP Professional correctly is to
    a. turn off the computer.
    b. click **Start**, then click   **Turn Off Computer**.

Problem Set II—Brief Essay

1. Describe the purpose and function of a pointing device. Then agree or disagree with the following statement and explain why you chose your position: *To use Windows XP Professional effectively, it is important to be able to use a pointing device*.
2. You may open, close, minimize, maximize, or move windows that are on the desktop. Briefly describe the purpose of each of the functions.

Problem Set III—Scenario

You have been directed to design a standard placement of items on the desktop for all newly purchased computers that come with Windows XP Professional. Wisely, you have decided to interview the users of these newly acquired machines to establish a standard organizational scheme so that, if one person needs to use another's computer, the transition will be easy and no time will be wasted with desktop reorganization. You must decide, among other things, what windows should be open and how the windows should be arranged. Prepare a plan for this investigation and include questions relating specifically to the desktop.

CHAPTER 2

Using Help and Dialog Boxes

Windows XP Professional provides extensive online help. Rather than having to look up how to accomplish a task in a printed manual, you can access the information directly from the computer. Help in Windows XP Professional is a hypertext utility; you can jump between logically connected items with the click of a mouse. You will use Help to find out how to install components that are missing from your Windows XP Professional installation.

Many tasks are performed the same way in all applications written for Windows XP Professional. Once you have learned how to complete a task in one application, you know how to do it in other Windows applications. Applications written for Windows XP Professional will also have an online help facility that looks and works the same way as Windows XP Professional Help.

Learning Objectives

1. Explain the purpose and function of online Help capabilities.
2. Explain the purpose and function of a hypertext utility.
3. Describe how to add missing Windows XP Professional components.
4. Compare and contrast the various ways to access Help.
5. Describe the purpose and function of the controls in a dialog box, such as command buttons, option buttons, list boxes, drop-down list boxes, check boxes, and spin boxes.
6. Explain the purpose and function of scroll bars and scroll boxes.
7. Explain the purpose and function of What's This?
8. Explain the purpose of troubleshooters.
9. Explain how to analyze a problem.

Student Outcomes

1. Access Help.
2. Use each of the different methods of using Help.
3. Print a Help topic.
4. Use Help to find information on a specific topic.
5. Use Help to find information related to a specific word or phrase.
6. Identify the different controls in dialog boxes.
7. Use a troubleshooter in Help to analyze and solve a problem.

2.1 • Touring Windows XP

For new and experienced users, Windows provides a built-in tour of the major new features of Windows XP Professional. If you are new to Windows, taking the tour will give you a nice overview of Windows XP. You may choose to use the animated tour that includes text, animation, music and voice animation. You may also choose to take the non-animated tour that has only text and images.

2.2 • Activity • Taking the Windows XP Tour

1   Click **Start**. Point to **All Programs**. Point to **Accessories**.

WHAT'S HAPPENING? Here in the Accessories menu is where you find the Tour Windows XP choice.

2 Click **Tour Windows XP**.

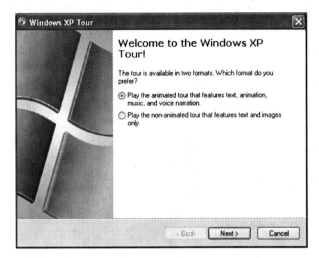

WHAT'S HAPPENING? You have a choice of the animated or non-animated version. Since most lab or school environments do not allow sound in their environment, you are going to choose the non-animated version.

3 Click **Play the non-animated tour that features text and images only**. Click **Next**.

WHAT'S HAPPENING? You may see more or less of the window depending on the size and resolution of your monitor. You may select any of the topics indicated by a colored button.

4 Click **Start Here**.

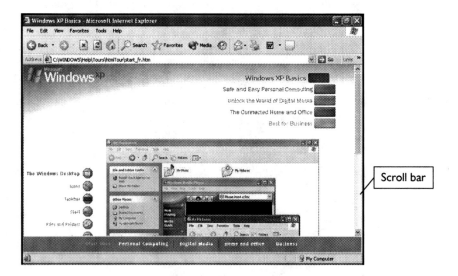

WHAT'S HAPPENING? You may change subjects by clicking either the color buttons on the top of the screen or choosing a topic by clicking the listed topics at the bottom of the screen. You can tell that Start Here has been selected because both the top button and the bottom screen choice are in a different color. Within the topic, you can tell what you are looking at as the topic is highlighted. Here The Windows Desktop is in a darker color.

5   Click the down arrow in the scroll bar until you reach the bottom of the window.

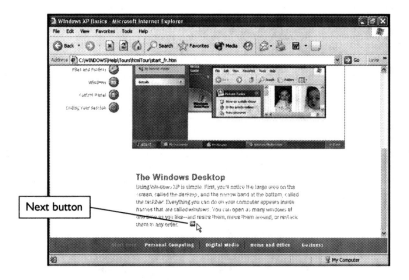

WHAT'S HAPPENING? You see a description of the desktop. Then, to see more, you click the right pointing arrow. This is the Next button.

6   Click the next button.

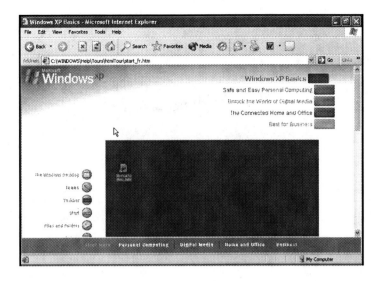

WHAT'S HAPPENING? ‣ Now Icons is highlighted. To see the textual description, you need to scroll through the window.

7   Scroll to the bottom of the window.

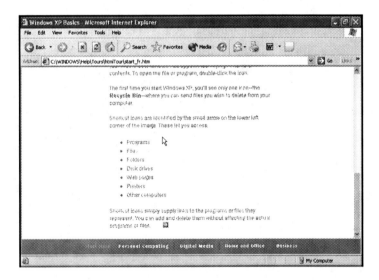

WHAT'S HAPPENING? ‣ If you continue to click the next button, you will be led through all the topics about the desktop.

8   Click the next button. Scroll until you can see all the topics.

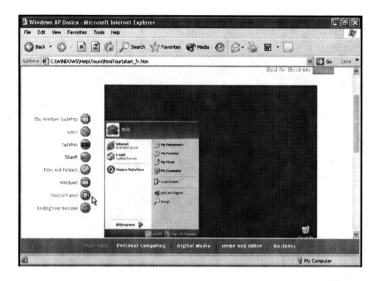

WHAT'S HAPPENING? You do not have to go through the list in order. You may click any topic to skip to that topic.

9   Click **Ending Your Session**. Scroll to the bottom of the window.

WHAT'S HAPPENING? As you can see, you have jumped to Ending Your Session. To exit the tour, you simply click the Close button.

10   Click the Close button.

WHAT'S HAPPENING? You have returned to the desktop.

2.3 • Help

It is difficult to know everything about your computer system, much less everything about the operating system (Windows XP Professional) and your programs. Windows XP Professional, as well as almost every program written for Windows XP Professional, comes with a built-in help system. The help system is *online*. Online has two meanings: (1) in a local sense, it means that the Help files you need are located on your hard disk and you can call them up and use them without having to refer to a printed manual, and (2) in a global sense, it means that you are on a network and connected to other computers. The network can be a company network or a worldwide network such as the Internet.

Windows XP Professional's help is a set of files on your computer that contain information about Windows XP Professional itself as well as the accessories that come with it. Help also offers Internet links, specifically to send Microsoft a problem report and view responses to other computer user's problems by Microsoft engineers. Help is presented as screens of information. It is organized in a Web-like browser. Help offers a large variety of ways to get help.. It has a Search function allows you to key in keywords and have Help search all of the available help pages for the occurrence of that word or words. It provides topics arranged in what Microsoft thinks is a logical order. It provides an index that lists all the available topics and provide tutorials that provide step-by-step instructions on how to perform a task. In the Help window are forward and backward arrows that can take you forward to the last areas you visited or back to previous areas you have visited. It includes a home button that takes you to the first page of help.

Windows XP Professional Help is a *hypertext* utility, which means that topics are linked together logically, allowing you to jump quickly from one topic to another. This means you can search Help in a nonlinear fashion; you don't have to follow a fixed path. Windows XP Professional also includes built-in troubleshooters. These troubleshooters can help you isolate and diagnose computer-related problems.

2.4 ● Activity ● Using Help

I   Click **Start**. Click **Help and Support**.

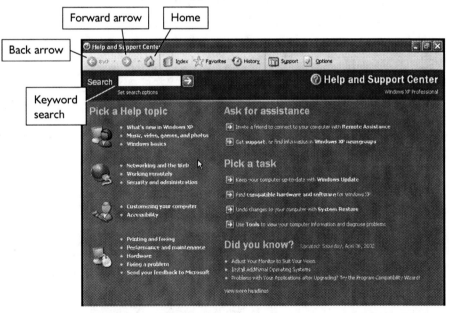

WHAT'S HAPPENING? Help and Support will normally fill the screen. You may place Help and Support in a smaller window by clicking the Restore button. In the Help window, a new mouse action is added. The mouse action uses a single-click feature. Rather than having to double-click an entry, you point and click. As you drag your mouse, you see topics highlighted by an underline and the mouse pointer changes to a hand. See Figure 2.1.

Figure 2.1 • Selected Topic in Help and Support

WHAT'S **HAPPENING?** An underline and hand pointer lets you know that you have selected that topic. This feature is called *hovering*.

2   Click **Windows basics**.

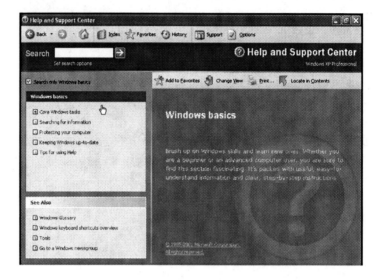

WHAT'S **HAPPENING?** You are taken to the screen listing topics about Windows basic. Now that you have selected a topic, your Back arrow is available.

3   Click the back arrow. Click the forward arrow.

WHAT'S **HAPPENING?** Using the back and forward arrows moved you back to the previous screen and then forward to the current screen. The back and forward arrows "stepped" you through your choices.

4   Click **Tips for Using Help**.

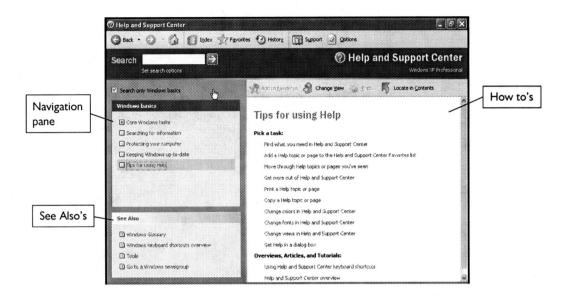

WHAT'S HAPPENING? The current topic is in indicated by reverse video in the navigation pane. Reverse video is simply a reversal of dark and light in the display of selected characters on a video screen. Reverse video is commonly used to highlight selected items. You have a See Also reference which provides other topics that might apply. The right pane includes Pick a Task that lists all the tasks that Help provides help on. Then you also have another section that lists general information about a topic and other places to go for help.

5 In the right pane, click **Get more out of Help and Support Center**.

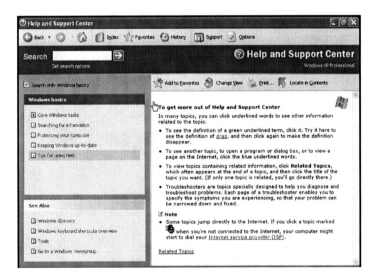

WHAT'S HAPPENING? The navigation pane remains the same. The right pane contains the information on the selected topic and is the topic portion of the window.

6 Click the underlined word, **drag**, in the right frame.

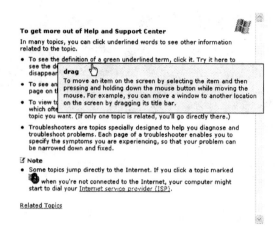

WHAT'S HAPPENING? Whenever you click an underlined term, you see a brief definition of the term. At the bottom of the topic pane, you often see a Note section that gives you further information. You also often see Related Topics, which is underlined. When you click a colored underlined topic, you will be taken either to the page of interest or to a display of further subjects.

7   Click **Related Topics**.

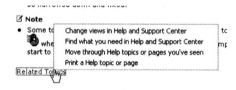

WHAT'S HAPPENING? By clicking the underlined phrase, you are presented with a menu that has menu choices that relate to your topic. To select an item from this menu, you would click your choice. If there is only one related topic, when you clicked Related Topics, you would be taken to that choice. However, the navigation pane remained the same.

8   Click **Change View** at the top of the topics window.

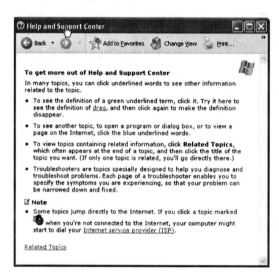

WHAT'S HAPPENING? You have now displayed the topics portion of the window only.

9   Click **Change View** to restore your previous view.

10 In the See Also, click **Windows Glossary**.

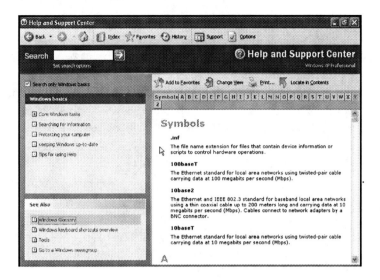

WHAT'S **HAPPENING?** The topics pane displays a list of terms you may find definitions for.

15 Click **Home**. Click **What's new in Windows XP**.

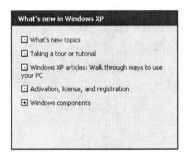

WHAT'S **HAPPENING?** The navigation pane lists several topics. One topic, Windows Components, is preceded by a box with a plus sign in it. The plus sign indicates that the topic can be expanded. If the topic has a minus sign, it can be collapsed.

11 Click the plus sign in the Windows components box.

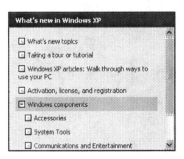

WHAT'S **HAPPENING?** The selected topic became highlighted in a different color or reverse video. In. You have expanded the topic. You now can click any item of interest. To collapse the selection, you click the box which now has a minus in it.

18 Close the Help window.

WHAT'S **HAPPENING?** You have returned to the desktop.

2.5 • Adding Windows XP Professional Components

Windows XP Professional is very customizable. How Windows XP Professional looks and what is installed depends on what choices you, or someone else, made when Windows XP Professional was installed. You may add the missing components later, but you must use the original CD-ROM to load them. If you purchased your computer with Windows XP Professional already installed on it and you did not get a Windows XP Professional CD-ROM, you have two choices: (1) contact the manufacturer of your computer to find out how you can get the missing components, or (2) purchase the Windows XP Professional upgrade.

The following activity will demonstrate how to identify and add missing components. If you are in a lab environment, read but do not do steps 11–14.

2.6 • Activity • Adding and Removing Windows Components

1   Click **Start**. Click **Help and Support**. Click the **History** button.

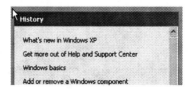

WHAT'S HAPPENING? You have opened the History window. Help remembers the topics that you viewed and lists them in the History window. If you wanted to access any of the topics you previously viewed, you would click it.

2   Click the Back button. Click **Music, Videos, Games, and Photos**.

3   Click **Games**.

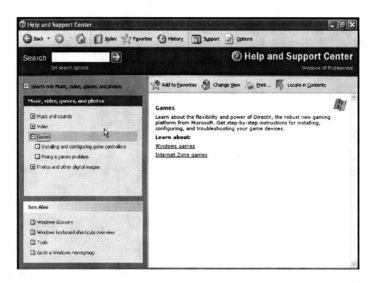

WHAT'S HAPPENING? You expanded the Games choice in the navigation pane. In the right pane, you see two topics, Windows games and Internet Zone games.

4   In the right pane, click **Windows games**.

WHAT'S HAPPENING? You see each game provided with a small box with a plus sign, indicating the topic can be expanded.

5 Click **FreeCell**.

WHAT'S HAPPENING? Here you see the object of the game as well as a link to the game. If you click the Open ▓ FreeCell. link you will be taken directly to the game. Under Notes, it tells you that if you do not see any Games on your All Programs menu, then click Related Topics.

6 Collapse Free Cell. Click **Related Topics**.

WHAT'S HAPPENING? There are two choices here—Playing Internet Zone games or to Add or remove a Windows component.

7 Click **Add or remove a Windows component**.

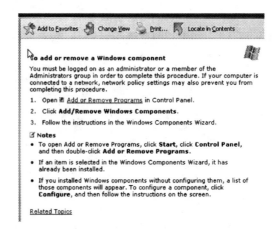

WHAT'S **HAPPENING?** Here are instructions for how to install a missing component. This procedure is an example of hypertext. Remember, hypertext allows you to jump from one logically related topic to another. You did not have to return to the categories as you would have had to do in a sequential search for information. In addition, when you see a link with a right-bent arrow, clicking it will take you to the appropriate place so you make your changes.

8   Click the right-bent arrow next to the Add or Remove Programs link.

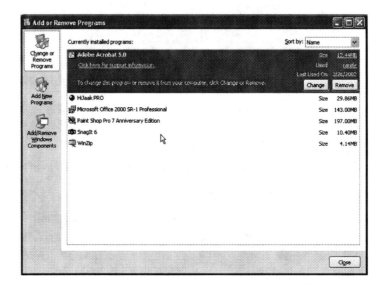

WHAT'S **HAPPENING?** Windows XP Professional took you to Add Remove Programs dialog box. The first page listed lists all of the programs installed on your system. The left column gives you three choices—Change or Remove Programs, Add New program and Add/Remove Windows Components.

9   Click the **Add/Remove Windows Components.**

WHAT'S HAPPENING? Windows XP Professional first looks to see what components are installed on your computer. When it determines this, you see the following screen:

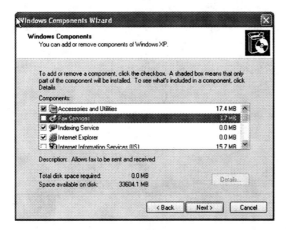

You were taken to the Windows Components Wizard that allows you to add or remove. If you look at the property sheet in this example, you see that the highlighted entry Fax Service has no check mark, indicating that this feature was not installed on this system. If installed, Fax Services would occupy occupies 3.7 MB of disk space. If you look in the Description box at the bottom of the dialog box, you see a description of the purpose of Fax Services.

In this example, if you look at the first entry, Accessories and Utilities, you see a check mark in the check box, but the check box is grayed, ☑ Accessories and Utilities. A check box with a check mark but grayed check indicates that some of the options were installed, but not all.

Working on your own computer. The following steps will demonstrate how to add missing Windows XP Professional components. If you want to take steps to add a component, you may need to have the Windows XP Professional CD-ROM available.

Working in a lab. If you are in a lab environment, you must not take these steps. Simply read the steps so that you understand how to complete the procedure.

10 Click **Accessories and Utilities**. Click **Details**.

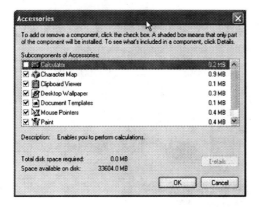

WHAT'S HAPPENING? In this example, the Description area tells the purpose of Calculator. In this example, Calculator is *not* installed. To install a component, you check it. To remove a component, you also click it to remove the check mark. The items to choose from are in a list box. A *list box* is exactly what you would think, a list of items from which you can select what interests you. Sometimes the list will not fit into one window. If the entries do not fit into one window, a scroll bar appears. The scroll bar allows you to move up or down through the list so you can see all the items. If you click the up arrow, you move up one entry, and, if you click the down arrow, you move down one entry. In addition, there is a scroll box that allows you to drag the box to move rapidly through the list, rather than move one item at a time.

I I   If you are in a lab environment or have no components to add, click **Cancel**. Click **Cancel**. Click **Cancel**. Click **Close**. Close the Help and Support window.

WHAT'S **HAPPENING?** Since you had no components to add or you are in a lab environment, you returned to the desktop. However, if you needed to add components, you would take the next steps, A through D.

A   Click the check box by Calculator (only if it is empty). Click **OK**. Click **OK**.

WHAT'S **HAPPENING?** You are returned to the Wizard. A wizard is a series of steps that are automatically taken to complete your task.

B   Click **Next**.

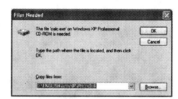

WHAT'S **HAPPENING?** Here is where you insert the correct CD.

C   Insert the Windows XP Professional CD-ROM and click **OK**.

WHAT'S **HAPPENING?** You will see a message box telling that files are being copied. When the task is completed, you will see the following dialog box.

D Click **Finish**.

WHAT'S **HAPPENING?** You have returned to the desktop.

2.7 ● Dialog Boxes

Windows XP Professional and Windows applications use dialog boxes to exchange information with you, the user. Dialog boxes give you a way to specify options and settings in a program. Although most dialog boxes ask you for information, others are only informational and either alert you to a problem or request confirmation for an action you are about to take.

Dialog boxes often have a question mark on the right side of their title bars. The question mark can provide a description of an item. When you see the question mark, you click it and point to the area you want explained. The question mark will then provide you with a *What's This?* pop-up description of the process in question. You may also right-click an item in a dialog box, and What's This? will pop up so that you can get a brief description of the item.

2.8 ● Activity ● Using Help to Learn about Dialog Boxes

1 Click **Start**. Click **Help and Support**. Click **Windows Basics**.

2 In the See Also section of the navigation pane, click **Windows keyboard shortcuts overview**.

3 Click **General keyboard shortcuts**.

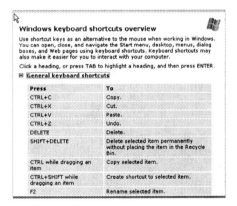

WHAT'S **HAPPENING?** You see information about the different keystrokes you may use, such as pressing the Ctrl + C to copy an item.

4 Collapse the General keyboard shortcuts. Click **Natural keyboard shortcuts**.

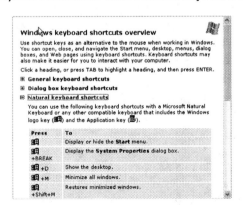

WHAT'S **HAPPENING?** Many new keyboards have a key or keys with the Windows logo. A *logo* is a distinctive signature or trademark that usually functions as a graphical representation of the company. The key with the Windows logo is , with an icon that looks like a waving flag. If you have such a key on your keyboard, this screen tells you how to use it. For instance, pressing the Windows key is a way to open the Start menu. If you scroll down, you will see that to get help, you press the Windows key and the **F1** key. If you are in an application program, pressing the **F1** key will usually bring up Help for that program.

5   In the See Also navigation area, right-click **Windows keyboard shortcuts overview**.

WHAT'S **HAPPENING?** You brought up a menu. One of the choices is to print. You could have also right-clicked in the topics area.

6   Right-click **Natural keyboard shortcuts**. Click **Print**.

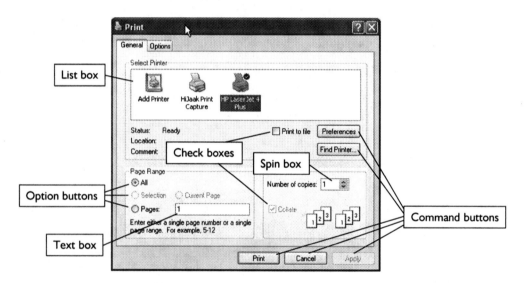

WHAT'S **HAPPENING?** This dialog box presents information about this print job. Your choices may differ depending on what printer you have installed. This dialog box has many elements common to most dialog boxes. The choices that are available are generically called controls. Remember, a control provides a way that a user can interact (provide input) with available choices. Usually a control is a way to initiate an action, display information, or set the values that you are interested in. The controls in this dialog box are as follows:

Command button   A *command button* carries out the command displayed on the button. In this case, the Print command button will cause printing to occur. The Cancel button will cancel the action and close the window. The Apply button will apply the changes without closing the dialog box. The Preferences and Find Printer buttons, when clicked, will open another dialog box.

List box   A *list box* contains a preferred (default) choice. In this case, the default printer is a Hewlett-Packard LaserJet 4 Plus. If you had other printers, you could click that icon to select it or you could click the Add Printer button to add a new printer. This would open the Add Printer wizard.

Option button   Option buttons present mutually exclusive choices; you may choose only one option at a time. The selected option contains a black dot. In this example, an option button under Pages allows you to print either a single page or a range of pages 1 to whatever number you wished. If you highlighted an area prior to choosing print, you could print only that selection.

Text box   A *text box* allows you to key in information. If you were working on a multiple page document, you could determine which pages you wanted to print by clicking the Pages option button and then keying in a range of pages in the from and to text boxes.

Check box   A check box provides a choice that may be enabled or disabled—turned on or off. You have many check boxes from which to choose. They are not mutually exclusive. In this example, the Collate check box is empty—not selected. If you had a multiple page document, you could choose to collate it. The other choices you have are linking when the document is attached in some way to other documents and printing when the document needs to be saved to a file. When you print to a file, you save the document so that it can be printed at a later time. You might choose this option if you do not have a printer available to you.

Spin box   A *spin box* is available in this dialog box for choosing the number of copies to print. A spin box allows you either to increase or to decrease the value in a text box. You may click the up or down arrow to increase or decrease the number of copies you wish to print. When you have to choose a numeric quantity, you usually see a spin box. You may also key a value directly into the text-box portion of the spin box. The Number of copies spin box may not be available to you, depending on the printer you have installed.

7   If your printer allows you to alter the number of copies printed, you will see a spin box. If the spin box is available to you, click the up arrow by Number of copies until you reach 5. If it is not available, read only (do not execute) steps 7 and 8.

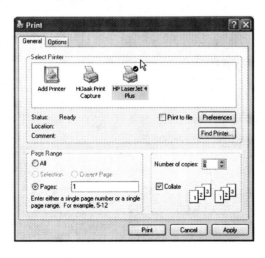

WHAT'S **HAPPENING?** By clicking the up arrow, you increased the number of copies that will be printed. The number 5 is highlighted. Windows XP Professional has a feature called *typing replaces selection* so that, when an item is highlighted (as the number 5 is), you may key in another number, replacing the old number with the new one, without having to delete the old one.

8   Key in the following: **1**

WHAT'S **HAPPENING?** When you keyed in the number 1, you replaced the number 5. You did not have to delete the 5 first. For this to work, the item to be replaced must be highlighted.

9   Click the **Preferences** command button.

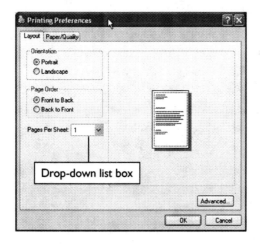

WHAT'S **HAPPENING?** You are looking at your preferences for the printer attached to your system. Your preferences may vary, depending on the printer installed on your system. In this example, there are two tabs from which to choose. Currently, the Layout tab is selected. This sheet has option buttons. You may either print in portrait or landscape; you cannot print in both. *Portrait* orientation is the typical way a document prints, in an 8½-by-11-inch mode. When you print in *landscape* orienta-

tion, you are printing in an 11-by-8½-inch mode (sideways). This property sheet provides a drop-down list box. A *drop-down list box* contains a preferred (default) choice. In this case, the default choice is 1 page per sheet.

10   If available, click the **Advanced** command button.

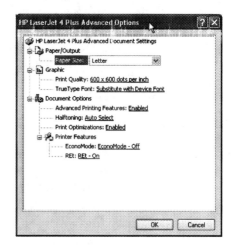

WHAT'S **HAPPENING?** This property sheet includes drop-down list boxes that allow you to choose the paper size as well as the media type. The paper source would select which tray paper is pulled from, if you had multiple trays. The media type would allow you to select from such items as regular paper or transparency paper.

11   Click **Cancel**. Click **Cancel**.

12   Click the question mark on the Print title bar. Click **Print to file**.

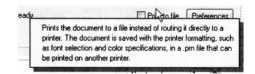

WHAT'S **HAPPENING?** A pop-up description appears telling you what Print to file does.

13   Click outside the pop-up window to close it. Right-click the Collate check box. Click **What's This?**

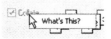

WHAT'S HAPPENING? You see the What's This? pop-up window. You may find out the purpose of an item in a dialog box by either clicking the mark and dragging it to the item in question or by right-clicking the item in question.

14 Click What's This?

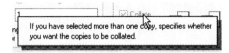

WHAT'S HAPPENING? Here is another way to see a definition or description of an item that you are interested in.

15 Click outside the definition to close it. Click **Print**.

WHAT'S HAPPENING? If you look quickly at the taskbar, you will see a printer icon, indicating that the printer is working. Now you have a hard (printed) copy of the Windows XP Professional shortcut keys.

16 Close all open windows.

WHAT'S HAPPENING? You have returned to the desktop.

2.9 ◦ A Summary of Dialog Boxes

As you can see, dialog boxes are an important part of the Windows XP Professional environment. The controls available will depend on the dialog boxes. A pictorial summary of the controls available in dialog boxes follows.

Check box   Check boxes allow you to turn a selection on or off (set or unset, enable or disable). If an item is set, there is a check mark in the check box. If it is unset, there is no check mark. See Figure 2.2.

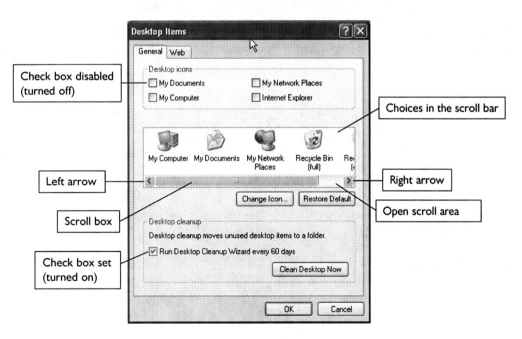

Figure 2.2 ◦ Scroll Bar and Check Boxes

Scroll bar   A scroll bar allows you to move through a document or window. A scroll bar appears automatically, vertically, horizontally, or both, whenever the information is too large to fit into the window. See Figure 2.2. Movement in the scroll bar is as follows:

Left arrow   When you click the left arrow, you move in small increments to the left. To scroll continuously, you hold down the mouse button on the left arrow.

Right arrow   When you click the right arrow, you move in small increments to the right. To scroll continuously, you hold down the mouse button on the right arrow.

Scroll box   When you drag the scroll box, you move quickly through the document. The *scroll box* indicates your relative position in the document. If the scroll box was halfway between the left and right arrows, you would be halfway into your document.

Open scroll area   Clicking the *open scroll area* to the right or left of the scroll box will move you in large increments through the document.

Choices in scroll bar   The selected choice is highlighted. When you click an icon, you make your choice.

Combo box   A *combo box* is a combination of a text box and a list box. You can select from the list or enter your own choice by keying it in. See Figure 2.3.

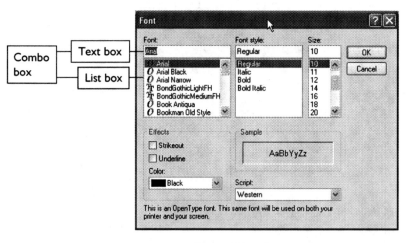

Figure 2.3 • Combo Boxes

Command button   A command button, when clicked, will cause the action on its label to occur. See Figure 2.4.

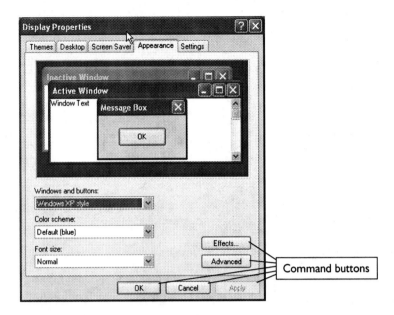

Figure 2.4 ◦ Command Buttons

Drop-down list box   A drop-down list box is a single-line list box. The default, or preferred, choice is in the box. Usually, you must select an entry; you may not leave the list box blank. If you want to see or change your other options, you click on the down arrow. See Figure 2.5.

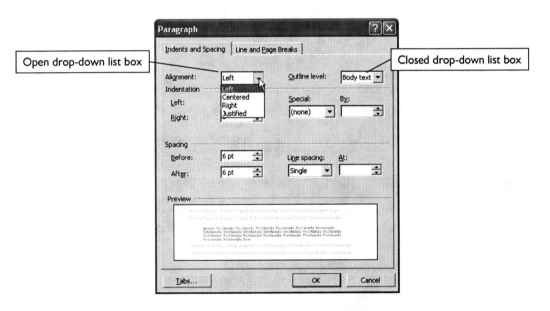

Figure 2.5 ◦ Drop-Down List Boxes

List box   A list box presents you with a list of many possible choices, but there is no preferred choice. Often in a list box, one of the choices is None, indicating that you do not want this option. Many list boxes are accompanied by a scroll bar so that you may scroll through the list. You make a choice by clicking it. See Figure 2.6.

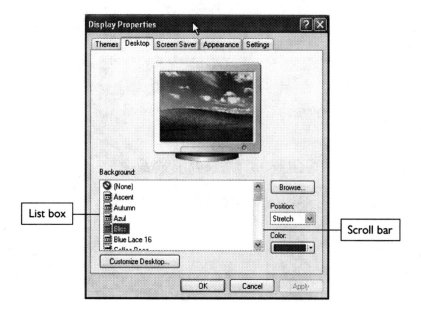

Figure 2.6 ◦ A List Box

Option button   Option buttons present you with a group of related choices from which you can select only one. Remember, an option button presents a group of mutually exclusive choices. See Figure 2.7.

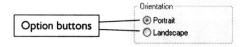

Figure 2.7 ◦ Option Buttons

Sample box   If a choice you make alters the appearance of an object, a *sample box* is displayed to show what will result from your choice. See Figure 2.8.

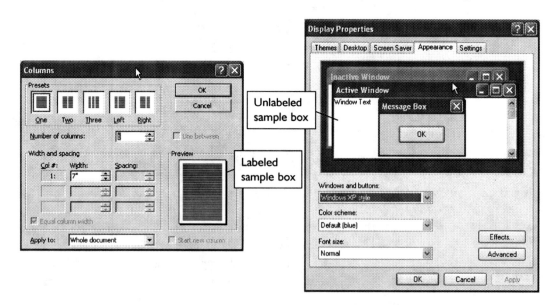

Figure 2.8 ◦ Sample Boxes

Scroll bar

When choices cannot be displayed in one screen, a *scroll bar* is presented either horizontally or vertically so that you may scroll through the choices. See Figure 2.6.

Slider bar

Figure 2.9 shows a slider bar. To make a change, place your mouse on the slider, hold the mouse button down, and slide in the desired direction.

Spin box or spinner

A spin box (or *spinner*) has arrows for increasing or decreasing the value in a text box. See Figure 2.9.

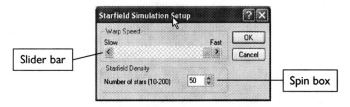

Figure 2.9 ◦ A Spin Box and a Slider Bar

Text box

A text box provides a place to key in your choices. Sometimes your choice will be limited to what already exists. For instance, if you were opening a file, you would need to key in a file name that already exists. On the other hand, if you were saving a new file, you would need to key in a unique new name. Often a text box will present and highlight text. If you wished to keep the highlighted selection, you would simply click OK. If you wanted a different choice, you would key in data over the highlighted choice. See Figure 2.10.

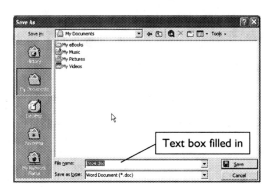
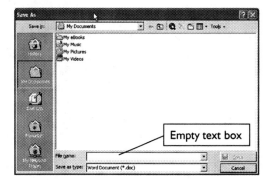

Figure 2.10 ◦ Text Boxes

2.10 ◦ The Help Index

Often when you want help, you are looking for a specific item. If you use the Home page, you have to guess in which area the information you want is located. The Index selection allows you to key in a specific word or phrase. If you wanted help with printing, it would probably be easier to look up printing in the Index sheet than to use the Home page. As in any index, you are limited to predefined words or terms that are listed in the Index.

2.11 ◦ Activity ◦ Using the Index

I   Click **Start**. Click **Help and Support**. Click the **Index** button, 📕 I̲ndex.

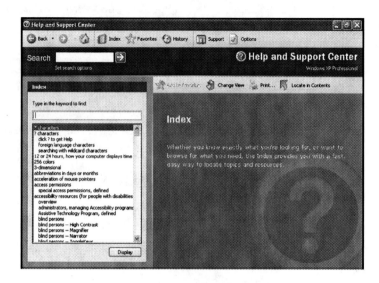

WHAT'S **HAPPENING?** There are two parts to the left frame—a text box and a list box. In the text box, you may key in the information you seek. As you start to key in letters, the list of terms in the list box will begin scrolling to match what you are keying in. Or you can scroll through the list box and select the item of interest. The topics (right frame) will display the help text when you locate it.

2   In the text box, key in the following: **h**

WHAT'S **HAPPENING?** When you keyed in the letter **h**, the items in the list box scrolled down to the first term that begins with the letter **h**. As you continue to key in letters, you will move through the list. Remember, in the next step, you have already keyed in the first letter, **h**.

3   Continue keying in the following: **elp**. Click the **Display** button.

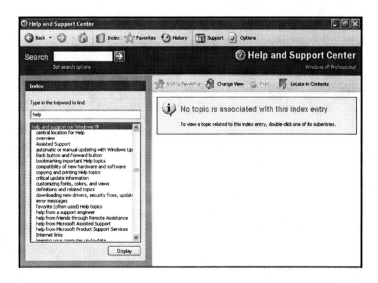

WHAT'S **HAPPENING?** You are at the topic, Help, but the right pane has no information on this general topic displayed. You need to click a subentry.

4   Click **Overview**. Click **Display**.

WHAT'S **HAPPENING?** You are presented with three topics that deal with Help.

5   Double-click **Support Overview**.

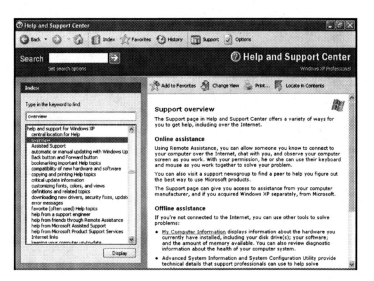

WHAT'S **HAPPENING?** The right frame has a link, indicated by the underlined text, that will take you to information you wish.

6   Click **My Computer Information**.

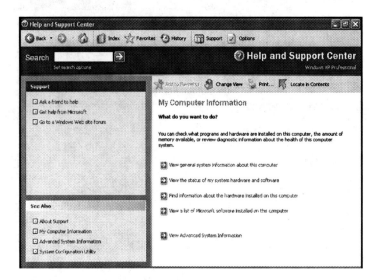

WHAT'S **HAPPENING?** > Now you are asked what it is you wish to do. In this case, you wish to find out information about your computer.

7   Click **View general system information about this computer**.

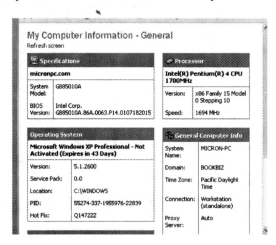

WHAT'S **HAPPENING?** > First information is gathered about your computer, then you see information about your computer.

8   Click the **Index** button.

9   In the text box, key in **Performance**. In the list box, double-click foreground and background programs.

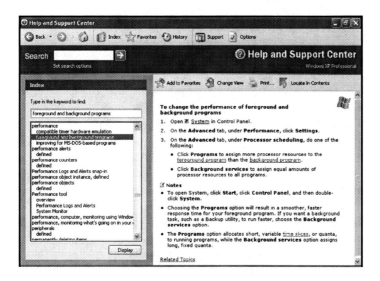

WHAT'S HAPPENING? There is only one topic associated with choice. The right frame has a link as indicated by the right pointing arrow and the underlined term, system, that will take you to the property sheet of interest. It also gives you alternate instructions for accessing this property sheet.

10 Click the link (**System**).

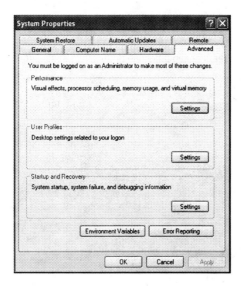

WHAT'S HAPPENING? You were taken to the System Properties property sheet. The Windows Help window remains open. The displayed sheet is Advanced, where Performance is located.

11 Click the **Settings** command button in Performance.

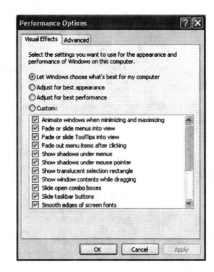

WHAT'S **HAPPENING?** Here is where you can choose how you best want your computer to perform.

12 Click **Cancel**. Click the **General** tab.

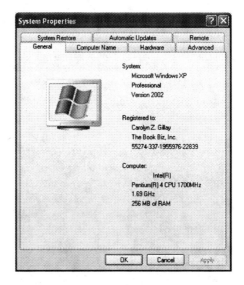

WHAT'S **HAPPENING?** The General property sheet tells you what operating system you are running (Microsoft Windows XP Professional) and the version number (2002). It states to whom the product is registered and the registration number (product identification). If you call Microsoft for technical support, you will be asked for your registration number. Here is where you find it. In addition, you can see what type of processor you have and how much memory is installed on the computer. Your properties will vary. In this example, you also see the manufacturer of the processor (Intel).

13 Click the **Hardware** tab. In the Device Manager section, click the **Device Manager** command button.

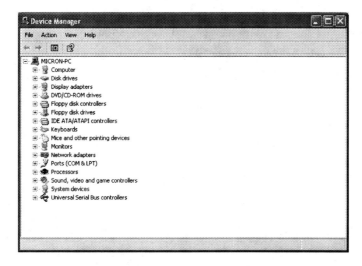

WHAT'S HAPPENING? The Device Manager sheet, which lists all your devices by type, has been selected. Here you can see a list of all the devices on the computer.

14 Click the plus sign in front of Display adapters.

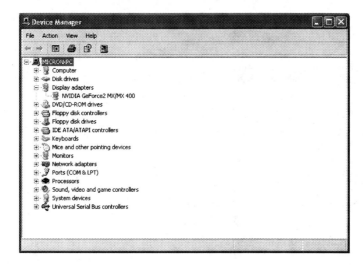

WHAT'S HAPPENING? Not only do you see that you have a device under Display adapters, but you now know which type of video card you have. Each item in the device manager, when expanded, will tell you the type of hardware you have.

15 Close the Device Manager window. Click **Cancel the System Properties sheet**.

16 In the text box, select foreground and background programs. Key in the following: **System Information**

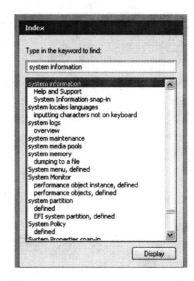

WHAT'S HAPPENING? You are interested in information about your computer system. What you are interested in is the System Information snap-in. A snap-in is a type of tool you can add to your system that is supported by Microsoft Management Console (MMC). A stand-alone snap-in can be added by itself.

17 Double-click **System Information snap-in**.

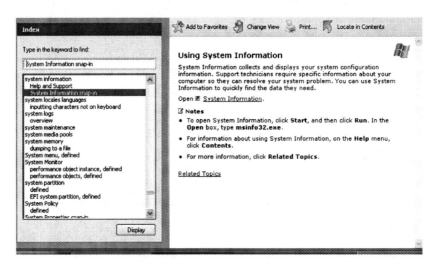

WHAT'S HAPPENING? Again you have a link.

18 Click the **System Information** link.

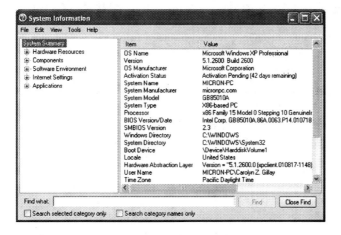

WHAT'S **HALF**PENING? Your system will take a few seconds to refresh the system information prior to displaying it. Again, you have a summary of information about the system.

19 Click the plus sign in front of Hardware Resources. Click **IRQs**.

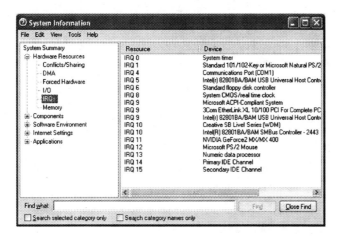

WHAT'S **HAPPENING?** You are currently looking at the interrupt request assignments for each device on your system. The *IRQ (interrupt request)* value is an assigned location where the computer can expect a particular device to interrupt it when the device sends the computer signals about its operation. For example, when a printer has finished printing, it sends an interrupt signal to the computer. The signal momentarily interrupts the computer so that it can decide what processing to do next. Since multiple signals to the computer on the same interrupt line might not be understood by the computer, a unique value must be specified for each device and its path to the computer. Prior to plug-and-play devices, users often had to set IRQ values manually (or be aware of them) when adding a new device to a computer.

If you add a device that does not support Plug and Play, its manufacturer, hopefully, will provide explicit directions on how to assign IRQ values for it. If you do not know what IRQ value to specify, you will probably save time by calling the technical support phone number for the device manufacturer and asking.

20 Close the System Information window. Close Windows Help.

WHAT'S **HAPPENING?** You have returned to the desktop.

2.12 ◦ The Search and Favorites Functions

When you use the Help and Support home page, you must locate information by general topic. When you use Index, you must locate information by a predetermined word or phrase. If you do not know what word or phrase you need, you can use the Search function. It will search for any occurrence of the word or phrase in the entire help file. You may search for any word or phrase in the Help file. Search is most effective when you key in the keywords you are looking for. The Search function is not case sensitive. It will look for either upper- or lowercase terms. The process of searching can be refined by setting options and knowing how to search. The phrase computer monitor will look for the phrase computer monitor before it will look for occurrences of computer then monitor. Hence, searching for monitor computer will find fewer occurrences.

Search also works with Boolean operators. ***Boolean operators*** are based on a mathematical system (Boolean algebra, named after George Boole) and are a cornerstone of logic. It concerns the two truth values (either something is true or something is false). When you key in a term, if the term is found, your query was true, but if it is not found, your query was false. Boolean operators also contain the functions of "and," "or," and "not." If you key in two or more terms and do not specify which operator you wish to use, Search assumes that you have used an "and" operator. An "and" operator search means that all words in your phrase must appear in order for Search to display a result. You may also use the "or" operator. An "or" operator search means that either one term or the other must appear in order for Search to display it in your results. A "not" search specifies that pages with that term will not be displayed in your results. Also, the order of the words in a multiple word query is important. Help and Support enhances the Boolean operators. Using them will narrow your search. See Table 2.1.

Boolean Operator	Search Results
AND	**File** and **Server** will find topics that contain both words. AND is the default.
NEAR	**File** near **server** will find any topics that contain both words near each other.
"Phrase"	The term **"file server"** will find only topics that contain exactly this term. You have quoted the phrase.
OR	The term **file or server** will search for topics that contain the word file or the word server. This expands your search.
NOT	The term file not server will find topics that contain the word file but does not contain the word server. This is a way to narrow your search.

Table 2.1 ◦ Boolean Operators

2.13 ◦ Activity ◦ Using the Search and Favorites Functions

1   Click **Start**. Click **Help and Support**.

2   Under the Search text box, click **Set search options**.

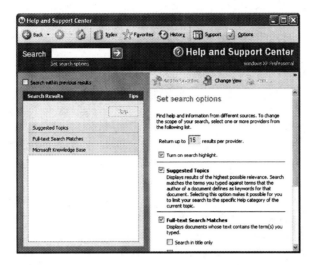

WHAT'S HAPPENING? Here is where you can set how you want to search. Turn on search highlights is selected. This will highlight the term you are searching for. In this example, your search is limited to 15 items.

3 Be sure Turn on search highlight is enabled. Scroll to the bottom of the help window.

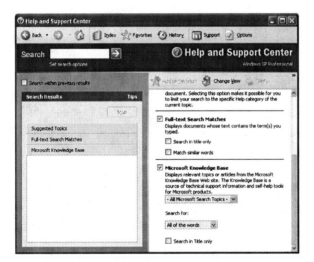

WHAT'S HAPPENING? By default, Search will search for all the words.

4 Click the down arrow in the Search for drop-down list box.

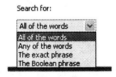

WHAT'S HAPPENING? Here is where you can set the options for the terms or keywords you wish to search for.

5 Click **The Boolean phrase**.

6 In the Search text box, key in the following: **system information**. Click the arrow next to the Search text box (the Go arrow).

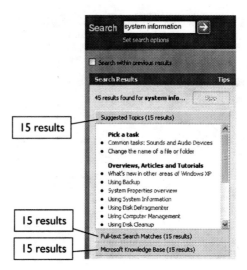

WHAT'S HAPPENING? You keyed in a multiple word search phrase. You are interested in help about your system.   There were a total of 45 results located, 15 in each area. Your results may differ.

7   In the Suggested Topics list box, click **Using System Information**.

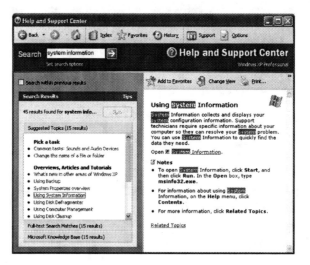

WHAT'S HAPPENING? The word System is highlighted wherever it appears. If you wanted to refer to this section of help again? Windows XP allows you to place it in Favorites so you can easily locate this topic again. It does not matter where you are in help, you can always add it to your Favorites.

8   Click the **Add to Favorites** button, .

WHAT'S HAPPENING? You are informed that this topic has been added to your Help and Support Favorites list.

9   Click **OK**. In the Search text box, key in **system or information**. Click the Go arrow.

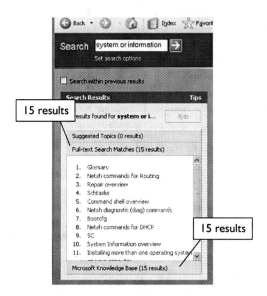

WHAT'S HAPPENING? You added an "or" operator to your search query. Now only 30 results are found. Your results may vary.

10 Click **System Information Overview**.

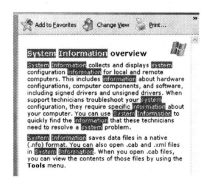

WHAT'S HAPPENING? Your search results now display both your search key words, system and information. You decide your previous view that took you to the system information window. You can use the Favorites that you added.

11 On the navigation bar, click the Favorites button, ☆ F<u>a</u>vorites .

WHAT'S HAPPENING? Your topic is listed. To go to the topic, you would double-click it or click it and then click the Display command button.

12 Click **Using System Information** to select it.

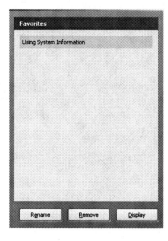

WHAT'S HAPPENING? Now that you have selected the topic, the command buttons, Rename, Remove and Display, are available.

13 Click **Remove**.

14 Close the Help and Support window.

WHAT'S HAPPENING? You have returned to the desktop.

2.14 • Using Help and Support to Solve Problems

You have learned that Help allows you to explore in different ways and to learn more about the features of Windows XP Professional. There is another aspect of Help and Support that is important: Help and Support as a problem solver.

When you work with computers, the chance that problems will occur is high, no matter whether you are a new or an experienced user. In fact, the only difference between a beginning and an experienced user is that an experienced user can get into more trouble faster! A fact of life in the computer world is getting into trouble and then getting out of trouble.

Help and Support is one tool that can assist you in solving your computer problems. Many users do not try to analyze what their problem is or try to get assistance; they simply repeat the same steps over and over again, to no avail. For instance, if a document will not print, repeatedly clicking the Print button will not magically make the document print. If the document did not print the first time you clicked Print, it will not print the 45th time you click it. In fact, you can create more problems for yourself by repeating the steps that did not work. A rule of thumb is that, if something does not work the first or second time you try it, you need to analyze the problem. One of the places you can go for assistance is Help. Furthermore, Windows XP Professional includes *troubleshooters* in its help. These are step-by-step guides to assist you in analyzing and solving a problem.

In the next activity, you are going to use the Print troubleshooter. You are going to open a document and try to print it. You are going to state that your document will not print and you do not know why. You will see the process that a troubleshooter (and you) should go through. You will take steps to determine the problem and then try solutions one at a time. You are analyzing the problem by breaking it down into each component and logically trying to find a solution.

2.15 • Activity • Using a Troubleshooter to Solve a Printing Problem

Note: If you are on a network and do not have a local printer, you will not be able to do this activity completely. If that is the case, just read steps 1 through 14, and begin the activity with step 15.

1   If you have a local printer, turn it off.

2   Place in Drive A the XPRODATA disk that came with this textbook.

3   Click **Start**. Click **My Computer**. Double-click the Drive A icon.

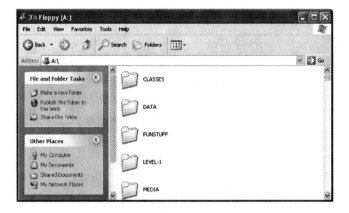

WHAT'S **HAPPENING?** You have "opened" the disk drive. Opening a drive means opening the drive window to see what files and folders are on the disk.

4   Click **View**. Click **Icons**.

5   Click **View**. Point to **Arrange Icons by**. Click **Name**.

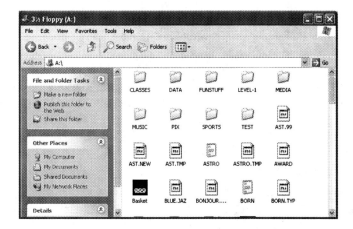

WHAT'S **HAPPENING?** The items that look like folders represent directories. They are shown first. The other icons represent files in the root directory of the disk in Drive A.

6   Scroll through the window until you locate the file called Dances.

7   Double-click **Dances**.

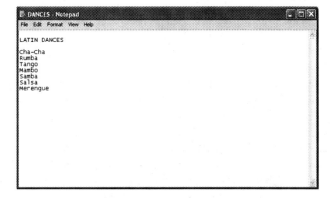

WHAT'S **HAPPENING?** You have opened the document (file) called Dances. Whenever you open a document, you must first open the application program that created the document. In most cases, when you have created a document with a program, the program has formatted the data in the document. This kind of formatting refers to information such as the size of the margins, the tab settings, the line spacing, and the size of the typeface. To display the document properly, the program places unique computer codes in the document for each formatting feature.

In this example, the program that created the Dances document is Notepad. Notepad is a *text editor*. A text editor may also be called an ***ASCII editor***. ***ASCII*** (American Standard Code for Information Interchange) is a standard format for documents created in a text editor. An ASCII file is one that has no embedded formatting codes. The file is only text.

Although Notepad is an ASCII editor, it is still a program. One of the features that all Windows applications have in common is a menu bar. A menu bar has choices. File is usually the first choice, with Help being the last choice. One of the advantages of working with application programs in Windows XP Professional is that, once you learn how to do a task in one program, you know how to do it in other programs. Tasks are accomplished the same way in the other programs. As you begin working with Windows XP Professional programs, you will begin to recognize these common elements.

8   Click **File**.

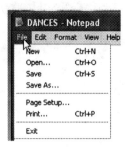

WHAT'S **HAPPENING?** The File menu lists the common tasks you use to manipulate a data file. The data file, your document, is called Dances. It is actually called Dances.txt. The .txt file extension indicates the program that created the data. If Windows XP Professional knows the program, it will not display the file extension unless you request it. The Notepad program allows you to create a new file (New), open a previously created file (Open), save your file to a disk (Save), save your file to a disk under a different name (Save As), change the way the document appears on the page (Page Setup), print a hard copy of the file (Print), and close the program (Exit). When you close the program, you close the file (document) as well.

9   Click outside the menu to close it.

10   In the Notepad window, click **File**. Click **Print**. Click **Print**. (Look at the status area in the taskbar. *Note:* If you are on a network with no local printer, the page will be printed on the network printer. Read the following steps, but do not do them.)

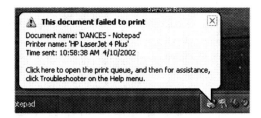

WHAT'S **HAPPENING?** You immediately get a message telling you that the document did not print. It also tells you what to do in order to solve the problem. If you look on the taskbar, you will also see that the printer icon has a question mark in a red circle, which is a visual representation of the problem. If you ignore the help and simply try and print the document again, you will see no message.

11   Click **File**. Click **Print**. Click **Print**.

12   Right-click the printer icon on the taskbar.

WHAT'S HAPPENING? You open the Printer menu. The bottom line tells you that there is an error on this printer.

13 Click **Open All Active Printers and Faxes**.

WHAT'S HAPPENING? When you clicked print a second time, all you did was line up the documents to be printed. Your document did not print but instead was placed in a queue. If you solve the printing problem, then all the documents would print that were in the queue. You can see that repeatedly clicking Print without solving the printer problem would simply print many copies of the same document.

14 Click the bottom copy of DANCES – Notepad to select it. On the menu bar, click **Document**.

WHAT'S HAPPENING? You may cancel the printing of this document. In this menu one of the choices is Cancel. Canceling a print document removes not the document, but its place in the print lineup. Windows XP Professional lines up (*queues*) print jobs. Since printing is a hardware-related process, it is much slower than any process that occurs in memory. Windows XP Professional manages the printing and feeds data to the printer as the printer becomes available. This print management feature frees up computer resources so that you may work on other tasks while Windows manages the printing.

15 Click **Cancel**.

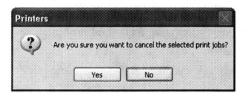

WHAT'S HAPPENING? You are asked if you are sure you want to cancel.

16 Click **Yes**. On the menu bar, click **Help**.

WHAT'S HAPPENING? One of the choices is Troubleshooter. This will help you diagnose your printing problem.

17 Click **Troubleshooter**. Maximize the Help and Support Center window.

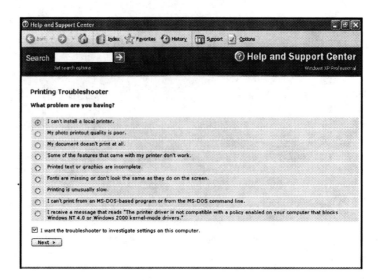

WHAT'S HAPPENING? You see a list of questions about what type of problem you are having and a list of options to determine the problem.

18 Click **My document doesn't print at all**. Click Next.

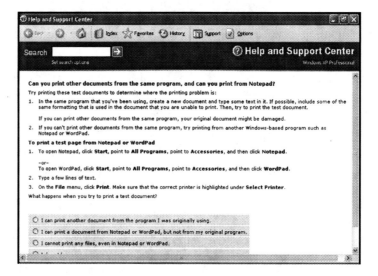

WHAT'S HAPPENING? You see another question that is trying to narrow the focus of the problem. It suggests that you create a document in the current program and then try to print. The troubleshooter is trying to determine if your document is the problem or if the program is the problem.

19 Scroll to the bottom of the window. Select **I cannot print any files, even in Notepad or WordPad**. Click **Next**.

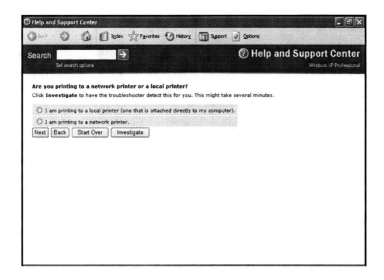

WHAT'S **HAPPENING?** It is asking a question about a local printer and a network printer and telling you how you can tell which is which. Your command buttons allow you to continue (Next), go back a step (Back), begin again (Start Over), or have the troubleshooter try to solve the problem (Investigate).

20 Click **I'm printing to a local printer (one that is attached directly to my computer).** Click **Next**.

WHAT'S **HAPPENING?** You see other questions that give you options to try.

21 Click **I want to skip this step and try something else.** Click **Next**.

WHAT'S HAPPENING? Again, the troubleshooter is trying to help you determine the cause of the problem. One of the items has a plus sign in front of it (To determine whether your printer is set to offline use) indicating that it can be expanded.

22 Click the plus sign.

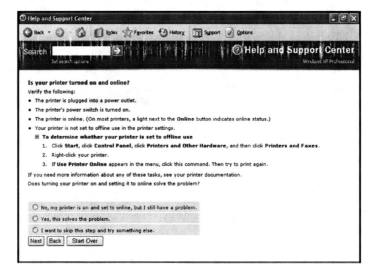

WHAT'S HAPPENING? You see a set of steps to see if your printer is set to offline use. But this window provided a solution to your problem—your printer is turned off. You have been performing an analysis of why you are having a problem. In this case, you knew why—you turned off the printer. Most often, you do not know what the problem is. Again, remember that a common problem users have when running into something that does not work is that they take the same steps over and over again, which simply compounds the problem. A good rule of thumb when having problems is that, if you take the same steps more than three times, you should stop and perform an analysis.

The first step in an analysis is to determine the problem. With computers, the cause of a problem is either hardware or software. By a process of elimination, try to determine which category the problem falls into. Ask the obvious first. In this example, the obvious is "Is the printer plugged in? Is it turned on? Is it online?" In this case, when referring to a printer, *online* means not only is the printer attached to the computer and to electric power, but it is also activated and ready to use. If all these items were true, it probably would not be a hardware problem, but a software problem. In the example you are using, you do have a hardware problem, not a software problem. You can carry your inquiry further by taking a different direction.

23 Click the minus sign to collapse the topic. Click **Yes, this solves the problem**. Click **Next**.

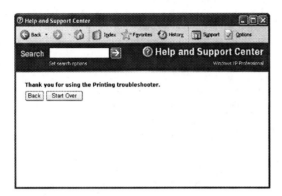

WHAT'S **HAPPENING?** ⇒ You have used the Troubleshooter. The objective of the troubleshooter is to try to analyze the different parts of the problem. It breaks down the problem into various aspects and tries different solutions to assist you. The lesson here is that, when you have problems, try to analyze them, use Help and Support, and use Troubleshooters.

24 Close the Help and Support window. Turn on the printer.

WHAT'S **HAPPENING?** ⇒ A few seconds will pass while the printer warms up. Then the document will print. The Printers window closes.

25 Close Notepad. Close the Drive A window. Remove the XPRODATA disk from Drive A.

26 Click **Start**. Click **Help and Support**. Click **Fixing a Problem**. Click **Troubleshooting Problems**.

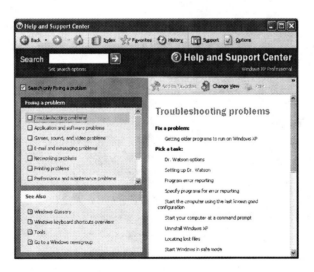

WHAT'S **HAPPENING?** ⇒ Here is a list of all the available troubleshooters.

27 Close the Help and Support window.

WHAT'S **HAPPENING?** ⇒ You have returned to the desktop.

Chapter Summary

This chapter introduced you to using the Help feature available in Windows XP Professional. You also learned how to install and remove Windows XP Professional components. To access Help and Support, you may click Start and then Help and Support.. You found that there are many ways to use Help: the Home page, the Index, Tours, and Search. The Home page is arranged by topic. The Index is arranged by keywords and phrases. You may go to different Internet sites to help research your problem. Tours demonstrates different features within Windows XP Professional. Search searches the database of all the words in the Help files. In addition, you can use the Boolean operators of "and," "or," or "not" to further refine your search technique.

You found that Help, in addition to providing the necessary steps to accomplish a task, will often have a Click here phrase that will take you to the window you need. You also learned that Help provides a What's This? feature that, when activated, presents definitions of a term. What's This? may be activated by clicking the question mark in a dialog box and dragging it to the item of interest or by right-clicking the item of interest.

You were introduced to the different types of dialog boxes and common controls in dialog boxes, and you learned about the controls that allow you to manipulate your actions. Common controls include list boxes, command buttons, option buttons, drop-down list boxes, text boxes, check boxes, spin boxes, combo boxes, scroll bars, scroll boxes, and sample boxes.

You used Troubleshooters in Help to solve a problem, and you found that, when you have a problem, you need to perform an analysis in order to solve it.

Key Terms

ASCII	landscape	scroll box
ASCII editor	list box	spin box
Boolean operators	logo	spinner
combo box	online	text box
command button	open scroll area	text editor
drop-down list box	portrait	troubleshooter
hovering	queue	typing replaces selection
hypertext	sample box	What's This?
IRQ (interrupt request)	scroll bar	

Discussion Questions

1. Describe how you could find out if you had any missing Windows XP Professional components.
2. List the steps to add or remove Windows XP Professional components.
3. Explain what is meant by online help capabilities.
4. Help in Windows XP Professional is a hypertext utility. Explain.
5. What is the purpose and function of the question mark icon in a dialog box?
6. Compare and contrast the ways Help is organized.
7. What purpose does an underlined term serve in the topics window?
8. What is a control?
9. Explain the purpose and function of command buttons and option buttons.
10. Explain the purpose and function of a check box and a spin box.
11. What is the purpose and function of a text box?
12. Compare and contrast a list box and a drop-down list box.

13. Compare and contrast portrait printing with landscape printing.
14. What types of information can be found on the System Properties property sheet?
15. Why is system information a useful utility?
16. What are Boolean operators? Identify each and describe its purpose.
17. Identify two Search options and their purpose.
18. If you have a problem with your computer, what might be the first step you should take?
19. What is a print queue?
20. What is a troubleshooter? How can it be used?

True/False Questions

For each question, circle the letter T if the statement is true or the letter F if the statement is false.

T   F   1. There is no way to add a missing component in Windows XP Professional. All features must be installed at the time of the original installation.

T   F   2. Help is a hypertext utility.

T   F   3. When you see check boxes in a dialog box, more than one check box may be selected.

T   F   4. All windows will automatically display a scroll bar.

T   F   5. If you attempt to print and are unsuccessful, continue clicking File and Print until your document prints.

Completion Questions

Write the correct answer in each blank space.

6. Windows XP Professional provides _____ Help, which minimizes the need for printed manuals.

7. If you click the _____ in a Help dialog box and then click a word or phase, you will see a brief definition of the item.

8. If you select _____, you are presented with a list of predetermined topics.

9. A(n) _____ has a set of arrows used to increase or decrease the value in a text box.

10. If you use the Search text box, you may use any of the three Boolean operators, _____, _____, or _____.

Multiple Choice Questions

Circle the letter of the correct answer for each question.

11. When adding or removing Windows XP Professional components, you see a grayed check box with a check mark in it, which means that
    a. the component you want is unavailable.
    b. all the components have been selected.
    c. some, but not all, of the components have been selected.
    d. none of the components has been selected.

12. If you click a phrase that has an underline in the topics window, you
    a. will open a menu.
    b. will open a pop-up window with a definition of the phrase.
    c. will note this item as extremely important.
    d. will open an annotation window.

13. If you knew the word or phrase you wanted help on, the fastest way to find what you needed in Help and Support would be to key in the phrase in the Search text box or use
    a. Index.
    b. the Home page.
    c. Favorites.
    d. Pick a Help Topic.
14. When Windows XP Professional is printing a document, a
    a. printer icon appears on the taskbar.
    b. menu appears on the taskbar with printing options.
    c. both a and b
    d. neither a nor b
15. Option buttons
    a. present choices that may be paired together.
    b. are available only in the Print menu.
    c. present mutually exclusive choices.
    d. are available in every dialog box.

Application Assignments

Problem Set I—At the Computer

Problem A

* Click **Start**.

* Click **Help and Support**.

* Click **Customizing your computer**.

* Click **Windows keyboard shortcuts overview**.

* Click **General Keyboard shortcuts**.

    1. Which key(s) do you press to cancel the current task?
        a. [Alt] + the underlined letter
        b. [Enter]
        c. [Esc]
        d. [Ctrl]

* Collapse General keyboard shortcuts. Click **Natural keyboard shortcuts**.

    2. You may display help and support by pressing the Windows key and the _____ key.
        a. [F1]
        b. H
        c. [F3]
        d. [Shift]

* Collapse Natural keyboard shortcuts. Click **Accessibility keyboard shortcuts**. Click **Related Topics**. Click **Change StickyKey options**.

    3. What is the purpose of StickyKeys?
        a. StickyKeys is designed for people who have difficulty holding down two or more keys simultaneously.
        b. StickyKeys is an instruction that tells your keyboard to ignore brief or repeated keystrokes.

    c. StickyKeys is an instruction that tells the computer to play a high sound when certain keys are turned on and a low sound when they are turned off.

    d. StickyKeys allows you to use the numeric keypad to move the mouse pointer and to click, double-click, and drag.

※ Close all open windows. Be sure Help and Support is closed.

Problem B

※ Right-click the desktop.

※ Click **Properties**.

※ Click the **Desktop** tab.

    4. To choose a background, you must use a(n)

      a. check box.

      b. drop-down list box.

      c. list box.

      d. option button.

※ Click the **Screen Saver** tab.

    5. *Settings* is an example of a(n)

      a. check box.

      b. command button.

      c. option button.

      d. slider bar.

※ Click the **Appearance** tab.

    6. *Color scheme* is an example of a(n)

      a. check box.

      b. drop-down list box.

      c. list box.

      d. option button.

※ Click the **Effects** button.

    7. *Use large icons* is an example of a(n)

      a. list box.

      b. text box.

      c. drop-down list box.

      d. check box.

※ Click Cancel. Click the **Settings** tab.

※ Click the question mark icon on the title bar and click **Screen resolution**.

    8. The higher the number of _____ you have, the more information you can display on your screen.

      a. colors

      b. velocity

      c. pixels

      d. 32-bit high color

* Close all dialog boxes.

Problem C

* Click **Start**.
* Click **Help and Support**.
* Click **Index**.
* In the text box, key in the following: **colors**
* Click changing on desktop. Click the **Display** command button.

   9. How many topics appeared?
       a. one
       b. two
       c. three
       d. four
       e. zero

* Click To customize a background color.
* Click the **Display** command button.
* Click the **Display** link.

   10. You are taken to a
        a. property sheet about Desktop.
        b. property sheet about Themes.
        c. property sheet about Settings.
        d. property sheet about Help.

* Return to the desktop by closing all dialog boxes and open windows.

Problem D

* Click **Start**.
* Click **Help and Support**.
* In the Search text box, key in the following: **desktop and appearance**
* Click the **Go** button.

   11. In Suggested Topics, how many topics appeared?
        a. 2
        b. 4
        c. 6
        d. 8
        e. 10

* In the Search text box, key in the following: **colors or desktop**

   12. In Suggested Topics, which is the first topic listed?
        a. Add web content to your desktop.
        b. Changing the color or size of items on the desktop.
        c. Use a picture as a desktop background.
        d. Change the number of colors displayed on a monitor.

* In the Search text box, key in the following: **colors not desktop**

13. In Suggested Topics, which is the first topic listed?
   a. Add web content to your desktop.
   b. Changing the color or size of items on the desktop.
   c. Use a picture as a desktop background.
   d. Change the number of colors displayed on a monitor.

❖ Return to the desktop by closing all dialog boxes and open windows.

Problem E

❖ Place the XPRODATA disk that came with this textbook in Drive A.

❖ Click **Start**.

❖ Click **My Computer**.

❖ Double-click the icon for Drive A.

❖ Locate the file called Astro that has the following icon:

❖ Right-click **Astro**.

❖ Click **Properties** on the menu.

14. The document, Astro, is a
   a. Write file.
   b. Text document.
   c. Word file.
   d. WordPerfect file.

15. In Attributes, Read-only is an example of a
   a. check box.
   b. drop-down list box.
   c. list box.
   d. text box.

❖ Close the property sheet.

❖ Double-click **Astro**.

❖ On the menu bar, click **Help**.

❖ Click **Help Topics**.

❖ Click **Index**.

❖ In the text box, key in **erasing text**.

❖ Click **Display**.

16. The window that you just opened has a title bar. The name in its title bar is
   a. Windows Help.
   b. Windows XP Professional Help.
   c. Notepad
   d. Note Help.

17. In order to delete text, you must first _____ it.
   a. copy
   b. edit
   c. paste
   d. select

❖ Close Help and Support.

* Close the document.
* Close all open windows and return to the desktop.
* Remove the XPRODATA disk.

Problem F

* Click **Start**.
* Click **Help and Support**.
* Click **Fixing a problem**.
* Click **Games, sound, and video problems**.
* Click **Sound Troubleshooter**.
* Click **I do not hear sound from my computer's speakers or headphones**. Click **Next**.
* Click **My speakers cannot play system sounds**. Click **Next**.

  18. How may you check your volume controls?
      a. click the Volume Control icon.
      b. Click Start. Point to All Programs. Point to Accessories. Point to Entertainment. Click Volume Control.
      c. either a or b
      d. neither a nor b

* Close Windows Help and Support.

Problem Set II—Brief Essay

1. You want to learn more about print queues. In Help and Support, use Pick a Help Topic, Search, and Index to try to locate this information.
   a. Compare and contrast the methods you used to locate help on this topic.
   b. Which method did you prefer and why?
   c. Which method gave you the best results and answered your question?
2. What steps would you take to find out which Windows XP Professional components were installed on your system? How could you find out which components are missing? How would you install the missing components? If you could not load all the components because of limited disk space, what components would you choose to install and why? Which would you choose to uninstall and why?

Problem Set III—Scenario

A friend of yours has just purchased a computer with Windows XP Professional installed on it. She does not understand the use of dialog boxes and the controls that are in dialog boxes. Write her a letter explaining the concepts of controls. Remember, controls are items such as command buttons, option buttons, text boxes, and so forth.

CHAPTER 3

Viewing Files and Folders in My Computer

In this chapter, you are introduced to program files and data files. You will learn about the hierarchical structure of disks. You will find that locating files and folders is an important part of using Windows XP Professional, and My Computer is one tool you use. You will learn how to manipulate the way your files and folders appear, and you will learn to differentiate between a program and a docucentric approach. You will find that the Documents menu gives you easy access to your data files. You will be introduced to the Registry, which allows Windows XP Professional to know which program to use to open a data file. You will learn the importance of file types and how the Registry uses them to determine the program used to open a data file. You will learn how to register your own file extensions.

Learning Objectives

1. Compare and contrast program files and data files.
2. List the file naming rules.
3. Explain the purpose and function of folders.
4. Describe the purpose of the hierarchical structure of disks and the root directory's role in this structure.
5. Explain the purpose and function of My Computer.
6. Describe the various ways to view and browse files and folders.
7. Explain the purpose and function of the Documents menu.
8. Compare and contrast the program method and the docucentric method of accomplishing a task.
9. Explain the purpose and function of file types.
10. Explain the purpose and function of the Registry.

Student Outcomes

1. Alter how files and folders are displayed.
2. Manipulate ways of browsing files and folders.
3. Clear the Documents menu.
4. Use Notepad to open a file.
5. Use the Documents menu to open a file.
6. Use the File Types dialog box.
7. Register a file extension with the Registry.
8. Remove a file extension's registration.

3.1 ● Files and Folders

Nearly all the work you do on a computer has do to with files. When you work with a file, it is stored in memory. When you are not working with a file, it can be permanently stored on a disk. There are two major types of computer files: program files and data files. *Program files* are applications that allow the user to solve some type of problem, such as a payroll application that lets the user create and maintain a payroll system for a company. Program files are step-by-step instructions that direct a computer to do something—resolve the user's problem. Program files are also called *application packages*, *software packages*, *software*, or just *apps*.

Generally, you purchase programs so you can create data files. *Data files* are files that contain information generated by the user, typically with an application program. Most often, only an application program can use data files directly. Data files are also called documents or *document files*.

You do not purchase a computer to run Windows XP Professional. You purchase a computer to write letters, manage your checkbook, prepare your taxes, or create a budget. Before computers, many individuals or small businesses would employ someone else to do these tasks. Often, the individual or business could not support a full-time employee for each job. Therefore, an employment agency would be used to hire temporary employees on an as-needed basis: a secretary to write letters, a bookkeeper to manage checkbooks, and an accountant to prepare taxes.

In the computer world, you have greater flexibility. Instead of contracting temporary employees, you purchase application packages—program files that help you do your work. These application packages fall into generic categories, such as word-processing and spreadsheet programs, similar to categories of employees, such as secretaries and accountants. You might have a favorite employee at the agency, so instead of requesting a secretary, you would specifically request Mr. Woo; or instead of requesting an accountant, you would specifically request Ms. Brown.

You do the same in the computer world. Instead of purchasing just any word-processing and spreadsheet programs, you ask for WordPerfect (the secretary) and Peachtree (the accountant). There are many choices of applications. To do word processing, you could choose WordPerfect, Microsoft Word, or Ami Pro. Your favorite money-management program might be Managing Your Money instead of Quicken. These application packages are "temporary employees" because you call on them specifically when you need to perform tasks that only they can accomplish. The ones that suit your needs are your favorites.

In order for these programs to do work, they must be placed in random access memory (RAM), the workspace of the computer. When they are not working, they are stored on a disk as files. Windows XP Professional is like the office manager of the temporary employment agency. You tell Windows XP Professional what work you want to do, and Windows XP Professional will go to the disk to get the correct program file and place it in RAM. Windows XP Professional then lets the work begin by *executing the program*.

Data files are the second part of the equation. Even though the secretary—Word—can create letters for anyone, you are interested only in *your* letters. Once you create the data, you want to keep it. Remember, all the work is occurring in RAM, which is volatile (temporary). In order to retain the information permanently, you direct Word to write (save) the information to a disk as a data file. Word does not actually save the data; it turns this task over to Windows XP Professional, which writes the file to a disk. When you need to retrieve the data file, Word again turns to Windows XP Professional, which then reads the disk to get the appropriate data file and delivers it to Word. The job of program files is to create and edit the data within a data file. One important job of Windows XP Professional is to read and write program and data files to and from disks and memory.

A name must be assigned to each file so that Windows XP Professional can identify and locate it. Certain rules must be followed when you name files. First, a file name must be unique. Second, the name length must range from 1 to 255 characters. Third, the file name is broken into two parts: a *file name* and a *file extension*. The file name describes or identifies the file, and the file extension identifies the type of data in the file. In Windows XP Professional, the file extension is referred to as the *file type*. Fourth, file names cannot contain the following characters: \ / : * ? " < > |.

Program files have predetermined names: Winword.exe for Word, Qw.exe for Quicken, and Excel.exe for Microsoft Excel. Data files, on the other hand, are named by the user. You may call a file anything you want, such as Letter to my sister, as long as you follow the naming conventions. You will find that, typically, a program such as Word will assign a file extension to your data file (document), so that the actual file name becomes Letter to my sister.doc. Now you, Word, and Windows XP Professional know what program created the data file.

Data files are generated by specific application programs, and the information or data in them can be altered or viewed only within the respective program. You do not give your tax information to the secretary to make changes. You would give the tax data to your accountant. A data file may be used only in conjunction with the application program that created it. Again, the job of Windows XP Professional is to fetch and carry both program and data files in and out of memory and to and from a disk (reading and writing).

To assist you in organizing your files, disks are divided into what are called *folders*. *Folder* is the Windows XP Professional name for a ***directory***. Folders are containers for objects, typically files. The objects in a folder may be opened into windows. Folders may have ***subfolders***. Subfolders is the Windows XP Professional name for ***subdirectories***. Folders allow you to group related objects such as program or data files so that they will be easy to locate at a later date.

A primary directory (the root) is automatically created when you prepare a disk to store information. It is called the root, but its symbol is \ (backslash). Under the root, you create additional folders and subfolders for storing related files. For example, all the program files related to a spreadsheet program such as Excel could be stored in a directory named Excel. You might then group any data files you created with Excel, such as Budget for 2000 and Budget for 2001, in another folder named Budgets, so that, when you wanted to locate Budget for 2000, it would be in the directory called Budgets. Office personnel have been using a similar organization process for years; related documents are filed in labeled file folders and then stored inside filing cabinets.

3.2 • The Hierarchical Structure: Files and Folders

My Computer is one way to locate files and folders on a disk. When you open My Computer, a window opens displaying the disk drives on your computer, such as Drive A, Drive C, and Drive D. Each disk drive icon in My Computer may be opened into another window which displays the files or folders on that drive. Folders may hold files and other folders, which may, in turn, hold other files and other folders.

If you double-clicked the Drive C icon, you would open a window showing all the folders and files on Drive C. One of the folders is usually called Windows. If you double-clicked the Windows folder, you would open another window showing the operating system files and folders. Each folder you open is dependent on the folder above it. This multiple-level structure forms a hierarchy. A *hierarchy* is a group of things ordered by rank; you begin at the top and work your way down through each subsequent level. In the Windows XP Professional hierarchy, you always begin at the root directory (the top-level directory) and work your way down through all the levels.

In Chapter 1, when you were seeking Notepad, you clicked Start, pointed at All Programs, pointed at Accessories, and then clicked Notepad. These steps led you through the hierarchical structure. A folder named Documents and Settings is under the root of C. Separate folders for each user name are under the Documents and Settings folder. (When you logged onto the system, you entered a user name. The user name is a label that identifies you to Windows XP Professional.) A Start Menu folder appears under each user name folder. Programs is a folder under each Start Menu folder. Accessories is a folder under each Programs folder. Then, finally, inside the Accessories folder you find a file named Notepad. In Chapter 2, when you accessed Help and Support, the files are kept in a folder called Help, which was under the folder called Windows, which was under the root of C. The root (\) is always the top of the hierarchy. Figure 3.1 illustrates a hierarchy.

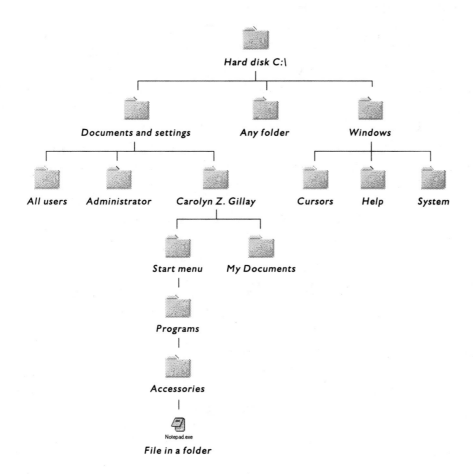

*Figure 3.1 * A Hierarchical Structure*

3.3 * Viewing Files and Folders

You constantly use My Computer to locate disk drives, files, and folders. Windows XP Professional provides you with many ways to view them. When you first open My Computer, the default settings for viewing and browsing your files and folders are already selected, if you have not set your own. The default settings for My Computer are Status Bar off, Standard Buttons toolbar on with Text Labels on with text labels appearing on the right, Address Bar toolbar on, Toolbars locked, Explorer Bar off, and Tiles arranged by Name with AutoArrange on.

How you browse folders is also preset. But you can customize the view and the browse settings. For instance, you can view the files as Tiles, Icons, as a List, by file Details, or by Thumbnails. You can choose to arrange your files by Name, Size, Modified (by date altered), or Type (file extension). You can have Windows XP Professional automatically arrange your icons in rows and columns along an invisible grid. You can also choose to browse the folders in different ways. In the next activity, you will learn how to customize your settings.

3.4 ● Activity ● Changing Views

Note 1: In order for the examples in this textbook to look and work the same, you must use the files and folders in the XPRODATA directory. These practice files and folders should be installed to the hard drive from the XPRODATA disk that comes with this textbook. You should not use the floppy disk for the activities. You must use the XPRODATA folder that has been installed on the hard disk.

Note 2: **Working in a lab.** If you are in a lab environment, the XPRODATA folder (directory) created from the XPRODATA disk probably has been set up for you. You will need to find out on which drive the XPRODATA folder has been installed. (It will probably not be Drive C.) Check with your lab instructor for the procedures in your lab environment.

Working on your own computer. If you are working on your own computer, you must first install the files from the XPRODATA disk to the hard disk before proceeding. Instructions for installing XPRODATA are located in Appendix A. You cannot just copy the folder from the disk to the hard disk; there is a special procedure you must follow.

I   Click **Start**. Click **My Computer**. Click **View**. Click **Tiles**.

2   Click **View**. Point to **Arrange Icons by:**. Click **Type**.

3   Click **View**. Point to **Arrange Icons by:**. If **Show in Groups** does not have a check mark by it, click it.

4   Click **View**.

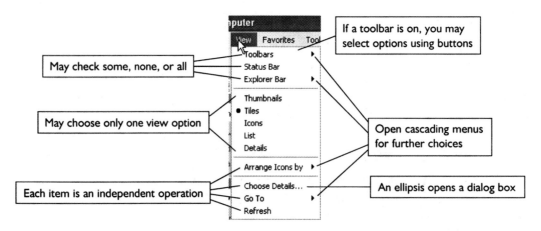

WHAT'S HAPPENING? ⟩ You have opened the View menu, which is divided into sections. If there is a check mark in a section, you may choose any number of the options (similar to check boxes that appear in dialog boxes). If there is a dot (an option button), you may make only one choice in that section (similar to option buttons that appear in dialog boxes). Any item with an ellipsis indicates that a dialog box will open. Any item without a symbol is a command. Any item with a right-pointing arrow opens another menu. You point to it to activate it.

5   On the View menu, point to **Toolbars**.

WHAT'S HAPPENING? You open the Toolbars submenu. Figure 3.2 identifies the available toolbars.

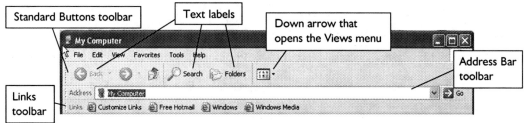

Figure 3.2 • Available Toolbars

The toolbars can have different looks as well. See Figures 3.3, 3.4, and 3.5 for some variations.

Figure 3.3 • Links Toolbar on the Address Bar

Figure 3.4 • Links Toolbar with a Closed Unfold Button

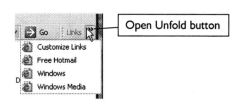

Figure 3.5 • Links Toolbar with an Open Unfold Button

WHAT'S HAPPENING? An unfold button allows you to drop-down a menu. Remember, a *toolbar* is a set of buttons you click to perform common tasks. The Standard Buttons toolbar displays buttons for commonly used commands in navigating My Computer, such as browsing forward and back, going up one level, and Search. In addition, you can change your view by clicking the Folders button so that you can see the structure of your disk. In addition, you have a Views button that will change how your display looks. The Address Bar toolbar can be used to locate Web pages, drives, or folders. By default, the Address Bar toolbar shows your current location, whether it's a folder or a Web page. Address Bar provides a method for opening files that are on the Internet or on your computer. The Links toolbar displays text or a picture that you click to jump from one location to another. You may also customize the toolbars by adding or deleting buttons from the toolbars.

6   On the View menu, point to **Toolbars**. Click **Customize**.

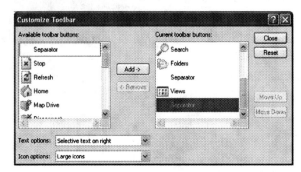

WHAT'S HAPPENING? You may customize how you want your toolbar to look. You may add or delete icons to match your needs.

7   In the **Text options** drop-down list box, click the down arrow.

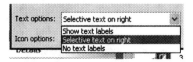

WHAT'S HAPPENING? You may choose to have text labels, have only a part of the label appear to the right of the button, or no text labels. If No text labels is selected, you may always place your pointer on the button to make a ToolTip appear. See Figure 3.6.

Figure 3.6 • No Text Labels Shown

8   Click **Show Text labels**. Click **Close**.

9   Click **View**. Point to **Explorer Bar**.

WHAT'S **HAPPENING?** No item should be selected. Search can be used to search for files and folders on your computer as well as on other computers on your network. It can search for people in your address book. It can extend your search to the Internet. Favorites will display items that you have specified as your favorite files, folders, and Web sites. In the navigation pane, Media will display all the different media types that are available, such as Music or Videos. History will list previously viewed Web sites and files, grouped by daily and weekly time periods. Folders will display in the left pane the hierarchical structure of the specified disk and in the right pane the contents of the default drive or folder. This is the same as clicking the Folders button on the Standard Toolbar. If you select Tip of the Day, a new tip for using Windows XP Professional will appear every time you open My Computer. Discuss allows you to initiate a discussion with a discussion server—a computer that allows interactive chatting. Now that you have set your toolbars, you are going to use these shortcuts for executing menu commands. You make choices by clicking on a button in the toolbar rather than accessing the menu. If you see two greater than signs (>>), there are more toolbar buttons that are hidden. To access those hidden buttons, click >>.

10 Click **Tools** on the menu bar. Click **Folder Options**. On the General page, click **Restore Defaults**. Click the **View** tab, click **Restore Defaults**, and then click **OK**.

11 Double-click the Drive C icon.

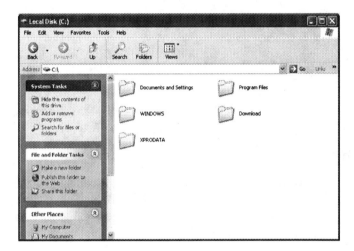

WHAT'S **HAPPENING?** You have opened the Drive C window and are looking at the root directory (C:\). You see the files and folders contained in the root directory. The left side of the window displays the tasks you might wish to accomplish as well as other places to look for files and folders.

12 Double-click the **XPRODATA** folder. (Remember, if you are in a lab environment, the **XPRODATA** folder may be on another drive.) Click **View**. Click **Tiles**.

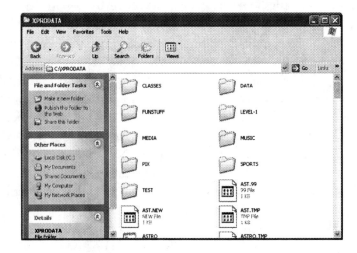

WHAT'S HAPPENING? You have opened the XPRODATA folder and can see its files and folders.

13 Click the down arrow next to the **Views** button, 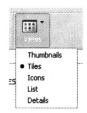 , on the Standard Buttons toolbar.

WHAT'S HAPPENING? You have dropped down the choices you have for viewing your files and folders.

14 Click **Thumbnails**.

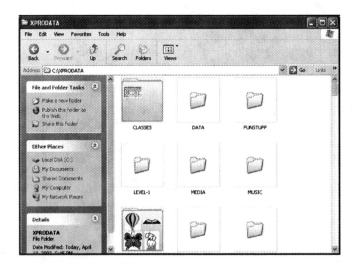

WHAT'S HAPPENING? You changed your view to Thumbnails. A thumbnail is a miniature version of an image. This option is most useful for graphic files.

15 Scroll through the window until you see a picture of a basket.

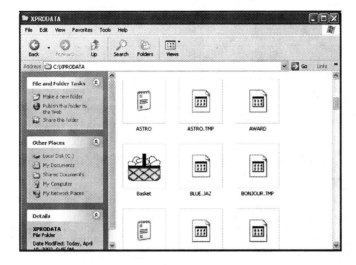

WHAT'S HAPPENING? You can see that the Thumbnails view is most useful when you are looking at a file that contains a graphic image.

16 Scroll to the top of the window. Click the **Views** button. Click **Icons**.

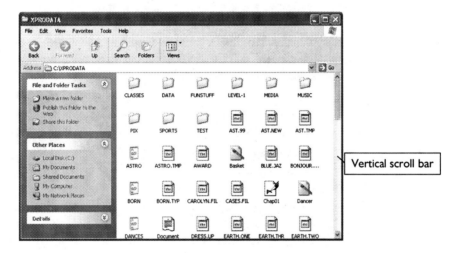

Vertical scroll bar

WHAT'S HAPPENING? You have changed your view of files and folders in the XPRODATA window to icons, in rows, in alphabetical order. The alphabetical order is from left to right in each row. There is a vertical scroll bar since all objects cannot be seen in this view.

17 Click the down arrow next to the **Views** button. Click **List**.

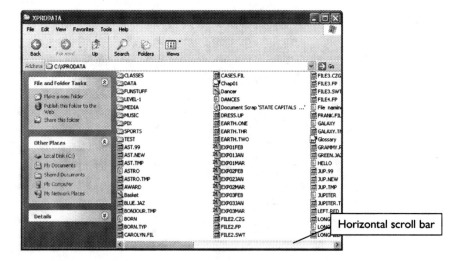

WHAT'S HAPPENING? You have changed the view to a list that appears in columns, in alphabetical order going down the columns. There is a horizontal scroll bar since you cannot see all objects in this window.

18 Click the down arrow next to the **Views** button. Click **Details**.

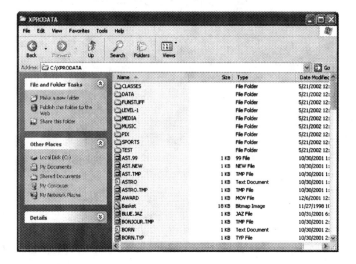

WHAT'S HAPPENING? You now see the details of the contents of the XPRODATA folder under the root of C. There is both a vertical and horizontal scroll bar since you cannot see all objects in this window. If your window is sized differently, you may not see the horizontal scroll bar. Scroll bars appear in a window when all items cannot be viewed at one time. The Details view is displayed in a list with column headings. Name, Size, Type, and Date Modified are the details given for each file and folder. You can adjust the width of the columns.

19 Place the pointer between **Name** and **Size** in the column headings.

WHAT'S HAPPENING? The cursor changed to a double-headed arrow.

20 Hold the left mouse button and drag the cursor to the left about an inch. Release the mouse button.

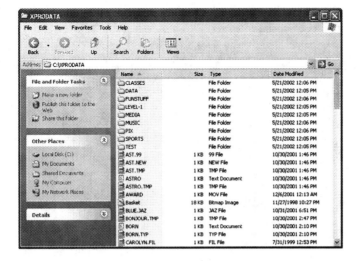

WHAT'S HAPPENING? You have changed the width of the columns.

21 Place the pointer between **Type** and **Date Modified** in the column headings. When the cursor becomes a double-headed arrow, double-click.

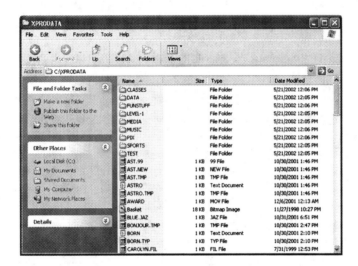

WHAT'S HAPPENING? You have used two ways to adjust the column width. Dragging is a manual adjustment to column sizes. Double-clicking adjusts the column's width based on the longest entry in the column. The column headings also allow you to rearrange the entries. When you click a column heading, you arrange that column in either ascending or descending order. This technique is a shortcut for clicking View, pointing to Arrange Icons, and selecting one of the items on the menu.

22 Click the **Name** button.

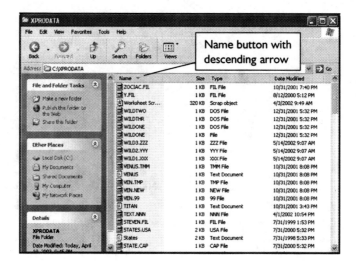

WHAT'S HAPPENING? Your file names are now arranged in descending alphabetical order—from Z to A. You can tell whether you are in descending or ascending order, as the triangle next to the column heading will be pointing either up or down. Up is ascending order, and down is descending order. In addition, files are listed first with folders listed last.

23 Click the **Name** button. Click the **Size** button. Click the **Date Modified** button.

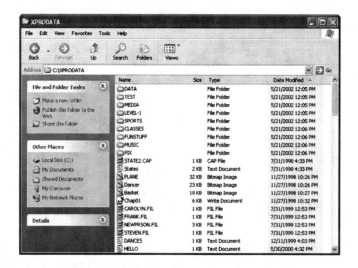

WHAT'S HAPPENING? As you clicked each column, your files and folders were arranged based on the column you chose. Since the triangle on the Modified column is pointing up, items are arranged in ascending order (oldest date first), with folders listed first, followed by files.

24 On the menu bar, click **View**. Point to **Arrange Icons by**. Click **Name**.

25 On the menu bar, click **View**. Point to **Arrange Icons by**. Click **Show in Groups**.

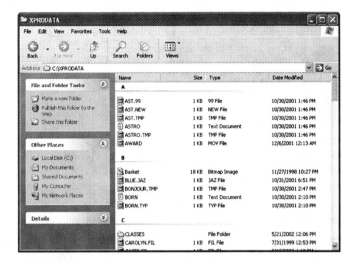

WHAT'S HAPPENING? When you set Show in Groups, your files and folders are arranged alphabetically—in a group.

26 Click the down arrow next to the **Views** button. Click **Icons**.

27 On the menu bar, click **View**. Point to **Arrange Icons by**. Click **Show in Groups**.

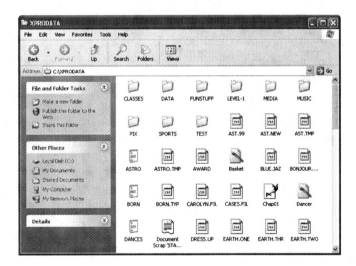

WHAT'S HAPPENING? The icons are now properly spaced and arranged by name. If AutoArrange were set, the icons would automatically adjust to fill the window and be in orderly rows and columns, based on an invisible grid.

28 Double-click the **Media** folder.

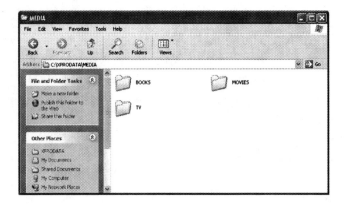

WHAT'S HAPPENING? You are moving down the Drive C hierarchy. Media is under the XPRODATA folder. The XPRODATA folder is under the root of C. If you look at the title bar, Media is displayed. If you look at the Address Bar, you see the hierarchy—C:\XPRODATA\MEDIA. Media also has folders.

29   Double-click **Books**.

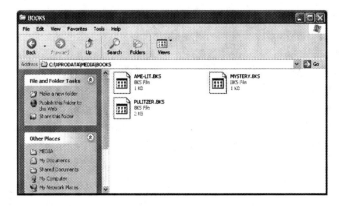

WHAT'S HAPPENING? Books is a folder under Media, which is under XPRODATA, which is under the root of C. The Books folder has only files, no folders. Again, the title bar states where you are in the hierarchy (BOOKS) and the Address Bar shows where Books is in the hierarchy (C:\XPRODATA\MEDIA\BOOKS).

30   Click the **Up** toolbar button, .

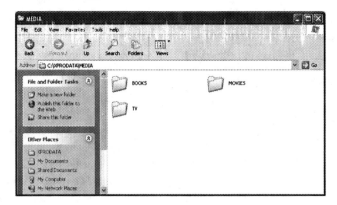

WHAT'S HAPPENING? You moved up the hierarchy. You made the Media window active. If you look at the taskbar, you will see a button for the Media window.

31 Press the ⌷Backspace⌷ key.

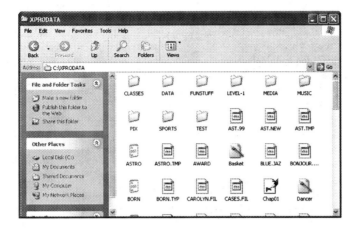

WHAT'S HAPPENING? Pressing the ⌷Backspace⌷ key is a keyboard shortcut that takes you to the parent of the active folder. The XPRODATA folder is the parent of the Media folder. If you want to see the hierarchy, you may change your view.

32 On the Standard toolbar, click the **Folders** button.

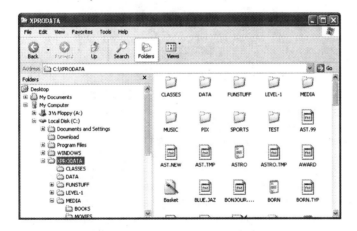

WHAT'S HAPPENING? Now you can see in the left pane where you are in the hierarchy. This is your default location. The right pane will display what files and folders are in the default directory.

33 In the right pane, double-click **Media**. Double-click **Books**.

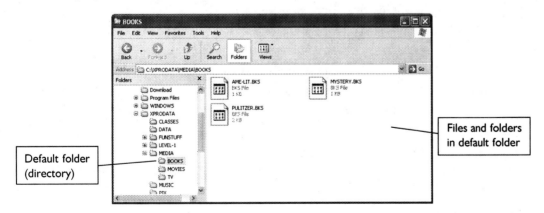

34 Press the ⌐Backspace⌐ key two times.

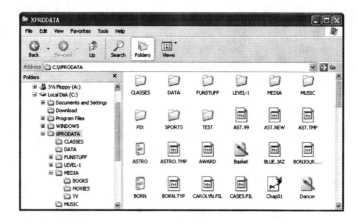

WHAT'S **HAPPENING?** You have made the XPRODATA window the active window. You can see the structure of the XPRODATA folder. Only one window can be active at a time.

34 Click **Tools**. Click **Folder Options**. Click the **View** tab. Click the **Restore Defaults** command button.

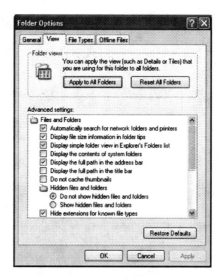

WHAT'S **HAPPENING?** These choices let you specify how your folders and their contents appear. Placing a check mark in a check box selects the choice. Removing a check mark deselects the choice. A click of the mouse either selects or deselects the choices. At any time, you can return to the default settings by clicking the Restore defaults command button. For Files and Folders, these choices are:

Automatically search for network folders and printers
When selected, specifies that Windows searches your network for any shared folders and printers. Any shared folders or printers that are found appear in My Network Places. The default is set (on).

Displays file size information in folder tips
When you place your pointer over a file, a tooltip will display with all the file details (type, date modified, and size). The default is set (on).

Display simple folder view in Explorer's Folders list

Will display not only the folder contents but will also display all subfolders within that folder. In addition, when you choose a different folder, all other folders are closed. Default is on.

Display the contents of system folders

System folders hold files that make your computer work. Default is off.

Display the full path in the address bar

When selected, the full path to the current folder appears in the Address Bar. The default is set (on).

Display the full path in title bar

When selected, the full path to the current folder appears in the title bar of the folder window. This duplicates the information in the Address Bar toolbar, if the Address Bar toolbar were selected. The path name will display the structure of the disk so that you know where you are in the hierarchy. The *path* is the statement that indicates precisely where a file is located on a disk. The default is not set (off).

Do not cache thumbnails

When you cache thumbnail images, Windows will reuse those images rather than creating new ones every time you open a folder. When caching is off, it may take a little longer for the thumbnail images to open. Default is off.

Hidden files and folders

You may see all files and folders (Show all hidden files and folders). The default is off—Do not show hidden files or folders.

Hide file extensions for known file types

The default, not set, will not display the file extensions that are registered with Windows. Most users want to see the entire file name, including its file extension (file type). The default is set (on).

Hide protected operating system files (Recommended)

The operating system files are hidden. This selection allows you to see these files. Enabling Hidden files and folders does not allow you to see the operating system files. The default is on.

Launch folder windows in a separate process

This specifies that each folder is opened in a separate part of memory. This can increase the stability of Windows, but your computer's performance may decrease somewhat. The default is off.

Remember each folder's view settings

When selected, each folder's setting is kept for use the next time you open that folder. When deselected, all folders return to their original states and your customization is not retained. The default is set (on).

Restore previous folder windows at logon

When set, any folder and browser windows you leave open when you log off will be restored the next time you log on to your computer. Default is off.

Show Control Panel in My Computer

Will display the Control Panel icon in the My Computer window as well as all your drives. Default is off.

Show encrypted or compressed NTFS files in color
I f you are using the NTFS file system and have compressed or encrypted any files, those file names will be displayed in a different color. Default is on.

Show pop-up description for folder and desktop items
A description of any selected folder or desktop item is displayed in a pop-up window. This allows ToolTips to appear. The default is set (on).

Use simple file sharing (Recommended)
When set, will allow you to share your folders and files with any one who is in your workgroups. Default is on.

35 Clear **Hide file extensions** for known file types. Click **Apply**. Click **OK**.

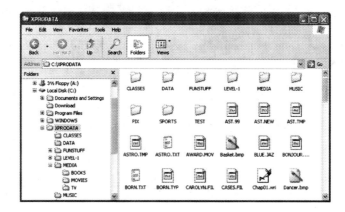

WHAT'S **HAPPENING?** You have set your options and returned to the XPRODATA folder in the My Computer window.

36 If you cannot see the **Dances.txt** file, scroll until you can. Place your pointer on the **Dances.txt** file.

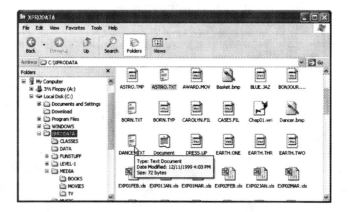

WHAT'S **HAPPENING?** In previous displays, you saw only the file name Dances. Since you changed the view options, you see the complete file name, Dances.txt. You also see a pop-up window containing a brief description of the selected file.

37 Close the XPRODATA window.

WHAT'S **HAPPENING?** You have returned to the desktop. The changes you made in Folder Options will remain. This textbook will assume these settings from now on. However, if you are on a network, your network may return the values to their defaults when you log off. You will need to alter them to the above settings each time you log on to your network.

3.5 ◦ **The My Recent Documents Menu**

Since Windows XP Professional is docucentric, one of the choices when you open the Start menu is the My Recent Documents menu. The My Recent Documents menu will display the last 15 documents you worked on. This approach fits into the docucentric model of Windows XP Professional. Prior to this docucentric model, which was introduced with Windows 95, the only way to view data was with the program approach: open the appropriate program, and then search for the particular data file from within the program. It worked the same way for every program and data file.

Using the older method, if you wanted to view the contents of a document called April.txt created in Notepad, you would have to take the following steps: click Start, point to All Programs, point to Accessories, and click Notepad. Then, in Notepad, you would have to click File, click Open, and locate April.txt. In the docucentric approach, if you had opened April.txt recently, you would click Start, point at My Recent Documents, and click April.txt. Notepad would open automatically, displaying April.txt. However, if you were creating a document, you would have to open the program. The docucentric approach is for documents that already exist.

The Taskbar and Start Menu Properties sheet contains all the options used to manipulate the Start and My Recent Documents menus.

3.6 ◦ **Activity** ◦ **Using the My Recent Documents Menu**

I   Right-click the taskbar in an empty spot. Click **Properties**. Click the **Start Menu** tab. Click the **Customize** command button. Click the **Advanced** tab.

WHAT'S HAPPENING? You have opened the property sheet that allows you to customize what appears on the Start menu. It has three areas to customize: Start menu settings, Start menu items, and Recent documents.

In Start menu settings, both choices are set as the default. These choices allow you to immediately see any submenus, and when you install a new program, it will be highlighted in the menus until you use it for the first time. In the Start menu items, you may select which items are on the Start menu. In the Recent documents section you can choose whether or not you want your Recent documents listed. The default is on. You can also clear the Recent Documents list. If the Clear button is dimmed, there are no documents in the Recent Documents menu.

2   Click **Clear List**.

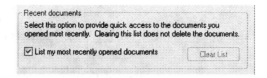

WHAT'S HAPPENING? The Clear button is dimmed, indicating that you have cleared the Recent Documents menu.

3   Click **OK**. Click **OK**.

4   Click **Start**. Point at **My Recent Documents**.

WHAT'S HAPPENING? Since you clicked Clear, no documents are available.

5   Point at **All Programs**. Point at **Accessories**. Click **Notepad**.

6   Click **File** on the Notepad menu bar. Click **Open**.

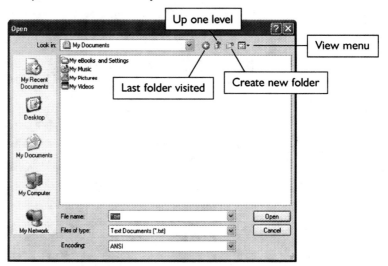

WHAT'S HAPPENING? You have opened the Open dialog box, which has a toolbar with a panel of controls. These controls provide quick access to options or commands. The buttons on the left allow you quick access to your most recently used documents, the Desktop, the My Documents folder, your drives on your computer, and any network you may have access to. The drop-down list box indicates which folder you are looking in; here, it is the My Documents folder. The dialog box also has icons that will perform an action when clicked. Since this dialog box contains a question mark icon, you may click the question mark, then click an item to display its definition.

7   Click the question mark icon. Drag it to **Look in**. Click it.

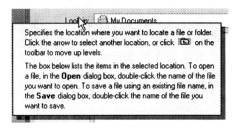

WHAT'S HAPPENING? A pop-up definition tells you the purpose of Look in and the function of the Up One Level button as well as how to use the Open dialog box.

8 Click to close the definition. Click the down arrow in the **Look** in drop-down list box.

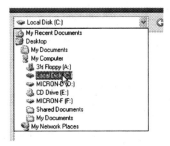

WHAT'S HAPPENING? You see the areas you can browse to locate a file. Your display may be different. You can choose to "look in" any disk drive or folder listed.

9 Click the Drive C icon in the drop-down list box.

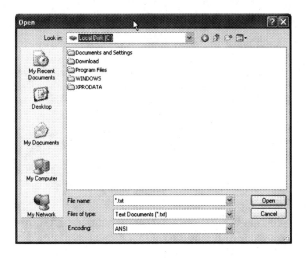

WHAT'S HAPPENING? You see the folders on Drive C.

10 Double-click the **XPRODATA** folder. (Remember, if you are in a lab environment, you may need to select a drive other than Drive C.) Click the down arrow next to the **Views** button and click **Details**.

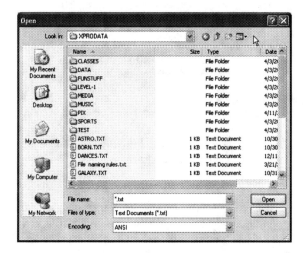

WHAT'S HAPPENING? Details displays information about the objects in the pane, including what the object is, its size, and the time and date it was last modified. You see the details of the objects in the pane—the files and folders in the XPRODATA folder on Drive C.

11   Click the down arrow next to the Views button and click **List**.

WHAT'S HAPPENING? You see a list of the files and folders in the XPRODATA folder. All subfolders in XPRODATA are listed, but only files with the .txt file extension are displayed. If you look at the File name text box, you see *.txt. If you look at the Files of type drop-down list box, you see that Text Documents is the default. Notepad will automatically assign the extension of .txt to any document created with Notepad, unless you state otherwise. The encoding is ANSI, which is the standard character set. Unless you are working with documents that use different character sets (such as Chinese or Cyrillic characters), you will not change the encoding.

Every time you install a program in Windows XP Professional, the program file tells the Windows XP Professional *Registry* what file extension the application program is claiming. The program registers a file extension or file type, much like a person checking into a hotel. When you register at a hotel, you are claiming a room. The hotel knows which guest is in which room by looking at the register. The hotel also knows that it cannot rent rooms that are already claimed. In the same way, Windows XP Professional registers file extensions (file types). The

Notepad program has claimed the file extension .txt. Any time Windows XP Professional sees this extension, it recognizes the file as a Notepad file. It will open Notepad automatically when you double-click the document icon.

When you register at a hotel and need more than one room, for example for another family member, you can claim additional rooms. In the same way, Windows XP Professional can register more than one file extension to a program. For instance, Notepad claims not only .txt, but also other extensions such as the .ini extension. Whenever you double-click a file with an extension claimed by Notepad, such as .txt or .ini, Notepad will open, and the file you double-clicked will be displayed in the Notepad window.

12 Click the down arrow in the Files of type drop-down list box.

WHAT'S HAPPENING? Your only other available choice is All Files.

13 Click **All Files**.

WHAT'S HAPPENING? Your display now includes every file and folder in the XPRODATA folder on Drive C.

14 Double-click **AST.99**.

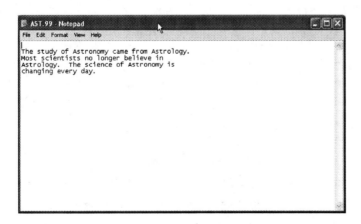

WHAT'S HAPPENING? You are looking at the contents (the data) of the AST.99 file. The .99 file extension is not registered to Notepad. However, you may always attempt to open a file with any file extension from the Open dialog box in Notepad. Beware that if the file is not a text file, it will not be readable in Notepad. The registration of files only affects what happens when you double-click an icon.

15   On the **File** menu, click **File**. Click **Open**.

WHAT'S HAPPENING? You have again opened the File Open dialog box. It returned you to your last open folder (XPRODATA).

16   Double-click **GALAXY.TXT**.

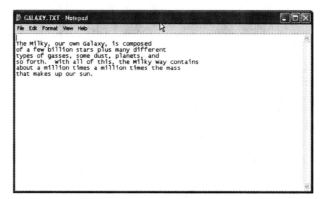

WHAT'S HAPPENING? When you opened the document GALAXY.TXT, you closed the document AST.99. Notepad can open only one document at a time. This procedure is called the *program approach* to opening files, which means you must locate and execute the program file before locating and opening the data file. There are many steps in the program approach. Windows XP Professional offers an easier way to access the last documents (data files) you worked on.

17   Close Notepad. Click **Start**. Point at **My Recent Documents**.

WHAT'S **HAPPENING?** The file you last looked at, GALAXY.TXT , is shown in the My Recent Documents menu.

18 Click **GALAXY.TXT**.

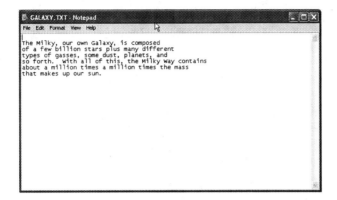

WHAT'S **HAPPENING?** You accessed your data file quickly. By using the My Recent Documents menu, you were able to open Notepad and the GALAXY.TXT data file in one step with the docucentric approach. You did not need to take all the steps required in the program approach.

19 Close Notepad.

WHAT'S **HAPPENING?** You have returned to the desktop. One thing to note is that, when you opened the Documents menu, GALAXY.TXT was listed but AST.99 was not because AST.99 is not a registered file type. In the next section, you will learn how to register AST.99.

3.7 ● **Registering File Types with the Registry**

As stated previously, Windows XP Professional uses a docucentric or document-centric model. This approach emphasizes the work you do, not the tool you use to do the work. For instance, you have drawn pictures without computers. How did you work? Typically, you probably got out a sheet of paper, selected your drawing tool, such as a pencil, and then began sketching your picture. Your focus was on your drawing—your document. To draw a picture using a computer, you first have to start a drawing program (your tool) before you begin drawing your picture. The software package is the container for your drawing. Your drawing is the document. You cannot even look at your drawing (document) without opening the container (software application).

In a program model, you always have to open your application program first, then search for your document in the application's Open dialog box. In a docucentric model, the process is much easier. It is more like the above example of drawing a picture without a computer. You can be less concerned with your tools and more concerned with your document. All you need to do is double-click a document icon. That will open the program and load the document with one step. In the computer world, you still must always open a program before you can edit, see, or use your document. The docucentric approach just makes it easier to do so.

How does Windows XP Professional accomplish this? It does so by associating a file with a specific application program. Windows XP Professional uses file extensions (the last characters following the last period in a file name) to designate what Microsoft calls file types. Your computer can take certain actions on files depending on their file type. Usually a program performs the actions. The actions include Open and Print for a text document or Play for a video clip. File types and their associated actions are defined (registered) in the Registry files. Windows XP Professional defines more than 100 file types and their actions.

The Registry is a database program that stores profiles for each property setting, such as the ones you set for the taskbar and Start menu, application program settings such as the options you set in My Computer, application program information, and information about the specific computer you are using. The Registry centralizes, then tracks, all this information, including the data file extensions that an application program assigns to its data files, the icons that represent a program and its data files, and other file-oriented information. The Registry tracks which data files belong to which programs. When you double-click a document icon, Windows XP Professional checks the Registry to know which program to open. Windows XP Professional also places any opened, registered data file on the My Recent Documents menu. The Registry bases its decision on the file extension (file type). When you install a program written for the Windows XP Professional interface, part of the installation process is the program informing the Registry what file extensions it plans to use for its data files.

There is a special Windows program called the Registry Editor (REGEDIT and REGEDT32) that allows a user to make changes directly to the Registry. However, it is very dangerous to edit Registry files directly. If you edited the files incorrectly, Windows XP Professional could not boot. Fortunately, you can register file types (extensions) easily without ever having to touch these important system files directly.

3.8 ● Settings

Each chapter in this textbook assumes you have the settings listed below. If you are working on your own computer, the changes you made in the default settings should have been retained from one work session to the next. However, if you are working in a computer lab, you may have to change your settings each time you log on to the network. The settings are as follows:

* In the View menu in My Computer, use these settings:
    * Toolbars—Standard Buttons on, Address Bar on, and Links off, and Lock Toolbar on.
    * In Toolbars, click Customize, click the Reset button for Text options to be set to Selective text on right.
    * Status Bar off.
    * Explorer Bar—none
    * Click Tiles.
    * Arrange Icons By Name and Show in Groups off.
    * On the Standard Toolbar, Folders view is off.
* In the My Computer window, in the Tools menu, select Folder Options.
    * General tab—Click Restore Defaults.
    * View tab—Click Restore Defaults. Then clear the Hide extensions for known file types.
    In Windows Explorer, the settings are identical to My Computer except that on the Standard Toolbar, the Folders view is on.

3.9 ● Activity ● Looking at File Types

Note 1: Different software applications, when installed, will claim file types (extensions) and make various modifications to the Registry. This impacts what is displayed on your screen and what choices you make when you take the steps in the following activity. If you follow the steps exactly and do not get the same results, it is probably a result of what software you have installed.

Note 2: In addition, if your settings do not match those outlined in Section 3.8, your displays may vary.

1 Click **Start**. Click **My Computer**. Double-click the Drive C icon. Double-click the **XPRODATA** folder.

2 Right-click **ASTRO.TXT**.

WHAT'S **HAPPENING?** When you right-clicked the document icon, you opened the shortcut menu, sometimes called the context or pop-up menu. The top section lists the actions defined for this file type. The default action is in boldface type. When you double-click the icon, bypassing the short-cut menu, the default action occurs.

This file was created with Notepad. The registered document icon for this file type resembles its program's (Notepad's) icon. The actions you can take on this file are Open (Open Notepad with this document), Print, Edit (Open Notepad with this document—in this case Edit and Open are the same), and Open With (open this document with a different program than the default). The other items on the menu relate to manipulating the entire file—not just its contents. These are file management commands. With these, you can send the file to a variety of locations such as another drive or folder (Send To), cut it (Cut), make a copy of it (Copy), delete it (Delete), change its name (Rename), or create a shortcut to it (Create Shortcut). You can also see the characteristics of this file (Properties). The file management commands are common to all files, but the actions depend on the file type. In addition, you may have other choices on this menu. Programs can add items to the shortcut menu when they are installed.

3 Click **Properties**.

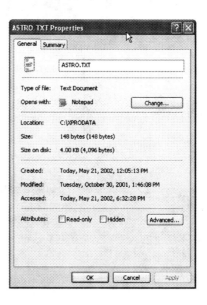

WHAT'S **HAPPENING?** You first see the file name, ASTRO.TXT. If you look at Type, it states Text Document. It then tells you what application program opens this document file (Notepad). It tells you the location of the file (C:\XPRODATA), the actual size of the file (148 bytes), and how much space it occupies on the disk (4,096 bytes). How much space it occupies on the disk depends on which file system you are using, FAT, FAT32, or NTFS. There is a minimum amount of disk space (known as a cluster) that must be assigned to each file. All files smaller than a cluster will still be assigned a full disk cluster—you may not place more than one file in a single cluster. You may also be puzzled that the file was modified on Tuesday, October 30, 2001, but created on Wednesday, April 3, 2002. How can a file be modified before it is created? Your dates may be different. The file creation date is the date the file was placed on your hard drive, not the date it was originally created. The Accessed date is the last time you opened the file.

4 Click **Cancel**. Double-click **Funstuff**. Double-click **BOG2**.

WHAT'S HAPPENING? This folder contains a game (BOG) and all the support files the BOG program needs to run. Notice that the icon is a program icon that tries visually to indicate what this program does.

5   Right-click **BOG.EXE**.

WHAT'S HAPPENING? This program file is a game that you play. Programs add the Run as.. and Pit to Start menu commands. When you choose Open, you will "open" the program so you can play the game. Pin to Start menu will place this item on your Start menu. Most programs will have this choice. This is one way that you can customize the Start menu to place programs that you use in the easiest location to get to. Again, note that the file management commands are the same.

6   Click **Run as ...**

WHAT'S HAPPENING? Remember, whenever you see a command with an ellipsis, you open a dialog box. Since Windows XP is a secure operating system, you can designate who may use this program.

7   Click **Cancel**. On the standard button toolbar, click **Back** twice. Right-click **AST.99**. Click **Open**.

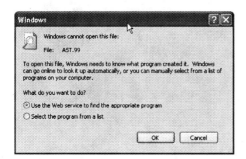

WHAT'S **HAPPENING?** Although this is a document icon, it has an unregistered file type. Windows does not know what program to open when it encounters a file with an extension of .99. Windows gives you two choices, to go online or to select a program from a list. This list is a list of all the programs that are installed on your computer system. The document icon for unregistered files is a page with a dog-eared corner and a generic Windows logo. Both Open and Open With are available.

8   Click **Cancel**. Right-click **AST.99**.

WHAT'S **HAPPENING?** Although your program choices are limited, the file management commands are the same.

9   Click outside the menu to close it. On the menu bar, click **Tools**. Click **Folder Options**. Click the **File Types** tab.

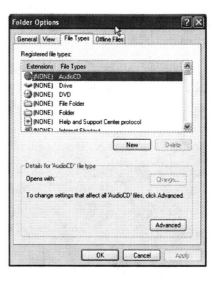

WHAT'S **HAPPENING?** This property sheet presents a list box with all the registered file types. The file types are sorted by extension in this list box. In the Details information, you are told what file types these are. This information appears on a file's property sheet in the Type field. The command buttons on the right show the actions you can take: create a new type, delete a type, change the program that opens files of this type, or modify the settings and icon assigned to this file type (Advanced). If you look at Details, you see the extension and what program is used to open this file type. Windows makes this decision based on the file extension.

10 Scroll in the list box until you locate **TXT**. Click it to select it.

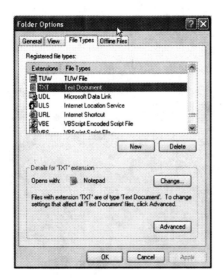

WHAT'S **HAPPENING?** In "Details for 'TXT" extension," you see that files with the extension TXT are of the file type "Text Document." Furthermore, you see the program icon for the program that opens TXT files.

11   Click the **Advanced** button.

WHAT'S **HAPPENING?** In Actions, you can see that there are three: open, print, and printto. Open is highlighted, so it is the default.

12   Click **open**. Click the **Edit** command button.

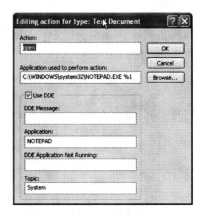

WHAT'S **HAPPENING?** Now you see the details of what program actually opens the data files with these extensions. You see the path and the name of the program, in this case, C:\Windows\System32\Notepad.EXE. The %1 represents the file name that will be used. The %1 is like the x in a formula—whatever file is selected, its name will be substituted for the %1. The other information relates to DDE (Dynamic Data Exchange). You normally will never use these other features.

13   Click **Cancel**. Click **Cancel**. Click **Cancel**.

14   Close all open windows.

WHAT'S **HAPPENING?** You have returned to the desktop.

3.10 ⬡ Registering File Types

The process of double-clicking an icon and automatically opening a program occurs because there is a lot of work going on in the background. Part of the process of installing an application program is registering the file extension with Windows. Windows registers the file extension to be associated with that program. Since Windows takes care of registering application program file extensions when they are installed, you may ask yourself why you would ever need to know this information and how you would use it?

How and why would you assign an unregistered file extension to a data file you create, rather than let the program assign the file extension? The "how" is fairly simple—when you save a file you created in a program such as Word, you could call it Myfile.let or you could let Word automatically add its extension of .doc so the file name becomes Myfile.doc instead of using your file extension of .let. The "why" is a little more complicated.

You will be creating many data files. The challenge in creating data files is organizing and retrieving them quickly. Word, for example, assigns the file extension .doc to each data file created with it. So every file you create in Word will have a different file name but the same extension (for example, Kathy letter.doc, Mr. Jones letter.doc, Finance plan report.doc, or Business plan report.doc). In terms of retrieving and identifying files, it would be helpful if files about similar topics had something in common. You could choose to have all files that were letters have a .let extension so that your file names would be (using the above examples) Kathy.let and Mr. Jones.let. All reports could have a .rep file extension so that your file names would be Finance plan.rep or Business plan.rep. You create an organizational scheme that helps you manage files. Then when you look at your files to alter, review, or print them, you can easily identify the kind of data in the files by the extensions you assigned.

Since you, not a program, assigned the file extension, Windows XP Professional will not know what application to open nor will it place any documents with unregistered file types on the My Recent Documents menu. Word, in the installation process, registered .doc. It did not register .rep or .let. You may register (inform Windows XP Professional of your preferences) your own file extensions in the Registry so that Windows XP Professional knows that, in this example, it should open Word when it encounters files not only with the .doc extension, but also with the extensions .let and .rep. However, there is an easier way. You could use your organizational scheme *and* use the program's assigned file extensions. Thus, you could name your letters Kathy.let.doc and Mr. Jones.let.doc. The files Finance plan.rep and Business plan.rep could become Finance plan.rep.doc and Business plan.rep.doc. By looking at these file names, you would know what data is in the files *and* what program created them.

In general, you will use the file extensions assigned by the application programs. However, there are instances when you do want to register a file type so that you may double-click its icon and Windows will know what program to open. For instance, in WordPerfect for DOS, you can assign any file extension to a document such as a project code or the initials of the author. You may now be using WordPerfect for Windows but still exchanging documents with some-one who is using WordPerfect for DOS and its old naming system. Another instance could be that you installed a new program and want a specific file type to be associated with the new program. For example, Windows XP Professional includes a graphics program—Microsoft Paint—that uses the bitmap file format and claims the .bmp file extension. If you want your new bitmap-viewing program to open instead of Paint, you will need to create a file-extension association. Another instance is that often a program comes with a Read.me text file that gives the latest information about itself. The extension .me is not associated with any program. You can register the .me extension, associating it with Notepad, so that you may double-click any .me file to open it and read it.

Not only may you register file extensions without using the Registry, but you can also easily register them without using the File Types dialog box. Windows XP Professional provides a *GUI (graphical user interface)* way of doing this.

3.11 • Activity • Registering File Types

1   Click **Start**. Click **My Computer**. Double-click the Drive C icon. Double-click the **XPRODATA** folder.

2   Double-click **AST.99**.

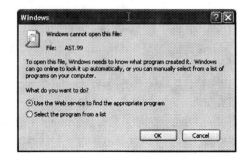

WHAT'S **HAPPENING?** The file called AST.99 does not have a registered file extension. Double-clicking a registered document icon will open the program that created that file. Since .99 is not registered, Windows XP Professional does not know what application program to open. Windows XP Professional presents you with two choices: Use the web service to find the appropriate program or Select the program from a list. The web service is a link to the File Association page on the Microsoft Web site. The second choice is that Microsoft will present a list of all the programs on your system and you will pick which program you want to use. *Note:* For the next step to work, you must be connected to the Internet.

3   Be sure Use the web service to find the appropriate program is selected. Click **OK**.

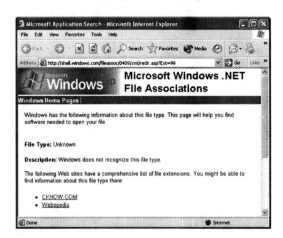

WHAT'S **HAPPENING?** Windows does not recognize this file type. However, even if it was a recognized file type, if you did not own the software, you would still have to purchase the software and install it on your system.

4   Click the Close button. Right-click **AST.99**. Click **Open**. Choose **Select the program from a list**. Click **OK**.

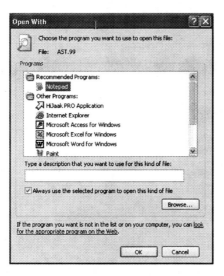

WHAT'S **HAPPENING?** You are presented with a dialog box listing all programs installed on your computer system. The dialog box asks you what program you wish to use to open AST.99. It also makes a recommendation that you try Notepad. What it is really asking you to do is to register (assign) the file extension .99 with a program so that in the future Windows XP Professional will know what program to open whenever it sees a .99 file extension

The registration of a file is based not on the file name but on the file extension. The dialog box has an empty text box for files of this type in which you can add descriptive information when registering a file type (extension). Thus, you can create file extensions that mean specific things to you and that clearly reflect your work. Also note that there is a check box that is set— Always use the selected program to open this kind of file. When that check box is set, it means that ALL files, forevermore, that have a .99 extension will be associated with whatever program you choose, in this case Notepad.

5   In the **Type a description that you want to use for this kind of file** text box, key in the following: **Class Files**

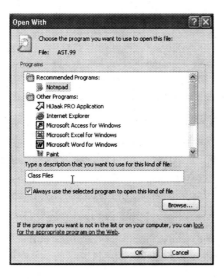

WHAT'S **HAPPENING?** You now have a general description of files with a .99 extension.

6 Click Notepad to be sure it is selected.

7 Be sure the Always use the selected program to open this kind of file check box has a check mark. Click **OK**.

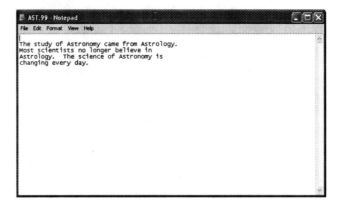

WHAT'S **HAPPENING?** Notepad opened, with AST.99 as the data file.

8 Close Notepad. Click **View**. Click **Icons**.

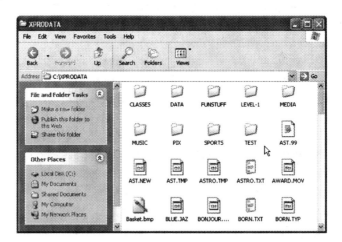

WHAT'S **HAPPENING?** In the C:\XPRODATA window, the AST.99 file now has the easily recognizable Notepad document icon. Table 3.1 shows common document icons.

AST.NEW

A generic document icon. Windows XP Professional does not know what program to use to open this file. If you double-clicked this icon, Windows XP Professional would present you with the Open With dialog box.

AST.99

A user-registered document icon. Windows XP Professional knows that Notepad is the program to use to open any file with a .99 extension. When you double-click this icon, Windows XP Professional will open Notepad and display the AST.99 document.

BORN.TXT

A program-registered document icon. Windows XP Professional knows that Notepad is the program to use to open any file with a .txt extension. When you create a file in Notepad, Notepad automatically assigns it the .txt file extension. When you double-click this icon, Windows XP Professional will open Notepad and display the April.txt document.

 A Paint document icon.

 A Word document icon.

 An Excel document icon.

 An Audio file.

Table 3.1 ∘ Common Document Icons

WHAT'S HAPPENING? Program icons try also to represent what kind of application they are. Table 3.2 shows some common program icons.

 The Paint program that comes with Windows.

 The Notepad program that comes with Windows.

 The Word program from Microsoft Office.

 The Excel program from Microsoft Office.

 A graphics program—Paint Shop Pro.

 A card game program called Solitaire.

Table 3.2 ∘ Common Program Icons

9 Scroll until you see **JUP.99**.

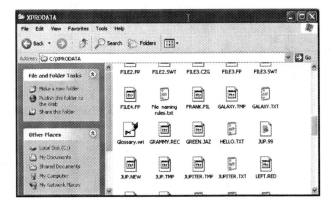

WHAT'S HAPPENING? Since you registered the .99 file extension with Notepad, *all* files with a .99 file extension are registered. You may double-click any of them, and Notepad will open along with the .99 data file.

10   Double-click **JUP.99**.

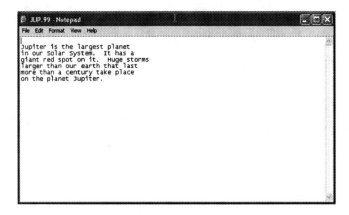

WHAT'S **HAPPENING?** Since this is a registered file, Notepad opened it.

11   Close Notepad. Scroll until you can see the **AST.99** icon.

12   Right-click **AST.99**.

WHAT'S **HAPPENING?** You have opened the shortcut menu. Notice that actions you can take are to Open, Edit, or Open With. However, the file management commands remain the same.

13   Click **Properties**.

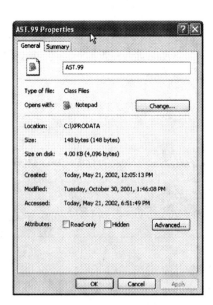

WHAT'S **HAPPENING?** You opened the property sheet for AST.99. Not only does the property sheet tell you the name of this file and when it was created, but also why it was created. In addition, it tells you that Windows Notepad is the program that will be used to open this file.

14 Click **Cancel**. Right-click **AST.TMP**.

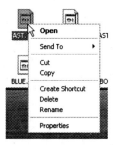

WHAT'S **HAPPENING?** Since AST.TMP is not a registered file, Windows XP Professional does not know what program to use to open the file. The only option available is Open.

15 Click **Open**. Click **Select the Program from a list**. Click **OK**.

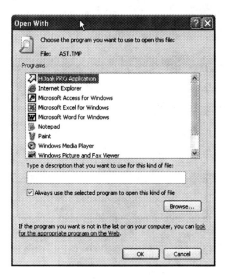

WHAT'S **HAPPENING?** You want to look at the contents of this file, but you DO NOT WANT to register it. To ensure that you do not register it, you must clear the **Always use the selected program to open this kind of file** check box.

16 Click **Always use the selected program to open this kind of file** to clear the check box.

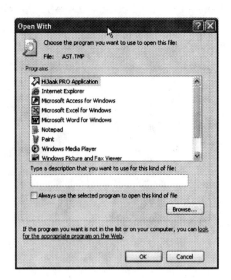

WHAT'S HAPPENING? The check box is clear. You are going to open this file this time only and not register or associate the file extension .new with Notepad.

17 If necessary, scroll until you locate **Notepad**. Click it. Click **OK**.

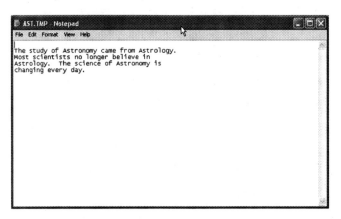

WHAT'S HAPPENING? You opened this file.

18 Close Notepad.

AST.TMP

WHAT'S HAPPENING? You did not register this file. The icon has not changed.

19 Right-click **AST.99**.

WHAT'S HAPPENING? When a file is registered, it will always open the program that it is registered to when double-clicked or when you select Open from the shortcut menu. Edit also allows you open the file so that you may edit it. Sometimes you may have different programs that use the same file extension for their data files. If a file extension is already registered to one program, it cannot be registered to another. For example, Word and WordPad both assign the file extension .doc to their data files; however, .doc is registered only to Word. Any file with a .doc extension automatically opens Word. By right-clicking and choosing the Open With menu, you can select WordPad to open the file instead of Word.

20 Click outside the menu to close it.

21 Click the **Start** button. Point at **My Recent Documents**.

WHAT'S HAPPENING? Every registered file that you used is listed on the Documents menu. Now that you have registered the .99 file extension, those files are listed here. If you want, you can open any file on this list.

22 Click outside the Start menu. In the XPRODATA window, click **Tools** on the menu bar. Click **Folder Options**. Click the **File Types** tab.

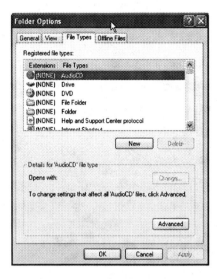

WHAT'S HAPPENING? You may add or remove file types at any time by selecting this property sheet under Folder Options from the View menu.

23 The list is alphabetically arranged. Scroll the list window until you locate **99**. Click that line to select it. (*Note:* If the 99 file extension is not available, go to Step 26).

WHAT'S HAPPENING? When you selected the 99 extension, Details for 99 told you the application program that opens it (Notepad). This method is one way to identify which extensions are registered to which programs. You are going to remove this extension from the registered list.

24 Be sure the 99 extension line is selected. Click the **Delete** command button. *Note:* If the 99 extension is not available, go to step 26.

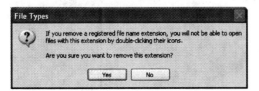

WHAT'S **HAPPENING?** You see an information message box warning you that, once you remove a registered file type, you will no longer be able to double-click to open it easily. You may still open it, but you will have to use the program approach with its many steps.

25 Click **Yes**. Click **Close**.

AST.99

WHAT'S **HAPPENING?** AST.99 is no longer registered, nor are any other .99 files. You can still open AST.99 and any other .99 file to edit it. To open a .99 file, however, you will first need to use the Open With dialog box to identify which program to use or use the program approach—use the Start menu's All Programs menu or submenus to open the Notepad application program and then use the File/Open command to locate and open the desired file. If you see the generic icon, go to step 29. But what if you did not see .99 in the File Types list box? If you do this activity more than once, Windows remembers that file registration and does not show this extension in the File Types list box. However, you can still remove file associations you no longer want.

26 Click **Tools**. Click **Folder Options**. Click the **File Types** tab. Click **New**.

WHAT'S **HAPPENING?** You are going to create the .99 file extension.

27 In the File Extension, key in **99**. Click **OK**.

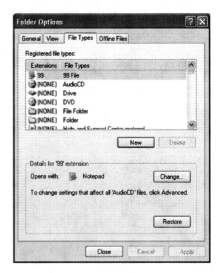

WHAT'S **HAPPENING?** You now have 99 listed but the Delete button is dimmed and not available.

28 Click the **Restore** button (or the **Advanced** button).

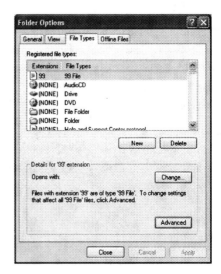

WHAT'S **HAPPENING?** Now the Delete button is available.

29 Be sure that **99** and **99** File is selected. Click **Delete**. Click **Yes**. Click **Close**.

AST.99

WHAT'S **HAPPENING?** You have eliminated the 99 file association with Notepad and now have the generic icon.

29 Click the Close button for the XPRODATA window.

WHAT'S **HAPPENING?** You have returned to the desktop.

Chapter Summary

In this chapter, you learned the difference between program files and data files. You learned that there is a hierarchical structure to a disk, and that every disk is structured around a root directory containing folders and files. You found that a file must have a unique file name of up to 255 characters plus a file extension.

You used the View menu in My Computer to alter how the files and folders are displayed, and you found that you can place a toolbar in a window and use it to execute menu commands. You found that Windows XP Professional remembers the last way you left a window. You changed view options, such as tiles, thumbnails, icons, icons, list, and details. You learned how to display the file extensions and the path in the address bar of the window.

You also found that the docucentric approach of the My Recent Documents menu provides an easy way to open an existing data file and the program it is registered to. However, a file must be registered before it will appear on the Documents menu. File extensions are registered with the Registry when you install programs. The Registry is the database that Windows XP Professional uses to keep track of what file extensions belong to what files. You may also register file extensions manually.

Key Terms

application package	file name	program file
app	file type	Registry
data file	folder	software
directory	GUI (graphical user interface)	software package
document file	hierarchy	subdirectory
executing the program	path	subfolder
file extension	program approach	toolbar

Discussion Questions

1. What is the purpose and function of a program file?
2. What is the purpose and function of a data file?
3. What does it mean to "execute a program"?
4. Since all work done in RAM is volatile, what must be done to permanently retain created data?
5. What is a folder? How is a folder used?
6. What is the hierarchical structure of a disk?
7. List and explain file naming rules.
8. Explain the difference between a file name and a file extension.
9. Who names data files? Program files? Why?
10. Why can data files only be used in conjunction with an application program?
11. How and why would you use the My Computer window?
12. What options can you change in the My Computer window?
13. Identify two changes you would make in the My Computer window and why.

14. Compare and contrast the toolbar and the menu in the My Computer window.
15. How can you quickly go to a parent of a folder?
16. What is the purpose and function of the My Recent Documents menu?
17. Explain the steps to open a file after you have opened Notepad.
18. Compare and contrast opening a file using the program approach versus using the docucentric approach.
19. Explain the purpose and function of the Registry.
20. How does the file extension play a key role in the Registry?

True/False Questions

For each question, circle the letter T if the statement is true or the letter F if the statement is false.

T   F   1. Application programs have user-selected names.
T   F   2. Data files are created with application programs.
T   F   3. The extension in a data file's name indicates what type of data is in the file.
T   F   4. The root directory is always the first directory on any disk.
T   F   5. If you double-click a registered document icon, Windows XP Professional will ask you which program you wish to open.

Completion Questions

Write the correct answer in each blank space.

6. The step-by-step instructions that direct a computer to perform the task that you require are called a(n) _____ file.
7. A file name consists of two parts, the file _____ and the file _____.
8. One way to see files and folders on a disk is to open the _____ window.
9. You may place a number of files in a subdirectory. Windows XP Professional calls this a(n) _____.
10. The Start button's My Recent Documents menu can be emptied by choosing the _____ from the Taskbar and Start Menu Properties sheet.

Multiple Choice Questions

Circle the letter of the correct answer for each question.

11. Folders are containers of objects. An object can be a
    a. document or a program file.
    b. device or folder.
    c. both a and b
    d. neither a nor b
12. If you open Notepad, click File, and then click Open, and the File name text box has *.txt in it, then
    a. all files and folders will be listed.
    b. only files with a .txt extension will be listed.
    c. only folders will be listed.
    d. only files beginning with an asterisk (*) will be listed.

13. Directly using the Registry Editor to edit Windows XP Professional system files
    a. is the recommended method for changing file types.
    b. could cause extreme, even fatal, damage to Windows XP Professional.
    c. is completely safe for any user.
    d. both a and c

14. You see the following icon in the XPRODATA window: 🗋. You know that this file
    a. will be opened by Notepad if you double-click the icon.
    b. cannot be opened.
    c. cannot be opened by double-clicking.
    d. is a program file.

15. On the My Computer toolbar, you see the following icon: 📂. If you click it, you will
    a. change the view to small icons.
    b. delete a file.
    c. change the way folders are browsed.
    d. move to the parent of the current folder.

Application Assignments

Problem Set I—At the Computer

Note 1: Be sure your settings match those listed in Section 3.8.

Note 2: You will be using the Windows directory. This folder typically is called Windows and is located on Drive C. If your Windows folder is called by another name and/or located on a drive other than C:, you will need to substitute the correct drive and directory.

Problem A

* Open My Computer.

* Open Drive C.

* Open the Windows folder.

* Click **Show the contents of this folder**, if necessary.

* Scroll until you see the icon labeled Notepad.exe.

    1. The icon for Notepad.exe is a
        a. program icon.
        b. document icon.

* Double-click the icon.

    2. The following occurred:
        a. An Open With dialog box appeared.
        b. The file April.txt opened.
        c. Notepad opened.

    3. What item *does not* appear on the Notepad menu bar?
        a. File
        b. Edit
        c. Bookmark
        d. Help

* Close Notepad.

* Move to the parent window.

   4. You may move to the parent window by
      a. clicking the **Back** button.
      b. clicking the **Up** button.
      c. both a and b
      d. neither a nor b

* Close all open windows.

Problem B

* Open My Computer.

* Open the Drive C window.

* Open the XPRODATA folder.

* Maximize the window.

* Click the down arrow next to the Views button.

* Click **Icons**.

* Click **View** on the menu bar.

* Point to **Arrange Icons by**.

* Click **Name**.

   5. The folders and files are arranged in alphabetical order
      a. and has a horizontal scroll bar.
      b. and has a vertical scroll bar.
      c. and show the file details.
      d. both a and c
      e. both b and c

* Select **Details** from the Views button.

   6. The folders and files are now arranged in alphabetical order
      a. and has a horizontal scroll bar.
      b. and has a vertical scroll bar.
      c. and are showing the file details.
      d. both a and c
      e. both b and c

* Select **List** from the Views button.

   7. The folders and files are now arranged in alphabetical order
      a. and has a horizontal scroll bar.
      b. and has a vertical scroll bar.
      c. and are showing the file details.
      d. both a and c
      e. both b and c

* Select **Tiles** from the Views button.

* Restore the window.

* Click **View** on the menu bar.

* Point to **Arrange Icons by**.

* Click **Name**.

* Be sure your settings match those in Section 3.8.

⁕ Double-click the **DATA** folder.

   8. The Address bar of DATA states:

      a. DATA

      b. C:\DATA

      c. C:\XPRODATA\DATA

      d. C:\XPRODATA\DATA\BONJOUR.TXT

   9. TEA.TAX.usa is an example of a(n)

      a. user-registered document icon.

      b. generic document icon.

      c. program-registered document icon.

      d. executable program.

   10. GOOD.TXT is an example of a(n)

      a. user-registered document icon.

      b. generic document icon.

      c. program-registered document icon.

      d. executable program.

⁕ Press the **Backspace** key once.

   11. You moved to the _____ window.

      a. C:\

      b. C:\XPRODATA

      c. C:\XPRODATA\DATA

      d. C:\WINDOWS

      e. MY COMPUTER

⁕ Scroll until you locate the Chap01.wri file.

   12. The Chap01.wri file is an example of a data file with which Windows XP Professional will

      a. know which application program to open.

      b. not know which application program to open.

⁕ Close all open windows.

Problem C

⁕ Open My Computer.

⁕ Click **Tools**.

⁕ Click **Folder Options**.

⁕ Click the **File Types** tab.

⁕ Locate the ANI file type.

⁕ Click **ANI** to select it.

   13. What file type is ANI?

      a. Annotated File

      b. Animated Cursor

      c. Agent File

      d. Animated Executable

14. This opens with which program?
    a. Windows Notepad
    b. Microsoft Media Player
    c. Microsoft Wordpad
    d. Microsoft Paint
    e. none of the above

* Locate AVI.

* Click **AVI** to select it.

15. This opens with which program?
    a. Notepad
    b. Windows Media Player
    c. Wordpad
    d. Paint
    e. none of the above

* Click the **Advanced** button.

16. What actions can you take?
    a. Open
    b. Play
    c. both a and b
    d. neither a nor b

* Click **Cancel**. Click **Cancel**.

* Close all open windows.

Problem D

* Clear the My Recent Documents menu.

* Open My Computer.

* Open the Drive C window.

* Open the XPRODATA folder.

* Click **View**.

* Click **Tiles**.

* Click **View**.

* Point at **Arrange Icons by**.

* Click **Name**.

* Locate the file called **Jupiter.txt**.

* Double-click it.

17. The following occurred:
    a. Notepad opened the file. Data appeared in the window.
    b. Notepad opened with an empty screen. There was no data in the window.
    c. You were presented with the Open With dialog box.
    d. You were presented with an error message stating that Windows cannot open the requested file.

* Close Notepad.

* Double-click the **Sports** folder.

* Double-click **Basketbl.tms**.

   18. The following occurred:
  - a. Notepad opened the file. Data appeared in the window.
  - b. Notepad opened with an empty screen. There was no data in the window.
  - c. You were presented with an dialog box stating that Windows cannot open the requested file and you must either choose which program to use from a list or use Microsoft's web service.
  - d. You were presented with a list of programs.

* Click **Cancel**.

* Close all open windows and return to the desktop.

* Click **Start**. Point at My Recent **Documents**.

   19. What file(s) appear(s) on the Documents menu?
  - a. JUPITER.TXT
  - b. BASKETBL.TMS
  - c. both JUPITER.TXT and BASKETBL.TMS.
  - d. No files appear.

* Close the menu.

Problem Set II—Brief Essay

1. In the Folder Options menu, the below views are set. Describe what would be displayed in a window you opened. Describe what would happen as you opened new windows. Would you choose these views? Why or why not? If they would not be your choices, describe your choices and explain what influenced your decision.

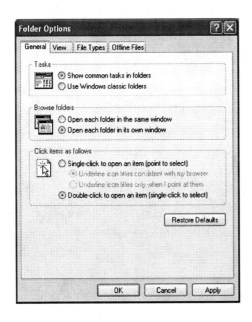
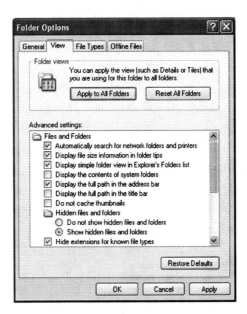

2. You see the following menu when you right-click a document icon. Compare and contrast the commands Open and Open With.

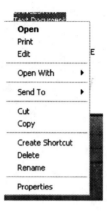

Problem Set III—Scenario

You have been asked to write an article for a newsletter for senior citizens about aspects of My Computer in Windows XP Professional. You have been using several view options, such as tiles, icons, list, thumbnails, and details. You decide that you will differentiate among them and explain when each option might be useful. In addition, you want to discuss and describe the various types of icons that appear in the My Computer window. Write the article.

CHAPTER 4

Windows Applications: Outlook Express, Notepad, WordPad, and Paint

Windows XP Professional provides some convenient tools with its desktop accessories. These applications are included with Windows XP Professional. They are called applications because they are small application programs. You can access them through the Start menu or the Start/All Programs/Accessories menu when you need them. Outlook Express is the Microsoft email program that you can use for emailing. You have already used another accessory, Notepad. You are now going to learn more about Notepad. Another accessory you will learn about is WordPad, a simple word-processing program. WordPad offers formatting capabilities that Notepad does not. The last tool you will learn about is Paint. Paint is a graphics application program that allows you to create and edit simple drawings and images.

In addition, Windows XP Professional includes some applications that are beyond the scope of this text. These include the Microsoft Windows Movie Maker, which can turn your computer into an audio and video editing center. It can be used to edit audio and video sequences from sources such as camcorders or digital cameras. Windows Media Player is another application included which can play all your digital media. Windows XP Professional includes an instant messaging program as well (Windows Messenger) that allows you to see who is online and allows you to communicate with others who are online. It also includes MSN Explorer. Both Windows Messenger and MSN Explorer are services that you must join to use them. Also included is the Scanners and Cameras icon, which appears in Control Panel when you install your first scanner or digital camera. You may then use the Scanners and Cameras feature to install other scanners, digital still cameras, digital video cameras, and image-capturing devices. Also included is the Microsoft Photo Editor application, which enables you to view, annotate, and perform basic tasks with image documents.

Learning Objectives

1. Explain the purpose and function of Outlook Express.
2. Explain email terminology and informal rules for interacting on the Internet.
3. Explain the purpose, function, and features of Notepad.
4. Explain how to open, save, print, and close files in Notepad.
5. Explain the purpose, function, and features WordPad.
6. Explain how to open, save, print, and close files in WordPad.
7. Compare and contrast WordPad and Notepad.
8. Explain the purpose, function, and features of Paint.
9. Explain how to open, save, print, and close files in Paint.
10. Name and explain the function of each item found on the Paint screen.
11. Explain the purpose and process of importing and exporting graphics.

Student Outcomes

1. Use Outlook Express to send and receive email and then send an email.
2. Use Notepad to create, save, apply page-level formatting to, and print a file.
3. Open WordPad, edit a WordPad document, apply character and page-level formatting to, and print a document.
4. Open Paint to manipulate an existing drawing.
5. Use Paint tools to draw and edit lines, curves, and geometric figures.
6. Import, export, and manipulate graphics.
7. Use Paint to create, edit, save, and print a drawing.

4.1 • Outlook Express

One of the most popular aspects of the Internet is the use of email. *Email (electronic mail)* allows you to exchange messages and files all over the world. Email is sent from one computer to another. In order to use email, you must have an email address, a connection to the Internet, and a program that handles email.

Many Web browsers, such as Netscape, provide these functions. Windows XP Professional includes a program called Outlook Express. Outlook Express is an email program and newsreader. It lets you create, manage, send, and receive email and newsgroup messages. If you have installed Microsoft Office, you may have installed Outlook. Outlook is the communications component of the Microsoft Office suite. It has many more features than Outlook Express, such as calendar scheduling and contact management.

Outlook Express has a message editor, a viewer, and an address book to keep your commonly used addresses. It includes a set of folders that allow you to organize your incoming and outgoing messages. It also provides access to several directories that you can use to find names and email and street addresses. Outlook Express can work with almost any type of email or news service, such as AOL and MSN.

4.2 • Outlook Express • Email Basics

Email is an exceedingly useful form of communication. You can send email at any time, and the recipient can read it at any time. The most common things you do when you run your email program are send email, read your email, reply to email, and delete email.

All email programs have a command to create a message. Once you begin to create an email message, you will be asked for the address of the person you wish to send it to. A person's address is in the form of *user name @address .domain*. *User name* is the name of the person. The *address* is that person's network and the *domain* is a code indicating whether that person is connected through a business (.com), a nonprofit group (.org), a university (.edu), and so on. An example of an email address is **czg@bookbiz.com,** which is pronounced "czg at bookbiz dot com." czg is the user name. The "at" (@) indicates which server is being referenced. Bookbiz is the address and .com indicates that it is a commercial site. Other common examples are shown in Table 4.1.

Network/Organization	User Name	Email Address
America Online	czg	czg@aol.com
Microsoft Network	czg	czg@msn.com
Saddleback College	cgillay	cgillay@saddleback.cc.ca.us
University of California at Irvine	cgillay	cgillay@uci.edu
Franklin, Beedle & Associates	cgillay	cgillay@fbeedle.com
The Book Biz, Inc.	czg	czg@bookbiz.com

Table 4.1 ⚬ Email Addresses

There are a variety of informal rules for politely interacting on the Internet. These rules are known as **netiquette**. Netiquette includes the principles of courtesy that you should observe when you send email or post messages to newsgroups. If you violate netiquette, you could be flamed. **Flaming** is the sending of abusive or personally insulting email messages or newsgroup postings. Examples of violating netiquette include such actions as insulting people, posting large amounts of irrelevant material, giving away the plot of a movie or book without warning, and posting offensive material.

You can have multiple email accounts. For instance, you could have a work email address and a personal email address. You could access all your email from Outlook Express. However, in order to set up your email account, you must have some information:

* Your email address and password. You usually receive this from your Internet service provider (ISP).
* Your local access phone number, if you connect through a dial-up account. Again, your ISP should provide this information.
* The names of the servers for incoming and outgoing email. Typically your incoming email is handled by a POP (Post Office Protocol) or IMAP (Internet Message Access Protocol) server, while your outgoing email is handled by an SMTP (Simple Mail Transfer Protocol) server. Again, you should receive all this information from your ISP.

4.3 ⚬ Activity ⚬ Setting Up Outlook Express

Note: In order to do this activity, you need to have a connection to the Internet, an email address, and Outlook Express.

1   Click **Start**. Click **E-mail**.

WHAT'S HAPPENING? In this example, Outlook Express has never been set up for the user on this computer. If Outlook Express has already been set up, you will see the screen following step 6. As each user sets up an email account, he or she will have to go through this process. This process is known as a wizard. A *wizard* is a program that uses step-by-step instructions to lead the user through the execution and completion of a Windows task.

2   Key in your name as you would like it to appear. Click **Next**.

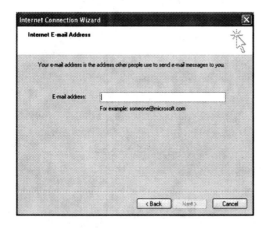

WHAT'S HAPPENING? Here is where you include your email address. You must use the email address that was given to you when you signed up for your Internet account.

3   Key in your email address. Click **Next**.

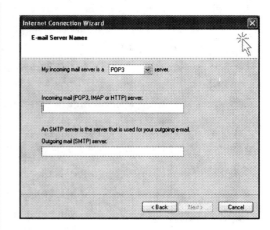

WHAT'S HAPPENING? The wizard needs to know your POP3, HTTP, or IMAP server as well as your SMTP server. They should look something like **pop3.bookbiz.com, pop.deltanet.com, smtp.deltanet .com,** or **mail.deltanet.com**.

4   Fill in the correct information from your ISP. Click **Next**.

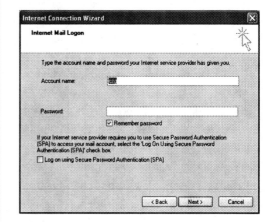

WHAT'S HAPPENING? Here you are asked for your logon name. Your POP account name could be different from your user name. It is not your email address. You may have different passwords for logging on to get your email and for logging on to your ISP.

5   Fill in the correct information. Click **Next**.

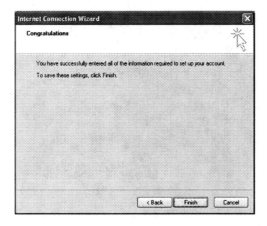

WHAT'S HAPPENING? You have established your Internet email account.

6 Click **Finish**.

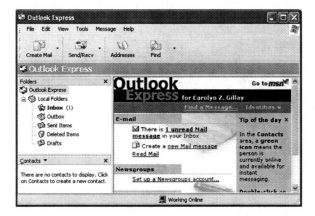

WHAT'S HAPPENING? The Outlook Express window opens now that you have set up your account.

7 On the menu bar in the Outlook Express window, click **Tools**. Click **Accounts**. Click the **Mail** tab.

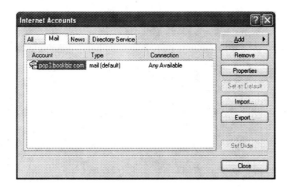

WHAT'S HAPPENING? Here you see the account that you just created or the account that was already created. Note that the account name simply reflects the POP name. You might prefer to have a more meaningful name.

8 Select the account. Click **Properties**.

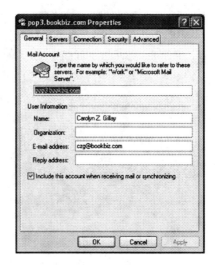

WHAT'S **HAPPENING?** In this example, you would highlight **pop3.bookbiz.com** and key in any user-friendly name you wish.

9   Key in a name you like. Click **OK**.

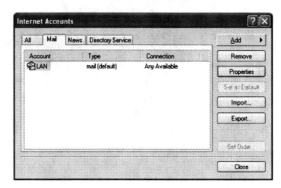

WHAT'S **HAPPENING?** Now you have a more identifiable name for your email account. You may have more than one email account if you have more than one email address.

10   Click **Add**. Click **Mail**.

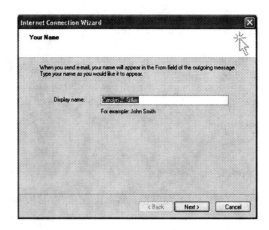

WHAT'S HAPPENING? When you selected Mail, Internet Connection Wizard opened again, allowing you to add additional email accounts. Figure 4.1 shows an example of multiple email accounts.

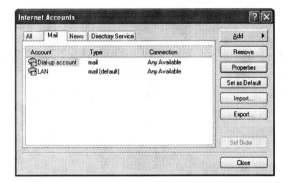

*Figure 4.1 * Multiple Email Accounts*

Notice that one account is the default. You can alter the properties of any account. You can add or remove any email account. To access any of these accounts from Outlook Express, click Tools and then point at Send and Receive. Figure 4.2 shows an example of the choices available with multiple email accounts.

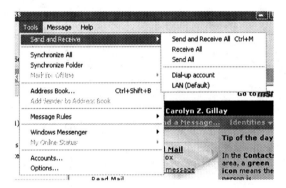

*Figure 4.2 * Using Multiple Email Accounts*

11 Click **Cancel**. Click **Yes**. Click **Close**. Close **Outlook Express**.

4.4 ◦ Sending, Receiving, and Organizing Email

Five folders are created in Outlook Express for your email. The structure of the folders is the tree structure that you have used in Windows Explorer. The five folders that are automatically created are Inbox, Outbox, Sent Items, Deleted Items, and Drafts. As you receive new messages, they are all placed in Inbox. Unread messages appear in boldface and the number of messages that are not read will be indicated in parentheses. All your outgoing messages that are to be sent are placed in Outbox temporarily. As they are sent, they are removed. In the Sent Items folder are copies of every message that you send. All items that you delete are placed in the Deleted Items folder. If you have any email that is not ready to send yet, you can store it in the Drafts folder until you are ready to send it. You can create folders and delete unwanted ones. You may use Inbox Assistant to sort your incoming email so that, for instance, when you receive email from a specific person, it can be sent directly to a folder that you create. Figure 4.3 shows these items in the Outlook Express window.

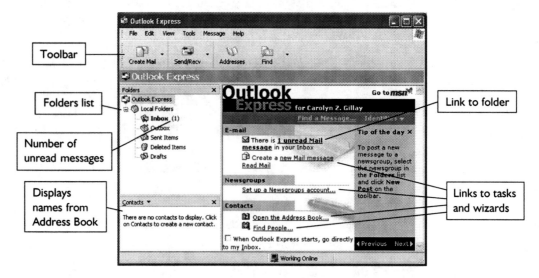

Figure 4.3 • *The Outlook Express Window*

You may send attachments. An ***attachment*** is a file that you attach to a message. You may also check your email regularly at some predetermined time or simply log on, get your email, and log off.

4.5 • Activity • Sending, Receiving, and Organizing Email

Note 1: If you are using Netscape or another email program, this activity will still work. However, these instructions are only for Outlook Express. You will need to get the directions for the email program that you are using.

Note 2: If you do not have an email address, check with your instructor to see if your school has one for you.

Note 3: You may need extra instructions for your environment. Check with your instructor.

I   Open Outlook Express.

2   Click the Create Mail icon, .

WHAT'S HAPPENING? You may also begin a new message from the menu bar or (File/New/Mail Message or Message/New Message). In the To text box, you will key in the email address of the recipient of your message. If you want this message to go to more than the one recipient, place the names in the Cc (carbon copy) line. Since email is sorted and saved by what is in the Subject line, be sure to fill this in. You will then key in your message.

3   Click the **To** line. Key in your email address.

4   Click the Subject line. Key in the following: **Email Test**

5   Click in the message area. Key in the following:

Today's date Enter

This is a test of sending email using a mail program. Enter

Your name

WHAT'S HAPPENING? You have created your message. You are sending a message to yourself. Now you need to send it. To send it, you need to be online.

5   Click **Send**.

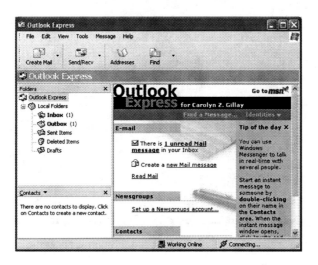

WHAT'S HAPPENING? In this example, you are already online, and your email is simply sent. Your environment may be different. If you had a dial-up connection, Outlook Express would begin dialing the number and making the connection.

The message is sent to the Outbox. You can see that (1) message is being sent. Once it is sent, (1) no longer appears next to the Outbox folder. Your connection may be so fast that the email is placed quickly in Outbox and is sent.

6   Click Tools. Point to Send and Receive.

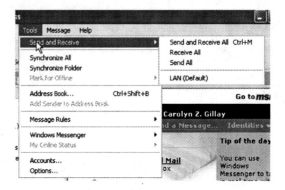

WHAT'S HAPPENING? Here you may choose not only to send and receive all, but also to only send or to only receive. You may also specify which account, if you have more than one account.

7   Click Receive All.

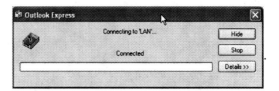

WHAT'S HAPPENING? You see a connection message box. If you had a dial-up account, you would see the dialing connection. When the connection is complete, you see the following window.

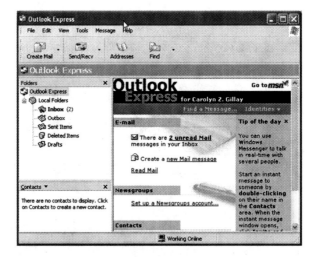

You see that you have two unread email messages. You may only have one, if you have previously used Outlook Express.

8   Click Local Folders.

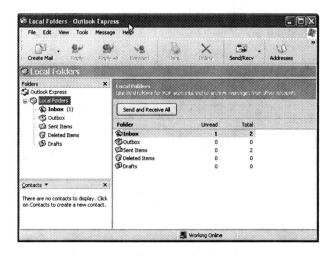

WHAT'S HAPPENING? You may also send and receive all your email from this location.

9 Click **Inbox**. Click your name in the right pane.

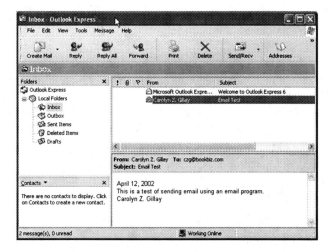

WHAT'S HAPPENING? As you selected your name, the bottom half of the screen showed your message.

10 Click the **Sent Items** folder.

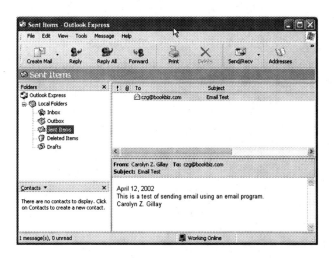

WHAT'S HAPPENING? You see the message you just sent.

11 Click your message to select it. Click the **Delete** button on the toolbar. Click **Inbox**. Click your message to select it. Click the **Delete** button on the toolbar.

12 Click the **Deleted Items** folder.

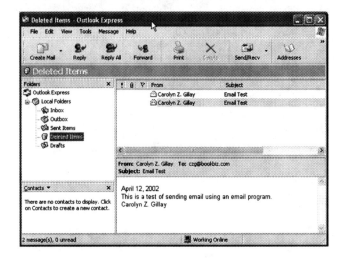

WHAT'S HAPPENING? You moved the messages from your Sent Items and Inbox folders to the Deleted Items folder. As you can see, as you increase your email correspondence, these folders become very crowded. In addition, you are taking up space on your hard drive saving old email. Beginning users have a tendency to keep all email. If you do this, your email becomes quickly overwhelming. Most email, once it has been read, can and should be deleted. Although you can do this manually, it is faster if you customize Outlook Express so the deletions happen automatically.

13 Click **Tools**. Click **Options**.

WHAT'S HAPPENING? You have many customization options. The default setting for how often to check your email is every 30 minutes. Obviously you must be online for this to occur. You can change this time period by using the spin box.

14 Click the **Maintenance** tab.

WHAT'S HAPPENING? One option that you might want to select is **Empty messages from the 'Deleted Items' folder on exit**. This selection will automatically eliminate deleted messages.

15 Set **Empty messages from the 'Deleted Items' folder on exit**. Click the **Send** tab.

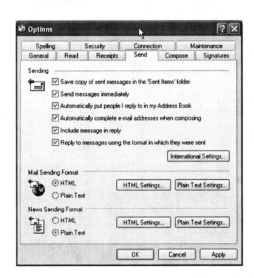

WHAT'S HAPPENING? Here you may choose not to save copies of your sent messages. In addition, you may also want to clear **Automatically put people I reply to in my Address Book**. If you do not clear this, your Address Book will become very large. You may also wish to clear **Include message in reply**. If you have a lengthy corre-

spondence with an individual, all the messages that you transmit will be included.

16 Clear **Save copy of sent messages in the 'Sent Items' folder**. Clear **Automatically put people I reply to in my Address Book**. Click **Apply**.

17 Click the **Connection** tab.

WHAT'S HAPPENING? If you have a dial-up connection, you can choose to hang up automatically if you simply want to connect to your email server, download your email, and hang up.

18 Click **OK**.

19 Click the **Deleted Items** folder. Click your name in the right pane. Click **Reply**.

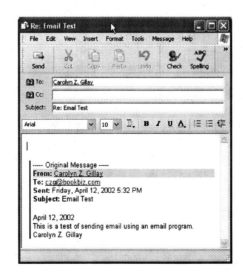

WHAT'S **HAPPENING?** Here you may reply to the author of the email message. When you reply, the email address and subject are automatically filled in. You need to type only your response. Notice that the entire message gets re-sent along with your comments, since you did not clear that check box.

20   Close the Re: Email Test window.

21   Right-click **Local Folders**. Click **New Folder**.

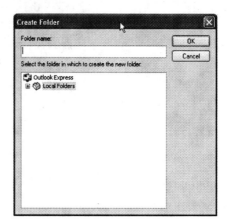

WHAT'S **HAPPENING?** Here you can create a new folder to further organize your email.

22   Key in **TEST**. Click **OK**.

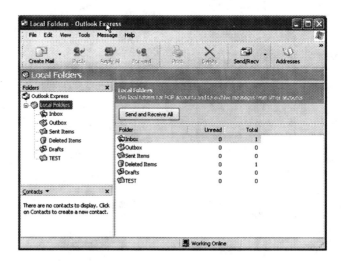

WHAT'S **HAPPENING?** You see your new folder.

23   Right-click **TEST**. Click **New Folder**. Key in **EMAIL**. Click **OK**.

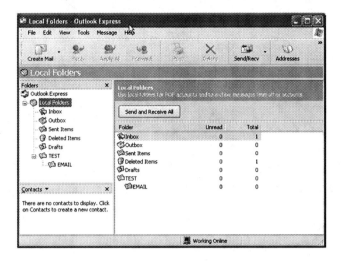

WHAT'S HAPPENING? You have created a new folder under Local Folders and under TEST.

24 Click **Deleted Items**. Right-click the message to yourself. Click **Move To Folder**. Choose **TEST**. Click **OK**. Click **TEST**.

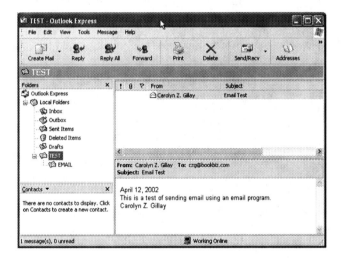

WHAT'S HAPPENING? You successfully moved your message.

25 Right-click **EMAIL**. Click **Delete**.

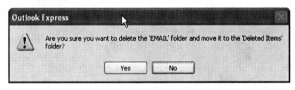

WHAT'S HAPPENING? You are asked if you are sure.

26 Click **Yes**. Right-click **TEST**. Click **Delete**. Click **Yes**.

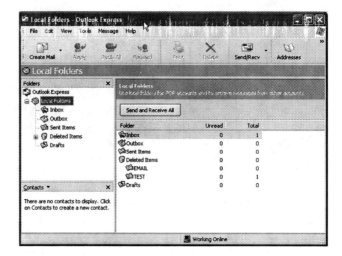

WHAT'S HAPPENING? You deleted the folders you created. You can also control how Outlook Express handles your email and newsgroups. You may specify that messages to or from a certain person be selected. You may choose to have messages selected by size or by account. You may choose to move or copy messages immediately upon their arrival. You can even block senders from whom you do not wish to receive email.

27 Click **Tools**. Point to **Message Rules**. Click **Mail**.

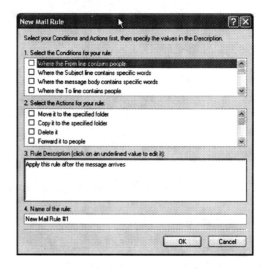

WHAT'S HAPPENING? Here is where you set up rules for your email.

28 Click **Cancel**. Click **Cancel**.

29 Click **Create Mail**. Click **Insert**.

WHAT'S **HAPPENING?** One common task people do with email is attach documents or pictures to email messages. Most documents and pictures are stored as files. To add an attachment to your email, you simply choose File Attachment, then tell Outlook Express where the file is located.

30 Click **File Attachment**.

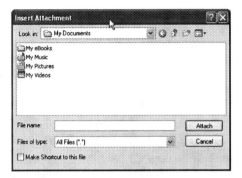

WHAT'S **HAPPENING?** The default location is My Documents.

31 In the Look in drop-down list box, locate and click the XPRODATA folder.

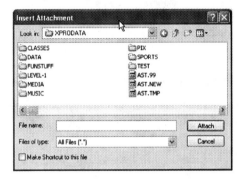

WHAT'S **HAPPENING?** In this case, this is the folder where your "attachment" is located.

32 Click **AST.99**. Click **Attach**.

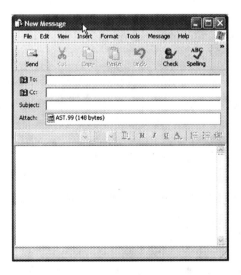

WHAT'S **HAPPENING?** In the Attach: text box, you see name of your attachment (file). You would simply fill out the email address, the subject, and your message and then click Send.

33 Click the Close button on the New Mail window. Click **No**. Close Outlook Express. If you have a dial-up account, disconnect.

WHAT'S **HAPPENING?** You have returned to the desktop.

4.6 ◦ Notepad

You have looked at the Notepad text editor. You used it to multitask and to open a file. Remember, a text document is one that has no embedded codes so that many formatting options, such as font selection and auto-format, are not available to you in the Notepad text editor. All word-processing programs have these embedded codes; all text editors lack them. As you will later see, at times you need to give direct instructions to Windows XP Professional itself, but Windows XP Professional can only recognize text files—those with no special embedded codes. This use is why you have Notepad. A text editor produces documents that are called text files, unformatted text files, or ASCII (American Standard Code for Information Interchange) files.

4.7 ◦ Activity ◦ Using Notepad

1 Place your MYDATADISK disk in Drive A (the disk that was formatted in Chapter 1, Section 1.19).

2 Click **Start**. Point at **All Programs**. Point at **Accessories**. Click **Notepad**.

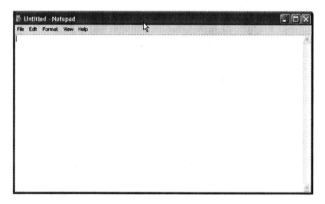

WHAT'S **HAPPENING?** You have opened Notepad. If you choose, you can adjust the size of the Notepad window by using the techniques you learned earlier.

3 Key in the following data. (*Note:* Where you see Tab press the Tab key. Where you see Enter, press the Enter key.)
Dream Machine Enter
Enter
Processor Tab Tab **Intel Pentium 4 at 1.8 GHz** Enter
RAM Tab Tab Tab **256 MB** Enter
Hard drive Tab Tab **80 GB** Enter
Floppy drive Tab Tab **3 1/2 inch** Enter
Removable Tab Tab **250 MB Zip drive** Enter
Monitor Tab Tab Tab **17-inch flat panel** Enter
DVD Tab Tab Tab **CD-RW/DVD Combo Drive** Enter

CD-ROM `Tab` `Tab` `Tab` **48 x CD-ROM Drive** `Enter`
Graphics `Tab` `Tab` **64 MB Video Card** `Enter`
Networking `Tab` `Tab` **Integrated 3Com 10/100 NIC** `Enter`
Sound Card `Tab` `Tab` **SB live Digital Sound Card** `Enter`
Speakers `Tab` `Tab` **Flat-panel speakers with subwoofer** `Enter`
Keyboard `Tab` `Tab` **Natural keyboard** `Enter`
Mouse `Tab` `Tab` `Tab` **Wheel mouse** `Enter`
System software `Tab` `Tab` **Windows XP Professional** `Enter`

WHAT'S **HAPPENING?** You have created a file with data. Now you wish to save it to disk. In order to save it, you have to name it.

4   Click **File**.

WHAT'S **HAPPENING?** You have two choices, Save and Save As. When you choose Save, your file is saved to a disk, overwriting the previous version of the file (if one exists). If you choose Save As, you preserve your original document by creating a new document. Since this document has never been saved, Save and Save As will behave in the same way.

5   Click **Save**.

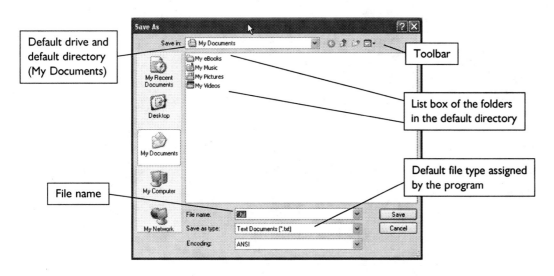

WHAT'S **HAPPENING?** Although you chose Save, you were presented with the Save As dialog box. A file must first have a name before it can be saved. Every time you save a new file, you see the Save As dialog box. Every time you save a named file, you skip this dialog box because the updated file is automatically saved under its original name. You also see the default directory. A file must have a name and a place to be saved. The default directory is My Documents on Drive C. (*Note:* If you are in a lab environment, the default may have been changed to a different directory.) In addition, the left column provides alternative locations to store your data. The My Recent Documents folder is a list of the documents that you have most recently used.

In the Save as type drop-down list box, Text Documents is the default. Text documents use the file extension .txt.

6   Click the down arrow in the Save in drop-down list box.

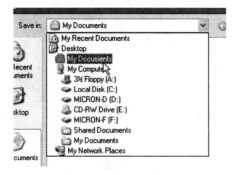

WHAT'S HAPPENING? You see all the drives on your system as well as some other locations that the document could be saved in, such as Shared Documents or a network drive (My Network Places).

7   Click the **3½ Floppy (A:)** icon.

WHAT'S HAPPENING? There are no folders or files on this disk.

8   In the File name text box, highlight ***.txt**. Key in the following: **DREAM**

WHAT'S HAPPENING? You have named your file. When you highlight text and then key in data, your typing replaces what was already there. This feature is called typing replaces selection. The extension .txt will automatically be added to the file name since this file is being created with Notepad.

9   Click **Save**.

10   Close Notepad. Open Notepad.

11   On the File menu, click **Open**.

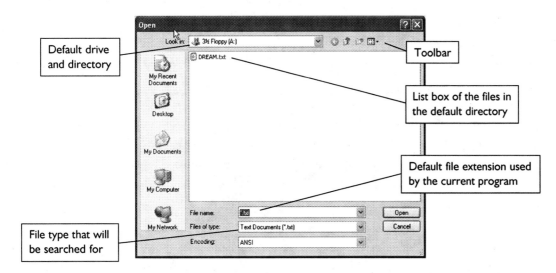

WHAT'S HAPPENING? The Open dialog box looks similar to the Save As dialog box. Because *.txt is shown in the File name text box, only files that have the .txt extension (but have any file name) will be displayed in the dialog box. Notepad is looking for files with its own default extension only. It is only looking in the default directory, My Documents. The documents in your directory may be different.

12   Double-click **DREAM.txt**.

WHAT'S HAPPENING? The file opens with the data that you created. You can see the name of the file (DREAM.txt) followed by the program name (Notepad) on the title bar. If the file extension .txt does not appear on the title bar (or in the Open dialog box's file name, you do not have your Folder Options set properly. See Section 3.8.

13   Press **Ctrl** + **End**

14   Key in the following:
     Printer ⌷Tab⌷ ⌷Tab⌷ ⌷Tab⌷ **HP LaserJet 2200D**

WHAT'S **HAPPENING?** ⟫ You have added text to the document.

15   Close Notepad.

WHAT'S **HAPPENING?** ⟫ Notepad knows that you have made changes but have not yet saved these changes to a disk. If you wanted to save the changes, you would click Yes. If you did not wish to save the changes, you would click No, and Notepad would close without saving the changes. If you wanted to save the changes but preserve your original document, you would click Cancel. This action would return you to the document where you could choose File/Save As and save the file under a new name. Then you would have your original file and an additional file with the new data in it. In this case, you only want one document with the changes.

16   Click **Yes**.

WHAT'S **HAPPENING?** ⟫ You have returned to the desktop.

4.8 ◦ Formatting with Page Setup and Printing in Notepad

To print a Notepad document, you may locate it with My Computer. Once the file is located and selected, you can use either the File/Print commands from the menu bar or the shortcut menus. Either choice will print the document immediately.

You may also open Notepad from the Start/All Programs/Accessories menu. From there, you can open your document. Once opened, you can print it. The advantage of opening Notepad to print a file is that you can apply page-level formatting to your document.

You can include a header, a footer, or both on each page. A *header* is text printed at the top of each page, while a *footer* is text printed at the bottom of each page. Typical items in headers and footers are file names, page numbers, and dates. You can also alter the top, bottom, left, and right margins of the document. In order to apply these formatting features, you must load Notepad and select File/Page Setup.

4.9 • Activity • Page Setup and Printing in Notepad

1 Your MYDATADISK disk is in Drive A. Open Notepad. Click **File**.
Click **Open**.

2 If **3½ Floppy (A:)** does not appear in the Look in drop-down list box, click the down arrow,
then click the Drive A icon.

3 Double-click **DREAM.txt**.

4 Click **File**. Click **Page Setup**.

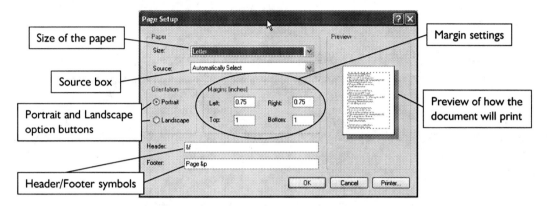

WHAT'S HAPPENING? Your options in the Size and Source drop-down list boxes will depend on which printer you have installed. You also may not have a Portrait or Landscape option. Portrait prints in the standard, vertical, 8½-by-11-inch format, whereas landscape prints sideways, in an 11-by-8½-inch mode. You can change the margin settings. There are default values in the Header and Footer text boxes. The symbol & indicates that something will be printed. In this case, &f means print the file name and Page &p means print the word Page and the page number. To see the available choices, drag the question mark down and click on the Header/Footer text boxes.

5 Click the question mark. Drag it over **Header:** and click.

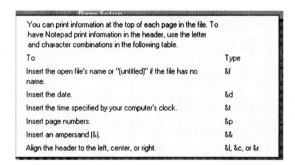

WHAT'S HAPPENING? You see the available options for use with the & symbol.

6 Click outside of the information box to close it. Select the text in the Header text box, then
key in the following: **&cCOMPUTER FILE**

7 Select the text in the Footer text box; then key in the following:
&l&f &rPage &p

8 Change the right and left margins to 1 inch.

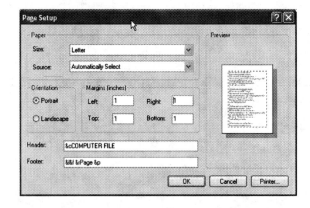

WHAT'S **HAPPENING?** You have set up how you want your document to print. When you changed the margins, the Preview picture in the Page Setup dialog box adjusted to show you the new look of your document. The &cCOMPUTER FILE centered those words at the top of the page (a header). The &l&f placed the file name at the left side of the bottom of the page (a footer). The &rPage &p inserted the word Page and the page number at the right side of the bottom of the page.

9　Be sure your printer is on. Click **OK**. Click **File**. Click **Print**.

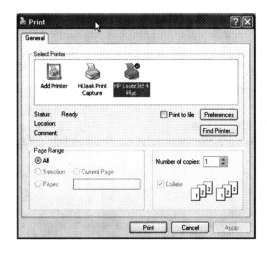

WHAT'S **HAPPENING?** You see your printer dialog box.

10　Click Print.

```
                      Computer File
   Dream Machine

   Processor            Intel Pentium 4 at 1.8 GHz
   RAM                  256 MB
   Hard drive           80 GB
   Floppy drive         3 1/2 inch
   Removable            250 MB Zip drive
   Monitor              17-inch flat panel
   DVD                  CD-RW/DVD Combo Drive
   CD-ROM               48 x CD-ROM Drive
   Graphics             64 MB Video Card
   Networking           Integrated 3Com 10/100 NIC
   Sound Card           SB live Digital Sound Card
```

```
Speakers             Flat-panel speakers with subwoofer
Keyboard             Natural keyboard
Mouse                Wheel mouse
System software      Windows XP Professional
Printer              HP LaserJet 2200D



DREAM.TXT                                    Page 1
```

WHAT'S **HAPPENING?** You have a hard copy of your document.

11 Save the file. Close Notepad.

12 Open My Computer. Double-click **Drive A**. Right-click **Dream.txt**.

WHAT'S **HAPPENING?** You may also print the document from the shortcut menu.

13 Click **Print**.

WHAT'S **HAPPENING?** You saw Notepad quickly open your document and then send it to the printer. This is a fast way to print

14 Close the Drive A window.

WHAT'S **HAPPENING?** You have returned to the desktop.

4.10 ● Features of Notepad

Notepad has some minimal editing features, such as word wrap, which you can turn on or off. *Word wrap* prevents text from running over into the margins, automatically moving text to the next line, so that you never need to press **Enter**. You can create a file, save it, and then reopen it to edit it. You can also create a time log to track your activities. You can cut, copy, and paste text within Notepad, as well as copy information to Notepad from other documents. You can also transfer Notepad text to other word-processing, text, or database documents.

4.11 ● Activity ● Using Features of Notepad

1 Your MYDATADISK disk is in Drive A. Open Notepad.

2 At the insertion point, key in the following exactly, making sure you use all uppercase letters. Also note that there is a period preceding the word LOG.

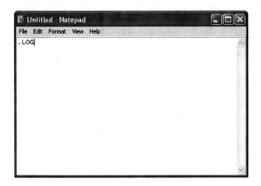

WHAT'S **HAPPENING?** You are going to keep a log of your work. The log will stamp the current date and time in your document every time you open it.

3   Click **File**. Click **Save**.

4   If Drive A is not already selected, click the down arrow in the Save in drop-down list box. Click **3½ Floppy (A:)**.

5   Select **Untitled** in the File name text box. Key in **LOG**. Click **Save**.

6   Close Notepad. Open Notepad. Click **File**. Click **Open**. If Drive A is not already selected, click the down arrow in the Look in drop-down list box. Click **3½ Floppy (A:)**, then select and double-click **LOG.txt**.

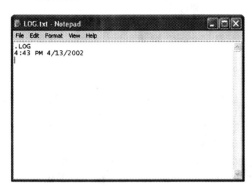

WHAT'S **HAPPENING?** You opened your log file. It is a log file because .LOG is the first line in the file. You see the current time and date displayed in the file. You are now logged in as opening this file at the current date and time.

7   Key in the following: **I am working with Notepad.**

8   Click **File**. Click **Save**.

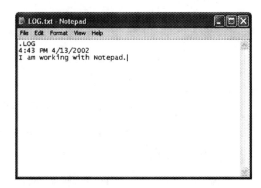

WHAT'S **HAPPENING?** You added data to the file and saved the updated information to the disk under the same file name.

9   Click **File**. Click **Open**.

10   In the Look in text box, click **(C:)**. Double-click the **XPRODATA** folder. (*Note:* Remember, if XPRODATA is on a drive other than C, you will have to select the correct drive.)

11   Double-click **States.txt**.

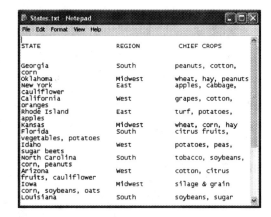

WHAT'S **HAPPENING?** When you open a file in Notepad, the previous file closes. You can only open one document at a time in Notepad. Depending on the size of your Notepad window, the text of this document may or may not fit in the window.

12   Size the Notepad window so it looks like the above example.

13   Click **Format**.

WHAT'S HAPPENING? In this example, Word Wrap is set so that the text will wrap in the window. Word Wrap is on by default.

14   Click **Word Wrap** to unset it.

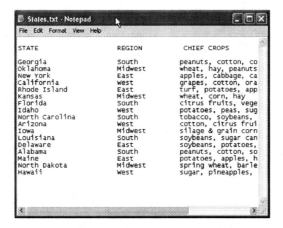

WHAT'S HAPPENING? When Word Wrap is off, all of the text does not fit into the window.

15   Click **Format**. Click **Word Wrap** to set it. On the Edit menu, click **Find**.

WHAT'S HAPPENING? The Find dialog box appears. In the Find what text box, you key in what you are looking for. You also have a check box that will, if set, make the search case sensitive. Using the two option buttons, you may search up or down through your document. Down is the default.

16   In the Find what text box, key in the following: **Wheat**

17   Click **Find Next**.

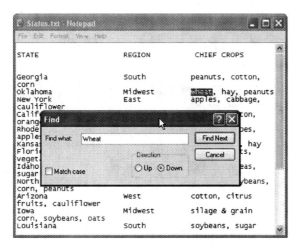

WHAT'S HAPPENING? The Find command located the first occurrence of the word wheat. If your dialog box is in the way and you cannot see the text, you may move the Find dialog box. If you desire, you can continue to search for the next occurrence of your selected text.

18 Click **Cancel**.

19 Click the insertion point in front of Oklahoma. Place the cursor after the **t** in **East**. Hold the [Shift] key and click.

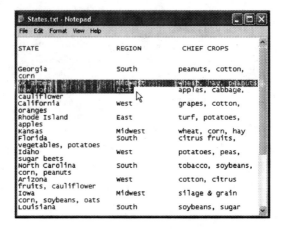

WHAT'S **HAPPENING?** In order to manipulate text, you must first select it. You know the text is selected because it is highlighted.

20 Click **Edit**. Click **Copy**.

WHAT'S **HAPPENING?** Windows XP Professional has a feature called Clipboard that uses an area of memory to store anything copied or cut from a file. Whatever is in Clipboard remains there until you clear the Clipboard, replace it with something else, or turn off the computer.

21 Click **File**. Click **Open**. In the File Name text box, key in the following: **A:\LOG.TXT**

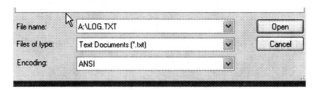

WHAT'S **HAPPENING?** If you know your file name and location, you can key it in the File Name text box.

22 Click **Open**.

23 Click **Edit**. Click **Paste**.

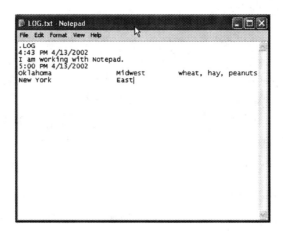

WHAT'S **HAPPENING?** Opening your existing LOG.txt file inserted the current date and time. You then selected Edit/Paste, which pasted the information that you copied from States.txt into LOG.txt.

24 Click **File**. Click **Save**.

WHAT'S **HAPPENING?** The new information in the file has been saved.

25 Close Notepad.

WHAT'S **HAPPENING?** You have returned to the desktop.

4.12 ⬝ WordPad

WordPad is a simple word-processing program that lets the user format a document. You can change the fonts, apply special character-level formatting such as boldface or underline, create margins, and insert bulleted charts. In addition, you can insert graphics and sound files. WordPad has both a menu bar and a toolbar, but it does not have powerful word-processing features such as the ability to create columns or check spelling.

If you have never used a word-processing program, there are some things you should know. You must not press **Enter** when a line of text reaches the right margin. A word-processing program will word wrap automatically when it encounters a right margin. This action is called a *soft return*. The only time you press **Enter** is to create a new paragraph. This action is called a *hard return*. Pressing **Enter** inserts a hidden character into the document known as a paragraph mark.

A paragraph in a word-processing context is different from the traditional paragraph that you were taught in a writing context. The traditional (English-style) paragraph is typically a group of several sentences. It begins with a topic sentence, is followed by two or more supporting sentences, and ends with a concluding sentence. It is usually indented by one tab. In word processing, however, a paragraph is any part of a document that is preceded by one paragraph mark and ends with another—text between two paragraph marks. A paragraph can be one character, one page, or several pages of text.

To WordPad, a paragraph is a unit of information that can be selected as a whole and given individual formatting instructions. The formatting information for a paragraph is contained in the invisible paragraph mark. For example, if you were keying in an address, you would press **Enter** at the end of each line. Each line, therefore, would be a separate paragraph.

When you open WordPad, the WordPad window appears as shown in Figure 4.4. See Table 4.2 for identification of the window's features.

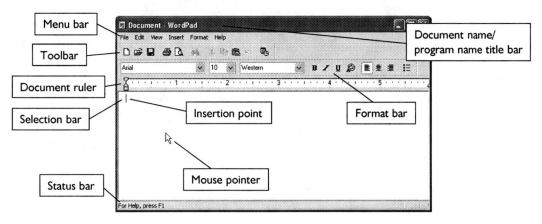

Figure 4.4 ⬝ The WordPad Window

Title bar	In applications designed for the Windows XP Professional docucentric approach, the name of the document appears first, followed by the name of the application. Until this document is named, it is assigned a generic name—Document.
Menu bar	The menu bar provides choices for the tasks you can accomplish within WordPad.
Toolbar	Each item on the toolbar is a shortcut to one of the menu choices. For instance, if you wanted to create a new file, you could click File/New, or you could click the first toolbar icon, ☐, which would accomplish the same task. If you are not sure what an icon represents, hold your pointer over the icon and a ToolTip will appear.
Format toolbar	The Format toolbar, like the standard toolbar, has shortcuts to the Edit and Insert menus. In addition, the Format toolbar provides special character formatting, such as boldface and italics.
Document ruler	The document ruler displays the margin and tab settings for a document.
Selection bar	The *selection bar* is an imaginary area just outside and to the left of the text in a document. When you are in the selection bar, your pointer changes shape from an I-beam to an arrow. When you are in the selection bar, you can take shortcuts with the mouse to select text.
Insertion point	Represented by an I-beam, the insertion point is the place where you begin keying in text. WordPad works in two modes. The default is the *insert* mode. As you key in or edit text, the existing text is pushed to the right. In the other mode, *typeover*, what you key in replaces what is already there. You toggle between these two modes by pressing the **Insert** key.
Status bar	The status bar tells you the status of the document.

Table 4.2 • WordPad Features

WordPad registers the default extension .rtf to any document you create in WordPad. ***Rich text format (RTF)*** is a file format that lets you exchange text files between different word processors in different operating systems. You could create a file in Word in Windows XP Professional, save it as an RTF file, and send it to someone who uses WordPerfect on Windows 3.1 and that person would be able to open the file and read it. As you know, if you are using My Computer and double-click a file with a registered file extension, you open the program that is registered to that extension as well as the document. Only one program can "own" a file extension. Microsoft Word also registers the .rtf extension. So if you have installed Microsoft Office and its word-processing component, Word, when you double-click a file with the .rtf extension, Word will open, not WordPad. This will happen even though you may have created the document with WordPad. This problem can occur with any registered file extension that is claimed by more than one program. Since you want to be able to open the program of your choice, and not necessarily the default program, you need to solve this problem. The following activity will present some alternatives.

4.13 ● Activity ● Choosing Your Program

1 The MYDATADISK disk is in Drive A. To open WordPad, click **Start**, point to **All Programs**, point to **Accessories**, and click **WordPad**.

2 Click **View**.

WHAT'S HAPPENING? If these items are not set in the View menu, check them now.

3 Click outside the menu to close it. Key in the following: **This is a test**.

4 On the toolbar, click the Save button, .

5 In the Save in drop-down list box, click the down arrow in the Save in drop-down list box., then click the **3½ Floppy (A:)** icon.

WHAT'S HAPPENING? Although you have files on the MYDATA DISK disk, you do not see any of them listed because WordPad is only looking at files that have the .rtf file extension. In the File name text box, Document.rtf is listed as the file name. In the Save as type drop-down list box, Rich Text Format (RTF) is displayed.

6 In the File name text box, select **Document.rtf**, then key in the following: **Test**

7 Be sure Drive A is selected. Click **Save**. Close WordPad.

8 Open My Computer. Double-click the **3½ Floppy (A:)** icon.

9 Right-click **Test.rtf**.

WHAT'S HAPPENING? The context menu will let you open this file. On this computer, Word has been installed and the icon for this document is a Word icon. Hence, if you clicked Open, Word would open, not WordPad. The Open With choice, however, offers you the opportunity to select which program you wish to use.

10   Point to Open With.

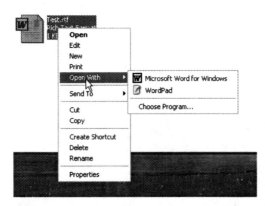

WHAT'S HAPPENING? The programs that will open this document are listed. In this example, the computer system has Microsoft Word for Windows and WordPad installed, both of which will open this document. You may have other choices. You may also choose a different program.

11   Click WordPad.

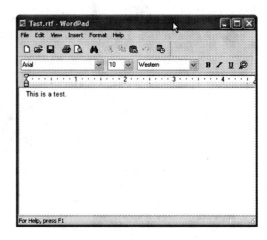

WHAT'S HAPPENING? Your Test.rtf file opened in WordPad, not in Word.

12   Click File. Click Save As.

WHAT'S HAPPENING? WordPad remembered your last location, A:\. In the File name text box is your file name, Test.rtf.

13   Select Test.rtf in File name and key in the following: Test2.new

14   Click the down arrow in the Save as type drop-down list box.

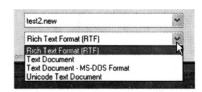

WHAT'S HAPPENING? You have other file types to choose from. If you choose any of the Text Document formats, you will strip out any formatting. Remember, Rich Text Format (RTF) is a text formatting standard that enables a word-processing program to create a file encoded with the document's formatting instructions but without any special codes. An RTF file can usually be read by another word-processing program without losing the formatting.

15   Click Rich Text Format (RTF). Click Save. Close WordPad.

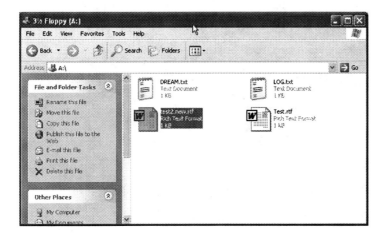

WHAT'S HAPPENING? In addition to your assigned file name, the extension .rtf was added so that your file name became Test2.new.rtf. If you double-clicked this file (and you had Word), Word would open. Word claimed the extension .rtf. If you have both Word and WordPad installed and you want to be able to double-click a document icon and open the program you created the data with, you can create a file extension just for WordPad and register it.

16 Right-click **Test2.new.rtf**. Point to **Open With**. Click **WordPad**.

17 Click **File**. Click **Save As**.

18 In the File name text box, select **Test2.new.rtf** and key in the following: **"test3.pad"**

WHAT'S HAPPENING? Again, WordPad remembered the last location and the last file type. By using quotation marks, you are telling WordPad to use only what you key in and to add no additional extensions.

19 Click **Save**. Close WordPad.

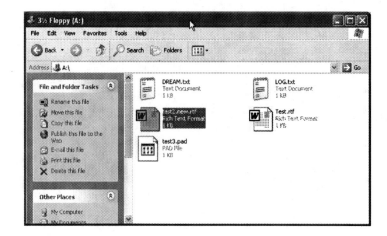

WHAT'S HAPPENING? Because you used quotation marks, your file name is exactly as you named it, test3.pad. When you enclose a file name with quotation marks, you are telling the application program to use exactly what you key in and not to add any other file extensions. Now you could register .pad as your extension for WordPad.

20 Double-click **test3.pad**. Click Select the program from a list. Click **OK**.

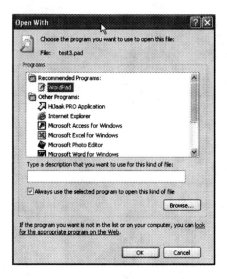

WHAT'S HAPPENING? The extension .pad is unknown to Windows XP Professional, so you are presented with the Open With dialog box. This time Always use this program to open these files check box is set. If you wanted to register this file extension so that every time you double-clicked a .pad file WordPad would open, rather than Word, you would leave this box checked. However, in this case, you are not going to register the extension.

21 Click **Cancel**. Close the 3½ Floppy (A:) window.

WHAT'S HAPPENING? You have returned to the desktop.

4.14 ● Editing and Printing a Document in WordPad

One of the many advantages to using a word-processing program is the ease of editing a document. You can edit a document using a combination of keyboard and mouse techniques. To edit text, you need to move the insertion point to the proper location in your document. You can move the insertion point using either the keyboard or the mouse. It is usually more convenient to use the keyboard when keying in data and the mouse when editing existing text. Taking your hands off the keyboard while you are typing can slow you down. When you use the mouse, you click at the desired location. If you cannot see the location, you can use the scroll bars or scroll boxes to move about your document. The keyboard method sometimes requires you to press two keys simultaneously. Table 4.3 lists ways to move the insertion point using the keyboard.

Keystroke(s)	Function
←	Moves the insertion point one character to the left.
→	Moves the insertion point one character to the right.
Ctrl + ←	Moves the insertion point one word to the left.
Ctrl + →	Moves the insertion point one word to the right.
Home	Moves the insertion point to the start of the line.
End	Moves the insertion point to the end of the line.
↑	Moves the insertion point up one line.
↓	Moves the insertion point down one line.
Ctrl + Home	Moves the insertion point to the beginning of the document.
Ctrl + End	Moves the insertion point to the end of the document.

Table 4.3 ● Using the Keyboard to Move the Insertion Point

Selecting text is fundamental when you work with WordPad. You must select text to modify it. You know when text is being selected because, as you select it, it becomes highlighted. For instance, if you wanted a word to be in italics, you would first have to select it before you could italicize it. Selecting also allows you to manipulate text. Instead of pressing the Backspace key repeatedly to delete a paragraph, you can select the paragraph and press the Delete key.

There are many ways to select text. Using the mouse is an easy method. You drag the mouse over the text you wish to select. You can also click the insertion point at the beginning of what you wish to select, move the mouse to the end of the text you wish to select, and hold the Shift key while you click the mouse.

When you are working with the mouse, remember that there is an important area on the screen called the selection bar. It is an unmarked column along the left edge of the document window. When you are in the selection bar area, the pointer becomes an arrow. This technique is most useful when you are selecting large amounts of text. Table 4.4 lists techniques for selecting text with the mouse.

Text to Be Selected	Technique
One or more characters	Click at the first character. Move the mouse to the last character and hold the **Shift** key while you click.
Word	Double-click the word.
Line	Move to the selection bar and click at the desired line. To select multiple lines, drag the mouse in the selection bar.
Paragraph	Move to the selection bar and double-click at the desired paragraph. To select multiple paragraphs, drag the mouse in the selection bar.
Document	Move to the selection bar, hold the **Ctrl** key, and click. You may also move to the selection bar and triple-click.

Table 4.4 ⬩ Using the Mouse to Select Text

There are also many ways to select text using the keyboard. Essentially, you use the same keyboard selection skills you have learned, but you hold down the **Shift** key. For instance, to move to the end of a line, you press the **End** key. To select to the end of a line, you press both the **Shift** and **End** keys. To select the entire document from the keyboard, hold down the **Ctrl** key and press A.

Remember, another benefit of the mouse is the ability to use the toolbars, which are shown in Figure 4.5.

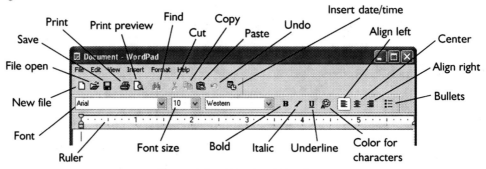

Figure 4.5 ⬩ WordPad Toolbars

4.15 ⬩ Activity ⬩ Editing and Printing a Document in WordPad

1   The MYDATADISK disk is in Drive A. Click **Start**. Point at **All Programs**. Point at **Accessories**. Click **WordPad**.

2   Click the **Open** icon. Click the **My Computer** icon in the left column. Double-click the Drive C icon. Double-click the XPRODATA folder. Double-click the **CLASSES** folder.

WHAT'S **HAPPENING?** It appears that there are no files in the C:\XPRODATA\CLASSES folder. However, in the Files of type drop-down list box, you see that it is only looking for .rtf files. If .doc is in the Files of type text box, you will see one file.

3 Click the down arrow in the Files of type drop-down list box. Click **All Documents (*.*)**.

WHAT'S **HAPPENING?** Now you can see all the available files.

4 Right-click **winxp.syl.doc**. Click **Open With**. Select WordPad. Click **File**. Click **Save As**.

5 Click the down arrow in the Save in drop-down list box. Click the **3½ Floppy (A:)** icon.

WHAT'S **HAPPENING?** You are ready to save the document called winxp.syl.doc to the MYDATADISK disk. You will keep the same file name but change the file extension to .wri. The .wri file extension, which was originally used for the Write program in Windows 3.1, will always open WordPad.

6   Change the file name to read **winxp.syl.wri**. Be sure Rich Text Format (*.rtf) is selected in the Files of Type text box. Click the **Save** command button.

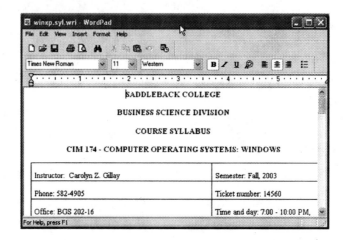

WHAT'S **HAPPENING?** You are looking at the document on the disk in Drive A.

7   Maximize the window. Click **Edit**. Click **Replace**.

8   In the Find what text box, key in **ASSIGNMENTS**. In the Replace with text box, key in **HOMEWORK**.

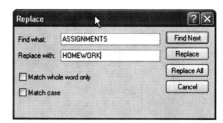

WHAT'S **HAPPENING?** You are going to replace every occurance of ASSIGNMENTS with HOMEWORK.

9   Click **Replace All**.

WHAT'S **HAPPENING?** WordPad has finished its replacement.

10   Click **OK**. Click **Cancel**. Press Ctrl + Home

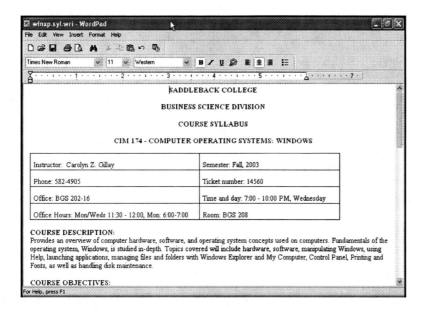

WHAT'S HAPPENING? You have replaced what you wanted and moved to the top of the document.

11 Click **Edit**. Click **Find**.

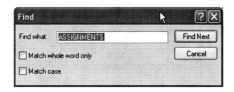

WHAT'S HAPPENING? Find remembers what you last keyed in.

12 In the Find what text box, key in **HOMEWORK**. Click **Find Next**. Click **Find Next**. Click **Cancel**.

> **HOMEWORK** (HOMEWORK): Although homev
> nor turn it in, you will lose 20% of your grade.
> **LATE HOMEWORK (HOMEWORK):** Homew
> homework in one week late, you will get "half" a pas
> have extraordinary circumstances and <u>only</u> if you hav

WHAT'S HAPPENING? When you made your global replacement, you did not delete the second (HOMEWORK). You want to delete this.

13 Click outside the text. Place the insertion point in front of the H in HOMEWORK and drag until **HOMEWORK** is highlighted. Do not include the parentheses.

> HOMEWORK (**HOMEWORK**): Al
> nor turn it in, you will lose 20% of your

WHAT'S HAPPENING? You have selected text.

14 Press the Delete key.

> HOMEWORK (): A
> will lose 20% of your c

WHAT'S HAPPENING? You have deleted the words between the two parentheses.

15   Click **Edit**. Click **Undo**.

HOMEWORK (HOMEWORK): A]
nor turn it in, you will lose 20% of your

WHAT'S **HAPPENING?** You just undid your deletion.

16   Press the ⌨Delete⌨ key again. Press the ⌨Backspace⌨ key twice. Press the ⌨Delete⌨ key once.

HOMEWORK: A

WHAT'S **HAPPENING?** Pressing the ⌨Backspace⌨ key deletes characters to the left. Pressing the ⌨Delete⌨ key deletes characters to the right.

17   Delete (HOMEWORK) in the next paragraph.

18   Move the insertion point into the selection bar area. It will assume an arrow shape. Point and click at the **MISSED TESTS:** line. Double-click.

Exam 2 - Chapters 6 through 10   20%

MISSED TESTS: Quizzes will be given periodically. No make-up quizzes will be given. Lowest three quiz gra
dropped. Tests will be given on dates shown. No make-up tests will be given. If any exam is missed, the total e
be divided among the other two exams.

WHAT'S **HAPPENING?** In the selection area, a single-click selects a line whereas a double-click selects a paragraph.

19   Click **Edit**. Click **Cut**.

20   Place the cursor on the line just above CELL PHONES. Click **Edit**. Click **Paste**.

HOMEWORK: Although homework is pass/fail, homework **is not** optional. If you do not do the homework nor turn it in, you
will lose 20% of your grade.
LATE HOMEWORK: Homework is due on the assigned dates. Homework is pass/fail. If you turn homework in one week late,
you will get "half" a pass. Homework will not be accepted after the second week due. Only if you have extraordinary
circumstances and only if you have prior permission from me, may you email your homework to me (czg@bookbiz.com) **before**
the class meeting when it is due. If some reason the email does not arrive, you will get a 0 on the homework. You may also have a
friend/classmate deliver it to me **before** the class meets.
MISSED TESTS: Quizzes will be given periodically. No make-up quizzes will be given. Lowest three quiz grades will be
dropped. Tests will be given on dates shown. No make-up tests will be given. If any exam is missed, the total exam per cent will
be divided among the other two exams.

CELL PHONE AND PAGERS - Please - no cell phones or pagers in class. It is extremely distracting to other students (and to
me) to have phones or pagers ring and answered in class.

HOMEWORK: Applications must follow this format to be accepted as homework:

WHAT'S **HAPPENING?** You removed the text from the file and copied it to the Clipboard. Then, whatever was on the Clipboard was pasted in the location you specified. When you selected the paragraph, you also selected the hard return, the invisible paragraph mark. A hard return is a character that can be deleted like any other character.

21   Press the ⌨Delete⌨ key once.

MISSED TESTS: Quizzes will be giver
dropped. Tests will be given on dates sho
be divided among the other two exams.
CELL PHONE AND PAGERS - Plea
me) to have phones or pagers ring and a

WHAT'S **HAPPENING?** When you pressed the ⌨Delete⌨ key, you deleted one character to the right of the insertion point. The character you deleted was a paragraph marker.

22   Select **MISSED TESTS:** Click the **Bold**, **Italic**, and **Underline** buttons on the Format toolbar. Click outside the selected area so it is no longer selected.

friend/classmate deliv
MISSED TESTS: Qu

WHAT'S HAPPENING? You have applied character formatting to the selected text. You made the text boldfaced, italicized, and underlined. Place your cursor in the underlined text. If you look at the buttons on the Format toolbar, you can see that they are highlighted (appear indented), which means that they are selected.

23 Highlight MISSED TEST. Click the Bold and Italic buttons on the Format toolbar. Click outside the selected area so it is no longer selected.

friend/classmate del
<u>MISSED TESTS:</u> Q
Tests will be given c

WHAT'S HAPPENING? You removed the boldface and italic character formatting, but left the underline character formatting. You can also change the font for a portion of the document or the entire document.

24 Place the insertion point in the selection bar area. Hold the Ctrl key and click.

25 Right-click the mouse.

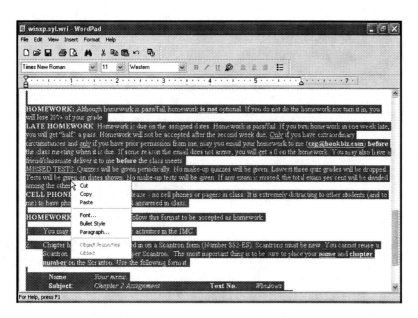

WHAT'S HAPPENING? You selected all the text in the document. It is all highlighted. You then opened the context menu. You can see the Cut, Copy, and Paste commands, which can also be found on the menu bar and the toolbar. Here you are interested in changing the font.

26 Click **Font**.

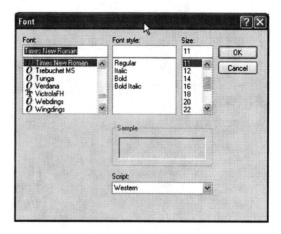

WHAT'S **HAPPENING?** You have opened the Font dialog box. Times New Roman is selected. It has four styles: Regular, Italic, Bold, and Bold Italic but since there is a mix of styles, that drop-down list box is empty. The selected size is 11 points.

27 Scroll towards the top of the Font list box. Locate **Arial**. Click it.

28 Locate **12** in the Size list box. Click it. Click **OK**. Click in the document window to deselect the text.

29 If you cannot see **MISSED TESTS:**, scroll until you can.

> MISSED TESTS: Quizzes will be giv
> grades will be dropped. Tests will be
> missed, the total exam per cent will b
> **CELL PHONE AND PAGERS** - Ple

WHAT'S **HAPPENING?** You have changed the type style of this document. The text that you underlined remains underlined, but now it is in Arial.

30 Place the cursor in the selection area. Double-click **HOMEWORK:**. Click the Bullets button, , on the toolbar.

> • **HOMEWORK**: Although homework is pass/fail, homework **is not** optional. If you do not do the homework nor turn it in, you will lose 20% of your grade.
> **LATE HOMEWORK**: Homework is due on the assigned dates. Homework is pass/fail. If you turn homework one week late, you will get "half" a pass. Homework will not be accepted after the second week due. Only if yo

WHAT'S **HAPPENING?** You selected text and formatted it in a bulleted style.

31 Click the Bullets button on the toolbar to remove the bullet. Click outside the text to deselect it.

32 Click **File**. Click **Page Setup**.

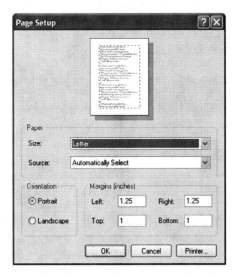

WHAT'S HAPPENING? Your options in the Size and Source drop-down list boxes will depend on the type of printer you have. You may not have the portrait and landscape options. You can change the margin settings. You can print a document from WordPad in the same manner that you printed from Notepad. You can use My Computer to locate the file. Once the file is located and selected, you can use either the File/Print commands from the menu bar or the context-sensitive menu. However, in WordPad, the only formatting you can apply to your document from Page Setup is the top, bottom, left, and right margins of the document. You cannot have headers or footers.

33 Change the right, left, top, and bottom margins to 2". Click **OK**.

34 Click **File**. Click **Print Preview**.

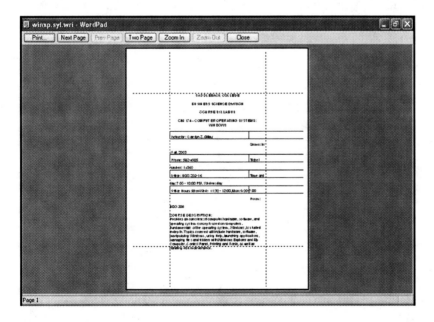

WHAT'S HAPPENING? Your display may or may not appear as shown above, depending on your installed printer and the screen fonts available to your system. Do not be concerned if your print preview is considerably different from the example here. Print Preview shows you what text will print on the page. The dotted lines represent the margins. You may see that the text at the bottom of the page is out of the margin.

35 Click the **Two Page** command button.

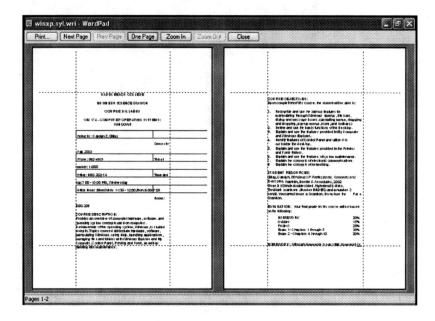

WHAT'S **HAPPENING?** You can see both pages of this document. Again, depending on your printer, you may not see this view. The bottom of the first page has an orphan. A *widow* occurs when the last line of a paragraph is at the top of the next page; an *orphan* occurs when the first line of a paragraph is at the bottom of a page. Sophisticated word-processing programs automatically fix widows and orphans for you, but WordPad has no such feature. You have to adjust margins manually. When you adjust the margins, you will often find that Print Preview in WordPad is not very accurate. How it appears in Print Preview and how it actually prints can vary.

36 Click the **Next Page** command button.

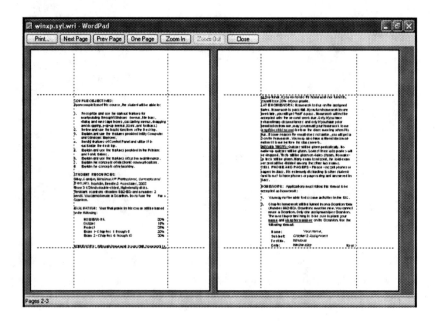

WHAT'S **HAPPENING?** By altering the size of the margins, you increased the number of pages to 4. Again, note that you cannot have a footer with the page number on it as you can in Notepad.

37 Be sure your printer is on. Click **Print**. Click **Print**.

WHAT'S **HAPPENING?** Your document should print. You can compare the hard copy to the way it appeared in Print Preview.

38 Click the **Save** button on the toolbar. Close WordPad.

WHAT'S **HAPPENING?** You have returned to the desktop.

4.16 • Paint

Paint is a graphics application program that allows you to create simple or complex drawings and images. Paint is an application that comes with Windows XP Professional. You can import or alter a picture or drawing in Paint. The images you create can stand alone, or you can copy them to other documents. You could purchase a sophisticated drawing program like Paint Shop Pro, but, if your drawing requirements are simple, Paint will meet most of your needs.

Drawing programs, like all programs, store the data you create in files. These files, generally called *graphic files*, come in a variety of formats identified by file extensions. Popular graphic file formats use the extensions .tif, .tiff, .gif, .pcx, .jpg, .jpeg, and .bmp. Paint creates bitmap graphics (.bmp). In general, graphic files consume a larger amount of memory and disk space than other forms of data. Even simple graphic files are large.

Paint can edit and create only bitmap graphics. Your computer screen is divided into small dots called *pixels*, also called *pels* (*p*icture *el*ements). A bitmap is collected bits of information that create an image when assigned (mapped) to the pixels on the screen. It works much like a theater marquee where a movie's name, a message, or a picture is displayed by turning light bulbs in the grid on or off. When you draw in Paint, you are turning pixels on or off in different colors. There are so many dots that they blend into a picture, much like the connect-the-dots images you may remember from childhood.

Bitmap graphics are detailed (and take a lot of storage space) because you control the placement and color of each dot. Because a bitmap graphic has a fixed number of dots, its resolution is fixed. You cannot make it look better by printing it on a high-resolution printer. The resolution is limited by your monitor and video card as well. If you have a color monitor and color printer, your drawing will appear and print in the colors that your computer system and printer support. If you have a noncolor printer, your drawings will appear in varying shades of gray.

If you have installed programs with appropriate graphic filters, such as Office, Paint can also read TIFF (tagged image file format), JPEG (Joint Photographic Experts Group), GIF (graphic interchange format), PCX, Targa, and Kodak Photo CD files. The filters supplied in Office also allow Paint to save files in GIF and JPEG format.

When you first load Paint, your screen will look like Figure 4.6.

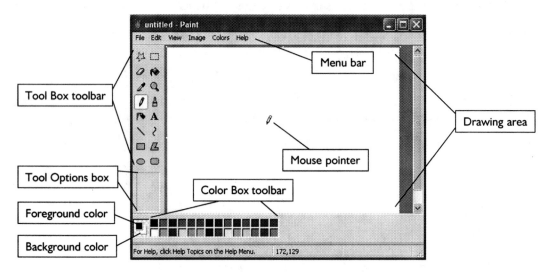

Figure 4.6 ∘ The Paint Window

The Paint menu bar has choices that you have seen in other Windows XP Professional applications, but it also has a new choice called Image. Throughout Windows XP Professional applications, the location of menu bar choices remains consistent, so File always appears on the left and Help on the right. All the other menu choices are found between File and Help. What they are depends on the program's purpose. Tasks in a drawing program differ greatly from those in a word-processing program, and the menu choices will reflect that.

The next area of importance in Paint is the *Tool Box*. The Tool Box is actually a toolbar from which you select your drawing tool. Below the Tool Box is an area called the *Tool Options box*. When a specific tool is selected, this box provides options for that tool. For instance, if you selected the line tool, your line thickness choices would be shown in this area.

The *Color Box* contains the colors you use in Paint. It is also a toolbar. In Paint you must distinguish between background and foreground colors. The *background color* is the color of your drawing area. The *foreground color* is the one with which you draw. The default color choices for Paint are a white background and a black foreground.

The *drawing area* is the canvas on which you create. There is a relationship between the mouse pointer (cursor) and the drawing area. When you open Paint, a default drawing tool is selected, the pencil cursor. When you click in the drawing area, you may begin to draw with that tool. In the Tool Box, you see the pencil icon button indented, indicating that it is the current drawing tool. When you click another tool icon in the Tool Box, your cursor will change to the shape of the selected drawing tool. The Tool Box icons and their names are listed in Figure 4.7.

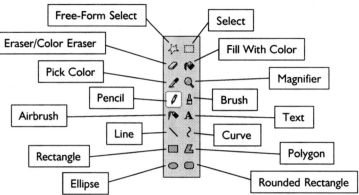

Figure 4.7 ∘ The Tools

Each tool in the Tool Box has a specific name and purpose. In the activities, the tools will be referred to by their names. If you want to know a tool's function, refer to this table. If you want to know a tool's name, place the pointer over the tool until its ToolTip appears. See Table 4.5.

Icon	Name	Purpose
	Free-Form Select	Defines or selects a free-form cutout in a drawing.
	Select	Defines or selects a rectangular cutout in a drawing.
	Eraser/Color Eraser	Changes the foreground color to the background color.
	Fill With Color	Fills a bordered area with the selected foreground color.
	Pick Color	Picks a color in your drawing to use as a foreground color. If you click a color in your drawing with the right mouse button, it will become the background color.
	Magnifier	Magnifies a selected area.
	Pencil	Creates a free-form line in the foreground color. Clicking the right mouse button creates a free-form line in the background color.
	Brush	Draws a free-form brush stroke in the foreground color. Clicking the right mouse button creates a brush stroke in the background color.
	Airbrush	Creates a spray can effect. The left mouse button sprays the foreground color, and the right mouse button sprays the background color.
	Text	Places text in the drawing for captions and titles.
	Line	Draws a line. You may select the width of the line in the Tool Options box. The left mouse button draws with the foreground color, and the right mouse button draws with the background color.
	Curve	Draws a straight line, then curves it. Each curve has a minimum of one arc and a maximum of two. The left mouse button draws with the foreground color, and the right mouse button draws with the background color.
	Rectangle	Creates a rectangle or square.
	Polygon	Draws a shape with an unlimited number of sides. You add sides to a configuration until you return to your starting point. You are essentially connecting straight lines in the selected foreground color.
	Ellipse	Creates a circle or an ellipse.
	Rounded Rectangle	Creates a round-cornered rectangle or square.

Table 4.5 • The Names and Uses of Tools

Rectangle, Polygon, Ellipse, and Rounded Rectangle are considered shape tools. When you select a shape tool, three choices appear in the Tool Options box. Since a shape encloses an area, each choice is considered a *fill style*. The color inside the shape is called the *fill*. Table 4.6 enumerates the choices available for shapes in the Tool Options box.

Tool Options Choice	Left Mouse	Right Mouse
	Outline in foreground color. No fill color. This option is highlighted, indicating that it is the default.	Outline in background color. No fill color.
	Outline in foreground color. Fill in background color.	Outline in background color. Fill in foreground color.
	Solid shape in foreground color. Has no outline.	Solid shape in background color. Has no outline.

Table 4.6 • Fill Styles

4.17 • Using Paint

You can use Paint to create a new picture. When you open Paint, it has standard settings for the characteristics of the picture you are about to create, like its size and whether it is in color. The default settings are the size of your screen (not the size of the window, but of the screen's resolution dimensions) and in color. In the next activity, you will look at your attributes and begin using tools.

4.18 • Activity • Creating a New Picture

1   Click **Start**. Point to **All Programs**. Point to **Accessories**. Click **Paint**.

2   Click **Image**. Click **Attributes**.

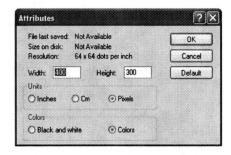

WHAT'S **HAPPENING?** Your default settings can be changed. In the example above, the image is in color and the screen resolution is 400 by 300 pixels. A standard screen resolution is 640 by 480. However, most people use higher resolutions such as 800 by 600 or 1,024 by 768.

3   Set Width to 800 and Height to 600. Click **OK**.

4   The Pencil should be your selected tool. Drag the mouse across the screen about two inches while holding down the left mouse button.

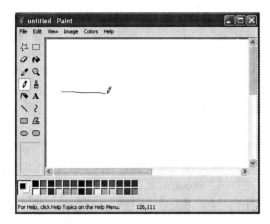

WHAT'S HAPPENING? You drew a free-form line.

5 Drag the mouse to create a second two-inch line, but do not release the left mouse button. Click the right mouse button once.

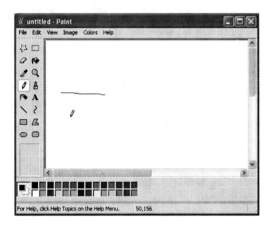

WHAT'S HAPPENING? Whenever you click the right mouse button without releasing the left mouse button, you remove from the screen what you just created.

6 Click the Brush tool.

WHAT'S HAPPENING? In the Tool Options box, you see the choices for shapes and widths of your Brush tool. The selected shape is highlighted.

7 Click the largest square in the Tool Options box. Position the pointer in the drawing area near your last line. Hold down the left mouse button and drag the mouse across the drawing area about two inches.

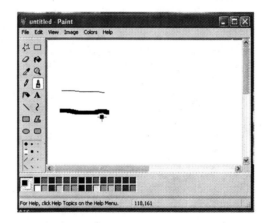

WHAT'S HAPPENING? You chose a wide brush to draw a wide line.

8 Click **Edit**.

WHAT'S HAPPENING? The drop-down Edit menu appears. Undo is not dimmed and is therefore available. You have three levels of Undo, which means you can reverse your last three changes.

9   Click **Undo**. Click **Edit**. Click **Undo**.

WHAT'S HAPPENING? You undid the lines you drew and now have a blank screen.

10   Click **Edit**.

WHAT'S HAPPENING? You cannot choose Undo, but Repeat is now available.

11   Click **Repeat**. Click **Edit**. Click **Repeat**.

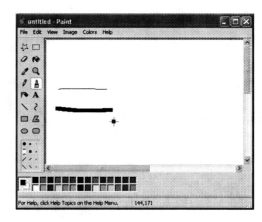

WHAT'S HAPPENING? The lines you erased returned to your canvas.

12   Click the Free-Form Select tool. Hold down the left mouse button and drag the cursor around the two lines in the canvas. Do not release the left mouse button.

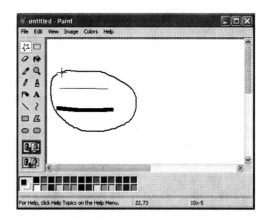

WHAT'S HAPPENING? The shape you created to encircle the two lines is irregular. Even though there are two items enclosed, when you work with them, they will be considered one object.

13   Release the left mouse button.

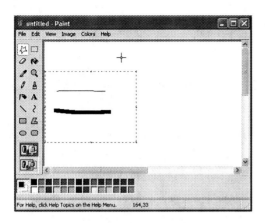

WHAT'S HAPPENING? A rectangular dotted line replaced your free-form line. Anything surrounded by a dotted line is selected. Since a dotted line is around your object, you have selected it. Once an object is selected, you can drag it around the screen or copy, cut, or paste it to a different location or even to a different document.

14 Place the cursor, now a four-headed arrow, inside the dotted rectangle. Drag the box to the right and down about an inch or two.

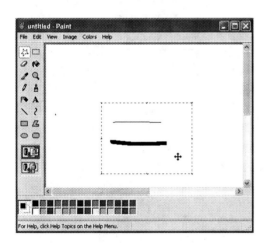

WHAT'S HAPPENING? While you were dragging your selection, the dotted line disappeared. When you reached your new location and released the left mouse button, the dotted line reappeared, indicating that your object (the two lines) is still selected. As long as an object is selected, it can be manipulated.

You have two select tools, the one you just used and the Select tool located next to it. Instead of a free-form shape, the Select tool uses a rectangular shape.

15 Click the Select tool. Holding down the left mouse button, drag the cursor around the two lines on the canvas. When you have selected them, release the left mouse button.

16 Click **Edit**. Click **Copy**. Click **Edit**. Click **Paste**.

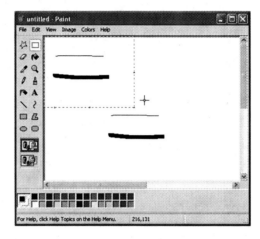

WHAT'S HAPPENING? You saved your object to the Clipboard. Then you pasted it. You now have two copies of your sketch. In the Paint program, Paste will always place whatever is on the Clipboard in the upper-left corner of the drawing area.

17 Click outside the box to deselect it.

18 Place the pointer on the color red, and click the left mouse button.

19 Place the pointer on the color green, and click the right mouse button.

WHAT'S HAPPENING? The left mouse click chose the foreground color, and the right-click chose the background color.

20 Click the Line tool. In the Tool Options box, pick the middle line for width.

21 Click the Rectangle tool. Click the middle fill style in the Tool Options box. In an empty area on the screen, hold the left mouse button and drag it down and to the right. As you drag it, you will see the outline of a green box bordered in red. When the box is about one and a half inches by one and a half inches, release the left mouse button.

WHAT'S HAPPENING? You should have a box filled with green (the background color) and outlined in red (the foreground color). You should have a box filled with green (the background color) and outlined in red (the foreground color). The rectangle's border matches the width you selected for the Line tool prior to drawing the rectangle. When drawing a rectangle, ellipse, or rounded rectangle, the border's width is based on the last line width you selected. This is also true when you are using the Line, Curve, or Polygon tools.

22 Place the pointer on the color blue, and click the left mouse button.

23 Click the Fill With Color tool. Your cursor becomes a paint can. Place the tip of the paint can in the green box. Click the left mouse button.

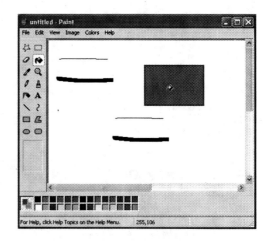

WHAT'S HAPPENING? The color inside the box changed from green to blue.

24 Click the Eraser/Color Eraser tool.

25 Hold the left mouse button down and drag across the box.

26 Hold the right mouse button down and drag across the box.

WHAT'S HAPPENING? The mouse pointer changed shape. You could pick a large or small eraser in the Tool Options box. The eraser was filled with green, the background color. The selected background color shows what color the eraser will leave behind. When you dragged the right mouse button, you changed only the foreground color to the background color. Since the fill was the single object in the foreground color (blue), this was the only area that the eraser changed to the background color (green). To limit your changes to a specific color (and nothing else), you change the foreground color to the color you want to erase and the background color to the color you want to replace it with. Click the eraser, and then right-drag the mouse across your selection.

27   Left-click green. Right-click yellow. Click the Eraser/Color Eraser tool. Right-drag it vertically over the box, being sure to drag it over part of the green line.

WHAT'S **HAPPENING?**   Your cursor changed anything green that it touched to yellow, but all other colors remained the same.

28   Click the Pick Color tool. Click the red border of the box.

29   Click the Fill With Color tool.

30   Move to the bottom black line. Position the tip of the paint can on the line and click.

WHAT'S **HAPPENING?**   The Pick Color tool let you select a foreground color from your drawing. If you look at the foreground color in the Color Box, you see your foreground is now red. You then clicked the next tool you wanted to use (the Fill With Color tool) and clicked on an object. The object, a black line, was changed to the foreground color (red).

30   Click on the color pink with the left mouse button.

31   Click the Airbrush tool.

32   Hold the left mouse button and drag the Spray Can cursor across the box. Then hold the right mouse button and drag the Spray Can cursor across the box.

WHAT'S **HAPPENING?**   When you dragged the left button a pink (foreground) color effect was produced, and, when you used the right mouse button, a yellow (background) color effect was produced.

33   Left-click the color black. Right-click the color white.

34   Click the Eraser/Color Eraser tool. Drag it across the box.

WHAT'S **HAPPENING?**   You are erasing your box. Actually, you are covering everything with the white background color.

35   Click the Pencil tool.

36   Click File. Click Exit.

WHAT'S **HAPPENING?**   Paint knows that you have not saved this drawing, and it is giving you an opportunity to do so. You do not want to save this drawing.

37   Click **No**.

WHAT'S **HAPPENING?**   You closed Paint and returned to the desktop.

4.19 • The Shape Tools

So far, you have been working with the Pencil, Brush, and Rectangle drawing tools. Pencil and Brush performed much like a pencil and brush you would hold in your hand. The Rectangle tool let you work with a predefined shape. In using all these tools, you have also worked with color. You have seen how the cursor changes to the shape of the selected tool. In addition, you worked with the Free-Form Select and Select tools to select, copy, and move an object. The other shape tools work just as easily.

4.20 • Activity • Using the Shape Tools

1   Open the Paint program.

2   Click the Ellipse tool. Click the top fill shape in the Tool Options box.

3   Anywhere in the drawing area, hold the left mouse button and drag. When you have an ellipse about one inch high and two inches wide, release the left mouse button.

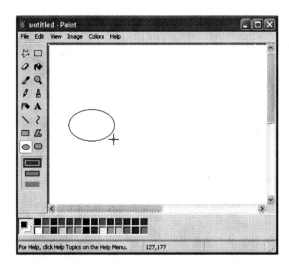

WHAT'S **HAPPENING?** You have an oval-shaped ellipse. If you want to use a shape tool to create a circle or a square, hold down the **Shift** key while dragging the mouse.

4   Next to your ellipse, hold down the **Shift** key and the left mouse button, and drag until you have a circle approximately one inch in diameter. (*Hint:* Release the left mouse button before releasing the **Shift** key. That way your circle—or drawing object—will not move.)

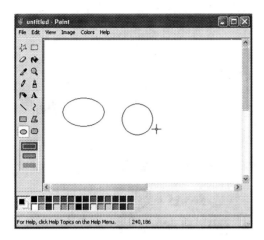

WHAT'S HAPPENING? You have a perfectly round circle instead of an ellipse. Holding the **Shift** key while using certain tools (such as the line, rectangle, rounded rectangle, and curved line tools) constrains the proportions of the object or makes the object straight.

5 Left-click the color blue. Right-click the color pink.

6 Left-drag to create a half-inch ellipse. Right-drag to create a half-inch ellipse.

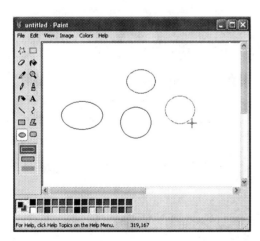

WHAT'S HAPPENING? The left-drag gave you a hollow ellipse with a blue (foreground) border. The right-drag gave you a hollow ellipse with a pink (background) border. In both instances, the first fill style (border with no fill) was selected.

7 Click the middle fill style. Left-drag to create a half-inch ellipse. Right-drag to create a half-inch ellipse.

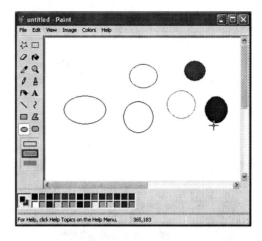

WHAT'S HAPPENING? The left-drag gave you a pink (background color) ellipse with a blue border, whereas the right-drag gave you a blue (foreground color) ellipse with a pink border. In this case, you chose the middle fill style (border and fill in two different colors) for both shapes. The border is very narrow. You can create a wider one.

8 Click the Line tool. In the Tool Options box, click the largest line. Click the Ellipse tool. In an empty area, left-drag to create a half-inch ellipse. Right-drag to create a half-inch ellipse.

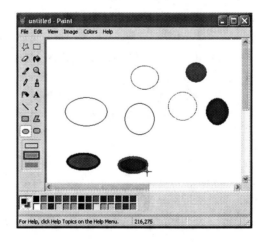

WHAT'S HAPPENING? You have the same shape and fill style, but the borders are larger. If you chose the bottom fill style and left-dragged, you would create an ellipse in the background color (pink) with no border. Right-dragging would create an ellipse in the foreground color (blue) with no border. The Rectangle and Rounded Rectangle tools work in the same fashion. Holding down the **Shift** key to "square" or "circle" your shape also works with all the shape tools.

9   Left-click the color red. Right-click the color green. Click the Curve tool.

10   In an open area, left-drag until you have about a two-inch vertical line. Release the left mouse button.

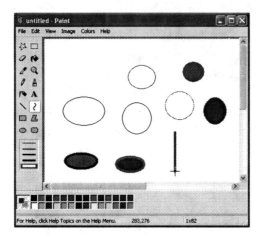

WHAT'S **HAPPENING?** So far, you have a red vertical line. If your line was not straight, you could have held down the **Shift** key. If you had wanted a green line, you could have right-dragged.

11   The pointer changes to a cross-hair. Place the cross-hair cursor in the middle of the line. Left-drag to the left about an inch. Click the left mouse button.

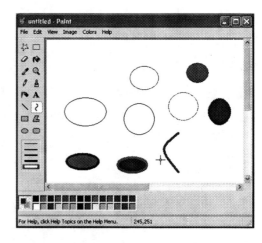

WHAT'S **HAPPENING?** You see your vertical line curving. When you clicked the mouse, you set the line in the curve. If you do not click the mouse, you can make one more curve.

12   In an open area, right-drag the mouse until you have a two-inch horizontal line. Release the mouse button. Place the cross-hair pointer in the middle of the line you just drew. Right-drag down about an inch.

13   Place the cross-hair cursor on the left end of the line. Right-drag up about an inch. Release the mouse button.

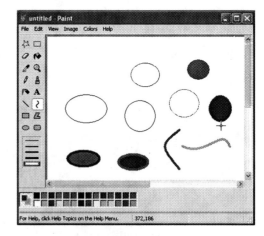

WHAT'S **HAPPENING?** You have made the line curve in two directions. You are limited to two curves and cannot curve it again.

14 Left-click the color brown. Right-click the color yellow. Click the Polygon tool. In the drawing
    area, left-drag to create a vertical one-inch line.

15 Place the cross-hair pointer at the bottom of the brown line. Left-drag one inch to the right.

16 Double-click on top of the first brown line you drew.

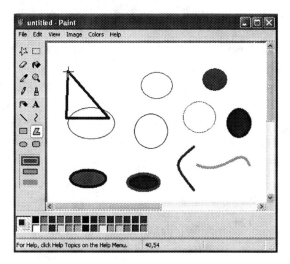

WHAT'S **HAPPENING?** You have drawn a triangle. You can also draw a filled polygon or a
polygon with many sides. You are going to draw a "W."

17 In the Tool Options box, click the middle fill style. Draw a W.

18 To connect all the lines, click at the end of the first line you drew.

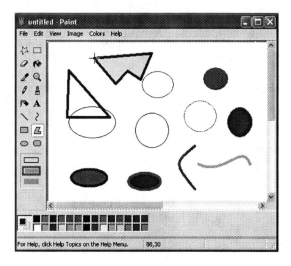

WHAT'S **HAPPENING?** You drew a yellow-filled shape with a brown border. The Polygon tool
lets you connect lines to create shapes.

19 Left-click black. Right-click white. Click the Pencil tool.

20 Close Paint. Do not save the drawing.

WHAT'S **HAPPENING?** You have closed Paint and returned to the desktop.

4.21 ● Importing and Exporting Graphics and Using the Text Tool

So far, you have used different Paint tools. None of the drawings has been a work of art. Not all of us have artistic talent. Don't be frustrated, because with Paint you can also *import* (open) or *export* (save to a disk) graphic files which have pictures created by people with artistic talent. Once you import a graphic, you may alter it. You may also purchase what is called *clip art*. Clip art provides many images (typically small) from which you can choose. You can alter the clip art and save it as a new drawing.

You may also take a graphic or an original drawing and select an area to create a cutout. A *cutout* can be any defined portion of your drawing area. Once you have defined it, you may copy it to the Clipboard for use in other programs, save it to a file, flip or rotate it, or copy it to another place in your current drawing. If you save it as a file, you can copy it into another document at any time. You can also add text to your drawing which can also be manipulated.

4.22 ● Activity ● Using a Graphic to Create a Cutout and Using the Text Tool

1   Open the Paint program.

2   Maximize your Paint window. If the drawing area does not fill the entire window, click **Image**. Click **Attributes**. Change the attributes to 800 by 600.

3   Click the Line tool. In the Tool Options box, select the widest line.

4   Click the Rectangle tool. In the middle of the drawing area, create a square with sides measuring approximately three inches.

5   Left-click green. Click the Fill With Color tool and click in the square.

6   Left-click black. Click the Pencil tool.

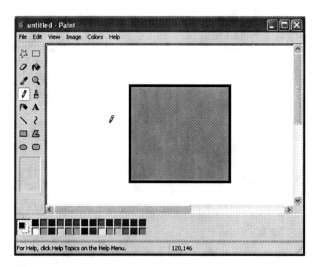

WHAT'S **HAPPENING?** You have a green square outlined in black.

7   Click **Edit**. Click **Paste From**. In the File name text box, key in **C:\XPRODATA\Dancer.bmp**.

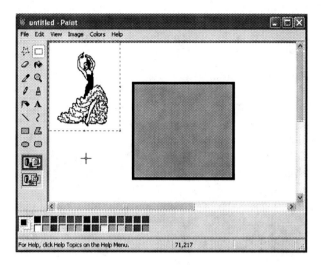

WHAT'S HAPPENING? You told Paint where to retrieve the file. When you Paste From, you copy an image into an existing drawing. The dancer is outlined by a dotted line, which means you can drag the image to a desired location. In addition, you can make the art opaque or transparent. Making it *transparent* means that it will not obscure the drawing in the background and will pick up the colors of that background. Making the drawing *opaque* means that it will retain its original colors and will obscure whatever is behind it. If you look in the Tool Options box, you will see buttons for these two choices. See Figure 4.8.

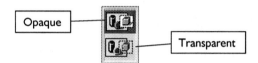

Figure 4.8 • Choices in the Tool Options Box

The top button (Opaque) is selected. If you drag the dancer to the green square now, the background color (white) around the dancer will obscure the green background.

8 Click the Transparent button—the bottom button. Drag the dancer into the green square. Click outside the square to deselect it.

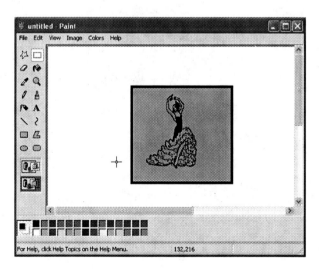

WHAT'S **HAPPENING?** Because you were in transparent mode, the dancer is completely green. In addition, she fits entirely into your square.

9   Click **Edit**. Click **Undo**.

10   Click **Edit**. Click **Paste From**. Double-click **Dancer.bmp**.

11   Click the Opaque button in the Tool Option box.

12   Drag the dancer into the box. Click to deselect.

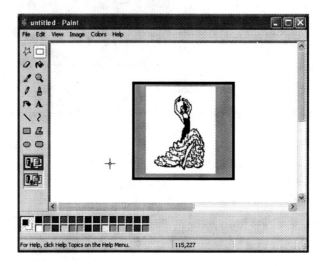

WHAT'S **HAPPENING?** The dancer and the surrounding white area now cover the green area and are within the outline of the square.

13   Left-click green. Click the Fill With Color tool. Click the white background around the dancer.

14   Left-click black. Click the Pencil tool.

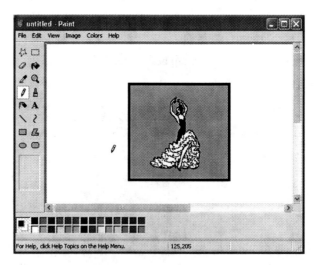

WHAT'S **HAPPENING?** The dancer is now in white and black with a green background.

15   Click the Text tool. In a blank area, right drag a rectangle.

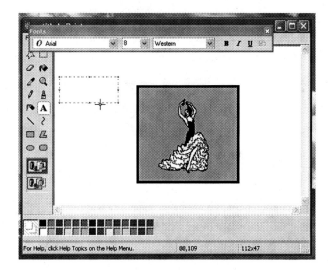

WHAT'S HAPPENING? You have created an area to key in text. If the Fonts box did not appear, you would click View and click Text Toolbar to activate it.

16   Select **Arial**. Select **12**. Click the **B** button. In the dotted rectangle, key in **DANCER**.

WHAT'S HAPPENING? You have keyed in text. You can manipulate text just as you would a drawing.

17   Click outside the text box. Click the Select tool. Encircle the word DANCER. Click **Image**. Click **Flip/Rotate**.

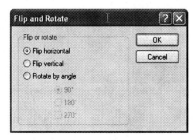

WHAT'S HAPPENING? You can flip or rotate your selected object.

18   Click **Rotate by angle**. Click **270°**. Click **OK**. Drag the dotted outline to the side of the dancer.

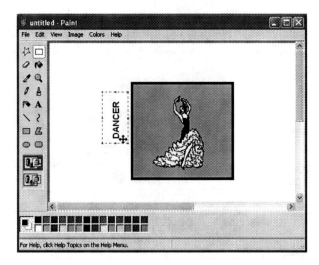

WHAT'S **HAPPENING?** > You manipulated the text.

19 Click outside the dotted area. Click the Select tool. Encircle the boxed dancer. Include the black border as well as the text.

20 Click **Edit**. Click **Copy To**.

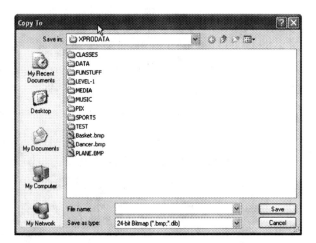

WHAT'S **HAPPENING?** > The Copy To dialog box is asking you where you want to file this cutout. Currently, the XPRODATA folder is the default directory. You want to save this to your MYDATADISK disk.

21 Be sure the MYDATADISK disk is in Drive A. Click the down arrow in the Save in drop-down list box. Click the **3½ Floppy (A:)** icon.

WHAT'S HAPPENING? You are ready to save your file. Graphic files are large, particularly bitmap files. The size of the file depends on the number of colors chosen when you set up your display properties. The more colors that are in your display, the larger the file will be. One of the ways to reduce the size of a bitmap file is to choose a small number of colors. How your monitor is set up depends on what capabilities your video adapter card and monitor support.

22 Click the down arrow in the Save as type drop-down list box.

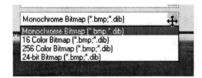

WHAT'S HAPPENING? The 24-bit Bitmap option will create the largest file, whereas Monochrome Bitmap will create the smallest file. In the middle ground is 16 Color Bitmap. Notice that you can only save the file in either the BMP format or the DIB (device-independent bitmap) format.

23 Click **16 Color Bitmap**.

24 In the File name text box, key in the following: **green.bmp**

25 Click **Save**. Restore the Paint window. Close Paint. If it asks if you want to save the picture, click **No**—you do not want to save the untitled picture.

4.23 • Printing in Paint

You can print any picture that you create in Paint. However, graphics print differently from text. If you have a dot-matrix printer, you will not get the resolution of a more sophisticated printer. Graphic images also take longer to print and use more toner and ink than text images. If you do not have a color printer, your drawing will be in shades of gray.

4.24 • Activity • Printing the Dancer Picture

1 Open My Computer. Double-click **3½ Floppy (A:)**. Right-click **green.bmp**. Click **Open With**. Choose **Paint**.

2 Click **File**. Click **Print Preview**.

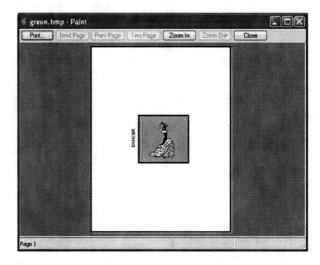

WHAT'S HAPPENING? Print Preview lets you see what your drawing will look like before you print it. In this example, you are satisfied. If you were not, you could close this window and click File and then Page Setup and adjust your margins.

3   Be sure the printer is on. Click **Print**. Click **Print**.

4   Close Paint. Close any open windows.

WHAT'S HAPPENING? You printed your drawing.

Chapter Summary

In this chapter, you learned about some of the accessories provided with Windows XP Professional. These include Outlook Express, Notepad, WordPad, and Paint.

You learned how to set up Outlook Express for email. Email is a major part of most users' lives now. You learned how to send and receive email.

Notepad is a simple ASCII editor for writing short text documents. It has no embedded codes, and therefore can be used to communicate with the computer system. Placing .LOG at the beginning of a file stamps the current date and time on your file whenever it is opened. You can also have headers and footers in a Notepad document. The default file extension for Notepad is .txt.

WordPad is a small word-processing program. The default file extension used with WordPad is .rtf. You hold down the **Shift** key while right-clicking a file to access the Open With option on the shortcut menu. Using quotation marks, you can give your file an exact name; for instance, you can customize a file extension or use none at all. You can register your own file extension for WordPad. WordPad has more editing capabilities than Notepad. WordPad has a toolbar as well as a menu bar. Toolbar buttons are shortcuts to menu commands. In WordPad, you can format characters and paragraphs in styles such as boldface or italic. In order to manipulate text, you must first select it. WordPad does not allow you to use headers and footers.

You also learned about Paint. You were introduced to different tools and used them to create and edit drawings. You created different shapes and used the color palette to change colors. You imported and exported clip art, which you edited and modified. You learned the difference between using File/Open, Edit/Paste From, and Edit/Copy To. You entered text into a drawing and manipulated that text. You learned how to save and print your drawings.

Key Terms

attachment	footer	pixel
background color	foreground color	rich text format (RTF)
clip art	graphic file	selection bar
Color Box	hard return	soft return
cutout	header	Tool Box
drawing area	import	Tool Options box
email (electronic mail)	insert	transparent
export	netiquette	typeover
fill	opaque	widow
fill style	orphan	wizard
flaming	pel	word wrap

Discussion Questions

1. What is email?
2. What form does an email address take? Give one example of an email address.
3. Define netiquette. Why is it important? Where is it used?
4. What is flaming?
5. Compare and contrast a logon name and a friendly name.
6. Why might you have more than one email account?
7. What five folders are created by Outlook Express?
8. What purpose does the Cc: line serve in an email message?
9. How do you send an email message? How do you receive your email?
10. What is an attachment? How may you include an attachment with your email?
11. Explain the purpose and function of Notepad.
12. What is a header? A footer?
13. What types of information would be found in headers and footers?
14. Define word wrap.
15. What is a log file? What would be the purpose of creating a log file?
16. Explain the purpose and function of WordPad.
17. Compare and contrast a soft return and a hard return.
18. Explain the purpose and function of the selection bar area. How is it used?
19. Compare and contrast printing a document using WordPad or Notepad.
20. In word processing terms, what is a widow? An orphan?
21. Explain the purpose and function of Paint.
22. What is a bitmap file? What is a bitmap file's resolution?
23. What is the drawing area?
24. What happens to the cursor in Paint when you change tools?
25. Compare and contrast background color with foreground color.
26. What is a fill style? How is it used?
27. Explain one way to cut out part of your drawing and drag it to a new location.
28. Explain how the Ellipse tool can be used to draw a circle.
29. What does it mean to import a graphic? Export a graphic?
30. Compare and contrast opaque and transparent copies.
31. How can you adjust the way your Paint picture prints?

True/False Questions

For each question, circle the letter T if the statement is true or the letter F if the statement is false.

T   F   1. If you do not have an email address, one will be assigned to you by Windows XP Professional.

T   F   2. In WordPad, each icon on the toolbar is a shortcut to one of the menu choices.

T   F   3. In WordPad, the selection bar area is an unmarked column along the left edge of the document window.

T   F   4. When you paste a selection in Paint, it will always appear in the upper-left corner of the drawing area.

T   F   5. Paint can combine text and pictures and save them in a single file.

Completion Questions

Write the correct answer in each blank space provided.

6. **czg@um.edu** is an example of a(n) _____ address.

7. If you have keyed in _____ at the beginning of a file, Notepad will stamp the current date and time when the file is opened.

8. In WordPad, boldface, italic, and underline are examples of _____ formatting.

9. If you don't have the time or talent to create drawings in Paint, _____ provides many images from which you can choose.

10. When you are using the Curve tool, a line may be curved a maximum of _____ times.

Multiple Choice Questions

Circle the letter of the correct answer for each question.

11. In word-processing terms, a paragraph is
    a. any text beginning and ending with a paragraph marker.
    b. any text between indents.
    c. any text that begins with an indent.
    d. text on a single line.

12. The last line of a paragraph printed at the top of a page is called a(n)
    a. child.
    b. orphan.
    c. parent.
    d. widow.

13. A header is
    a. text printed on the top of each page.
    b. text printed at the bottom of each page.
    c. always a page number.
    d. not available as an option in Notepad.

14. The following are shape tools except
    a. Select.
    b. Rectangle.

    c. Rounded Rectangle.

    d. Polygon.

15. To change the foreground color in Paint,

    a. click the left mouse button on the new color.

    b. click the right mouse button on the new color.

    c. double-click the left mouse button on the new color.

    d. double-click the right mouse button on the new color.

Application Assignments

Problem Set I—At the Computer

Note: The application answers assume you have worked through the chapter and retained the settings.

Problem A

* If necessary, go online.

* Open Outlook Express.

* Compose a message to yourself.

* The subject is **TEST**.

* The message states: **This is a test.**

* Send the message.

* Retrieve your messages.

    1. The TEST message appears in

        a. the Inbox folder.

        b. the Sent Items folder.

        c. both a and b

        d. neither a nor b

* Delete the message.

* Compose another message to yourself.

* The subject is **ATTACH**.

* The message states: **There is an attachment.**

* You want to attach the file called BLUE.JAZ located in the XPRODATA folder.

    2. In order to attach the file, you must first click

        a. Attach.

        b. Insert.

        c. Tools.

        d. View.

* Click the Close button.

* Click **No**.

* Close Outlook Express.

Problem B

* Open Notepad.

* Open the Page Setup dialog box. (*Hint:* Remember What's This?)

3. To insert the current date, use
   a. &d.
   b. %d.
   c. @d.

* Click **Cancel**.

* Open Help for Notepad.

* Click **Help Topics**.

* Click the **Contents** tab.

* If necessary, expand the book Notepad.

* Click **Insert the Time and Date in a document.**

4. Is there an entry for a log?
   a. yes
   b. no

* Close Notepad Help.

* Close Notepad.

Problem C

* Open WordPad.

* Open the document called Personal.fil in the XPRODATA directory. (*Hint:* Remember file type.)

5. What street does Tai Chan Tran live on?
   a. Lemon
   b. Lakeview
   c. Miller
   d. Wick

6. On what toolbar can you discover information about the font?
   a. toolbar
   b. format toolbar
   c. status bar
   d. ruler bar

7. What font is the document presented in?
   a. Times New Roman
   b. Arial
   c. Courier (or Courier New)

* Close WordPad.

* Do not save the document to the disk.

Problem D

* Open Paint.

* Click the Line tool.

* Choose the middle line for your line width in the Tool Options box.

* Left-click blue.

* Right-click red.

* Click the Ellipse tool.

* Choose the top fill style in the Tool Options box.

* Draw an ellipse using the left mouse button.

8. The ellipse is
    a. a blue outline with a white interior.
    b. a red outline with a white interior.
    c. a solid blue ellipse.
    d. a solid red ellipse.

* Choose the bottom fill style in the Tool Options box.

* Draw another ellipse using the left mouse button.

9. The newly drawn ellipse is
    a. a blue outline with a white interior.
    b. a red outline with a white interior.
    c. a solid blue ellipse.
    d. a solid red ellipse.

* Draw another ellipse using the right mouse button.

10. The newly drawn ellipse is
    a. a blue outline with a white interior.
    b. a red outline with a white interior.
    c. a solid blue ellipse.
    d. a solid red ellipse.

* Left-click black.

* Right-click white.

* Click **Edit**.

* Click **Paste From**.

* In the File name text box, key in **C:\XPRODATA\Basket.bmp**.

* Click **Open**.

11. What color is the basket?
    a. red
    b. yellow
    c. white
    d. black

* In the Tool Options box, choose the bottom style.

* Drag the basket and the eggs over both ellipses.

12. The basket is
    a. opaque.
    b. transparent.

* Drag the basket to a blank spot on the screen.

* Click outside the basket to deselect it.

* Left-click yellow.

* Right-click pink.

* Click the Eraser/Color Eraser tool.

❋ Right-drag the eraser across the entire basket, including the eggs.

    13. What happened?

        a. Only the yellow basket became pink.

        b. The yellow basket and all the eggs became pink.

        c. The basket remained yellow, but the eggs became pink.

        d. The basket and eggs became white.

        e. Everything that the eraser touched became pink.

❋ Left-drag the eraser across the entire basket, including the eggs.

    14. What happened?

        a. Only the yellow basket became pink.

        b. The yellow basket and all the eggs became pink.

        c. The basket remained yellow, but the eggs became pink.

        d. The basket and eggs became white.

        e. Everything that the eraser touched became pink.

❋ Left-click black.

❋ Right-click white.

❋ Close Paint.

❋ Do not save the picture.

Problem E

For the following assignment, use Notepad.

❋ Open Notepad. Create a .LOG file.

❋ Key in your name, your class information, and **Chapter 4 Problem** E. Save the document to the MYDATADISK disk as LOGGING.TXT.

❋ Close the LOGGING.TXT file.

❋ Open the STRAITHITS.TXT file in the MUSIC folder in the XPRODATA directory.

❋ Copy the first three song titles to the Clipboard.

❋ Click **File**. Click **Open**. If asked, do not save the existing file.

❋ Open LOGGING.TXT on the MYDATADISK disk.

❋ Paste the song titles from the Clipboard into this document.

❋ Save the document.

❋ Print the document.

❋ Close Notepad.

Problem F

For the following assignment, use WordPad.

❋ Open WordPad.

❋ Open the DREAM.txt file (on the MYDATADISK disk) created in Section 4.7. If you did not create it, create it now.

❋ Save it with the exact name DREAMING, choosing RTF as the file type, to the MYDATADISK disk.

- Make the following changes:
  - Place your name, your class information, and Chapter 4 Problem F at the top of the document.
  - Change the font to Times New Roman, 12 point, for the entire document.
  - Make the words DREAM MACHINE 14 point, boldface, and italic. Center it.
  - Change System Software to Operating System.
  - Add a line after Operating System that reads Software - Quicken.
  - Add and remove tabs as needed to line up the columns.
- Save the document.
- Print the document.
- Close WordPad.

Problem G

For the following assignment, use Paint. Graphic files are very large. It is recommended that you reduce the resolution to 16 Color Bitmap.

- Open Paint and recreate the above drawing. The plane is a "Paste from" and is located in the XPRODATA folder. It is called PLANE.BMP.
- Key in your name, your class information, and **Chapter 4 Problem G** at the top of the picture.
- Save it as READ.BMP to your Book disk. Remember to change the File Type to 16 colors.
- Some hints on drawing the picture:
  - Fill all the areas with color first.
  - Use any typeface and size you want for your letters. Remember to make the text box big enough so the letters fit. To move text, it is best to key in the words first and use the Select tool to encircle the words. You can then drag them to the desired location.
  - Use any colors or gray tones you wish.
- Print the drawing if you have a laser or ink jet printer. Do not print if you have a dot-matrix printer.
- This document will print on two pages.

* Save the drawing.
* Close Paint.

Problem Set II—Brief Essay

For all essay questions, use Notepad or WordPad for your answer. Print your answer. Be sure and include your name and class information.

1. *Having an email address is just as important as having a phone number*. Agree or disagree with this statement and give your rationale for your answer.
2. Compare and contrast WordPad and Notepad. Describe what features you prefer in each. When would you want to use Notepad? WordPad? Justify your decisions.
3. What purpose does Paint serve? Do you think it was important for Windows XP Professional to include it as an accessory? Why or why not?

Problem Set III—Scenario

Use Notepad or WordPad for your answer. Print your answer. Be sure and include your name and class information.

You are in a study group for your Windows XP Professional class. Each member of your group has the assignment of outlining a section of this chapter. Select and outline one section for your group. Include keywords and their definitions. Make the document as attractive as possible by using different fonts and font sizes, and bulleted lists. Use boldface, italic, or underline for emphasis. If possible, create a drawing in Paint that you could use with your document.

CHAPTER 5

Exploring Files and Folders

In this chapter you will learn that files and folders must follow specific naming rules. You will also see that there are strategies in naming files and folders so that you may locate them easily. All files have properties that may be viewed using property sheets. You will learn about the Search command, located on the Start menu, which will assist you in locating files and folders by name, modification date, or a keyword or phrase.

You will discover that you can create shortcuts—pointers to objects, files, folders, and devices. You will find that you can create a folder to keep your files and shortcuts in. You will also discover the convenience of dragging and dropping objects to the Recycle Bin to eliminate them.

Learning Objectives

1. Explain the purpose and function of files and folders.
2. Compare and contrast DOS and Windows XP Professional file-naming rules.
3. Evolve strategies for developing naming conventions.
4. Compare and contrast the purpose and function of files and folders.
5. Explain the purpose and function of Search.
6. Describe the purpose and function of wildcards.
7. Describe the features available in the Search Results window.
8. Explain the purpose and function of shortcuts.
9. Explain the purpose and function of drag-and-drop operations.
10. Explain the purpose and function of the Recycle Bin.

Student Outcomes

1. List rules for naming files in Windows XP Professional.
2. View and manipulate the properties of a document.
3. Use Search to locate a file by its name, modification date, size, or type.
4. Use wildcards with the Search command.
5. Use Search to locate a folder.
6. Create and use shortcuts to devices, files, and folders.
7. Print a document using a shortcut.
8. Create a folder on the desktop.
9. Delete and retrieve items placed in the Recycle Bin.

5.1 ● File Systems

Windows XP Professional supports the major hard disk file systems: *FAT16*, *FAT32*, and *NTFS (New Technology File System)*. A *file system* defines the structure and the rules used to read, write, and maintain information stored on a disk. The decision on which file system you should use is based on your hardware, software, and security needs and if you need a dual-booting system. A *dual-booting* system allows you to have more than one operating system on the same computer but you may only use one operating system at a time. Although a computer could have more than two operating systems installed on it *(multibooting)*, dual-booting is most common. Dual-booting is necessary when you use application programs that require different operating systems or you wish to experiment with different operating systems. Dual-booting saves you the cost of an additional computer because you may place both operating systems on your current hard drive in separate *volumes*. A physical hard disk can be *partitioned* (divided) into one or more volumes. Each volume then functions as if it were a physically separate drive and is assigned a logical drive letter. You do not need to have a dual-booting system in order to use multiple volumes. The decision on which file system to use on a hard drive is determined when Windows XP Professional is installed, when an existing disk volume is formatted, or when a new disk is installed.

Of the three file systems listed, FAT16 is the oldest and was originally created for file systems based on the DOS operating system. This file system is still supported by many operating systems, including DOS, Windows 3.x, Windows 95/98, Windows NT 4.0, Windows for Workgroups, Windows 2000 Professional, Unix, and Linux. Its major disadvantage is that it cannot be installed in partitions greater than 2 GB (gigabytes).

Windows 95 OSR (Operating System Release) 2.1 introduced the FAT32 file system. FAT32 supports disks from 512 MB to 2 TB (terabyte, one trillion bytes) in size and a smaller cluster size (which means smaller files take up less room on a disk). It is compatible with Windows 98 and Windows 2000 Professional.

NTFS, the most recent file system, introduced with Windows NT 3.1, offers many advantages over the other two file systems, including better file security, disk compression, logging features, reliability, and stability. NTFS's major disadvantage is that if you are using a dual-booting system, the other operating system may not be able to access files on the NTFS volume.

FAT16 and FAT32 volumes can be converted to NTFS volumes without formatting, however NTFS volumes cannot be converted to FAT16 or FAT32 volumes without formatting (erasing) the desired volume. Conversion to the NTFS file system is not a decision to be taken lightly. Prior to a conversion decision, thoroughly research the consequences of that decision on your existing files on your computer system.

5.2 ⬦ File and Folder Names

Files and folders are the most fundamental concepts in Windows. No matter what you use your computer for, you will deal with files and folders. Files and folders will come on your computer or will be added to your computer when you install software. The minute you decide to save your work, you will create files. When you want to organize your files, you will create folders.

A *file* is any collection of related information that is given a name and stored on a disk so it can be retrieved when needed. A file is a named collection of information, such as a program, a set of data used by a program, or a user-created document. A file is the basic unit of storage that enables a computer to distinguish one set of information from another.

Because of all the files that come with Windows and the different application programs you use, not to mention the files that you create, your hard disk can contain hundreds, if not thousands, of files. If you are on a network, you could have access to millions of files. There would be no way to keep track of all these files if they were not organized in some way. The fundamental way to organize and track files in Windows XP Professional is with the use of folders.

A folder is a means of organizing programs and documents and can hold both files and additional folders. It is a container that holds objects. Technically, a folder is just a special kind of file that contains a list of the locations of other files.

If everything to do with computers has to do with files and folders, it is a self-evident truth that all files and folders must be named. All operating systems have rules for how files and folders may be named. File and folder names follow the same rules because a folder is just a special type of file.

Prior to Windows 95, names fell under what is called the FAT (file allocation table) file system, or more commonly, the DOS 8.3 rule. Under the FAT file system, a *file name* is technically a *file specification*. A file specification is comprised of two parts, a file name and a file extension. Often people use the term file name to mean what is actually the file specification. The DOS rules are:

⬦ The name of a file must be unique within a folder.
⬦ No file name can be longer than eight characters.
⬦ File extensions are optional, but an extension cannot be longer than three characters.
⬦ A file name must be separated from its extension with a period, called a dot. The dot is an example of a delimiter. A *delimiter* is a punctuation mark that marks the end of one thing

and the beginning of another. Delimiters are very specific; the dot (period) can be placed only between a file name and its extension. There are no spaces within a file name or between a file name and its extension. If a file is called Myfile.txt, it cannot be keyed in as My file . txt.

* File names are not case sensitive. MYFILE.TXT and myfile.txt signify the same file.
* All alphanumeric characters can be used in a file specification except the following illegal characters:

[Print Screen] [PgDn] [Alt] [Ctrl] [Space Bar] . " / \ : ; [ ] ¦ < > + = , * ?

* The total length of a path and file name is limited to 80 characters.

Windows 95 introduced a major new feature provided by the **VFAT** *(virtual file allocation table) file system.* It is an extension of and compatible with the older FAT system. It was designed for backward compatibility with DOS and Windows 3.1 programs still being used. FAT32 and NTFS follow the same rules.

This feature has the ability to handle long file names. **Long file names,** also referred to as **LFN**s, allow files (and folders) to have names with up to 255 characters. In this scheme, every file has two names, a long file name and a short file name that complies with the 8.3 rule. Nearly identical to the DOS rules, the Windows XP Professional rules are:

* The name of a file in a folder must be unique.
* No file name can be longer than 255 characters. However, that length includes the path name. For instance, a file called myletter.doc stored in the My Documents folder on Drive C has the full path name of C:\My Documents\myletter.doc. Thus, the length of the file name is not 12 characters (myletter.doc) but 28 characters.
* File extensions are optional, but practically speaking, most file names include a file extension (file type). File extensions, or file types as they are called in Windows XP Professional, are always the last characters following the last period in a file name. As you saw in Chapter 3, file types are heavily utilized by the Registry.
* A file name is separated from its extension with a period, called a dot. The characters following the last period are the file type. In the FAT32 and NTFS file systems, you may use spaces and more than one dot. Thus, a file legally could be named MY FILE NAME.SECOND.TXT.
* File names are not case sensitive. MYFILE.TXT and myfile.txt are the same file. Windows XP Professional allows you to use any combination of case; you could have a file name of MyFILE.tXt and Windows would retain that capitalization. But that would still be an identical file name to MYFILE.TXT.
* All alphanumeric characters, including spaces, can be used in a file specification except the following illegal characters:

\ / : * ? " < > ¦

* The quotation mark (") is not a valid character in naming a file but can be used to specify long file names, especially those with spaces, such as "My file for you.doc".
* If you use long file names, a short file name is automatically created for you. To create this short file name, the operating system takes the first six characters of the long file name (ignoring spaces), adds ~1 (or a larger number), and sets the file extension as the first three letters after the last period in the long file name. If you had two files, one called My file text.doc and a second called My file for handling taxes.doc, Windows XP Professional would assign Myfile~1.doc to the first file and Myfile~2.doc to the second. Windows XP Professional uses a slightly different method for creating short file names when there are five or more files that can result in duplicate file names. For every file after the fifth file, Windows XP Professional uses only the first two letters of the LFN. It then mathematically manipu-

lates the remaining letters of the LFN to generate the next four letters. Then it appends ˜1 (or another unique number) to avoid a duplicate file name.

* You should never rename system folders, such as System or System32, because they are required for Windows to run properly.

5.3 • File-Naming Strategies

The files you create must be named by you, the user. You do not name program files; these have predetermined names such as Winword.exe for Microsoft Word, Qw.exe for Quicken 2000, and Excel.exe for Microsoft Excel. You must name the data or document files you create.

Programs that were not designed to work with Windows XP Professional still typically follow the DOS file-naming rules (the 8.3 rule). If you attempt to save a file with a long name within an older application, the application will present an error message telling you that the file name is too long.

Even when you have new applications written for Windows XP Professional that support long file names, you have to think about what you name your files. You are going to want to retrieve your files, and you should have a logical naming scheme to facilitate your search. This method is known as a *naming convention*. If you name files randomly, locating them will become a problem. As the number of files increases, remembering all the names you have assigned becomes next to impossible.

For instance, if you were corresponding with Mr. Bob Wong, you could name one file Letter to Bob and another file Response to Mr. Wong's letter. These would both be valid file names, but when you wanted to locate all the correspondence with Bob Wong, how would you find these files? Although the Start menu provides a Search command for locating files (that you will learn to use later in this chapter), you would have to look for each file individually. Locating similar files would be easier if you gave all the file names some element in common, such as Wong.letter and Wong.response. When you wanted to find all the correspondence relating to Bob Wong, you would know they all have an item in common.

Even though you are no longer shackled to the DOS 8.3 rule, you must be careful not to get carried away with long file names for a number of reasons. First of all, you are going to be the one keying them in. The longer the file name, the better the chance of making a typographical error and not locating your file. Second, in My Computer, if your file name is too long, it will be truncated, and you will not be able to read the complete name anyhow. Third, if you are saving files to the root directory of a floppy disk, there is a 224-file limit in the directory table. Long file names take up more than one entry in the table. Thus, you could get an error message that the disk was full when the disk was not full but the directory table was. When the directory table is full, you cannot save any more files to the floppy disk. By using shorter file names, you eliminate this problem. Last, there is an old programming principle—KISS (Keep It Simple, Stupid). This principle is very appropriate to file names. The more complicated you make your file name, the less likely you are to remember it. Anyone who has spent hours looking for a file can appreciate this fact. The rule of thumb is use long file names, but do not make the file names too long.

There is a further consideration. Operating systems are very literal. If you name a file MYFILE.DOC and later look for a file called MY FILE.DOC, Windows XP Professional will not locate it. It will look for an exact match. Spaces are very difficult to work with. Even though Windows XP Professional allows you to use spaces in file names, there are many utility programs such as backup programs that "choke" on spaces in file names. In other words, these programs will not recognize spaces in a file name and will not run. But more importantly, it is important for users to be consistent in how they name their files. It is difficult, as a user, to remember whether or not you put spaces in a file name. The simplest rule, which most computer users opt for, is never use spaces in a file name.

As far as case goes, again, it is difficult for a user to remember if one used uppercase letters or a combination of upper- and lowercase letters. Windows XP Professional does not differentiate between case; e.g., it treats MYDOC.TXT, MyDoc.TXT, and mydoc.txt as identical file names. Regardless of how you named a file, in whatever case you key it in, Windows XP Professional will locate it. However, if you are an Internet user, you are sometimes dealing with a different operating system. The Internet runs on an operating system called Unix. Unix *does* care about case and wants all lowercase letters for file names. Again, to keep it simple, many users opt for all lowercase file names only.

Today, most application packages will assign predetermined file extensions to data files unless you tell them otherwise. For example, Word assigns .doc. Using the earlier example of letters to Bob Wong, if the data files were created with Word the file names would actually be Wong.letter.doc and Wong.response.doc because Word would add the file extension .doc. Although the .doc extension is a common element that you could use for your naming convention, you would still have a problem locating files by .doc because every file you created with Word would have the .doc extension. You want a more distinctive way to locate files with similar subjects.

Whether or not a data file has an extension depends on the rules of the program that it was created in. Word, as mentioned, assigns .doc; Microsoft PowerPoint assigns .ppt; Excel assigns .xls; all by default. An application program may have more than one file extension registered. For instance, Microsoft Access uses many file extensions, such as .mdb and .mdn.

Typically in Windows XP Professional, the file name tells you about the subject and the extension tells you about the type of data. If you had a data file called Sister letter.doc, Sister letter would tell you that the file was a letter to your sister and .doc would tell you (and Windows XP Professional) that the file was created with Word. In Windows XP Professional, file extensions are referred to as file types. Programs are identified by the file types .exe and .com; Windows XP Professional recognizes them as program files. The extension .exe stands for executable code. The extension .com stands for command file. There are other file types reserved for programs, such as .dll for dynamic-link libraries and .sys for system files. Table 5.1 lists those file extensions.

Extension	Meaning
.com	Command file
.exe	Executable
.bat	Batch
.cmd	Command script file
.vb	VBScript file (Visual Basic)
.vbe	VBScript Encoded Script file (Visual Basic)
.js	JScript file (Java)
.jse	JScript Encoded Script
.wsf	Windows Script File
.wsh	Windows Script Host Settings file

Table 5.1 • *The Search Order for Extensions.*

5.4 • Activity • File Properties

Note: There are assumed settings for each chapter. If you are working on your own computer, the changes you made in the default settings should be retained from one work session to the next. However, if you are working in a computer lab, you may have to change your settings each time you log into the network. Check Section 3.8.

1 Open My Computer.

2 Double-click the **Drive C** icon. Double-click the **XPRODATA** folder.

3 Scroll until you see Glossary.wri. Place the pointer on the **Glossary.wri** icon.

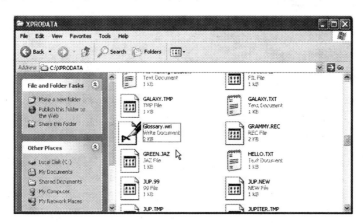

WHAT'S **HAPPENING?** The document icon represents Write, the program that created this document. Write was the word-processing program that came with Windows 3.1. It has since been replaced by WordPad. This file will open with WordPad. Since Hide file extensions for known file types is not set, you can see the complete file name, Glossary.wri. By placing the pointer on the icon, you can see additional information: type, author, title, and size. The file's property sheet displays additional information.

4 Right-click the icon for the document called **Glossary.wri**.

WHAT'S **HAPPENING?** You have opened the shortcut menu for this object. Remember, the shortcut menu is also called a context, pop-up, or right-click menu. In this case, the object is a document file. This menu lets you manipulate the document without changing the data it contains. From this shortcut menu you can initiate such object-oriented tasks as opening, deleting, copying, renaming, or printing the document (the object).

All objects have properties, such as settings and parameters. Each object has a property sheet that displays a collection of information about it. You can tell what an object is by looking at its properties.

5 Click **Properties**.

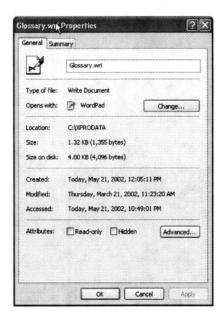

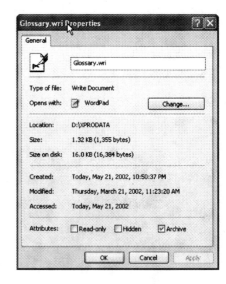

NTFS File System   *FAT 32 Property Sheet*

WHAT'S HAPPENING? The type of property sheet you see will depend on what file system you are using. If you have Word installed, other tabs may appear. If the General tab is not on top, click it. By looking at the properties, you know the document's name is Glossary.wri. Both property sheets display the Type of file statement. It tells you that Glossary.wri was created with the Write program (Write Document), and the Location of the file is Drive C in the XPRODATA folder (C:\XPRODATA). You know the document's size. You also know when the document was created, modified, or accessed. Your dates may vary. The created date is the date the files were copied to the hard disk. Check boxes indicate file attributes. A *file attribute* is a flag that is attached to a file that describes and regulates its use. In FAT32, a file can have three attributes: (1) It may be Read-only (it cannot be modified or deleted). (2) It can be Hidden (the file name does not display in a file listing). Often program files are hidden so that you do not accidentally move or delete them. (3) It can have an Archive attribute, also called an archive bit, which is used by some programs to determine which files are to be backed up. If the Archive attribute is set, either the file has never been backed up or it has changed since you last backed it up. If your file system is NTFS, the archive attribute does not appear on this sheet.

6 If you have the NTFS file system, click the **Advanced** button.

WHAT'S HAPPENING? Here you see that the file is ready for archiving, which means that Glossary.wri either has never been backed up or has changed since the last time it was backed up. The NTFS file system also shows check boxes for Compressed or Encrypted files.

7 Click the **Cancel** command button to close the property sheet. Click **Cancel**.

8 Right-click **Glossary.wri**. Click **Open**.

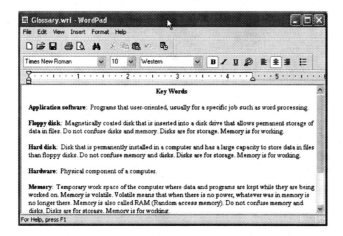

WHAT'S HAPPENING? In order to see the data in the document Glossary.wri, you had to open the application program. In this case, the WordPad program opened. The Write program was the program bundled with Windows 3.1. In Windows XP Professional, WordPad has replaced Write as the word-processing program. Operating systems such as Windows 3.1 and Windows XP Professional come *bundled* with some software applications. These smaller programs, such as Write, WordPad, and Calculator, have been included with the operating system package to make it more attractive or functional.

WordPad opened as an application window with Glossary.wri as the document. The Control-menu icon, in the upper-left corner of the title bar, is the icon for WordPad. Since this program was written for Windows XP Professional, Glossary.wri, the file name, appears first in the title bar and is followed by WordPad, the name of the program. This organization reflects the docucentric approach, where the document is more central than the application that created it.

Your screen might look different, depending on how WordPad is customized. However, you will have a window that you can size. You can minimize, maximize, or close the application. Most Windows applications also have a separate document window so that you can open multiple document windows. Since WordPad is a less powerful application, it does not have a separate document window. If you wanted to make changes to the data now, you would do so here in the application program.

9 Double-click the Control-menu icon on the title bar, 🗐.

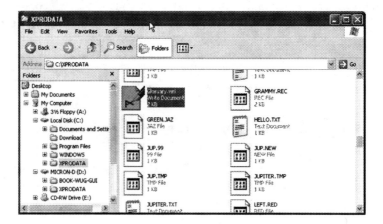

WHAT'S HAPPENING? You now know two ways to close a program, single-click the Close button or double-click the Control-menu icon. Since you opened this document by double-clicking its icon in the XPRODATA window, you were returned to that window when you closed the program. If you wanted to print the document, you could do so by using the shortcut menu.

10 Be sure the printer is turned on. Right-click **Glossary.wri**. Click **Print**.

WHAT'S HAPPENING? You saw WordPad quickly open. Then a message box appeared, telling you that WordPad is printing your document. You can print a document only from within an application. In other words, to print a document, you must first open the program that created it. By choosing Print on the shortcut menu, you automatically opened the program so that the document could be printed. The Print command automatically opens the application, prints the document, and closes the program.

11 Close all open windows.

5.5 ● Folders

Folders are another tool to help you organize your files. A folder is a special type of file. The DOS term for folder is directory. A folder within a folder is called a subfolder or in DOS terms, a subdirectory. Folder and directory are synonymous terms; they can be used interchangeably. Folder and subfolder and directory and subdirectory are also used interchangeably. A folder is a container in which you can place related files or folders. The only folder that is automatically created for you on a disk is the root directory. Otherwise, either you create folders or they are created for you by the installation of a program. Windows XP Professional is a program and does create folders.

When you install a program, it will usually create folders and place all of the files necessary to run the program within them. Programs consist of many files. More than likely a program is not just one executable file. It may be comprised of several, even hundreds, of support files. These support files can include help files, font files, template files, and .dll files. Windows allows executable routines to be stored as *DLL (dynamic-link library)* files and loaded only when needed. A dynamic-link library has several advantages. First, it does not consume any memory until it is used. Second, because a dynamic-link library is a separate file, a programmer can make corrections or improvements to that module without affecting the operation of the program or any other dynamic-link library. Finally, a programmer can use the same dynamic-link library with other programs. All of a program's support files are needed to execute that program. They are the working program files. The program files are the tools you use to create your data.

You do not want to store your data files in the same place as your program files. Before there were computers, people used tools like typewriters to create documents. A typewritten letter to Ms. Hall and a typewritten chapter in a book would not be filed together under T for type-writer. In the computer world, the same logic applies. If your tool is Word, a folder called C:\Program Files\Microsoft Office contains all the program files that make Word work. You do not want to store the Hall letter and the Chapter 1 document in the C:\Program Files\Microsoft Office folder. Therefore, you want to create your own folders. Chapter 1 and the Hall letter are not related documents. You want to place these documents in their own folders. You might have a folder called Book in which you place the Chapter 1 file, and you might have another folder called Letters in which you place the Hall document. When you need to locate either of these documents, you can go directly to the appropriate folder and know that related documents are in the folder.

The Windows XP Professional docucentric paradigm assumes that you are interested in your own documents, not the tools that created them. It is much more efficient to create folders for different topics than to search for documents among the program files. Besides helping you locate the document you need, folders allow you to back up your data and manipulate your files easily.

5.6 ● Finding Documents

As you work, you will create many documents, which is no different from working in any office environment, although in offices of the past, you used paper, filing cabinets, and typewriters. In the computer age, your tool is a software application package, and you store your files electroni-cally. Your tasks, however, are the same.

In the old office environment, people realized that they had to organize information in some fashion so that they could store and retrieve it. They used filing cabinets to store documents. They placed documents in folders and arranged them in some sort of order, usually numerical or alphabetical. They might have placed several files in a larger folder, grouping related informa-tion together. For instance, instead of filing the electric bill under Electric and the gas bill under Gas, they might have put them both in a folder called Utilities. In Windows XP Professional terms, Electric.doc and Gas.doc would be the files that contained the information. The con-tainer or folder where these objects were stored would be called Utilities. To find anything, they needed to search their memory and recall where it had been filed. Windows XP Professional has a Search feature you can use to search your disks (your electronic filing cabinets) for the files and folders, printers, people, and other computers on your network. It also can assist you in searching the Internet. When you first open Search, it presents a browser-like window. See Figure 5.1. The Search Results window is divided into two vertical panes. The left pane (the Search Companion) queries you on what it is you want to search for. Once you choose what it is you are searching for, you will be presented with additional dialog boxes where you enter your search specification while the right pane (the Search Results pane) displays your search results.

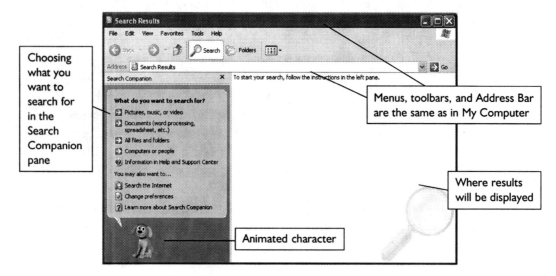

Figure 5.1 • The Search Results Window

The menus, toolbars, and Address Bar are the same as in My Computer. In the Search Companion Pane, you choose what it is you wish to search for. The Search Results Pane will display the results of your search. The Animated Character will provide extra help and even do a trick. It can also be turned off.

5.7 • Activity • Using Search

1   Click **Start**. Click **Search**.

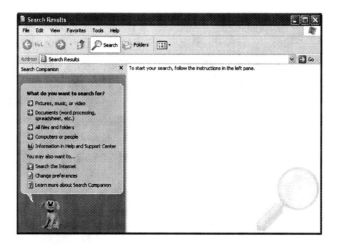

WHAT'S HAPPENING? If you cannot see all the choices, size the window so you can. You need to decide what you want to look for. The choices you see are picture, music, or video. If you choose this option, search will look for files but specific types of files. Documents will only look for document files whereas All files and folders will look for all, regardless of whether or not the file is a document. Computers and people will look for computers on your network or people in your address book. It will also lead you to help. Your further options include searching the Internet, changing your preferences, or using help to learn more about the Search Companion.

2   Click the animated character.

WHAT'S **HAPPENING?** You can choose another character, turn off the character, or have the character do a trick.

3 Click **Do a trick**.

WHAT'S **HAPPENING?** The animated character did a trick for you. The tricks will vary.

4 Click **Back**. Click **All files and folders**.

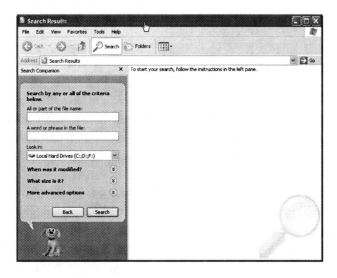

5 Click **View**. Point to **Toolbars**.

WHAT'S **HAPPENING?** The Search Results' View menu and Folder Options dialog box closely resemble My Computer's.

6 On the View menu, check the following settings:
Toolbars—Standard Buttons and Address Bar on, Links is off with Lock Toolbar on.
Status Bar—Off
Explorer Bar—only Search on
Tiles is the selected display and Arrange Icons by Name is selected and Show in Groups is off.

7 Click **View**. Click **Details**. Then click **View** and click **Choose Details**.

WHAT'S **HAPPENING?** You changed your view to Details. When you are looking for files and folders, it is useful to have as much information as you can displayed. Choosing Choose Details allows you to specify which file and folder details you wish to see. You use the check boxes to specify which file details you wish to view in the right pane. You can also use the Move Up and Move Down buttons to arrange the columns in the Search Results pane from left to right.

8 The default is Name, In Folder, Size, Type, and Date Modified. Each of these check boxes is selected. If they are not, check them to select them. Click **OK**.

9 Click **View**. Point to **Toolbars**. Click **Customize**. Ensure that Text options is set to Show selective text on right and Icon options is set to Large Icons. Click **Close**.

10 Click **Tools**. Click **Folder Options**. On the View tab, be sure Display the full path in the address bar and Do not show hidden files and folders are set and the Hide file extension for known file types check box is cleared.

11 Click **OK**.

12 In the left pane, click the **More Advanced Options** unfold button to open it.

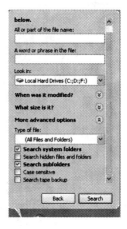

WHAT'S **HAPPENING?** In More advanced options, by default it is set so that Search System folders and Search subfolders are all enabled. Remember, a *default* is a setting that a program applies in the absence of any specific instructions from the user. A computer must always have instructions. The defaults change for each option. For instance, if you had selected Documents (word processing, spreadsheets, etc.), the Advanced Options would search subfolders by default but not System folders or hidden files and folders.

13 Be sure **Search System Folders** and **Search Subfolders** are set and all other check boxes are clear. Click in the All or part of the file name text box. Key in the following: **Computer.xls**

14 Click the down arrow in the Look in drop-down list box.

WHAT'S HAPPENING? The Look in drop-down list box is asking you to choose where you want to look. In this example, Local Hard Drives (C:, D: F:) is the default choice since this computer has more than one hard drive. Your default could be different. If you choose My Computer, Search will look on all your drives for your named file, including your floppy disk drive, your CD-ROM drive, and any removable drives such as a Zip drive. Choosing Local Hard Drives directs Search to look on all your hard drives. You can also select individual drives.

15 Click **Browse**.

WHAT'S HAPPENING? The Browse For Folder dialog box opens. Searching even one hard disk for a file can take a long time, particularly in this day and age of very large hard drives. Search will search the entire hard disk literally from top to bottom. If you can narrow your search to a drive and then to a folder on that drive, you will decrease the search time. My Computer is the default selection. My Computer will search for your file on every drive attached to your computer (all hard drives, all floppy drives, and any CD-ROM drives). If you choose My Network Places, Search will search every drive on the network, which can take a really long time.

16 In the list box, click **My Computer**. Click **(C:)**. Click the **XPRODATA** folder. (Remember, if you are in a lab environment, the XPRODATA folder could be on a drive other than C.)

WHAT'S HAPPENING? You have selected the XPRODATA folder on Drive C.

17 Click **OK**.

WHAT'S HAPPENING? In this example, you know both the name of the file you will be looking for and its approximate location. You have entered the information in each text box. The Search system folders and Search subfolders check boxes are set, which means Search will look in the XPRODATA folder and any subfolders in the XPRODATA folder for your named file.

18 Click the **Search** button.

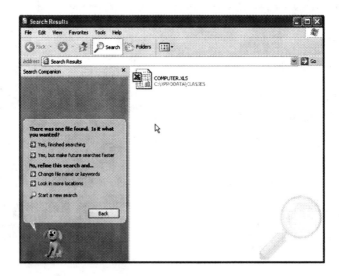

WHAT'S HAPPENING? The file, COMPUTER.XLS, was found in Drive C in the XPRODATA folder in the Classes folder. This document was created with Excel. However, this window is not displaying the file details. You may still see those details.

19 Place your mouse pointer on **COMPUTER.XLS**.

WHAT'S HAPPENING? Now you can see the type, date, time the file was last modified, and size of the file as well as information that Microsoft Excel provides.

20 Click **View**. Click **Details**.

WHAT'S HAPPENING? Now you can see all the information. If you cannot see all the information, you can alter the size of this window and size the columns. To size the columns double-click or drag the lines separating the column names.

21 On the menu bar, click **File**.

WHAT'S HAPPENING? Most of the choices are dimmed and thus unavailable. First you have to select a file in order to manipulate it. If you choose Save Search, Search will allow you to save your search in a specified location so that you may quickly find the same file or files again.

22 On the menu bar, click **Edit**.

WHAT'S HAPPENING? Your Undo choice may vary. Undo remembers the last action you took. Cut, Copy, Paste, Paste Shortcut, Copy to Folder, and Move to Folder are all dimmed because you have not selected a file. You have the choice of Select All, which would select all the files. Invert Selection would reverse the choice of items.

23 In the Search Results window, click **COMPUTER.XLS** to select it.

24 On the menu bar, click **File**.

WHAT'S HAPPENING? Now that you have selected a file, you can choose actions such as Open or Print. You can perform file management tasks such as Delete or Rename. You also have a new choice, Open Containing Folder.

25 Click **Open Containing Folder**. Click **View**. Click **Tile**.

WHAT'S HAPPENING? You were taken to the folder window that contains this file.

26 Close the window.

27 In the list box, right-click **COMPUTER.XLS**.

WHAT'S HAPPENING? Now that you have located the file, you can manipulate it with the right-click shortcut menu. If you have the Excel program installed on your system, you can also double-click the file to open it or choose Open.

28   Click **File** on the menu bar. Click **Save Search**.

WHAT'S HAPPENING? You are presented a dialog box asking you where you want to save the file. The default location is the My Documents folder. The type of file is Saved search files. These file will have the extension of .fnd.

29   Click **Save**. Close the Search Results window.

30   Click **Start**. Click the My Documents folder.

WHAT'S HAPPENING? Your saved search is located in the My Documents folder. The contents of the My Documents folder will vary.

31 Double-click **Files named Computer.xls.fnd**.

32 In the All or part of the file name text box, click after **Computer.xls**. Key in **, astro.txt, dress.up**.

33 Click the down arrow in the Look in text box. Click **Browse**. Click **My Computer**. Click **Drive C**. Click the **XPRODATA** folder. Click **OK**.

WHAT'S HAPPENING? You were returned to the Search Results window with the information filled in for this search. You then added two more files, separating the names with commas. You may search for more than one file at a time with the use of commas. In this case, you are going to search for three files that have no common elements in their file names but are all located in the XPRODATA folder or one of its subfolders.

34 Click the **Search** button.

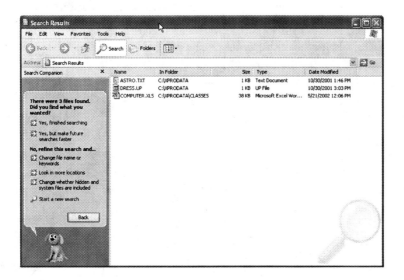

WHAT'S **HAPPENING?** Search found all the files you asked it to search for.

35 Close the Search Results window.

36 In the My Documents folder, drag the icon labeled **Files named Computer.xls.fnd** to the Recycle Bin on the desktop.

37 Close the My Documents window.

WHAT'S **HAPPENING?** You deleted your saved search and have returned to the desktop.

5.8 ● Improving Your Searches with Wildcards

In the above activity, the file Computer.xls was easy to locate because you knew the file specification and the approximate folder location. The same was true of Astro.txt and Dress.up. However, as you work, you will create many documents. Remembering what you specifically called every document becomes difficult.

If you create naming conventions—plans for how you name your files—you can locate a group of files that relate to a specific topic easily. For instance, if you created a series of documents that were reports, your naming convention could have your file names look as follows: Gillay.rep.doc, Sanchez.rep.doc, and Ho.rep.doc. If you needed to see all your reports, it would be easy to remember that you included rep as part of their file names.

Search allows you to use the * and ? characters in your search criteria. *Search criteria* are search instructions. The * and ? characters are called wildcards. A *wildcard* character represents one or more unknown characters. The asterisk (*), called "star," can represent any number of characters. The asterisk is the most commonly used wildcard. The question mark (?) replaces a single character in your criteria.

For instance, if you wanted to find all your files that had a .doc extension, you could search for *.doc, which would tell Search to locate any file that has .doc as a file extension, no matter what appears before the file extension. If you wanted to locate all your rep files, you could specify *rep*.* in your search criteria. When you use *.* (called "star dot star"), you are asking for every file whether it has a file extension or not.

The question mark represents a single character in your search criteria. If your search request was ??rep.dat, you would be asking Search to locate files that have any two characters in front of rep and that end in .dat. Search would locate MYrep.dat and 12rep.dat but not YOURrep.dat because YOUR has four characters, not two. It also would not find Myrep.xls because .xls does not match .dat. If your search request was ??rep.*, you would be asking Search to locate files that have any two characters in front of rep and that end in any file extension. Search would locate MYrep.dat, 12rep.dat, and Myrep.xls, but not YOURrep.dat because YOUR has four characters, not two. Table 5.2 gives some more examples of using wildcards.

Search	Results
*	All files and folders.
.	All files and folders.
.doc	All files and folders with an extension of .doc.
doc	All files and folders with doc in their name (including the file extension).
exe	All files and folders with exe in their name (including the file extension).
*.exe	All files and folders with .exe as the file extension. Since .exe stands for executable code, this would locate all of your program files.

doc	All files and folders with doc in their name.
*doc	All files and folders with doc as the last letters in their name (not including the file extension).
*doc?	All files and folders with any number of characters before doc and one character between doc and the end of their name (not including the file extension).
?doc	All files and folders with doc one character from the beginning of their name.

Table 5.2 ◦ Search Criteria

5.9 ◦ Activity ◦ Using Wildcards with Search

1   Click **Start**. Point to **Search**. Click **All files and folders**.

2   Choose **C:\XPRODATA** in the Look in drop-down list box, using the techniques you learned in the last activity.

3   Click **View**. Click **Status Bar** to set it.

4   In the Search for files or folders named text box, key in the following: **c**

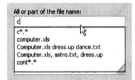

WHAT'S HAPPENING? As you keyed in the letter c, a drop-down list box opened showing you your previous selections. If the selection you wanted was there, you could click it to select it.

5   Click the **Search** button.

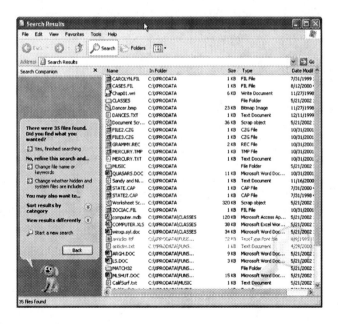

WHAT'S HAPPENING? The search criteria were extremely vague. You asked for any file or folder that has the letter c anywhere in its name, not just for files that begin with c. You got the folder Classes, but also a total of 35 files that had the letter c somewhere in their name. If you look at the bottom of the windows, you see how many files you found. Turning on the status bar gives you that information. You need to be more specific. The file you are looking for was created with Excel. You should know that data files in Excel have an .xls file extension. If all you can remember about the file name is that it begins with c, you may use a wildcard, *, to represent an unknown group of characters.

6   Click the **Back** button. In the Search for files or folders named text box, key in the following: **c*.xls**

7   Click the **Search** button.

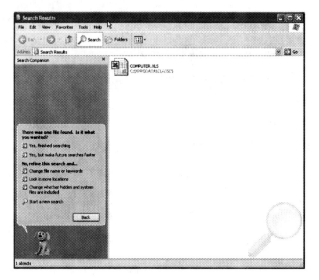

WHAT'S HAPPENING? This approach worked. You asked to see every file that begins with the letter c, has any number of characters following the c, and has an extension of .xls (c*.xls). You used * to represent all the characters you did not know.

8   Click the **Back** button. In the All or part of the file name, drag the mouse over **c*.xls** to select it.

9   Key in the following: ***fil***

WHAT'S HAPPENING? When you highlight a word or phrase and then key in another word or phrase, you replace what was there with what you keyed in.

10   Click the **Search** button.

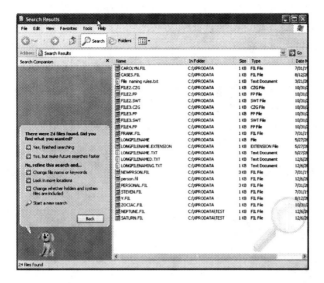

WHAT'S HAPPENING? You asked for a file with fil somewhere in its name. Look in the status bar; 24 files were found. These found files include files that have the extension .fil and names that contain fil. When you name files that are related by subject, you like their names to contain a common element.

11 Click the **Back** button. In the All or part of the file name text box, select ***fil*** and then key in the following: ***.fil**

12 Click the **Search** button.

WHAT'S HAPPENING? In this case, your "in common" feature was the file type, .fil. When you keyed in your query, you asked for files with any name (*) but only the .fil extension. You included * in your search phrase for a very specific reason.

13 Click the **Back** button. In the All or part of the file name text box, select ***.fil** and then key in the following: **.fil** [Enter]

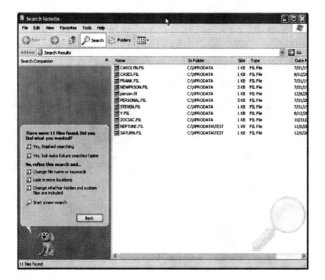

WHAT'S **HAPPENING?** Pressing ⌨Enter serves the same purpose as clicking the Search button. You found all files that have an extension of .fil. Remember when you asked for *fil*, you found all the files with fil anywhere in their names. Each time, you have asked for different information and have received different answers.

14 Click the **Back** button. In the All or part of the file name text box, select **.fil** and then key in the following: **ca*.fil** ⌨Enter

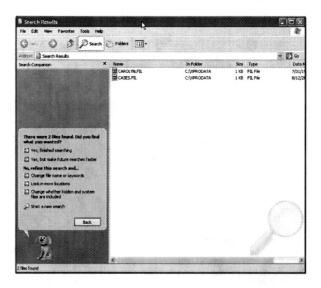

WHAT'S **HAPPENING?** You found two files that begin with ca and have a file extension of .fil. You can further refine your search.

15 Click the **Back** button. In the All or part of the file name text box, select **ca*.fil** and then key in the following: **ca*lyn.fil** ⌨Enter

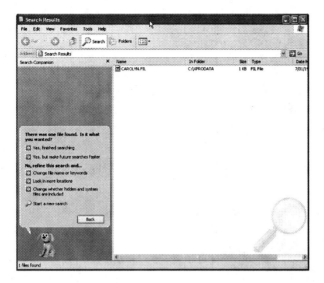

WHAT'S HAPPENING? In this case, you asked Search to locate every file that begins with ca, ends with lyn, has characters in the middle, and has a file extension of .fil. Case did not matter. You used lowercase letters, but the search results still found CAROLYN.FIL.

16 Click the **Back** button. In the All or part of the file name text box, select **ca*lyn.fil** and then key in: **exp*.*** [Enter]

WHAT'S HAPPENING? You found nine files that begin with exp followed by no specific number of characters and any file extension. What if you were only interested in the files that begin with exp and have feb in them?

17 Click the **Back** button. In the All or part of the file name text box, select **exp*.*** and then key in the following: **exp*feb*.*** [Enter]

WHAT'S **HAPPENING?** You found three files that meet your search criteria.

18 Click the **Back** button. In the All or part of the file name text box, select **exp*feb*.*** and then key in the following: ***.??** [Enter]

WHAT'S **HAPPENING?** Your search criteria found 13 files. You asked for file names of any length, but the files could have only two-character file extensions.

19 Close the Search Results window.

5.10 ● Other Features of Search

Search has other options for finding files. You have used both all or part of the file name and Look in. You have not used the text box A word or phrase in the file. This text box is allowing you to look for files with a specific word or phrase within the document. The other options include When the file was modified, the type of file (File extension) and What size is the file. When the file was modified has to do with the date and time stamp on a file. Every time you modify a file, the current date and time are stamped on the file folder. If you know when you created or modified a document, you can search by different date criteria. The other choices allow you to look for files by type or by size. The default is Don't remember. See Figure 5.2.

*Figure 5.2 * Finding Files Using Search Options*

If you scroll to see the Types of Files and open the drop-down list box, you will display a list of programs stored on your hard drive. See Figure 5.3.

*Figure 5.3 * Using Type of Files*

You may set criteria in all areas. For instance, you could specify a search for a file named Myfile.txt located in C:\XPRODATA that contains the text string Carolyn's Shopping List. Then you could specify that it was created last month and that the file is no larger than 4800KB. All these specifications or search criteria would have to be true in order for a file to be located. A file that met all other criteria but its size was 4900KB would not be found. A file that met all the other criteria except it only contained the text string Shopping would not be found. It would have to meet all the criteria that you specified.

Finding files is easiest when you plan for how to name them or when you use a naming convention. For instance, if you worked in a law office, you could have a naming scheme that made all pleadings start with PL. If you were looking for the documentation of a pleading from the previous month concerning your client Panezich, you could specify a search for all files that begin with PL, that were created last month, and that contain the text Panezich.

5.11 ● Activity ● Using Other Search Options

1   Click **Start**. Point at **Search**. Click **All files and folders**.

2   Choose **C:\XPRODATA** in the Look in drop-down list box, using the techniques you have learned.

3   Expand **When was it modified?**.

WHAT'S HAPPENING? You have limited your search to the XPRODATA folder and all the folders beneath it. You are now going to specify a date for your file.

4   Click the **Specify dates** option button.

WHAT'S HAPPENING? The current date is placed in the from and to text boxes. You can search among files created between two dates. You can look within the last week, last month, or last year.

5   In the from text box, click each portion of the date one by one (month, day, and year) to select it and key in the appropriate portion of the following date: **7-31-2000**

6   In the to box, click the down arrow.

WHAT'S HAPPENING? You opened a calendar. You can click ◄ for previous months and ► for later months.

7   Scroll through the calendar until you locate August 2000. Click **31** in the calendar.

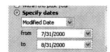

WHAT'S HAPPENING? You have selected your search criteria. You want to locate files created between 7/31/2000 and 8/31/2000 that are in the XPRODATA folder on Drive C.

8 Click the **Search** button. Click **View**. Click **Status Bar** to set it.

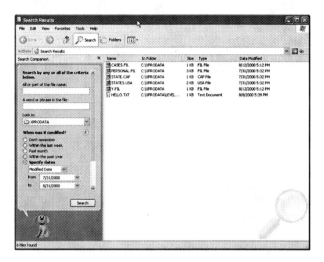

WHAT'S HAPPENING? Six files met your criteria. Now you want to locate specific text within a document. If you remember some phrase or word in a document, you can key it in.

9 Click **Back**. Click in the **A word or phrase in the file** text box and key in the following:
Tuttle

WHAT'S HAPPENING? You are ready for your search.

10 Click the **Search** button.

WHAT'S HAPPENING? It seems that no file met your criteria. You did not clear the dates when you asked to find a file with Tuttle in it. Your request was to find a file with Tuttle in it that was created between 7/31/2000 and 8/31/2000. Both criteria had to be met.

11 Click **Back**. Click **Don't Remember** in When was it modified? Click the **Search** button.

WHAT'S HAPPENING? Apparently one document on this disk, in the XPRODATA folder, has the word Tuttle in it. In reality, the phrase Tuttle appears in six files (person.fil, personal.fil, computer.mdb, grades.wri, phone.wri, and computer.xls). These six files were created for this textbook with the phrase "Tuttle" in each. If this is so, why then was only one file located? For a file to be included in the search for a word or phrase, the program that created the data must be registered. The file types, .wri and .fil, are not registered file types. In addition, although Office is registered, the feature of Search also does not include the Access component of Microsoft Office. In order to see the data in the documents, you must have the programs that created the documents. If you double-clicked Computer.xls and did not have Excel, you would not be able to see the document. If you do not have Microsoft Office installed on your computer, you will not be able to open the file.

12 In the right pane, double-click **computer.xls**.

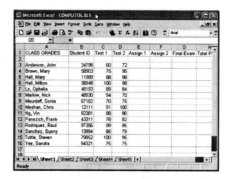

WHAT'S HAPPENING? You were interested in the document called computer.xls, which was created with Excel, so you opened Excel. Indeed, the word Tuttle appears toward the end of the document. The problem with looking for text in a document is that it is the most time-consuming way to look for files and you are also limited to registered file types. In this case, you were only looking in one folder on the hard drive. If you were looking on an 80-GB hard disk or on a network, the search for text could take minutes, even hours, and therefore would not be the most efficient way to locate text. If you were going to search for text often, you should turn on the Indexing Services.

13 Close Excel.

14 Click **Back**. Click **Back**. Click **Change Preferences**. Click **With Indexing Services** (for faster local searches).

WHAT'S HAPPENING? This is where you turn on this service.

15 Click **Cancel**. Click **Back**. Click **All files and folders**.

16 Clear **Tuttle** from the **A word or phrase in the file** text box.

17 Collapse **When was it modified?** Click **What size is it?**. Click **Specify size (in KB)**. **At least** should be selected. In the KB text box, key in **200**.

WHAT'S HAPPENING? You are going to search for any file in the C:\XPRODATA folder that is at least 200KB in size.

18 Click the **Search** button.

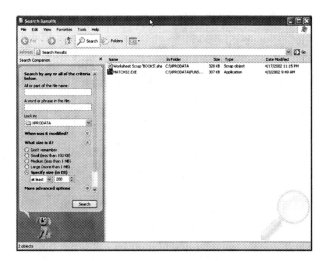

WHAT'S HAPPENING? Two files in the XPRODATA folder and subfolders meet the criteria.

19 Close the Search Results window.

5.12 • Finding Folders

One advantage to grouping your files in folders is the ability to limit your searches for these files later. When first using an application package to create documents, many people have no idea where their data files are being saved. Most application packages set a default folder where all data files are stored. For instance, Microsoft Word uses My Documents for saving files if you do not specify otherwise, whereas WordPerfect uses My Files. As you continue to create new files, however, the contents of this folder grow at a rapid pace, making it increasingly harder to locate a specific file. An easier method is to create folders that will hold similar files. If you were writing a mystery book, you could create a folder called MysteryBook and keep all your chapters in that folder. As you will see in the next activity, if you know the folder name, it is easier to locate files. In this activity, the folders were created for you. You will learn how to create your own folders later.

5.13 • Activity • Using Search to Find Folders

1   Click **Start**. Click **Search**. Click **All files and folders**.

WHAT'S HAPPENING? If you have been using Search often, you may be taken directly to this criteria window as Windows tries to remember what you often use without clicking All files and folders.

2   Choose **C:\XPRODATA** in the Look in drop-down list box, using the techniques you have learned.

3   In the All or part of the file name text box, key in the following: **Classes**

WHAT'S HAPPENING? You are looking for the folder called Classes. Classes is a folder that was created for you in the XPRODATA folder. A folder called Classes would logically store any files that deal with classes. When Search searches the XPRODATA folder, it is looking for both files and folders with Classes in their names. Search does not distinguish between files and folders. If you remember, a folder is just a special type of file.

4   Click the **Search** button.

WHAT'S HAPPENING? You found the Classes folder under the XPRODATA folder. What is in the folder?

5   In the right pane, double-click the **Classes** folder.

WHAT'S HAPPENING? Your window size and shape may vary. You can size it to see all the files. There are five files in the folder.

6   Close the Search Results window.

WHAT'S HAPPENING? You have returned to the desktop.

7   Click **Start**. Click **My Computer**. Double-click the **Drive C** icon. Double-click the **XPRODATA** folder. Click **View**. Click **Tiles**.

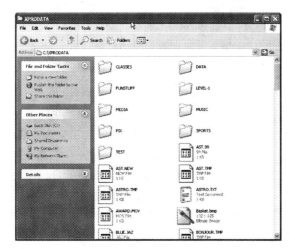

WHAT'S HAPPENING? An icon helps you differentiate between a folder and a file. A folder icon looks like an actual folder. If the folders are not visible, scroll up until they are.

8   Double-click the **Classes** folder.

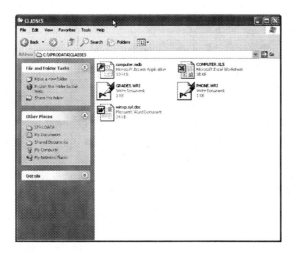

WHAT'S **HAPPENING?** You are looking in the container (folder or directory) called Classes. In Classes are five documents (data files) that deal with classes. You can see that, although Search is useful in helping you locate files, it is faster and more efficient to have an organizational scheme that allows you to access files quickly on your own. It is easier to remember a folder name than to remember all the individual file names and use Search.

No organizational scheme, however, is perfect. As you work with computers, you will create more files, and it is inevitable that you will "lose" files. They will not really be lost, just misplaced somewhere on a drive. If you name like files with similar names and if you place like files in a folder that has a meaningful name, you will have a much better chance of locating a needed document.

9   Close the C:\XPRODATA \Classes window.

WHAT'S **HAPPENING?** You have closed all the open windows.

5.14 • Shortcuts and the Drag-and-Drop Feature

Windows XP Professional offers a feature called a *shortcut*. A shortcut is a pointer to a resource located elsewhere on the computer or network. The resource can be a file, folder, device, or program. A shortcut is a way to place a commonly used object on the desktop (or in other convenient locations) for easy access. A shortcut has a small right-pointing arrow on an icon to identify it as a shortcut. It usually has the word "shortcut" in its name, but not always. However, the right-pointing arrow is always there. See Figure 5.4.

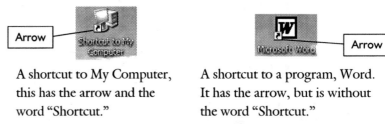

A shortcut to My Computer, this has the arrow and the word "Shortcut."

A shortcut to a program, Word. It has the arrow, but is without the word "Shortcut."

Figure 5.4 • Shortcut Icons

For instance, if you had an address book and needed to look up telephone numbers constantly, it would be most productive to have the address book on your desk instead of filed away in a filing cabinet. However, the address book takes up space on the desk. One solution to the problem would be to place the address book in the filing cabinet but to have a string on the desktop that you could pull to grab the address book quickly when you needed it. A shortcut is somewhat like that string.

In Windows, a shortcut is a pointer to the actual object. The shortcut merely contains information about the location of the object. It is not the object itself. The shortcut appears on the desktop. It points to the object so that you can access it quickly. The desktop is not the only location where you can place a shortcut.

Since one of the most common tasks you perform is using My Computer, having a shortcut to My Computer on the desktop would be useful. Therefore, creating a shortcut to My Computer would be most convenient. Another common task you perform, printing a document, would be easier to have a printer shortcut on the desktop. Having the printer quickly available to you would be convenient. Therefore, you may want to create a printer shortcut.

With the drag-and-drop feature, you can select an object, drag it with the mouse, and reposition it somewhere else (drop it). Drag and drop has some powerful components and can simplify many tasks in Windows XP Professional. You may drag items off the Start menu. And if you drag a document and drop it on a printer icon, you issue a command to open the program and print the document.

5.15 ● Activity ● Creating and Using a Shortcut

I   Click **Start**. Place the mouse pointer on **My Computers**. Begin to drag it to the desktop.

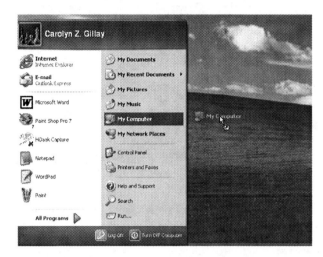

WHAT'S **HAPPENING?** As you begin to drag My Computer off the Start menu, you see that a shortcut is being automatically created.

2   Release the mouse button.

WHAT'S **HAPPENING?** You now have a shortcut to My Computer on the desktop.

3   Click **Start**. Click **Printers and Faxes**.

WHAT'S **HAPPENING?** You have opened the Printers and Faxes folder. The window displays all the printers and faxes available on your system. If you are using your own computer, there is probably only one printer icon. If you are on a network, you could have many choices. Only one printer is the default printer. The default printer is indicated by a checkmark on the printer icon. See Figure 5.5. Another way to determine the default printer is to right-click each printer icon. The default printer is indicated by a checkmark next to Set as Default Printer, as shown in Figure 5.5.

Icon indication of the   Menu indication of the
default printer.   default printer.

Figure 5.5 • Indications of the Default Printer

4   Click your default printer to select it.

5   Hold the right mouse button down and begin to drag the icon out of the Printers and Faxes folder onto the desktop.

WHAT'S **HAPPENING?** As you begin to drag the icon across the open window, it may acquire the international symbol for No, a circle with a line through it, which tells you that you cannot move the printer. As you drag the object onto the desktop, a shortcut symbol appears. The shortcut icon has a right-pointing, bent-back arrow on top of the object's normal icon. The bent arrow helps distinguish it from a normal icon and indicates that it is a pointer to the object.

6   Release the right mouse button.

WHAT'S **HAPPENING?** A shortcut menu appears, giving you the choice to create a shortcut or to cancel the operation.

7   Click **Create Shortcuts Here**.

8   Close all open windows.

9   Right-click the desktop. Point to **Arrange Icons by**.

WHAT'S **HAPPENING?** Here you can arrange your desktop icons in the usual ways. Show Desktop Icons should be set. If it is not, you will see no icons on your desktop.

10   Click **Name**.

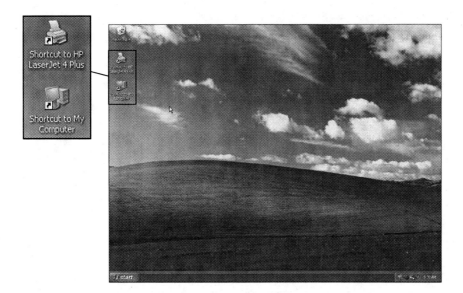

WHAT'S HAPPENING? On the desktop is a shortcut to the printer and a shortcut to My Computer. The icon represents My Computer and the printer, and both shortcuts have a shortcut symbol (the right-pointing arrow) and the words "Shortcut to."

11 Double-click the **Shortcut to My Computer**. Double-click the **Drive C** icon. Double-click the **XPRODATA** folder.

12 Click **View**. Click **Icons**. Scroll through the window until you locate **Glossary.wri**. Click it.

WHAT'S HAPPENING? You should be able to see both Glossary.wri and the shortcut to the printer. If you cannot, move the window until you can.

13 Be sure the printer is on. Right-drag **Glossary.wri** out of the XPRODATA folder and position it on top of the shortcut to the printer.

WHAT'S HAPPENING? When Glossary.wri is poised over the printer shortcut, you see that the document acquires a plus symbol. The plus symbol means copy. You are going to "copy" the document to the printer—which is printing it.

14 Drop **Glossary.wri** onto the shortcut to the printer.

WHAT'S HAPPENING? A shortcut menu appears, giving you the choice to print or cancel the operation.

15 Click **Print**.

WHAT'S HAPPENING? Right-dragging the document file to the printer displays a shortcut menu. Left-dragging the document file to the printer shortcut will quickly load WordPad, and display a message box informing you that the document is being printed.

What happens to the document depends on where you drop it. If you had released the mouse button (dropping the document) on the desktop instead of on top of the printer shortcut, you would have opened a different shortcut menu. See Figure 5.6.

*Figure 5.6 * The Right-Drag Shortcut Menu*

If the file is on the same drive as the desktop, the default operation is Move Here. (*Note:* If your XPRODATA folder is on a drive other than C, the default operation will be Copy Here.) If you had left-dragged, you would have moved the Glossary.wri file to the Desktop folder. The difference between a left-drag and a right-drag is that a left-drag will perform the default operation, and a right-drag will open a shortcut menu containing other choices before it completes the operation.

The Copy Here choice places another copy of Glossary.wri on the desktop while retaining the file in the XPRODATA folder. The Create Shortcuts Here choice maintains the one copy of Glossary.wri in the XPRODATA folder and places a pointer to it on the desktop.

The default operation depends on whether you are working on the same drive or going from drive to drive. Table 5.3 lists the operations for a left-drag. A right-drag will always open a shortcut menu with the default operation in boldface type.

A file or folder on the same drive	Move Here
A file or folder from one drive to another	Copy Here
A device (a printer, drive, etc.)	Create Shortcuts Here

*Table 5.3 * Default Operations When Left-Dragging*

16 Close all open windows.

WHAT'S HAPPENING? You have returned to the desktop.

5.16 ● Creating Shortcuts for Documents and Folders

As you have seen, shortcuts are not limited to devices. You can create shortcuts for program files, data files, and folders. You can place a shortcut on the desktop or in a folder, but the actual file will not move from its original location. When you create a shortcut for a file or a folder, you are creating a pointer that indicates where the file or folder is located, giving you quick access to a frequently used document or program or folder. You might think of a shortcut as an alias for the actual file or folder. As your work changes, you can add new shortcuts and delete shortcuts that you no longer use. It is safe to do because all you are doing is removing a pointer or creating a pointer. You are doing nothing to the actual file or folder object.

5.17 ● Activity ● Creating Shortcuts for Documents and Folders

1   Double-click the **Shortcut to My Computer**. Double-click the **Drive C** icon. Double-click the **XPRODATA** folder.

2   Double-click the **Classes** folder.

3   Right-click and drag **grades.wri** onto the desktop. Release the right mouse button.

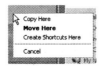

WHAT'S HAPPENING? Since you right-dragged the document icon, the shortcut menu appeared. Moving or copying an object is much different from creating a shortcut. If you selected Move Here, you would be removing the document from the XPRODATA folder and placing it in Drive C in an actual folder (directory) called C:\Documents and Settings*username*\Desktop. If you selected Copy Here, you would have two copies of grades.wri, one in the XPRODATA folder and one in the Desktop folder. The problem with having two copies is that, if you added or changed data in grades.wri on the desktop, you would not change the data in grades.wri in the XPRODATA folder. If you create a shortcut, however, there is still only one grades.wri file, the one in the XPRODATA folder. (*Note:* If the XPRODATA folder is on a drive other than C, the default operation is Copy Here.)

4   Click **Create Shortcuts Here**.

WHAT'S HAPPENING? You now have a shortcut to your document on the desktop.

5   Close the Classes window.

6   Double-click **Shortcut to GRADES.WRI**.

WHAT'S HAPPENING? You quickly opened the WordPad program, with grades.wri as the open document. You can also create a shortcut for a folder.

7   Close WordPad.

8   Double-click the **Shortcut to My Computer**. Double-click the **Drive C** icon. Double-click the **XPRODATA** folder.

9   Right-click and drag the **Classes** folder onto the desktop. Release the right mouse button.

WHAT'S HAPPENING? Since you used the right mouse button to drag the folder icon, the shortcut menu appeared. Again, you could move or copy the folder with all the documents in it, but you want only one version of the folder and you want it to remain where it is. (*Note:* If the XPRODATA folder is on a drive other than C, the default operation is Copy Here.)

10   Click **Create Shortcuts Here**.

11   Close all open windows.

WHAT'S HAPPENING? You now have shortcuts to both the document called grades.wri and the folder called Classes.

12   Double-click **Shortcut to CLASSES**.

WHAT'S HAPPENING? You now have immediate access to the CLASSES folder. When you boot Windows XP Professional, you can immediately access the Classes folder, which contains all your class-related documents. Look carefully at the document icons. There are no shortcut icons. These are the actual files in the C:\XPRODATA\CLASSES folder. You created a short-cut to the folder, not a shortcut to the documents in the folder.

13   Close the C:\XPRODATA\CLASSES window.

5.18 • Creating Folders

A convenient method to access quickly the files and folders you use regularly is to create a folder on the desktop. In this folder, you may place shortcuts to the programs and files you use most often and yet maintain an uncluttered desktop. You can then quickly access what you need, bypassing the Start menu. Since you place shortcuts in this folder, you can alter what is in the folder as your work needs change. You never have to worry about deleting or moving actual objects because you are dealing with pointers to the objects, not the actual objects. This process allows you a great deal of flexibility with no danger of accidentally removing files or folders.

5.19 ● Activity ● Creating Folders on the Desktop

I   Right-click the desktop. Point to **New**.

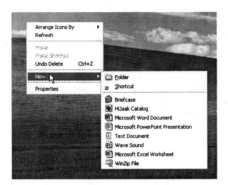

WHAT'S **HAPPENING?** The New menu has appeared. You can now create a new folder, shortcut, or document. You create documents with programs. That is why many of the programs that you have installed on your system are shown here. You may select the program you want to use to create a new document. Your menu choices will vary, depending on what programs you have on your system and which programs place entries on this menu. In this case, you are going to create a new folder.

2   Click **Folder**.

WHAT'S **HAPPENING?** You have just created a new folder. You can key in your folder name where the cursor is blinking.

3   Key in the following: **EVERYDAY**

4   Click outside the text box.

WHAT'S **HAPPENING?** You have named your folder. Since you keyed in uppercase letters, the folder is displayed with uppercase characters.

5   Double-click the **EVERYDAY** folder icon.

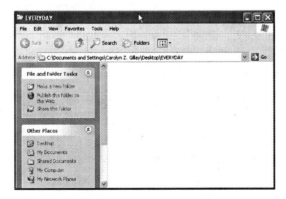

WHAT'S **HAPPENING?** It is an empty folder. The title bar states EVERYDAY and the Address Bar toolbar display the path to the folder. The Everyday folder is in the Desktop folder that is under the Carolyn Z. Gillay (the user name) folder, which is under the Documents and Settings folder on Drive C. The user name is the specific name of the user that is currently logged on to the computer system, such as Carolyn Z. Gillay.

6   Left-drag and drop all your shortcuts except the Shortcut to My Computer into the EVERYDAY window. These include the shortcuts to Classes, grades.wri, and the printer.

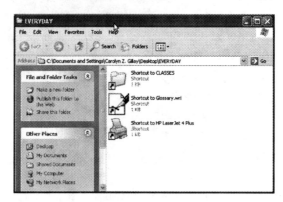

WHAT'S **HAPPENING?** You have placed nearly all the shortcuts in a folder on the desktop. You did not create new shortcuts but moved the existing shortcuts from the desktop to the folder called EVERYDAY. Remember, when you left-drag on the same drive, the default operation is to move objects rather than to copy them.

7   In the EVERYDAY folder window, on the menu bar click **View**. On the View menu, click **Icons**. On the View menu, point to **Arrange Icons By**. Click **Auto Arrange** if it does not have a checkmark in front of it.

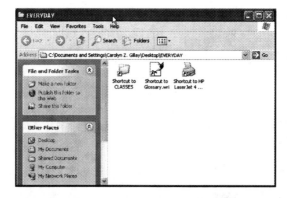

WHAT'S **HAPPENING?** Since you have used the Auto Arrange feature, the icons will automatically be arranged along an invisible grid each time you open the Everyday folder.

8   Close the EVERYDAY window.

WHAT'S **HAPPENING?** The objects on your desktop are not arranged in any particular order.

9   Right-click the desktop. Point at **Arrange Icons By**.

WHAT'S **HAPPENING?** You have the same choices for arranging your icons on the desktop as in any folder: by Name, Size, Type (file extension), by Date. The desktop is just a special folder. In this example, Auto Arrange is not set. If you have a checkmark in front of Auto Arrange, remove it by clicking it.

10 Click **Modified**.

WHAT'S **HAPPENING?** The folders and documents are arranged by date. You could confirm this by right-clicking on each object and clicking Properties to see the date.

11 Right-click the desktop. Point at **Arrange Icons By**. Click **Name**.

WHAT'S **HAPPENING?** You now have your icons arranged by name. If your icons were already arranged, you would see no change on the desktop.

5.20 ● The Recycle Bin

One of the advantages of Windows XP Professional is its flexibility. As you work, your priorities change. You may work on one project for a week and then a new project the next week. You could create a shortcut for each new project. As you can imagine, your desktop could become very cluttered with shortcuts. You may want to eliminate old shortcuts. When you delete a shortcut, you are not deleting the object, document, or folder, only the pointer to the object, document, or folder.

In Windows XP Professional, an easy way to eliminate objects is to send them to the Recycle Bin. The advantage of the Recycle Bin is that items do not get permanently deleted until you empty the Recycle Bin. It is much like putting items in a wastebasket. If you need an item back, you can go through your wastepaper basket and recover what you need. Once you take your wastepaper basket to the trash bin and a truck hauls the trash away, you cannot recover the item. The same is true with the Recycle Bin, but only for items on the hard disk. If you delete an item on a removable disk such as a floppy disk or a Zip disk, the item is not moved to the Recycle Bin, it is deleted permanently.

5.21 ● Activity ● Using the Recycle Bin

1 Right-click the **Recycle Bin** icon. Click **Properties**.

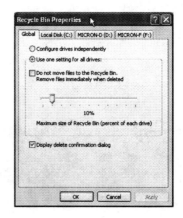

WHAT'S HAPPENING? The Recycle Bin is an object and has properties. The default size of the Recycle Bin is 10 percent of the hard disk, in this example. Ten percent is the default value. If you have more than one hard drive, you may have different settings on each (the Configure drives independently option). If you have multiple drives, there will be a tab for each drive. If you did not want the ability to recover deleted files, folders, and shortcuts, you would set the check box **Do not move files to the Recycle Bin. Remove files immediately when deleted.** If you did not want every deletion confirmed, you would not set **Display delete confirmation dialog.**

2   Click Cancel.

3   Right-click the Recycle Bin icon.

Menu When Items Are   Menu When the Recycle
in the Recycle Bin   Bin Is Empty

WHAT'S HAPPENING? As you see, if there are no items in the Recycle Bin, the Empty Recycle Bin choice is dimmed and not available. You can also look at the icon itself to determine if the Recycle Bin is empty or full. The paper protruding out of the Recycle Bin indicates items in the Recycle Bin. The absence of paper indicates an empty Recycle Bin. See Figure 5.7.

Full Recycle Bin Icon   Empty Recycle Bin Icon

Figure 5.7 • The Recycle Bin Icon

The empty bin has no paper in it whereas the full bin has paper in it. Your Recycle Bin icon should resemble the full Recycle Bin icon. Earlier in this chapter you placed the File named Computer.xls.fnd in the Recycle Bin. Generally, it is a good idea to open the Recycle Bin and check to see what is inside before emptying it, however you already know what is inside so you may empty it.

4   If your Recycle Bin has items in it, click Empty Recycle Bin. Click Yes.

5   Double-click **Everyday**. Drag **Shortcut to grades.wri** to the Recycle Bin. Drop it onto the Recycle Bin.

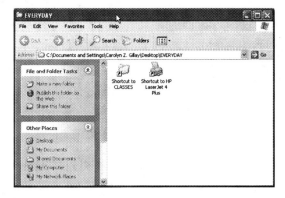

WHAT'S HAPPENING? The shortcut to grades.wri is no longer in the Everyday folder.

6   Double-click the **Recycle Bin** icon.

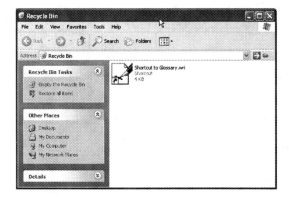

WHAT'S HAPPENING? You opened the Recycle Bin window and can see your shortcut inside. You can take your shortcut out of the Recycle Bin or undo its deletion or Restore it. In addition, you may click Empty Recycle Bin to remove all of the objects.

7   Drag **Shortcut to grades.wri** to the desktop.

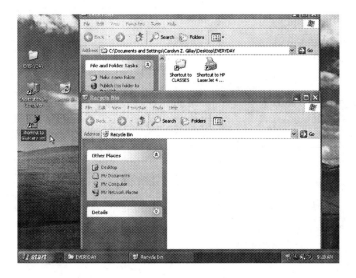

WHAT'S HAPPENING? If you had no other files in the Recycle Bin window, it should be empty. The shortcut has been retrieved and is on the desktop. You may also retrieve files in the Recycle Bin by right-clicking the desktop and choosing Undo Delete or by opening the Recycle Bin window, clicking Edit, and choosing Undo Delete.

8   Drag and drop **Shortcut to grades.wri** back to the Recycle Bin window.

9   Click **Edit** in the Recycle Bin window.

WHAT'S HAPPENING? As you can see, the Undo Delete command is available.

10   Click outside the menu to close it. Right-click **Shortcut to grades.wri**.

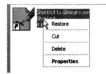

WHAT'S HAPPENING? You can restore, cut, delete, or look at properties for individual items in the Recycle Bin window.

11   Click outside the menu to close it. Right-click the desktop.

WHAT'S HAPPENING? The desktop also has a menu that will allow you to undo your last action.

12   Click outside the menu to close it. Close the Everyday window. Drag and drop the **Everyday** folder to the Recycle Bin.

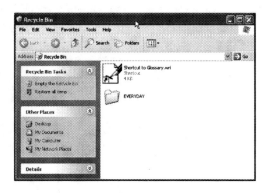

WHAT'S HAPPENING? You see the shortcut you dragged to the Recycle Bin and the folder EVERYDAY.

13   Double-click the **EVERYDAY** folder icon.

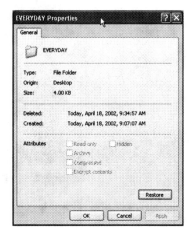

WHAT'S HAPPENING? You only see the properties of the file folder but nothing that was in the folder. You cannot retrieve individual items from this folder, but you can retrieve the entire folder.

14   Click **Cancel**. On the Edit menu, click **Undo Delete**. Double-click the **Everyday** folder.

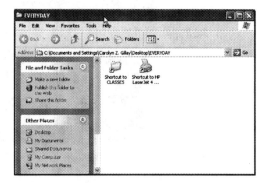

WHAT'S HAPPENING? Now you have recovered the items in the folder. However, on the desktop, you can only undo the last action you took. Hence, you cannot undo from the desktop if you have taken other actions since your deletion.

15 On the Recycle Bin's menu bar, click **File**.

WHAT'S HAPPENING? You have dropped down the menu. One of the choices is Empty Recycle Bin. When you choose this menu item, you delete everything in the window. When the Recycle Bin window is closed and is an icon, you may right-click the icon.

16 Click **Empty Recycle Bin**.

WHAT'S HAPPENING? Since Display delete confirmation dialog was set, a message gives you one more chance to save what is in the Recycle Bin. Remember, when you delete shortcuts, you are not deleting the objects, only the pointers to these objects. However, if you have the search results file in the EVERYDAY folder, it will be deleted. In this case, you do want to empty it.

17 Click **Yes**.

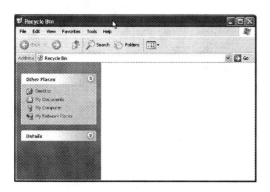

WHAT'S HAPPENING? The Recycle Bin is empty.

18 Close the Recycle Bin window.

WHAT'S HAPPENING? You have returned to the desktop. The EVERYDAY folder is still on the desktop. In this case, you are *sure* you want to delete it, so you do not want to send it to the Recycle Bin.

19 Close the EVERYDAY folder. Click the **EVERYDAY** folder to select it.

20 Hold the **Shift** key down, and press the **Delete** key.

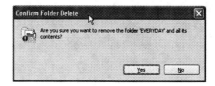

WHAT'S HAPPENING? You are presented with a dialog box asking you to confirm the removal of the EVERYDAY folder. Notice there is no mention of the Recycle Bin.

21 Click **Yes**.

22 Double click the **Recycle Bin**.

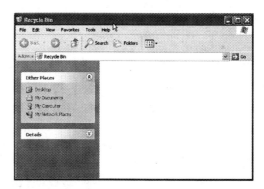

WHAT'S HAPPENING? The Recycle Bin is empty. The EVERYDAY folder has indeed been deleted. When you select an object and press **Shift** and **Delete** keys the file or folder is deleted permanently, skipping the Recycle Bin.

23 Close the Recycle Bin window.

WHAT'S HAPPENING? You have returned to the desktop.

Chapter Summary

You learned that files and folders follow specific naming rules. You also learned that although Windows XP Professional allows long file names (LFNs) of up to 255 characters, there are shortcomings in using long file names. You learned that you should develop a naming convention for your files so you can more easily locate them. You learned that folders are created by application programs or by users. Folders typically contain files, other folders, or shortcuts.

You learned how to locate the properties of files using shortcut menus. You found that the Search command allows you many ways to locate files. You may search for files by name, date, size, or type. These choices allow you to search for files by different search criteria. You learned about wildcards, * and ?, that let you find files using different search criteria.

You learned that if you drag an object from one location to another on the same drive, the default operation is a move. You learned that if you right-drag an object, you see a shortcut menu that allows you to choose whether you want to move, copy, or create a shortcut for the object. You created shortcuts for a device, a file, and a folder. You found that a shortcut is a pointer to an object. You created a folder on the desktop. You used the Recycle Bin to delete the shortcuts you created, and you found that you could retrieve items from the Recycle Bin, if you had not emptied it.

Key Terms

bundled	file attribute	partitioned
default	file name	search criteria
delimiter	file specification	shortcut
dual-booting	file system	VFAT file system
dynamic-link library (DLL)	long file name (LFN)	volume
FAT16	multibooting	wildcard
FAT32	naming convention	
file	New Technology File System (NTFS)	

Discussion Questions

1. List four file-naming rules in Windows XP Professional.
2. A file specification consists of a file's name and its extension. Compare the purpose and function of a file's name and its extension.
3. Windows XP Professional gives both a long and short file name to each file. Why?
4. What is a naming convention? Why would you want to create one?
5. What can be learned about an object by looking at its properties?
6. Explain the purpose and function of folders.
7. Why do programs create folders? Why do computer users create folders?
8. Data files should not be put in the same folder as program files. Why?
9. What is the difference between a folder and a document?
10. Explain the purpose and function of the Search command.
11. What are search criteria?
12. What is a wildcard? How are wildcards used in locating files?
13. Compare and contrast the two characters that are used for wildcards.
14. Name two ways Search can be used to locate files and folders.
15. What is a shortcut?
16. Explain the purpose and function of shortcuts. How can a shortcut be created?
17. What would be the purpose of placing a shortcut on the desktop?

18. How can you identify a shortcut icon?
19. When dragging a document on the desktop, what happens to the document depends on where you drop it. Explain.
20. What is the difference between a right-drag and a left-drag?
21. What happens to a file when it is moved? When it is copied? When a shortcut is created to the file?
22. List two ways icons can be arranged on the desktop.
23. Explain the purpose and function of the Recycle Bin.
24. Why is it advantageous to use the Recycle Bin when eliminating an object?
25. List and explain the features that can be set for the Recycle Bin. Where can these settings be configured?

True/False Questions

For each question, circle the letter T if the statement is true or the letter F if the statement is false.

T   F   1. Windows XP Professional and DOS have identical file-naming rules.

T   F   2. Data files and program files should be placed in the same folder for easy access.

T   F   3. A property sheet is a collection of information about an object.

T   F   4. In order to use Search to locate a file, you must know the exact file name and folder location.

T   F   5. Shortcuts may be placed only on the desktop.

Completion Questions

Write the correct answer in the blank space provided.

6. A file specification is composed of a file _____ and a file _____ .

7. A collection of information about an object is located in the object's _____ .

8. A file that cannot be modified has its _____ attribute set.

9. A right-pointing, bent arrow over an icon signifies that the object is a(n) _____ .

10. Deleting a document shortcut does not delete the document, but only the _____ to the document.

Multiple Choice Questions

Circle the letter of the correct answer for each question.

11. Dragging a registered document and dropping it on a shortcut to a printer will
    a. result in an error message.
    b. print the document.
    c. open a shortcut menu.
    d. create a shortcut that prints the document when double-clicked.
12. You may Search for files or folders named by
    a. file name.
    b. file size
    c. date modified.
    d. all the above

13. You may create shortcuts for
   a. devices.
   b. data files.
   c. folders.
   d. all of the above
14. Which of the following search criteria may you use in Search?
   a. file name
   b. file extension
   c. both a and b
   d. neither a nor b
15. In Windows XP Professional, a shortcut
   a. is a pointer to an object.
   b. is a copy of an object.
   c. cannot be used with devices.
   d. can be placed only in a folder.

Application Assignments

Problem Set I—At the Computer

Note: Check that your settings match those listed in Section 3.8.

Problem A

❖ Double-click the **Shortcut to My Computer**.

❖ Double-click the Drive C icon.

❖ Double-click the **XPRODATA** folder.

❖ Scroll until you locate the document called Chap01.wri.

❖ Open the property sheet for the file.

❖ Click the **General** tab.

   1. What is the entire name of the document?
      a. Chapter 1 document
      b. Chapter01.doc
      c. Chap01.wri
      d. Chapter 01 write

   2. What is the size of the document in kilobytes?
      a. 6.00
      b. 6,144
      c. 32,768

   3. The type of the file is
      a. Microsoft Word Document.
      b. Write Document.
      c. WordPad Document.
      d. text document.

❖ Click **Cancel**.

❖ Right-click **Chap01.wri**.

4. Is Print an available action?
   a. yes
   b. no

* Close any open windows.

Problem B

* Create a shortcut for your default printer and place it on your desktop.

* Locate the file called File naming rules in the XPRODATA folder.

* Locate and use the property sheet for this file.

5. What is Windows XP Professional's name for this file?
   a. File naming rules
   b. Filenamingrules
   c. File naming rules.txt
   d. Filena~1.txt
   e. Filename.txt

* Close the Property dialog box.

* Be sure the printer is on.

* Drag and drop this file onto the printer shortcut. (Be sure you drop the file on the shortcut to the printer and not on the desktop.)

* Read the printed document.

6. Spaces are allowed in file names
   a. only in DOS or applications written for DOS.
   b. only in Windows applications.
   c. in both DOS and Windows applications.

7. According to this document, Windows XP Professional allows a maximum of _____ characters in a file name.
   a. 215
   b. 255
   c. 8.3
   d. 83

* Close any open windows.

Problem C

* Use Search to locate the file called Mer.99 in the XPRODATA folder.

* In the Search window, click **View**. Click **Details**.

8. In the Search Results window, in the Size column, what file size is displayed for this file?
   a. 1 Byte
   b. 1 KB
   c. 1 MB

9. What date is displayed for this file in the Date Modified column?
   a. 10/31/19999
   b. 10/31/2000
   c. 10/31/2001
   d. 10/31/2002
   e. 10/31/2003

* Begin a new search.

* In the XPRODATA folder, including all subfolders, locate all the files that have 99 as their file extension.

10. How did you limit your search?
    a. I used wildcards in the All or part of the file name text box.
    b. I used wildcards in the A word or phrase in the file text box.
    c. I used wildcards in the Look in drop-down list file

11. How many files did you locate?
    a. one
    b. two
    c. three
    d. four
    e. zero

* Begin a new search.

* Clear the **Search for files or folders named** text box. Set the **Specify Date** check box.

* In the XPRODATA folder, including all subfolders, find all the files that were modified between 7/31/1999 and 12/31/1999

12. Among the files found,
    a. only Carolyn.txt is listed.
    b. only Dances.txt is listed.
    c. both Carolyn.txt and Dances.txt are listed.
    d. neither Carolyn.txt nor Dancers.txt is listed.

* In the "When was it modified" area, click **Don't Remember**. Begin a new search.

* In the XPRODATA folder, including all subfolders, find any file that has the word "star" in its contents.

13. The word "star" was found in
    a. the Born.txt file.
    b. the Mystery.bks file.
    c. both the Born.txt and the Mystery.bks files.
    d. neither the Born.txt nor the Mystery.bks file.

* Close all dialog boxes and windows.

Problem D

* Double-click **Shortcut to My Computer**.

* Double-click the Drive C icon.

* Double-click the **XPRODATA** folder.

* Double-click the **Media** folder.

14. Does the Media folder display any document icons?
    a. yes
    b. no

* Double-click the **Movies** folder in the Media window.

15. Does the Movies folder display any document icons?
    a. yes
    b. no

16. Does the Movies folder display any folder icons?
    a. yes
    b. no

* Close all open windows.

Problem E

* Create a new folder called Today on the desktop.
* Double-click **Shortcut to My Computer**.
* Double-click **(C:)**.
* Open the XPRODATA folder.
* In the Today folder on the desktop, create a shortcut to the Level-1 folder. Remember to right-drag the folder or file and choose Create Shortcuts Here.
* In the XPRODATA folder, there is a file called Astro.txt. Create a shortcut to this file and place it in the Today folder on the desktop.
* Close My Computer (XPRODATA).
* Open the Today folder.
* Open the Level-1 shortcut.

17. How many document icons are in the Level-1 shortcut?
    a. one
    b. two
    c. three

18. How many folder icons are in the Level-1 shortcut?
    a. one
    b. two
    c. three

* On the desktop, create a shortcut to the Hello.txt file that is in the C:\XPRODATA \level-1 folder. Remember to right-drag the folder or file and choose Create Shortcuts Here.

19. Is there still a document icon for Hello.txt in the Level-1 folder?
    a. yes
    b. no

* Close all open windows.

Problem F

* Empty the Recycle Bin.
* Drag and drop **Shortcut to Hello.txt** (created in Problem E) on the desktop onto the Recycle Bin.
* Drag and drop the shortcut to the printer (created in Problem B) onto the Recycle Bin.

* Drag and drop the **Today** folder onto the Recycle Bin.
* Open the Recycle Bin window.
* Click **View**.
* Click **Icons**.
* Click **Shortcut to Hello.txt** in the Recycle Bin window.
* Click **File**.
* Click **Delete**.

> 20. What is the name (title) of the message box?
>   a. Empty Recycle Bin
>   b. Confirm File Delete
>   c. Confirm Multiple File Delete

* Click **Yes**.
* Empty the Recycle Bin.
* Close all open windows.

Problem Set II—Brief Essay

For all essay questions, use Notepad or WordPad to create your answer. Be sure to include your name, your class information, and the problem number. Then print your answer.

1. On your computer, you have two folders. One is named Letters. In it are the files Mom.letter.doc, Mom.doc, and Mom.birthday.txt. The other folder is named BusinessLetters. In it are the files Modern Electric Company.doc and Mortgage.txt. You want to locate the following files:

   Modern Electric Company.doc

   Mortgage.txt

   Mom.letter.doc

   Mom.doc

   Mom.birthday.txt

   Using Search, describe what strategies and search criteria you used to locate all the business letters. Using Search, describe what strategies and search criteria you used to locate all the letters to your mother. Using Search, describe any strategies and search criteria you used to locate all the files at once. If you did not use Search, describe what other ways you located the files.

2. DOS follows the 8.3 file-naming rules. Windows XP Professional allows the use of LFNs. Compare and contrast these two sets of rules. Which set of rules do you prefer? Is there any reason to continue to use the 8.3 rules? Explain your answer.

Problem Set III—Scenario

For the next week, you will be writing and printing letters and resumes to help your brother with his job search. Your brother's documents are in a folder called Brother. In addition, you are writing a research paper for your history class, Civilwar.doc, located in a folder called History. You decide that the easiest way to access these documents would be to create shortcuts to files, folders, and the printer. Describe what shortcuts you would create, how you would create them, and where you would place them. At the end of the week, you want to remove these shortcuts. Describe what steps you would need to take to eliminate the shortcuts.

CHAPTER 6

Using My Computer
and Windows Explorer

In this chapter you will further examine the hierarchical structure of folders and files in Windows XP Professional. You will discover the importance of a path in locating a file or folder. You will learn to move around in the My Computer/ Windows Explorer window. You will find that opening multiple windows can assist you in locating files and folders, and you will discover the difference between a logical view and a physical view of your computer system. You will learn to determine which view best suits your needs. You will find that My Computer and Windows Explorer are in fact the same program. You will find that you can alter menus, but only if you can locate the correct folders and files.

Learning Objectives

1. Describe the hierarchical structure of a disk.
2. Describe the role the path plays in locating files.
3. Explain the purpose and function of My Computer/Windows Explorer.
4. Compare and contrast logical views with physical views.
5. Explain the purpose and function of copying disks.
6. Explain the purpose and function of copying files to a compact disc.

Student Outcomes

1. Open My Computer/Windows Explorer to examine the hierarchical structure of folders and files on your disk.
2. Set folder options in the My Computer/Windows Explorer window.
3. Open and maneuver in the tree side and the contents side of My Computer/Windows Explorer.
4. Use Windows XP Professional's multitasking ability to open multiple Windows Explorer and My Computer windows.
5. Add and remove a printer from the Send To menu.
6. Make a copy of a disk.
7. Make a Compact Disc-R, if possible.

6.1 ● A Disk's Hierarchical Structure

As you have seen, all files are stored on and retrieved from disks. A disk can be a floppy disk in Drive A, a hard disk in Drive C, a disk in a removable Zip drive that might be Drive F, or a network disk in a drive such as Drive Y. A hard disk or network disk has a much larger capacity to store files than any floppy disk. CD-ROMs also have a large capacity to store files. Unless you have a read/write CD-ROM drive, you can usually only retrieve, or read, files from CD-ROMs. You cannot save files to CD-ROMs. However, most new computers today come with a CD-RW drive. Windows XP Professional assists you in assigning drive letters so it can differentiate among drives. This way you know which drive has your files on the disk. Letters of the alphabet followed by a colon (like A:, B:, and C:) are reserved for disk drives. If you do not tell your program on which drive to save a file, it will assume the default drive. There is always a default drive because Windows XP Professional has to look to a disk to retrieve or store files.

So that you may manage your files easily, you may also organize a disk with folders. Remember, the DOS name for *folders* is *directories*. *Folder* and *directory* are synonymous terms and can be used interchangeably. Every disk has a hierarchical, tree-shaped structure. The tree begins with what is called the *root directory*, which is created when a disk is formatted. The root (\) is the top of the structure. Then, like an upside-down tree growing branches, other folders branch out from the root. Each of these folders can have folders of its own. Within folders are files (documents or programs). You can start at the root and "burrow" down the tree to a folder or subfolder, or you can start at the last subfolder and climb your way up to the root. Remember, it is all connected. You cannot jump from folder to folder whenever you are within a hierarchical structure. You must follow a path to a file. See Figure 6.1.

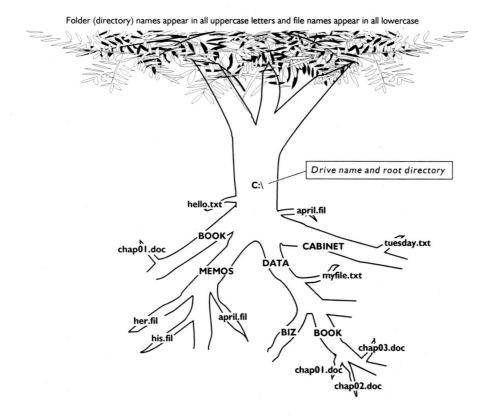

Folder (directory) names appear in all uppercase letters and file names appear in all lowercase

Figure 6.1 ◦ The Tree-shaped, Hierarchical Directory Structure

A file is saved to or retrieved from a specific location on a disk. Although a file can be saved to the root directory, it is best saved to a folder. To locate the file later, you will need to know the name of the drive and the folder where the file is stored. A path specifies the drive and the folder in which the file is located.

If you had a file called myfile.txt on the disk in Drive C in the folder called DATA, the path to the file would be C:\DATA. If you were using an application program and wanted to retrieve the file, the application would present you with a dialog box into which you would key the file name. You would need to key in C:\DATA\myfile.txt. The first \ indicates the root directory. The second backslash (\) is a delimiter that separates one folder or file name from another. A backslash may *never* be used as a part of a file name. If you look at Figure 6.1, you see a file called tuesday.txt in the CABINET directory on Drive C. If you key in the name as \CABINET\tuesday\txt, you are asking to locate a file called txt in a folder called tuesday in a folder called CABINET that is under the root. This path is incorrect. Your file name is tuesday.txt, not txt.

File and folder names must be unique so that the correct file may be identified. Thus, in Figure 6.1, C:\april.fil is clearly identified as a different file from C:\MEMOS\april.fil. Each can be identified because of the path. The same would hold true for C:\BOOK\chap01.doc and C:\DATA\BOOK\chap01.doc. Although the folder and file names appear identical, they are not because each follows a different path in the tree.

As you begin to create files and add new programs, a tool called Windows Explorer allows you to browse your drives and network drives to locate files and folders. This program is not to be confused with Microsoft Internet Explorer, a Web browser that may appear as an icon on your desktop:

Internet Explorer is a program that is used to explore the World Wide Web. Typically, to distinguish between the two Explorers, one is called Internet Explorer and the other, which primarily is used for your local machine, is called Windows Explorer.

In Chapter 3, you used My Computer to view the contents of several disks and folders. In Chapter 5, you used a powerful tool, Search, to quickly locate a file that met your specifications. Both tools are useful and serve their own unique purposes. Windows Explorer is My Computer with a different view and a different starting location. When you are in Folders view, My Computer/Windows Explorer provides the best of both worlds; you can browse through a drive or folder to see what files it contains, and if you have organized your files and folders, you can quickly locate the drive, folder, and file you need. Browsing through your drives is useful when you want to evaluate which files or folders are candidates for deletion or backup. You may even find that you wish to reorganize your files and folders for easier access. You can use My Computer and Search to launch application programs and open data files.

6.2 ⬤ Windows Explorer

When you open Windows Explorer, you will find that it looks nearly identical to My Computer. The major difference between the My Computer and the Windows Explorer window is that the Windows Explorer window opens by default in Folders view and starts with My Documents as the starting location. The left pane shows the hierarchical structure of the selected disk. The right pane displays the contents of the left pane's default drive or folder. In fact, the right pane is exactly like My Computer. Figure 6.2 shows Windows Explorer with the new items identified. In this instance, you are looking at Drive C. This view is Tiles.

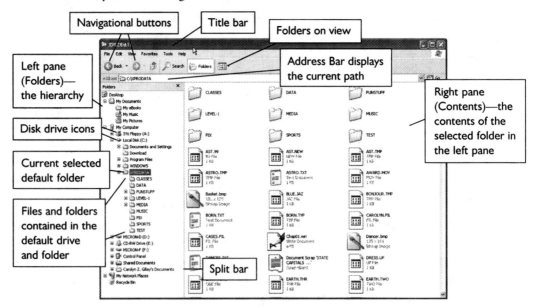

Figure 6.2 ⬤ Windows Explorer

The following elements appear in Windows Explorer:

Folders pane	The *Folders pane* is the hierarchical tree of folders, also called the tree pane.
Contents pane	The files and folders currently in the selected default drive and folder.
Current default path	The files and folders in the current default drive and directory.
Disk drive icon	Represents a drive on your computer system. The drive letter follows each icon.
Default folder	The *default folder* is the folder that currently appears in the title bar of the window. Every disk has one root folder, \. The folders branch from the root and are located under the root.
Split bar	The *split bar* is the line between the left and right panes of Windows Explorer that changes the panes' dimensions. To resize the panes, use the mouse to drag the split bar.

6.3 • Activity • Customizing and Viewing Folders in Windows Explorer/My Computer

Note: Settings are assumed for each chapter. If you are working on your own computer, the changes you made in the default settings should be retained from one work session to the next. However, if you are working in a computer lab, you may have to adjust your settings each time you log into the network. See Activity 3.8.

I Click **Start**. Point to **All Programs**. Point to **Accessories**. Click **Windows Explorer**. If necessary, click **View**. Click **Tiles**.

WHAT'S **HAPPENING?** You have opened Windows Explorer. It looks identical to My Computer except the left pane shows the hierarchy of the disk. In addition, the default location that it opens at is My Documents. Your folders may vary.

2 Open My Computer. On the navigation bar, click **Folders**.

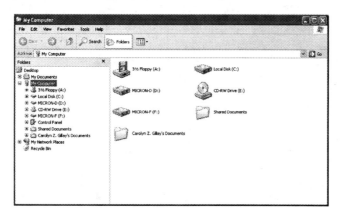

WHAT'S **HAPPENING?** By choosing Folders, My Computer now looks exactly like Windows Explorer with the only difference being that My Computer opens with My Computer as the default location whereas Windows Explorer opened with My Documents as the default location.

3 Right-click the taskbar. Click **Tile Windows Horizontally**.

WHAT'S **HAPPENING?** In this example, My Computer is the top window and Windows Explorer is the bottom window. By enabling the Folders option, the two windows look identical, except for their starting location. However, Windows Explorer opens with Folders view on but My Computer open with Folders view off.

4 Right-click the taskbar. Click **Undo Tile**. Close the My Computer window.

5 In the My Documents window, in the left pane, click the **My Computer** icon. Click the **C:** icon.

6 Click the **XPRODATA** folder icon in the **Folders** pane (the left pane). If you cannot see the **XPRODATA** folder, scroll until you can. (*Hint:* Click the icon for XPRODATA, not the folder name or the plus or minus sign.)

7 Click **View**. Click **Icons**.

WHAT'S HAPPENING? You are looking at the Icons view of folders and files in the right pane and the hierarchical structure in the left pane. The Address Bar now shows C:\XPRODATA as the default folder. You may customize the way a folder looks.

8   Right-click the **Classes** folder in the right pane. Click **Properties**. Click the **Customize** tab.

WHAT'S HAPPENING? Since this folder has an Excel document in it, a small picture of the Excel document appears on the folder in the preview. You have three areas to make choices: What kind of folder do you want? (which concerns templates), Folder pictures, and Folder icons. When you choose a template, you apply specific features to your folder such as viewing options for working with pictures and music files.

Thumbnails view will display miniature versions on the folder icon. In Thumbnails view, you can choose a picture to help identify the contents of the file. This is very useful when you need to quickly browse through multiple images. When you restore the default, the last four image files you modified in the folder will be used to identify it.

The Change Icon option allows you to change the graphic that is displayed for the folder except in Thumbnails view.

9   Click **Choose Picture**.

WHAT'S HAPPENING? The dialog box is asking for image files. There are no image files in the Classes directory.

10   Click the Up button. Double-click the **PIX** folder.

WHAT'S **HAPPENING?** In the PIX folder are image files. You are going to choose the student.jpg file.

11 Click **student.jpb**. Click **Open**.

WHAT'S **HAPPENING?** You see a picture of a student.

12 Click **OK**.

13 Click **View**. Click **Thumbnails**.

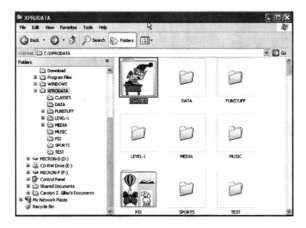

WHAT'S **HAPPENING?** Only in Thumbnails view can you see your picture on the folder. Note that the PIX folder shows four images that are located in this folder.

14 Right-click **Classes**. Click **Properities**. Click the **Customize** tab. Click **Restore Default**. Click **OK**.

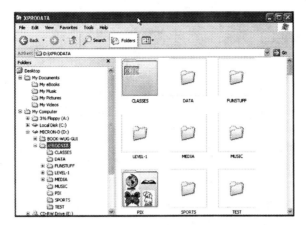

WHAT'S HAPPENING? The CLASSES folder displays an Excel picture. Since this folder contains other types of documents than Excel documents, you do not want to have the Excel picture on the folder. You want it to be a plain folder like the other folders.

15 Right-click **CLASSES**. Click **Properties**. Click the **Customize** tab. Click **Choose Picture**.

16 In the File name text box, key in the following: **%systemroot%\SYSTEM32\Shell32.dll**

WHAT'S HAPPENING? The %systemroot% refers to the location of the Windows folders with all the various system files that are needed to run Windows. The %systemroot% is a system variable. You provide the "formula" for what you want and Windows will supply the value. On this system, %systemroot% is C:\WINDOWS but if your Windows files were in a directory called WINNT, then the value for %systemroot% would be C:\WINNT. SYSTEM32 is a folder within the Windows system files and shell32.dll is a file that contains the standard window icons.

17 Click **Open**. Click **Change Icon**.

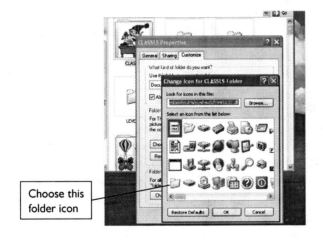

Choose this folder icon

WHAT'S HAPPENING? You have opened shell32.dll, the file that holds the standard icons for Windows.

18 Click the bottom folder. Click **OK**. Click **OK**.

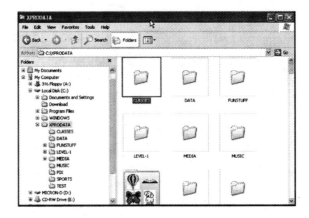

WHAT'S HAPPENING? You have changed the folder icon back to the Windows default folder icon. You may look at your window in many different views.

Step 19   Click the **XPRODATA** folder in the left pane. Click **View**. Click **Tiles**.

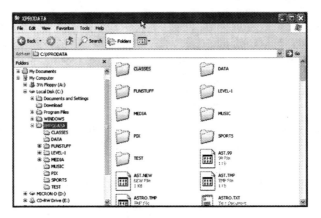

WHAT'S HAPPENING? You have changed your view so that you see a tile representing each file and folder.

20   Click the **XPRODATA** folder in the left pane. Click **View**. Click **Icons**.

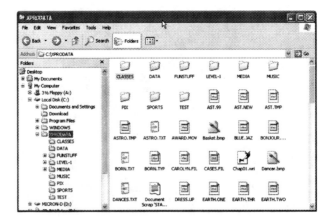

WHAT'S HAPPENING? You have again changed your view so that each file and folder in the right pane is represented by an icon which is supposed to represent what the object is.

21 Click the **XPRODATA** folder in the left pane. Click **View**. Click **List**.

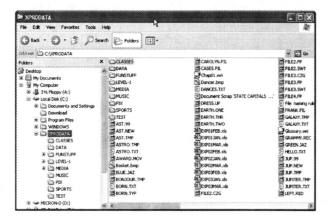

WHAT'S HAPPENING? Again, you have changed your view to List. The List view lists the files and folder names as well as the small icons. Again, an icon is supposed to indicate what is in the file.

22 Click **View**. Click **Details**.

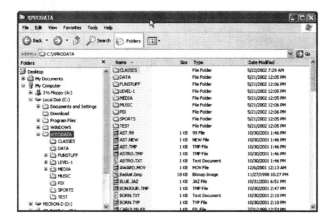

WHAT'S HAPPENING? When you are in Details view, you see the file and folder names and file and folder details. Although you can choose many details to display, the default details are file/folder name, size, file type, and date and time the file was last modified. Your choice of views allows you to look at the files and folders in a way that is most useful to you.

23 Click **View**. Click **List**.

24 Click **Tools**. Click **Folder Options**.

WHAT'S HAPPENING? You are looking at Folder Options, which is identical to the My Computer Folder Options dialog box. The settings that you chose in My Computer are retained.

25 Click the **View** tab.

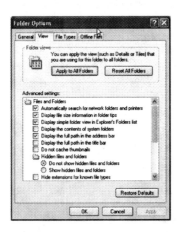

WHAT'S HAPPENING? Your choices are the same as those you selected in the My Computer Folders Options dialog box, which makes sense as these are the same programs.

26 Right-click the **Apply to All Folders**. Click **What's This?**.

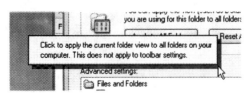

WHAT'S HAPPENING? Once you have a folder setting you are satisfied with, you can set it here for all your folders. This is called

setting it globally. However, your changes will not apply to any toolbars you have set up.

27 Right-click **Reset All Folders**. Click **What's This?**.

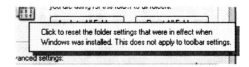

WHAT'S HAPPENING? What's This? tells you that you may return to the default settings for folder options.

28 Click outside the definition to close it. Click **Restore Defaults**. Clear **Hide extensions for known file types**.

29 Scroll until you can see **Remember each folder's view settings**.

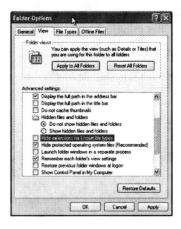

WHAT'S HAPPENING? You cleared one check box because as you work with Windows, you will find that you will want to see the file extensions (types). By default, **Remember each folder's view settings** is on. This option will retain your settings for each folder. For example, if this box were checked, you could set one folder to be in Icons view and another to be in List view. Then, each time you opened the folder window, it would remember the selected view. If the procedure did not work every time it would be considered a bug. A *bug* is an error in a program that causes it to malfunction or to produce incorrect results.

30 Click **OK**. Close all open windows.

6.4 • Moving Around the Tree Pane

In Windows Explorer or My Computer with Folders on, you can expand or contract the folders. If you see a plus sign in front of a folder on the tree side, there are subfolders beneath it that are not visible. If you see a minus sign in front of a folder, you are seeing the expanded hierarchy of that folder. You can use the mouse or the keyboard to move around the hierarchy. You can maneuver in the tree (folders) side or the contents side. You can also use the navigational arrows in the Standard Buttons toolbar to move back and forth between folder windows that you have previously viewed.

6.5 • Activity • Moving Around the Windows Explorer Tree Pane

1   Click **Start**. Point to **All Programs**. Point to **Accessories**. Click **Windows Explorer**.

2   In the left pane, click the **My Computer** icon. Click the **C:** icon. Click the **XPRODATA** folder icon to select it. (Remember, if your XPRODATA is on a drive other than C:, you will first have to select the drive.)

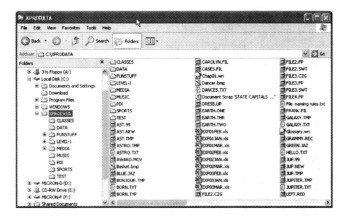

WHAT'S HAPPENING? This window should have been left in List view. If it has returned to another view, change it back to List view by clicking View and then List.

3   Click **Tools**. Click **Folder Options**. Click the **View** tab.

4   Click the **Apply to All Folders** command button.

WHAT'S HAPPENING? You see a dialog box informing you that all your folders will now be set to match the current folder's view settings except any toolbars and folder tasks. This means all Windows Explorer will be in List view each time you open a window.

5   Click **Yes**. Click **OK**. Close Windows Explorer.

6   Click **Start**. Point to **Programs**. Point to **Accessories**. Click **Windows Explorer**. Click the **My Computer** icon. Click the **C:** icon. Click the **XPRODATA** folder icon.

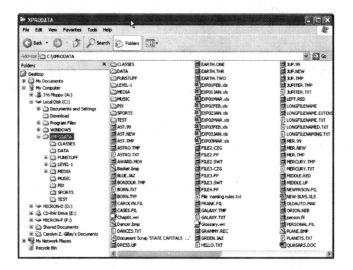

WHAT'S HAPPENING? Now your List view is remembered.

7   Close the Explorer window. Open My Computer.

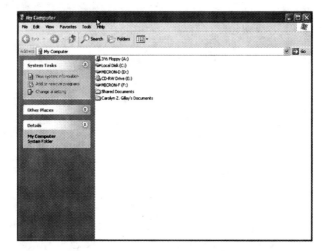

WHAT'S HAPPENING? The global change ensures that the My Computer window will be in List view. However, since Remember each folder's view settings is set, you can change the My Computer window's settings and it will not affect the Explorer window's settings.

8   Click **View**. Click **Icons**. Click **View**. Click **Arrange Icons by**. If **Show in Groups** has a check mark, click it to clear it.

9   Close My Computer. Open Windows Explorer. Click the **My Computer icon**. Click the **C:** icon. Click the **XPRODATA** folder icon.

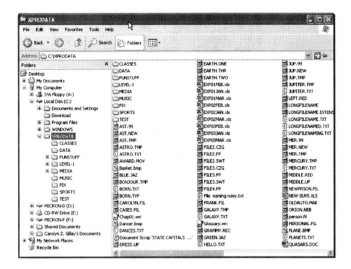

WHAT'S HAPPENING? Windows Explorer did remember the setting. Furthermore, when you clicked XPRODATA, it expanded to show all the folders in it. This is because in folder options, the default is Display simple folder view in Explorer's Folder List. This means each time you click a folder, if it has subfolders, they will be displayed. Each time you change a view in a window, Windows will remember the setting.

10 Click **View**. Click **Details**.

11 Click **AST.99** in the contents pane.

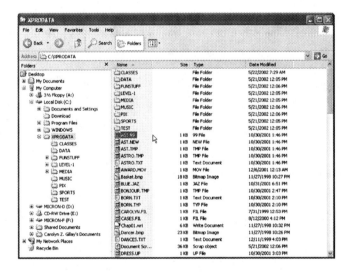

WHAT'S HAPPENING? If you look for the sizes of the folders, you will not see any. Unlike files, a folder is a container and has no specific size of its own. A file description (Type and Size) appears briefly as you rest the mouse pointer on the file icon. A message does not appear if the mouse pointer rests on a folder icon. The brief description indicates AST.99 is 148 bytes in size, while the Size column to the right of the file name indicates it is 1KB in size. In fact, it seems many of the subsequent files are 1KB. Can all these files be the same size? It is possible, but unlikely. Windows Explorer rounds off the size and shows it in kilobytes. To find out the actual size of a file, you must rest the pointer on the file icon or open the file's property sheet.

12 Right-click **AST.99**. On the shortcut menu, click **Properties**.

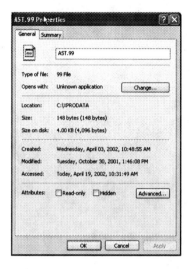

WHAT'S HAPPENING? Apr.99 is only 148 bytes in size. When files are this small, Windows Explorer rounds them off to 1KB. However, the amount of disk space used to store the file varies depending on your file system (FAT16, FAT32, or NTFS). Files are assigned a storage area of at least one cluster. Cluster sizes vary depending on the disk's file system. On a FAT16 system, this file would be assigned 32,768 bytes. On a FAT32 system, this file would be assigned 16,384 bytes. On a NTFS file system, as is this system, this file is assigned 4,096 bytes. In addition to actual file size, the property sheet gives you full information about the file.

13   Click **Cancel**. Press the letter **g**.

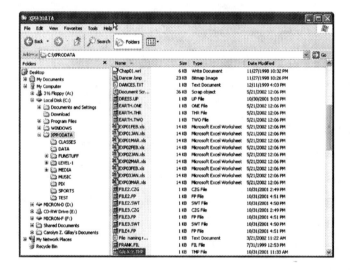

WHAT'S HAPPENING? You arrive at the file that begins with the letter g. Pressing a letter on the keyboard will move you to the first folder or file that begins with that letter in the active pane. In this case, GALAXY.TMP is shown as 1KB.

14   Press the letter **g** until you see **Glossary.wri**. Right-click **Glossary.wri**. Click **Properties**. Click the **General** tab if necessary.

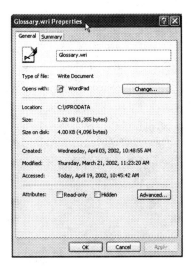

WHAT'S HAPPENING? The file is about 1.32KB, which Windows Explorer rounded off to 2KB. The actual file size is 1,355 bytes but it occupies one cluster (4,096 bytes) because this computer system is using the NTFS file system.

15 Click **Cancel**. Make sure **NumLock** is off. Press the **Home** key.

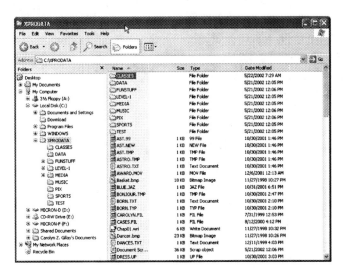

WHAT'S HAPPENING? Pressing the **Home** key is a quick way to move to the top of a document, window, or pane. If you look at XPRODATA in the Folders pane (the left pane), you will see a minus sign (-) by the XPRODATA folder, indicating that the XPRODATA folder can be collapsed.

16 Click the minus sign in the folder icon for **XPRODATA** in the Folders pane.

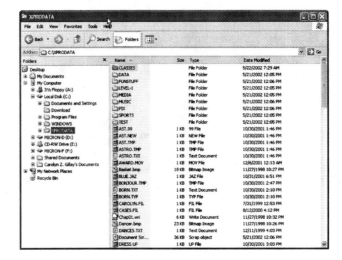

WHAT'S **HAPPENING?** By clicking the minus sign you collapsed the XPRODATA folder. It is still the default folder. In the right pane, you can see the files and folders that are contained in XPRODATA.

17 Click XPRODATA in the left pane to expand it.

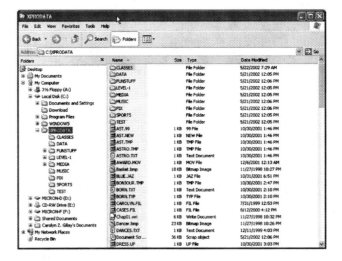

WHAT'S **HAPPENING?** You can expand a folder by either clicking the plus sign or clicking the folder name. The XPRODATA folder now has a minus sign in front of it. The minus sign serves two purposes. The first is to show you that the XPRODATA folder can be collapsed, and the second is to indicate that there are no hidden folders beneath it. In the list of folders beneath XPRODATA, three folders have plus signs, indicating that they also have subfolders.

18 Click the plus sign to the left of the folder named Level-1 in the tree pane. Click the **Level-1** folder to select it.

WHAT'S HAPPENING? Both the left and right panes have changed. The hierarchical tree shows that Level-1 has beneath it the Level-2 and Level-3 folders. The right side of the pane shows that the Level-1 folder contains one file (Hello.txt) and one folder (Level-2).

19 Click the **Level-2** folder icon in the hierarchical tree (the left pane) to select it. Click **Level-2** to make it the default folder.

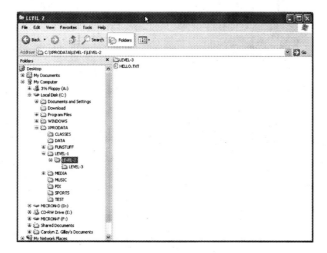

WHAT'S HAPPENING? Both the left and right panes changed. The hierarchical tree shows that Level-2 has the Level-3 folder beneath it. Since Level-3 has no plus sign, it cannot be expanded further. The right pane shows that the Level-2 folder contains one file (Hello.txt) and one folder (Level-3).

20 Click the **Back** button on the toolbar.

WHAT'S **HAPPENING?** You returned to your last view.

21 Click the **Forward** button on the toolbar.

WHAT'S **HAPPENING?** You returned to Level-2. The Forward and Back buttons move you through the actions you have taken.

22 Click the **Up** button on the toolbar.

WHAT'S HAPPENING? You moved to the parent of Level-2, which is Level-1. Thus, Level-2 is a child folder to Level-1 and a parent folder to Level-3. It is helpful to remember that a parent can have many children, but a child can have only one parent.

23 Click the **Up** button on the toolbar.

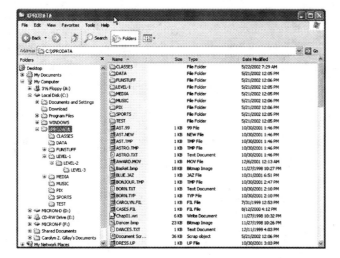

WHAT'S HAPPENING? You moved to the parent of Level-1, which is XPRODATA. Level-1 is a child folder to XPRODATA, but a parent to the Level-2 folder. A folder can be a child to another folder and have children of its own. This parent-child analogy shows the hierarchical nature of the directory tree. Notice that, as you moved up the tree in the left pane, the right pane also changed to show the contents of the currently selected (default) folder.

24 Click the minus sign in front of the folder icon Level-1 in the left pane.

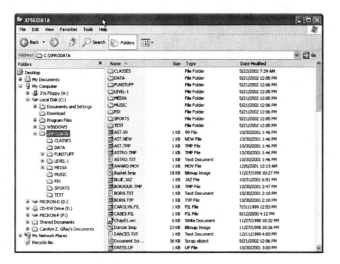

WHAT'S HAPPENING? You collapsed all the children of Level-1. If you had not collapsed the Level-1 folder, the next time you opened this view, it would have remembered the expanded look.

25 Click the minus sign (-) in front of the folder named **XPRODATA** in the left pane. Click **View**. Click **List**.

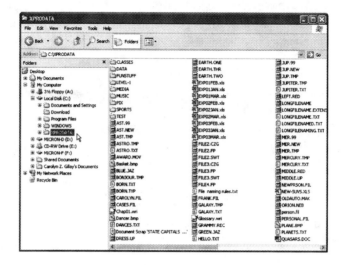

WHAT'S **HAPPENING?** You collapsed XPRODATA to its highest level. The XPRODATA folder is a child to the root directory. You also changed the view of the right pane to List.

26   Press the ⊞ key on the numeric keypad.

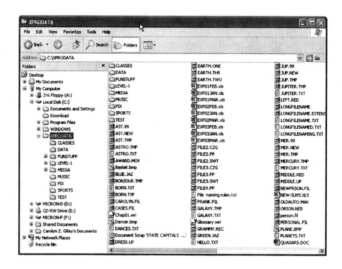

WHAT'S **HAPPENING?** Pressing the ⊞ key on the numeric keypad is a keyboard shortcut for expanding the hierarchical tree. You can see all the branches of the XPRODATA folder in the left pane.

27   Press the ⊟ key on the numeric keypad.

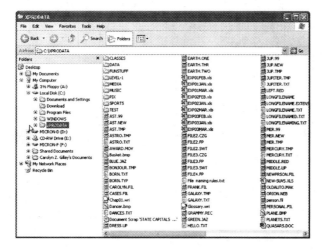

WHAT'S HAPPENING? Pressing the ⊟ key is a keyboard shortcut for collapsing a branch to its highest level.

28 Close Windows Explorer.

6.6 ◦ Opening More than One Folder Window

One of the advantages of using a graphical interface to manage files and folders is that you can see more than one file and folder at a time and you can compare the contents of files and folders on the same disk drive or different disk drives. This feature allows you to analyze your organizational scheme and manipulate files and folders from one directory window to another. In Windows XP Professional, one way to see more than one folder with its files is to launch multiple copies of Windows Explorer or My Computer. You can then tile or cascade the open windows. Although you may open multiple copies of Windows Explorer, in the same location, you must move to a different directory to open another copy of My Computer.

6.7 ◦ Activity ◦ Using Multiple Copies of Windows Explorer and My Computer

1 Click **Start**. Click **My Computer**.

2 Click **Start**. Open **My Computer**.

WHAT'S HAPPENING? Although you opened My Computer twice, only one copy is open. If you look at the taskbar, you see only one taskbar for My Computer.

3   Double-click the Drive C icon.

4   Click **Start**. Click **My Computer**.

WHAT'S HAPPENING? After you opened Drive C and displayed another view of My Computer, you could open another copy of it. If you If you look at the taskbar, you see only two taskbar buttons, one for Local Disk (C:) and one for My Computer.

5   Close all open windows.

6   Click **Start**. Point to **All Programs**. Point to **Accessories**. Click **Windows Explorer**.

7   Click **Start**. Point to **All Programs**. Point to **Accessories**. Click **Windows Explorer**.

WHAT'S HAPPENING? You are still in list view. Note that you can open two copies of Windows Explorer in the same default location. If you look at the taskbar buttons, you have two buttons, one for each copy of My Documents that is open.

8   In the left pane, click **My Computer**. Click **Drive C:**. Click **XPRODATA**. Click **Media**. Click **Movies**.

WHAT'S HAPPENING? You are looking at the documents located in the Movies folder, which is under the Media folder, which is under the XPRODATA folder, which is under the root of Drive C. An easier way to state the structure is to use the path name. You would say that the path is C:\XPRODATA\MEDIA\MOVIES. Now you also want to look at the files in the Books folder.

9   Click the **My Documents** taskbar button. In the left pane, Click **My Computer**. Click **Drive C:**. Click **XPRODATA**. Click **Media**. Click **Books**.

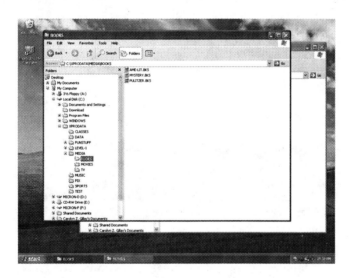

10   Right-click in an empty spot on the taskbar. Click **Tile Windows Horizontally**.

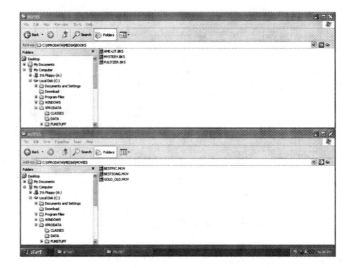

WHAT'S HAPPENING? Now you can compare what files you have in the Books folder and what files you have in the Movies folder.

11   Right-click the taskbar. Click **Cascade Windows**.

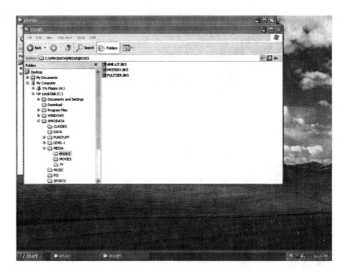

WHAT'S HAPPENING? The Windows Explorer windows are cascaded, layered, or stacked upon one another. You are not limited to opening two folder windows. You can keep adding copies of Windows Explorer.

12   Close all the open Explorer windows.

6.8 • Logical and Physical Views

Windows XP Professional emphasizes a logical rather than a physical view of your computer. The desktop is a *logical view* of your computer system. On a default Windows installation, the only icon placed on your desktop is the Recycle Bin. Some installations of Windows will place more objects on your desktop, represented by icons. Common icons that may appear by default on your desktop can include My Computer (a way to see what is on your computer system), My Network Places (a way to see what is on your network), the Recycle Bin (your waste basket), and Internet Explorer (a way to connect to the Internet) on the desktop. This logical view adheres to the docucentric paradigm. As the user, you are interested in your documents, not the programs that created them. Indeed, you can place any icon on the desktop you choose, such as a document icon, but without the program, you cannot create, edit, or view the document.

My Computer, with the Folders option off, is a classic example of a logical view of a computer system. When you open My Computer, the contents that are displayed are not the physical contents of your computer (the circuit boards, memory chips, etc.), but its logical contents. The My Computer window contains icons that look like physical items—all your disk drives. The drive icons represent the logical contents (the files, folders, documents, and programs) that are stored on these drives. In addition, the My Computer window usually contains a Shared Documents folder and a folder named *your name* Documents, e.g., Carolyn Z. Gillay Documents. There may also be other folders with other user names (Frank Panezich Documents, Steven W. Tuttle Documents and so on). My Computer is not stored as an executable file that you can run. To run it, you run Explorer.exe.

By default, Windows Explorer, for the most part, affords a ***physical view*** of what files and folders are on your system and where they are located (Folders on). Windows Explorer is stored as a program in the Windows folder that can be executed. By default, if you opened My Computer, clicked the XPRODATA folder, and clicked the Media folder, you would see the files and folders displayed in a window with the tasks you could accomplish listed in the left pane. By default, if you opened Windows Explorer, XPRODATA, and Media (C:\XPRODATA\MEDIA), you would still see a two-paned window. But now, instead of tasks, the hierarchical structure would be displayed in the left pane and the contents would be displayed in the right pane. Windows Explorer provides a map to the physical locations of folders and files.

To understand the difference between a physical and a logical view of objects, consider the way you use a telephone. You know that there are physical telephone lines that connect your phone with all the other telephones in the world. When you want to call your mother, you simply dial her number. You probably realize that there is not just one physical telephone line that directly connects your phone to your mother's phone, but you do not really care. You are using the telephone logically.

If, however, your telephone does not work or you want to add another telephone line, you have to call a telephone repair person. When the telephone repair person arrives at your home, she or he needs a map that shows where the telephone line that comes into your house is located. The repairperson is going to track the actual telephone wires and may need the map of telephone lines for your neighborhood or your city to do this. These maps are the physical views of your telephone.

Both logical and physical views are important and necessary, and for this reason by default Windows XP Professional opens My Computer in the logical view and opens Windows Explorer in the physical view. The view you use depends on what task you are trying to accomplish; however, these views are not absolute. Although Windows Explorer, for the most part, shows you the physical view of your computer and its resources, it also displays a logical view. See Figure 6.3.

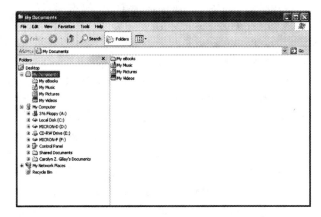

Figure 6.3 ∘ Windows Explorer in a Logical View

This view shows the Desktop folder at the top of the hierarchy. The dotted lines coming down from Desktop indicate that all items are subservient to Desktop. My Documents, My Computer, My Network Places, and the Recycle Bin are all contained within Desktop. My Computer, branching off Desktop, has all of your disk drives and a special folder (Control Panel) attached, and subservient, to My Computer. The Control Panel folder gives you access to important system functions such as setting up your printers (Printers) and changing hardware and software settings for your computer. There are special folders in Control Panel such as the Printers and Faxes folder and the Network Connections folder. They are unlike most other folders. They have special functions and their contents are not stored in the My Computer folder. For instance, the contents of Control Panel are actually stored in the \Windows\System32 folder in files that have a .cpl extension. If, in Folder Options, Show Control Panel in My Computer is not on, it will not appear in this view.

But, in reality, each drive is a separate physical device with its own hierarchical structure. Ordinary files and folders are stored on each disk, and the folder icons are connected to the drive icon. The My Documents and Recycled folders are located under the Desktop. As you can see in Figure 6.4, the My Documents folder under Desktop and the My Documents folder under My Computer contain the same folders (My eBooks through My Videos). This is true because the My Documents folder is physically stored on Drive C:.

Figure 6.4 ∘ The My Documents Folder

There is also a Desktop folder. Actually, there will be several Desktop folders, one for each user. There is also a folder for the Administrator and for All Users. All Users is where the default settings are set for each user initially. Each user's Desktop folder is a subfolder, physically located under the user name folder. For instance, Figure 6.5 shows the exact physical location of user Carolyn Z. Gillay's Desktop folder (C:\Documents and Settings\Carolyn Z. Gillay\Desktop). This folder contains any document or program shortcuts that are on the user Carolyn Z. Gillay's desktop.

Figure 6.5 * The Desktop Folder, Located in Explorer in a Physical View

The logical view is useful for certain types of tasks. If you wanted to open a drive window, launch a program, or open a document, the logical view presented by My Computer would be an easy way to use your computer. However, when you want to accomplish some tasks, you cannot use a logical view. When you want to add or delete items to the Start menu, add something to a shortcut menu, or copy or move files and folders, you must know the physical locations of files and folders. Therefore, a physical view is appropriate for making these types of changes.

6.9 • Activity • Looking at the Hierarchical Structure

1   Click **Start**. Point to **All Programs**. Point to **Accessories**. Click **Windows Explorer**.

2   Click **My Computer**. Click **Drive C**.

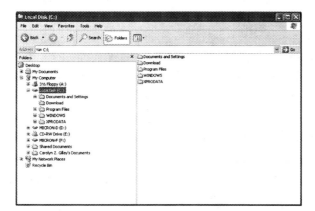

WHAT'S HAPPENING? The left pane is the hierarchical, somewhat logical view described earlier. You may have more folders than are listed here. Documents and Settings, as the folder name indicates, contains the documents and settings for each person that has a user account on the system. In this example, Download was a folder created by the user. Program Files are the folder where programs are installed. Windows is the folder that holds the Windows XP Professional files and folders that make your system usable. These are the operating system files. This folder is usually called Windows. However, if you upgraded from a previous version of Windows, the folder could be called WINNT. It could also have another name such as Windows XP Professional or something similar, depending on how it was installed. This text will use *Windows* to refer to the folder that holds the Windows XP Professional files and folders. You should know where the Windows files are located.

3   Click **Documents and Settings**. Click the folder **All Users**. Click the folder showing the user name you used to log onto the computer (Carolyn Z. Gillay, for example).

WHAT'S **HAPPENING?** When you expand a folder by clicking its folder icon, the other folder that was expanded collapses.

4   Click the plus sign next to **All Users**.

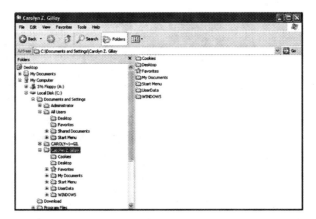

WHAT'S **HAPPENING?** When you used the plus sign, you kept the hierarchical structure open for both folders. Both All Users and your user name have a Desktop folder.

5   Click **Desktop** under your user name.

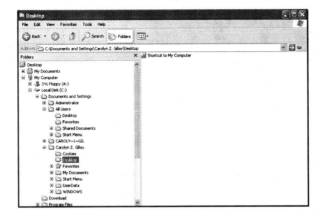

WHAT'S HAPPENING? In this example, Carolyn Z. Gillay has one item on her desktop, a shortcut to My Computer. Your display may be different.

6   Under **All Users**, click **Desktop**.

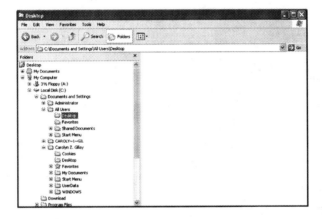

WHAT'S HAPPENING? In this example, All Users have nothing on the desktop. Your display may be different. The settings and items in All Users are those that each user gets when logging on for the first time. Then, as each user makes changes to their environment, those changes are kept in each user's own folder. Windows XP Professional uses information stored in your user name folder and the All Users folder to define your work environment. Note that the My Computer icon does not appear. My Computer is a *virtual* container that holds everything about your computer system. Anything that is virtual is a computer representation of what is real on your system. Thus, if you right-click My Computer and click Properties, you are taken to the System Properties property sheets. The System Properties property sheets *are* real and allow you to view and manipulate every device on your system.

7   Below your user name, click the plus sign in front of the **Start Menu** folder icon. Below **All Users**, click the plus sign in front of the **Start Menu** folder icon.

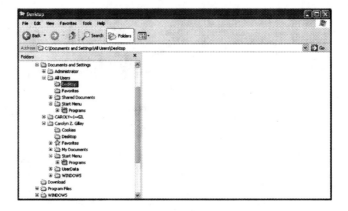

WHAT'S HAPPENING? You see the Programs folder under both Start Menu.

8   Click the plus sign in the **Programs** folder under your user name and under **All Users** in the left pane.

WHAT'S HAPPENING? If you look at the left pane, some of the folders listed on the Start menu are listed here. There is a difference between what is on the Start Menu for Carolyn Z. Gillay and All Users. Windows XP Professional also uses information stored in the C:\Documents and Settings\All Users\Start Menu\Programs folder. What appears on your Start menu is a combination of what is in your personal folder and the All Users folder. Remember, the left pane shows the hierarchical, or tree, structure of a folder. The right pane shows the selected folder's contents.

9   Click the **Accessories** folder under your user name and under **All Users** in the left pane.

WHAT'S HAPPENING? If you look at the left pane, some of the folders listed on the Accessories menu are listed here. Again, what appears on your menus is a combination of what is in your personal folder and the All Users folder. Note that the programs in the right pane are shortcuts to the program files, not the actual program files. Remember that icons representing shortcuts have a right-bent arrow. Note that in your personal user folder, the menu items Games does not appear but it does appear in the All Users folder.

10 In the left pane, click the **Games** folder under the **All Users** folder.

WHAT'S HAPPENING? These are the games you see when you click the Start button, point to All Programs, point to Accessories, and, lastly, point to Games. All of the objects in the Games folder are shortcuts to the program files.

11 Under **All Users**, collapse the **Accessories** folder. Collapse the **Programs** folder. Collapse the **Start Menu** folder. Collapse the **All Users** folder.

12 Under your user name, collapse the **Accessories** folder. Collapse the **Programs** folder. Collapse the **Start Menu** folder. Click your user name folder.

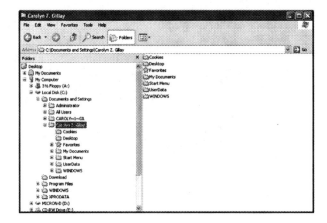

WHAT'S HAPPENING? You have collapsed all items in the All Users folder. However, there are folders and files that are hidden from you. If you want to make changes to your system, you need to see all the files and folders. To do this, you must change the options in the Tools/Folder Options window.

13 On the menu bar, click **Tools**. Click **Folder Options**. Click the **View** tab.

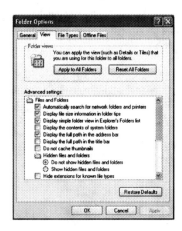

WHAT'S HAPPENING? There is an option for Hidden files and folders. Do not show hidden files and folders is set.

14 Click **Show hidden files and folders**. Click **Apply**. Click **OK**. Click your username.

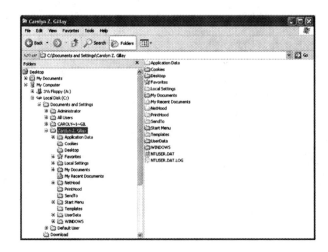

WHAT'S HAPPENING? Now you see any file or folder that was hidden. You should see a few folders and files in the right pane that appear to be more subdued (lighter in color) than the other folders. These are the folders and files that were hidden before. The NTUSER.DAT and NTUSER.DAT.LOG are files that keep the settings for you. All users will have their own copy of these files. Now that you know how to see all your files and folders, as well as understand the hierarchical structure, you are going to use this information to customize your system.

15 Close all open windows.

WHAT'S HAPPENING? You have returned to the desktop.

6.10 ● Manipulating Windows

Now that you know where to locate the physical files and folders, you can manipulate items. You can add programs, files, and folders to the Start menu or to any of the program folders, and you can remove programs, files, and folders from these areas.

6.11 ● Activity ● Using My Computer and Windows Explorer to Add a Printer to a Menu

1 Right-click the **Start** button.

WHAT'S HAPPENING? When you right-click the Start button, you open a shortcut menu that allows you to perform several critical tasks: open the My Computer window showing your (user name) Start Menu folder (Open), open the Windows Explorer window with your user name's Start Menu folder selected and the hierarchical structure displayed in the left pane (Explore), open the Search window (Search), and open the Taskbar and Properties property sheet, open the My Computer window showing the Start Menu folder for all users (Open All Users), and last open Windows Explorer with the Start Menu folder for all users selected and the hierarchical structure displayed in the left pane (Explore All Users). Some application programs add items to this menu, such as Paint Shop Pro and Norton AntiVirus.

2 Click **Explore**.

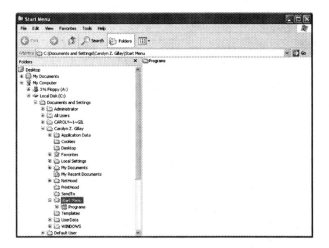

WHAT'S HAPPENING? You are taken to Windows Explorer. Instead of being at the top of the hierarchy, you are in your user name's current default drive and directory, which is Start Menu. Remember that the user name will vary from computer system to computer system. You also see all the files and folders since you chose that option in the last activity.

3   Scroll until you locate the **XPRODATA** folder. Click the **XPRODATA** folder icon.

4   Right-click **ASTRO.TXT** in the contents (right) pane. Point to **Send To**.

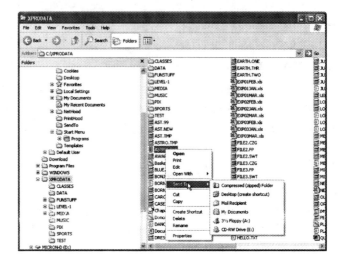

WHAT'S HAPPENING? You have selected a file. You may send (copy) the file to a Compressed (zipped) Folder, to the desktop as a shortcut, to a Mail Recipient which will open your electronic mail program, to the My Documents folder, to your floppy disk, and to your CD-ROM drive, if you have one. The choices that appear on this menu depend on what programs have been installed on the system. You may remove items you do not use, and you may add items you would like to use. For instance, you would like to be able to send a file to the printer, but that choice is not listed here. You may add a printer shortcut to this menu. You do this by locating the Send To folder for your user name and dragging a printer shortcut to this folder.

5   Click a blank area of the desktop to close the shortcut menu. On the tree side, click the minus sign in front of **XPRODATA** to collapse it to its highest level.

6   Locate the SendTo folder icon under your user name folder (**C:\Documents and Settings\user name**). On the tree side, click the **SendTo** folder icon.

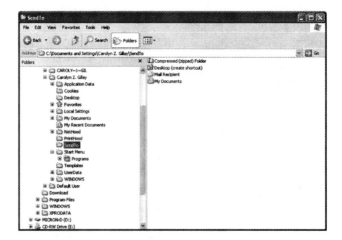

WHAT'S HAPPENING? You can see all the objects in the SendTo folder on the contents side. The one that you want to add here is the printer shortcut.

7 Click **Start**. Click **Printers and Faxes**. Click **View**. Click **Tiles**.

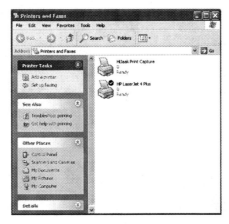

WHAT'S HAPPENING? You see the printers on your system.

8 Move your open windows until you can see both of them. Make the **Printer and Faxes** window the active window.

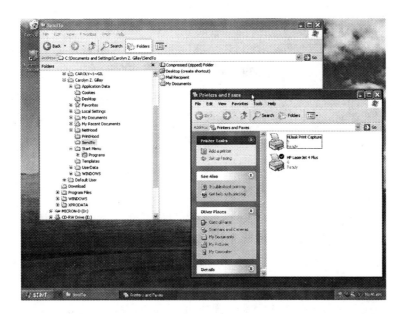

WHAT'S HAPPENING? You are going to drag your default printer in the your user's name SendTo folder.

9 Right-drag your default printer (the one with a checkmark) into the right pane of the **SendTo** folder in Windows Explorer. Release the right mouse button.

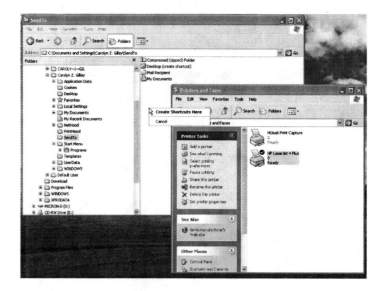

WHAT'S HAPPENING? Now that you right-dragged and dropped, you see the pop-up menu. Since a printer is a device, you are asked if you want to create a shortcut.

10   Click **Create Shortcuts Here**.

11   Close the **Printers and Faxes** window. If necessary, click the **SendTo** window in Windows Explorer to make it active.

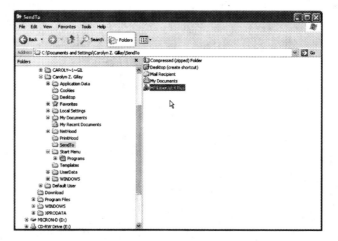

WHAT'S HAPPENING? You now have a shortcut to your printer in the SendTo folder.

12   On the tree side of Windows Explorer, scroll until you see the **XPRODATA** folder. Click it.

13   In the contents pane, right-click **ASTRO.TXT**. Point to **SendTo**.

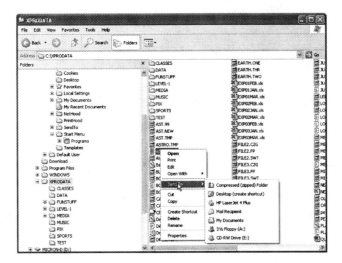

WHAT'S HAPPENING? You have added a shortcut to your Send To menu. If you have other users, since this choice is not in the All Users folder, they would not have it available. By right-clicking, you can print your document. Although you added a shortcut to a device in this case, you can add a shortcut to a drive, a folder, or wherever you might want to send an item. The one tricky task is placing a shortcut to a folder on the Send To menu. If you later used this shortcut to send a file that was on the same drive as the folder, you would be moving it from one location to another instead of copying it. You can also remove items from the Send To menu by reversing the process you followed when you added the printer shortcut.

14   Locate and click the **SendTo** folder icon located under your user name folder.

15   Click the printer shortcut to select it. Drag the printer shortcut and drop it on the Recycle Bin on the desktop.

16   On the tree side, click your user name folder icon to collapse it to its highest level.

17   On the tree side, click the **Documents and Settings** folder icon to collapse it to its highest level.

18   On the tree side, scroll until you locate the **XPRODATA** folder icon and click it.

19   Right-click **ASTRO.TXT**. Point to **Send To**.

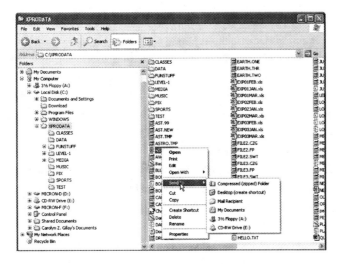

WHAT'S **HAPPENING?** You have removed the printer from the Send To menu.

20   Collapse the XPRODATA to its highest level.

21   Click **Tools**. Click **Folder Options**. Click **View**. Click **Do not show hidden files or folders**. Click **Apply**. Click **OK**.

22   Close Windows Explorer. Close any open windows.

WHAT'S **HAPPENING?** You have returned to the desktop.

6.12 • Managing Disks with Windows Explorer

You have been using Windows Explorer and My Computer to search for files, look at different details about files and folders, and manipulate folders. As you have seen, you may use either Windows Explorer or My Computer to accomplish these tasks. The tool you use will be the one that works best for you. Both My Computer and Windows Explorer let you perform operating system functions, such as copying floppy disks and preparing a disk for use. Even though you perform file-related tasks most often in Windows XP Professional, you still need to know how to perform disk-related tasks.

6.13 • Copying Floppy Disks

Although you will work primarily on and with hard disks does not mean you will never use a floppy disk drive and floppy disks. You may make a copy of a floppy disk—an exact copy. One of the original purposes of floppy disk drives was installing program files from the floppy disks that came with application software. Computer software manufacturers instructed you to make copies of the disks that you purchased and then install from the copies. This procedure protected you if something happened to the original disks. Today, this occurrence is rare. Most software today comes on a CD-ROM because of compact discs' storage space and reliability.

You can make a copy of a floppy disk. You can make backup copies of any data disks you create, which can be useful if you must transport files between work, home, and school. Or you may want to use a floppy disk if you have a digital camera and have saved your pictures to a disk. If you make a copy of the disk, you can give it to friends and family so they can view your pictures. You can copy floppy disks, but not hard disks or removable cartridges. You will learn how to copy files from a hard disk to a floppy disk, but this method is not the same as copying the actual disk.

When you copy one floppy disk to another floppy disk, the disk media type must be identical. For instance, if you have a 3½-inch high-density disk, you must have a blank 3½-inch high-density disk. You cannot copy a 5¼-inch disk to a 3½-inch disk. You can copy the files from a disk of one media type to a disk of another type, but you must copy the files individually, not as an entire disk. Today, you rarely see any floppy disk size other than 3½-inch.

You will learn how to copy a disk by making a copy of the XPRODATA disk. Then, if you have a problem with the XPRODATA disk later, you will have another copy. Since in the lab environment you will be saving all your files to a floppy disk, you can use this technique to make a copy of your MYDATADISK disk at the end of each chapter. This way, if you made an error in a chapter, you would not have to go back to the beginning chapters to redo your work. You could merely use your backup copy of the MYDATADISK disk.

6.14 • Activity • Making a Copy of the XPRODATA Disk

1   Place the XPRODATA disk that came with this textbook in Drive A.

2   Click **Start**. Point to **All Programs**. Point to **Accessories**. Click **Windows Explorer**. In the left pane, click **My Computer**. Click **View**. Click **Tiles**. If you cannot see the Drive A icon, scroll until you can. Click the Drive A icon in the left pane.

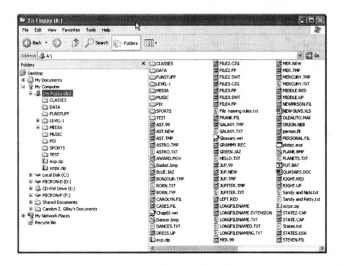

WHAT'S HAPPENING? The left pane, Folders, shows you the floppy disk drives on your computer system. The contents pane shows you the files and folders that are located in the disk's root directory in Drive A.

3   Right-click the Drive A icon.

WHAT'S HAPPENING? The shortcut menu appears listing the tasks you can accomplish with this object—the disk in Drive A. Explore shows you what files and folders are on the disk in Drive A. If you select Open, you will open a Drive A window. Depending on how Windows XP Professional was installed, you may see another choice, Sharing and Security. Sharing and Security allows you to determine whether or not to permit anyone else access to your files and folders and what access they may have.

4   Click **Open**.

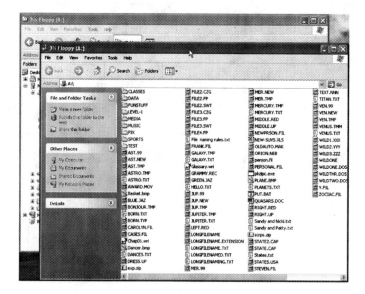

WHAT'S **HAPPENING?** You open another copy of the Drive A window but this time without folders on (My Computer).

5   Close this window. Right-click the Drive A icon in the tree. Click **Properties**.

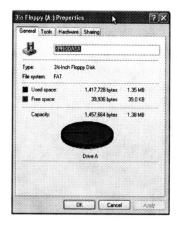

WHAT'S **HAPPENING?** You are looking at the properties of the disk in Drive A. Windows XP Professional gives you a graphical view of how much free space there is on a disk. As you can see, there is very little free space for files and folders on this disk. Notice that the Label entry is highlighted. This entry is an internal label, not an external label that you affix to a disk. You may change the label on any disk using this property sheet. The property sheet also tells you that this is a 3½-inch disk. When you see a capacity of 1,457,664 bytes, you know that it is a high-density disk. The file system used on this disk is FAT.

There are four tabs on the top of this property sheet: General, Tools, Hardware, and Sharing. Tools includes the abilities to back up your disk and improve disk performance. You will learn more about Tools later. Hardware displays a list of physical storage devices on your system. Sharing allows you to determine whether or not to permit anyone else access to your folder (disk).

6   Click the **Cancel** button.

7   Right-click the **Drive C** icon. Click **Properties**.

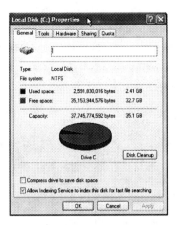

Figure 6.6 • An NTFS Properties Dialog Box

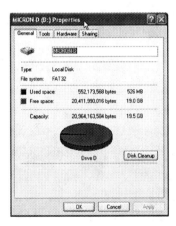

Figure 6.7 • A FAT32 Properties Dialog Box

WHAT'S HAPPENING? You are looking at the amount of space available on the hard drive. Figure 6.6 shows that a disk not named (C:) has very little on it. The file system used for this disk is NTFS. The MICRON-D (D:) disk in Figure 6.7 is also almost empty. The NTFS file system was used for Drive C hard disk. In the two check boxes at the bottom of the dialog box, drive compression is not set but the Indexing Service is enabled. An additional property sheet, Quota, also appears in NTFS drives' Properties dialog boxes.

8 Click **Cancel**.

9 Right-click the Drive C icon.

WHAT'S HAPPENING? For the hard drive, there is no choice to copy the disk. You may back up the hard disk, but you cannot copy it.

10 Right-click the Drive A icon. Click **Copy Disk**.

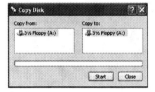

WHAT'S HAPPENING? You have opened the Copy Disk dialog box. Both the Copy from and the Copy to panes indicate Drive A as the default source and destination. If you had two floppy drives and both Drive A and Drive B contained the same type of disk, you could disk-copy from Drive A to Drive B. The disk you want to copy is in Drive A, so you can begin.

11 Be sure Drive A is selected in each pane. Click **Start**.

WHAT'S HAPPENING? The Copy Disk dialog box tells you to insert your source disk, which you have done.

12 Click **OK**.

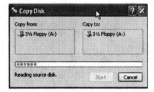

WHAT'S HAPPENING? At the bottom of the dialog box, you see the *progress bar indicator,* also known as the *progress bar control.*

A progress bar indicator usually appears when you are doing an operation that can be lengthy. It gives you some idea where you are in the task. You also see the message, Reading source disk. When you copy a disk, the contents of the disk are copied to RAM (memory), which is called reading. When that task is complete, you see the following information message box:

This message instructs you to remove your original disk and insert the disk on which you want the information copied (the destination disk). When you copy a disk, whatever is on the destination disk is overwritten with the information in memory. You are going to use the MYDATADISK for the copy. You will overwrite the information currently on the MYDATADISK disk. You will have a backup copy of the XPRODATA disk when you are finished.

13   Remove the XPRODATA disk from Drive A and place the MYDATADISK disk in Drive A. Click **OK**.

WHAT'S HAPPENING? What was in RAM (memory) is being copied, or written, to the disk in Drive A. When the copy is complete, you see the following message in the Copy Disk dialog box:

The message in the dialog box, Copy completed successfully, states that your operation succeeded.

14   Click **Close**.

15   Right-click the Drive A icon. Click **Open**.

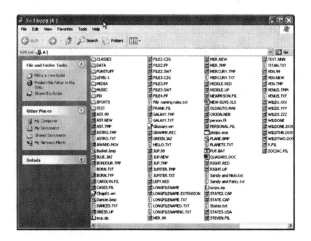

WHAT'S **HAPPENING?** The contents of this disk are identical to those of the XPRODATA disk. You now have a copy of the disk as well as the original.

16 Close all open windows.

WHAT'S **HAPPENING?** You have returned to the desktop.

Chapter Summary

In this chapter, you learned more details about the hierarchical structure of folders and files. You found that you can identify the location of a file by its path. You found that My Computer presents a logical view of your system, and Windows Explorer presents both a logical and a physical view. You learned that the difference between the two is that My Computer does not have the Folders button on by default and presents you with the contents of a disk in the right pane and possible tasks you might wish to accomplish in the left pane. Windows Explorer presents two panes, the hierarchical and the contents panes. You learned how to set the different folder options and how they impact My Computer as well as Windows Explorer.

You discovered that when you want to accomplish tasks such as adding an item to a menu, you need to know the physical location of a file or folder in order to make changes. You found that copying a disk requires the two disks to be identical media types.

Key Terms

bug	logical view	progress bar indicator
default folder	physical view	split bar
Folders pane	progress bar control	virtual

Discussion Questions

1. Explain the purpose and function of the root directory.
2. Explain the purpose and function of a path.
3. Compare and contrast the left pane with the right pane of the Windows Explorer window.
4. When you are looking at the Folders hierarchical tree, the size of the folders is not given. Why?
5. What is the purpose and function of the ⊞ and ⊟ keys on the numeric keypad in Windows Explorer?
6. Objects in Windows XP Professional can be viewed physically and logically. Explain.
7. When changing items on the Start menu the physical view is used. Why?
8. How are My Computer and Windows Explorer similar?
9. List and explain two advantages of using Windows Explorer over My Computer.
10. List and explain two uses of floppy disks.

True/False Questions

For each question, circle the letter T if the statement is true or the letter F if the statement is false.

T   F   1. Windows Explorer presents objects in a physical rather than a logical fashion.

T   F   2. Every hierarchical tree begins with a root directory.

T   F   3. If you have customized your folders with pictures, you will see the pictures in both My Computer and Windows Explorer, regardless of the view you have selected.

T   F   4. If you want to see the date a file was modified, use the Details view.

T   F   5. My Computer and Windows Explorer are two very different programs that accomplish different tasks.

Completion Questions

Write the correct answer in the blank space provided.

6. When using Windows Explorer, the left pane displays the _____ structure of a disk.

7. If you see a minus sign next to a folder, and you click the minus sign, you will _____ the folder.

8. To know the actual size of a specific file, you should view the _____ of the file.

9. The _____ folder is where the default settings are initially set for each user.

10. When copying floppy disks, both disks must be the _____ media type.

Multiple Choice Questions

Circle the letter of the correct answer for each question.

11. When using My Computer, you double-click on the Next folder. Inside the Next folder is the One folder.
    a. Next is the child of One.
    b. One is the child of Next.
    c. One is the parent of Next.
    d. none of the above

12. One advantage of opening more than one copy of Windows Explorer is that you may
    a. compare the contents of two folders.
    b. open as many copies of Windows Explorer as you need.
    c. both a and b
    d. neither a nor b

13. When you first open Windows Explorer, it shows Desktop at the top of the hierarchy because
    a. Desktop is the top of the hierarchy.
    b. Desktop is the most important folder in the tree.
    c. Windows Explorer is presenting a logical view of your system.
    d. none of the above

14. You have opened Windows Explorer. The contents pane is active. You press the letter N. The following occurs:
    a. All files and folders beginning with N are selected.
    b. All files and folders are arranged by name.
    c. The first file or folder beginning with N is selected.
    d. The cursor moves to the next file or folder.

15. When you make a copy of a disk, the newly copied disk
    a. retains any files that were on the disk and includes all the new files.
    b. is blank.
    c. is identical to the original disk.
    d. none of the above

Application Assignments

Problem Set I—At the Computer

Note: You should be in list view and arranged by name.

Problem A

* Open Windows Explorer.

* In the left pane, expand My Computer and Drive C:.

* Select the **XPRODATA** folder icon on the Folders side.

    1. The XPRODATA folder has _____ folder(s) displayed beneath it on the tree side.
       a. zero
       b. one
       c. three
       d. six
       e. nine

* Collapse the XPRODATA folder to its highest level in the tree pane.

    2. The XPRODATA folder has _____ folders displayed beneath it on the tree side.
       a. zero
       b. two
       c. three
       d. six
       e. nine

* Click in the contents pane.

    3. The first file on the contents side that begins with C is
       a. Classes.
       b. Carol.fil.
       c. Carolyn.fil.
       d. Cases.fil.

* Close Windows Explorer.

Problem B

* Open Windows Explorer.

* In the left pane, expand My Computer and Drive C:.

* Click the **XPRODATA** folder icon on the Folders side.

* Arrange the icons by name and use the Details view.

    4. The file called BLUE.JAZ has a last modification date of
       a. 10/1/1999.
       b. 1/30/2000.
       c. 10/31/2001.
       d. 11/22/2002.

    5. Is the file called BLUE.JAZ a document file or a program file?
       a. a document file
       b. a program file

* Move to the top of the window on the contents side.

6. What key could you press to move to the top of the window?
   a. Home
   b. Ctrl
   c. End
   d. Shift

* Arrange the icons by type.

7. Which file (not folder) appears first?
   a. AST.99
   b. AST.NEW
   c. STATE2.CAP
   d. Glossary.wri

* Arrange the icons by date.

8. Which file (not folder) appears first?
   a. AST.99
   b. AST.NEW
   c. STATE2.CAP
   d. Glossary.wri

* Arrange the icons by name and use List view.

* In the tree pane, expand the FUNSTUFF folder.

* In the tree pane, click the BOG2 folder.

9. The BOG2 folder is a _____ to the FUNSTUFF folder.
   a. parent folder
   b. child folder

10. The XPRODATA folder is a _____ to the FUNSTUFF folder.
    a. parent folder
    b. child folder

* Click the minus sign by the FUNSTUFF folder to collapse it.

* Collapse the XPRODATA folder to collapse it to its highest level.

* Close Windows Explorer.

Problem C

* Open Windows Explorer.

* In the left pane, expand My Computer and Drive C:.

* Open the XPRODATA folder on Drive C so you can see the subfolders. Remember that if in your lab the XPRODATA folder is on a drive other than C, first choose that drive.

* Click **View**. Click **Status Bar** to enable it.

* Place the XPRODATA disk in Drive A.

* Open another copy of Windows Explorer.

* Open My Computer and Drive A.

* Click Drive A in the new copy of Windows Explorer.

* Click **View**. Click **Status Bar** to enable it.

* Tile the windows horizontally.

* In the C:\XPRODATA window, click the Funstuff folder on the tree side.

* In the Drive A:\ window, click the Funstuff folder on the tree side. Look at the status bar for both windows.

    11. Both Explorer windows have the same number of objects in them.
        a. true
        b. false

* In the Drive C:\XPRODATA\Funstuff window, right-click the Anticlim.txt file on the contents side.

* Click **Properties**.

* Click the **General** tab.

    12. The anticlim.txt file size in bytes is
        a. 646
        b. 4.0.
        c. 4,096.

* Click **Cancel**.

* In the C:\XPRODATA\Funstuff folder, click XPRODATA to select it.

* In the Drive C:\XPRODATA window, right-click BONJOUR.TMP on the contents side.

* Point to **Send To**.

    13. You may send BONJOUR.TMP to
        a. 3½ Floppy (A).
        b. Printer.
        c. XPRODATA folder.
        d. all of the above

* Right-click the taskbar.

* Click **Undo Tile**.

* Collapse Funstuff and XPRODATA to its highest level in each window.

* In the left pane, locate and right-click the Drive A icon.

* Click **Properties**.

    14. In what color is free space shown?
        a. pink
        b. blue
        c. green

* Close the property sheet.

* Close all Explorer windows.

* Remove the XPRODATA disk from Drive A.

Problem Set II—Brief Essay

For all essay questions, use Notepad or WordPad to create your answer. Place your name, class information, and which question you are answering. Print your answer.

1. Compare and contrast My Computer and Windows Explorer. Give examples and reasons for when you might use each.
2. The following is a Windows Explorer window. Identify and explain the purpose of each labeled item.

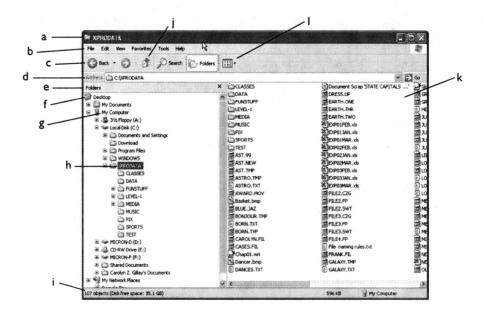

Problem Set III—Scenario

Your friend sees that when you right-click a document, the Send To menu has your Zip drive listed (Drive G:). Your friend wants to know how she could add her Zip drive to her Send To menu. Briefly explain to her the steps she needs to take. Include an explanation of the Documents and Settings folder, both All Users and the login name.

CHAPTER 7

Managing Files

You have been using Windows Explorer and My Computer to search for files and look at different details about files and folders. Another function of these tools is launching programs. However, not all files in a program folder are programs; many are support files that allow the program to be executed.

You can perform similar tasks in Windows Explorer and My Computer. Both My Computer and Windows Explorer let you perform operating system functions, such as creating directories, removing directories, copying files, moving files, renaming files, and deleting files. You manage your files and folders with Windows Explorer and My Computer.

341

Learning Objectives

1. Determine if a file is a program file, a data file, or a support file.
2. Explain the purpose of program files and support files.
3. Explain the purpose of file management commands.
4. Compare and contrast copying files and moving files to a floppy disk and a CD.
5. Explain why it is important to delete files and folders.

Student Outcomes

1. Launch programs from Windows Explorer and My Computer.
2. Create and use shortcuts to accomplish various tasks such as renaming files and folders.
3. Use file management commands to manipulate files and folders.
4. Copy and move files from one drive to another and on the same drive.
5. Create and delete files.

7.1 ◦ Program Files

As you continue to use your computer, you will find yourself accumulating programs for different purposes. You will find that today, most programs, when you install them, will automatically appear on the Start/All Programs menu. As you may recall, your frequently used programs automatically appear on the Start menu. It is important to remember that programs are files, and you should be able to recognize a program file. In some cases, however, not all your programs will appear on the Start/All Programs menu. You may always access a program from My Computer or Windows Explorer when you need to use it. To do these tasks, you need to be able to recognize a program file from a data file as well as understand what other files belong to a program. You can use either My Computer or Windows Explorer to launch programs.

7.2 ◦ Activity ◦ Using My Computer to Launch a Program

1   Click **Start**. Click **My Computer**. Double-click **Drive C**.

2   Double-click the **XPRODATA** folder. Click **View**. Click **Icons**.

3   Right-click on an empty area in the menu bar of XPRODATA.

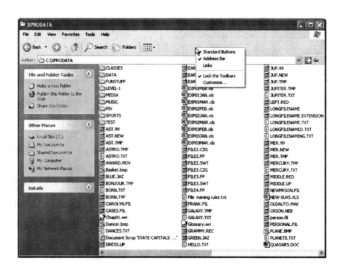

WHAT'S **HAPPENING?** You can check your settings at any time by right-clicking the menu bar, the Address Bar, or the toolbar. You will then see a shortcut menu where you can adjust your settings.

4   Double-click the **FUNSTUFF** folder. Click **View**. Click **Icons**.

WHAT'S **HAPPENING?** The name of this folder indicates that it contains things that are supposed to be fun activities. The window shows the objects in the FUNSTUFF folder. (If you cannot see all the objects, size or maximize the window.) Each file name has an icon. What are these objects, and how can you identify the programs? Sometimes you can recognize a program by its icon. There are three games—ARGH.EXE, MLSHUT.EXE, and LS.EXE—and three fonts—grunge.ttf, astronbw.ttf, and anticlim.ttf.

You know which icons represent programs because they have the .exe file extension. The extension .exe stands for *executable* code and always indicates a program file. The games listed were written for DOS, but it can still be run under Windows XP Professional . Not all programs written for DOS, Windows 3.1, Windows 9x, or Windows Me will run under Windows XP Professional. Windows 9x means Windows 95 and Windows 98. When purchasing a new program, be sure to look at the program's documentation to verify that it runs in the Windows XP Professional environment. Generally, a program's container will list the compatible operating system(s).

In this window, you also see several files with the .doc extension. Often, programs with a .doc extension explain the rights and rules of the program in question. Read-me.txt files also often explain rights and rules.

5   Double-click **READ_ME.TXT**.

WHAT'S **HAPPENING?** This text document is about the one of the fonts included in this directory. The file automatically opened in Notepad because .TXT is a registered file extension.

6   Close Notepad.

7   On the menu bar, click **Tools**. Click **Folder Options**. Click the **View** tab.

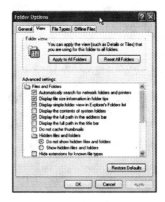

WHAT'S HAPPENING? You have been instructed to clear the check box for Hide file extensions for known file types although the default is set. There is a very good reason for wanting to see the file extensions.

8   Click **Restore Defaults**. Click **Show hidden files and folders** to set it. Click **OK**.

WHAT'S HAPPENING? Now you no longer see the file extensions of .exe, .ttf, .txt, and .doc. These are all registered file extensions. It is common practice for programmers to name files with the same name only differentiating their purpose by the file extension. The only way to recognize a program is by its icon. Sometimes you can recognize and sometimes you cannot. This folder also has three subfolders: BOG2, HANG2, and MATCH32. Each of these folders also contains games. In addition, you are also elected to display any hidden files or folders.

9   Double-click **BOG2**. Click **View**. Click **List**.

WHAT'S HAPPENING? There is one BOG.GID file. If you had not turned on Show all files and folders you would not see the BOG.GID file. You know it is hidden because its icon is gray. In addition there are three BOG files—which is the program?

10 Click **View**. Click **Icons**.

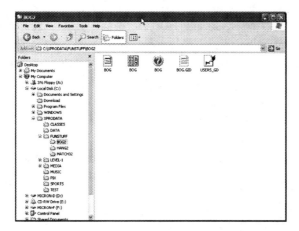

WHAT'S **HAPPENING?** In Icons view, the objects are a little larger and you might guess that the icon, , is the program since it is the most colorful icon.

11 Click **View**. Click **Tiles**.

WHAT'S **HAPPENING?** In Tiles view, you see descriptive information for the listed files. And again, you see the grayed out hidden file. But if you have your file extensions available, it is always easier to know which is a program.

12 On the menu bar, click **Tools**. Click **Folder Options**. Click the **View** tab. Clear the check box for **Hide extensions for known file types**. Click **OK**.

WHAT'S **HAPPENING?** The file with the .HLP extension is the help file for this program. BOG.EXE is the program itself. But what are the other files? Are they candidates for deletion? They are not. The .hlp file and the other nonprogram files are support files. Remember, support files can vary from program to program but are needed to execute a program properly.

13   Double-click **BOG.GID**.

WHAT'S **HAPPENING?** Windows XP Professional does not know what to do with this file. The extension .GID is not registered to a program. Windows XP Professional presents the message box so you may choose how to open this program. If you choose Select the program from a list, you will see the Open With dialog box, which lists all the programs on your system. Windows XP Professional is hoping that you know what program it should open for a .GID file and helps you by providing a list of programs. The .GID file, which is normally hidden, as well as the .DAT file is not a program or a document file. However, the BOG program needs all of these files to execute or run.

14   Click **Cancel**. Double-click **BOG.EXE**. Click **Start Game**.

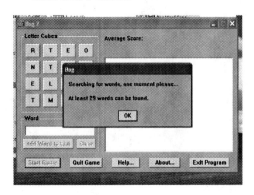

WHAT'S **HAPPENING?** You have opened (executed) the game called BOG, which is a variation on a word search game. BOG is *shareware*, a version of a program that is not distributed through commercial channels, saving the programmer the costs of marketing and distribution. You may try out shareware to see if you like it. If you decide to keep a program and use it, you pay a registration fee to the programmer (or company) that owns it. If you do not like the program or do not use it, you delete the program files from your disk and do not owe anyone anything. As you will see with BOG, an executable program is usually not just a single file, such as BOG.EXE. Programs have support files and BOG has its own support files.

15   Click **OK**.

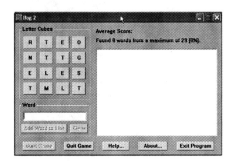

WHAT'S **HAPPENING?** Now you can play the game. If you wanted to know how to play this game, you could click Help. If you had deleted the .hlp file, you would receive no help and if you deleted any of the other support files, you would not be able to play the game at all. Like any executable program (.exe), nearly all programs have a multitude of files to support them. If it were a word-processing program, the support files could include a spelling checker, different fonts, and templates (samples of documents). The support files vary from program to program, but they are critical to being able to use a program.

16   Click **About**.

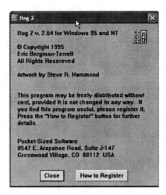

WHAT'S HAPPENING? The author of this program is telling you that this program is shareware and may be distributed freely.

17 Click **How to Register**.

WHAT'S HAPPENING? The author is asking for a $10.00 registration fee if you like his game and want to keep it. He supplies his name and address. If, when you are finished with this class, you would like to keep this game, please send him the fee.

18 Close the Help window. Click **Close**. Click **Exit Program**.

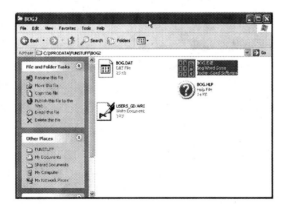

WHAT'S **HAPPENING?** You have returned to the BOG2 window. The address bar tells you the entire path name or location of this folder—C:\XPRODATA\FUNSTUFF\BOG2.

19   Click **Tools**. Click **Folder Options**. Click **Folder Options**. Click the **View** tab. Click **Do not show hidden files and folders** to set it. Click **OK**.

20   Close the open window.

WHAT'S **HAPPENING?** You have returned to the desktop.

7.3 ● Creating a Shortcut and Formatting the Floppy Disk

One of the advantages to Windows XP Professional is the ability to customize the desktop to meet your needs. You have created shortcuts for devices, files, and folders. You can also create shortcuts for programs. When you create a shortcut for a program, you must know where the .exe file is physically located. You must be careful when creating a shortcut for a program; be sure not to move or copy the program by mistake. As you have seen, support files are necessary for executing a program. If you moved a program instead of created a shortcut, you would need to move all the support files, including the hidden ones. These moves would not be reflected in the Registry, possibly causing programs not to run.

In addition, you want to format the floppy disk, MYDATADISK, so it will be blank and ready to accept new data. You are going to be copying files and folders to your floppy disk.

7.4 ● Activity ● Creating a Shortcut for Windows Explorer and Formatting a Disk

1   Click **Start**. Point to **All Programs**. Point to **Accessories**. Right-drag Windows Explorer to the desktop. Release the right mouse button.

WHAT'S **HAPPENING?** When you dragged My Computer off the Start menu, you created a shortcut. Here, your only choice is to move or copy the program to the desktop. You do not want to do this. You can create a shortcut but you must find the .exe program in order to do so.

2   Click **Cancel**.

3   Click **Start**. Point to **All Programs**. Point to **Accessories**. Click Windows Explorer.

4   Click **My Computer**. Click **Drive C**. Scroll down the tree side and locate and click the Windows folder. (Remember, on your system, the Windows folder could have a different name and could be on a different drive.)

5   Click **View**. Click **List**.

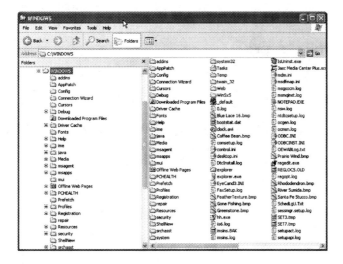

WHAT'S **HAPPENING?** You will be using Windows Explorer a great deal in the next activities. The fastest way to access Windows Explorer is to create a shortcut. In order to do this, you must locate the program file called Explorer.exe. Since this program file is a Windows XP Professional program, it will be located in the Windows folder.

6   Click the contents side of the window. Press the letter **E** on the keyboard.

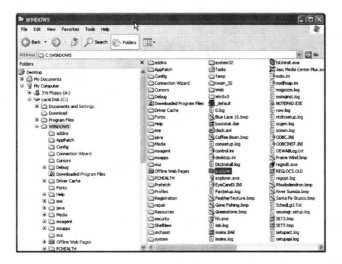

WHAT'S **HAPPENING?** You were taken to the first object that begins with the letter e in the active pane. You want the program, so it must be an .exe file.

7   If you cannot see **Explorer.exe**, scroll until you can. Right-drag the **Explorer.exe** object to the desktop. Release the right mouse button.

WHAT'S **HAPPENING?** You are presented with a shortcut menu that gives you choices. You can move, copy, or create a shortcut. Since program files often have support files that they must access, moving program files to a different location can cause them to malfunction. Copying a program file such as Explorer.exe is also undesirable because having two copies of the program would take up disk space. Creating a shortcut is ideal in this situation. If you were on a different drive, the default choice would be Copy Here.

8   Click **Create Shortcuts Here**.

9   Close all open windows.

10 Double-click **Shortcut to Windows Explorer**. Click **My Computer**. Click **View**. Click **Tiles**.

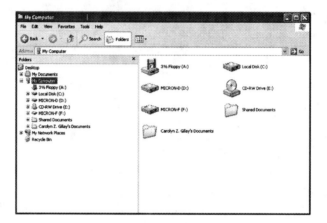

WHAT'S **HAPPENING?** Because you created a shortcut, Windows Explorer is readily available to you.

11 Place your MYDATADISK in Drive A. Right-click **Drive A**. Click **Format**.

WHAT'S **HAPPENING?** Your disk is ready to format. You are going to change the Volume label to MYDATADISK, Because this disk has been previously formatted, you may select Quick Format.

12 Change the label to MYDATADISK. Click **Quick Format** to set it.

WHAT'S **HAPPENING?** You have altered the dialog box.

13 Click **Start**. Click **OK**. The disk formats and you see the following:

WHAT'S **HAPPENING?** You can see how much faster enabling Quick Format is. Your disk is ready and will be used for the remainder of the text.

14 Click **OK**. Close all open windows.

WHAT'S **HAPPENING?** You have returned to the desktop.

15 If you are finished, remove the MYDATADISK from Drive A.

7.5 • Manipulating Files with Windows Explorer

Some of the most common tasks Windows Explorer handles are file management tasks. The ability to see the hierarchical structure of your disk allows you to more easily know what files you are dealing with and where they are. Windows Explorer enables you to copy, rename, delete, or move files and folders, as does My Computer. These are tasks you perform daily. Typically, most of your time is spent manipulating your data files. You are constantly working with your files to maintain control over your hard disk. You want backup copies of your current data files. You want to delete out-of-date files to free space on your hard drive and create new folders as your work changes. Except for backing up files, most of your file management occurs on the hard disk. You will now practice file management on a floppy disk. This activity will allow you to learn how to use the commands and yet preserve the integrity of your hard drive.

7.6 • Activity • Copying Files with Windows Explorer

1 If you removed the MYDATADISK from Drive A, insert it now into Drive A.

2 On the desktop, double-click **Shortcut to Explorer.exe**.

3 Click **My Computer** in the Folders pane. Click the Drive C icon. Click the **XPRODATA** folder. Click **View**. Click **List**.

4 Click the contents side of the pane. Press the [Home] key. Press the **G** key once.

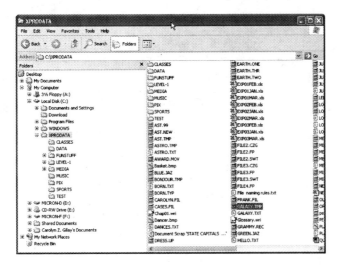

WHAT'S HAPPENING? By making the contents side active and pressing the [Home] key once, you moved to the top of the window. Then, when you pressed the g key, you moved to Galaxy.tmp, the first document that began with the letter g. You might want to copy galaxy.tmp from the hard disk to the floppy disk, either because you are transporting the file from one computer to another or because you want a backup copy of this file.

5   Right-click **Galaxy.tmp**. Point to **Send To**.

WHAT'S HAPPENING? When you select Send To, you are given a list of places to send the file. When you use Send To, you are making a copy of the file.

6   In the Send To menu, click the **3½ Floppy (A:)** icon.

7   When the task has been completed, click the **3½ Floppy (A:)** icon in the **Folders** (left) pane.

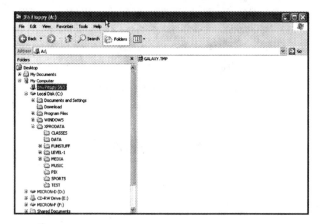

WHAT'S HAPPENING? You can see that the file was successfully copied from C:\XPRODATA to A:\. If you wished to copy more than one file, you might find it tedious to copy the files one at a time. You can copy, delete, or move a group of files at the same time by selecting them. Whether you are in My Computer or Windows Explorer, you select multiple files the same way. You will find some interesting features when you select multiple files.

8   You should be in List view. Click **View**. Click **Status Bar** to set it. On Drive C, click the **XPRODATA** folder in the Folders pane. Click in the contents side. Press the [Home] key.

9   Click the **Ast.new** document. Hold the [Shift] key and click the **Astro.tmp** document.

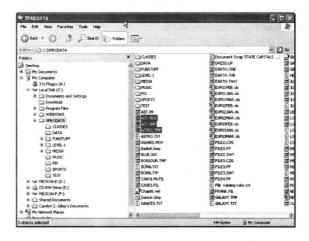

WHAT'S HAPPENING? When you click an object, hold the **Shift** key, and click another object, you are selecting contiguous, or adjacent, objects. The status bar at the bottom of the window tells you that you have three objects selected, for a total of **444** bytes. You may still use the Send To command with a group of objects.

10 Right-click within the highlighted area of the selected files.

WHAT'S HAPPENING? When you click one object, then hold the **Shift** key, and click another object, you select all objects between the first and the second click. Once the objects were selected, right-clicking opened the shortcut menu.

11 Point to **Send To**. Click **3½ Floppy (A:)**.

WHAT'S HAPPENING? As each file is copied, you will see the Copying message box.

12 When the copying is complete, click the **3½ Floppy (A:)** icon in the tree side (left pane).

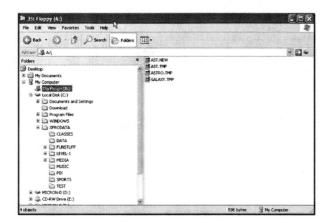

WHAT'S HAPPENING? As you can see, you now have copies of these files on the MYDATADISK. Selecting contiguous files with the **Shift** key is straightforward. There is another technique to select objects. You may *lasso* them. You can use the mouse to draw an imaginary lasso around objects. The lasso appears as a dotted line. You may lasso in any view. You are going to lasso in Icon view.

13   Click the **XPRODATA** folder in the tree (left) pane. Click **View**. Click **Icons**. Size your window to look like the following:

14   Scroll in the contents side (right pane) until you can see both the **AST.TMP** file and the **BONJOUR.TMP** file.

15   Place the mouse pointer just above the **AST.TMP** file, not on the file. Hold down the left mouse button and drag in a downward direction. Drag down and to the right until **AST.TMP** and **BONJOUR.TMP** are selected. Keep holding the mouse button.

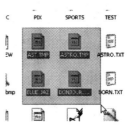

WHAT'S HAPPENING? You see a square box that is an inverse color (highlighted) which is your lasso. The lasso must be rectangular. When you have lassoed the files you want, you release the mouse button.

16   Release the left mouse button.

WHAT'S HAPPENING? You have lassoed these four objects. They are contiguous by column. Once you have selected objects, you can manipulate them—copying, moving, or deleting them or performing other types of file maintenance tasks.

17 Right-click one of the highlighted icons. Point to **Send To**. Click the **3½ Floppy (A:)** icon.

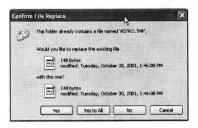

WHAT'S HAPPENING? Windows XP Professional knows that you have a file on Drive A called ASTRO.TMP. When you copy a file from one location to another and the file already exists in the new location, you *overwrite* the existing file. When you overwrite a file, you replace what was there with new information. The old information will no longer exist. Normally, you want to overwrite files because you want to have the most current information in your file. However, because you may not have known that you had a certain file, Windows XP Professional confirms your intentions before it overwrites, preventing you from destroying data accidentally.

You have several command buttons: Yes, Yes to All, No, and Cancel. If you choose Yes, you are giving permission to overwrite only this specific file and will be queried for any other duplicate files. If you choose Yes to All, Windows XP Professional will overwrite any files that have duplicate names. Choosing No will prevent the computer from copying this specific file, but it will continue to copy any files that do not have duplicate names. Cancel allows you to change your mind and copy no files.

18 Click **Yes to All**.

WHAT'S HAPPENING? Your files are being copied and all duplicate files are being overwritten. You may also may select files that are not contiguous by holding the **Ctrl** key when you click a file.

19 Scroll in the windows until you can see both **ASTRO.TXT** and **CAROLYN.FIL**.

20 Click **ASTRO.TXT**. Hold the **Ctrl** key and click **CAROLYN.FIL**.

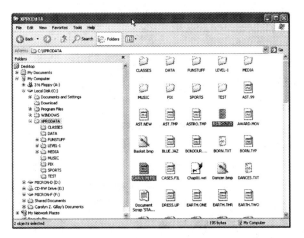

WHAT'S HAPPENING? You have selected two files by clicking them while using the **Ctrl** key. This technique for selecting noncontiguous files will work in all views. After you have selected your files, if you right-click any selected file, you will open a shortcut menu.

21 Right-click **CAROLYN.FIL**. Point at **Send To**. Click the **3½ Floppy (A:)** icon.

22 Click the **3½ Floppy (A:)** icon on the tree side.

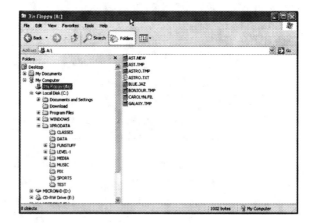

WHAT'S **HAPPENING?** You can see that your files have been copied.

23 Close all open windows.

WHAT'S **HAPPENING?** You have returned to the desktop.

7.7 ● Other Ways to Copy Files

As you can see, you can select files in a variety of ways. There are many ways to copy files as well. You may want to copy many files to the MYDATADISK, perhaps because you are transporting data from a home computer to a computer at work or school. Instead of merely selecting and using the Send To shortcut menu, you want to see both your source (what you are copying) and your destination (the place to which you're copying items). A Drive A shortcut on your desktop is the easiest way to accomplish these goals.

7.8 ● Activity ● More Techniques for Copying Files

Note: The MYDATADISK disk is in Drive A.

1 Click **Start**. Click **My Computer**. Click **View**. Click **Tiles**.

2 In the My Computer window, right-drag the Drive A icon onto the desktop. Release the right mouse button.

WHAT'S **HAPPENING?** The default choice is Create Shortcuts Here. If you chose Copy Here, you would copy all the files on Drive A to the desktop which would be placed in folder called 3½ Floppy (A). Its location would be C:\Documents and Settings\Carolyn Z. Gillay\Desktop\3½ Floppy (A) where Carolyn Z. Gillay would be replaced by your user name. If you chose Move Here, then all the files on Drive A would be removed from Drive A and placed in a folder on the desktop called 3½ Floppy (A). Its location would be C:\Documents and Settings\Carolyn Z. Gillay\Desktop\3½ Floppy (A) where Carolyn Z. Gillay would be replaced by your user name. You simply want a shortcut to Drive A.

3 On the shortcut menu, click **Create Shortcuts Here**. Close the My Computer window.

WHAT'S **HAPPENING?** You have created a shortcut to Drive A.

4 Double-click the **Drive A** shortcut. Double-click the **Windows Explorer** shortcut. In the My Documents window, click **My Computer**. Click **Drive C**. Click **XPRODATA**.

5 Right-click on an empty spot on the taskbar. Click **Tile Windows Horizontally**.

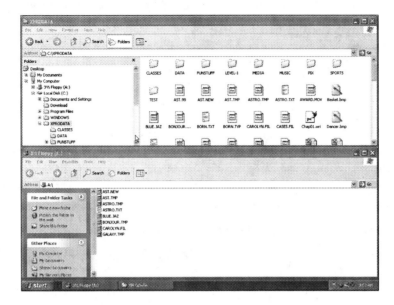

WHAT'S **HAPPENING?** In this example, the Drive A window is open on the bottom with the Windows Explorer window (XPRODATA) open on the top.

6 In the Drive A window, click **View**. Click **Icons**.

7 In the XPRODATA Windows Explorer window in the contents side, select **AWARD.MOV**. Begin to left-drag **AWARD.MOV** to the Drive A window. Keep holding the mouse button.

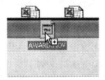

WHAT'S **HAPPENING?** As you drag the file AWARD.MOV out of the XPRODATA Windows Explorer window and into the Drive A window, you see an outline of the document with a plus sign. Whenever you see a plus sign as you drag an object, it indicates that you are doing a copy operation. When you left-drag files across drives (from one drive to another drive), as you are doing now, the default operation is to copy.

8 Drop the **AWARD.MOV** icon into the Drive A window.

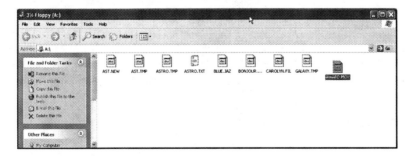

WHAT'S **HAPPENING?** The file from Drive C was copied to Drive A.

9   In the **C:\XPRODATA** window, locate the file called Cases.fil on the contents side of the Windows Explorer window. Left-drag and drop it into the Drive A window.

WHAT'S HAPPENING? You saw the Copying message box as the file was copied. Remember, you are dragging from one drive to another, so the default operation is to copy.

10   Right-drag **Blue.jaz** from the **C:\XPRODATA** Windows Explorer window to the **Drive A** window. Release the right mouse button.

WHAT'S HAPPENING? Whenever you right-drag an object, you will display the shortcut menu. The default choice is highlighted. When you right-drag an object across drives, Copy is the default. The only difference between a right-drag and a left-drag is that the right-drag displays a menu whereas a left-drag simply performs the default operation. In this case, it is a copy.

11   Click **Copy Here**. Click **Yes** in the Confirm File Replace dialog box.

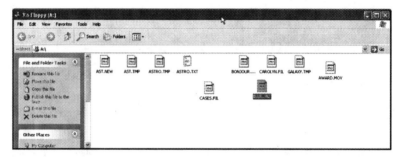

WHAT'S HAPPENING? You have copied BLUE.JAZ from the XPRODATA folder on Drive C to the root of Drive A. You have also overwritten the existing BLUE.JAZ file.

14   In the contents side of the **XPRODATA** Windows Explorer, locate the file called **BORN.TYP** and click it. Locate the file called **Chap01.wri**. Hold the Ctrl key and click it. Locate the file called **DANCES.TXT**. Hold the Ctrl key and click it. Holding the Ctrl key, locate and click the file called **DRESS.UP**.

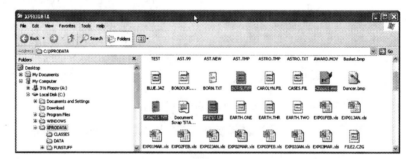

WHAT'S HAPPENING? Remember, when you hold the Ctrl key and click, you can select noncontiguous files. You may deselect a file without canceling your selection by holding the Ctrl key and clicking the selected file.

12   Holding the Ctrl key, click **DRESS.UP**.

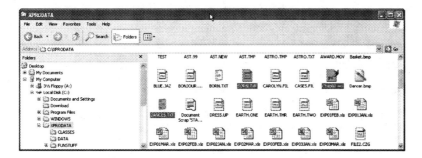

WHAT'S **HAPPENING?** You deselected DRESS.UP without canceling your other choices. You could right-drag or left-drag the selected files to copy them to the floppy disk in Drive A, but there is also another method. You may use the drop-down menus.

13 On the **C:\XPRODATA** menu bar, click **Edit**.

WHAT'S **HAPPENING?** You dropped down the Edit menu. The Undo Copy choice is available. If you wanted to undo the last copy, you could make this selection. If Undo Copy were dimmed, it would be unavailable. If you had cut or copied any items, the Paste and Paste Shortcut choices would be available. If you had neither cut nor copied anything, the Paste and Paste Shortcut choices would be dimmed. Notice that there are keyboard shortcuts next to the menu choices. If you wanted to cut an object, you could select it and then press the **Ctrl** key and the letter X simultaneously. If you wanted to copy an object, you could use the keyboard shortcut the **Ctrl** key plus the letter C. If you wanted to paste a selected object, you could press **Ctrl** and V. You will find these keyboard shortcuts almost universal, not only in Windows XP Professional, but also in the application world. These keyboard shortcuts are especially valuable because, some-times, although you have selected an object or text, there is no Edit menu. However, you can almost always use these keyboard shortcuts. Copy to Folder and Move to Folder are also available. Copy to Folder allows you to copy selected files to a folder. Copy will leave the original files where they were. The Move to Folder will copy the selected files to a folder and delete the files from their original location. The menu also has a Select All choice, which is self-explanatory, but what is the Invert Selection choice?

14 Click **Invert Selection**.

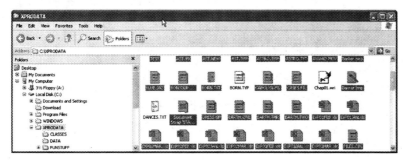

WHAT'S HAPPENING? When you chose Invert Selection, your selection was reversed. Now every object is selected *except* the ones you originally selected. This method is a quick way to select files when there are only a few files you do not want to manipulate. It saves you the trouble of holding the **Ctrl** key and clicking many times.

15 On the menu bar, click **Edit**. Click **Invert Selection**.

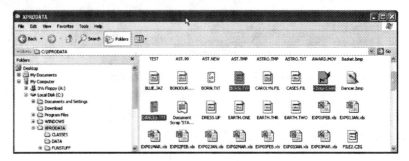

WHAT'S HAPPENING? Now the C:\XPRODATA window show the three files you originally selected.

16 On the **C:\XPRODATA** menu bar, click **Edit**. Click **Copy**.

17 On the 3½ Floppy (A:) menu bar, click **Edit**.

WHAT'S HAPPENING? Undo Copy is available. Both the Paste and Paste Shortcut options are available because you have copied something to the Clipboard. The *Clipboard* is a special memory resource maintained by Windows XP Professional. It stores a copy of the last information that was copied or cut. A paste operation passes data from the Clipboard to the current program. If you selected Paste Shortcut, the actual files would not be copied from Drive C to Drive A. Instead, Drive A would only have a pointer to the files on Drive C. You want to take this floppy disk back and forth between two computers, so having a pointer to Drive C would do you no good. You need copies of the files, not pointers to the files.

18 Click **Paste**. Click **View**. Click **Icons**.

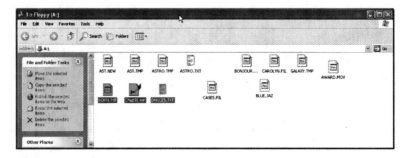

WHAT'S HAPPENING? As each file was copied, you saw the Copy message box. All three files are now on the MYDATA disk.

19 Right-click the taskbar. Click **Undo Tile**.

20 In the 3½ Floppy (A:) window, click **View**. Point to **Arrange Icons by**. Click **Name**. Click **View**. Click **List**.

21 Close all open windows.

WHAT'S HAPPENING? You have returned to the desktop.

7.9 • Folders and Files

You can select files in a variety of ways. You can use these same techniques to select folders. Once a folder is selected, you can copy it, move it, delete it, or use any of the other file manipulation commands. However, be aware that when you manipulate a folder you are also manipulating all the files and subfolders in that folder. For example, if you copy a folder to a different drive or directory (folder), you are recreating the folder and its files in the new location. Likewise, you can select contiguous and noncontiguous folders. You may drag and drop files and folders and use the menu commands to copy and paste. You may also use the Copy to folder and Move to folder commands on the Edit menu. These commands allow you to selective copy files and folders to an existing folder or to a new folder.

7.10 • Activity • Copying Folders and Files

1 Double-click the **Drive A** shortcut. Double-click the **Windows Explorer** shortcut. In the My Document window, click **My Computer**. Click the **Drive C** icon. Click the **XPRODATA** folder.

2 Right-click on an empty spot on the taskbar. Click **Tile Windows Horizontally**.

3 In the **C:\XPRODATA** window, in the tree pane, left-drag the **Level-1** folder and drop it in the **A:** window.

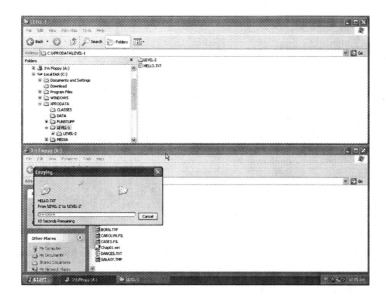

WHAT'S HAPPENING? You left-dragged across drives (copying from one drive to another), so no shortcut menu appeared. Copying occurred as the default operation. As you read the Copying message box, you see that not only folders are being copied, but also files.

4 On the tree side of the **C:\XPRODATA** window, click the **Level-1** icon. Then press the [✱] (asterisk) key on the numeric keypad.

5   In the 3½ Floppy (A:) window, click the **Level-1** folder. In the **A:** window, hold the [Shift] key and double-click the **Level-1** folder.

WHAT'S HAPPENING? Pressing the * (asterisk) key is a keyboard shortcut for expanding a branch of the tree, as you did in the C:\XPRODATA window. If necessary, move the A:\LEVEL-1 window so that you can see the tree structure of the C:\XPRODATA window. You can see that when you dragged the Level-1 folder from XPRODATA on Drive C to Drive A, you recreated the hierarchical structure with folders and files on Drive A. Your Folder Options are set so that, when you open one window, you close the previous window. Sometimes you may want to leave the current window open and open another window. Rather than having to go back to Tools/Folder Options, you can use the keyboard shortcut of holding the [Shift] key when you double-click a folder. This action leaves the previous window open and opens another window.

6   Close the **Level-1** window.

7   In the **C:\XPRODATA\LEVEL-1** window, click the **Level-1** folder icon in the tree (left) pane. Press the [−] (minus) key on the numeric keypad.

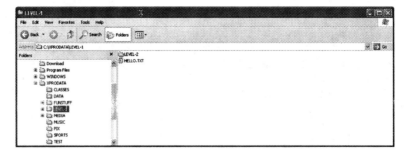

WHAT'S HAPPENING? You used the keyboard shortcut to collapse the Level-1 folder to its highest level.

8   In the tree pane of the **C:\XPRODATA** window, scroll up to the **3½ Floppy (A:)** icon. Click this icon. Click the **Level-1** folder in the tree pane. Press the [*] key on the numeric keypad.

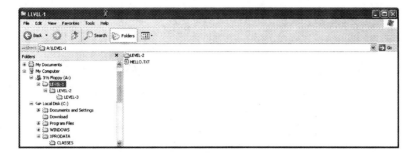

WHAT'S HAPPENING? The A:\LEVEL-1 window indicates that the entire Level-1 folder with its subfolders and files was copied to the disk in Drive A.

9 In the **A:\LEVEL-1** window, click the **Level-1** folder on the tree. Press the ⊟ (minus) key on the numeric keypad.

10 Click **XPRODATA** to select it. Double-click the **DATA** folder in the right pane.

11 Select the files **GOOD.TXT** and **THANK.YOU**. Click **Edit**. Click **Copy**. Click **Edit**.

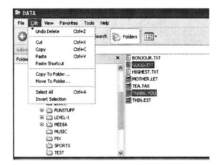

WHAT'S HAPPENING? One of the choices is Copy to Folder. You can take these selected files and copy them to a folder.

12 Click **Copy to Folder....**

WHAT'S HAPPENING? You are asked where you want to copy these files.

16 Click **3 ½ Floppy (A:)**. Click **Make New Folder**.

WHAT'S HAPPENING? You have selected the disk in Drive A. When you clicked Make New Folder, an icon appeared with an empty box. You key in the name of your folder within that empty box.

18 In the New Folder text box, key in the following: **DATA2**. Click outside the box.

WHAT'S HAPPENING? You have created a new folder, DATA2, where you are going to copy these two files. DATA2 on Drive A is selected as your destination folder.

20 Click **Copy**.

22 In the 3½ **Floppy (A:)**, double-click **DATA2**.

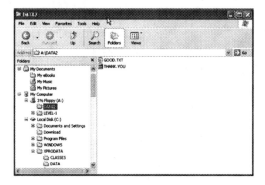

WHAT'S HAPPENING? You have created a folder on the 3½ Floppy (A:) disk called DATA2 and copied two files from the C:\XPRODATA\DATA directory.

24 Right-click the taskbar in an empty spot. Click **Undo Tile**.

25 Close all open windows.

WHAT'S HAPPENING? If you did not click Undo Tile, the next time you opened Windows Explorer or My Computer window, each would retain the current tiling shape. In that case, Windows XP Professional would have "remembered" that each window occupied half the screen the last time the program was accessed. Another way to eliminate the horizontal tiling is to right-click the taskbar and click Cascade.

7.11 • Copying and Moving Folders and Files

When you drag and drop files from one drive to another, the default operation is always Copy. If, however, you are on the same drive and use drag and drop, your default operation becomes Move. Remember, when you copy a file, you are leaving the original where it was and creating a duplicate. A Move operation, on the other hand, removes a file from one location and places it in another. You start with one file and end with one file. When you use the Copy and Paste choices in the Edit menu, you are copying a file. When you use the Cut and Paste choices in the Edit menu, you are moving a file.

As you continue copying and moving files, you must remember that every file in a folder (directory) must have a unique name. If you have two files on Drive A called Myfile.txt, with one located in the Data directory and the other in the root directory, the file names are unique. The real file names are A:\Myfile.txt and A:\Data\Myfile.txt. The paths make these names unique. A path is a drive and then a folder location. Thus, A:\Data is considered the path to the file Myfile.txt. Windows XP Professional allows you to have the same file name in different folders. The folder name, or path to the file, makes it a unique file name. If you tried to copy A:\Data\Myfile.txt to A:\Myfile.txt, Windows XP Professional would give it the name of A:\Copy of Myfile.txt, enforcing the unique file name rule.

7.12 ● Activity ● Copying and Moving Files on the Same Drive

1   Double-click the **Explorer** shortcut on the desktop. Click **My Computer** in the left pane. Click **3½ Floppy (A:)**.

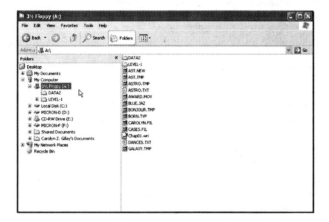

WHAT'S HAPPENING? You have opened 3½ Floppy (A:) window. The title bar displays 3½ Floppy (A:) and the Address bar displays A:\. You have also expanded the tree. One advantage to using the folders view in Windows Explorer or My Computer is that you can see a disk's structure. When you are in Folders view, although the two panes are connected, they are independent. You can view, and thus manipulate, the contents of a folder in the right pane and, without disturbing that view, expand the view in the left pane to find another folder. In Folders view, you can drag a file from the contents pane to the tree pane without having to open multiple windows.

2   Click **View**. Click **Icons**. Click **View**. Set the **Status Bar** on.

3   Click **Tools**. Click **Folder Options**. Click the **View** tab.

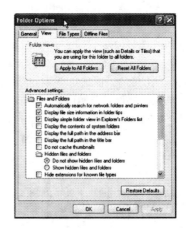

WHAT'S **HAPPENING?** Display the full path in the title bar is not set. That is why you have been seeing only the folder title in the title bar.

4   Click **Display the full path in the title bar**. Click **OK**.

WHAT'S **HAPPENING?** You have changed your view to icons, changed your title bar so it displays the path information, and turned the status bar on. As you can see, your view does not matter in terms of accomplishing work. You choose what works best for you. If your view on your computer screen does not match the textbook, you may change it if you wish. If a specific view is important to an exercise or an activity, you will be instructed to change your view to the appropriate view. Otherwise, you can use whatever view pleases you.

5   Begin to drag **BORN.TYP** from the contents side to the tree side over the **Level-1** folder under the Drive A icon.

WHAT'S HAPPENING? As the file icon passes over the border between the two windows, you see its outline but no symbol. If you dragged the file over the Drive C icon, you would see a plus sign, indicating a copy. The window above shows that if you pause too long over the Level-1 folder or the DATA2 folder before dropping the BORN.TYP icon, it will automatically expand and display the Level-2 subfolder. Since you are over the Drive A icon (not Drive C), you do not see the plus sign, which means that you are moving, not copying.

6   Drop the **BORN.TYP** icon onto the **Level-1** folder under the Drive A icon on the tree side.

WHAT'S HAPPENING? You removed the file from the root of Drive A and placed it in the Level-1 folder. The file BORN.TYP is no longer located in the root of Drive A.

7   Click the **Level-1** folder on the tree side.

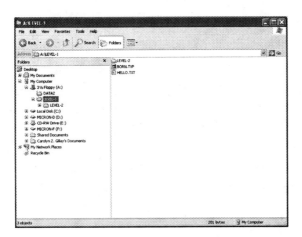

WHAT'S **HAPPENING?** The file is now located only in the Level-1 folder. Its name is now A:\LEVEL-1\BORN.TYP instead of A:\BORN.TYP.

8   On the contents side, right-drag **BORN.TYP** to the **3½ Floppy (A:)** icon on the tree side. Release the right mouse button.

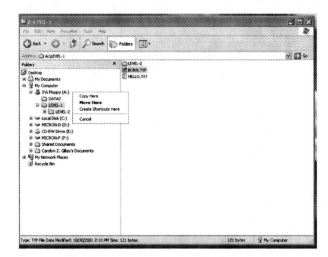

WHAT'S **HAPPENING?** You see a shortcut menu, but now the default choice is Move Here. Since you are on the same drive, when you drag and drop, the default is a move operation.

9   Click **Move Here**.

10   Click the Up button on the toolbar.

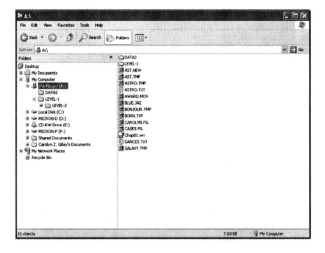

WHAT'S **HAPPENING?** You have moved the file BORN.TYP back to the root directory of A. You may have noticed that the view is in List view. Although you changed the view to icons, and you selected Remember each folder's view settings in Folder Options, the view shifted back to List view. Thus, this program did not behave the way it was supposed to. This is known as a *bug*. Later releases of Windows XP Professional may correct this problem.

11   Left-drag **BORN.TYP** from the contents pane and drop it on the **3½ Floppy (A:)** icon in the tree pane.

WHAT'S HAPPENING? You get an error message. You cannot move a file to the same location with the same name.

12 Click **OK**.

13 Right-drag **BORN.TYP** from the contents pane and drop it on the **3½ Floppy (A:)** icon in the tree pane.

14 On the shortcut menu, click **Copy Here**.

WHAT'S HAPPENING? Using this technique, you were allowed to copy the file, but Windows XP Professional gave it a new name, Copy of BORN.TYP. Remember, files must have unique names if they are in the same drive and folder.

15 In the contents pane, click **BORN.TYP**. Click **Edit**. Click **Copy**.

16 Click **Edit**. Click **Paste**.

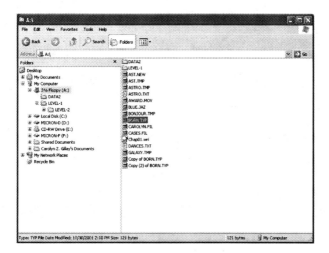

WHAT'S **HAPPENING?** Once again, you were allowed to copy the file BORN.TYP to the same drive and folder, but Windows XP Professional assigned the file a different name, Copy (2) of BORN.TYP. You can never have duplicate file names in the same drive and directory.

17 In the contents pane, right-click **born.typ**. Click **Copy**.

18 Right-click an empty area in the contents pane. Click **Paste**.

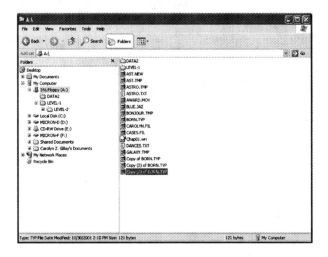

WHAT'S **HAPPENING?** Once again, you were allowed to copy the file BORN.TYP to the same drive and folder, but Windows XP Professional assigned the file another new name, Copy (3) of BORN.TYP. You can never have duplicate file names in the same folder. Using the right-click menus saved you a step. You did not have to click Edit, then Copy.

19 Close the window.

WHAT'S **HAPPENING?** You have returned to the desktop.

7.13 • Making Folders and Other File Management Commands

There are many commands that you can use in Windows Explorer or in My Computer. You have been copying and moving files and folders from one drive to another and on the same drive. Other commands enable you to rename files and folders and create folders so you can store similar files in one location as well as copy or move folders.

When working with your computer, you will work primarily on the hard disk. You are going to learn to accomplish tasks using the floppy disk rather than the hard disk. Since you are in a learning environment, using a floppy disk to learn file management skills will allow you to practice without harming files or folders on your hard disk.

7.14 • Activity • Creating Folders and Copying Files

1 Double-click the shortcut to Explorer. Click **My Computer** in the window. Click the **Drive A** icon on the tree. Click **View**. Click **List**.

2 Right-click an empty area on the contents side. Point to **New**.

WHAT'S HAPPENING? You have opened the submenu for the New command. If you select one of the top two commands, Folder or Shortcut, you can create a new folder or shortcut on the contents side. In this case, the folder or shortcut would be located in the root of A (the default). Below Folder and Shortcut the list of programs will vary, depending on what programs are installed on your system. At the very least, Text Document will appear as a choice. If you choose that option, you will open the application program Notepad. You wish to create a folder to hold files.

3 Click **Folder**.

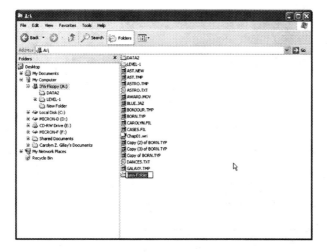

WHAT'S HAPPENING? You see a folder icon with a box around the words New Folder. Here you key in the name of the folder.

4 Key in the following: **TEST** Enter

WHAT'S HAPPENING? You have a new folder called TEST with no files. You now decide that you would like a more descriptive name. You may rename files and folders any time.

5   Right-click the TEST icon. Click Rename.

WHAT'S HAPPENING? The box appears around Test. You can key in your new name.

6   Key in the following: MY TEST FILES [Enter]

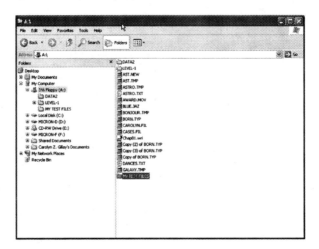

WHAT'S **HAPPENING?** You have renamed your folder. You can rename files just as easily with the same technique. You can also use another method.

7   Click **Award.mov**.

WHAT'S **HAPPENING?** You have selected a file.

8   Click **Award.mov** again. Be sure to click on the file name, not the icon.

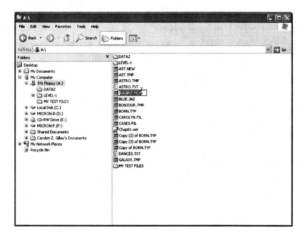

WHAT'S **HAPPENING?** Now Award.mov has a box around it within which you can key in the new file name.

9   Key in the following: **ACADEMY AWARD MOVIES** Enter. Click **Yes** if necessary.

WHAT'S HAPPENING? You renamed a file. You did not include an extension. If .mov was assigned to an application program, you were warned that changing the extension could make it unstable. That is why you clicked Yes.

10 In the contents pane, click on an empty area to deselect the file. Point and rest the mouse pointer on **Academy Award Movies**.

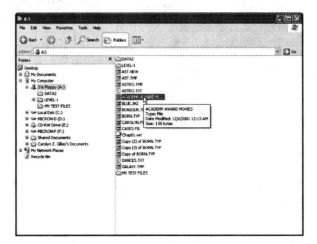

WHAT'S HAPPENING? You renamed your file, and Windows XP Professional maintained your capitalization. However, you cannot see the entire file name unless you rest the mouse pointer on the file. You can also change the view to display the entire file name.

11 Click **View**. Click **Icons**.

12 Click **View**. Point to **Arrange Icons by**. Click **Name**.

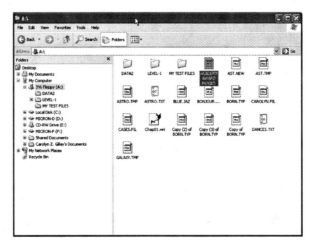

WHAT'S HAPPENING? You can see the entire file name. Windows XP Professional *wrapped* (created additional lines for the text) your file name, making it easier to read. Windows XP Professional in Icons and Tiles views contains an invisible *grid of cells*, and each icon is placed in a cell. The size of the grid depends on the size of the icons, the font size, and the resolution of your monitor. You can snap your icons to the center of the cells by right-clicking and clicking Line Up Icons. This procedure is available in Windows Explorer and My Computer.

13 Click **View**. Click **List**.

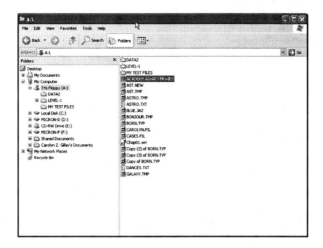

WHAT'S HAPPENING? When you changed to List view, Windows XP Professional adjusted the window so you could see the complete file names.

14 In the tree pane, click the **Drive C** icon and then click the **XPRODATA** folder. Click **FUNSTUFF**.

15 In the contents side, click the **HANG2** folder. Click **Edit**. Click **Copy to** Folder.

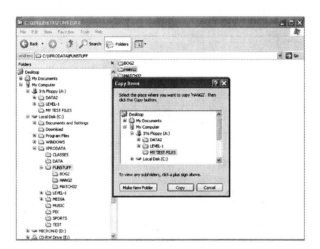

WHAT'S HAPPENING? You have selected a folder, HANG2, with all of its files. You want to copy the folder and the files to the MY TEST FILES folder on Drive A.

16 In the Copy Items dialog box, select **MY TEST FILES** under **3½ Floppy (A:)**. Click **Copy**.

17 After the files are copied, click the 3½ Floppy (A:) icon on the tree side. Expand **MY TEST FILES**. Click **HANG2**.

18 Right-drag and drop **HANGMAN.EXE** to the **3½ Floppy (A:)** icon on the tree side. Release the right mouse button.

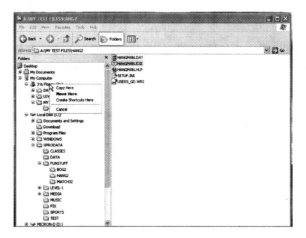

WHAT'S HAPPENING? The default choice is Move Here. Remember, many programs have support files. If you moved just the executable program (the file with .exe), the program would not work because it would not be able to find the support files it needed. HANGMAN.EXE is a shareware program.

19 Click **Create Shortcuts Here**.

20 Click the **3½ Floppy (A:)** icon on the tree side.

WHAT'S **HAPPENING?** You can see your shortcut. You can tell it is a shortcut because it has the bent arrow next to its icon and its file name is Shortcut to HANGMAN.EXE.

21   Click **DANCES.TXT** to select it.

22   Hold the Ctrl key and drag the file across the split bar to **MY TEST FILES** in the tree pane.

WHAT'S **HAPPENING?** Although the default operation for a left-drag on the same drive is Move, when you hold the Ctrl key and left-drag, you are making the default operation Copy. You can tell because you can see a small plus sign next to the cursor, ![cursor].

23   Drop the **DANCES.TXT** file onto the **MY TEST FILES** folder.

24   Open **MY TEST FILES**. Select **DANCES.TXT**. Drag the file to the root of the **MYDATADISK** disk. Click **Yes** in the **Confirm File Replace** dialog box.

WHAT'S **HAPPENING?** You moved the DANCES.TXT file to the root of the MYDATADISK disk and overwrote the existing DANCES.TXT file.

25   Close all open windows.

WHAT'S **HAPPENING?** You have returned to the desktop.

7.15 ● Copying Files to a CD

Since CDs typically hold 600 K of data, so much more than a floppy disk or a Zip disk, they are a preferred choice for backing up data. But in order to be able to do this, you need a CD burner. Today, on most computer system's sold, rather than just a CD-ROM drive, recordable and rewritable compact disk drives are common hardware. These drives allow you to copy files and folders (back up your data), or play or copy music CDs. These drives, in general, are called CD burners. Although DVD-RAM drives are available, they tend to be more costly and less common. Most CD drives sold today are *CD Rewritables (CD-RW)* that can also burn *CD-Recordable (CD-R)* discs. Rewritable discs have the advantage of being able to be erased and thus, reused. However, they may not play in other devices. If your goal is to create music CDs, Windows XP Professional offers a tool in Media Player (Start/All Programs/Accessories/Entertainment). Creating music CDs is beyond the scope of this text. However, if you want to create music CDs, you may open Media Player and use Help to find out how to accomplish this task. Many people opt for third party software, such as Adaptec Easy CD Creator. In fact, many computer manufacturers, such as Dell, include this software when you purchase a computer from them.

But, as you will see, copying files to a CD is not too much different from copying files to a floppy disk. If you do not have a CD burner, you will not be able to do the next activity. You may also not want to do the next activity, since you are going to put very little data on the CD, and chances are you will throw away the CD when you are done. Although blank CDs are fairly inexpensive (about 50 cents per CD), you still may not want to use a CD for this purpose. If this is so, simply read through the next exercise and look at the screen captures, so that if you ever do want to do this, you will know how.

7.16 ● Activity ● Copying Files to a CD

Note: This is an optional activity.

I   Place a CD-R or CD-RW in your CD-ROM drive.

WHAT'S **HAPPENING?** You may see this dialog box if Autoplay is turned on. As you can see, it will open a writable CD.

2   If this dialog box opened, click **Cancel**. Open My Computer. Double-click your CD Drive.

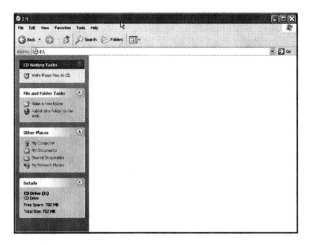

WHAT'S **HAPPENING?** In My Computer, one of the tasks is to write files to a CD. At this moment, you have no files selected. Although you are going to write data files to the CD, music is also simply a file.

3   Close My Computer. Open Windows Explorer. Click **My Computer**. Click **Drive C**. Click the **XPRODATA** folder. Click **View**. Click **List**.

4   In the contents pane, click the **CLASSES** folder. Hold the Shift key and click **DANCER.BMP**.

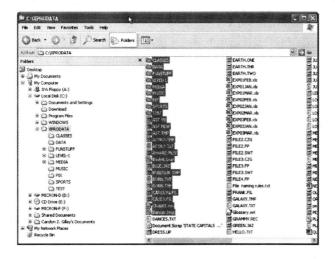

WHAT'S HAPPENING? You have selected the files and folders you are going to copy to the CD.

5   Click **Edit**. Click **Copy**. Click your CD drive. Click in the contents pane of the CD drive. Click **Edit**. Click **Paste**.

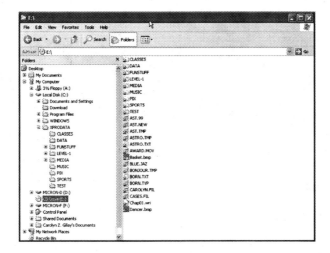

WHAT'S HAPPENING? You have just copied the selected files and folders to your CD. You do need free space on your hard disk to copy files. Windows creates temporary files that are created during the CD writing process. For a standard CD, Windows reserves up to 700 MB of available free space on the drive. If you are using a high-capacity CD, Windows reserves up to 1 GB of free space.

6   Click the **XPRODATA** folder on Drive C. Click **DANCER.BMP**. Then, holding the [Shift] key, click **DRESS.UP**.

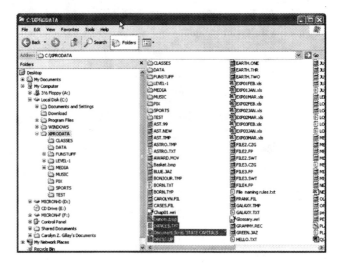

WHAT'S HAPPENING? You have selected more files to copy. DANCER.BMP is already on the CD. Will Windows overwrite it?

7   Right-click the selected files. Click **Send To**. Choose your CD drive.

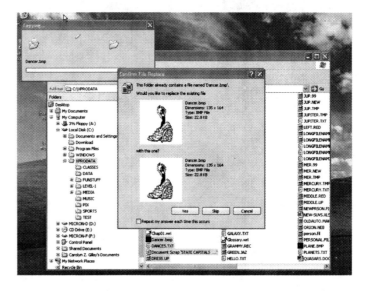

WHAT'S HAPPENING? The CD acts just like the floppy disk. You are asked if you want to overwrite the file on the CD.

8   Click **Yes**.

WHAT'S HAPPENING? Your files are copied. You may also see the following item on your taskbar—that files are waiting to be written to the CD.

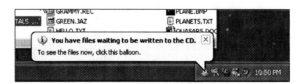

9   Click the balloon.

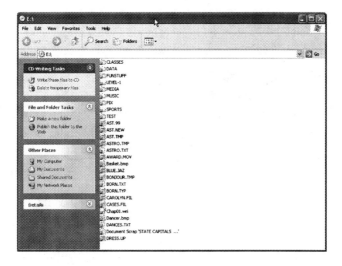

WHAT'S HAPPENING? You are taken to the My Computer window with a list of tasks you can accomplish. One of the tasks is Write these files to CD.

10   Click **Write these files to CD**.

WHAT'S HAPPENING? You are taken to a CD writing wizard. A wizard will lead you through the steps you need to take to accomplish your desired task. You may name your CD.

11   In the **CD Name:** text box, key in the following: **BACKUP**. Click **Next**.

WHAT'S HAPPENING? You see your files being written to the CD. When the wizard is finished writing the files, it ejects the CD automatically and presents the next window.

You could put another blank CD in and write the same file to the CD.

12 Click **Finish**. Close the window.

13 Reinsert the CD.

WHAT'S **HAPPENING?** You see many more choices. Since the files on the CD are only data files, none of the choices are appropriate, except Open folder to view files.

14 Click **Open folder to view files**. Click **OK**.

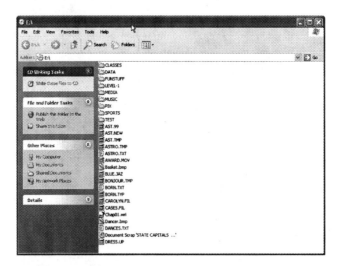

WHAT'S **HAPPENING?** You see your files.

15 Close all open windows.

16 Open My Computer. Right-click your CD drive. Click **Properties**.

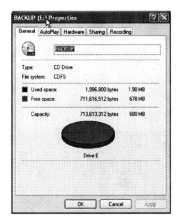

WHAT'S HAPPENING? You have used less than 2 MB on this CD. You will be able to write more files to this disk.

17 Click **Cancel**.

18 Remove the CD from the drive.

19 Close all open windows.

WHAT'S HAPPENING? You have returned to the desktop.

7.17 ● Removing Files and Folders

One of the most important tasks handled by My Computer and Windows Explorer is deleting files and folders you no longer need. Keeping these files on a disk is problematic because you use up valuable disk space and it is more difficult to find the files you want. It becomes time-consuming to search all the files you no longer want along with those you do want.

There is a difference between deleting files on a hard disk and on a floppy disk, removable disk, or network drive. When you delete files on a hard disk, they are not really deleted. They are copied to the Recycle Bin instead, so you can retrieve them in case you change your mind. If the Recycle Bin directory gets too full, Windows XP Professional begins deleting files, with the oldest files first. When you delete a file or folder, most of the time you do want to get rid of it. When you delete files from a floppy disk, removable disk, or network drive, however, they do not get copied to the Recycle Bin. They are deleted, and you cannot recover them except with special utility programs.

You will find that deleting files one at a time is laborious. You have learned previously that using Search from the Start menu is a good way to locate folders that you want to manipulate. In a lab environment, you do not want to delete files from the hard disk. If you are on a network, you may not have deleting privileges. You are going to delete files and folders from the MYDATADISK disk. You cannot delete files from a CD with these techniques.

7.18 ● Activity ● Deleting Files and Folders

1 On the desktop, right-click the **Recycle Bin**. Click **Empty Recycle Bin**. Click **Yes**, if necessary.

2 Open Windows Explorer. Click **My Computer**. Click **3½ Floppy (A:)** on the tree side.

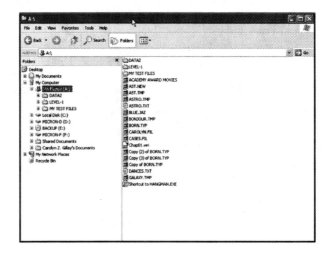

WHAT'S HAPPENING? You are looking at the files and folders on the MYDATADISK disk. You want to see how much available space is on the disk. You could right-click the disk-drive icon on the tree side, but there is a keyboard shortcut to reach the property sheet.

3   Press [Alt] + [Enter].

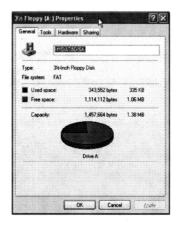

WHAT'S HAPPENING? Whenever an object is selected, pressing [Alt] plus [Enter] will bring up a property sheet. This disk has a large amount of unused space, but assume you need more. You want to delete files and folders you no longer need.

4   Click **Cancel** on the property sheet.

5   Left-drag **Copy of BORN.TYP** and drop it on the Recycle Bin on the desktop.

WHAT'S HAPPENING? You get a dialog box asking you to confirm that you want to delete this file. Notice that the message does not say it will send the file to the Recycle Bin.

6   Click **Yes**. Double-click the Recycle Bin on the desktop.

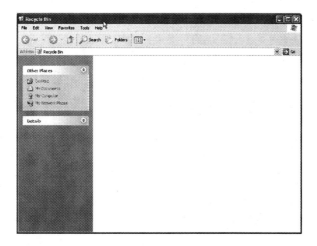

WHAT'S HAPPENING? The Recycle Bin window is empty. The Copy of BORN.TYP file was deleted. It did not go to the Recycle Bin. When you delete a file from any disk other than a hard disk, dragging it to the Recycle Bin on the hard disk does not save a copy of the file.

Total deletion can be advantageous, since files in the Recycle Bin take up disk space. If you know you want to delete a file without sending it to the Recycle Bin, even on your hard drive, you can use a keyboard shortcut. By holding down the **Shift** key while pressing the **Delete** key, you will bypass sending the file to the Recycle Bin. When you delete a file and it does go to the Recycle Bin, you then have to empty the Recycle Bin to delete the file. If you always want files to bypass the Recycle Bin, you can unset the option to Display delete confirmation dialog box in the Recycle Bin property sheet.

7   Close the Recycle Bin window.

8   Click **Copy (2) of BORN.TYP** on the contents side of Windows Explorer.

9   Hold the **Shift** key and press the **Delete** key.

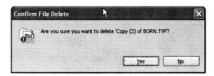

WHAT'S HAPPENING? The Confirm File Delete message appears. Again, it does not say that the file is being sent to the Recycle Bin.

10   Click **Yes**.

WHAT'S HAPPENING? The file is gone. You do not see an additional message box showing the file being copied to the Recycle Bin. Typically, you want to delete many files. Selecting and deleting files one at a time is very labor intensive. You can delete many files simultaneously. A quick way is either to use Search from the Start menu or to use a keyboard shortcut.

11   Press **F3**.

WHAT'S HAPPENING? Pressing **F3** is a keyboard shortcut to switch Explorer bars from Folders to Search in the left pane. Since you are in Drive A, the Look in drop-down list box reflects that. The Look in text box used the default drive and directory.

12   If necessary, click **All files and folders**. In the **All or part of the file name:** text box, key in the following: **Ha*.***

WHAT'S HAPPENING? You are asking Search to locate all the files that have names beginning with Ha and are in Drive A.

13   Click **Search**.

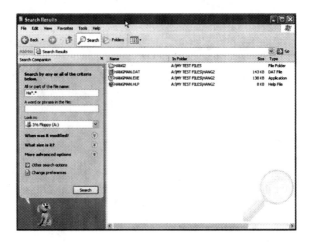

WHAT'S **HAPPENING?** Search has located all the files that begin with Ha in any folder on the MYDATADISK disk.

14 Click the first file. Hold the $\boxed{\text{Shift}}$ key and click the last file.

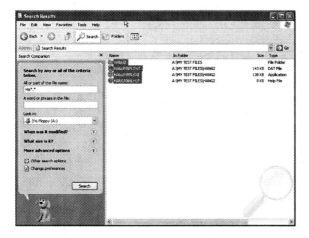

WHAT'S **HAPPENING?** You have selected all the files in the list box.

15 Press the $\boxed{\text{Delete}}$ key.

WHAT'S **HAPPENING?** The Confirm Multiple File Delete message window tells you two items will be deleted.

16 Click **Yes**.

WHAT'S **HAPPENING?** The dialog box cannot find a file it wished to delete because it is a folder.

17 Click **OK**.

18 Click **HANG2**. Right-click it. Click **Delete**. Click **Yes**.

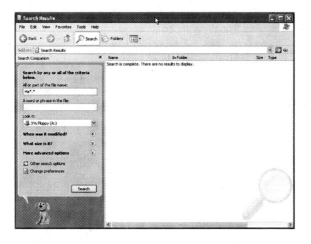

WHAT'S **HAPPENING?** Your files have been deleted.

19 On the toolbar, click the **Folders** button. Scroll to the Drive A icon and click it to select it.

20 Click **MY TEST FILES** on the tree side.

WHAT'S **HAPPENING?** MY TEST FILES is an empty folder. You decide that you want to delete the MY TEST FILES folder. If there were any files or folders in MY TEST FILES, they would also be deleted. When you delete a folder, you delete all the files in it as well as any folders that are beneath it.

21 Right-click **MY TEST FILES** on the tree side. Click **Delete**.

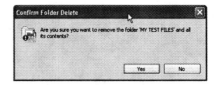

WHAT'S **HAPPENING?** The Confirm Folder Delete message appears, warning you that are about to delete the folder and all its contents.

22 Click **Yes**.

WHAT'S **HAPPENING?** The folder is not going to the Recycle Bin. The MY TEST FILES folder is gone. If it had contained any files or subfolders, they also would be gone.

23 Close all open windows. Remove any disks from any drive.

WHAT'S **HAPPENING?** You have returned to the desktop.

Chapter Summary

In this chapter, you learned that many files comprise a program. Although you launch a program with an executable file, programs also need support files. You can execute a program by locating it and double-clicking the file name.

You found that you can copy and move files across drives and within the same drive by using such techniques as drag and drop, copy and paste, and the Send To option on the shortcut menu. You may also use the Copy to Folder and Move to Folder choices on the Edit menu. You learned that every file must have a unique name. You learned that when you drag a file on the same drive, the default operation is Move, but if you drag a file to a different drive, the default operation is Copy. You can copy files and folders to a CD, if you have a writable CD.

You found that you can create a new folder by right-clicking the desktop and choosing New. You name your folder by keying in its name in the selected box. You may rename a file or folder at any time by using the shortcut menu or selecting the file and keying in the new name. You can eliminate files and folders by pressing the $\boxed{\text{Delete}}$ key, dragging them to the Recycle Bin, or using the shortcut menu. When you delete files on a floppy disk, removable disk, or network drive, they are not kept in the Recycle Bin. You cannot delete a file or folder from a CD.

Key Terms

bug	executable	overwrite
CD-Recordable (CD-R)	grid of cells	shareware
CD Rewritables (CD-RW)	lasso	wrapped
Clipboard		

Discussion Questions

1. Explain the purpose of a support file.
2. List two ways to launch a program.
3. What would be the purpose of creating a desktop shortcut to Windows Explorer? To a drive?
4. What is the purpose and function of file management commands?
5. List three tasks that can be accomplished with file management commands.
6. Describe one way to select contiguous objects and one way to select noncontiguous objects.
7. Explain what it means to lasso objects. How do you lasso objects?
8. What does it mean to overwrite a file?
9. Why would you want to overwrite a file?
10. When would you use the Invert Selection menu choice?
11. Describe two ways that files and folders can be copied.
12. What is the difference between copying and moving a file or folder?
13. Compare and contrast dragging and dropping files from one drive to another and dragging and dropping files on the same drive.
14. When using the Edit menu, compare and contrast Copy and Paste with Cut and Paste.
15. What happens if you try to copy a file to a folder that already contains a file by that name?
16. How can you create a folder?
17. List two ways to rename a file or folder.
18. List two ways to delete a file or folder.
19. If you drag a file from a floppy disk to the Recycle Bin, what happens?
20. Why is it important to be able to delete files and folders?

True/False Questions

For each question, circle the letter T if the statement is true or the letter F if the statement is false.

T   F   1. Support files can be deleted because they take up valuable space.

T   F   2. Moving a file brings about the same results as creating a shortcut.

T   F   3. When you drag a file from one drive to another, the default operation is Copy.

T   F   4. Only contiguous files and folders can be selected at one time.

T   F   5. To bypass sending a file to the Recycle Bin, hold down the [Shift] key when you press the [Delete] key.

Completion Questions

Write the correct answer in each blank space provided.

6. The extension .exe stands for _____ and always indicates that a file is a program file.

7. A trial version of a program that is not distributed through commercial channels is called _____.

8. The default action when dragging an object between folders on the same drive is a(n) _____ operation.

9. If you hold down the left mouse button and drag, you create a square of an inverse color. This is called a(n) _____.

10. Copying over an existing file is called _____.

Multiple Choice Questions

Circle the letter of the correct answer for each question.

11. To create a folder, right-click the desktop and choose
    a. New.
    b. Properties.
    c. Create folder.
    d. Create file.

12. If you drag a file from one drive to another and see a plus sign, you know that
    a. it is a program file.
    b. there is already a copy of this file on the new drive.
    c. this file will be copied.
    d. none of the above

13. To select contiguous files, hold the _____ key when you select the files.
    a. [Ctrl]
    b. [Shift]
    c. [Alt]
    d. [Delete]

14. Is it possible to have a file called First.one in the Apps folder and another file named First.one in the Files folder?
    a. Yes, file names do not have to be unique.
    b. No, files must have unique names, and these names are not unique.
    c. Yes, these files have unique names because of the paths.
    d. No, First.one is not a valid file name.

15. You may move a file to a new location on the same drive in one step without using the shortcut menu by
    a. left-dragging and dropping.
    b. right-dragging and dropping.
    c. clicking Copy and then Paste from the Edit menu.
    d. either a or b

Application Assignments

Problem Set I—At the Computer

Problem A

* Open Windows Explorer. Open the XPRODATA folder on Drive C so you can see the subfolders.
* Change to Icons view.
* Click the Funstuff folder in the tree pane.
* Click the MATCH32 folder in the tree pane.
* Open MATCH32.
* Click **Help** on the menu bar. Click **About Match**.

    1. The author of the program is
        a. Eric Bergman-Terrell.
        b. Steve R. Hammond.
        c. Yuntong Kuo.

    2. The version number is
        a. 1.0.
        b. 1.1.
        c. 2.1.

    3. MATCH32 is a
        a. maze game.
        b. concentration game.
        c. word game.
        d. variation of Solitaire.

* Click **Close** to close About Match. Close MATCH32.
* Click the **BOG2** folder in the tree pane.
* Open BOG.
* Click **About**.

    4. The author of the program is
        a. Eric Bergman-Terrell.
        b. Steve R. Hammond.
        c. Yuntong Kuo.

* Click **Close**.

    5. BOG is a
        a. maze game.
        b. concentration game.
        c. word game.
        d. variation of Solitaire.

* Close BOG.
* Close all open windows.

Problem B

* If you do not have a shortcut to Windows Explorer on the desktop, create it now.

* Double-click the Explorer shortcut. Expand My Computer and Drive C.

* Click the XPRODATA folder on the tree side.

* Click the Funstuff folder on the tree side.

* Change to Icons view.

* On the contents side, you see this icon: READ_ME.TXT

    6. This icon represents a
        a. document file that can be opened by double-clicking.
        b. program that will open with an empty document window.
        c. document that cannot be opened by double-clicking.
        d. program file.

* On the contents side, you see this icon: MLSHUT.EXE

    7. This icon represents a
        a. document file that can be opened by double-clicking.
        b. program that will open with an empty document window.
        c. document that cannot be opened by double-clicking.
        d. program file.

* Change to List view.

* Close Windows Explorer.

Problem C

* Open Windows Explorer.

* Place the MYDATA DISK in Drive A.

* Open My Computer. Open Drive C. Select the XPRODATA folder on the tree side.

* Change to List view.

* Arrange the icons by name in ascending order (A–Z).

* Locate EARTH.ONE on the contents side of the window.

* Click **EARTH.ONE**.

* You wish to select EARTH.TWO and EXP01FEB.XLS along with EARTH.THR.

    8. The quickest way to select all adjacent (contiguous) files is to hold the _____ key when you click EXP01FEB.XLS.
        a. **Shift**
        b. **Ctrl**
        c. **Alt**

* Copy the selected files to the root of the MYDATADISK disk.

    9. You may copy the selected files by
        a. using the Send To command.
        b. dragging the files to a Drive A shortcut.
        c. either a or b
        d. neither a nor b

* Click in the contents side to deselect the files.

❋ Select the files LEFT.RED, MERCURY.TXT, States.txt, STEVEN.FIL, and ZOCIAC.FIL.

10. To select these noncontiguous files, you had to hold the _____ key when you clicked each file.

a. [Shift]

b. [Ctrl]

c. [Alt]

❋ Copy the selected files to the root directory of the MYDATADISK disk.

❋ Select the Media folder and copy it to the MYDATADISK disk.

❋ Select the Sports folder and copy it to the MYDATADISK disk.

❋ Use Windows Explorer to open the Drive A window.

11. Media and Sports appears as _____ icons in the Drive A window.

a. file

b. folder

c. document

❋ Select the Media folder on the tree side of Windows Explorer.

12. Media has _____ subfolder(s).

a. zero

b. one

c. two

d. three

❋ Select the Sports folder on the tree side of Windows Explorer.

13. Sports has _____ subfolder(s).

a. zero

b. one

c. two

d. three

❋ Select 3½ Floppy (A:) in the tree pane of Windows Explorer.

❋ Create a folder in the root of A called Games.

❋ Open another copy of Windows Explorer. Expand My Computer. Click Drive C. Select the XPRODATA folder on Drive C.

❋ Horizontally tile the two open Windows Explorers.

❋ Place both windows in List view.

❋ In the C:\XPRODATA window, click the Funstuff folder (in the tree pane) once to select it.

❋ In the contents pane of C:\XPRODATA\Funstuff window, select HANG2, Mlshut.exe, and Mlshut.doc.

❋ Click **Edit**. Click **Copy**.

❋ Click the A:\ window to make it active.

❋ Click GAMES on the tree side. Click an empty spot on the contents side.

❋ Click **Edit**.

14. Is Paste available to use?

a. yes

b. no

* Copy the selected files into the GAMES folder on the Drive A window.
* Click **3½ Floppy (A)** on the tree side.
* Right-click the contents side of the Drive A window.
* Arrange the icons by type.
    15. What folder appears first?
        a. DATA2
        b. GAMES
        c. LEVEL-1
        d. MEDIA
        e. SPORTS
* Right-click the taskbar.
* Click **Undo Tile**.
* Close all open windows and return to the desktop.

Problem D

* Double-click the Windows Explorer shortcut.
* Open My Computer in Windows Explorer. Select the 3½ Floppy (A:) on the tree side.
* Make the contents side active.
* Use List view.
* Click **View**. Click **Arrange Icons by:** Choose **Name (in ascending order)**.
* Rename the file ZOCIAC.FIL to ZODIAC.FIL.
    16. You may rename a file by
        a. right-clicking it and choosing Rename.
        b. Clicking the file once to select it and then clicking the file name again until the file name text box opens.
        c. both a and b
        d. neither a nor b
* In the root, create a folder called Presentation files.
* Arrange the icons by name.
* Move the MERCURY.TXT file, copied to the MYDATADISK disk in Problem C, to the Presentation files folder without using a shortcut menu.
    17. To move these items without the shortcut menu, you had to
        a. left-drag the items.
        b. right-drag the items.
* Rename the Presentation files folder to Samples.
* In the contents pane, open the Samples folder on the MYDATADISK disk.
* Select the file Mercury.txt. Hold the **Ctrl** key and drag it to the 3½ Floppy (A:) icon on the tree side.
* Before you release the left mouse button, look for any symbols.
    18. Did any symbol appear?
        a. The bent arrow appeared.
        b. The + symbol appeared.
        c. No symbol appeared.

❋ Release the left mouse button while on top of the Drive A icon on the tree side.

   19. The file _____ to the root directory of A.
      a. was copied
      b. was moved
      c. had a shortcut created

❋ Delete the Samples folder.

   20. What is the first message box titled?
      a. Confirm Folder Delete
      b. Confirm File Delete

❋ Delete the Games folder.

   21. Does a Confirm File Delete message box ever appear?
      a. yes
      b. no

❋ Click Yes or Yes to All in any dialog box.

❋ Open the Recycle Bin.

   22. Is the GAMES folder, MLSHUT.DOC, and MLSHUT available to you in the Recycle Bin window?
      a. Yes
      b. No

❋ Open the Sports folder created on the MYDATADISK disk in Problem C.

❋ Double-click the Foot-col.tms file icon.

   23. In the dialog box, the first line states:
      a. Windows cannot open this file.
      b. Windows cannot open the Foot-col.tms file.
      c. No dialog box opened.

❋ If any dialog box opened, click **Cancel**.

❋ Change the name of Foot-col.tms to College football teams.txt.

❋ Double-click the College football teams.txt file.

   24. What is the nickname of the Michigan team?
      a. Bruins
      b. Tigers
      c. Wolverines

❋ Close all open windows.

❋ Remove the MYDATADISK from Drive A.

Problem Set II—Brief Essay

For all essay questions, use Notepad or WordPad to create your answer. Include your name and cloass information as well as the problem number you are answering. Then print your answer.

   1. Compare and contrast moving and copying files and folders. Explain when you would choose to copy files and folders and when you would choose to move files and folders.

   2. *Deleting files and folders can have serious consequences.* Agree or disagree with this statement, and explain your answer. In addition, describe the differences, if any, between deleting files and folders from a hard disk and from a floppy disk.

Problem Set III—Scenario

You see the following display:

You do not want any files in the Biz directory, just folders. Describe what folders you would create or rename. Explain your rationale. Are there any files that you feel you could delete? Explain your rationale. Describe the steps you would take to create, move, copy, or delete any files or folders.

CHAPTER 8

Organizing and Managing Your Disk

You do not purchase a computer exclusively to use Windows XP Professional. You purchase a computer to help you do work more efficiently. Computer work is comprised of two aspects—the application programs that perform the work and the data files that you create to store your information. As you work with a computer, you accumulate many programs and data files. If you are going to be an efficient user, you must have a way to manage those files. An operating system such as Windows XP Professional helps you manage them. You have already used several tools to help you locate files and folders such as Windows Explorer, My Computer, and Search.

As you have learned, folders allow you to group files together in a logical manner. The root directory, created when a disk is formatted, is limited in the number of entries it can contain. Although the number of possible entries is increased significantly if you are using FAT32 or NTFS, there is a limit. Folders that are created can contain any number of entries, limited only by the available disk space. You may add, delete, or rename folders as your needs change. These actions help you manage a large number of files efficiently, but it is best if you have an organizational scheme when manipulating files and folders.

In this chapter, you will learn common pitfalls you should avoid when organizing your disk. You will continue to work with Windows Explorer and My Computer. You will also learn several ways to customize the Start menu as well as see what programs are running with Task Manager. In addition, you will find that you may add, alter, and remove desktop toolbars based on the work you do.

Learning Objectives

1. Explain how Windows XP Professional can be used to manage program and data files.
2. Explain the importance of having an organizational scheme for a disk.
3. List and explain criteria that should be considered when organizing a hard disk.
4. Explain how to customize the Taskbar and Start menu.
5. Explain the purpose and function of toolbars.
6. Explain the purpose and function of Task Manager.

Student Outcomes

1. Copy and move data and program files and create folders for files.
2. Use Windows Explorer to organize the MYDATADISK disk.
3. Change Start menu settings to customize your Start menu.
4. Add a toolbar to the desktop.
5. Create a new toolbar.
6. Use Task Manager.

8.1 • Getting Organized

You will accumulate many programs, and with each program you usually generate many data files. What you have is an information explosion. Organization of information is a constant process in the world; whether in a library or an office, items need to be organized so that information can be found. People have been managing paper files and folders with many office-related tools such as file cabinets, folders, and other organizational labels. However, managing files and folders on a computer system is a much neglected topic of discussion. No one would think of taking paper files and folders and throwing them into a room, yet that is exactly what happens with a computer system. People "throw" their files and folders on the computer system with no thought of organization or the ability to retrieve the information they need. You need to manage these programs and data files so that you can not only locate what you need but also be able to identify what is located.

Imagine you own 10 books. Reading each cover, you can quickly peruse the authors and titles to locate the book you wish to read. Suppose your library grows and you now have 100 books. You do not want to have to read each author and title looking for a specific book, so you classify your books. A common classification scheme is to arrange the books alphabetically by the author's last name. If you want a book by Gillay, you quickly go to G. You may have more than one book by an author whose name begins with G, but by going to the letter G, you narrow your search. By reading the title, you have some idea of the contents of the book.

Now, imagine you have 10,000 books. Organizing them alphabetically by author is not good enough. You may have 200 books by authors whose last names begin with G, so you further classify your books. You first divide them into categories like Computer and Fiction. Then, within each category, you arrange them alphabetically by the author's last name. If you want a computer book by Gillay, you first go to the Computer section, then to the letter G. If you want a novel by Grafton, you first go to the Fiction section and then to the letter G. As you can see, you are classifying and categorizing information so that you can find what you want quickly.

You want to organize files in the same manner. Remember, you have many program and data files. You want to be able to locate them quickly. Grouping files logically is the best way to organize. With Windows XP Professional, you create folders (subdirectories) for storing related files. In addition, you want to name your files and folders in some meaningful way so that you can identify what is in each.

8.2 ◦ Organizing a Hard Disk

When Windows XP Professional is installed, certain folders are created. These include at the very least My Documents, with its subfolders of My eBooks, My Music, and My Pictures, and sometimes My Videos, Documents and Settings, Program Files, and Windows (or WINNT). Each of these folders holds other folders and files. Windows is used for the operating system files; Program Files is used for different programs you may install, as well as programs included with Windows such as Outlook Express. Documents and Settings is used to hold your preferences for your system. My Documents is the default folder for data files with specifically named folders for types of documents, e.g., My Pictures. As you can see, if you have nothing on your computer but Windows XP Professional, there is an organizational scheme using folders to hold significant files needed for the operating system and the utility programs that come with Windows. There are also critical files and folders placed in the root directory that Windows needs to boot the system. These files and folders are normally hidden from view.

Obviously, you did not purchase a computer to have only an operating system to use. You purchase programs that you will use in your work. People often purchase or receive with their computer purchases some kind of integrated program that provides tools for the most common types of work. Integrated programs, sometimes called suites, usually include a program for word processing, a spreadsheet program, a database program, some kind of presentation software, and other related tools.

The two most popular choices are Microsoft Office (which includes Word, Excel, Access, PowerPoint, and other office-related programs) or WordPerfect Office (which includes WordPerfect, QuattroPro, Paradox, Corel Presentations, and other office-related programs). Sometimes, people choose individual programs rather than a suite, particularly if they do not need all the programs in the suite. For instance, you might choose to use Word as your word-processing program but Lotus 1-2-3 as your spreadsheet program. Other critical programs that users should absolutely purchase or download include virus-checking programs such as Norton AntiVirus or McAfee VirusScan and a file compression utility such as WinZip. After these programs, you will purchase programs that meet your needs—graphics, games, Web-related software, financial management software, etc. The list is endless as to the kinds of tools (software) you will want to have on your computer.

When you purchase these additional programs for your computer system, you must install them on your hard disk in order to use them. In general, most people use the installation program that comes with their new program. In general, most programs today come on a CD. The CD will have an installation program, usually with a file with a name like SETUP or INSTALL. You may double-click that file name to start the installation process. Often, when you insert the CD into the CD-ROM drive, the program will automatically ask you if you want to install it.

An installation program creates a folder or folders for the application program you are installing and then copies the files from the CD-ROM (or floppy disks) to the named folders. Many of these application programs have such huge files that, when they are placed on the disk by the manufacturer, the files are compressed. In the process of copying the files to the named subdirectory, the setup or install programs must first decompress those program files. As part of the installation, these programs may or may not create a directory for data. If not, your data files may, by default, end up being saved to the directory that holds the application program files or to the My Documents folder. In addition, the installation program will usually make entries in the Windows Registry that accomplish such tasks as adding the program name to your menus, registering file extensions, and so forth. However, if you do not tell the installation program where you want the files and folders located, the program will decide what the folders are called and where the files and folders are to be located. Many programs, including Microsoft programs, will install their program folders under the Program Files folder. Other programs will install the program folders and files to the root directory.

If you do not control how programs are installed, when you use Windows Explorer or My Computer to view your files and folders, the file and folder names in the root directory or in the Program Files folder seem endless. Furthermore, in many cases, you will look at a folder name and have no idea if it contains a program you use. If you look inside the folder, you also will have no idea if the files in it are your data files or program files. You do not know what you can safely delete or what you should back up. To further complicate the organization of your hard drive, the installation of programs is only the beginning. You will be creating data files and the location of those data files will be critical to you and your work. If you do not have some organizational scheme, you will spend your time looking for data files instead of working with them.

The use of long file names on floppy disks, which are sometimes used for backing up files from the hard disk, can be a problem. Remember, floppy disks always use FAT. Thus, if you are using a 1.44-MB floppy disk, the root directory table is limited to 224 entries. Disks were originally designed to hold files that complied to the old 8.3 naming convention. Even if the files are very small (not much data in them) and there is still ample room in the data sectors for new information, once the directory table is filled you can no longer place more files on the disk. Once the root directory table is full, as far as the operating system is concerned, the disk is full, regardless of how much actual space remains on the disk. On the hard disk, you do not have this problem unless you are using FAT16 as your file system. In that case, the root directory table on your hard disk has a limit of 512 entries. If every folder or file was located in the root directory, you would ultimately get a message that the disk was full. The root directory table would be what was actually full, not the disk, but you would still not be able to place anything else on the disk. However, today, most hard disks use either FAT32 or NTFS. If you are using FAT32 as your file system, your root directory table on the hard disk has a capacity of 65,535 entries. Although this number may seem sufficient, it is still not a good idea to place all your folders and data and program files in the root directory. Just think of scrolling through 65,535 entries to find a file of interest. Although the NTFS file system does not have these limitations, organization of a disk is still a concern for ease in locating files and folders. You still do not want to be scrolling through the root directory looking for files and folders.

Most programs written for the Windows environment install themselves to the C:\Program Files subdirectory. As you can imagine, this directory fills rapidly. Other setup programs handle it differently. For example, when you install a program like WordPerfect using the setup program, a subdirectory is created called C:\Corel, and all products written by Corel are installed in that same directory. Most setup programs allow you to change the directory you wish to install in. If you have a second drive or partition with extra space on it, you may want to install your software to a subdirectory of your own choosing. Perhaps you have three drawing and graphics programs, PCDraw, PCPaint, and Paint Shop Pro. You might want to create a subdirectory called DRAW, and then install the programs in C:\DRAW\PCDraw,

C:\DRAW\PCPaint, and C:\DRAW\PSP, respectively. In this way, all your drawing programs would be in one location.

There can be, however, one disadvantage to choosing your own installation location. If you have technical problems with an installed program and need to call that company's tech support, the person you speak to will undoubtedly expect the software to be installed to the setup program's default directory. If you have installed it somewhere else, the support person may have difficulty helping you.

You probably have more than one program on your computer system. The programs may have come with the computer when you purchased it, or you may have purchased additional programs. For instance, you might have a word-processing program (Word), a spreadsheet program (Lotus 1-2-3), a database program (Access), a checkbook-management program (Quicken 2000), a program that creates greeting cards (Greeting Card Maker) a virus-checking program (McAfee VirusScan), a file compression program (WinZip), and your operating system (Windows XP Professional). Figure 8.1 shows what your hard disk might look like.

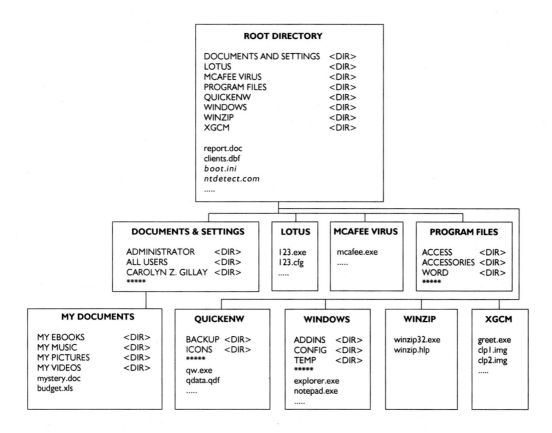

Figure 8.1 ◦ A Typical Hard Disk Organization

In the figure, the names in uppercase letters are folders and ***** represents additional folders. The names in lowercase letters are files and ..... represents additional files. Items in italics are hidden items. The installation programs create folders for each application and place the program and support files in the named subdirectory. As you can see, sometimes you can recognize what program the folder contains (LOTUS); other times, you have no idea what the program is by the folder name (XGCM—Greeting Card Maker). It is also difficult to differentiate between support files that the program uses and data files that you created. There is also the critical question of what the data files are called and where they are kept.

Some programs automatically create a separate folder for data files. Others, by default, save data files to the program's subdirectory. Others use the My Documents folder created by Windows as the location to save data files. Every data file from most Microsoft programs such as Word or Excel will, by default, be saved to the **My Documents** folder. Microsoft is telling users that the root directory is no place to save files; but a folder called **My Documents** that holds *all* your data files is also problematic. Even Microsoft knows this and added folders called My eBooks, My Pictures, My Pictures, and perhaps My Videos to categorize and classify your data files.

Using the **My Documents** folder for all of your data files is the equivalent of storing all of your paper documents in a filing cabinet folder called **Miscellaneous**. When you wanted to locate a document, you would have to go through all of your files, hardly an efficient organizational scheme. The same is true if you use one of the subfolders, such as My Pictures. This is the equivalent of taking all of your photographs and throwing them into a shoebox. The pictures are all in one place, but how are you going to find the one picture you want to look at without having to go through every picture in the shoebox?

The point is, you want to use programs to do work. As an example, say you are a salesperson selling widgets and bangles. You use Word to write letters to clients and make proposals, Lotus to do budget projections, Quicken to manage expenses, Access to manage client names and addresses in a database, Greeting Card Maker to create cards for your clients, and Windows XP Professional to manage your files and disks. In addition, you have other programs to help you manage and protect your system (McAfee Virus Scan and WinZip). Each data file you create needs to be named and saved. You will end up creating hundreds if not thousands of data files. You understand that you do not want data files such as **report.doc** and **clients.mdb** in the root directory, nor do you want all of your data files in the **My Documents** folder. Thus, the question becomes where are you going to place the data files?

First and foremost, you do not want to save your data files to the program folders. Placing data files in the program folders is not a good organizational technique for several reasons. Program files do not change, while data files change as often as you add or delete information. You also add and delete files. You will want to back up your data files from the hard disk to a floppy disk, a tape, a CD, or a Zip drive to ensure you do not lose your data. If you have placed your data files in the program folders, you will have to sort through many program and support files to back up your data and identify which is a program file and which is a data file. Furthermore, part of the rationale for folders is to categorize information; data files are information.

Part of a good organizational scheme is creating meaningful names for your data files so you can identify at a later date what they contain without having to open each file. Naming data files requires more thought than most beginning users realize. Having a *naming convention*, a scheme for naming your files, helps you determine what is in files. It also requires knowledge of how your application programs work. In the next example, the programs you are using are Word and PowerPoint. You need to know that Word automatically assigns the file extension of .doc to each file you create in Word, and PowerPoint assigns the file extension of .ppt to each file you create in PowerPoint. With that knowledge, you now can name your files. For instance, if you were writing a book on Windows XP Professional, your naming convention could be to preface every file name with a code to indicate that it had to do with that book. Thus, your file names could be **wxpch01.doc** (Windows XP Professional Chapter 1 document) and **wxpch02.doc** for the chapter documents and **wxpch01.ppt** (Windows XP Professional Chapter 1 PowerPoint presentation) and **wxpch02.ppt** for your presentations and **wxppub1.doc** (Windows XP Professional publisher document 1) and **wxppub2.doc** for your correspondence with your publisher. With this convention, it would be easy to locate all your files that dealt with the book or only the files that dealt with your correspondence to your publisher.

Because Windows XP Professional allows up to 255 characters for a file name, it might seem easy to create meaningful names. In fact, you might ask why not call the document **Windows XP Professional Chapter 1.doc** rather than wxpch01.doc? Certainly reading the file's name will tell you what is in it and what program created it (Word because of the .doc file extension). However, the availability of long file names can actually be problematic, and not only because of the limitations of the root directory table. Certainly, if you are using older programs, you must still use the 8.3 file-naming rule. Windows XP Professional creates an MS-DOS alias for a long file name which is a truncated version of the long file name. Thus, Windows XP Professional Chapter 1.doc will have an MS-DOS name of window~01.doc and Windows XP Professional Chapter 2.doc would have an MS-DOS name of window~02.doc. Although, when using long file names, it is helpful to know the 8.3 file name, it is not too critical today as most people will have programs written for the Windows world that do support long file names. But there are other reasons for using an 8.3 name. Some utility programs will not work with long file names. *Utility programs* include such types of programs as virus-scanning programs and disk-repair utilities. Many of these types of programs cannot work with long file names. A strong recommendation is also to not use spaces in file names, although Windows XP Professional allows you to do so. There are two primary reasons for this. Again, you will find that sometimes utility programs, the Internet, and even Windows XP Professional itself do not like spaces in file names, even though spaces are allowed characters. A program could "choke" (not work) if it finds a file name with spaces. But more importantly, as a user, it is difficult to remember whether or not you placed spaces in a file name and where you placed the spaces. My new file.doc, mynew file.doc, and mynewfile.doc are all considered unique file names by Windows XP Professional. If you never use spaces, you never have to remember where and what spaces you used. For this reason, another recommendation is always to use lowercase letters.

Long file names can pose a problem in Windows XP Professional. Although a file name can be up to 255 characters in length, the full file name also includes the path name. Remember that the folder name is part of the file name so that a file called BOG.EXE's full name is C:\XPRODATA\FUNSTUFF\BOG\BOG.EXE. Another consideration is that file names that are too long make browsing a list of files in Windows Explorer very difficult. If you have any older application programs, you will be able to give the documents long file names only in Windows Explorer or My Computer. The application program will not let you save a long file name. However, even if you only use Windows XP Professional programs that allow long file names, there is still a problem. You are the user who is going to key in the file name. The more characters you have to key in, the more likely it is that you are going to make a typographical error. It is also difficult to remember your naming strategy when you use very long file names.

An added difficulty in creating meaningful names is that you often have similar file names. As an example, if you were a salesperson who sold two products, widgets and bangles, you would want to name your files by the product. You could track your clients for the bangles product line in a database and save the information in a file called **Clients for the Bangles product line.mdb**. When you created a client list for the widgets product line, you could call it **Clients for the Widgets product line.mdb**. These file names, although consistent with a naming convention, are long and unwieldy. You could instead call one **Bclients.mdb** and the other **Wclients.mdb**. Both of these names clearly state what data is in the files and are also easy to remember and to key in. An even more efficient way to distinguish one file from the other would be to create two folders, **Bangles** and **Widgets**, and to place each client file in the appropriate folder. Both files could be called **Clients.mdb**. Figure 8.2 shows a hard disk organizational scheme for programs with folders for data.

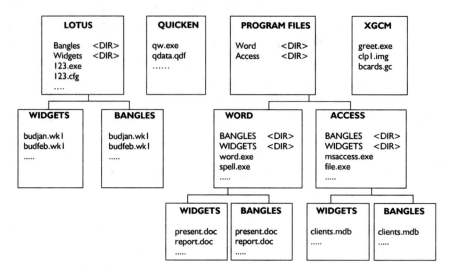

Figure 8.2 ◦ A Sample Organizational Scheme

Although this organizational scheme is better than placing the data files in the root directory, in the program folders, or in the **My Documents** folder, it is still very inefficient. There are too many repeated folder names. In addition, every time you wanted to use a data file, you would have to remember what application was used to create the file and where the appropriate data file was located. You would have to key in long path names such as C:\Program Files\Word\Widgets\Report.doc and have to remember if there were spaces in the name.

You can use data files in conjunction with different programs. For instance, you could use the **clients.mdb** file in Access to generate a mailing list and in Word to send out a form letter. When you begin doing this, you end up with data in two places: the word-processing folder and the database folder. If you purchased a new program, you would need to add a new folder for that program and further folders for your products, bangles and widgets. What if you picked up a new product line, such as beads? Then you would have to create a **Beads** folder under each application program folder. Finding out where files are located and deciding what data files to keep would be a logistical nightmare.

The real problem with this typical organizational scheme is the logic behind it. Remember, programs are tools. When using tools such as a pencil, calculator, or typewriter, would you file documents according to the name of the tool you used? If you wrote a letter using a typewriter, would you file it in a folder labeled **Typewriter**? Of course not, but in the above organizational scheme, that is exactly what was done.

It makes much more sense to organize a hard disk by the way you work rather than by the application package (the tool). An efficient organizational scheme makes it easier to save, locate, back up, add, and delete data files, as well as to add and delete program files. The following section will recommend some guidelines to assist you in organizing your hard disk. You must keep in mind, however, that what is a good organizational scheme for one user may not work for another.

8.3 ◈ Methods of Organizing a Hard Disk

The following guidelines can give a hard disk an efficient and logical organization:

◈ The root directory should be a map to the rest of the disk. Look at the root directory as the index or table of contents of your entire hard disk. Ideally, when you open Windows Explorer and expand My Computer, then Drive C, you should be able to see all the folders and files in the root of Drive C without scrolling.

◈ Plan the organization of your hard disk.

◈ Create as many folders and subfolders as you need before copying files into folders and subfolders.

◈ Keep folder names short but descriptive. Stay away from vague folder names such as Data, Misc, My Files, or My Documents.

◈ Avoid placing data files in the folder with program files.

◈ Create folders that are shallow and wide instead of compact and deep. You should have several folders branching from the root directory, rather than one folder, with a subfolder beneath it, and another subfolder beneath that, and so on. Shallow and wide makes it easier to find files. If you create folders that are compact and deep, you will have files buried several levels down. See Figure 8.3.

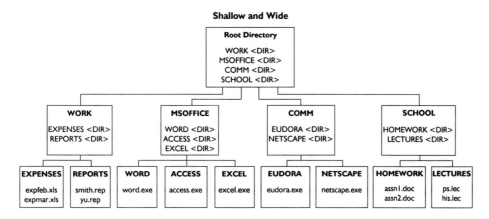

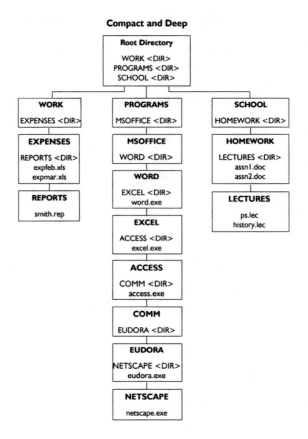

Figure 8.3 • Shallow and Wide Versus Compact and Deep

* Many small folders with a few files in each are better than a large folder with many files. If you begin to get too many files in a folder, think about breaking the folder into two or more subfolders. On the other hand, if a folder has only one or two files, think about combining it with another folder. Again, use the rule of thumb that if you cannot see all your files in a folder without scrolling, then you probably have too many files in that folder.

* There is no risk in creating or deleting folders for data files. Nor is there any risk in moving, copying, or deleting data files. However, if your application software has already been installed on your computer for you, you *cannot* and *must not* rename or move program files or any program support files. If you do either, the program will not work!

* When you are installing new software or you have a new hard disk, create a separate folder containing all the application software you will be using. This program subdirectory will be a map to all the software programs on the disk. Windows XP Professional encourages this plan with a folder called Program Files. When you install software designed for Windows XP Professional, a subdirectory is created under Program Files by default. For instance, if you installed a program like Paint Shop Pro, it would install its files to C:\Program Files\Paint Shop Pro unless you specified another directory.

* Before you install a program, read the installation directions. See where it will place the folder and files. Most installation programs today allow you to choose where you want a program installed and what you want the folder called. For instance, if you were using Paint Shop Pro, version 7, you might want to call the program folder PSP7 instead of Paint Shop Pro. Or if you were using a greeting card program that installed its program files in a folder called XGM, you might want to call it CARDMAKER, allowing you to easily identify what the program does.

* Before you install applications, think about how you might group them. For instance, rather than having all of your application software installed under the Program Files folder, it can make sense to group them by program type. If, for instance, you have several application packages that deal with communications such as Eudora (an email program), Netscape (a browser and mail program), Acrobat Reader (a program that allows you to view, navigate, and print files in the PDF file format—a universal file format used on the Internet), WS_FTP (a file-transfer program), and CuteFTP (another file-transfer program), creating a subdirectory called Communications with a folder for each program will help you identify your software. If you installed WS_FTP under the Program Files folder, you could conceivably not remember its purpose, but if you installed it under the Communications folder, you would at least know that it has something to do with communications. Again, remember that if you choose another location than Program Files, you could have problems getting advice from technical support.

* Learn how to use the application package and how the application package works. Know what file extensions are assigned for the data files you create.

* Develop a naming convention for files and folders. It should be easy to follow so that when you create new files or folders, you can logically name them to fit your convention and when you look at a file name, you will know approximately what data is in it.

* Analyze the way you work. If you always use a program's default data directory when you save and retrieve files, then you might want to create data directories under the My Documents folder. Figure 8.4 shows another way to organize your hard disk. The advantage to this scheme is that many programs when you open or save files will default to the My Documents folder. This way you have the folders that you need in the default directory.

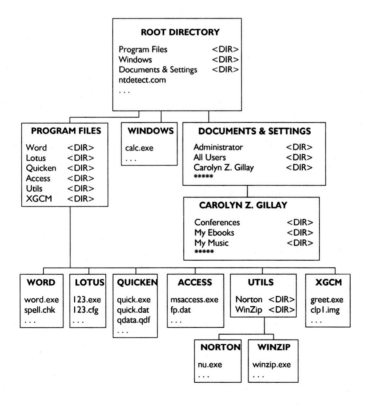

*Figure 8.4 * Another Organizational Scheme*

* Analyze your environment. If, for instance, you are in an educational environment, organizing your disk by application package is logical.
* A scheme organized by project and based on the salesperson scenario could look something like Figure 8.5.

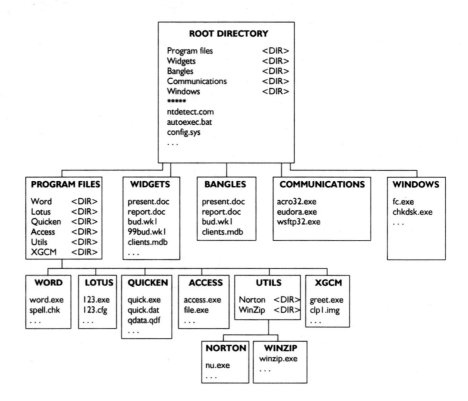

Figure 8.5 ∗ Organization by Project

This organizational scheme has many advantages. You know where all your software applications are located. In addition, it is much easier to add a new software package or to update an existing software package because all the program files are located in one place. For instance, if you wanted to add a Web authoring tool such as Dreamweaver, you could create a folder called **C:\Program Files\Dreamweaver**. All the files would be installed in that location. If you had many Web authoring tools such as Dreamweaver, Adobe PageMill, Microsoft FrontPage, HotDog, and NetObjects Fusion; instead of placing all the programs under Program Files, you might want to create a folder called WebTools and then install all your Web authoring tools under the WebTools folder. This way all of your Web tools would be in one location. Since this scheme is organized by project, it is also easy to add a new project or delete an old one. If, for example, you are now selling beads, you create a folder called **C:\Beads**. If you no longer are selling widgets, you eliminate the Widgets folder entirely. This scheme makes it easy to tell which data files belong to which projects.

You can also tell what data file belongs to which program by virtue of the file extension. In this example, if you look at the subdirectory called Widgets, you know that the data files **Present.doc** and **Report.doc** were created with Word, that the data files **Bud.wk1** and **99bud.wk1** were created with Lotus, and that **Clients.mdb** was created with Access. The same is true for the Bangles folder.

You can organize your hard disk any way you wish, but there should be some logic to your organization. Although it may take some time in the beginning, organization will ultimately make more effective use of the hard disk and of your time. The two major considerations for any organizational scheme are How do you work? and How do your programs work?

8.4 ◦ Organizing Files

When working with your computer in an office environment, you will work primarily on the hard disk. Since you are in a learning situation, you are going to learn to accomplish tasks using a floppy disk rather than the hard disk. In this way, you will not harm files or folders on your hard disk as you learn and practice. You are using the MYDATADISK disk instead of the hard disk, but the organizational techniques you learn are the same.

You want to organize the MYDATADISK disk so that files and folders are logically organized. You want to be able to see what is on the disk quickly. As you know, there are many commands to help you with these tasks in Windows Explorer and My Computer. You can create folders and copy or move files from one location to another easily. In order to exemplify the process, you are going to work with both program and data files.

8.5 ◦ Activity ◦ Creating Folders and Copying Files

Note: The examples will be easier to follow if you do this: In Windows Explorer, click **Tools**. Click **Folder Options**. Click the **View** tab and place a check mark by **Display full path in the title bar.**

1   Place the MYDATADISK disk in Drive A.

2   Open Windows Explorer. Expand My Computer and Drive C. Click the **XPRODATA** folder to select it.

3   In the contents side, select the following folder and files:
MUSIC, EXP01FEB.xls, EXP01JAN.xls, EXP01MAR.xls, EXP02FEB.xls, EXP02JAN.xls, EXP02MAR.xls, EXP03FEB.xls, EXP03JAN.xls, EXP03MAR.xls, GALAXY.TMP, GALAXY.TXT, GRAMMY.REC, JUPITER.TMP, and **JUPITER.TXT.**

4   Right-click in a selected (highlighted) area. Point to Send To. Click **3½ Floppy (A)**. Overwrite any files.

5   Select the **FUNSTUFF** folder. In the contents pane, click **HANG2, MLSHUT.DOC,** and **MLSHUT.EXE.** Right-click in a highlighted area. Point to **Sent To.** Click **3½ Floppy (A:).**

6   Collapse the **FUNSTUFF** folder. Collapse the **XPRODATA** folder. Click **3½ Floppy (A:)** to select it. Arrange the files by name in a list view in ascending order.

7   Click **View.** Turn the **Status Bar** on.

WHAT'S **HAPPENING?** You have copied folders and files to the MYDATADISK disk so you may emulate organizing your hard disk. You should have 44 objects in the root of the MYDATADISK disk (6 folders and 38 files). You can see that the files are scattered about. There is no particular organization to this disk.

8   Right-click on the contents side. Point to **New**. Click **Folder**.

9   Key in the following: **FUN** [Enter]

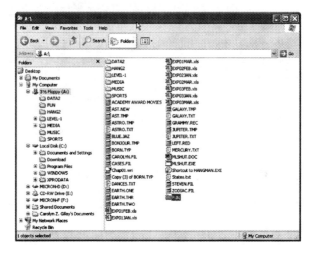

WHAT'S **HAPPENING?** You have a new folder called FUN with no files in it. You decide you would like a more descriptive folder name. You may rename files and folders any time.

10   Be sure that the **FUN** folder is still selected. Press the [F2] key.

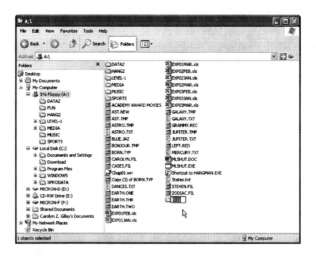

WHAT'S **HAPPENING?** Pressing the [F2] key is a keyboard shortcut to renaming files and folders. A box appears around FUN. You can directly key in your new name.

11   Key in the following: **GAMES** [Enter]

WHAT'S **HAPPENING?** You have renamed your folder.

12   Click **View**. Point to **Arrange Icons by**. Click **Name**. If you are in descending order (Z to A), click **View**. Point to **Arrange Icons by**. Click **Name**. Be sure you are in List view. If necessary, scroll so your window looks as follows:

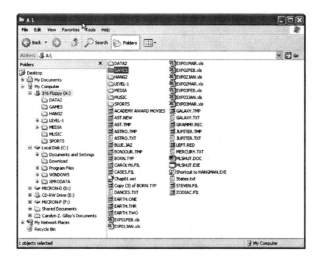

WHAT'S HAPPENING? You have arranged your files and folders by name. You may have noticed that each time you arrange your icons, they will be in either descending or ascending order. You may need to rearrange them by using the View menu again.

Note: If you did not work through the chapter activities and/or did not do the homework, there will be files and folders missing. You can either return to Chapter 7 and do the activities and the homework, or create the missing folders and copy the missing files from the XPRODATA folder on Drive C.

13 In the contents pane, drag **MUSIC** to the **MEDIA** folder in the tree pane. Then expand the MEDIA folder in the tree pane.

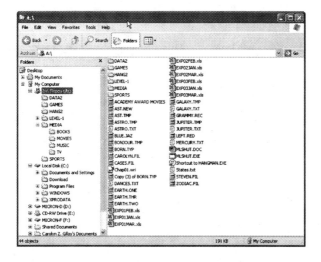

WHAT'S HAPPENING? Now the MUSIC folder is with all your different media types.

14 Be sure 3½ Floppy (A:) is selected in the tree pane. Right-click in the contents side. Point to **New**. Click **Folder**. Key in the following: **ASTRONOMY** [Enter]

15 In the contents pane, select the following files: **AST.NEW, AST.TMP, ASTRO.TMP, ASTRO.TXT, BORN.TYP, EARTH.ONE, EARTH.TWO, EARTH.THR, GALAXY.TMP, GALAXY.TXT, JUPITER.TMP, JUPITER.TXT, MERCURY.TXT**, and **ZODIAC.FIL**.

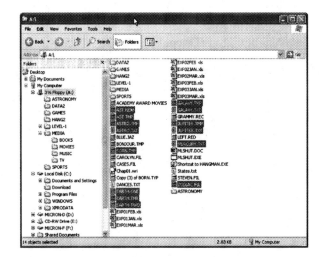

WHAT'S **HAPPENING?** You have selected all the files relating to ASTRONOMY.

16 Drag the selected files to the **ASTRONOMY** folder.

17 Select and drag **HANG2**, **MLSHUT.DOC**, and **MLSHUT.EXE** to the **GAMES** folder.

18 Click **MEDIA** to expand it. Click **3½ Floppy (A:)** in the tree pane. Select and drag **ACADEMY AWARD MOVIES** to the **MOVIES** folder.

19 Select and drag **BLUE.JAZ** to the **MUSIC** folder.

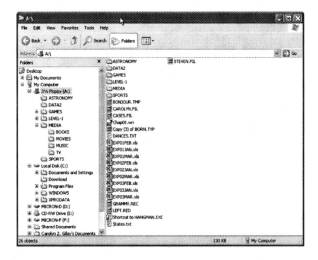

WHAT'S **HAPPENING?** As you can see, your disk is becoming less cluttered.

20 Create a new folder called **BIZ**. Select **BONJOUR.TMP**, **CAROLYN.FIL**, **Chap01.wri**, **CASES.FIL**, **LEFT.RED**, **States.txt**, **STEVEN.FIL**, and all the files that begin with **EXP**.

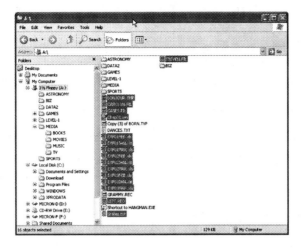

WHAT'S HAPPENING? You are going to move these files to the BIZ folder.

21   Drag the selected files to the **BIZ** folder.

22   Move **DANCES.TXT** to the **DATA2** folder.

23   Move **GRAMMY.REC** to the **MUSIC** folder under MEDIA.

24   Delete Copy (3) of **BORN.TYP** and **Shortcut to HANGMAN.EXE**.

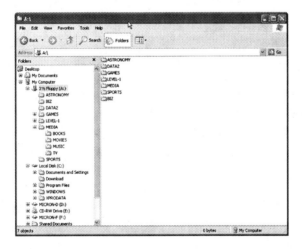

WHAT'S HAPPENING? Your disk is now much neater. But neatness is not the objective—being able to quickly locate files and folders is the goal.

25   Collapse the **MEDIA** folder. Close all open windows.

8.6 • A New Model

You have reorganized your floppy disk as a model for reorganizing your hard disk. The question now becomes how are you going to use this organized disk. Organizing your disk is not simply an exercise in keeping your system neat and tidy. It has a much more practical application, which is to allow you to become a more efficient user of your own computer system. Once again, remember that your computer is a tool that you use to perform work. You use the programs you have to create new data files. When you do, using the Start menu is an appropriate way to access those tools. However, much of the time you will be using existing data files to revise them, copy them, back them up, and other such types of tasks. You want quick and easy access to those files.

For instance, if you are a student writing a report, you will be using a word processor such as Word. You will be accessing your data file, your report, many times. If you are using Word, you can click Start, point to All Programs, and click Word. Then you can click File and then Open. Then you have to locate your data file. As you can see, you will have taken many steps to simply get to the file you wish to alter. This is not efficient. Since Word documents are registered file types, if you had immediate access to the file, you would need to only double-click the file to open Word with your document ready to edit.

When it comes to organizing your programs, it becomes a little more complex. If you have a new hard disk or a new computer and you are the person who is going to install your programs, you can follow the guidelines suggested in Section 8.3. If you are adding new software to your computer, you can also follow the guidelines. However, often when you purchase a computer, you find that much of the software has already been installed, which presents a problem for organizing your disk. If you move an installed program to another location, many problems can occur. The major problem is the probability, if not certainty, that the program will no longer work.

When a program is installed (as opposed to when program files are copied), certain critical events happen, among which is the updating of the Registry. The Registry is the key for the path to the program as well as the location of all support files and the registration of any file types associated with that program. When you move program files, the Registry is not updated. The Registry still has the old information and cannot locate the program files in their new locations. The programs then will not run.

The problem is solvable but the solutions are complex. One solution is to edit the Registry with the new information, which is not an easy task or for the faint of heart. If you edit the Registry and make any errors, then your computer will not even boot. Editing the Registry is *not* recommended. The other solution is to uninstall the program and then reinstall it in the location you wish. Most programs have an uninstall routine, or you can use the Windows XP Professional Add/Remove Programs utility. Although this solution is not that dangerous, it is time consuming, and there is a small risk that the newly installed program will not work. For most users, it is best to leave existing program organization as it is on the computer and only use the organizational criteria when installing new programs. The solution is to organize the data files and use shortcuts for program files. There are few problems with moving or copying data files or creating shortcuts.

8.7 ● Activity ● Using an Organized Disk

1   Be sure the MYDATADISK disk is in Drive A. Open Windows Explorer. Expand My Computer. Expand Drive C. Click the **3½ Floppy (A:)** on the tree side.

2   Click the **GAMES** folder on the tree side. Click **HANG2**.

3   On the contents side, select **HANGMAN.EXE** and right-drag it to the **3½ Floppy (A:)** icon on the tree side.

WHAT'S HAPPENING? Since this is a file and you are manipulating it on the same disk, the default choice is Move Here. It does not matter that it is a program—a program is a file. You want to choose Move Here.

4   Click **Move Here**. Click the **3½ Floppy (A:)** icon on the tree side. Click the **3½ Floppy (A:)** on the tree side to make it active.

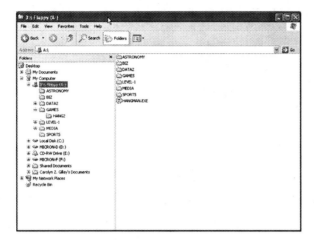

WHAT'S HAPPENING? You moved a program file. There is only one copy of it on the MYDATADISK disk, in the root directory folder. It is not a shortcut.

5   Double-click **HANGMAN.EXE** on the contents side.

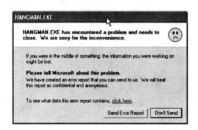

WHAT'S HAPPENING? This dialog box tells you that the program will not run. As you can see, you cannot and should not move program files.

6   Click **Don't Send**. Drag **HANGMAN.EXE** back to the **HANG2** folder.

7   If necessary, move the **3½ Floppy (A:)** window so you can see the desktop. On the desktop, create a new folder called **Daily**.

8   On the **3½ Floppy (A:)**, click **HANG2** on the tree side. In the contents side, right-drag **HANGMAN.EXE** to the **Daily** folder. Click **Create Shortcuts Here**.

9   Double-click the **Daily** folder on your desktop.

WHAT'S **HAPPENING?** You created a shortcut to the HANGMAN program. You did not move it. There is no danger in creating, moving, or deleting shortcuts since a shortcut is only a pointer to a file. You placed the shortcut in a folder on your desktop for easy access. Thus, if you wanted to play this game every day, it is quickly and easily available to you.

10 Double-click **Shortcut to HANGMAN.EXE**.

WHAT'S **HAPPENING?** Since this is a shortcut, the program can find the support files it needs. The shortcut is a pointer to the file. You are now ready to play the game.

11 Click **Exit Program**. Close the **Daily** window. Collapse the **GAMES** folder in the 3½ **Floppy (A:)** window. Click 3½ **Floppy (A:)** to select it in the tree pane.

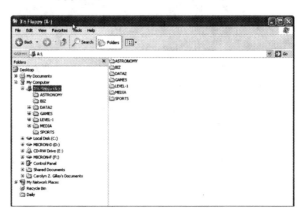

WHAT'S **HAPPENING?** You have returned to the 3½ Floppy (A:) window. You now see that a shortcut to a program is an effective way to access a program you use all the time. But what about data files? Suppose you are working on a report and you are going to be working on it for several days. You will first use the program approach.

12 Click **Start**. Point to **All Programs**. Point to **Accessories**. Click **Notepad**. Click **File**. Click **Open**.

13 In the File Name text box, key in the following: **A:\MEDIA\MUSIC\BALLAD1960.TXT**. Click **Open**.

WHAT'S **HAPPENING?** You opened the file of interest. In this case you knew the exact file name and location. If you did not, you would have needed to search your computer system for this file.

14 Click **File**. Click **Open**.

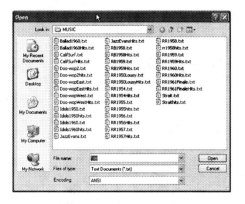

WHAT'S **HAPPENING?** Notepad remembers the last location—A:\MEDIA\MUSIC.

15 Click **Ballad1960Hits.txt**. Click **Open**.

WHAT'S **HAPPENING?** In order to open this file, Notepad had to close the other file. If you wanted both files open at the same time—perhaps to copy text from one file to another, you would have to repeat the steps you just did to accomplish this task.

16   Close Notepad. In the tree pane on the 3½ Floppy (A:), click **MEDIA**. Click **MUSIC**. In the
      contents pane, select **Ballad1960.txt** and **BalladHits1960.txt**.

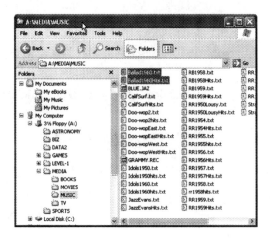

WHAT'S **HAPPENING?** These are the files of interest. You are going to create shortcuts to them
in your Daily folder on the desktop for easy access.

17   If necessary, move the 3½ Floppy (A:) window so you can see your Daily folder on the desktop.
      Right-drag these files to the **Daily** folder. Be sure to drop them on the Daily folder, not the
      desktop. Click **Create Shortcuts Here**.

18   Close the 3½ Floppy (A:) window. Open **Daily**.

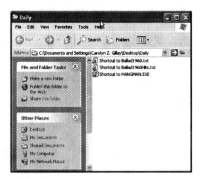

WHAT'S **HAPPENING?** You now have shortcuts to your often used data files. You did not want
to copy the files. If you copied the files, you would have used valuable disk space. But more
importantly, when you edited a file, you would not know which was the current version—the
one on the Desktop or the one on the floppy disk. By creating a shortcut, you are only dealing
with the original file—any changes will be made to one and only one file.

19   Double-click **Shortcut to Ballad1960.txt**. Double-click **Shortcut to BalladHits1960.txt**.

WHAT'S HAPPENING? You quickly opened both files. Depending on your screen layout, you may not see all open windows, but if you look at the taskbar, you can see a button for each file. To access the file of interest, you only need to click the taskbar button of the file you are interested in. There is another tool you can use to see what programs are running. It is called Task Manager. Windows Task Manager gives you information about your computer's performance and displays the details about the programs and processes that are running on your computer. Task Manager also allows you to end programs or processes, switch to a different program, and even start programs.

20 Right-click the taskbar. Click **Task Manager**.

WHAT'S HAPPENING? You have opened Task Manager. In this dialog box you see which programs are running. You have three command buttons: End Task, Switch To, and New Task. If you select an object in the window and click End Task, you will close the program. If you have a program that "hangs"—quits working—you can open this dialog box and close the offending program without having to reboot. Another way to open this dialog box is to press the Ctrl + Alt + Delete keys at the same time. This is sometimes referred to as the "three-fingered salute." If you select an object and click Switch To, you will switch to that open program. New Task allows you to open a new program.

21 Click the **Users** tab.

WHAT'S HAPPENING? On this system, only one user is logged on. If you look at the available command buttons, you have Disconnect and Logoff command buttons. The Disconnect button allows you to disconnect from a network. If your system hangs, you can open this dialog box and click Logoff. This will allow you to log off in an orderly fashion. This is much better than simply turning off your computer. You may not be able to access all features of Task Manager if you do not have Administrator privileges.

22 Click the **Applications** tab. Select **Ballad1960.txt – Notepad**. Click **End Task**.

WHAT'S HAPPENING? Now only one copy of Notepad is open.

23 Close the Task Manager window. Close Notepad.

WHAT'S HAPPENING? You have returned to your Daily folder. You can easily remove or add file shortcuts to your desktop, making it efficient and easy to access the files of interest.

24 Close the Daily window.

WHAT'S HAPPENING? You have returned to the desktop.

8.8 • Taskbar and Start Menu Options

Although you are very safe in organizing your data files by creating folders and moving files, it has already been mentioned that altering the location or changing the names of your programs, once installed, is a very risky operation. Fortunately, you generally access your programs from the Start menu either from the most frequently used list or from the All Programs menu. Since the Start/All Programs menu is comprised of shortcuts, you may freely change the way your Start menu operates so that you can arrange your programs to your liking. You will find that as you install new programs, nearly every program will place an entry on the All Programs menu. Soon your All Programs menu is overwhelming and difficult to use. Thus, altering the Start menu and what is on it allows you to tailor the menu to meet your needs.

You can choose how you view your menus, either cascading (see Figure 8.6) or menus that scroll (see Figures 8.7 and 8.8).

Figure 8.6 • The Programs Menu in Columns

The menu displayed in columns will increase the number of columns to accommodate the number of programs that you have.

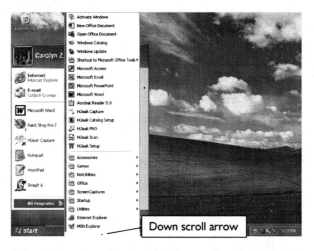

Figure 8.7 • A Scrolling Programs Menu with a Down Scroll Arrow

Figure 8.7 shows a scrolling menu with a down scroll arrow. In a scrolling menu, there is only one column. To access your programs, you click either the up or down arrow to scroll to see items that are not immediately visible on the menu.

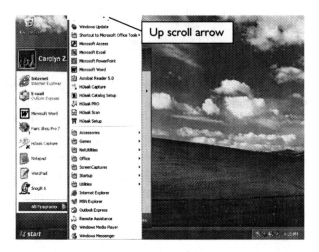

Figure 8.8 • A Scrolling Programs Menu with an Up Scroll Arrow

Figure 8.8 shows a scrolling menu with an up scroll arrow.

8.9 • Activity • Changing Start Menu Options

I   Right-click the taskbar. Click **Properties**.

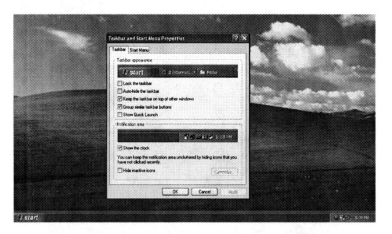

WHAT'S HAPPENING? You have opened the property sheet. Look at the taskbar. Quick Launch is a toolbar that allows you easy access to Internet Explorer, the desktop, and Windows Media Player. The Notification area, on the far right, also known as the System Tray, will display icons that indicate some system state such as documents waiting to print. Show the clock is on but Hide inactive items is off.

2   Click **Hide inactive items** to set it. Click the **Customize** command button.

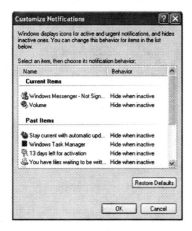

WHAT'S HAPPENING? You can choose which items you want displayed and how you want them displayed. The list is divided into items that currently appear in the notification area and those that have appeared in the past in the notification area. What is on the Past List will vary, depending on what tools you have used.

3   Click **Volume** to select it. Click the down-arrow in the drop-down list box for Volume. (If you do not have Volume listed, select another item.)

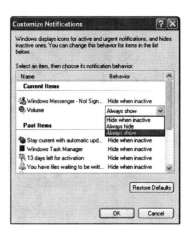

WHAT'S HAPPENING? You can always hide the icon, always show it, or only hide it when it is inactive (not being used).

4   Click **Restore Defaults**. Click **OK**.

5   Click **Show Quick Launch** to set it. Clear **Show the clock**. Click **OK**.

WHAT'S HAPPENING? The taskbar has the Quick Launch toolbar next to the Start button. The notification area no longer shows the clock. You can also alter the Start menu settings in the area where you have access to your resources (My Computer, My Recent Documents, and so on).

6   Right-click the taskbar. Click **Properties**. Click the **Taskbar** tab. Set **Show the clock**. Clear **Show Quick Launch and Hide inactive icons**.

7   Click the **Start Menu** tab. Click **Start Menu**. Click **Customize**. Click the **Advanced** tab.

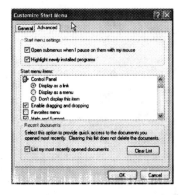

WHAT'S HAPPENING? In the Start menu settings, both check boxes are selected. These choices affect behavior. Because Open submenus when I pause on them with my mouse is selected, you need only to point to a submenu and it opens. If you did not enable this choice, then you would have to click the submenu. Figure 8.9 shows an example of how newly installed programs are highlighted. These programs are highlighted until you use them for the first time.

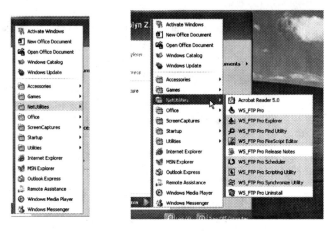

Figure 8.9 • Newly Installed Programs

In Figure 8.9, you see that both the menu item and the expanded menu items are highlighted. The items in the list box allow you to choose what resources are displayed on the Start menu. You may display them as a link, as a menu, or not at all.

8   In Control Panel, click **Display as a menu**.

9   Click **Favorites menu** to set it.

10 Scroll to the bottom of the list, looking at how each menu item is classified.

WHAT'S HAPPENING? Here is where you set Scroll Programs, if you wish to enable this feature. If you are not an Administrator, you will not be able to set System Administrative tools.

11 Click **OK**. Click **OK**. Click the **Start** menu. Point to **Control Panel**.

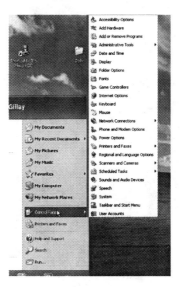

WHAT'S HAPPENING? Favorites now appears on the menu. The content of the Favorites menu varies; it displays links to important Internet addresses. Now when you point to Control Panel, it displays the choices in a menu form.

12 Click outside the Start menu to close it.

13 Right-click the taskbar. Click **Properties**. Click the **Start Menu** tab. Click **Start Menu**. Click **Customize**. Click the **Advanced** tab.

14 Under Control Panel, click **Display as link**.

15 Clear the check box for **Favorites**.

16 Click **OK**. Click **OK**. Click the **Start** menu. Point at **Control Panel**.

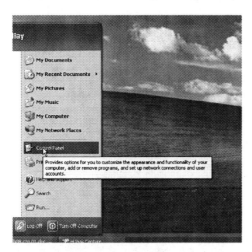

WHAT'S HAPPENING? Favorites no longer appears and Control Panel does not display a menu. If you clicked Control Panel, it would take you to the Control Panel window.

17 Click outside the menu to close it.

WHAT'S HAPPENING? You have returned to the desktop.

8.10 ● Customizing the Start Menu

In the Start menu, you can pin links (shortcuts) to the programs you always want to appear on the menu. You can rearrange pinned programs by dragging them into whatever order you want. You can delete items as well. You may also sort your menus by name as well as do drag-and-drop operations to add items to the menus.

8.11 ● Activity ● Customizing the Start Menu

1   Right-click the taskbar. Click **Properties**. Click the **Start menu** tab. Click **Customize**. Click the **General** tab. Click **Clear List**. Click **OK**. Click **OK**.

2   Click the **Start** menu.

WHAT'S **HAPPENING?** ⟩ You have cleared the Start menu so you can place and remove items.

3   Click **Start**. Point to **All Programs**. Point to **Accessories**. Click **Notepad**. Close Notepad.

4   Click **Start**. Point to **All Programs**. Point to **Accessories**. Click **Calculator**. Close Calculator.

5   Click **Start**. Point to **All Programs**. Point to **Games**. Open **Solitaire**. Close Solitaire.

6   Click **Start**. Point to **All Programs**. Point to **Games**. Open **FreeCell**. Close FreeCell.

7   Wait a second or two, then click the **Start** menu.

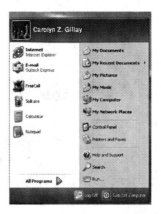

WHAT'S **HAPPENING?** ⟩ You have opened some programs that now appear on the program list.

8   Right-click **Calculator**.

WHAT'S HAPPENING? There are many things you can do with this object as listed in the menu.

9 Click **Pin to Start menu**.

WHAT'S HAPPENING? You have pinned Calculator to the top of the menu. Now, no matter what programs you use, Calculator will remain there at the top of the menu.

10 Click outside the menu to close it. Open Windows Explorer. Open My Computer. Open Drive C. Select the **XPRODATA** folder.

11 In the right pane, drag **ASTRO.TXT** and drop it on top of the **Start** menu button.

12 Click **Funstuff** to select it. Click **HANG2** to select it. In the right pane, right-click **HANGMAN.EXE**.

WHAT'S HAPPENING? Any program (a program with a .exe extension) will provide you a menu choice of Pin to Start menu.

13 Click **Pin to Start menu**.

14 Click **BOG2** in the left pane. In the right pane, drag and drop **BOG.EXE** on the Start menu button.

15 Collapse **FUNSTUFF**. Close Windows Explorer. Click the **Start** button.

WHAT'S HAPPENING? You "pinned" several programs to the Start menu. You also pinned a document. Since this is a registered file type (a Notepad file), you could drag a copy of it to the Start menu. If you right-clicked any document icon, you would not have the choice of Pin to Start menu but you can always drag a document icon there. You are simply placing shortcuts to programs and files on the Start menu.

16 Right-click **Calculator**. Click **Unpin from Start menu**.

17 Right-click **ASTRO.TXT**.

WHAT'S HAPPENING? When you have a document icon, you do not unpin it but simply remove it from the list.

18   Click **Remove from This List**.

19   Unpin **HANGMAN.EXE** and **BOG.EXE**.

WHAT'S **HAPPENING?** Your menu is clear.

20   Point to **All Programs**. Click **Accessories**. Place your mouse pointer on **Windows Messenger** and begin to drag it up the menu.

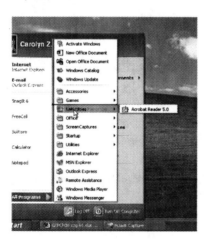

WHAT'S **HAPPENING?** As you begin to drag it, you see its outline.

21   Drop it right above **Accessories**.

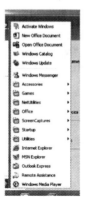

WHAT'S **HAPPENING?** You have rearranged the All Programs menu. It is no longer in alphabetical order.

22   Right-click somewhere in the **All Programs** menu.

WHAT'S **HAPPENING?** Again, the right-click menu brought up many choices that control how this menu looks. The choice you are interested in is Sort by Name.

23   Click **Sort by Name**.

WHAT'S **HAPPENING?** Your menu is in alphabetical order, with folders followed by programs.

24   Click outside the menu to close it.

WHAT'S **HAPPENING?** You have returned to the desktop.

8.12 ● Toolbars

Toolbars are collections of icons that you can click to launch common tasks. Quick Launch is a toolbar that Windows provides that you may add to your taskbar. Quick Launch provides an icon for two programs: Internet Explorer, Microsoft's Web browser, and Windows Media Player. A *Web browser* is software that you use to navigate the World Wide Web (WWW). The Web, part of the Internet, is a set of hypertext documents called Web pages. Hypertext is text or pictures you can click to jump from one location to another. For instance, in an online (on the Web) encyclopedia, an entry for *dish* could allow you to jump to both an entry for dinnerware and an entry for satellite dish. The two most popular Web browsers are Netscape Navigator and Microsoft Internet Explorer. Internet Explorer, referred to as IE, comes with Windows XP Professional. The Show Desktop icon allows you to toggle between your documents and the desktop. Windows XP Professional also provides some built-in toolbars that you can activate or deactivate. These are Address, Links, and Desktop. You can also create your own toolbars.

The Address toolbar is the same as the Address Bar in Windows Explorer. The Address toolbar allows you to key in an Internet address or the location of a file or folder. The Links toolbar provides shortcuts to selected Internet sites. The Desktop toolbar places whatever objects are on your desktop onto the taskbar. You may also customize the size of the toolbars on the taskbar as well as their position. You may anchor the toolbars to any edge of the desktop or you may float them anywhere on the desktop.

8.13 ● Activity ● Using Toolbars

1 Right-click the taskbar in an empty spot. Point to **Toolbars**.

WHAT'S **HAPPENING?** Here the available toolbars are displayed. None are active.

2 Click **Quick Launch** to select it.

3 Open Windows Explorer. Expand **My Computer** and **Drive C**. Open the **XPRODATA** folder. Double-click **Astro.txt**. Maximize Notepad.

WHAT'S **HAPPENING?** You can no longer see your desktop. Other programs also allow you to have toolbars. When you work with application programs, you normally work in full-screen view to give yourself as much area as possible to work. There are times when you wish to access objects on your desktop. By using the Show Desktop icon on the Quick Launch toolbar, you can quickly toggle between your document and the desktop.

4   Click the **Show Desktop** icon in the Quick Launch toolbar.

WHAT'S **HAPPENING?** Both open windows became minimized and are now buttons on the taskbar.

5   Click the **Show Desktop** icon.

6   Restore the Notepad window to its original size. Close Notepad. Close Windows Explorer.

7   Right-click the taskbar. Point to **Toolbars**. Click **Address**.

WHAT'S **HAPPENING?** You are looking at the Address toolbar incorporated into the taskbar. It is a small button. You can change the size of the toolbar, float it on the desktop, or anchor it to an edge of the desktop. You use the handles to manipulate the toolbar.

8   Place your mouse over the left dotted line of the Address button until it turns into a double-sided arrow.

WHAT'S **HAPPENING?** You have "grabbed" the handle for the toolbar.

9   Press the left mouse button and slowly drag your mouse to the left about five inches. Release the mouse button.

WHAT'S **HAPPENING?** You have changed the size of the toolbars. You made the Address larger. You could do the same for the Quick Launch toolbar.

10   Place the pointer on the **Address** label and hold down the left mouse button.

WHAT'S **HAPPENING?** When you see the mouse pointer assume the shape of a four-sided arrow, you can move the toolbar.

11   Drag the Address toolbar up about three inches.

WHAT'S **HAPPENING?** The Address toolbar is now floating. In this example, it is quite large. It can be sized just like any window.

12 If necessary, make the Address toolbar smaller. Then click in the Address toolbar and key in the following: **C:\XPRODATA\FUNSTUFF**

WHAT'S **HAPPENING?** You have selected a location to go to. If you have used this folder before, Windows XP Professional will display a drop-down list of recently accessed locations and will automatically fill in the words for you, if you wish.

13 Press **Enter** or click **Go**.

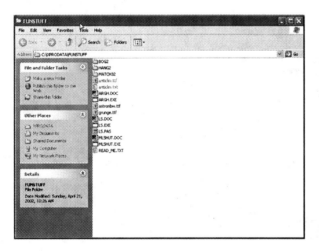

WHAT'S **HAPPENING?** You were taken to the Funstuff folder in the XPRODATA folder. Your view could be different.

14 Close the window. In the Address toolbar key in **C:**

WHAT'S **HAPPENING?** The drop-down list box will list any locations you have visited, whether they were Internet addresses or folder or file locations. You may have only one location if you have not used the Address toolbar before.

15 Click the Close button on the Address toolbar.

WHAT'S HAPPENING? The dialog box is telling you that you are closing the toolbar. It will not appear on the taskbar again, unless you choose it to. You could have also closed the drop-down list box and dragged it back to the taskbar. Then you would have re-anchored it and incorporated it into the taskbar. The other toolbars work in a similar fashion.

16   Click **OK**. Right-click on an empty spot on the taskbar. Point to **Toolbars**. Click **New Toolbar**.

WHAT'S HAPPENING? You may key in an Internet address or choose a folder. My Documents is the default choice.

17   Click **My Computer**. Click Drive **C**. Click the **XPRODATA** folder. Click **OK**.

WHAT'S HAPPENING? Now the XPRODATA folder is a toolbar button. If you wanted, you could make it larger, as you did with the Address toolbar. The double arrow (> >) on the right allows you to display the contents of the folder.

18   Click the right arrow.

WHAT'S HAPPENING? You see a list of your folders and files in a scrolling list. You may access your files and folders through this toolbar.

19   Click **ASTRO.TXT**.

WHAT'S HAPPENING? You quickly opened Notepad with ASTRO.TXT as the document.

19   Close Notepad.

20   Make the **XPRODATA** toolbar larger by grabbing the handle and moving to the left so the toolbar is about four inches.

21   On the taskbar, right-click the **XPRODATA** label.

WHAT'S **HAPPENING?** You have a new taskbar menu. You can choose to see the title of the folder you are looking at. If you choose to unset Show Text, you will not see the names of your folders and files; you will only see unmarked folder and file icons.

22 Point to **View**. Click **Large Icons**.

WHAT'S **HAPPENING?** Your taskbar is larger as well as your folders and their names. To open any folder, you only need to click it.

23 On the taskbar, right-click the **XPRODATA** label. Click **View**. Click **Small Icons**.

24 Double-click the XPRODATA's left handle.

WHAT'S **HAPPENING?** Double-clicking the toolbar's handle is a quick way to expand or contract the toolbar.

25 Right-click the taskbar. Point to **Toolbars**. Click **XPRODATA** to deactivate it.

26 Right-click the taskbar. Point to **Toolbars**. Click **Quick Launch** to deactivate it.

WHAT'S **HAPPENING?** You have returned to the desktop. You may still have toolbars for other programs. You will need to adjust the height of the taskbar.

27 Size the taskbar's height as needed.

WHAT'S **HAPPENING?** You have completed your introduction to toolbars.

Chapter Summary

In this chapter, you learned that all disks should be organized. Program and data files should not reside in the same directory. Many users organize their disks by program, focusing on the tools rather than the data. In general, it is best to focus on your data files. Once organized, it is then easier to move, copy, save, back up, and accomplish the other necessary data management tasks.

You also learned that part of an organizational scheme is naming your files. If you will be working with older programs that use the 8.3 file-naming rule, you must be cautious in using long file names. Even if your application program recognizes long file names, you should still plan how you will name your files so that you may locate them easily.

You learned about a new model to access your programs and data files. Instead of always using the Start menu to access your files and folders, you learned that you can create shortcuts to files and folders and place them on your desktop for quick and easy access. This is an efficient way to use shortcuts. You also learned about Task Manager. This gives you information about your computer's performance and displays the details about the programs and processes that are running on your computer. Task Manager also allows you to end programs or processes, switch to a different program, and even start programs.

You may also customize the Start menu. Windows XP Professional will remember your most often used programs and place them on the Start menu. In addition, Windows XP Professional offers different toolbars on the desktop as well as on the taskbar. You may add toolbars such as the Address or Desktop toolbars as well as create your own custom toolbars.

Key Terms
naming convention
utility program
Web browser

Discussion Questions

1. Explain the relationship between program files and data files.
2. Why would it be important to group your files in a logical manner?
3. Explain why it is important to organize a disk.
4. Why is it recommended that you create or use folders?
5. Why is it important to avoid placing data files in program folders?
6. Why should file and folder names be chosen with care?
7. What is a naming convention? Give two examples of a naming convention you might use.
8. Identify two advantages in using long file names.
9. Identify two disadvantages in using long file names.
10. Explain how having the root directory serve as a map to the rest of your disk would be helpful in organizing your disk.
11. List and explain five criteria that should be considered when organizing your disk.
12. Why would you place shortcuts to data files or programs on the desktop? How could you use them?
13. Identify the purpose of Task Manager. Give two examples of how you might use it.
14. Identify two disadvantages to using the Start menu to access your data files.
15. Name three items you may customize in the Start menu.
16. What does the term pinned to the Start menu mean? Identify two ways to pin an item to the Start menu.
17. In the Customize Start menu dialog box, you may choose to display Control Panel as a link or a menu. Explain the purpose of each of these choices.
18. If you set Scroll Programs menu in the taskbar's property sheet, what would happen to your menus?
19. What is the purpose of the Quick Launch toolbar? How would you use it?
20. Other than Quick Launch, identify and describe the functions of one toolbar provided with Windows XP Professional.

True/False Questions

For each question, circle the letter T if the statement is true or the letter F if the statement is false.

T	F	1. A folder in the root directory can contain many files, limited only by the size of the disk.
T	F	2. There is no risk in moving or renaming program files.
T	F	3. It is not wise to place data files in program folders because data files are constantly changing while program files rarely change.
T	F	4. Many small folders with few files is a better organizational scheme than one large folder with many files.

T   F   5. When you click the Show Desktop icon in the Quick Launch toolbar, you toggle between the desktop and your open program window.

Completion Questions

Write the correct answer in each blank space provided.

6. In Windows XP Professional, a file name can have up to _____ characters in its name.

7. A good rule of thumb to use when naming folders is to make the folder name _____ and descriptive.

8. When organizing your disk, _____ files are safe to move.

9. The _____ toolbar allows you to key in an Internet address or the location of a file or folder.

10. A quick way to access Task Manager is to press the _____, _____, and _____ keys.

Multiple Choice Questions

Circle the letter of the correct answer for each question.

11. If you have a file called Run.exe and you right-drag the file to a different folder on the same drive, the default action will be
    a. a move.
    b. a copy.
    c. the creation of a shortcut.
    d. none of the above

12. Which of the following types of files should not be moved?
    a. program files
    b. data files
    c. shortcuts
    d. all of the above

13. Usually, when you install a program to the hard drive,
    a. the newly installed program registers the program's data file type.
    b. the newly installed program creates an entry for it under the Start menu.
    c. both a and b
    d. neither a nor b

14. To rename a folder or file, after you select the object, press _____ to rename it.
    a. Alt + R
    b. F2
    c. Ctrl + N
    d. none of the above

15. You have a program called MY.EXE. You drag and drop it on the Start button. What have you done?
    a. You have pinned it to the Start menu.
    b. You have added it to the All Programs menu.
    c. You have executed it.
    d. none of the above

Application Assignments

Problem Set I—At the Computer

Note: If you did not work through the chapter, you will be missing files and folders that you need to complete the homework. You will need to go back through the chapter and locate where the files and folders are created.

Problem A

❋ Place the MYDATADISK disk in Drive A. Open Windows Explorer. Expand My Computer. Select the 3½ Floppy (A:) folder.

❋ Create a folder on the root of the Homework disk called PEOPLE.

❋ Use Search to locate all the files in the XPRODATA folder on Drive C that begin with FI and have any file extension. (*Hint:* Remember wildcards.)

❋ Copy them to the newly created PEOPLE folder on the MYDATADISK disk.

    1. How many files were copied?
        a. 2
        b. 4
        c. 6
        d. 8

❋ On the MYDATADISK disk, in the PEOPLE folder, rename **FILE2.CZG** to **CAROLYNFILE2.TXT**. Click **Yes** if any dialog box appears.

❋ After completing the above instructions, on the MYDATADISK disk, in the PEOPLE folder, rename **FILE2.FP** to FRANKFILE2.TXT. Click **Yes** if any dialog box appears.

❋ Close any open dialog boxes.

❋ Open **FRANKFILE2.TXT** by double-clicking.

    2. The title bar of Notepad states
        a. FRANKFILE2.TXT - Notepad.
        b. Notepad - FRANKFILE2.TXT.
        c. Notepad - FRANK ~ 01.TXT.
        d. FRANKFILE2.TXT.

    3. For the file you just opened, you can say that Notepad
        a. supports long file names.
        b. does not support long file names.
        c. when you opened it, presented you with a dialog box that offered you the choice of using the long file name or the MS-DOS file name.
        d. both a and c

❋ Close Notepad.

❋ In Activity 8.5, you created folders and copied files. Move **carolyn.fil** and **steven.fil** from the **BIZ** directory of the MYDATADISK disk to the **PEOPLE** folder using drag and drop. You do not want to see a shortcut menu.

    4. To accomplish this task, after you selected the files, you _____ the files.
        a. held the **Ctrl** key and left-dragged
        b. left-dragged
        c. held the **Ctrl** key and right-dragged
        d. right-dragged

5. The file STEVEN.FIL is now located
   a. only in the BIZ of the MYDATADISK disk.
   b. in both the BIZ directory of the MYDATA disk and in the PEOPLE folder.
   c. only in the PEOPLE folder.

* Hold the [Ctrl] key and drag the file called **Steven.fil** from the PEOPLE and drop it on the 3½ Floppy (A:).

6. The file Steven.fil is now located
   a. only in the root directory of the MYDATADISK disk.
   b. in both the root directory of the MYDATADISK disk and in the PEOPLE folder.
   c. only in the PEOPLE folder.

* Close Windows Explorer.

* Remove the MYDATADISK from Drive A.

Problem B

* Open the property sheet for the Taskbar and Start Menu.

* In the Start menu item, for My Computer, choose Display as a menu.

* Click **OK**. Click **OK**.

7. Click **Start**. Point to **My Computer**. What has occurred?
   a. My Computer now has a cascading menu.
   b. My Computer no longer has a cascading menu.
   c. My Computer is no longer available in the Start menu.
   d. none of the above

* Close the menu.

* Open the property sheet for the taskbar.

* In the Start menu item, for My Computer, choose Display as a link.

* Click **OK**. Click **OK**.

8. Click **Start**. Point to **My Computer**. What has occurred?
   a. My Computer now has a cascading menu.
   b. My Computer no longer has a cascading menu.
   c. My Computer is no longer available in the Start menu.
   d. none of the above

* Create a toolbar for the Media folder in the XPRODATA folder.

* Create a toolbar for the Sports folder in the XPRODATA folder.

9. Click the double arrow for Media. The Media folder toolbar displays
   a. only folder icons.
   b. only file icons.
   c. both folder and file icons.
   d. only file or folder names. No icons are displayed.

10. The Media folder
    a. has cascading menus.
    b. does not have cascading menus.

11. The Sports folder toolbar displays
   a. only folder icons.
   b. only file icons.
   c. both folder and file icons.
   d. only file or folder names. No icons are displayed.

* Remove the Media and Sports toolbars.

Problem Set II—Brief Essay

For all essay questions, use Notepad or WordPad to create your answer. Be sure to include your name, your class information, and the number of the question you are answering. Then print your answer.

1. List five criteria that can be used for organizing a hard disk. Explain the rationale for each.
2. One way to organize a hard disk is by project. Another way to organize it is by program. Which way do you prefer? What advantages/disadvantages do you see to each method? Explain your answer. Is there another method you prefer? If so, describe it and explain your rationale.

Problem Set III—Scenario

You are currently enrolled in college. You are taking political science, history, and Windows XP Professional classes. You have been using your computer for your lecture notes, assignments, and other classroom requirements. You have created the following files:

File Name	Purpose of File
PS - Lecture 1.txt	Notes for first week's lectures in political science.
Lecture 2 - PS.txt	Notes for second week's lectures in political science.
History lecture	Notes for first week's lectures in history.
2ndHlec.txt	Notes for second week's lectures in history.
1WinXP.doc	Notes for first week's lectures in the Windows XP Professional class.
XP-2.txt	Notes for second week's lectures in the Windows XP Professional class.
history.rep	Beginning of a history research paper.
Assn1.winXP	First assignment for the Windows XP Professional class.
Assn1 for history.doc	First assignment for the history class.

You decide you need to organize your information efficiently. You need to create folders. You may rename your files. You may use long file names for any or all of your files, if you choose. Write a brief paper discussing your organizational scheme. Include the following information in your report:

1. A drawing showing your folder structure.
2. The purpose of each folder.
3. The location of each file and why you placed it there.
4. If you rename a file, the old name and the new name.
5. If you use a long file name, your rationale for the new name.
6. A file-naming convention for the new files that you anticipate creating for your classes. Explain your rationale for your file-naming plan.

CHAPTER 9

Fonts and Printers

In this chapter, you will begin to understand what fonts are and why they are so important. You will begin with an overview of basic terminology that deals with fonts and typefaces. Then you can see what fonts are installed on your system, install new fonts, and arrange fonts by similarities. You will also look at Character Map, an accessory that assists you in using different fonts, as well as use Calculator to help you convert hexadecimal numbers to decimal numbers. There are fonts that provide special characters such as © and ™ or even special pictures like ☎ and ✆ that are not normally accessible from the keyboard. You will look at Windows XP Professional's printing features, which allow you to add a printer, look at and manage a print queue, and create logical printers. You will see how to install a new printer and remove an existing printer.

Learning Objectives

1. Explain the purpose and function of fonts.
2. Compare and contrast fonts and typefaces.
3. Identify and define basic font terminology.
4. Explain how to resolve screen and printer inconsistencies.
5. Explain the purpose and function of Character Map and Calculator.
6. Explain the purpose and function of a print driver.
7. Explain how to add or remove a printer.
8. Explain the purpose and function of the printer window.

Student Outcomes

1. Use the Fonts window to identify and compare the fonts on your system.
2. Arrange fonts by similarity and type.
3. Add and delete a font.
4. Use Character Map to insert special characters into WordPad and Paint.
5. Use Calculator to convert a number.
6. Add and remove a printer.
7. Add and remove documents in the print queue.

9.1 ◦ Introducing Fonts

When Windows XP Professional was installed on your computer, it installed basic fonts so that you could view your work on the screen as well as print your work as it appears on your monitor. Many software packages, when they are installed, also add fonts to your system. In addition, Windows XP Professional most likely installed a default printer. You are not limited to these fonts, nor are you limited to the installed printer. Choices allow you more control, not only over your system, but also over your documents.

9.2 ◦ Fonts

Any text that appears on the screen or is printed on paper appears in a font and typeface. A *typeface* is a specific design for a set of printed characters. Each typeface has an assigned, copyrighted name, such as Arial, Times New Roman, or Courier. A *font* is a set of characters of a given size, weight, and style in a specific typeface, such as 12-point Arial or 10-point Times New Roman. A font can also refer to a specific style (such as italic) or thickness, called a *stroke weight* (such as bold). Font refers to all the characters available in a particular size, style, and weight in any type design. Typeface refers to the design itself. As an example, Times New Roman is a typeface that is made up of a collection of fonts such as Times New Roman Bold, Times New Roman Italic, and Times New Roman Bold Italic. Windows XP Professional and most computer users use the term *font* to refer to both font and typeface. In fact, in general, only the term *font* is used when referring to a typeface.

Windows XP Professional uses fonts to display and print characters. Fonts can be *scaled* (made bigger or smaller). With typewriters, type sizes are measured in characters per inch. A measurement such as 10 CPI means that 10 characters fit horizontally into one inch. On computers, you work with fonts that are measured vertically in *points*, with one point equaling $1/_{72}$ of an inch. The font size really only refers to the printed size. On the screen, point size has little significance because of the differences in size and resolution of monitors. A 10-point font on a 21-inch monitor at 640-by-480 resolution will probably look larger than a 12-point font on a 15-inch monitor at 800-by-600 resolution, even though 10-point is smaller than 12-point.

Typefaces, also referred to as fonts, are either monospaced or proportional. *Monospaced typefaces* give all characters (numbers, letters, and punctuation marks) the same width. Monospaced fonts are useful when you need to align columns of text or numbers in a simple text editor such as Notepad or when sending email. Courier is an example of a monospaced font. *Proportional typefaces* vary the space given to each character so that, for instance, an "M" will take more space than an "I." An example of a proportional font is Times New Roman. In a typical word-processing environment, proportional fonts are used because these fonts are easily read and are much more visually attractive.

Fonts are divided into two main categories, serif and sans serif. Both serif and sans serif fonts are usually proportional fonts. *Serif fonts* have a small line at the end of each main line in a character, called a serif. Serif fonts, like proportional fonts, are used for most word-processing activities. *Sans serif fonts* (*sans* is French for *without*) don't have these small lines. Sans serif fonts are used primarily for emphasis in headings, titles, and subtitles. Figures 9.1 and 9.2 give examples of serif and sans serif fonts.

Galliard 12 Point	Arial 12 Point
Galliard 10 Point	**Arial 14 Point**
Times New Roman 12 Point	Verdana 12 Point
Times New Roman 8 Point	**Verdana 16 Point**

Figure 9.1 ◦ Serif Fonts   *Figure 9.2 ◦ Sans Serif Fonts*

The technology that places text on a computer screen differs from the technology that prints the characters on a printer. Your computer and your printer each have fonts, appropriately called *screen fonts* and *printer fonts*.

Windows XP Professional supports three basic font technologies: raster fonts, vector fonts, and outline fonts. Raster fonts, stored in files as bitmap images and also referred to as *bitmap fonts*, are supported because a number of older programs require them and because Windows uses them to display text in dialog boxes, message boxes, and so on. A raster font uses a series of dots to create characters. These dots are called pixels (picture elements). A pixel is the smallest point of light that can be displayed on a monitor. You cannot successfully scale bitmap fonts because they come in predetermined sizes. Different sizes of each font must be stored separately on the hard disk. These fonts are used for Windows XP Professional menus and icon labels. Since some of these fonts are used for Windows XP Professional functions, never delete them. In fact, Windows tries to prevent you from accidentally deleting these system fonts by assigning the hidden attribute to them. This means that you will not see many of the system fonts in the Fonts window unless you enable the viewing of hidden files and folders (Tools/Folder Options). Windows XP Professional raster fonts include Courier, MS Sans Serif, MS Serif, Small Fonts, and Symbol.

With raster (bitmap) fonts, what you see on your screen may not exactly match what is printed on your printer. The variance between screen fonts and printer fonts can have a tremendous impact on your documents. You may format your document in a particular fashion, decide that it looks perfect on the screen, and print it only to find that the printed copy looks nothing like what appeared on the screen.

Vector fonts are scalable fonts that draw characters by using line segments rather than dots. Vector fonts are often used for output to plotters and some types of printers. A *plotter* is a special kind of printer used to draw charts, diagrams, and other line-based graphics. Typically, plotters use pens to draw on paper or transparencies. Windows XP Professional comes with three vector fonts: Modern, Roman, and Script.

Outline fonts are fonts that are rendered from line and curve commands. Each outline font file contains formulas and algorithms on how to draw each character outline, and how to smooth the character lines and curves. The shapes of the characters are defined in terms of mathematically generated lines and curves rather than patterns of dots. Outline fonts are designed to be *WYSIWYG* (pronounced wissiwig)—"what you see is what you get." These fonts are scalable, viewable fonts that resolve the appearance inconsistency between screen and printer. Windows XP Professional supports three types of outline fonts: *Adobe Type 1*, *TrueType*, and *OpenType*.

Type 1 fonts, created by Adobe Systems, Inc., were developed for use with PostScript printers. PostScript printers require a computer inside the printer to calculate the PostScript font formulas and then render the fonts on paper; this in turn makes PostScript printers expensive. However, Windows XP Professional with OpenType technology fully supports Type 1 fonts.

TrueType, the original Windows fonts format, was first introduced in Windows 3.1 (1991) and Macintosh's System 6.0 operating system. TrueType was a joint effort between Microsoft and Apple. All calculations required to render a TrueType font are done in the computer, rather than the printer, and then necessary commands are passed to the printer. This allows sophisticated printing to be done on an inexpensive printer.

OpenType is an extension of TrueType. Microsoft and Adobe in collaboration developed the OpenType technology. OpenType is not only a font file format, it is also a new font-rendering technology that allows you to use Type 1, TrueType, and OpenType fonts on all output devices supported by Windows XP Professional. Windows XP Professional provides a selection of OpenType fonts including Arial, Courier New, Lucida Console, Times New Roman, Symbol, and Wingdings.

You can identify font types by their icons. See Figure 9.3.

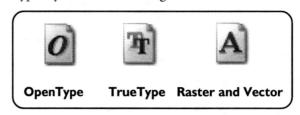

OpenType   TrueType   Raster and Vector

Figure 9.3 ▪ Font File Icons

Printer fonts give directions to your brand of printer. When you install a printer, you are installing the correct printer driver. A *printer driver* is a software program designed to enable application programs to work with a printer without concern for the specifics of the printer's hardware and internal language. Different printers require different codes and commands to operate properly. You communicate with your printer by installing the correct printer driver to manage all the subtleties of that printer.

Printers come with *built-in fonts*, sometimes called *resident fonts*. If you use a printer's built-in font in your application, Windows XP Professional will try to match that font on the screen as closely as it can with one of its bitmap screen fonts. If the match is not exact, your printed document will be different from the screen display. TrueType and OpenType fonts are scalable, viewable fonts and resolve the inconsistency between screen and printer. There are other manufacturers of scalable, viewable fonts such as Bitstream, PostScript, and Speedo.

These fonts are also supported by Windows XP Professional (and have their own file type icons), ensuring that their display on the screen is identical to what is printed by your printer.

9.3 ● Activity ● Looking at Fonts

I   Click **Start**. Click **Control Panel**. Click **Switch to classic view** if necessary. Double-click the **Fonts** folder. Click **View**. Turn the Status Bar on. Click **View**. Click **Large Icons**.

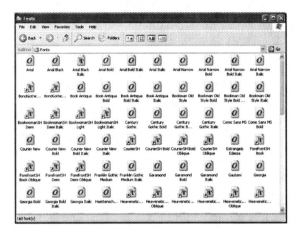

WHAT'S **HAPPENING?** You have opened the Fonts window, which displays the fonts on your system. The number of available fonts varies from computer to computer depending on the installed hardware and application software. The window above contains 160 fonts. Each font is contained in a separate file and is represented by an icon.

The icon for bitmap fonts (raster and vector) is a red A:

The TrueType fonts have a gray and blue TT:

The OpenType fonts have a blue/green O:

2   Double-click the Arial font icon.

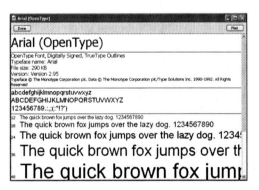

WHAT'S **HAPPENING?** You see information about Arial (the font type, the typeface name, the file size, and the version number) and samples of the font. The sentence "The quick brown fox jumps over the lazy dog" is used to display the font sample because it displays every letter of the alphabet. This sentence has been used for years for showing typefaces for that reason.

3   Scroll until you see the last point size.

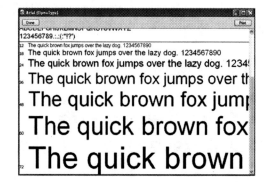

WHAT'S HAPPENING? Since this is an OpenType font, you can see how sharp and clear the letters are. If you wanted a hard-copy sample of this font, you could print it by clicking the Print button.

4   Click **Done**. Click **Tools**. Click **Folder Options**. Click the **View** tab. Set the **Show hidden files and folders** option. Click **OK**.

5   On the menu bar, click **View**. Click **Details**.

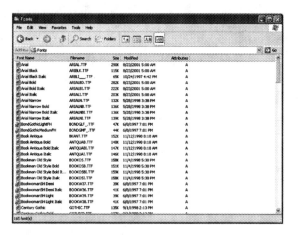

WHAT'S HAPPENING? On the toolbar, you have a button for each view. The Details button is indented, indicating that it is the current choice.

6   In the window, click the **Attributes** column heading.

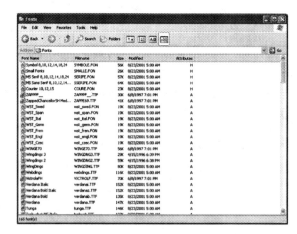

WHAT'S HAPPENING? In the Attributes column, all files assigned the hidden attribute appear at the top of the window in descending sequence by font name. The majority of these files contain a bitmap font and are used by Windows. They are ordinarily hidden so that you do not accidentally delete them. In the Fonts window, the first column displays the font names while the second column displays the actual file names. You may see multiple fonts with the same font names but with different file names. For example, MS Sans Serif 8, 10, 12, 14,… appears twice in the window above, but the file names are unique, SSERIFF.FON and SSERIFE.FON. The SSERIFE.FON is available for use on a VGA monitor. The FON file extension is assigned to all bitmap font files, while TTF is assigned to OpenType and TrueType font files.

7   Locate the MS Sans Serif (SSERIFF.FON) icon. Double-click it. Scroll to the bottom of the window.

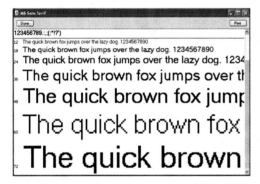

WHAT'S HAPPENING? Since MS Sans Serif is a bitmap font, you see jaggies. Unlike outline fonts, the edges of the characters cannot be rounded because bitmap characters are formed with pixels.

8   In the MS Sans Serif window, click **Done**. Click **File** on the menu bar.

WHAT'S HAPPENING? Here you can open an existing font by a menu rather than by double-clicking it. You can print your font selection. You can install any new fonts you purchase or receive. You may also delete fonts from this menu. Be very cautious when deleting fonts because you do not want to delete a font that Windows XP Professional relies on, such as MS Sans Serif. However, you may want to delete fonts that you do not use. Fonts take up a lot of space on a disk. With the advent of large hard disks, this is not as much as an issue as it used to be. But a disadvantage of having many fonts is that when you use a program and want to select a font, scrolling through 40 or 50 fonts that you never use can be quite time consuming. You can look at the properties of a font, which can help you identify file names. Font files are typically kept in the Windows\Fonts directory.

9   Click **Properties**.

WHAT'S HAPPENING? Here you see the location of the file (C:\Windows\Fonts) and the name of the file (SSERIFF.FON). Bitmap fonts have a .FON file extension. The Hidden attribute is set.

10   Click the **Version** tab. Click **Product Name**.

WHAT'S HAPPENING? Additional version information appears on this page. The selected item in the Item name list (Product Name) is described in the Value box (Microsoft Windows Operating System). Some fonts will have a Summary page where you could add comments or key words.

11   Click **Cancel**. Click the **Font Name** column heading. Locate Arial. Right-click the icon. Click **Properties**.

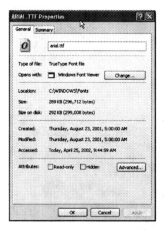

WHAT'S HAPPENING? Here you see the location of the file (C:\Windows\Fonts) and the name of the file (ARIAL.TTF). TrueType fonts have a .TTF file extension. There are tools that can help you determine which fonts might be candidates for deletion. Some fonts are similar in appearance, and at times it can be difficult to distinguish among them. In this situation, the Fonts viewer will assist you. Many fonts have what is called a **_PANOSE file_**, which supplies information about the font. Windows XP Professional can compare fonts that have PANOSE files and list the similar ones. If a font has no PANOSE file, Windows XP Professional cannot compare it to other fonts.

12   Click **Cancel**. Deselect the Arial icon. Press $\boxed{\text{Ctrl}}$ + $\boxed{\text{Home}}$. On the toolbar, click the icon for List Fonts by Similarity, $\boxed{\text{AB}}$.

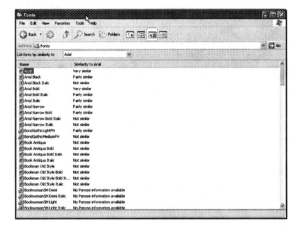

WHAT'S **HAPPENING?** You see a list of fonts, which varies based on the fonts installed on your system. They are listed by similarity to Arial as indicated in the drop-down list box. You also see that all styles of Arial are listed, such as Arial Italic. You can simplify your display. You are currently, on this system, looking at 165 fonts. Your display could be different.

13 Click **View**. Click **Hide Variations (Bold, Italic, etc.)** to set it.

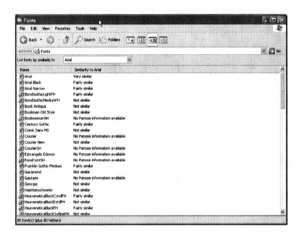

WHAT'S **HAPPENING?** By hiding the variations, it is easier to see what fonts are similar to others. You have limited your display. In this example, the status bar indicates you have reduced the number of fonts that you are looking at to 85 (with 85 hidden). Now you can see how many fonts are similar without viewing several variations of the same font.

14 In the **List fonts by similarity to** drop-down list box, click the down arrow. Locate and click **Times New Roman**.

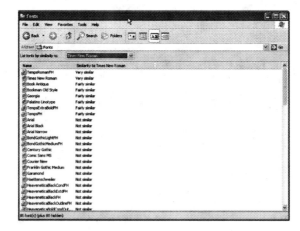

WHAT'S HAPPENING? Now you are comparing fonts to Times New Roman.

15 Click the Large Icons toolbar button, ▣ .

16 Click **View**. Click **Hide Variations (Bold, Italic, etc.)** to unset it.

17 Click **File**. Click **Install New Font**.

WHAT'S HAPPENING? Windows has found no fonts in the root of C. Normally Windows wants to copy any fonts to the Fonts folder, so the default Copy fonts to Fonts folder check box is set. You may have fonts in any folder on your hard drive. If you uncheck the Copy option, Windows XP Professional will place a shortcut in the Windows\Fonts folder and not copy the file there. There are reasons for not copying font files to the Fonts folder. If your hard disk space is at a premium and the font files exist elsewhere on the disk, there is no point to creating an extra copy. If the font files you want to use are on a network drive, there is no reason to store the font files on your hard drive. If you have special fonts that you wish to keep isolated, such as fonts for a specific graphics program, you would not want to copy the fonts here. Also, if you have purchased a CD-ROM with hundreds of fonts, you really do not want all of those fonts on your hard drive. You may use a selected font without installing it to the hard drive although you will need to insert the CD when you wish to use that font. There are three fonts in the XPRODATA\Funstuff folder. You are going to install shortcuts to the Grunge font in the Fonts folder.

18 Clear the **Copy fonts to Fonts folder** check box.

19 In the Folders list box, double-click the Drive C icon. (If your XPORDATA folder is on a drive other than C, you will need to select the drive in the Drives drop-down list box.) Double-click **XPRODATA**. Double-click **Funstuff**.

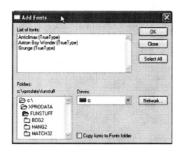

WHAT'S HAPPENING? Three fonts were found: Anticlimax, Astron Boy Wonder, and Grunge. These are fonts that are in the public domain. Many fonts are copyrighted. If a font is copyrighted and you do not purchase it, it is illegal to copy or use it.

20 Click the Grunge font.

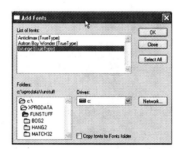

WHAT'S HAPPENING? You have selected the font you want installed. Since the Copy fonts to Fonts folder check box is empty, only a shortcut to the Grunge font file will be placed in the Fonts folder.

21 Click **OK**. If necessary, scroll until you locate **Grunge**. Click it to select it.

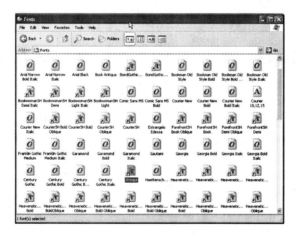

WHAT'S HAPPENING? The Grunge font has a shortcut arrow, indicating that it is a pointer to the file in the XPRODATA\FUNSTUFF folder.

22 Double-click **Grunge**.

WHAT'S **HAPPENING?** You see what the Grunge font looks like. This font will now be available in any program that uses fonts.

23   Click **Done**. Right-click **Grunge**. Click **Delete**.

WHAT'S **HAPPENING?** A dialog box asks you to confirm your request to delete the font. You can safely delete this font because you are only deleting the shortcut, not the font file.

24   Click **Yes**. Click **Tools**. Click **Folder Options**. Click the **View** tab. Set the **Do not show hidden files and folders** option. Click **OK**.

WHAT'S **HAPPENING?** All fonts that have the hidden attribute set are hidden from view.

25   Close the Fonts window.

WHAT'S **HAPPENING?** You have returned to the desktop.

9.4 ● Using Special Symbols ● Character Map

Keyboards are an important part of using a computer. There are four primary keyboard types that are used with desktop computers. The older 83-key PC and XT keyboard and the 84-key AT keyboard are rarely used. Most users have the 101-key Enhanced keyboard or the new 104-key Enhanced Windows keyboard. The 101-key Enhanced keyboard has four major sections: the typing area, the numeric keypad, the cursor and screen control, and the function keys. The 104-key Enhanced Windows keyboard adds Windows keys and an application key plus additional Tab and Backspace keys. The Windows keys are used for Windows XP Professional functions. For instance, if you press the Windows key, 🪟, the Start menu appears. Many new software programs are starting to take advantage of these new keys. However, when you use notebook computers, keyboard layouts can be very different from desktop keyboard layouts. In order to save space, many functions keys or auxiliary keys are not in standard locations. In addition, new keyboards are being introduced that are programmable and include such features as being able to surf the Web with a press of a key.

How does this impact you? There is a relationship between the characters you see on the keyboard and the characters that appear on your screen. The characters that appear on your screen are stored in font files. Each font file has at least 224 character definitions, known as *character sets*. You know that every key on the keyboard serves at least double duty, such as the lowercase a and the uppercase A or the ' and the ". You get the alternate character by holding down the **Shift** key. It may seem very simple to you—you press the letter a and the letter a appears. In reality, what is going on is that a keyboard consists of a set of switches mounted in a grid called a key matrix. When you press a key, a processor in the keyboard identifies which key is pressed and maps it to the grid. Identifying which key is pressed, however, does not tell the operating system which character or symbol to display on the screen.

To solve this problem, a coding scheme was developed to assign numeric values to letters, numbers, and other characters. This coding scheme is called ASCII (American Standard Code for Information Interchange). There are 256 characters available for each font. ASCII divides the 256 characters into two sets—standard and extended—with 128 characters each. The standard set is universal. It uses the first 32 values for communication and printer control codes. The remaining 96 codes are assigned to common punctuation marks, the digits 0 through 9, and the uppercase and lowercase letters of the Roman alphabet. The extended set codes, the remaining 128, are assigned to variable sets of characters provided by computer manufacturers and software developers. This scheme is also referred to as the extended ASCII character set or the IBM extended character set used by most character-based programs.

Now most Windows fonts use the ***American National Standards Institute (ANSI)*** character set. Although in the United States, at least, the ANSI and IBM extended sets are identical for the characters numbered between 32 and 127, which correspond to the letters, numbers, and symbols on the standard keyboard, the two sets differ when it comes to other characters. For instance, the British pound symbol (£) in ANSI uses the number 163, whereas the extended character set uses the number 156. However, you do not need to worry about whether it's ANSI or ASCII; you simply need to know the number for the character you wish to use.

Windows XP Professional also supports the character set called Unicode developed by the Unicode Consortium. ***Unicode*** is an international standard that represents the characters that are in common use in the major languages of the world. It allows almost all characters of the written languages of the world to be represented. Unicode is a 16-bit character encoding system where each character is stored as two bytes of data. This permits tracking of 65,536 characters. This lets languages with more than 256 characters be tracked. The traditional character sets are only single-byte and thus can define only 256 characters per set. To date, approximately 39,000 Unicode characters have been assigned with 21,000 alone being used for Chinese ideographs. Some programs, however, do not understand Unicode and cannot read a file saved in Unicode format.

Each character in a character set is assigned a unique numeric code. Thus, both a and A have a unique code. However, there are more character codes available than keys on the keyboard. For instance, if you want to use ½ instead of 1/2, that character is not available on your key-board, but it is typically available in a font set. So how do you access this character? The trick is to know the assigned code. Then you make sure the **NumLock** key is turned on, hold down the **Alt** key, and press the correct number on the numeric keypad (do not use the numbers across the top of the keyboard). For instance, in the font Century Schoolbook, ½ has been assigned the number 0189. To access this character, you would hold down the **Alt** key; press 0, then 1, then 8, and then 9 on the numeric keypad; and then release the **Alt** key.

Unicode characters often give their numeric value in hexadecimal. Hexadecimal is a base-16 number system represented by the digits 0 through 9 and the uppercase or lowercase letters A (equivalent to decimal 10) through F (equivalent to decimal 15). Decimal, the number system you are most familiar with, is a base-10 number system. A base-10 number system uses only 10 digits—0 through 9. You can convert numbers from one system to another. A simple tool that is provided with Windows that allows you to do so is Calculator.

There are many special symbols available, such as the copyright symbol (©), the registered symbol (®), foreign characters (like â), and even pictures (&). As you can imagine, it would be very difficult to remember all these numbers. Here is where Character Map can assist you. Character Map is an accessory that gives you access to special symbols and characters used in application programs. Character Map shows you the character set of each font installed on your system. It displays the assigned keystrokes required to create each character from the keyboard. You can easily copy a character from Character Map into an application.

9.5 • Activity • Using Character Map and Calculator with WordPad

1 Open WordPad.

2 Click **Start**. Point at **All Programs**. Point to **Accessories**. Point at **System Tools**. Click **Character Map**.

3 In the **Font** drop-down list box in Character Map, locate **Times New Roman**. Click it.

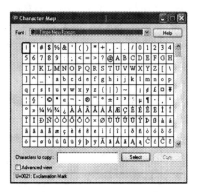

WHAT'S HAPPENING? You have opened both WordPad and Character Map. The selected character, the exclamation mark (!), has a dark border surrounding it. The Unicode character code for that character appears in the lower-left corner of the window (U+0021).

All the characters available in this set are in the grid. Each one is tiny. You can view a character in a larger format by placing the mouse pointer over it and clicking the mouse button.

4 Click the lowercase **a** (fourth row, fifth column).

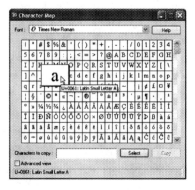

WHAT'S HAPPENING? You see the lowercase a. As you hover over the letter, you see a tool tip indicating the Unicode number. The keystroke necessary to display the letter a is, of course, the a key, referred to as Latin Small Letter A. This simply means to press the a on the keyboard.

5 Click the cell in the seventh row, fifth column.

WHAT'S HAPPENING? You have selected the ¾ character. The keystroke to insert it into your document appears in the lower-right corner of the window. It is **Alt** + 0190 and the Unicode number in hexadecimal is 00BE.

6 Click WordPad to make it active. Choose Times New Roman as the font. Be sure the **NumLock** is on. Hold down the **Alt** key. Press 0, then 1, then 9, then 0 on the numeric keypad. Then release the **Alt** key.

WHAT'S HAPPENING? You inserted the ¾ character by using the **Alt** key and the correct number code. Notice that the font size is 10 points, which is the WordPad default. Besides telling you keystroke

combinations, Character Map can be even easier to use.

7 Make the Character Map window active. Click ¾. Click the **Select** command button. Click the **Copy** command button.

WHAT'S HAPPENING? You have selected the character you want to copy. It appears in the Characters to copy text box.

8 Click WordPad. If the insertion point moved to the next line, press **Backspace**. On the toolbar, click **Paste**.

WHAT'S HAPPENING? You pasted ¾ into the document. Notice the font size has changed to 12 points and you have moved to the next line. Characters in the Character Map grid are sized at 12 points. Windows XP Professional also supplies two fonts that provide pictures instead of characters. The fonts are Wingdings and Webdings.

9 In the taskbar, click Character Map. In the Font drop-down list box, locate and click the OpenType font **Wingdings**. Click the "happy face" character in the third row, second column.

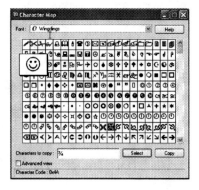

WHAT'S HAPPENING? An Alt keystroke combination to insert this character in your document does not appear in the right corner of the window. You can use Character Map's Copy command button and WordPad's Paste command to insert this character in your document or you can drag and drop.

10   Tile the windows horizontally. In Character Map, place your mouse pointer in the middle of the happy face character. Drag the character to the WordPad document.

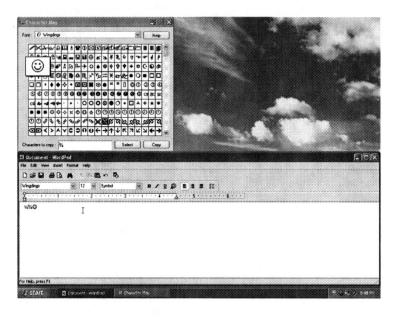

WHAT'S HAPPENING? By tiling the windows, you see both the Character Map and WordPad windows. When you dragged and dropped, you copied the happy face into WordPad. You have a happy face, but it is quite small.

11   In WordPad, select the happy face character. Change the font size to 36. Click next to the character to deselect it.

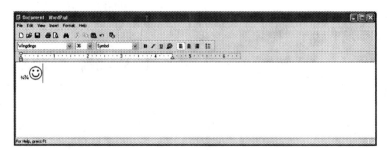

WHAT'S **HAPPENING?** Now the character is more visible because it is larger.

12 Key in the following: **test**

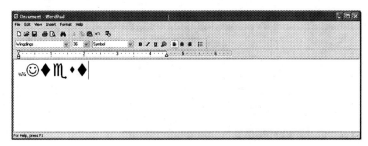

WHAT'S **HAPPENING?** Instead of letters, you see different symbols. You are still using the Wingdings font.

13 Select the four characters you just keyed in. Select Times New Roman as the font. Click outside the text to deselect it.

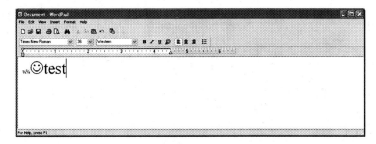

WHAT'S **HAPPENING?** Now you can see your characters as letters rather than pictures because Times New Roman shows letters whereas Wingdings displays pictures.

14 Right-click the taskbar. Click **Undo Tile**. Close WordPad. Do not save the document.

15 In the Character Map window, select the Arial font. Click the Advanced view check box to set it.

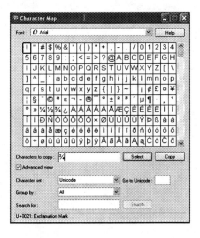

WHAT'S **HAPPENING?** You can use this view to search for characters by Unicode character name or by Unicode subgroup. For instance, suppose you want to use the currency symbol for the Italian lira but you have no idea what the keystrokes are for that currency symbol. You can use the Search for text box to locate the symbol.

16 The Character set is Unicode and the Group by is **All**. In the Search for text box, key in **lira**. Click **Search**.

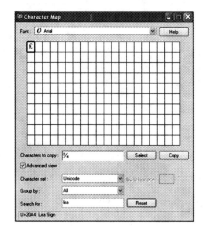

WHAT'S HAPPENING? Since the selected font, Arial, contains the lira currency symbol, it appears in the window. What if you didn't know the name of the character you were searching for?

17 Click **Reset**. Click the **Group by** drop-down list box. Click **Unicode Subrange**.

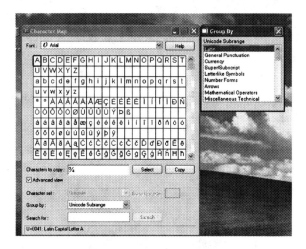

WHAT'S HAPPENING? A Group By dialog box appears listing all the ways you can look for characters.

18 In the Group By dialog box, click **Currency**.

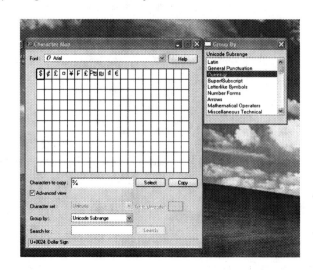

WHAT'S HAPPENING? All currency charac-ters in the Arial font, including the lira currency symbol, appear in the window.

19 Click the seventh character, the Lira symbol.

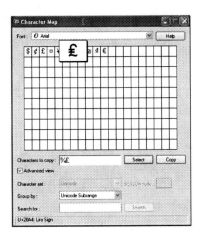

WHAT'S HAPPENING? The Lira sign shows as Unicode hexadecimal number of 20A4. To use the [Alt] key and the numeric keypad, you need to know the decimal number.

20 Click **Start**. Point to **All Programs**. Point to **Accessories**. Click **Calculator**.

WHAT'S HAPPENING? You opened Calcula-tor, which, by default, is in its standard arithmetic mode. The Calculator tool is an arithmetic and scientific calculator. An arithmetic calculator provides basic math-ematical functions, such as addition, subtraction, and division. A scientific calculator provides additional mathematical functions, such as calculating the sine or cosine of trigonometric functions and converting decimal numbers into binary, hexadecimal, or octal numbers. Calculator does not provide any business functions such as calculating interest rates, rates of return, or future values.

21 Click **View**. Click **Scientific**.

WHAT'S HAPPENING? You are now looking at the scientific mode of the calculator. In the scientific mode, you can perform a number of scientific functions, such as squaring a number or identifying the reciprocal of a number. You may also view numbers in four number systems – hexa-decimal, decimal, octal, and binary. You are going to convert the hexadecimal number to decimal.

22 Click **Hex**. Click **2**, then click **0**. Click **A**, then click **4**.

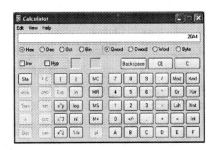

WHAT'S HAPPENING? You have keyed in the hexadecimal Unicode number for the Lira sign. You want to know its decimal equivalent.

23 Click **Dec**.

WHAT'S HAPPENING? Now you could open WordPad, hold the [Alt] key, and key in 8536 and you would display the Lira sign.

24 Click **View**. Click **Standard**. Close Calculator.

25 In Character Map, clear the **Advanced view** option.

26 Close Character Map. Close Notepad.

WHAT'S **HAPPENING?** You have returned to the desktop.

9.6 • The Printers and Faxes Folder

The Printers and Faxes folder, located on the Start menu and in the Control Panel folder, is a special kind of folder. It is a container that, instead of showing files on a disk, contains an icon for every printer driver installed on your computer system. Nearly everything to do with printers can be managed from the Printers and Faxes folder. You can install new printer drivers, delete printer drivers you are no longer using, change the characteristics of a printer driver, set the default printer, and view and manage the print queue of jobs that are printing.

A printer is a physical device that is much slower than a computer. A printer cannot print as fast as a computer can send it data. So that you do not have to wait to use your computer until the printer is done printing, Windows XP Professional uses print queues. A print queue is a special part of computer memory, called a buffer. *Buffers* are regions of memory that are reserved for data that is being temporarily held while waiting to be transferred between two locations, in this case, between the computer and the printer. When an application places a document into a print queue, the document is held in a line (a queue), where it waits until the printer is ready to print it.

If you are on a stand-alone system, it is most likely that you have only one printer, which is connected by cable directly to your parallel port or USB port. This is considered a *local printer*. *Local* is not just used to refer to printers. A local device is one that can be accessed directly rather than by some type of communication line. A local operation is one performed by the computer at hand rather than by a remote computer. A network printer is one that is connected physically to another computer or to a server on a network. You can print across the network to the printer once you have the correct printer driver installed on your computer. There is one more aspect to a so-called network printer. Today, many homes and businesses have several computers and printers. It is no longer necessary to have a printer physically attached to a print server—a computer that is dedicated fully or partially to manage printers. Instead, one can purchase a hub. A hub is a device that is used to connect several computers and other devices, such as a printer. The hub is responsible for directing the communication among computers and devices. A hub is a place of convergence where data arrives from one or more directions and is forwarded out in one or more other directions. Computers and devices all have ports. A port is a specific place for being physically connected to some other device, usually with a socket or plug of some kind. With a hub, the computers and devices attach to a network cable which is attached to the hub that directs the traffic. This technology is rapidly changing as the new wave of technology is wireless. The principle is still the same, but now you no longer need physical cables to be connected to the hub. And again, there are other choices today such as purchasing a device that simply acts as a print server but is not actually a stand-alone computer. This device also attaches to a hub. However, if you have a low-end (inexpensive) printer, it usually will not be able to be hung on a hub as it will not have the ability to have a network card installed in it.

In reality, what the Printers and Faxes folder is showing you is not the printer physically attached to your system, but instead all the printers for which printer drivers have been installed. Remember, a printer driver is a mini-program that lets Windows control the printer and the applications that print to it. A printer driver can be associated with a local or network printer. When you install a printer what you are really doing is installing a printer driver for that brand of printer. This terminology can be confusing because it would seem that to install a printer means to attach the printer cable to the computer and plug the printer into a power source. In the Windows XP Professional Printers and Faxes folder, installing a printer means installing software—the printer driver.

If you have a new computer or add a new printer to your computer, the installation of the printer driver is done automatically by Windows. When you add a new printer and you boot your system, Windows XP Professional normally detects the new hardware and will install the correct driver for that printer brand. This procedure is part of the *plug and play* that Windows XP Professional promises; you "plug" in a device, and Windows XP Professional knows how to install it correctly—how to "play" it. However, sometimes Windows XP Professional will not install your printer automatically. You must then go the Printers folder and add your printer manually by using the Add Printer wizard. You may have acquired a more recent printer driver for your printer and wish to install it. You may have added another printer to your system and need to install the driver that came with it. In addition to installing printer drivers for printers that are either local or networked, you may wish to install printer drivers for printers that you do not own or are not connected to.

A frustrating problem for users is a printed page that does not match what is seen on the screen. If the printer does not have access to the same fonts that are on the screen, the font that is substituted likely has minute differences that will throw off spacing in items like columns or page numbers. One way to solve this problem is to use only outline fonts. There are circumstances where you would want to use printer fonts. For instance, say you have a special printer at work with special printer fonts. You create a document that is heavily formatted and requires the printer fonts from that printer. If you install that printer driver and select that printer as your default printer on your home computer, the document will not print correctly on your printer, although it will print correctly on the printer at work.

You may also create a logical or virtual printer which will point to one physical printer. A virtual printer is a logical representation of a physical device. A virtual printer has many uses. For instance, if you were an administrator, you could configure different settings for each named virtual printer such as assigning different permissions or hours of use. Each of these configurations could be saved as a separate printer even though it was the same physical printer. You might also want to create a virtual printer for a printer that is not installed on your system. For instance, when you create a document in a word-processing program, it is configured to your local printer specifications. If you wanted to send this document out so that anyone could print it, you might want to install a more generic type printer so that your document would print on any printer.

In the Printers and Faxes folder, Windows uses different icons to represent different types of printers. See Figure 9.4.

Figure 9.4 • Printer Icons

A printer may be represented as an icon in your Printers and Faxes folder, but not available to use. It could be that there is a problem with the printer, that there is a problem with the printer driver, or simply that you are not on the network, and thus, the printer is not available to you. You can tell if one is not available either by being in Tile view or by placing your mouse pointer on the printer icon. In Figure 9.5, the message indicates that the printer cannot be found. In this case, it is because the computer to which that printer is attached is not turned on.

Figure 9.5 • An Unavailable Printer

9.7 • Activity • Adding a Printer

Note: If you are in lab environment, check with your instructor to see if you should do this activity.

I   Click **Start**. Click **Printers and Faxes**.

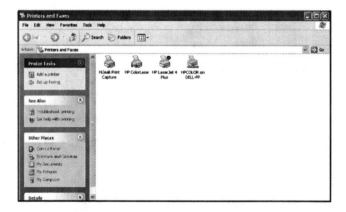

WHAT'S **HAPPENING?** Your Printers and Faxes window will be different depending on what printers you have on your system. In this example, there are three local printers and one network printer. The default printer in this example is an HP Laser Jet 4 Plus. You know it is the default printer because there is a checkmark over the icon. You may delete a printer icon and then reinstall the printer driver from this window. You would delete an icon if you were having trouble with that printer or you bought a new printer and wanted to delete the old printer.

2 Click **Add a Printer**.

WHAT'S HAPPENING? You have begun Add Printer Wizard. The wizard will lead you through the steps you need to take to install a printer driver. Windows XP Professional provides many such wizards for different tasks. Remember, a wizard is a mini-program that uses step-by-step instructions to lead you through the execution and completion of a task in Windows XP Professional.

3 Click **Next**.

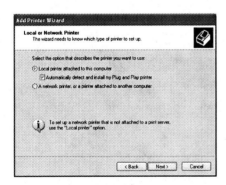

WHAT'S HAPPENING? Here you choose either a local or a network printer. If you had a hub and a printer that was "hanging" off the hub, you would choose Local printer.

4 Be sure Local printer is selected. Clear **Automatically detect and install my Plug and Play printer**. Click **Next**.

WHAT'S HAPPENING? You must choose which port the printer is going to be connected to. Normally, for a local printer, you use the printer port, called LPT1. This is the connection where your printer is physically connected. If you had a hub, you would create a new port where the network connection existed.

5 Click **Next**.

WHAT'S HAPPENING? The wizard highlights the last printer driver you installed. Printer drivers are very specific. They not only require that you know your brand name but also your specific model. If you install the wrong printer driver for your printer, your printer will not only print your documents incorrectly but may also print "garbage" characters, send multiple blank pages to the printer, or create general havoc. In fact, many printer problems that users have result from an incorrect printer driver being installed.

You are going to install a generic text printer, which is a minimally functioning printer driver that you can use when nothing else works as well as allow you to print to a printer that is "generic" so that any document can be printer on any printer.

6   Scroll in the Manufacturers list box until you locate **Generic**. Click it.

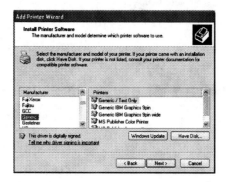

WHAT'S HAPPENING? Generic/Text Only is the most basic driver that Windows XP Professional offers.

7   Click **Generic/Text Only**. Click **Next**.

Note: You may go directly to the screen following step 8.

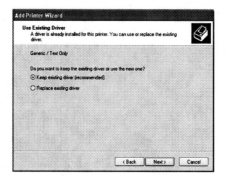

WHAT'S HAPPENING? If you already have an existing driver for this printer installed on your system, you will be asked if you wish to keep the existing driver. If you did not have a driver for the printer you selected, you would see the following dialog box.

Figure 9.6 ◦ Missing Printer Driver

You would have to acquire the correct driver. Usually, if you purchase a new printer, it has a CD with it with proper drivers. If it is a network printer, you have to contact your network administrator to install it.

8   Be sure **Keep existing driver (Recommended)** is selected, then click **Next**.

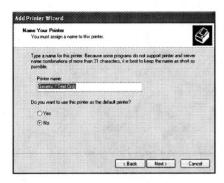

WHAT'S HAPPENING? You may give the printer any name you wish. You can also choose to make it the default printer, but in this case you do not wish to do so.

9 Be sure **No** is selected. Click **Next**.

WHAT'S HAPPENING? You are asked if you wish to share this printer with other users on the network. In this case, you do not wish to share it.

10 Be sure **Do not share this printer** is selected. Click **Next**.

WHAT'S HAPPENING? Although you can print a test page, you do not wish to do so.

11 Be sure **No** is selected. Click **No**. Click **Next**.

WHAT'S HAPPENING? A summary of your printer specifications appears. To correct any printer setting, click the Back button until you reach the step containing the incorrect information.

12 Click **Finish**.

WHAT'S HAPPENING? If this printer has not been installed before, Windows may need the CD-ROM to locate the correct printer driver file. After you place the CD-ROM in the drive, you will see a message that it is copying files. If the printer driver is already on your computer, the printer is simply installed, and you see the following in your Printers window:

Now that you have created your printer, you may use it for printing generic documents.

13 Open WordPad. Click **File**. Click **Print**.

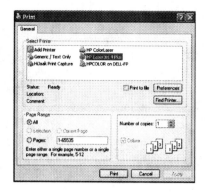

WHAT'S HAPPENING? Your normal default printer is selected. In order to format your document, you must select the Generic/Text Printer.

14   Click **Generic/Text Only**. Click **Apply**.

WHAT'S HAPPENING? You just selected the Generic/Text Only printer as your default printer. Now you would click Cancel and create your document and it would be formatted correctly for this printer. Another example would be, for instance, if you have a printer at work that will print 11-by-17-inch paper such as an HP 1220. At home, you have another printer, say an HP4000 that does not print 11-by-17 paper. If you created a document at home on the HP 1220, it would not adjust margins or length or anything to do with a bigger piece of paper. To solve the problem, you would "install" the HP 1220 at home. Take the above steps and when you took your document to work, it would print properly on the HP4000.

15   Click your default printer. Click **Apply**. Click **Cancel**. Close WordPad.

16   In the Printers window, select **Generic/Text Only**. Press the ⟮Delete⟯ key.

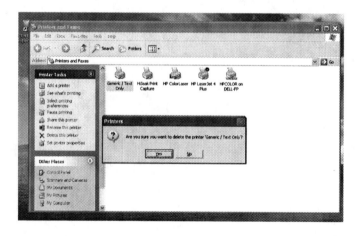

WHAT'S **HAPPENING?** You are asked if you want to delete the Generic/Text Only. Remember, all you are deleting is the icon.

17 Click **Yes**.

18 Close the Printers and Faxes window.

9.8 ◦ Managing Your Printer

In reality when you choose to print a document in a Windows program, Windows creates a temporary file on your hard disk called a *spool file*. While this spool file is being prepared, your application is busy and not available to use. When you see the hourglass icon, the program is telling you to wait. If your files are small, as has been the case with the documents you have been printing in this textbook, the process is so fast you do not have to wait. If, however, you had larger files, you would see the hourglass. Once the spool file is created, it is considered a *print job* and sent to the print queue.

You can check the status of the print queue by opening the printer in the Printers and Faxes window or, if the printer is already printing, opening the printer by clicking the printer icon on the taskbar. Once the window is open, you may view what documents are printing. In addition, by using the commands available in the Printer and Faxes window, you may pause and resume printing some or all of the documents, rearrange the order of documents printing, or remove some or all of the documents from the print queue. These commands are effective only if you have a local printer that you can control and if you have the proper permissions. By default, you must be a member of the Administrators or Power Users group to have full access to the printer and to manage the printer.

If you are using a printer on a network, the spool file is sent to the hard disk of the network computer where the printer is attached. This is typically called a print server. On a network printer, if you are not the network administrator or do not have administrator privileges, you are often very limited in what you can do to the print queue. Usually, you cannot in any way manage the print queue, except to cancel your own print jobs.

If you have a notebook computer, you often do not have a printer with you. You may then choose to print offline. This feature allows you to save your spool files. When you reconnect your computer to a printer, or go online, your documents will print. You may also choose to print offline with a network printer.

9.9 ◦ Activity ◦ Managing the Print Queue

Note 1: If you do not have a local printer, you will not be able to do these activities.
Note 2: Check with your lab instructor for any special instructions for these activities.

I   Open the Printers and Faxes folder. Right-click your default printer.

WHAT'S HAPPENING? From this menu, you can perform the usual tasks such as Open, Create a Shortcut, Rename, or Delete. In addition, you can perform special printer tasks such as pausing the printer (Pause Printing), Sharing it (Sharing…), or using the printer offline. Using a printer offline, means that, for instance, if you had a notebook computer and did not have immediate access to a printer, you could still print your documents. The documents would go to a spool file. Then, when you connected your notebook to a printer, all the documents would print.

2   Click **Open**.

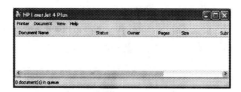

WHAT'S HAPPENING? Since you have not selected any document to print, your printer window is empty.

3   On the menu bar, click **Printer**.

WHAT'S HAPPENING? You can pause the printer from this menu. When you pause the printer, no documents will be sent to the printer until you indicate that you wish them to be sent. In addition, you can cancel all the documents waiting to print, if there are any.

4   Click **Pause Printing** to set it. On the menu bar, click **Printer**.

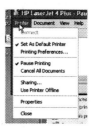

WHAT'S HAPPENING? Your printer is now paused and no documents will print. You are pausing the printer because the documents you are going to place in the queue are so small, they would all print before you could open the printer window. This activity will allow you to queue up many documents to print and experiment with the features of the printer window without having to waste paper by printing the documents.

5   Click outside the menu to close it.

6   Click **Start**. Click **Search**. Click **All files and folders** if necessary. Click **View**. Click **Status Bar** to set it.

7   In the All or part of the file name text box, key in ***.txt**.

8   In the Look in text box, click the down arrow. Click **Browse**. Click **My Computer**. Click **Drive C**. Choose the XPRODATA folder. Click **OK**.

9   Click **More Advanced Options**. Clear **Search subfolders**.

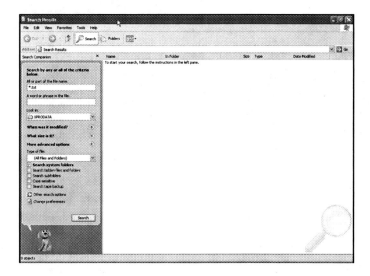

WHAT'S HAPPENING? You want to select only files with the .txt extension in the XPRODATA folder, not in all the subfolders beneath the XPRODATA folder.

10   Click **Search**.

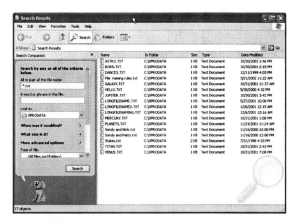

WHAT'S HAPPENING? Seventeen files were found. In this example, the Status Bar was on.

11   Click the first file in the list (**ASTRO.TXT**). Scroll to the last file, hold the Shift key and click.

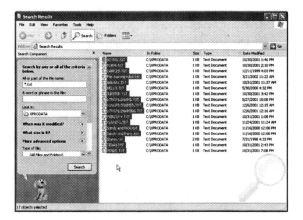

WHAT'S **HAPPENING?** You have selected all the files.

12 Click File. Click Print.

Note: If you do not see Print on the File menu, click outside the selected files. Then double-click each file to open it. When each file is open in Notepad, click File. Click Print. Click Print. Then close Notepad. Do this for each file in the Search Results window.

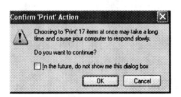

WHAT'S **HAPPENING?** You may see the following message box as Windows is warning you that it may take a long time to print these documents as you are lining up your documents to print (queuing). If you had to open and print each file individually because Print did not appear on the menu, you have run into a bug in Windows XP Professional. For some unknown reason, the right-click menu for certain registered file types will cease to work correctly. This bug may be fixed in later releases of Windows XP Professional. However, what you did by opening Notepad and printing each document from within Notepad is known as a work-around. If you cannot get something to work that is supposed to work, you have to find another solution—a work-around.

13 Click OK.

WHAT'S **HAPPENING?** You will see Notepad opening and closing 17 times, once for each file. Wait until no more Notepad windows open.

14 Close the Search Results window.

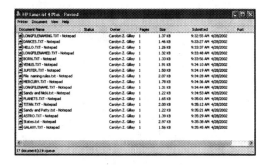

WHAT'S **HAPPENING?** Your file order may be different. If you cannot see all the files, size the window so it looks like the above example. You can see much information about your files—their names, what programs created them, who owns them, how long they are, and what date and time they began printing. If you were printing a long document and you opened the printer window, it would tell you which page it was printing.

15 Right-click ASTRO.TXT. Click Properties.

WHAT'S **HAPPENING?** There are two ways to specify when this document will print. First, you can drag the Priority slider to raise or lower the document's printing priority. The lowest priority is 1, and the highest priority is 99. Second, you can use the Schedule section to specify an exact time period for the document to print. If you are on a network, you may not be able to change the document's printing priority because as a user you may not have permission to manage documents.

16 Click **Cancel** to close the dialog box. Click **GALAXY.TXT**. Click **Document** on the menu bar.

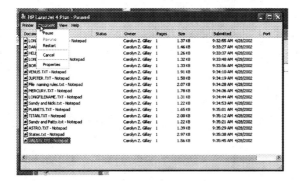

WHAT'S HAPPENING? You can restart the printer or cancel the printing of this one document.

17 Click **Cancel**.

WHAT'S HAPPENING? You are asked if you are sure.

18 Click **Yes**.

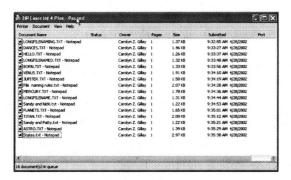

WHAT'S HAPPENING? GALAXY.TXT is no longer in the print queue.

19 Click **BORN.TXT**. Hold the Ctrl key and click **Sandy and Patty.txt**. Press the Delete key. Click **Yes**.

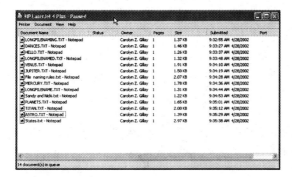

WHAT'S HAPPENING? You have removed two files from the print queue. You can also cancel all print jobs.

20 On the menu bar, click **Printer**. Click **Cancel All Documents**.

WHAT'S **HAPPENING?** You are asked to verify that you want to cancel all documents.

21 Click **Yes**.

WHAT'S **HAPPENING?** You have emptied the print queue. There are no longer any documents waiting to be printed.

22 Click **Printer**. Click **Pause Printing** to return the printer to an active state.

23 Close the printer window. Close any open windows.

WHAT'S **HAPPENING?** You have returned to the desktop.

Chapter Summary

In this chapter you learned about fonts. The terms *font* and *typeface* are used interchangeably, though technically they are different. You discovered that there are screen and printer fonts. Fonts are either monospaced or proportional. They are also either serif or sans serif. You learned that in some instances the technology to display fonts on the screen differs from the technology required to print fonts. You learned that outline fonts print the same as they appear on the screen. You learned to use the Fonts folder, install and uninstall a font, as well as compare fonts.

You learned that Character Map is a tool that provides you access to special characters and symbols, which you may use in programs such as WordPad. Character Map shows you the character set for each font you have installed on your system. It displays Unicode for all characters and the assigned keystroke combination for some characters and allows you to copy a character from Character Map into another application. If you use the keyboard to press the **Alt** key and key in a number to insert a character, you must be sure to use the numeric keypad. You must also convert a Unicode hexadecimal number to decimal to be able to use the **Alt** plus number on the numeric keypad. You may use the calculator tool to perform this conversion.

You also learned about the Printers and Faxes folder. The Printers and Faxes folder shows you all the printers installed on your system, local and network. You learned that installing a printer really means installing the printer driver for that printer. You learned that you can create logical printers that perform different functions on the same printer. You also learned that, if you have a local printer, you can manage the documents in the printer window by changing the priority of the print job, removing individual documents from the print queue, or clearing the print queue altogether.

Key Terms

Adobe Type 1

American National Standards
  Institute (ANSI)

bitmap font

buffer

built-in font

character set

font

local printer

monospaced typeface

OpenType

outline font

PANOSE file

plotter

plug and play

point

print job

printer driver

printer font

proportional typeface

resident font

sans serif font

scale

screen font

serif font

spool file

stroke weight

TrueType

typeface

Unicode

vector font

WYSIWYG

Discussion Questions

1. Compare and contrast fonts and typefaces.
2. What is the difference between serif and sans serif fonts?
3. Compare and contrast a screen font and a printer font.
4. What is a bitmap font? A vector font?
5. What are outline fonts? What are some of the advantages of using outline fonts?
6. Explain the purpose and function of the Fonts folder.
7. What directory normally stores fonts? How can you access this directory?
8. What tasks can be accomplished in the Fonts window?
9. Explain the purpose and function of Character Map.
10. A character set is not limited to the keys displayed on the keyboard. Explain.
11. What is the ASCII character set? The ANSI character set? A Unicode character set?
12. Explain two ways you may use Character Map to insert the © symbol in a WordPad document.
13. How might you use Calculator with Character Map? Why would it be necessary to use Calculator?
14. What is a local printer?
15. Explain why you might install a printer driver for a printer not physically attached to your system.
16. Compare and contrast a local printer and a network printer.
17. What is a print buffer?
18. List the necessary steps to install a new printer.
19. Why do you have less control over a network printer than a local printer?
20. You are printing 14 documents on a local printer. You open your default printer window. Identify three tasks you can accomplish in this window.

True/False Questions

For each question, circle the letter T if the statement is true or the letter F if the statement is false.

T   F   1. You may safely delete the MS Sans Serif font if you never use it in your documents.

T   F   2. In the computer world, the terms font and typeface are used interchangeably.

T   F   3. If you wanted to use ¾ instead of 3/4 in your document, Character Map could assist you.

T   F   4. The Printers and Faxes folder can show you icons only for printers that are physically attached to your system.

T   F   5. If you open your default printer window for your local printer, you may selectively delete documents from the print queue.

Completion Questions

Write the correct answer in each blank space.

6. A(n) _____ font gives all characters the same width.

7. The smallest point of light that can be displayed on the screen is called a(n) _____.

8. A(n) _____ font creates characters with a pattern of dots.

9. To insert the character , which has a number of 0191, you would hold down the _____ key and press 0191 on the _____ keypad.

10. If you see a printer icon that looks like

HP LaserJet 4 Plus

you know that it is a(n) _____ printer.

Multiple Choice Questions

Circle the letter of the correct answer for each question.

11. A character appearing in 12-point Times New Roman is an example of a
    a. font.
    b. bitmap graphic.
    c. both a and b
    d. neither a nor b

12. A font that varies the space given to each character is known as a _____ font.
    a. bitmap
    b. monospaced
    c. proportional
    d. serif

13. Windows XP Professional supplies a font that presents pictures instead of letters. The font is
    a. Webdings.
    b. Wingdings.
    c. both a and b
    d. neither a nor b

14. A Windows XP Professional mini-program that leads you through the steps of a task is a
    a. task manager.
    b. wizard.
    c. helper program.
    d. none of the above

15. If you have printer icons that point to the same physical printer, these printers are considered _____ printers.
    a. virtual
    b. local
    c. network
    d. none of the above

Application Assignments

Problem Set I—At the Computer

Problem A

* Open Calculator.

* Choose the Scientific mode. Click the **Dec** option button.

* Multiply 19 by 37.

* With the results still visible, click the **Hex** option button.

    1. The hexadecimal (Hex) equivalent of 19 * 37 is
        a. 703.
        b. 11.
        c. 1010111111.
        d. 2BF.

* Click the **Bin** option button.

    2. The binary equivalent of 19 * 37 is
        a. 703.
        b. 11.
        c. 1010111111.
        d. 2BF.

* Return Calculator to the Standard mode.

* Close Calculator.

Problem B

* Open Fonts in Control Panel.

* Double-click **Courier New**.

    3. The smallest font displayed is _____ points.
        a. 12
        b. 14
        c. 18
        d. 24

* Close the window.

* Click **View**. Click **List**.

* Click **View**. Click **Hide Variations (Bold, Italic, etc.)** to set it.

* Click **View**. Click **List Fonts by Similarity**.

* In the List fonts by similarity to drop-down list box, choose **Courier New**.

* In the Name list box, locate Arial.

    4. Arial
      a. is similar to Courier New.
      b. is not similar to Courier New.
      c. has no PANOSE information.

❋ Click **View**. Click **Hide Variations (Bold, Italic, etc.)** to deselect it.

❋ Click **View**. Click **Large Icons**.

❋ Locate the Modern font.

    5. The Modern font is a(n) _____ font.
      a. raster and vector
      b. TrueType
      c. unknown

❋ Close the Fonts window.

Problem C

❋ Open Fonts in Control Panel.

❋ Install the font called Astron Boy Wonder located in the XPRODATA\Funstuff folder. Be sure the **Copy fonts to Fonts folder** check box is clear.

❋ Install the font called Anticlimax located in the XPRODATA\Funstuff folder. Be sure the **Copy fonts to Fonts folder** check box is clear.

❋ Open the Astron Boy Wonder font.

    6. The year that Astron Boy Wonder was copyrighted was
      a. 1990.
      b. 1994.
      c. 1998.
      d. 2000.

    7. A sample of the Astron Boy Wonder font looks like which of the following?
      a. The quick brown fox jumps over the lazy dog.
      b. *The quick brown fox jumps over the lazy dog.*
      c. THE QUICK BROWN FOX JUMPS OVER THE LAZY DOG.
      d. *The quick brown fox jumps over the lazy dog.*

❋ Open the Anticlimax font.

    8. A sample of the Anticlimax font looks like which of the following?
      a. The quick brown fox jumps over the lazy dog.
      b. *The quick brown fox jumps over the lazy dog.*
      c. THE QUICK BROWN FOX JUMPS OVER THE LAZY DOG.
      d. *The quick brown fox jumps over the lazy dog.*

❋ Close the fonts window.

❋ Delete the Astron Boy Wonder and Anticlimax fonts.

    9. When you deleted these fonts, you
      a. deleted the font files from the XPRODATA\Funstuff folder.
      b. deleted the font file from the Windows\Fonts folder.
      c. retained the shortcut to the font in the Windows\Fonts folder but removed the font file in the XPRODATA\Funstuff folder.
      d. removed the shortcut to the font in the Windows\Fonts folder but retained the font file in the XPRODATA\Funstuff folder.

❋ Close the Fonts window.

❋ Close Control Panel.

Problem D

❋ Open WordPad.

❋ Open the document called Personal.fil in the XPRODATA directory.

    10. What street does Tai Chan Tran live on?

        a. Lemon

        b. Lakeview

        c. Miller

        d. Embassy

    11. What font is the document presented in?

        a. Times New Roman

        b. Arial

        c. Courier (or Courier New)

        d. Tahoma

    12. What is the font size?

        a. 10

        b. 12

        c. 14

        d. 16

❋ Close WordPad.

❋ Do not save the document to a disk.

Problem E

❋ Open Character Map.

❋ Locate and choose the OpenType Wingdings font.

    13. What is the picture in the last column, third row from the bottom? (Do not scroll the character list.)

        a. a computer

        b. a disk

        c. a clock

        d. a monitor

        e. a spider web

❋ Locate and choose the Webdings font.

    14. What is the picture in the second column, first row from the top?

        a. a computer

        b. a disk

        c. a clock

        d. a monitor

        e. a spider web

❋ Locate and choose the Times New Roman font.

15. The number for © is
    a. 0139.
    b. 0149.
    c. 0159.
    d. 0169.
    e. 0179.

  * Close Character Map.

Problem Set II—Brief Essay

For all essay questions, use Notepad or WordPad to create your answer. Be sure to include your name and your class information and which question you are answering. Then print your answer.

1. Compare and contrast fonts and typefaces. Identify the major categories of fonts that Windows XP Professional uses. Include in your discussion what the fonts are and how and why they are necessary. Describe the purpose and function of outline fonts.
2. What is the purpose and function of print queues?

Problem Set III—Scenario

You are at work and have been working on a report. You are ready to print your document. You open the Printers and Faxes folder and see the following window:

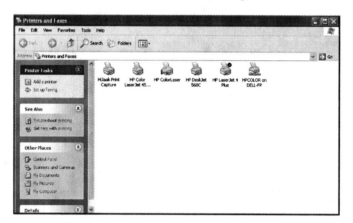

1. Only the HP Laser Jet 4 Plus printer is physically attached to your computer. The HP ColorLaser is hanging from your hub. The HP Color Laser Jet 45 is a printer you have at home that provides special printing capabilities. A fellow co-worker is at your desk when you open the window. He asks you what each one of the icons represents. Explain the purpose and function of these icons to your co-worker.
2. Your co-worker has purchased a printer for home use that has the ability to print 11-by-17-inch paper—HP LaserJet 1220 Series PS (MS). He does not understand why when he creates a document at work using the HP Laser Jet 4 Plus Printer, which does not allow any paper size other than 8 ½ by 11, and then tries to print the document on his new printer at home, he cannot use the larger paper. Explain what he has to do to be able to print properly at home. In other words, explain to your co-worker what a virtual printer is and the steps he needs to take to set up the HP LaserJet 1220 Series PS (MS).

CHAPTER 10

Customizing Your System

This chapter will demonstrate Windows XP Professional options that allow you to customize your computer based on your needs. You will use some of Control Panel's features to accomplish this customization. You will be able to save time by setting features so that they behave the way you want. You can change the themes, colors, and backgrounds for your desktop. You will learn about screen savers and power management features that help you protect your monitor and drives. You will learn about Active Desktop and different effects you can choose. Depending on your hardware, you will be able to make changes to your monitor's resolution. You can adjust your mouse and keyboard to better meet your needs. If you have a sound card, you can assign sounds to computer events as well as assign a theme to your entire desktop. You can adjust the date, time, and regional settings. You will learn about user accounts. You will learn how each of these customization features can be applied to meet your needs.

Learning Objectives

1. Explain the purpose and function of Control Panel and objects found in the Control Panel.
2. Explain how to customize your desktop by using themes and backgrounds.
3. Explain the purpose and function of screen savers and power management features.
4. Explain how to further customize your desktop by using the desktop's property sheet to determine how your desktop behaves and looks.
5. Explain how Active Desktop is used to integrate the desktop with the Internet.
6. Explain the purpose and function of screen resolutions.
7. List reasons for and ways of customizing the mouse and keyboard.
8. Describe an event and explain why sounds are assigned to it.
9. Describe the purpose of the system date and the system time.
10. Explain the purpose of regional settings.
11. Explain how to make more efficient use of menus.
12. Explain the purpose and function of user accounts and passwords.

Student Outcomes

1. Use themes, backgrounds, and colors to customize your desktop.
2. Customize your screen saver and power management options.
3. Use Control Panel to customize and adjust screen elements.
4. Identify the resolutions and colors available on your monitor.
5. Customize the functions of the mouse and the keyboard.
6. If a sound card is available, assign sounds to computer events.
7. Set the date and time.
8. View regional options.
9. Make more efficient use of menus by adding, moving, and rearranging folders, programs, or documents on the Start menu.
10. Create new user accounts that preserve settings for each computer user on the system and set passwords for a user, if possible.

10.1 • Introducing Control Panel

When Windows XP Professional was installed on your computer, it gave you a standard configuration for your desktop, keyboard, and mouse. The setup program chose standard colors, screen resolution, button and icon sizes, and icon locations. The way the keyboard and mouse operate was also established by the setup program.

You are not limited to these default choices. Control Panel allows you to make changes to the default settings. You can change the appearance and behavior of different elements of your workspace. For instance, you can control how much information fits on the screen by changing the resolution of your monitor (depending on the kind of monitor and video card you have). You can change the colors, add wallpaper, and change the size of the font for icons, toolbars, or any other items that appear on your screen. You can also speed up or slow down the movement of your mouse or keyboard. If you have the correct software, you can select larger, smaller, or animated pointers.

Besides providing ways to change some of the features of your system, Control Panel provides ways for you to maintain your system. Maintaining your system means adding or removing hardware or programs. Through Control Panel you can support networks, modems, and multimedia devices. Windows XP Professional also provides special support to physically challenged individuals so that they can have better control of their computers.

In order for Windows XP Professional to know what type of peripherals you have, such as which monitor or keyboard, and what choices you have made in regards to personal preferences, such as the desktop colors or what is on the Start menu, it must keep track of this information. This information is tracked in the Registry. When you install Windows XP Professional, your preferences are written to the Registry. After Windows XP Professional is installed, you may use Control Panel to make changes to your system. Control Panel allows you an easy way to make changes through wizards and dialog boxes. When you use Control Panel, the changes you make are written to the Registry, allowing you to configure your system easily without having to edit the Registry directly.

You may have more choices in Control Panel than those presented here. Some programs add items to Control Panel so that you can make alterations to them. The following is a list of what Windows XP Professional places in Control Panel.

Accessibility Options	To accommodate varying hearing, vision, and motor challenges, this option presents choices that make Windows XP Professional easier to use. You can alter the display, mouse, and keyboard settings and utilize sound to improve ease of use.
Add Hardware	Windows XP Professional detects and installs new plug-and-play hardware with this option.
Add or Remove Programs	You may add or remove Windows XP Professional components with this option. Components refer to Windows XP Professional programs that you may choose to install or not. You may also install other software that you purchase with this option.
Administrative Tools	This folder contains shortcuts to several tools that configure administrative settings for your computer.
Date and Time	Use this to change the system date or time.
Display	Use this option to alter nearly every setting for your desktop visual display. It also controls monitor type and monitor-related settings, including device drivers for your video card. A *device driver* is a special piece of software that drives, or controls, another device.
Folder Options	Use this option to change the way your folders appear as well as how you view your files. You can also change and alter file types. This is the same as choosing Folder Options from the Tools menu in the My Computer or Windows Explorer.
Fonts	Use this folder icon to see what fonts you have on your system and to add or remove fonts.

Game Controllers	You may have special devices such as a joystick or game paddles. These devices are popular pointing devices primarily used for playing computer games. If you have a device of this type installed, you can control its settings. You may also control how much disk space you allow for games.
Internet Options	This icon has all the controls for your Internet connection and lets you configure a variety of settings for Internet Explorer. Here you can change your home page, set up security options, and perform other tasks such as determining your email program and newsreader.
Keyboard	Use this Keyboard icon to change keyboard settings such as the cursor blink rate or the repeat rate of keys (how quickly characters repeat when you hold down a key). You may also update keyboard drivers here.
Mouse	Use this icon to alter the characteristics of your mouse. You can alter the double-click speed and the speed of the mouse as you drag it.
Network Connections	Use this icon to create new connections. You can also view, add, remove, and modify LAN components as well as dial-up connections.
Phone and Modem Options	Use this icon to identify the properties of your modem (a device to transmit data over phone lines), to install a new modem, and to configure or remove your existing modem. You can specify the dialing properties Windows uses when it dials using your computer's modem. You can also identify dialing rules for outside lines for local and long distance calls and disable call waiting.
Power Options	Power Options provides power schemes, which are a set of preset power options, such as how long the computer must be inactive before the monitor and/or disk drives are turned off. This feature helps you configure any power-saving features your computer may have. Power Management can also be accessed from the Display icon.
Printers and Faxes	Printers and Faxes will display the printers and faxes that are on your system. It will let you modify the property settings for those items. You may add or delete a printer or fax, choose paper size, and perform other printer or fax-related tasks. You may also access it from the Start menu.
Regional and Language Options	The Regional and Language Options icon accommodates the use of Windows in different countries. You can, for instance, change currency symbols or the date format.

Scanners and Cameras	This folder allows you to add any scanners or digital cameras you may have. This allows you to control these devices as well.
Scheduled Tasks	Use this icon to schedule computer tasks to run automatically.
Sounds and Audio Devices	Use this icon to enable or disable the beeping the computer makes to inform you of errors or events. If you have a sound card, you may assign prerecorded sound files to keyboard or mouse actions. For instance, you could have the computer make a chime sound every time you open a file. You may configure and troubleshoot any audio equipment you might have.
Speech	The Speech icon opens a dialog box where you can control the settings for any text-to-speech translations.
System	The System icon provides information about all your system resources such as the CPU and your disk drives. The controls for all these devices are also located here. Here you can view hardware settings, configure devices, remove devices, and configure general performance settings.
Taskbar and Start Menu	This icon will open the Taskbar and Start menu property sheet where you can customize your taskbar and Start menu. This can also be accessed by right-clicking the taskbar and clicking Properties.
User Accounts	This object allows you to manage user accounts. All user accounts currently on your computer system are listed here. You may add users, delete users, change settings for users, and create and change logon passwords with this icon. A *password* is a security measure used to restrict access to files and programs. It is a unique string of characters that a user keys in as an identification code. Here is also where you may enable or disable pressing Ctrl + Alt + Delete when you log on. However, you must be an Administrator to create accounts and make other changes.

In this chapter, you will use many, but not all of, these objects. You have already used Folder Options, Fonts, Printers and Faxes, and Taskbar and Start Menu objects. Since some of these objects are quite complicated, such as the Network or depend on the availability of hardware that you may not have, they will either be reserved for later chapters or not covered.

10.2 ◦ Themes

A *theme* is a coordinated look for your desktop, which affects your background, fonts, colors, sounds, mouse pointers, and so on. All the items that affect your desktop that are associated with a theme are preselected items. Thus, by one click of your mouse, you can change your entire desktop. Windows XP Professional provides only two desktop themes, Windows XP and

Classic. Its other choices take you to Microsoft's web site where you can browse online for other themes. There are also many other websites that offer different themes.

10.3 • Activity • Using Themes

1   Click **Start**. Click **Control Panel**. If you are not in Classic View, click **Switch to Classic View**.

2   Click **View**. Click **Tiles**. Place the pointer on the **Taskbar and Start menu** object.

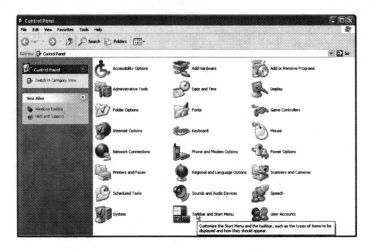

WHAT'S **HAPPENING?** A tooltip appears next to the Taskbar and Start Menu icon. A brief explanation appears next to the Taskbar and Start Menu icon. You have already worked with this object.

3   Place Control Panel in Details view. Size the Comment column so that you can read the comments.

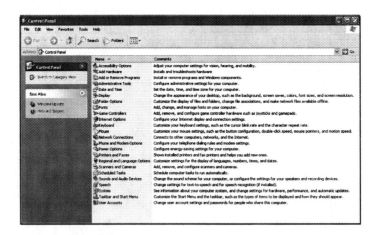

WHAT'S **HAPPENING?** A brief comment appears for each icon. You may have more or fewer objects. Your display will vary.

4   Click **Switch to Category View**.

WHAT'S HAPPENING? Category view groups the various elements of Control Panel into the categories that it thinks you might be interested in.

5   Click **Appearances and Themes**.

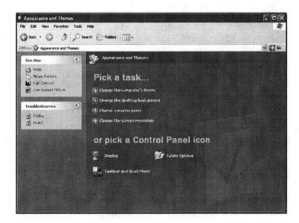

WHAT'S HAPPENING? You have opened up a new category window with more specific choices.

6   Click **Change the computer's theme**.

WHAT'S HAPPENING? You have arrived at the correct property sheet to change the theme. Most users find the Category view annoying as it involves a lot of clicking to get where you want to go. However, if you did not know which icon to pick in Control Panel, then Category View can assist you.

7   Click the down arrow in the drop-down list box.

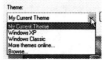

WHAT'S HAPPENING? Your choices are Windows XP, Windows Classic, My Current theme, More themes online, and Browse. Currently, on this system, there is no Current Theme. If you chose Browse, it would take you to a dialog box where you could search for files that have a .THEME extension. Your other choice is to go online.

8   Click **Windows Classic**. Click **OK**.

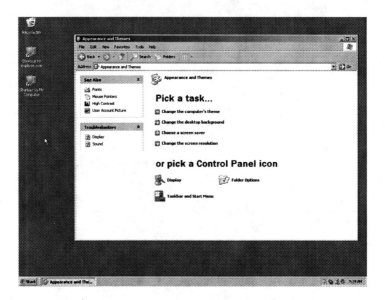

WHAT'S HAPPENING? If you have used previous versions of Windows, such as Windows Me, Windows 2000 Professional, or Windows 98, this view is familiar to you. The classic view is much more streamlined with less graphic elements.

9   Click **Change the computer's theme**. In the drop-down list box, click **Windows XP**. Click **Apply**.

WHAT'S HAPPENING? The advantage to choosing Apply rather than OK is that if you choose OK, the dialog box would close. By choosing Apply, you can change your results and not close the dialog box.

10 If you have a connection to the Internet, click the down-arrow in the drop down list box and choose **More themes online.**

WHAT'S HAPPENING? Your display may be different. Web sites change daily. In this example, Microsoft is advertising a product that provides "extras" for your Windows XP environment. If you clicked Themes, you would be shown samples of what is available in the package that you purchase. There are sites on the Internet that provide free themes.

11 Close the browser window. Close the **Appearance** dialog box. Click the back button.

12 Click **Switch to Classic view.** Click **View.** Click **Tiles.** Close the Control Panel window.

WHAT'S HAPPENING? You have returned to the desktop.

10.4 ● Wallpaper

You can customize your system by changing the background of your desktop. You may choose a wallpaper. A *wallpaper* is a graphic image that is stored as either as a bitmap graphics file in the standard .bmp (bitmap) format or in the Joint Photographic Experts Group (.jpg), pronounced J-Peg. The .bmp files are simple images whereas the .jpg files are photographic images that are much more powerful graphic images. Windows XP Professional comes with several wallpapers, which are stored in the Windows folder. You can also create your own wallpaper with a graphics program such as Paint. You can scan in an image and modify it, or you can modify an existing wallpaper. You can purchase different wallpaper files as well. In addition, if you have any .bmp, .jpg, .jpeg (JPEG bitmap) and .gif (Graphics Interchange Format) files in your My Pictures folder, Windows will also display those as choices for you in selecting a wallpaper. All of these extensions or file types refer to different types of graphic images.

10.5 ● Activity ● Using Wallpaper

1 Click **Start.** Click **Control Panel.** Click **View.** Click **Icons.**

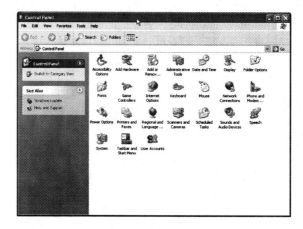

WHAT'S **HAPPENING?** ≫ You know the object you wish to use—Display.

2   Double-click Display.

WHAT'S **HAPPENING?** ≫ Everything to do with your display in contained in this dialog box. You can access this dialog box by right-clicking an empty space on the desktop and choosing Properties. Each tabbed item in Display Properties controls some aspect of your display. The Themes tab is active.

3   Click the Desktop tab.

WHAT'S **HAPPENING?** ≫ The current choice is Bliss. Your selection may be different.

4   In the list box, locate and click on **Coffee Bean**. In the Position drop-down list box, choose **Center**. Click **OK**.

5   Close the Control Panel window.

WHAT'S HAPPENING? When a wallpaper image is centered, only one copy of the image appears. Note that you are in Classic view as well.

6   Right-click the desktop. Click **Properties**. Click the **Desktop** tab. In the Background drop-down list box, choose **Tile**. Click **OK**.

WHAT'S HAPPENING? Tiling an image repeats the image until the desktop is covered.

7   Right-click the desktop. Click **Properties**. Click the **Desktop** tab. In the Background drop-down list box, choose **Stretch**. Click **OK**.

WHAT'S HAPPENING? Stretching takes the image and stretches it to fill the screen. You see that the image is not as sharp and clear since you are expanding a smaller picture.

8   Right-click the desktop. Click **Properties**. Click the **Desktop** tab. In the Background list box, choose **Azul**. In the Position drop-down list box, choose **Tile**.

WHAT'S HAPPENING? In the sample box, you see a photographic image. Windows XP Professional includes some very beautiful photographic images that you can use as wallpaper.

9   Locate and click **Bliss** for background. In Position, choose **Stretch**. Click **OK**.

10   Open Windows Explorer. Open My Computer. Open Drive C. Open the XPRODATA folder. Select **BASKET.BMP**. Click **Edit**. Click **Copy**.

11   Click **Start**. Click **My Pictures**. Click **Edit**. Click **Paste**.

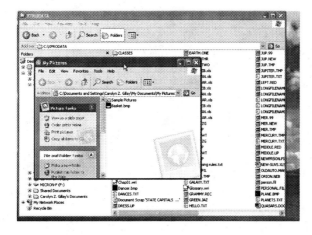

WHAT'S HAPPENING? In the My Pictures folder, you just copied the file Basket.bmp.

12   Make the XPRODATA folder active. Double-click **PIX**. Click **Student.jpg**. Click **Edit**. Click **Copy**. Close the XPRODATA window.

13   In the My Pictures window, click **Edit**. Click **Paste**.

WHAT'S HAPPENING? You now have two graphic files in the My Pictures window, one a .bmp file and the other a .jpg file.

14   Close all open windows.

15   Right-click the desktop. Click **Properties**. Click the **Desktop** tab. In the Background drop-down list box, choose **Basket**. Click **Tile**. Click **OK**.

WHAT'S **HAPPENING?** You now have a picture of your choosing as your background.

16   Right-click the desktop. Click **Properties**. Click the **Desktop** tab. In the Background drop-down list box, choose **Student**. Click **Tile**. Click **OK**.

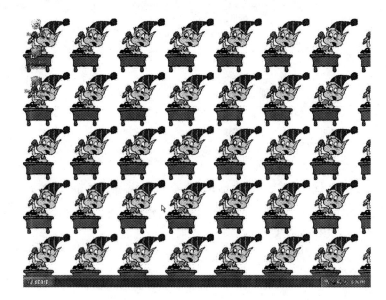

WHAT'S **HAPPENING?** You now have another picture of your choosing as your background. As you can see, you can customize the background with any graphic image you like—a picture you draw in Paint, a photo that you scan in and so on.

17   Right-click the desktop. Click **Properties**. Click the **Desktop** tab. In the Background drop-down list box, choose **Bliss**. Click **Stretch**. Click **OK**.

18   Click **Start**. Click **My Pictures**. Select **basket.bmp** and **student.jpg**. Right-click. Click **Delete**. Click **Yes**. Close the My Pictures window.

WHAT'S **HAPPENING?** You returned your desktop background to the default Bliss. You then deleted the graphic files you copied to the My Pictures and returned to the desktop.

10.6 ◦ Other Features of Customizing the Desktop

You can customize how your desktop behaves and looks using the Customization feature of the Desktop tab. You can choose to display the icons for the My Computer, My Documents, My Network Places or Internet Explorer on the desktop like earlier versions of Windows did. You can choose different icons for these objects, including the Recycle Bin. You can choose to automatically have your desktop cleared of all icons and moved to a folder if they have not been used in 60 days.

Active Desktop integrates your desktop and the Internet. Active Desktop is how Microsoft describes the ability of Windows XP Professional to display Web pages and other content downloaded from the Internet. It is an implementation of push technology. *Push technology* brings requested Internet content to you instead of making you retrieve it. You can choose to receive Internet content that is tailored to your interests. For instance, if you are interested in the stock market, you could subscribe to a service or link to a site on the Internet that displays stock market prices. You could then place that link on your desktop. If you had a continuous connection to the Internet, that window would constantly be reflecting changing stock prices. If you had to dial in to the Internet, each time you made a connection, your Active Desktop object would be updated. You can make your home page your desktop so that you can just click on your desktop to go to any Web site you wish. This is most useful if you have a cable or DSL (constant) connection to the Internet. To add items to the desktop, you may use the Web tab in the Display Properties/Customize Desktop/Web dialog box. You may toggle Active Desktop on or off as well in this property sheet.

10.7 ● Activity ● Effects and the Web

1   Right-click the desktop. Click **Properties**, Click the **Desktop** tab. Click the **Customize Desktop** command button.

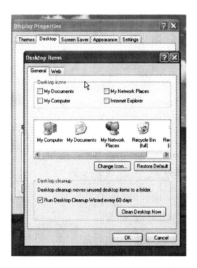

WHAT'S **HAPPENING?** The Desktop cleanup wizard, which in this example is selected, by default, every 60 days, any desktop icon that has not been used will be moved to a folder. If the checkbox is cleared, then your desktop icons will not be cleared. In addition, you have four check boxes, which in this example are not set (My Computer, My Documents, My Network Places, and Internet Explorer. By choosing these items, you will see each of these items on your desktop for easy access.

2   Click in each check box to set it. Click **OK**. Click **OK**.

WHAT'S HAPPENING? Now you see the four icons you selected, My Documents, My Computer, My Network Places, Recycle Bin and Internet Explorer on the desktop. Now, instead of using the Start menu, you have these objects always available to you. In this example, there is also a shortcut to explorer.exe and to My Computer. By placing the icons on the desktop, you do not need to create a shortcut.

You may also change the desktop icons. You are not limited to the icons that are displayed on your desktop. Icons are stored in files. Individual icons are usually stored in the program files or they may have a separate file has the .ico file extension. Groups of icons are stored in .exe files or in .dll files. Two collections of icons that come with Windows XP Professional are stored in the Explorer.exe and shell32.dll file. Each icon also has its own icon file.

3   Right-click the desktop. Click **Proper-ties**, Click the **Desktop** tab. Click the **Customize Desktop** command button.

4   In the scroll box, click **My Computer**. Click the **Change Icons** command button.

WHAT'S HAPPENING? These are the avail-able choices stored in the file Explorer.exe.

5   Click **Browse**. Double-click **System32**. Locate and click **shell32.dll**.

WHAT'S HAPPENING? You are in the Windows\system32 folder and have selected the shell32.dll file.

6   Click **Open**.

WHAT'S HAPPENING? You now see a larger collection of icons from which you can select.

7   Click the icon that is a monitor with a moon in it (second row at right end). Click **OK**.

8   Click **My Documents**. Click **Change Icon**.

WHAT'S HAPPENING? You see that the My Documents icon is kept in a file called mydocs.dll in the System32 folder. If you wanted another icon, you could browse or use Explorer.exe or shell32.dll.

9 Click **Cancel**. Click **OK**. Click **OK**.

WHAT'S HAPPENING? Now you have different icon, the one you selected for My Computer.

10 Right-click the desktop. Click **Proper-ties**, Click the **Desktop** tab. Click the **Customize Desktop** command button.

11 Click the **My Computer** icon. Click **Restore Defaults**. Clear all the check boxes (**My Computer**, **My Documents**, **My Network Places**, and **Internet Explorer**).

12 Click the **Web** tab in Desktop items.

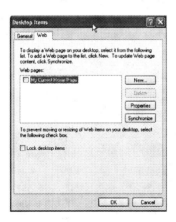

WHAT'S HAPPENING? Here is one place you may enable or disable Active Desktop. You can show any Web content on your desktop. In this example, My Current Home

Page is not selected. If you upgraded from Windows 98, you may have an entry for Internet Explorer Channel Bar. If Windows XP Professional was originally installed on your computer, you will not have this choice. If you choose Lock desktop items, any web pages that are placed on your desktop will not be able to be moved.

13 Click **Properties**.

WHAT'S HAPPENING? This property sheet tells you about your home page, if you had it selected. There are three tabs, Web document, Schedule and Download. You can update the content manually or auto-matically.

14 Click the **Schedule** tab.

WHAT'S HAPPENING? Here you can set a schedule to synchronize (get the latest update to your Web page) either manually or on a predetermined schedule.

15 Click the **Download** tab.

WHAT'S HAPPENING? Here you can have multiple levels of Web pages sent to your computer. This means that you will get the initial page of the site you choose as well as all the pages that it is linked to. You can go up to three levels deep. You can also be notified when the page changes.

16   Click **Cancel**. Click **Cancel**. Click **OK**.

WHAT'S HAPPENING? You have returned to the desktop that no longer has icons on it.

10.8 ● Screen Savers

There has always been a debate among computer users about whether or not you should turn your computer off when you finish working. Some schools of thought believe you should turn off the computer and monitor to save energy and prevent wear on the electronic components. Others feel that the energy savings are minimal compared with the risks related to turning the computer on and off. The items most likely to break on a computer are the mechanical parts, such as the switch. Furthermore, when you turn on the power, there is a slightly higher power surge that could damage electronic components. If you are in a lab or work environment, there is probably a policy for whether computers should be turned off after each work session. If you are in charge of your own computer, it is up to you. Most people decide that if they are going to be gone a short while—an hour or two—they will leave the computer on. If they are going to be gone for a longer period of time, however, they will turn off the computer.

One point on which everyone agrees is the importance of caring for the monitor. In the early days of monitor technology, if a monitor were left on for a long time displaying the same image, the image could "burn in," and a ghostly shadow would remain on the screen forever. *Screen savers* were developed to prevent this. Early screen savers were actually blank screens. When a user did not have any keyboard or mouse activity, the screen would go blank until the user reactivated the system by pressing a key or moving the mouse. Since blank screens are rather boring, people developed screen savers comprised of constantly moving images.

In today's monitor technology, burn-in is not usually a problem, and screen savers are fun. They do offer some security by providing passwords so that if you leave your computer for a time, no one can see your work. In addition to all the commercial screen savers available, Windows XP Professional comes with a choice of screen savers. You can locate screen savers with the same techniques you have been using.

However, the latest computers and their high power, high-resolution video and other available components consume large amounts of energy. As an assistance in reducing energy consumption, many monitors support the VESA Display Power Management Signaling (DPMS) specification. In order for your system to support this feature, you must have an Energy Star–compliant monitor and a video card that supports Advanced Power Management (APM) or VESA BIOS Extensions for Power Management (VBE/PM). Windows XP Professional supports VBE/PM. All these standards combine in ways to manage the power on your system, to perform what is referred to as *power management*. Power management, depending on your system, can perform such tasks as automatically turning off your computer and your monitor and automatically switching to standby, which reduces power consumption by your computer after some selected time period. Standby can also make your monitor blank, turn off your hard drive, and in general perform tasks that reduce power consumption.

10.9 ● Activity ● Using Screen Savers and Power Management

I   Right-click the desktop. Click **Properties**. Click the **Screen Saver** tab.

WHAT'S HAPPENING? You opened the Screen Saver tab in the Display Properties sheet. The number of screen savers available to you depends on the software you have installed. Here you can also enable energy saving features for your monitor, if available.

2   Click the down arrow in the **Screen Saver** drop-down list box. Click **Mystify**.

WHAT'S HAPPENING? In the sample screen, you see a preview of what the screen saver will look like. In the Wait spin box, you can choose how much time elapses before the screen saver goes into effect. In this example, it is set to 10 minutes, which means that, if there is no activity for

10 minutes, the screen saver will be activated. If you set the On resume, password protect, when you click, the screen saver will ask for a password which is your logon password.

3 Click the **Preview** command button.

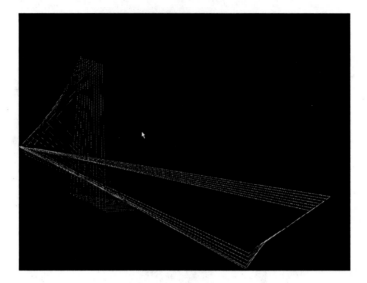

WHAT'S HAPPENING? You see a full-screen view of your choice.

4 Click to return to the dialog box. Click the **Settings** command button that is next to the **Preview** button.

WHAT'S HAPPENING? You can customize this screen saver by altering the number of polygons, the number of lines for each polygon, and the colors.

5 Click **Cancel**. If you have an Energy Star–compliant monitor, click the **Power** command button in the energy savings area.

WHAT'S HAPPENING? Power Management Properties may also be accessed from Control Panel with its own Power Options icon. In this case, you have selected your power scheme. A *scheme* is a set of predetermined options. In this example, the power scheme is always on. If available,

System standby reduces the power consumption of your monitor. You may have your monitor turned off after a specified time limit. This action would override your screen saver. You can also turn off your hard disk's spinning after a preselected length of time. Again, these are all features to conserve energy as well as reduce wear on your computer system.

The options and pages available in the Power Options Properties dialog box vary based on your computer hardware. For instance, an Alarm page may appear in this dialog box if you are using a laptop computer with a recognized battery system.

6 Click the **Advanced** tab.

WHAT'S HAPPENING? You can directly activate this window if you place an icon on the taskbar. You can also provide some security by enabling password protection and specifying what happens when you press the power button on your computer. Again, depending on your hardware and settings, you may have more different choices on this property sheet.

7 Click the **Hibernate** tab.

WHAT'S HAPPENING? Hibernation will save anything in memory to the hard disk and then shut down the computer. When you come out of hibernation, everything is returned to memory. Many notebook or laptop computers use hibernation to maximize their battery life. In this example, hibernation is enabled.

8 Click the **UPS** tab.

WHAT'S HAPPENING? If your system is connected to a UPS (Uninterruptible Power Supply) instead of directly to a power source (wall plug or power strip), the UPS service would not be stopped. This computer does not have an UPS.

9 Click **Cancel**. In the Screen Saver list box, choose **(None)**. Click **OK**.

WHAT'S HAPPENING? You have returned to the desktop.

10.10 ◦ Changing the Appearance of the Desktop

In addition to wallpapers and patterns, the desktop may be further customized. You may choose a color scheme for your desktop or select specific colors for elements of the desktop. You can use different fonts in different styles for icons and alter icon spacing. All these changes can be made in the Appearance tab in the Display Properties property sheet.

10.11 ◦ Activity ◦ Customizing the Desktop

1   Right-click the desktop. Click **Properties**. Click the **Appearance** tab.

WHAT'S **HAPPENING?** There are three areas you can alter—Windows and buttons, the color scheme, and the size of your fonts. The sample window previews your choices. If you want a coordinated theme, you may choose a the Themes page.

2   Click the down arrow in the **Windows and buttons:** drop-down list box. Choose **Windows Classic Style**.

WHAT'S **HAPPENING?** You only had two choices—Windows XP style and the one you chose.

3   Click the down arrow in the **Windows and buttons:** drop-down list box. Choose **Windows XP Style**.

4   Click the down arrow in the **Colors** drop-down list box. Choose **Olive Green**.

WHAT'S HAPPENING? In the Sample box, you see how you desktop would look if you made these choices. You could choose to click Apply and you would see the background on the desktop.

5 Click the down arrow in the **Colors** drop-down list box. Choose **(Default) Blue**.

6 Click the down arrow in the **Font** size drop-down list box. Choose **Extra Large Fonts**.

WHAT'S HAPPENING? Again, by looking in the Sample box, you could check the results of your choices. One thing you might note is that by choosing Extra Large Fonts, the entire title or icon title would not appear. However, you can change each element of the desktop to meet your specifications.

7 Click **Advanced**.

8 Click the **Color** drop-down list box next to **Desktop**. Click the color green.

WHAT'S HAPPENING? You still have Extra Large Icons enabled, which you can see in the Sample box. In addition, the desktop background is green.

9 Click the down arrow in the **Item** drop-down list box. Click **Menu**.

WHAT'S HAPPENING? The item you selected, Menu, has a size of 21 points, which is the actual size of the menu in pixels. Since the menu object has a size, you may make the size of the menu itself larger or smaller.

The Font drop-down list box also has a Size entry near it, so you may alter the point size for the text in the menu. The currently selected font for menus is Tahoma at 12 points in black.

10   Click the down arrow in the **Item** drop-down list box.

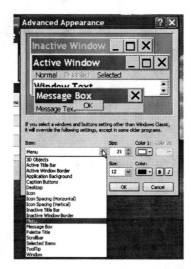

WHAT'S **HAPPENING?** As you can see, you can customize almost any element of the desktop. There are three Icon choices. Icon allows you to change the grid space an icon requires, in pixels. Icon Spacing allows you to adjust the vertical or horizontal spacing between icons, in pixels. Thus, if you choose to use Large Icons or Extra Large Icons, you could then adjust the size of the icons and their spacing so that you could read the entire icon title.

11   Click **Desktop**. Click the **Color 1:** drop-down list box and choose blue. Click **Cancel**.

12   In the **Font** drop down list box, choose **Normal**. Click the **Effects** command button.

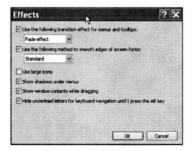

WHAT'S **HAPPENING?** Here you can set different visual effects, such as using large icons, or using a fade technique for which has your menus and windows fading and dissolving. Your other choice would be scrolling. You smooth the edges of your fonts as well as have shadows under your menus and showing or not showing the window contents as you are dragging a window. You may also turn on or off the underlined letters. A keyboard navigation indicator underlines a letter in each menu choice. On the Start menu, you merely press the underlined letter of your menu choice. In windows with menu choices, you press the **Alt** key and the selected underlined letter. Once you open a menu, you need only press the underlined letter. If this option is off, you must first press the **Alt** key to display the underlined letters.

13   Click **Cancel**. Click **Cancel**.

WHAT'S **HAPPENING?** You have returned to the desktop. As you can see the desktop can be extraordinarily customized to meet your tastes.

10.12 • Screen Resolution Settings

Standard VGA, the default screen configuration, has a grid that is 640 pixels horizontally by 480 pixels vertically and a 16-color palette. The 640–by-480 configuration (*pixels* is understood) is the resolution of your screen. Standard VGA is the most basic setting and provides limited colors and resolution. When Windows XP Professional was installed, the setup program determined what type of monitor and video adapter your computer uses, and made the appropriate settings. Sometimes, Windows XP Professional does not take advantage of all the settings your video card and monitor can support. You can optimize your video settings, if you know what your video card and monitor can support.

Today, one of the most popular monitor sizes is 19 inches, with 21 inches gaining popularity in a full-size monitor. Monitors can be even larger. These are the traditional CRT (Cathrode Ray Tube). But with advances in technology, most people would prefer a flat screen or an LCD (Liquid Crystal Display). These new monitors weigh much less than the old style monitors and take up much less desk space. A 17 inch flat panel monitor has a bigger viewing area that a traditional CRT 17 inch monitor.

Typically most people use settings of at least 800 by 600 for working with text and 1,024 by 768 or higher for working with graphics. If you choose a higher resolution, you gain more workspace on the desktop. Since higher resolutions require more pixels, your display will be sharper but much smaller. In fact, icons on the display may become so small that you cannot identify them in high resolution. However, you can change the size of the fonts to make them more visible and customize your desktop to make them more visible.

Depending on your monitor and video card, you may also change how many colors you can display. The two choices are medium (16 bit) and Highest (32 bit)

There are drawbacks to increasing the resolution and number of colors. With a higher resolution, your system has to work much harder to manage the display when there are more pixels to process and when there are a higher number of colors. This is why most people purchase a video card with its own memory to handle the color display. Both your monitor and video card limit the resolution and color settings of your system. Once you know your hardware limitations, you can decide what works best for you.

10.13 • Activity • Viewing Your Resolution

1   Right-click the desktop. Click **Properties**. Click **Settings**.

WHAT'S **HAPPENING?** The ways you may alter your display depend on the choices your hardware supports. This system is currently set to 1024 by 768 resolution. Its color choice is Highest (32 bit). If you had an older monitor and video card, you would not have additional choices and would not be able to do the following steps.

2   Move the slider to the right as far as you can.

WHAT'S **HAPPENING?** In this example, this computer can be increased to 1280 by 1024 pixels. If you look at the sample area, you will see that you have more desktop area available because the resolution was raised. You can usually click OK and make the resolution change without having to restart Windows XP Professional. However, if you attempt to change the color palette *and* the resolution, you may have to restart Windows XP Professional.

3   Click **Cancel**. Right-click the desktop. Click **Properties**. Click the **Settings** tab. Click the **Advanced** button.

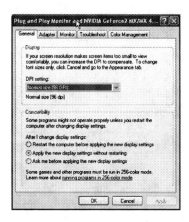

WHAT'S **HAPPENING?** You should have the tabs General, Adapter, Monitor, Troubleshooting, and Color Management. You may have other tabs, depending on your video card. The Adapter tab allows you to change drivers if you get a new video card, and it also allows you to alter the refresh rate. The *refresh rate* is the frequency with which the entire screen is redrawn to maintain a constant, flicker-free image. From the Monitor tab you can set options for plug-and-play monitors or change the driver if you get a new monitor. Color Management allows you to set individual color preferences in user profiles. If you are having problems with your graphic hardware you can use the Troubleshooting tab to adjust the levels of hardware acceleration controlled by device drivers.

4   Click the down arrow in the **DPI settings** drop-down list box.

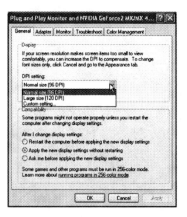

WHAT'S **HAPPENING?** The current setting is Normal size (96 DPI). DPI means dots per inch. If you wanted to use Large size, you would select it and then click OK. You can also scale your fonts to a custom size that is more specific than these preset sizes.

5   Click the **Troubleshoot** tab.

WHAT'S **HAPPENING?** Windows XP Professional tries to get the best performance out of your video card, but this sometimes may actually cause problems. If you experience problems with your mouse, unexpected crashes in application programs, or strange things such as the Start button becoming black, you may want to reduce the hardware acceleration.

6   Click **Cancel**. On the **Settings** page, click the **Troubleshoot** command button.

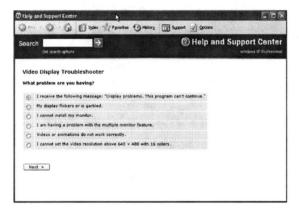

WHAT'S **HAPPENING?** The Windows XP Professional help feature opens and takes you to the correct troubleshooter for display.

7   Close the **Windows XP Professional help** window. Click **Cancel**.

WHAT'S **HAPPENING?** You have returned to the desktop.

10.14 • The Mouse and the Keyboard

You can also customize the mouse and the keyboard. Although it is generically referred to as the mouse, it can be any type of pointer. You can adjust such pointer-related items as the double-click speed, the pointer movement, the pointer size, and the *tracking speed*, which is the rate the pointer moves across the screen. You can also enable *pointer trails*, which leave images tracking the mouse's path. This feature is particularly useful on any computer with a where the pointer is difficult to see. You can switch the left and right pointer buttons, which is useful for left-handed users. If you have a special mouse, such as the new and popular wheel mouse, a different mouse driver will be installed with more features for mouse control. In fact your mouse icon will have the features of what pointing device you installed.

The keyboard can be adjusted as well. Your keyboard repeats a character after you have held a key down for a period of time, which you can specify. You can also adjust the rate at which the cursor blinks. You can install keyboard support for different languages, but you must have your original Windows XP Professional CD-ROMs in order to do so. When you install Windows XP Professional, it installs only one language.

10.15 • Activity • Customizing the Pointer and the Keyboard

Note: If necessary, switch to Classic view.

1   Click **Start**. Click **Control Panel**. Double-click the Mouse object.

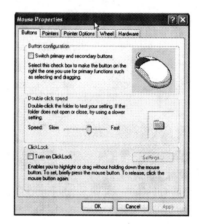

WHAT'S HAPPENING? Your property sheet and choices will vary, depending on the type of mouse you have installed. The wheel mouse is a popular alternative to a standard mouse and is the property sheet shown here. In this example, the left mouse button is for normal dragging and dropping, which technically is called the primary button, whereas the right mouse button is used for right-clicking which is technically called the secondary button. Right-clicking opens a pop-up menu, also called a context menu, which you used when you right-clicked the desktop and chose Properties. There is a slider that sets the speed—the amount of time it takes to double-click. You may also set ClickLock on which relieves you of holding down the mouse button.

Note: In the steps that follow, you may not have the same property sheets so you will have to see if your pointer has these options.

2   Click the **Pointers** tab.

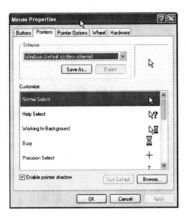

WHAT'S HAPPENING? Here you see each pointer symbol and its meaning. Your choices may be different, depending on what pointers were installed on your system.

3   Click the down arrow in the Scheme drop-down list box.

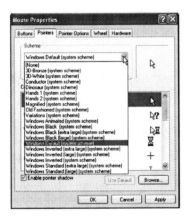

WHAT'S HAPPENING? Again, you may not have as many choices or you may have more choices, depending on what pointers have been installed. The 3D Pointers choices gives pointers a three-dimensional look. The Windows Animated choice displays animated pointers such as an hourglass that fills and turns whenever the computer is busy performing a function, such as saving a file. If you do not like the size of your pointers, you can change their size.

4   If available, click **Conductor (system scheme)**. Click **Busy**.

WHAT'S HAPPENING? If you look in the sample box, you should see the metronome moving back and forth.

5   Click the down arrow in the Scheme drop-down list box. Click **Windows Default (system scheme)**.

6   If available, click the **Pointer Options** tab.

WHAT'S HAPPENING? Here you can adjust the tracking speed and acceleration of your pointer. When activated, the Snap to default option automatically moves the mouse point to the default button when a dialog box opens.

7   Click **Cancel**. Double-click the **Keyboard** object in Control Panel.

WHAT'S HAPPENING? The Keyboard Properties sheet has two tabs: Speed and Hardware. Speed controls the *repeat rate*, which is how fast a key repeats when held down, and the *repeat delay*, which is the length of time that Windows XP Professional waits before it repeats the key. You can also adjust the cursor blink rate.

8   Click the **Hardware** tab.

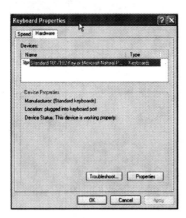

9   Click the **Properties** command button.

WHAT'S HAPPENING? The Troubleshoot command button opens a help window to guide you through troubleshooting your keyboard problems.

10   Click the **Driver** tab.

WHAT'S HAPPENING? If you were having trouble with your keyboard, you could update your driver or roll it back to a previous version that worked or you could even uninstall it.

11   Click **Cancel**. Click **Cancel**. Close all open windows.

10.16 ● Sounds and Audio Devices and Speech

The Sounds and Audio Devices icon is where you control all the audio devices on your system, your speakers, microphones, recording, and music controls. What you control, of course, depends on the hardware that you have. If you have any of these special devices such as a microphone or MIDI devices, you can change the settings of those devices. In this activity, you will only look at a few items that are common to most users.

Windows XP Professional provides many sounds for you. These sounds are related to certain events. An *event* is an action performed by you or a program that your computer can notify you about. For example, your computer can beep when you press an incorrect key. There are sounds assigned to many events, such as when you start or exit Windows XP Professional or when you empty the Recycle Bin. Although most computers today do have a sound card, if you are in a lab, school, or business environment, you may either not have a sound card or it may be disabled. Sometimes a school environment will provide headphones so you may use sound, but not disturb other users.

If your environment allows, you may change the sounds assigned to events or add a sound to an event that does not have one. You can also choose to have no sounds at all. Windows XP Professional provides sound schemes, much like the color schemes you saw when changing the desktop's appearance. Sound schemes are entire collections of sounds grouped together under a specific name. Many sound files have a .wav file extension or other type of extensions such as WMA (Windows Media Audio File) . If your environment does not allow the use of sounds, you will not be able to do the next activity, but you should read through the steps to understand how sounds are assigned.

The speech capabilities refers to the ability to play back text in a spoken voice (referred to as text-to speech or TTS), or to convert a spoken voice into electronic text (referred to as speech recognition or SR). The two capabilities are independent of each other. Many systems will have only TTS. SR may be installed later either by loading a special speech application program or by installing a software application which includes speech. In general, speech-enabled applications will use Speech icon in Control Panel to control those speech features.

10.17 ● Activity ● Using Sounds and Audio Devices and Speech

I   Click **Start**. Click **Control Panel**. Double-click **Sounds and Audio Devices**.

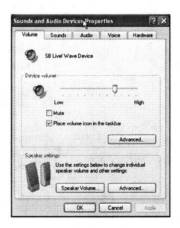

WHAT'S HAPPENING? In the Volume property sheet, you can control the volume of the sound and whether the volume control icon appears on the taskbar. You may also control your speaker settings here.

2   Click the **Sounds** tab. In Sound scheme, be sure **Windows Default** is selected.

WHAT'S HAPPENING? In the Schemes drop-down list box, Windows Default is the selection. You are looking at the sound assigned to the all the events of Windows XP Professional.

3   Click **Critical Stop**.

WHAT'S HAPPENING? In the Sounds drop-down list box, the file name Windows XP Critical Stop.wav appears. To preview the sound, you could click the play button or you can use Media Player to play this or any sound. You may access Media Player by choosing Start. Pointing All Programs and Choosing Windows Media Player. You may also double-click any .wav file.

4   Click **Start**. Click **My Music**. Double-click **Sample Music**.

WHAT'S HAPPENING? Your view may be different and you may not have any sample files. However, by default, two music files are shown.

5   Double-click **Beethoven's Symphony No. 9**.

WHAT'S HAPPENING? You have opened Media Player and it is playing the file that you double-clicked. To play another file, you must select the file you wish to play.

6   Click **File**. Click **Open**. Click the **My Computer** icon. Double-click **Drive C**. Double click **Windows**. Double-click **Media**.

WHAT'S **HAPPENING?** Here are all the Windows System sound files you can listen to.

7 Double-click **Windows XP Critical Stop.wav**.

WHAT'S **HAPPENING?** You should have heard the a very quick sound that is associated with a having a problem with Windows.

8 Close **Media Player**. Close the **Sample Music** window.

9 The **Sounds** tab should be available in **Sound and Audio Devices** and **Windows Default** is the scheme.

10 Click **Close Program**.

WHAT'S **HAPPENING?** In the list box, the Close program event has no assigned sound. You can tell because there is no sound icon next to its name. In the Name drop-down list box, (None) is selected. To assign a

sound to this event so that every time you close a program, you will hear a sound, you need to assign a sound file to it.

11 Click the arrow in the **Sounds** drop-down list box. Choose **ringin.wav**. Click the Play Sound button.

WHAT'S **HAPPENING?** You should have heard the sound of a ringing phone. Now, every time you close a program such as Notepad or this property sheet you would hear this sound.

12 Click **OK** to close the **Sounds and Audio Devices Properties** property sheet.

WHAT'S **HAPPENING?** When you closed the Sounds and Audio Devices Properties property sheet, you heard the sound you selected. You assigned a sound (ringing phone) to an event (closing a program).

13 Double-click **Sounds and Audio Devices** in Control Panel. Click the **Sounds** tab.

WHAT'S HAPPENING? In the Scheme text box, no scheme is listed. When you assigned a sound to the Close program event, you changed the sound scheme. Once it is altered, it is no longer the Windows Default sound scheme.

14 Click the down arrow in the **Scheme** drop-down list box. Choose **Windows Default**.

WHAT'S HAPPENING? You created a scheme based on Windows Default. If you do not save it under a new name, you cannot choose it as an option later. In this case, you do not want to save it. You do not want Close program to have a sound associated with it.

15 Click **No**. Click **Apply**.

16 Click the **Audio** tab.

WHAT'S HAPPENING? Here you may see a list of your audio devices, control the quality of a device's performance, and troubleshoot any audio problems you may be having.

17 Click the **Voice** tab.

WHAT'S HAPPENING? Here you control all of your voice devices and you can test your hardware as well.

18 Click the **Hardware** tab.

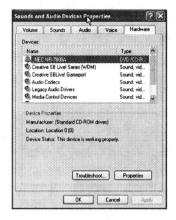

WHAT'S HAPPENING? Here is where you may alter the settings for your device drivers and troubleshoot hardware problems.

19 Click **OK**. Click the **Speech** icon.

WHAT'S HAPPENING? Here is your text to speech availability.

20 Click **Preview Voice**.

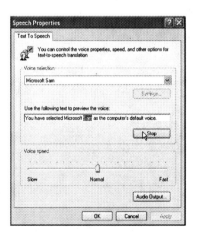

WHAT'S HAPPENING? As each word is highlighted, you hear it spoken by "Sam."

21 Click **Cancel**. Close all open windows.

WHAT'S HAPPENING? You have returned to the desktop.

10.18 • Date, Time, and Regional and Language Options

Your computer has a clock that indicates the current date and time, called the *system date* and *system time*. All programs use the system date and system time. Whenever you save a new file or modify an existing file, the date and time "stamped" on the file comes from the system date and system time. Any activity that relies on the date or time such as sending faxes or scheduling tasks uses the system date and time.

The date and time are set to the geographic area in which you live. How they are displayed relates to the country in which you live. Many programs support international settings. When you alter Regional and Language Options, you may affect the way programs display and sort dates, times, currency, and numbers. For instance, in the United States, dates are displayed in the format of mm/dd/yy. The long form of the date, for example, is written as August 1, 2002, and the short form appears as 8/1/02. Many other countries use the format of dd/mm/yy, so that the long form of the date is written as 1 August 2002, and the short form appears as 1/8/02. Currency symbols also vary. In the United States, the $ sign is used. In Great Britain, the £ sign is used. With Control Panel, you can customize the way the date, time, currency, and numbers are displayed, based on either a country's setting or your preferences. Since Windows XP Professional sets the regional preferences appropriate for your country, you will rarely need to change these settings.

10.19 • Activity • Using Date, Time, and Regional Options

1   Click **Start**. Click **Control Panel**. Double-click the **Date and Time** object.

WHAT'S HAPPENING? You have opened the property sheet for the system date and time. Here you can reference and, if needed, correct the date and time.

2   Click the **Time Zone** tab.

WHAT'S **HAPPENING?** In the drop-down list box, you see that the time zone for this computer is Pacific Time. You also see GMT-08:00, which tells you that Pacific Time is Greenwich mean time minus eight hours. Greenwich mean time is the mean solar time of the meridian of Greenwich, England, which is used as the basis for standard time throughout most of the world. The check box is set for Automatically adjust clock for daylight saving changes. Arizona, for instance, does not participate in daylight saving time. If you lived in Arizona, you would not check the Automatically adjust clock for daylight saving changes check box. If you were in a network environment, you most likely would not check this box, because most file servers adjust for daylight saving time. If you did check it under that circumstance, you would either get a two-hour adjustment instead of the one-hour change that was needed or your change would have no impact because only the administrator of the network has permission to change the date and time.

3   Click the **Internet Time** tab.

WHAT'S **HAPPENING?** This options specifies whether the date and time is automatically checked against an Internet time server. This checks your internal computer clock against an external time source. If you are on a network, this is done for you. In this example, the accuracy of your internal computer clock will automatically be checked with a connection to a web site—time.windows.com.

4   Click **Cancel**. Double-click the **Regional and Language Options** object.

WHAT'S **HAPPENING?** Regional Options is the top property sheet. The default setting is English (United States) in this example.

5   Click the arrow in the top drop-down list box.

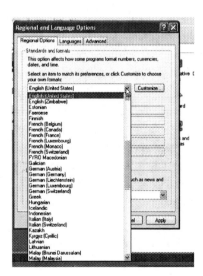

WHAT'S HAPPENING? As you can see, there are many countries to pick from. When you select another country, you are changing the way data such as currency, date and time is formatted.

6   Scroll up and select **English (United Kingdom)**.

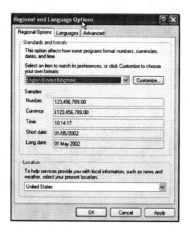

WHAT'S HAPPENING? You see that the currency symbol is the British Pound sign and the date is expressed in the European fashion (dd/mm/yy). The other tabs (Languages and Advanced) are options that allow you to have multilanguage support. If you use the United States English version of Windows XP Professional, you can still work in other languages in your applications. However, your application menus, help files and so on will still be displayed in English. You can add a taskbar icon that will allow you to switch between languages. There are non-English versions of Windows XP Professional—at last count—24 versions. If you have, for instance, the Italian version of Windows XP Professional, everything is displayed in Italian. If you need to work in another language, you can do so with the Regional and Language Property sheet.

7   Click **Cancel**.

8   Close all open windows.

WHAT'S HAPPENING? You have returned to the desktop.

10.20 • Customizing the Start Menu

When you install a program, the program's installation process, among other tasks, can place items on the Start menu as well as on the All Programs menu. If you install many programs, your menus can become large and unwieldy. The idea behind menus is that by clicking and pointing, you can quickly choose the program of interest. When you have dozens of programs on these menus, it defeats the purpose. To make more efficient use of menus, you may add items to the Start menu by pinning applications. You may also alter the All Programs portion of the Start menu. Here, you may place, rearrange, or remove whatever folders, programs, or documents you wish. By adding a frequently used item to the All Programs menu, you can avoid the extra step of using the cascading menus. You can remove programs that you seldom use and you organize existing program choices, grouping logically related items under one heading.

Frequently, when new programs are installed, they receive a separate entry on the All Programs menu. This creates a long and cluttered All Programs menu. In Figure 10.1, you can see that the Microsoft Office installation created an entry for each program (Word, Excel and so on) in the Office suite. The user created a folder called Other for seldom used program and then moved programs used on an occasional basis to it to create a cascading menu. There are also separate entries for some screen capture programs (HiJaak Pro, JASC and Snagit) and there are separate entries for some utility programs that are used with the Internet such as Acrobat Reader and WS_FTP Pro. By creating folders and moving items, you can create a more organized, easily accessible menu. See Figure 10.2.

*Figure 10.1 * A Cluttered Menu*   *Figure 10.2 * An Efficient Programs Menu*

Here all the office programs have been grouped under Office, all the graphics or screen capture programs have been grouped under ScreenCaptures, all the Internet type programs have been grouped under NetUtilities and all other utility programs have been grouped under Utilities. Figure 10.3 shows the cascading Office menu and Figure 10.4 shows the cascading NetUtilities menu.

*Figure 10.3 * An Efficient Programs Menu * Microsoft Office*   *Figure 10.4 * An Efficient Programs Menu * NetUtilities*

In this example, instead of 21 separate items on the Programs menu, the user has logical, cascading menus reducing the menu items to 13. Those items are logically arranged so that you can quickly access the program of interest.

In order to make changes to the Start menu, you will need to go to the Documents and Settings menu under your user name (profiles). Sometimes, the changes have to be made to the All User profile under Documents and Settings. If you are on a network, you may not be able to make any changes to your user name (profile) or to the All Users profile. If this is so, then simply read the activity to see how you could make those changes.

10.21 • Activity • Altering the Start Menu

1   Open Windows Explorer. Click **My Computer**. Click **Drive C**. Click the **Documents and Settings** folder. Locate your user name. Under your user name, click **Programs**. Click **Start Menu**.

2   Open another copy of Windows Explorer. Click **My Computer**. Click **Drive C**. Click the **XPRODATA** folder. Click the **FUNSTUFF** folder. Click **BOG2**.

3   Right-click the Taskbar. Click **Tile Windows Horizontally**.

4   In the left pane of the C:\Documents and Settings*yourusername*, click **Programs** under the **Start Menu** folder.

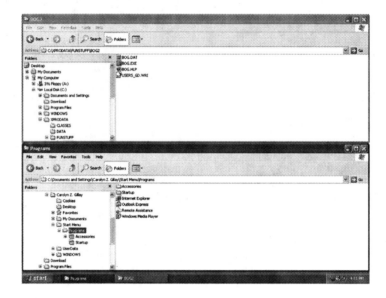

WHAT'S HAPPENING? By creating a shortcut of BOG.EXE, from the C:\XPRODATA folder to the C:\WINDOWS\Documents and Settings\Carolyn Z. Gillay\Start Menu\Programs folder, this item will appear on the Start/All Programs window.

5   Right-drag **BOG.EXE** from the **C:\XPRODATA** window to the **C:\WINDOWS\Documents and Settings\yourusername\Start Menu\Programs** window. Release the mouse button and click **Create Shortcuts Here**.

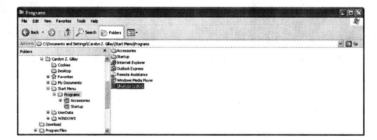

WHAT'S HAPPENING? You now have a shortcut in the Programs folder.

6   Click **Start**. Point to **All Programs**.

WHAT'S HAPPENING? BOG has been added to the menu.

7 Click outside the menu to close it. Click the up arrow in the BOG2 window. Click **MATCH32.** Right-drag **MATCH32.EXE** from the C:\XPRODATA\FUNSTUFF\MATCH32 window to the C:\WINDOWS\Documents and Settings*yourusername*\Start Menu\Programs window. Release the mouse button and click **Create Shortcuts Here.**

8 Click the up arrow in the MATCH32 window twice. In the right pane, select **BORN.TXT** and **DANCES. TXT**. Right-drag the files from the C:\XPRODATA window to the C:\WINDOWS\Documents and Settings*yourusername*\Start Menu\Programs window. Release the mouse button and click **Create Shortcuts Here.**

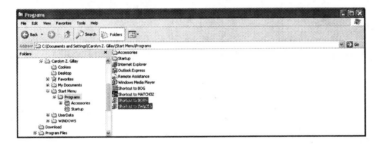

WHAT'S HAPPENING? You now have shortcuts the BOG game, the MATCH32 game, the BORN.TXT and DANCES.TXT file in your Programs folder.

9 Right-click the taskbar. Click **Undo Tile**. Close the XPRODATA window.

10 Click **Start**. Point to **All Programs.**

WHAT'S HAPPENING? All your shortcuts are at the end of the All Programs menu. You could sort them but a better way is to logically arrange them and place them in folders.

11   In the right pane of the Programs window, create two new folders, one called MyGames and the other called School.

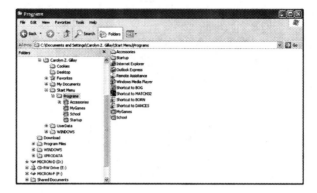

WHAT'S **HAPPENING?** Now you are going to move your shortcuts into the appropriate folder. You can rename your shortcuts as well.

12   Rename **Shortcut to BOG** to **BOG**. Drag **BOG** into MyGames.

13   Drag the **Shortcut to Match32** to the **MyGames** folder.

14   Drag **Shortcut to BORN** and **Shortcut to DANCES** to the **School** folder.

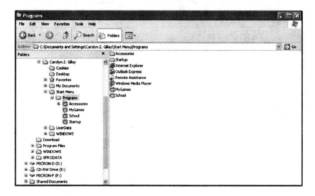

WHAT'S **HAPPENING?** You have organized your files and folder in your Start/All Programs menu.

15   Click the **Start** button. Point to **All Programs**.

WHAT'S **HAPPENING?** You have grouped your files and placed them into folders, creating cascading menus. You could sort this menu if you wanted.

16   Point to **School**.

WHAT'S HAPPENING? You have set up your menu so you may quickly access those data files that pertain to your school work. Remember, however, that if you want to be able to open a document from this menu, it must be a registered file and associated with an application. Both of these files are associated with Notepad.

17 Click **Shortcut to DANCES**.

WHAT'S HAPPENING? You quickly opened the file of interest from the Start menu.

18 Close **Notepad**.

19 In the Programs window, delete **MyGames** and **School**.

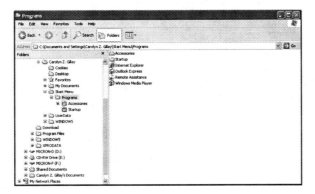

WHAT'S HAPPENING? You have removed the folders and files you created. Since all of these items were shortcuts, removing them did not affect the program or data files. As you can see, you can customize the Start menu, adding or removing items that pertain to your needs.

20 Close the Programs window. Click **Start**. Point to **All Programs**.

WHAT'S **HAPPENING?** > You have removed what you added to the Start menu.

21 Click outside the menu to close it. Close all open windows.

WHAT'S **HAPPENING?** > You have returned to the desktop.

10.22 • Creating User Profiles and Passwords

The Users Accounts object is used to add and remove users' access to your computer, grant specific permissions and user rights to groups of users, and change passwords. Each time someone logs onto a computer, Windows XP Professional will restore the individualized working environment that was in place when that user logged off. If your computer is a stand-alone computer or if you are a member of a workgroup, there are three types of accounts, Computer Administrator, a Limited Account and a Guest account.

The computer administrator account is the most powerful account. A computer administrator is a user who can make changes to the entire computer system, is allowed to install new hardware and programs and is allowed to access all files on the computer. An administrator can create and delete user accounts. He can create password for other user accounts on the computer. He can alter other user's account names, pictures, passwords and account types. There must be at least one user who is an administrator on the computer system.

A limited account, as it names suggests, is for user who will be allowed to make few changes to the computer system. He cannot install programs or hardware. However, he can access programs that are already installed on the computer system. He can change his account picture and create, change or delete his password but he cannot change his account name or account type.

The guest account has no password so he can log on quickly to the system. He could use the computer to check his email or browse the Internet. But a guest has even fewer privileges than a Limited Account. He can use software that is already installed but cannot add hardware or software. He cannot change the Guest account type but he can change the guest account picture. Table 10.1 summarizes the difference in the account types.

Privileges	Computer Administrator	Limited User	Guest
Install hardware and software	Yes	No	No
Make system wide changes	Yes	No	No
Access and read all non-private files	Yes	No	No
Create and delete other user accounts	Yes	No	No
Change your own or other user's names or account types	Yes	No	No
Change your own picture	Yes	Yes	Yes
Change or create your own password	Yes	Yes	No
Make files private	Yes	Yes	No

Table 10.1 • User Privileges

You may make your own files private so that other users may not access them. In addition, When you installed Windows XP Professional, there was an account created called Administrator. This account uses the password you used when you installed Windows XP Professional.

If you are on a network, Windows XP Professional will already be set up with specific users and groups that the network administrator determines. In that case, you may customize your system as much or as little as the network administrator allows in that working environment.

10.23 ◦ Activity ◦ Creating Users and Using Passwords

Note: Check with your lab instructor to see if you can do this activity in your lab. If you cannot do it in your lab environment, then read the steps.

1   Click **Start**. Click **Control Panel**. Switch to category view. Double-click **User Accounts**.

WHAT'S HAPPENING? You bring up a wizard that lets you accomplish three major tasks, Change an account, create a new account or change the way users log on or off. In this example, there is only one user, Carolyn Z. Gillay, who is the Computer administrator. The Guest account is off.

2   Click **Change the way users log on or off**.

WHAT'S HAPPENING? There are two options, which on this system are set. Because this is a single user computer, when the system is booted, there is no welcome screen. Instead, one is immediately taken to the Windows desktop. If the option is unset, then when the system is booted, there would be a dialog box where the user would have to press **Ctrl** + **Alt** + **Delete** and then key in their user name and password. This option would provide more security for the system. Use Fast User Switching is also set. When additional users are added to this system, rather than having to log off or turn off the computer to access a new account, one could simply switch to another user. This has the advantage that the current user's work is saved and when you switch back, your work is exactly as you left it. If this option is off, then you will have to log off or turn off the computer so another user can log on. Your work would not be in the same place as you left it.

3   Be sure both check boxes are set. Click **Apply Options**.

4   Click **Create a new account**.

WHAT'S **HAPPENING?** ⟩ You must name your user. User name is what the user will log on as and what is displayed in the Start menu. Having a user name is mandatory.

5   In the **Type a name for the new account** text box, key in **Bambi**. Click **Next**.

WHAT'S **HAPPENING?** ⟩ You have two account types from which to choose. In this case, you will make Bambi a Computer administrator.

6   Be sure **Computer administrator** is selected. Click Create Account.

WHAT'S **HAPPENING?** ⟩ You see that Bambi has been added as a user.

7   Click **Create a new account**.

8   In the **Type a name for the new account** text box, key in **Thumper**. Click **Next**.

9   Click **Limited**.

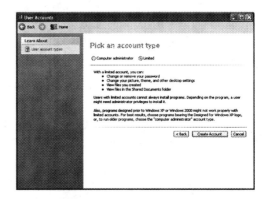

WHAT'S **HAPPENING?** ⟩ Bambi is an administrator but Thumper will have fewer privileges as a limited user.

10   Click **Create Account**.

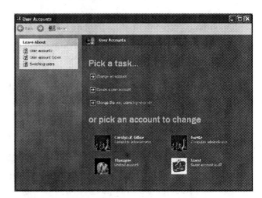

WHAT'S **HAPPENING?** ⟩ All your users are listed.

11 Close all open windows.

12 Open Notepad. Open Calculator.

13 Click **Start**. Click **Log Off**.

WHAT'S **HAPPENING?** Since fast user swithing is on, you see both a Switch User button and a Log Off button.

14 Click **Switch User**.

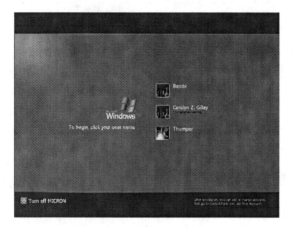

WHAT'S **HAPPENING?** All of your available users are listed. Since you choose to switch users, you see that there are two programs running for the current user.

15 Click **Bambi**.

16 Open **Windows Explorer**. Open **My Computer**. Open **Drive C**. Open **Documents and Settings**.

WHAT'S **HAPPENING?** When you selected Bambi, your personalized settings were loaded. Then you were taken to the desktop. When you opened Documents and Settings, you see all your users except Thumper. You may not see the Administrator account if you never logged on as Administrator. A user account is created the first time you log in.

17 Close Windows Explorer. Open Control Panel.

WHAT'S HAPPENING? Your Control Panel window opens in the Category view—the default settings. The changes you made to your view as your original log on name, were not retained since Bambi is a new user.

18 Click **User Accounts**. Click **Change an account**.

WHAT'S HAPPENING? Since you are an administrator as Bambi, you can change all the accounts listed.

19 Click **Bambi**.

WHAT'S HAPPENING? All the tasks listed are those that you can accomplish.

20 Click **Create a password**.

WHAT'S HAPPENING? You must key in a password and then key it in again to confirm it. You will not see the password, only a series of asterisks. Since a password is being used for security reasons, you want to be careful what your password is. You do not want to pick obvious items like your name, your logon name, or your birthday, nor do you want to place your password on a note taped to your computer. Passwords can be a maximum of 127 characters—this includes characters, numbers, or symbols. But if you are on a network that uses Windows 95 or 98, do not exceed 14 characters as those versions of Windows allow a maximum of 14 characters.

Passwords are case sensitive. A good password is one that is at least seven characters in length. A mix of characters, numbers, and symbols is the hardest to break. One way to create a password that is hard to guess and yet easy for you to remember is to select some item like a favorite poem and use the first letter in each line. For instance, if you could easily remember the line "How do I love thee, let me count the ways," your password could be HDILTLMCTW.

21 Key in **deer** in the Type a new password text box.

22 In the Type the new password again to confirm text box, key in **deer**.

23 In the Type a word or phrase to use as a password hint, key in **disney**.

WHAT'S HAPPENING? Now you have your password, which is encrypted—you cannot see it. But your password hint, as the screen states, will be visible to everyone who users this computer. The purpose of a password hint is to help you remember your password.

24 Click **Create Password**. Close the window.

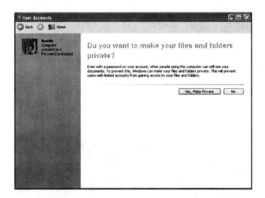

WHAT'S HAPPENING? Simply having a password does not make your files inaccessible to other users. You may choose to make them private by enabling the private files options. In this case, you will not have private files. If you do not see this window, then just close all open windows.

25 Click **No**. Close all open windows.

26 Right-click the desktop. Click **Properties**. Click the **Desktop** tab. Choose **Wind**. (If wind is not available, choose another background.) Click **OK**.

27 Click **Start**. Click **Log Off**. Click **Switch Users**. Choose **Thumper**.

28 Click **Start**. Click **Control Panel**. Double-click **User Accounts**.

WHAT'S HAPPENING? When you selected Thumper, Thumper's personalized settings were loaded. Then you were taken to the desktop. You saw the default desktop, not the desktop for your original user nor for Bambi. You then opened Control Panel and choose User Accounts. Since Thumper is a limited account, he cannot create users—he can only change his own account.

29 Close all open windows. Open **Windows Explorer**. Open **My Computer**. Open **Drive C**. Open **Documents and Settings**.

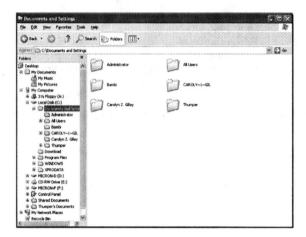

WHAT'S HAPPENING? Since you logged in as Thumper, he now has an account.

30 Close all open windows. Click **Start**. Click **Log Off**. Click **Switch Users**. Choose **Bambi**.

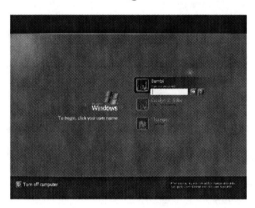

WHAT'S HAPPENING? Since you created a password for Bambi, you must use it to log on.

31 Key in the following: **deer** Enter

32 Open Windows Explorer. Click **My Computer**. Click **Shared Documents**.

WHAT'S **HAPPENING?** You see Bambi's personalized desktop. In additon, in the Shared Document folder, there are subfolders for each user on this system. Even though you, as Bambi, made your personal files private, any files you wanted to share, you could place them in the Shared Folder folder.

33 Close all open windows. Click **Start**. Click **Log Off**. Click **Switch Users**. Choose your original login name.

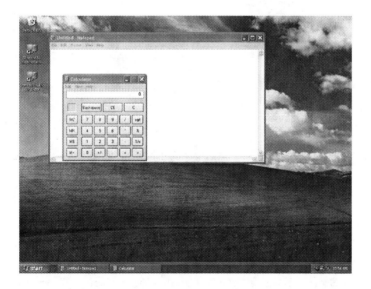

WHAT'S **HAPPENING?** Because you used Switch users, the programs you left running are still open and in the spot where you left them.

34 Close all open windows. Right-click the taskbar. Click **Task Manager**. Click the **Users** tab.

WHAT'S **HAPPENING?** Task Manager lets you know who the users are on the system and what their status is.

35   Close the Task Manager window. Click **Start**. Click **Control Panel**. Click **User Accounts**. Choose **Change an account**. Choose **Thumper**.

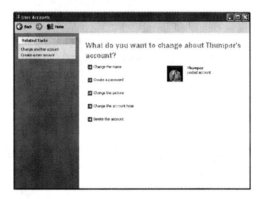

WHAT'S **HAPPENING?** You want to delete this account. Since you are an adminstrator, you may do this. If you had logged in as Thumper, a limited user, you would not be able to delete or create an account.

36   Click **Delete the account**.

WHAT'S **HAPPENING?** You switched users so Thumper is still active. You need to return to Thumper and Bambi and Log off.

37   Click **OK**. Click **Start**. Click **Log Off**. Click **Switch User**. Choose **Thumper**. Click **Start**. Click **Log Off**. Click **Log Off**.

38   Choose **Bambi**. Key in the password. Press [Enter]. Click **Start**. Click **Log Off**. Click **Log Off**.

39   Choose your current login name. Right-click the taskbar. Choose **Task Manager**. Click the **Users** tab.

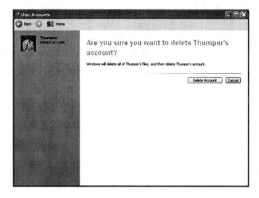

WHAT'S HAPPENING? Now only your user name should be active. You cannot delete a user who is currently logged on.

40 Close this window. In the User Accounts window, Thumper should be the selected user. Click **Delete the account**.

WHAT'S HAPPENING? You get one more chance to save Thumper.

42 Click **Delete Account**.

WHAT'S HAPPENING? You can save some of Thumper's information. In this case you do not want to do so.

41 Click **Delete Files**.

WHAT'S HAPPENING? You have returned to the User Accounts window. Thumper is no longer there as a user.

43 Choose **Bambi** and delete her account. Then close all open windows.

WHAT'S HAPPENING? You have returned to the desktop.

Chapter Summary

In this chapter, you learned about the different resolutions and colors available on your system. You looked at the different color schemes you could use when you select the Display properties. You learned to access the Display properties from the Control Panel and by right-clicking the desktop. Display provides many options for altering the screen including using a theme, using a wallpaper, , using a screen saver, changing color schemes, and adjusting elements of the desktop. You looked at the system date and time by accessing the Date/Time object in Control Panel. You learned about Regional and Language Options and how to change them. You learned that you can alter the keyboard and mouse to meet your needs with the Keyboard and Mouse objects. By accessing the Sounds and Audio Devices object, you can assign sounds to computer events, control your audio devices, and work with your multimedia devices. You found that you can have text read to you by using the Speech object. You found that you can customize the Start menu by going to the Start menu foldr in Windows Explorer. You can add or remove programs and documents from the Start menu according to your needs. You can drag and drop programs and documents to the Start menu. You learned how to use the User Accounts icon to manage the user accounts on your system.

Key Terms

Active Desktop	push technology	system date
device driver	refresh rate	system time
event	repeat delay	theme
password	repeat rate	tracking speed
pointer trail	scheme	wallpaper
power management	screen saver	

Discussion Questions

1. Explain the purpose and function of Control Panel.
2. List and explain three objects that Windows XP Professional places in Control Panel.
3. What is a theme? A wallpaper? Compare and contrast themes and wallpapers.
4. Compare and contrast tiling and centering a background.
5. Explain how and why you would use a background.
6. What is power management? What functions can it perform?
7. Explain the purpose and function of a screen saver.
8. Why would you use a password with a screen saver?
9. What is a scheme? How can you use it?
10. Describe the steps to change the font of icons or menus.
11. Describe the purpose of push technology. How is it implemented in Windows XP Professional?
12. What are effects? How might you use them?
13. Can you change the icons on the desktop? If you can, how would you do so?
14. What are some of the advantages and disadvantages of using a higher resolution setting for your monitor?
15. What does Standard VGA refer to?
16. What are the advantages and disadvantages of having more colors displayed on your monitor?
17. What factors must you take into account to determine what resolution you can use?

18. List reasons for and ways of customizing the mouse and keyboard.
19. Explain the terms repeat rate and repeat delay.
20. Explain the purpose and function of the system date and system time.
21. What impact does a regional setting have on the system date and time?
22. What is a scheme? Where are schemes used in Windows XP Professional?
23. What is an event? How may a sound be assigned to an event?
24. Describe how to to add a document to the Start menu.
25. Explain the purpose and function of user accounts.

True/False Questions

For each question, circle the letter T if the statement is true or the letter F if the statement is false.

T   F   1. Control Panel includes an object for adding new users.

T   F   2. Logging off as a user is the same as shutting down the computer.

T   F   3. You may never change the icon for any desktop item such as My Computer.

T   F   4. Screen savers can be assigned a password.

T   F   5. You may only add programs to the Start menu.

Completion Questions

Write the correct answer in each blank space.

6. If you want to have more than one user on a computer, you must create a(n) _____.

7. The smallest point of light that can be displayed on the screen is called a(n) _____.

8. In the Desktop tab in the Display Properties sheet, Bliss, Azul and Tulips are all examples of _____.

9. A predetermined set of options, including sounds, icons, and so forth, is referred to as a(n) _____.

10. Sound files used by Windows XP Professional may have the extension _____.

Multiple Choice Questions

Circle the letter of the correct answer for each question.

11. When using Themes tab from the Display Properties sheet, you may
    a. only choose from the listed schemes.
    b. choose from the listed themes and search the Internet for more themes.
    c. alter power management settings from this property sheet.
    d. determine users from this property sheet.

12. You can set all of the following in Regional and Language Options except
    a. an automatic adjustment of the clock for daylight saving time.
    b. the way the date is displayed.
    c. the way the time is displayed.
    d. the currency symbol used.

13. The main factor in determining the monitor resolution you can use is the
    a. version of Windows XP Professional you are using.
    b. monitor you have.
    c. video card you have installed.
    d. both b and c

14. The Programs folder within the Start Menu folder
    a. contains all the programs available on your computer.
    b. contains all shortcuts and folders found on the Programs submenus.
    c. contains programs that require a password.
    d. cannot be modified.

15. In order to change any user password in any user account, you must
    a. be an adminstator.
    b. be logged on as that user.
    c. cannot change a password once it has been created.
    d. both a and b

Application Assignments

Problem Set I—At the Computer

Problem A

* Open the Display Properties sheet.
* Click **Desktop**.
* In the drop-down list box for backgrounds, select **Blue Lace 16**.
* Select **Tile**.
* Click **Apply**.
* Close the Display Properties window. If the Control Panel window is open, close it.

    1. The wallpaper on the desktop has a _____ background.
        a. red
        b. black
        c. green
        d. blue

* Open the display property sheet.
* Click **Desktop**.
* Click **Browse**. Locate and choose **Plane.bmp** located in the C:\XPRODATA folder. Click **Open**.
* Click **Center**. Click **Apply**.

    2. The plane image is
        a. a repeated image on the desktop.
        b. displayed one time on the desktop.
        c. cannot be displayed.
        d. none of the above.

* In the drop-down list box for backgrouns, select **Bliss**.
* Click **Apply**.
* Close the Display Properties sheet. If it is open, close Control Panel.

Problem B

* Open the Display Properties sheet.

* Click the **Screen Saver** tab.

* Choose the **3D FLYING OBJECTS** screen saver. Preview it.

  3. What appears is a picture of
     a. a file.
     b. the Windows XP Professional logo.
     c. a blank screen.

* Click the **Settings** button. Click the **Style** drop-down arrow in **Settings**.

  4. In Style, one choice is
     a. One Ribbon.
     b. Two Ribbons.
     c. One Thread.
     d. Two Threads.

* Be sure Windows Logo is selected. Click **Cancel**.

* Choose **None** for screen savers.

* Click the **Power** button.

  5. In the Power Schemes drop-down list box, _____ appears as a choice.
     a. Home/Office Desk
     b. Portable/Laptop
     c. both a and b
     d. neither a nor b

* Click **Cancel**. Click **OK**.

* Close the Display Properties sheet.

* If it is open, close Control Panel.

Problem C

* Open the Display object.

* Choose the **Appearance** tab.

* Choose **Olive Green** in the Color Scheme drop-down list box.

  6. In the sample box, the Inactive Window title bar has what background color?
     a. olive
     b. tan
     c. white
     d. black

* Choose **Silver** in the Color Scheme drop-down list box.

  7. In the sample box, the desktop has what color?
     a. green
     b. dark gray
     c. white
     d. silver

* Click **Advanced**.

* Locate ToolTip in the Item drop-down list box. Click it.

8. Does ToolTip have a font and a font size assigned to it?
    a. yes
    b. no
    c. ToolTip is not listed.

* Click **Cancel**.

* Click the **Desktop** tab.

* Choose **Customize Desktop**.

* Click the **My Documents** icon in the Desktop icons window to select it.

* Click the **Restore Default** command button.

* Click the **Change Icon** command button.

9. What file name is listed?
    a. Explorer.exe
    b. Explorer.dll
    c. Mydocs.exe
    d. Mydocs.dll

* Click **Cancel**. Click **Cancel**. Click **Cancel**.

* Close Control Panel, if necessary.

Problem D

* Open Control Panel.

* Open the Mouse object.

* Click the **Pointers** tab.

* Select **Dinosaur (System scheme)**. Click the **Busy** icon to select it. Look in the samples portion of the dialog box.

10. The dinosaur
    a. rotates.
    b. is running.
    c. is jumping.
    d. all of the above

* Select **Windows Default (system scheme)** in Schemes.

* Click the **Pointer Options** tab.

11. The Pointer Speed control, under Motion, is a(n)
    a. check box.
    b. option button.
    c. slider.
    d. command button.

* Click **Cancel**.

* Open the Keyboard object. Click the question mark on the title bar. Drag it to the clock icon and click.

12. Which tip appears?

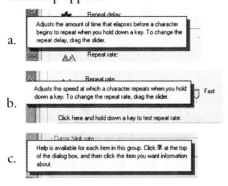

a.

b.

c.

* Close the Keyboard Properties sheet.
* Close Control Panel.

Problem E

* Open Control Panel.
* Open the **Date and Time** object.
* Click the **Time Zone** tab.
* Click the down arrow on the drop-down list box.
* Drag the scroll box to near the end of the list until you see Auckland, Wellington.

13. The number of hours after Greenwich mean time for Auckland, Wellington, New
     Zealand is
     a. 4.
     b. 8.
     c. 12.
     d. 16.

* Be sure your correct time zone is selected. Click **Cancel**.
* Close the Date and Time Properties dialog box.
* Open the Regional and Languages object.
* Click **Norwegian (Bokmal)**.

14. The currency symbol that appears is
     a. zł
     b. €
     c. kr
     d. L

* Click **Cancel**.
* Close Control Panel.

Problem Set II—Brief Essay

For all essay questions, use Notepad or WordPad to create your answer. Be sure to include your
name and class information and the number of the question you are answering. Then print your
answer.

1. Why do you think Windows XP Professional provides multiple options for changing fonts,
    colors, the desktop background, and other screen elements? Discuss the advantages and
    disadvantages of these multiple options.

2. You may create a password with your user account. What purpose does a password serve? What guidelines would you use to establish a password? Give examples of good passwords and reasons why they are good passwords.

Problem Set III—Scenario

When you click the **Start** button and point to **Programs**, you see the following:

* HP Install Network Printer Wizard is a utility program that allows you to quickly install an HP Network printer.

* Acrobat Reader is a commercial program from Adobe that converts a document created on a computer with the Windows XP Professional or any other operating system into a portable document format (PDF) file that can be sent electronically to anyone. The recipient does not need the original program to read the document but must have Acrobat Reader, which is available for free. Typically PDF is used for documents that will be downloaded from the Internet.

* Hearts is a card game.

* Microsoft Access, Excel, PowerPoint, and Word and Microsoft Office tools are all programs that come with Microsoft Office.

* Shanghai is a game.

* WinZip is program that allows you to combine one or more files into a compressed file and to open any file compressed with WinZip.

* Shortcut to WS_FT Pro is a program that allows you to upload and download files to and from computers on remote systems.

* SnagIt 6 is a screen capture utility program.

* You also have two files, Dances.bmp and February.txt, that you use every day but are not on the menu.

* You have just installed a game you like playing every day called GOLF.EXE which is not on the menu.

Create a plan to alter this menu scheme so that it assists you in working more efficiently. List the steps you would take to alter these menus. Include in your answer the folders you would create, if any, and what items you would remove, if any. State which items you would move and where you would move them. Discuss your rationale.

CHAPTER 11

File and Disk Maintenance

By running programs designed to keep your hard disk in good working order, you can learn much about your system and optimize the performance of your disk. You can repair disk errors, gain more disk space by removing unneeded files, store files more efficiently, run regular maintenance routines, schedule programs to run at specific times and dates, synchronize your files, back up and restore files, and learn other ways to gain more space on your disk.

In this chapter, you will learn to use different file and system programs. You will learn how to use the Check Disk program to check for system errors and bad sectors on your disks. You will learn how Disk Cleanup can delete unnecessary files. You will use Disk Defragmenter to optimize the storage space of a disk. You will see that you can set up a regular maintenance routine as well as use Task Scheduler to run programs. The Backup program will allow you to back up and restore files for data protection and create an ASR (Automated System Recovery Disk. If you have problems starting your computer, the ASR can assist you in trying to fix the problems.

The Registry keeps track of all of your object linking and embedding (OLE) operations. It stores all the configuration information about the hardware on your specific computer. It also tracks and contains all the preferences for each user of the computer system. Typically, you do not have to deal directly with the Registry. The preferred method for making changes is to use tools such as Control Panel. However, if your Registry becomes corrupt, there are methods to restore it. You can use System Restore. If you add new hardware or software that causes your computer to become inoperable, System Restore allows you to roll back your computer system to a time when your computer was working properly. You will use plug and play as well as Device Manager to determine if all your devices are working properly. Windows XP also offers information about your system in a tool called System Information that tells you about your computer system. In addition, Windows XP Professional provides a set of Administrative Tools to help you manage your system. You will use the Computer Management tool to look at different aspects of your computer system.

537

Learning Objectives

1. Explain conditions that can cause hardware problems and how to avert these problems.
2. Explain what lost clusters and cross-linked files are.
3. Explain conditions that can cause data errors and how to avert these errors.
4. Explain the purpose and function of Check Disk.
5. Explain the purpose and function of Disk Cleanup.
6. Compare and contrast contiguous and noncontiguous files.
7. Explain how Disk Defragmenter can help optimize a disk's performance.
8. Explain the purpose and function of Task Scheduler.
9. Compare and contrast full, differential, and incremental backups.
10. Explain the importance of and procedures for backing up and restoring files.
11. Explain the purpose and function of the ASR (Automated Recovery System).
12. Explain the purpose and function of initialization files.
13. Explain the purpose and function of the Registry.
14. Explain the purpose and function of System Restore.
15. Explain the purpose and function of a paging file.
16. Explain the purpose and function of plug and play.
17. Explain the purpose and function of Administrative Tools.

Student Outcomes

1. Use Check Disk to repair disk problems.
2. Use Disk Cleanup to remove unneeded files.
3. Use Disk Defragmenter to optimize a disk's performance.
4. Use Task Scheduler to add and remove a scheduled task.
5. Back up and Restore files.
6. Create a restore point with System Restore
7. Use Device Manager to review your driver settings.
8. Use System Information.
9. Use the Computer Management tool.

11.1 • Detecting and Repairing Errors with Check Disk

It is a truism in the computer world that it is not *if* you will have problems with your hard drive but *when*. Hard drives can have physical problems for many reasons. Some of these are:

* Wear and tear on the hard disk. When your computer is on, the hard disk is always spinning. Eventually your hard disk can wear out. This fate of all hard disks is one reason users like computers that support power management. If you use power management features, you can place your computer on standby when it is idle. While on standby, your monitor and hard disks turn off, and your computer uses less power. You can also put your computer in hibernation. The hibernation feature turns off your monitor and hard disk, saves everything in memory on the disk, and turns off your computer. Typically, you use these features to conserve power. You can also use power management features, if your computer supports them, to minimize wear on your system.

* Head crash. The read/write heads of the hard disk float on a cushion of air just above the spinning platters. A severe jolt can cause the heads to crash onto the disk, which can destroy the disk as well as the data on the disk. This event is called a ***head crash***. To minimize this problem, place your system unit in a location where it will not get knocked around.

In addition to physical problems, there are also software-related problems. For instance, you can infect your computer with a virus by using an infected floppy disk, unzipping and installing an infected program, using a data file that has a virus embedded in it, or receiving email that has a virus embedded in it. With email, opening a document from an unknown source can infect your computer with a virus.

Viruses are programs that have damaging side effects. Sometimes these side effects are intentionally damaging, sometimes not. Some viruses can destroy a computer's hard disk or the data on the disk. To minimize this problem, you should purchase an antivirus program that will always check your drive for viruses. Popular virus protection programs include Norton AntiVirus and McAfee VirusScan.

The following conditions can cause errors to your data that you may be able to repair. In some cases, these are errors that you have no control over. These include:

* Power surge. Although the current supplied to your computer is usually fairly constant, there can be a sudden and possibly damaging increase in line voltage. This event can occur, for instance, during a severe electrical storm or when the power company has a huge demand such as during a heat wave. To minimize this problem, plug your computer into a surge protector or surge suppressor. A *surge protector (surge suppressor)* is a device that prevents surges from reaching your computer.

* Power outage. If the power suddenly goes out, you will, of course, lose everything in memory, and that could also damage your hard disk. To minimize this damage, use a surge suppressor. There is a more expensive solution—purchase a UPS (Uninterruptible Power Supply). This device provides a backup power supply, usually by battery, so that you can shut down the system properly.

* Improperly closed program or locked system. If you simply turn off your computer without closing application programs or going through the Windows XP Professional shut-down process, information is not properly written to the disk. To minimize this problem, you should always close any open programs and always go through the Windows XP Professional shut-down procedure. However, sometimes your computer will "lock." In other words, your keyboard, mouse, and program become frozen and your only choice is to go through a power cycle (physically turn the computer off, wait at least five seconds, and then turn it back on again).

Windows XP Professional comes with a program called Check Disk, which can check your hard disk for problems and repair those problems. Check Disk checks for logical errors in the file system, such as invalid entries in the tables that keep track of file location and problems that involve the physical disk, lost clusters, or cross-linked files.

Lost clusters are not uncommon. They occur because the file allocation table (FAT) and directory work in conjunction. Every file has an entry in the directory table. This entry points to the starting cluster in the FAT. If the file is longer than one cluster, which it usually is, the FAT has a pointer that leads it to the next cluster, and the next cluster, and so on. These pointers *chain* together all the data in a file. If the chain is broken (a pointer is lost), the disk ends up with lost clusters. Lost clusters are incorrectly marked as used in the FAT and unavailable for new data. A *lost cluster* then is marked by Windows XP Professional as being in use but not representing any part of the chain of a file. In other words, the FAT knows that the clusters are occupied by data, but does not know to which file the clusters belong. Look at Figure 11.1. The FAT looks normal. Clusters 3, 4, and 6 are a chain, but the FAT does not know to which file this chain belongs. There is no entry in the directory. Hence, these are lost clusters.

Root Directory Table

File Name	File Extension	Date	Time	Other Info	Starting Cluster Number

File Allocation Table

Cluster Number	Status
1	in use
2	in use
3	4
4	6
5	in use
6	end

Clusters 3, 4, and 6 have data, are linked together,
but have no file entry in the directory table.

Figure 11.1 ∘ Lost Clusters

Since these lost clusters belong to no file, they cannot be retrieved or deleted. The data becomes useless. Windows XP Professional cannot write other data to these lost clusters, so you lose space on the disk. This phenomenon occurs for a variety of reasons. The most common explanation is that a user did not exit a program properly. Often, when a user interrupts this process, the data will not be properly written to the disk. Other times, power failures or power surges cause clusters to be lost.

Check Disk will fix these lost clusters automatically or save them to disk as files. It converts lost file fragments into files so that you may view the contents to determine whether there is any data in them that you want. The files are stored in a directory and have names such as File0000.chk, File0001.chk, and so on.

A cross link occurs when two or more files claim the same cluster simultaneously or twice in the same file. The files that are affected are called *cross-linked files*. The data in a cross-linked cluster is usually correct for only one of the cross-linked files, but it may not be correct for any of them. Figure 11.2 gives an example of what happens when two files claim the same cluster.

Root Directory Table

File Name	File Extension	Date	Time	Other Info	Starting Cluster Number
MY	FIL	4-15-94	11:23		1
HIS	FIL	4-15-94	11:23		3

File Allocation Table

Cluster Number	Status
1	MY.FIL
2	MY.FIL
3	HIS.FIL
4	MY.FIL HIS.FIL
5	HIS FIL
6	MY.FIL

Figure 11.2 ∘ Cross-Linked Files

In the example above, My.fil thinks it owns clusters 1, 2, 4, and 6. His.fil thinks it owns clusters 3, 4, and 5. Both My.fil and His.fil think that cluster 4 is part of their chain. Either one or both of these files are bad.

Figure 11.3 shows an example of a file with two FAT entries that refer to the same cluster. EOF stands for the end-of-file marker.

Cluster number	100	101	102	103	104
Pointer to the next cluster with data	101	102	103	103	EOF

Figure 11.3 ∘ Another Cross-Linked File

In the above example, the pointer in cluster 100 says to go to cluster 101 (where there is more data in the chain); the pointer in cluster 101 says to go to cluster 102; the pointer in cluster 102 says to go to cluster 103, but the pointer in cluster 103 says to go again to cluster 103 which is not possible; so again, here is a cross-linked file.

Check Disk can check and repair local hard drives, floppy disks, and removable drives, but cannot find or fix errors on CD-ROMs or network drives. Check Disk can only be used on actual physical drives connected to your computer system. In addition, the system must have exclusive access to the disk to complete its job. If any disk files are in use, you will see an error message asking you if you want to reschedule the task to automatically occur the next time you start your computer. This is true if you are using FAT32 as a file system. It is recommended that Check Disk be run on a regular basis to prevent errors. Remember, before you run Check Disk, you should close any programs that are open, including screen savers, toolbars such as the Microsoft Office toolbar, and virus-checking programs. Since Check Disk is dealing with the disk structure, open programs or open files can cause data loss, corrupt files, and a host of other catastrophic errors.

If the disk or volume (disk partition) is formatted as NTFS (New Technology File System), Windows XP Professional automatically (without running Check Disk) logs all file transactions, replaces bad clusters, and stores copies of key information for all files on the NTFS volume.

11.2 • Activity • Using Check Disk

Note: The MYDATADISK disk should be in Drive A.

1   Open Windows Explorer. Click **My Computer**. Right-click the Drive A icon. Click **Properties**. Click the **Tools** tab.

WHAT'S **HAPPENING?** You are interested in error-checking. When you choose error-checking, you execute the Check Disk program.

2   Click **Check Now** in the Tools property sheet.

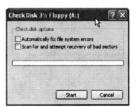

WHAT'S **HAPPENING?** The Automatically fix file system errors option directs Windows to fix file system errors. The Scan for and attempt recovery of bad sectors option attempts to locate bad sectors, record them as bad, recover data from them, and write the recovered data to good sectors on the disk. If this option is selected, it is unnecessary to activate the first option because it is included automatically.

3   Click Start.

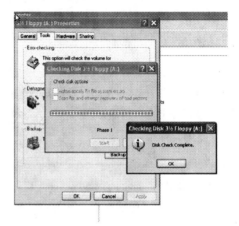

WHAT'S **HAPPENING?** The status bar indicated the program's progression. When the program has completed its task, a dialog box appears, informing you of the disk's condition. In this case, Check Disk has completed and found no errors.

4   Click OK. Click OK. Close all open windows.

11.3 • Cleaning Up Your Disk

How well your computer system performs depends a great deal on your hard drive. Remember, all your files (programs and data files) primarily are stored on the hard disk. You need to access these files easily and quickly, and you need space for new files, both program and data files. In addition, many programs create temporary files while they are working. You must have sufficient disk space to allow the creation of these files. When you print a document, it is sent to the hard disk, where it is queued in a temporary file until the printer is ready. If you use the Internet, Web browsers cache files on the hard disk to improve your access speed to the sites you frequently visit. A *cache* is a storage area for often-used information. When you delete files from the hard disk, they are sent to the Recycle Bin which, again, is an area on the hard disk.

As you can see, you need hard disk space. You will find that many programs do not delete their temporary files. You will forget to empty the Recycle Bin or delete your cached Internet files. All of these items will not only cause your hard disk to run out of space, but will also slow down your system's performance. Windows XP Professional provides a tool to help you maintain your disk. It is a utility called Disk Cleanup. Disk Cleanup is intended to be run on your hard drives. Disk Cleanup gives you several options to assist you in recovering disk space.

11.4 • Activity • Using Disk Cleanup

1   Click Start. Point to All Programs. Point to Accessories. Point to System Tools. Click Disk Cleanup.

WHAT'S **HAPPENING?** A message box appears, asking you which drive you want to clean up. If you have only one drive, go to Step 3, as you have no selection to make.

2 Click the down arrow in the drop-down list box.

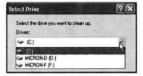

WHAT'S **HAPPENING?** Your list will be different depending on how many hard drives you have. If you have only Drive C, you will see no other choices. Notice that no CD, DVD, or floppy drives appear.

3 Click outside the drop-down list to click it. Click **OK**.

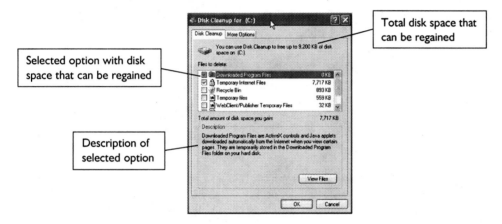

WHAT'S **HAPPENING?** A quick message box appears, telling you that your system is being analyzed. Then the Disk Cleanup property sheet appears with the complete analysis. Your computer's analysis will be different. In the example, 9,200 KB can be regained in disk space. You have a choice of seven types of files to remove.

4 If Recycle Bin is not selected, check it now. Then click the **View Files** command button.

WHAT'S **HAPPENING?** Before you delete the files, you can look at them to confirm that you do want to delete them. Your files will vary; you may even have no files to delete. In this example, the Recycle Bin has not been emptied in quite a while.

5   Close the Recycle Bin window. Click the **More Options** tab.

WHAT'S **HAPPENING?** Other options are available to free up disk space. The first option is to remove Windows XP Professional components that you seldom or never use.

6   Under Windows Components, click **Clean Up**.

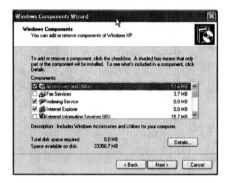

WHAT'S **HAPPENING?** You are taken to Windows Components Wizard. You may remove Windows components that you do not use. For instance, if you are using Netscape Navigator as your browser, you could choose to remove Internet Explorer.

7   Click **Cancel**.

8   In the **Disk Cleanup** window, under Installed Programs, click **Clean Up**.

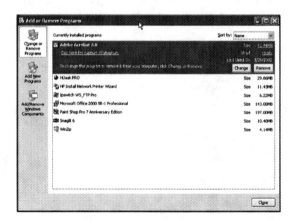

WHAT'S HAPPENING? You are taken to the Add or Remove Programs utility. Here is a list of programs that are installed on this system. Your list will be different. If you had a program that you installed but found you did not use or did not like, you can remove it here.

9   Click **Close**.

10   In the Disk Cleanup window, under System Restore, click **Clean Up**.

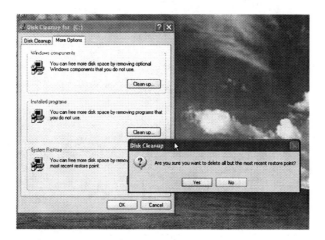

WHAT'S HAPPENING? System Restore is a utility that you can use to restore your computer to a previous state, if a problem occurs with Windows XP Professional. System Restore works with the Windows XP system files and the Registry. Restoring a system does not affect your data files. You will learn to create your own restore points but Windows XP normally creates a restore point daily and at the time of significant events such as when you install a new program or a new device driver. These system restore points can take up much room on your hard disk. Thus, you can opt to keep only the most current restore points. In this case, you do not want to run this utility.

11   Click **No**. Click the **Disk Cleanup** tab.

12   Click **OK**.

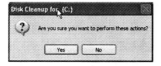

WHAT'S HAPPENING? You are asked to confirm the Disk Cleanup.

13   Click **Yes**.

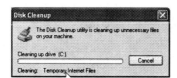

WHAT'S HAPPENING? You see a progress report on your Disk Cleanup. When it is finished, you are returned the desktop.

14   Click **Start**. Point to **All Programs**. Point to **Accessories**. Point to **System Tools**. Click **Disk Cleanup**. Click **OK**.

WHAT'S HAPPENING? Space was gained on the disk in this example. Your results will be different. In this example, there is still space to be regained as every check box was not selected.

15 Click **Cancel**.

WHAT'S HAPPENING? You have returned to the desktop.

11.5 ● Contiguous and Noncontiguous

Contiguous means in contact or touching. What does this have to do with files? Windows XP Professional keeps track of data by grouping it into files. In order to store and retrieve files, Windows XP Professional divides a disk into numbered blocks called sectors. Sectors are then grouped into clusters. A cluster is the smallest unit that Windows XP Professional will handle. A cluster is always a set of contiguous sectors. The number of sectors that make up a cluster on a hard disk varies, depending on the size of the hard drive and how it was installed.

Usually, a file will take up more than one cluster on a disk. Thus, Windows XP Professional has to keep track of the location of all the file's parts on the disk. When files are edited and need more space, the file is broken into fragments and stored in open space on the disk. Furthermore, if you are using FAT or FAT32, when a file is deleted, only the entries in the file allocation table (FAT) are deleted and the space the file occupied is marked as open and available for new data.

Windows XP Professional writes data to the disk based on the next empty cluster. It attempts to write the information in adjacent clusters. Windows XP Professional wants all the parts of a file to be next to each other (tries to write to adjacent clusters) because it is easier to retrieve or store information when it is together. When this occurs, the file is considered to be contiguous. When the file is broken up and is no longer stored in adjacent clusters, it is a noncontiguous or *fragmented file*. If a disk is comprised of many noncontiguous files, it can be called a *fragmented disk*. Windows XP Professional will take longer to read a noncontiguous file because the read/write heads must move around the disk to find all the parts of the file.

11.6 ● Optimizing the Performance of Disks

To fix a fragmented disk, you need a defragmenting utility program, sometimes called a *defragger* or a *disk optimization program*. Sometimes these programs are called disk compression programs, but that is a misnomer. These programs do not compress data. Defragmenting programs literally move data around on a disk to make files contiguous. In System Tools, Windows XP Professional provides a utility called Disk Defragmenter.

The Disk Defragmenter program rearranges files, programs, and empty space on the hard drive. Individual files are stored as a complete unit on the disk. Files are moved around on the disk until all files are stored contiguously on the disk with no space between them.

You should run both Check Disk and Disk Cleanup prior to running Disk Defragmenter. Before you optimize your hard disk, you want to remove all lost or cross-linked clusters and all unnecessary files. Before you run any disk optimizers, it is recommended that you close all open programs, including screen savers and virus-checking programs. In addition, you should be sure to have plenty of time to run Disk Defragmenter. A good time to run the program is overnight when you are away from the computer. If you run it every couple of weeks, depending on your computer use, the program will not take as long to run, because it will have less to do.

You must use the Disk Defragmenter program that comes with Windows XP Professional. Although Disk Defragmenter is safe, it directly manipulates your disk. Therefore, you should back your disk up before beginning Disk Defragmenter. You may use Disk Defragmenter on local drives only, but you cannot run it on floppy disks. You also cannot use it on network drives. In addition, you must have administrator privileges to use this utility program.

11.7 ● Activity ● Using Disk Defragmenter

1   Place the MYDATADISK disk in Drive A.

2   Click **Start**. Click **My Computer**. Right-click the Drive A icon. Click **Properties**. Click the **Tools** tab. Click **Defragment Now**.

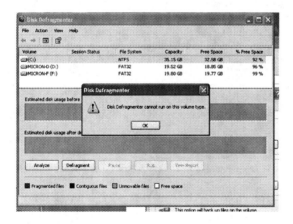

WHAT'S **HAPPENING?** Floppy disks cannot be defragmented. Again, usually you are trying to improve performance on a hard disk. You can start any of these operations from this property sheet, or you can use menus (Start/All Programs/Accessories/System Tool/Disk Defragmenter).

3   Click **OK**.

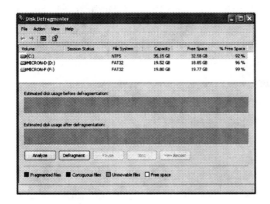

WHAT'S **HAPPENING?** The Disk Defragmenter window opens and displays a list of available hard drives.

4   Click Drive C to select it. Click the **Analyze** command button.

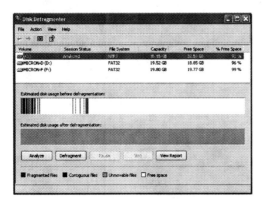

WHAT'S **HAPPENING?** While your hard disk is being analyzed, vertical lines slowly appear along the Analysis display bar. The line color indicates a file's current status. To interpret the Analysis display bar, refer to the legend along the bottom of the window.

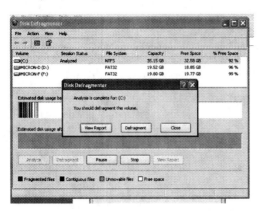

WHAT'S **HAPPENING?** Since this volume (Drive C) uses the NTFS file system, you see the report on the fragmentation of the Master File Table.

After a few minutes, a dialog box appears indicating whether you should defrag the disk or not. In this example, the analysis determined that defragmenting the disk was necessary.

5   Click the **View Report** command button.

WHAT'S **HAPPENING?** The volume information reports statistics describing the volume size, cluster size, and the used, free, and percentage of free space. The most fragmented files list box describes the most fragmented files, including the file's name, the file's size, and the number of fragments that make up the file. Four command buttons allow you to print the report, save it as a file, go ahead and defrag the disk, or close the Analysis Report dialog box.

6   Scroll to the bottom of the **Volume Information** list box.

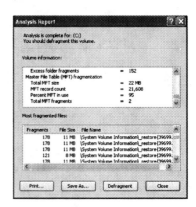

WHAT'S **HAPPENING?** Since this volume (Drive C) uses the NTFS file system, you see the report on the fragmentation of the Master File Table.

7   Click **Close**.

8   If you have another drive, select it and click **Analyze**. When the analysis is complete, click **View Report** and scroll to the bottom of the Volume information list box.

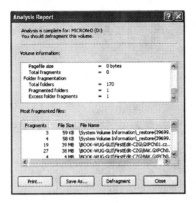

WHAT'S HAPPENING? Because this volume (Drive D) was formatted as FAT32, there is no information about the MFT (Master File Table). The MFT is only used on NTFS volumes.

9   Click **Close**.

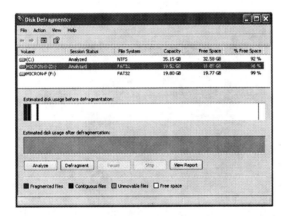

WHAT'S HAPPENING? In the Disk Defragmenter window, you see that both Drive C and D, in this example, have been analyzed.

10   Close all open windows.

WHAT'S HAPPENING? You have returned to the desktop.

11.8 ● Starting Programs Automatically

Windows XP Professional has a wizard for scheduling any program to run at any time. It is called Task Scheduler. For example, you can schedule such programs as Disk Cleanup and Backup to run at a predetermined time when it is most convenient for you. As another example, you might use Task Scheduler to dial into an online service during off hours, look for certain topics, download the results, and then hang up. You would, of course, need a program that could do that task before you could schedule it. Just be sure that you leave the computer on, and that any task you schedule to run when you are not around can operate without user input and can exit cleanly when completed.

11.9 • Activity • Using Task Scheduler

1   Click **Start**. Point at **All Programs**. Point at **Accessories**. Point at **System Tools**. Click **Scheduled Tasks**. Click **View**. Click **Tiles**.

WHAT'S **HAPPENING?** In this example, there are no tasks scheduled. Your display may vary.

2   Double-click **Add Scheduled Task**.

WHAT'S **HAPPENING?** You are presented with Scheduled Task Wizard.

3   Click **Next**.

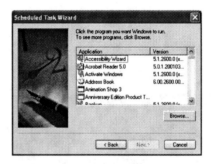

WHAT'S **HAPPENING?** You are presented with a list of programs on your system.

4   Locate **Disk Cleanup**. Click it.

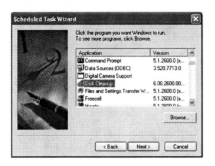

WHAT'S HAPPENING? You are interested in scheduling Disk Cleanup.

5 Click **Next**.

WHAT'S HAPPENING? As you can see, you can schedule the program to run at almost any interval.

6 Click **Weekly**. Click **Next**.

WHAT'S HAPPENING? Your task is scheduled for once a week. The start time is set to whatever the current time is, although you can change that as well. You must pick a day of the week that you want the task to run.

7 Click **Sunday**. Click **Next**.

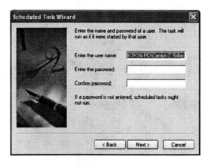

WHAT'S HAPPENING? You must identify the user responsible for starting this task by entering the user's name and logon password. By default, your user name appears in the first text box.

8 Enter your password in the second and third text boxes. Click **Next**.

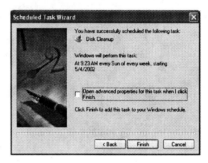

WHAT'S HAPPENING? Your task is scheduled. You can open the advanced properties when you are done. In this case you do not need to see them.

9 Click **Finish**.

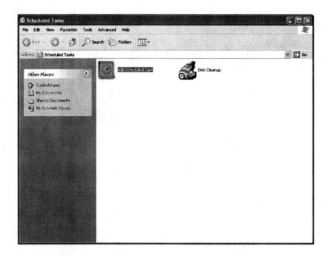

WHAT'S HAPPENING? Your task has been added to the list of scheduled tasks.

10 Click **Advanced** on the menu bar.

WHAT'S HAPPENING? Not only can you pause or stop using Task Scheduler, but you can also look at a log of the tasks that have been done, as well as be notified of any missed tasks. The AT Service account is a program (the "at" program, which can be run at the command line by the administrator.

11 Click somewhere off of the menu to close it. Click **Disk Cleanup** to select it.

12 Press the Delete key.

WHAT'S HAPPENING? You are asked to confirm your deletion. Notice that Task Scheduler files have the extension of .job. Windows considers any file with a .job file type to be registered to Task Scheduler.

13 Click **Yes**.

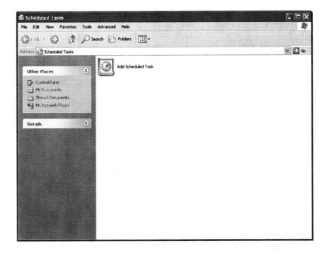

WHAT'S **HAPPENING?** You no longer have any tasks scheduled.

14 Close the **Scheduled Tasks** window. Close all open windows.

WHAT'S **HAPPENING?** You have returned to the desktop.

11.10 ● Backing Up Your Data

Backing up data is a critical task that users too often neglect. When things go wrong, either through your error or the computer's, rather than having to try to recreate data, you can turn to your backups, but only if you have created them. A *backup* is nothing more than a duplicate of files that are on a disk copied to a medium such as a floppy disk, a CD-R, a CD-RW, a Zip disk, or a tape. You retrieve the files by restoring them, which means copying them back to the original medium. When you copy a file to a floppy disk, you are in effect backing it up. You usually want to back up your entire hard disk, which includes all your files and all your folders. Although you can back up your entire hard disk to floppy disks, it is a very laborious and time-consuming process in this era of 15-gigabyte or larger hard drives. Thus, most users opt to have a tape backup unit or a removable drive with removable media such as a CD-RW, Zip, or Jaz drive. Special tapes must be purchased for use in a tape drive; cartridges for a removable drive. One of the many advantages of using Backup instead of the Copy command is that a backup file can span multiple backup disks. When one disk is full, you are directed to insert another empty disk into the drive.

As you use your computer and programs, you create data. For instance, imagine you are writing a book and you create your first chapter and save it as a file to the hard disk. You back up in January. It is now April, and you have completed 10 chapters. You accidentally delete the folder that contains your chapters. You do not want to rewrite those chapters and, furthermore, you cannot. You turn to your backup, but you have a major problem. The only file you can restore is that first chapter you created in January. The rest of your work is gone. To say the least, backing up your data files regularly is critical. The reason for backing up your entire hard drive may not be as obvious, but it is equally important.

As you work with Windows XP Professional, you create settings, install new programs, and delete old programs. You are also adding and making changes to the system Registry that controls the Windows XP Professional environment. If the Registry becomes corrupt, you will not be able to boot Windows XP Professional. The system itself is ever-changing. If, for instance, you install a new program and it does something to your hard drive, such as cause another program not to work (or worse), you want to return to the working system you had prior to your installation. If the problem is serious, you might have to reformat your hard drive. It can literally take hours, if not days, to reinstall all of your software. If you have backed up your system, you can simply restore what you had before, and a major catastrophe becomes a minor inconvenience. The Backup program supplied with Windows XP Professional supports five methods of backups: Copy Backup, Daily Backup, Differential Backup, Incremental Backup, and Normal Backup.

A *normal backup*, sometimes called a *full backup*, copies all the files from the hard drive to the backup medium, regardless of when or whether anything has changed. Full backup is the "back up everything on my computer" option. In addition, a normal backup will mark each file as having been backed up. Every file has attributes. One of these attributes, also called a flag, is the archive attribute or archive bit. This bit is either off or on. When a file has been backed up using the Normal backup option, the bit is cleared, indicating that the file has been backed up. When you alter the file, the bit is turned back on, indicating that the file has changed since the last backup. When you simply copy a file, the attribute is not altered by the copy routine. Although, the copy operation has "backed" up the file, Windows is not aware of this. The archive bit is only altered by certain programs such as Backup.

An *incremental backup* only copies or backs up the files that have been created or changed since the last normal or incremental backup. Incremental backups mark files as having been backed up by clearing the archive bit.

Backup uses the archive bit to determine whether or not a file needs to be backed up when you are performing incremental backups. If the bit is on, the file needs to be backed up. After the file is backed up, the archive bit may be set to off so that Backup knows that the file has been backed up. When you make create a new file or make any changes to an existing file, the archive bit is automatically turned on, indicating that the file has changed since the last backup.

A differential backup backs up files created or changed since the last normal or incremental backup. However, it does not mark the files as having been backed up. It does not clear the archive bit.

A daily backup backs up all files that have been created or modified the day the daily backup is performed. Again, these files are not marked as having been backed up. The archive bit is not cleared. The daily backup is a quick and dirty way to back up your current work.

A copy backup backs up the files that you select but does not mark each file has having been backed up. The archive bit is not cleared. A copy backup does not affect normal or incremental backups since file attributes are not affected. A copy backup is really no different than simply copying the file to another drive or disk.

You usually backup using a combination of full backups and incremental backups or full backups and differential backups. The choice you make usually has to do with whether you would rather spend less time backing up and more time restoring or more time backing up and less time restoring. You can always do a full backup every time you backup your system but a full backup is slower to perform than an incremental backup because you are backing up your entire system. However, it is faster to restore as you only need the most current full backup storage.

If you use a combination normal (full) backups and incremental backups, when you restore, this method requires that you restore the most recent full backup media, and all incremental media that have changes on them. However, this method requires the least amount of storage space and is the quickest method to use for backing up. Restore will take longer because you will need all the tapes or disks.

Backing up your data using a combination of normal backups and differential backups is more time-consuming, especially if your data changes frequently, but it is easier to restore the data because the backup set is usually stored on only a few disks or tapes.

If you use a combination of normal (full) backups and differential backups, the backup will take more time but it is much easier and faster to restore because your backup data is stored on fewer disks or tapes. This method requires that when you restore your files, you restore the most recent full backup media, and all incremental media that have changes on them. A *differential backup* backs up all selected files that have changed since the last normal or incremental backup. All files that have the archive bit on are backed up. When the backup is complete, the archive bit is left on.

You should have a regular backup schedule. The timing of your backups depends on how much you use your computer and how often you change things. A typical backup schedule might be that once a week you perform a full backup and every day you perform an incremental backup. If you need to restore your data, you need all of the backups, both the full and the incremental. If you are on a network, the network administrator will take care of the full backup; you need to be concerned about your data files only.

When you do backups, it is a good idea to have more than one copy of your backup or backup set. For instance, if you did a full system backup once a week and incremental backups daily, you would want at least two sets of backups. One week, you would back up on one set; the following week you would use the other set. Thus, if Murphy's law was in effect for you— your hard disk and your backup were both corrupted—you would be able to restore files from the other week's backup. The files would not be the most current, but at least you would not have to recreate everything from scratch. Another word of warning: Store at least one copy of your backup away from your computer. If you have your backup tapes at the office and you have a fire or theft, you will lose everything. If you have another set at home, you can recover what was lost at work. The most important thing about backing up is to **DO IT**. Not only do it, but do it on a regularly scheduled basis.

To access Backup, you may right-click a drive, choose Properties, choose the Tools tab, and select the Backup Now command button. You may also access Backup from the Programs submenu. Backup also has other uses. You can use Backup to *archive data*. If your hard disk starts filling up and you want to make more room on it, you can use Backup to copy seldom-used files to a backup medium and then delete them from the hard drive. If you need these files at a later date, you can restore them.

11.11 ◦ Activity ◦ Using Backup

Note 1: Since Backup requires writing information to the hard disk, and since each system is unique, these steps are only one example of how to use Backup. Should you choose to complete this activity on your own computer, be aware that you are going to do only an incremental backup of some files. Under no circumstances should you do this activity if you are on a network, nor will you be able to do it on a network.

Note 2: Place the MYDATA disk in Drive A.

1   Click **Start**. Point at **All Programs**. Point at **Accessories**. Point at **System Tools**. Click **Backup**.

WHAT'S HAPPENING? You are welcomed to the Backup and Restore wizard.

2 Be sure **Always start in wizard mode** has a check mark. Click **Next**.

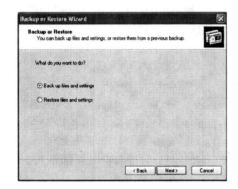

WHAT'S HAPPENING? You are asked if you want to Backup or Restore.

3 Click **Back up files and settings**. Click **Next**.

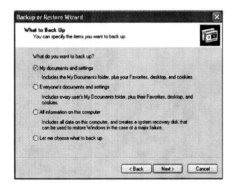

WHAT'S HAPPENING? Four choices are listed. You may back up your personal documents and settings. You may back up the documents and settings of everyone who is a user on this system. You may choose to back up all information on this computer. This includes the creation of an

ASR (Automated System Recovery) disk. When you choose this option, you include the Registry and other key system files. The last choice is what you want to backup. The default setting is to back up My Documents and settings. Since this is just a learning activity, you are going to choose the other option, **Let me choose what to backup.**

4 Click **Let me choose what to backup**. Click **Next**.

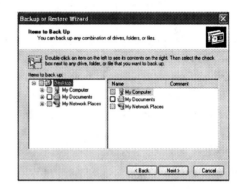

WHAT'S HAPPENING? You see your desktop objects.

5 Click the plus sign next to My Computer. Click the plus sign next to Drive C: to expand it. Scroll in the left pane until you locate the XPRODATA folder. Click on the plus sign to expand it. Click XPRODATA in the left pane. Be sure not to place a check mark in the box.

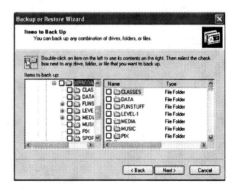

WHAT'S HAPPENING? The Backup Wizard window looks somewhat like Windows Explorer. The left pane shows the structure of your disk, and the right pane shows the files in the folders. In front of each item is an empty check box. To select an item for backing up, click in its check box. To

expand an entry, double-click it or click the plus sign next to it. In this example, the left pane shows the structure of the XPRODATA directory. The right pane shows the contents of the XPRODATA directory. Placing a checkmark in the check box next to XPRODATA would indicate that you want to back up the entire XPRODATA folder.

6 Scroll in the right pane until you can see the file that begins with AST. Click the check boxes in front of **AST.99**, **AST.NEW**, **AST.TMP**, **ASTRO.TMP**, and **ASTRO.TXT**.

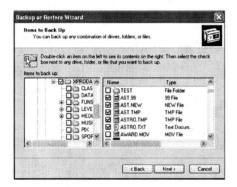

WHAT'S **HAPPENING?** You have selected the files you wish to back up by placing a checkmark in the box preceding each file.

7 Click **Next**.

WHAT'S **HAPPENING?** The wizard wants to know where to back up to. If you had a tape drive or another backup media type, you could select it here. You could choose to back up to another computer by choosing Browse and selecting My Network Places. You can back up to a CD-R or CD-RW

drive but it is a bit more complicated as the files are saved as temporary files so they are saved as "files ready to write to CD"—it is a two step operation. Also, you must have a lot of free disk space. However in this case, since you are backing up to a floppy disk, your only choice is File. Backup creates a file, and you need to tell it what device and what name you are going to use.

8 Select **Backup** and key in the following: **ASTRO**

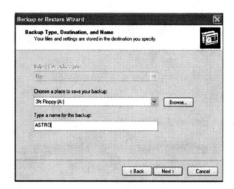

9 Click **Next**.

WHAT'S **HAPPENING?** You have completed your backup of these files. Note that they are saved as ASTRO.BKF on Drive A.

10 Click **Advanced**.

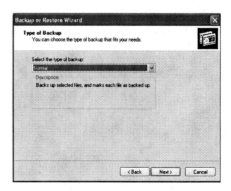

WHAT'S HAPPENING? You may select your type of backup.

11 In the drop-down list box, click the down arrow.

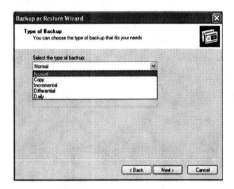

WHAT'S HAPPENING? You see your five backup types.

12 Click **Next**.

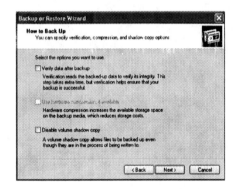

WHAT'S HAPPENING? You are asked to make a few more decisions. Windows can verify the data after the backup by reading it and comparing it to the original data, and it can save space on the backup media by compressing the data. In this example, hardware compression is not available, because the drive being backed up is not compressed. You may also disable volume shadow copy. With this option on, you may backup files, even as you are currently using them.

13 Clear all options. Click **Next**.

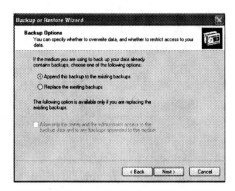

WHAT'S HAPPENING? You must decide if you want this backup set to be appended at the end of the data on the backup disk or if it should replace the data on the disk.

14 Click **Next**.

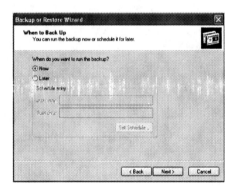

WHAT'S HAPPENING? You can do your backup now or schedule it for later.

15 Be sure **Now** is selected. Click **Next**.

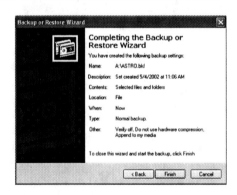

WHAT'S HAPPENING? A revised summary appears that includes your new options.

16 Click **Finish**.

WHAT'S HAPPENING? A window tells you that Backup is getting ready to do its job. Another window shows the progress of the backup. When it is complete, you see the following information box:

17 Click the **Report** button.

WHAT'S HAPPENING? You have opened a document in Notepad that has all the information about your backup.

18 Close Notepad. Click **Close**.

WHAT'S HAPPENING? You have returned to the desktop.

19 Open Windows Explorer. Open Drive A.

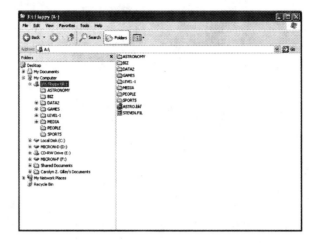

WHAT'S HAPPENING? You see your backup file, ASTRO.BKF. However, you cannot use this file or open it except with the Restore portion of the Backup utility.

20 Close the Drive A window.

WHAT'S HAPPENING? Your backup is complete. You have returned to the desktop.

11.12 • Restore

Backup, although called Backup on the menu, is called the Backup or Restore Wizard. You may use the Restore wizard to copy some or all of your files to your original disk, another disk, or another directory. Restore lets you choose which backup set to copy from. Restoring files is as easy as backing them up with the Backup program. You merely choose Restore option and choose the kind of restoration you want. You can use the Restore Wizard, which will lead you through the process of restoring your system.

11.13 • Activity • Restoring Files

Note: Since using Restore requires writing information to the hard disk and since each system is unique, these steps are one example of how to restore. Should you choose to complete this activity on your own computer, be aware that you are only going to do an incremental restoration of some files. Under no circumstances should you do this activity if you are on a network, nor will you be able to do it on a network.

1 Click **Start**. Point at **All Programs**. Point at **Accessories**. Point at **System Tools**. Click **Backup**.

WHAT'S **HAPPENING?** You saw this screen in the last activity. In this case, you are going to restore the files on the floppy disk to the hard disk.

2 Click **Next**.

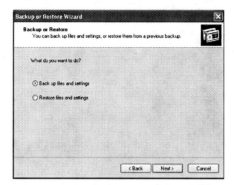

WHAT'S **HAPPENING?** Now you choose Restore files and settings.

3 Click **Restore files and settings**. Click **Next**.

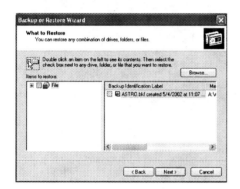

WHAT'S **HAPPENING?** The Backup or Restore Wizard is asking you what you want to restore. If the Backup program was previously run on your computer, you may have several items listed.

4 Be sure the MYDATADISK is in Drive A. Click the plus sign in the left pane. In the right pane, scroll to the end of the list and click the last entry in the list.

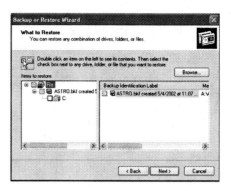

WHAT'S **HAPPENING?** The last entry in the list is selected and expanded. Since there is only one item (backup) in the right pane, you can continue.

5 In the left pane, click the check box next to Drive C. Click **Next**.

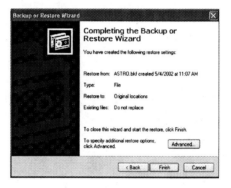

WHAT'S **HAPPENING?** The Completion window appears. The choices are preselected in that you are going to use Astro.bkf and restore it to the original location and you are not going to replace any existing files on Drive C.

6 Click the **Advanced** command button.

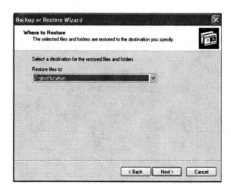

WHAT'S **HAPPENING?** Now you can change your options if you wish.

7 Click the down arrow in the **Restore files to** drop-down list box.

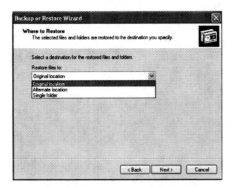

WHAT'S HAPPENING? You can restore the files to their original location, an alternate location, or a single folder.

8 Click **Original location**. Click **Next**.

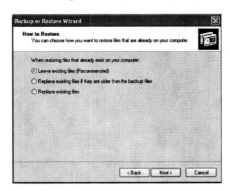

WHAT'S HAPPENING? Three option buttons allow you to select how to restore files that are already on the disk: Leave existing files (Recommended), Replace existing files if they are older than the backup files, and Replace existing files.

9 Click **Replace existing files**. Click **Next**.

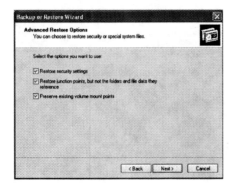

WHAT'S HAPPENING? Since you want all the files to appear in the same locations with the same security, you will leave the defaults on.

10 Click **Next**.

WHAT'S HAPPENING? The revised settings summary information appears and indicates that existing files are always replaced.

11 Click **Finish**.

WHAT'S HAPPENING? Restore is gathering the information it needs. Since there was only one file on the disk in Drive A to restore, it is using that file. If you had multiple backup files, it would ask you to confirm the name of the file to restore. When it is completed restoring files, you see the next window.

12 Click the **Report** command button.

WHAT'S **HAPPENING?** The report indicates that the backup set has been restored.

13 Close Notepad. Close the Restore Progress dialog box.

14 Click **Start**. Point to **All Programs**. Point to **Accessories**. Point to **System Tools**. Click **Backup**.

WHAT'S **HAPPENING?** You do not have to use the wizards to back up and restore files. If you clear the Always start in wizard mode check box, the next time you open Backup and Restore, you will see many more choices. For instance, you can also schedule when Windows will perform the Backup task. To open the Advanced Options, click the underlined phrase.

15 Click **Advanced Mode**.

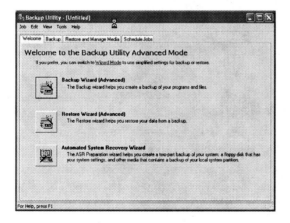

WHAT'S **HAPPENING?** Here are the advanced options.

16 Click the **Restore and Manage Media** tab.

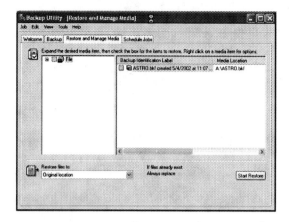

WHAT'S **HAPPENING?** You can change how you want your restore to function.

17   Click the **Schedule Jobs** tab.

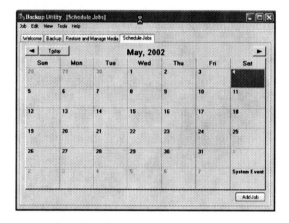

WHAT'S **HAPPENING?** Clicking the Add Job command button starts Backup Wizard so that you can enter your backup settings and schedule the backup job.

18   Close the Backup window.

WHAT'S **HAPPENING?** You returned to the desktop.

11.14 • Automated System Recovery (ASR)

Windows XP Professional has a built-in repair system for a catastrophic failure of your system. Although the name states it is automated, the process really requires a fair amount of preparation. The purpose of ASR is to restore your system partitions. It saves the contents of your system drive (where Windows is installed) to some backup media. You do not want to use floppy disks for storing your system information. Although the ASR wizard will prompt you to insert other floppy disks, it would take many floppy disks and many hours to back up the system information to floppy disks. Thus, you should choose a location such as a Zip disk, another drive on a network, or someplace that can handle large files. ASR saves information about your arrangement of disk partitions, system files, and detected hardware. ASR does not save your program files or any of your data files. During the process you also create a floppy disk that is pointing to the location of your backup files. This feature is not available on Windows XP Home Edition. This process is used to solve problems such as when you have a corrupt Registry or when your system will not boot. This repair system relies on the creation of an Automated System Recovery (ASR). It is created in the Advanced Mode of Backup. This disk, and the files that are stored on some media type other than a floppy, along with the CD-ROM used to install Windows XP Professional, repair a corrupted system. The ASR is not a substitute for backing up your data. The ASR is for system problems. It can only restore the system as it was when the ASR was made. It is like a snapshot of your system at a specific point in time. Any time that you make a change to your system, such as installing new programs or hardware, you should update your ASR. The emergency repair process also relies on data saved in the %SystemRoot%\Repair folder. The notation %SystemRoot% indicates a variable name. Windows will substitute the name of your Windows folder, such as \Windows\Repair or \WINNT\Repair.

To repair a damaged version of Windows XP Professional, you would need both the ASR, the availability of those backed up system files, *and* a Windows XP Professional installation CD. You would boot the system from the CD (or from a setup floppy disk). You would then be asked if you wanted to install Windows XP Professional or repair a damaged version. To repair, you would press the F2 key and follow the instructions on the screen. You would be instructed when to insert the ASR disk.

11.15 The Registry

As you are aware, the Windows XP Professional environment is very customizable. You may have different users for one computer, each with his or her own desktop settings, menus, and icons. When you install new hardware, the operating system must know about the new hardware and any drivers for those hardware devices. You can double-click a document icon in Windows to open the correct application program, because, when you install an application program, the program registers its extension with Windows. As you can see, the operating system has much information to keep track of. All this information is the *configuration information*.

In previous versions of Windows, the operating system and most application programs used .INI files to store information about the user environment and necessary drivers. The .INI extension was derived from *initialization files*. Initialization files were broken into two types: system initialization files and private initialization files. Windows itself created the system .INI files such as WIN.INI and SYSTEM.INI, and application programs would also create private .INI files. These configuration files contained the information that Windows needed to run itself, as well as run the programs that were installed on a specific computer. The private .INI files were often added to the Windows directory and kept track of the state of the application, containing such information as the screen position or the last-used files.

The .INI files could specify many items that varied from one computer to the next. Thus, there could not be one set of .INI files that was common to all users. These files contained such items as the name and path of a specific file that is required by Windows, some user-defined variable, or some hardware or software configuration.

Windows itself had two primary initialization files, WIN.INI and SYSTEM.INI. WIN.INI was the primary location for information pertaining to the software configuration and system-wide information added by application software. The SYSTEM.INI file was the primary location for system information that had to do with the computer hardware. One might say that WIN.INI had information for how your system behaved, whereas SYSTEM.INI pointed the Windows operating system to the correct hardware and software components such as device drivers. In order to run Windows, these two files had to be present.

Another file that Windows used was a file called REG.DAT. This file was the *registration database*, but was not an ASCII file and could only be edited by a special application program, REGEDIT. It contained information about how various applications would open, how some of them would print, the information that was needed about file extensions, and how OLE (object linking and embedding) objects were handled.

Instead of using SYSTEM.INI for hardware settings, WIN.INI for user settings, REG.DAT for file associations and object linking and embedding, and all the various private initialization files, Windows XP Professional uses a single location, called the Registry, for hardware, system software, and application configuration information. Windows XP Professional does retain support for both WIN.INI and SYSTEM.INI, although Windows no longer uses these files, so they are available to any legacy application programs that might need to refer to them. Registry information comes from the installation of Windows XP Professional, the booting of Windows XP Professional, applications, and system and user interaction. Every part of Windows XP Professional uses the Registry, without exception. The Registry files are kept in the directory %SystemRoot%\System32\Config. The Registry files that are backed up are kept in %SystemRoot%\Repair\Back.

If you use the ASR disk, there are choices available that do allow you to restore the Registry by using the Recovery Console. The Recovery Console is a text-based command interpreter that allows the system administrator to access the hard disk and files. This process is beyond the scope of this text.

However, you may use some options an alternate method, what is called "Last Known Good Configuration." This option starts Windows XP Professional with the Registry settings that were saved at the last shutdown. This does not solve problems caused by missing or corrupt drivers, but it can be useful in overcoming problems caused by changes you might have made in the current session.

It is always smart to have an ASR so that if something goes wrong, you can always boot and recover. In addition, if you have a problem, you can boot to what is called safe mode. You access safe mode by pressing and holding the **F8** key after your system finished displaying startup messages such as Keyboard installed but before the Windows logo appears. When you go to safe mode, you are presented with the Startup menu. See Figure 11.4.

```
Microsoft Advanced Options Menu
Please select an option.

_____

Safe Mode
Safe Mode with Networking
Safe Mode with Command Prompt

  Enable boot logging
  Enable VGA Mode
  Last Known Good Configuration (your most recent settings that worked)
  Directory Services Restore Mode (Windows domain controllers only)
  Debugging Mode

 Start Windows normally
 Reboot
 Return to OS Choices menu

Use the up and down arrows to move the highlight to your choice
```

Figure 11.4 ◦ *The Startup Menu*

This feature allows you to troubleshoot different types of problems. For instance, if you choose an incorrect video driver, you cannot open the property sheet for Display in order to correct your error. You can boot into the Advanced Options menu and choose Enable VGA mode. This would load only the most basic video drivers so that you could then open the property sheet for Display and correct your settings. Safe mode itself loads the minimum amount of drivers and functionality that allows Windows XP Professional to run. If you wanted to return to the last time the system worked, you would use the arrow keys to highlight **Last Known Good Configuration**, and then press **Enter**. However, Windows has included an easier way to solve some of these problems. It is called System Restore.

11.16 ● System Restore

If you make changes to your hardware, such as adding new hardware, installing a new driver for your hardware, or installing or removing software, you are making changes to your system settings. Any of these changes can cause your computer or your devices to no longer work or to work incorrectly. Sometimes, even removing the hardware, the drivers or uninstalling a program still does not solve your problem. As Microsoft XP Professional states, your computer is now in an "undesirable state." You would like the ability to be able to go back in time to when your system was working properly, when you were in a "desirable state." System Restore allows you to undo the changes you made to your computer. System Restore does all of the following:

Rolls back your computer to a more stable state because System Restore keeps track of changes made at specific times. It also tracks certain events such as when you install a new software program. These times are called *restore points*. You may also create your own personal restore points. Restore points allow you to "roll back" your computer system to a time when you know that everything was working correctly.

System Restore will save your email messages, browsing history and so on. However, be forewarned—System Restore DOES NOT save or restore your documents. System Restore is not a substitute for backing up your data files. System Restore is for your "computer" system, not for your data files. System Restore restores Windows and your programs to a restore point—not your data files.

System Restore saves about one to three weeks of changes depending on how much you use your computer, your hard disk size and how much space has been allocated to store the System Restore information.

You may select which dates you want to restore to by use of a calendar.

System Restore provides several restore points. It creates an initial system checkpoint when you upgrade or install Windows XP Professional. Even if you have not made any changes to your system, regular checkpoints are created daily and at significant events such as when you install a new device driver. If you use Windows Automatic update, restore points are created prior to the update.

All system restores are reversible, so that if the restore point you selected is not successful, you can undo it.

11.17 ● Activity ● Using System Restore

Note: If you are in a lab environment, you will not be able to do this activity.

I   Click **Start**. Point to **All Programs**. Point to **Accessories**. Point to **System Tools**. Click **System Restore**.

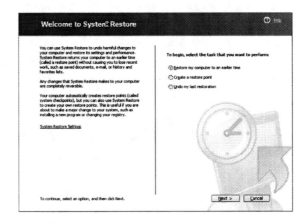

WHAT'S **HAPPENING?** The System Restore wizard window opens. You may either create a restore point or restore your computer to an earlier time.

2   Click **Create a restore point**. Click **Next**.

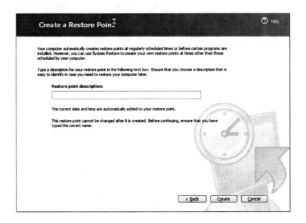

WHAT'S **HAPPENING?** Here you name your restore point. The date and time are automatically added. Make your description brief but meaningful. For instance, if you wanted to install a new program, called Wonder Program, you would want to create a restore point prior to your installation and you might call this Pre-Wonder.

3   Key in **Pre-Wonder**. Click **Create.**

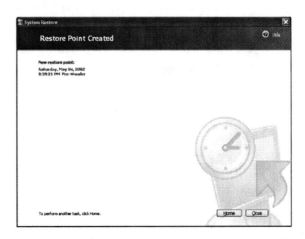

WHAT'S **HAPPENING?** The system took a few minutes to create the restore point then presented you with a confirmation window. You may either go back to the opening screen of the System Restore wizard (Home), or close the window.

4   Click **Close**.

WHAT'S **HAPPENING?** You are returned to the desktop.

5   Click **Start**. Point to **All Programs**. Point to **Accessories**. Point to **System Tools**. Click **System Restore**.

WHAT'S **HAPPENING?** You again opened the System Restore wizard. Now you are going to look at your restore points.

6   Be sure that **Restore my computer to an earlier time** is selected. Click **Next**.

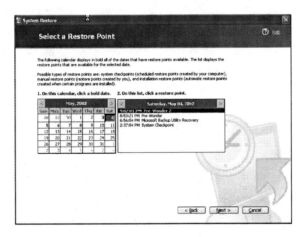

WHAT'S **HAPPENING?** You are presented with a calendar with available restore points. In this example, there are three restore points created by this user (Pre-Wonder, Pre-Wonder 2, and Microsoft Backup Utility Recovery) and a System CheckPoint created by Windows XP Professional. Your display will vary depending on what restore points have been created. Only dates that are bold have a checkpoint.

7   Click the **Show previous month** button to look at an earlier month.

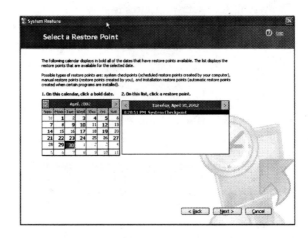

WHAT'S **HAPPENING?** In this example, there is only one restore point, one created by Windows XP Professional. However, any date that is in bold on the calendar holds a restore point. You would select the date you wanted to restore to and then click Next.

8   Click Cancel.

WHAT'S **HAPPENING?** You have returned to the desktop. System Restore is another way to protect your system.

11.18 ● Plug and Play and Device Drivers

Prior to Windows 95, adding new hardware to your system could be a nightmare. If you wanted to add a new piece of hardware such as a sound card, not only would you have to take the cover off the computer and physically add the card, but you would also need to make software changes. Each hardware component needs access to system resources such as IRQ and DMA channels. An IRQ (interrupt request line) signals the CPU to get its attention. DMA (direct memory access) devices use DMA channels to access memory directly, rather than going through the CPU. If different devices contend for the same IRQ or DMA channel, you can have a hardware conflict, which means that the hardware does not work. Furthermore, most hardware devices need software support, contained in driver files that must also be installed. They are called drivers because they "drive" the hardware. A user needs a fair amount of technical expertise to adjust these settings so that the hardware devices work.

Plug and Play is an industry standard developed by Intel and Microsoft, with help from other computer industry leaders, that automates adding new hardware to your computer. Plug and Play in Windows XP Professional is even better than in Windows 95, Windows 98, or Windows 2000 Professional. Windows XP Professional's Plug and Play makes adding new hardware to your system truly user friendly. You install the hardware. Then, when you boot the system, Windows XP Professional detects that you have added a new hardware device and makes the appropriate adjustments to your system. Hence, the name—you plug it in and it plays. Occasionally, like any new standard, Plug and Play does not work, so sometimes it is called "Plug and Pray." Windows has also added support for new types of devices, including universal serial bus (USB) devices and IEEE 1394 devices. USB devices share a common connector (port) and do not need to be configured manually. IEEE 1394 is a high-speed serial bus that is used by some devices that require fast data transfer, such as scanners or video cameras.

In order for Plug and Play to work, you must have a computer that has a Plug and Play–compatible BIOS (Basic Input Output System). The device you are going to install also needs to be Plug and Play–compatible. Windows XP Professional is Plug and Play–compatible. Full support in Windows XP Professional requires an Advanced Configuration and Power Interface (ACPI)–compliant system board and BIOS, Windows XP Professional as the operating system, the device you want to install, and the drivers for that device. Most computers manufactured after 1998 have an ACPI BIOS. Most computers manufactured between 1995 and 1998 instead use an Advanced Power Management (APM) BIOS or a Plug and Play BIOS. If you have one of these computers, the Plug and Play setting in your BIOS needs to be set to off. See your computer's documentation on how to do this. Hardware that is not Plug and Play–compatible is called *legacy hardware*. If you have an older computer or an older device, you still can get help from Windows XP Professional in resolving hardware conflicts. The Add/Remove Hardware wizard in Control Panel will attempt to assist you in solving hardware conflicts. You may also use Device Manager to add updated drivers or help you identify problems as well as roll back a driver that does not work correctly.

11.19 ● Activity ● Looking at Plug and Play

1 Click **Start**. Right-click **My Computer**. Click **Properties**.

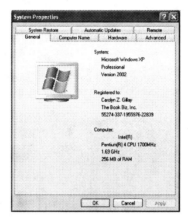

WHAT'S **HAPPENING?** You are looking at the system properties for your computer.

2 Click the **Hardware** tab. Click the **Device Manager** command button. Expand the Computer entry.

WHAT'S **HAPPENING?** This computer has ACPI.

3 Collapse the Computer entry. Scroll to the bottom until you see **System devices**. Double-click **System devices**.

WHAT'S HAPPENING? You see that on this system, one of the entries is Plug and Play Software Device Enumerator. This computer is compatible with Plug and Play. You may see an ISA Plug and Play BIOS or an ISA Plug and Play bus on older systems.

4   Right-click **Plug and Play Software Device Enumerator**. Click **Properties**.

WHAT'S HAPPENING? This device is working properly. If it were not working properly, you could click the Troubleshoot command button to open Windows' Help program's Troubleshooter feature. Not all devices will have a Driver tab, because devices may or may not have drivers. This is another place you can search to solve problems.

5   Click the **Driver** tab, if available.

WHAT'S HAPPENING? Here is the piece of software that drives this device. Here you may look at the details of the driver (Driver Details), update the driver (Update Driver), and, if the driver you installed did not work, roll it back to the previous driver version (Roll Back Driver). You may also, if it is available, uninstall the current driver (Uninstall). In this example, because this is a Windows system function, uninstalling is not an option. You can look at each device on your system and review its properties and attributes as well as update it or roll it back.

6   Click **Driver Details**.

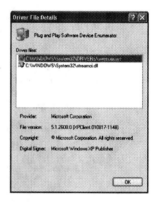

WHAT'S HAPPENING? This feature tells you what driver file is being used and where it is located.

7   Click **OK**. Click **Cancel**. Click the minus sign (–) next to **System devices**.

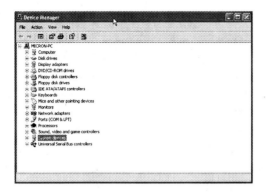

WHAT'S **HAPPENING?** You have returned to Device Manager. This window tells you if devices are working properly. If there is a ? next to a device's icon, it means that you have a problem and the device has been disabled. If you have an exclamation point with a circle around it, it means that the device has a problem. The type of problem will be displayed in the Properties dialog box for the device.

8 Click **Sound, video and game adapters** to select it. Click the plus sign (+) next to it to expand it.

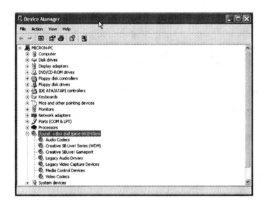

WHAT'S **HAPPENING?** You see what sound card you have. In this case, a Creative Labs Sound Blaster Live is the sound card installed (your sound card may be different).

9 Right-click your sound card to select it. Click **Properties**.

WHAT'S **HAPPENING?** You see further details about this sound card. In Device status, you are informed that the device is working properly. If it were not or if you had an updated driver, you could install it.

10 Click the **Driver** tab.

WHAT'S **HAPPENING?** By clicking the Update Driver button, you could install a new driver. If you clicked the Roll Back Driver, you could return to a previous version of the driver. In this example, you could uninstall the driver altogether.

11 Click **Cancel**. Collapse the entry. Close all open windows.

WHAT'S **HAPPENING?** You have returned to the desktop.

11.20 ◈ The Paging File

One of the items that has the most impact on the performance of your computer system, other than the processor itself, is the amount of physical memory you have installed. To improve performance, Windows XP Professional uses space on the hard drive as virtual memory. When you run out of physical memory, Windows writes data from physical memory to a hidden file on your disk. When it needs that information again, it reads it back from what used to be called the *swap file* and is now called the ***paging file***. The name *swap file* came from the fact that Windows "swaps" information to and from the hard disk when needed. This process is called ***demand paging***. This file is dynamic—it can shrink and grow as needed. Perhaps you are writing a book and have an 80-page chapter with color pictures. Such a document can be 20 to 24 MB in size. Even a computer with 128 MB of RAM does not have enough memory available—with the drivers, the running program, and other overhead—to keep a document of that size in memory. So, while you are looking at pages 7 and 8, pages 60 through 80 may be written out to the swap file to free up needed RAM. The swap does slow down performance, but it gives the user more "room" in which to operate.

However, paging does impede performance; any activity is slower when it uses a disk rather than memory. It is possible to set the place and size of the paging file yourself, but it is strongly recommended by Microsoft that you let Windows manage the paging file. There are, however, some instances when it may be advisable to specify where you want the swap file to be. Perhaps you have a second hard drive that is free of executable programs. There would be little I/O (input/output) to this drive. You may want to place your paging file on that drive, freeing up the read/write heads on your main drive. Also, if you elect to modify the placement of your swap file, be sure you place it on your fastest hard drive (the drive with the fastest access time). You may also have a large hard drive that has little information on it. In that case, you may wish to place the swap file on that drive and increase the paging file size.

11.21 ◈ Activity ◈ Looking at Setting Up Your Paging File

Note: This activity is specific to the machines used for the demonstration.

1   Click **Start**. Right-click **My Computer**. Click **Properties**. Click the **Advanced** tab.

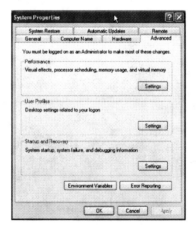

WHAT'S HAPPENING? You are looking at the property sheet that deals with Performance, User Profiles, and Startup and Recover.

2   Click the **Settings** command button in **Performance Options**. Click the **Advanced** tab.

WHAT'S HAPPENING? The Virtual memory area tells you the current total paging size for all drives. You can change this.

3   Click the **Change** command button.

WHAT'S HAPPENING? You can set the paging file size.

4   Click the question mark in the title bar, then click the **Initial size (MB)** text box.

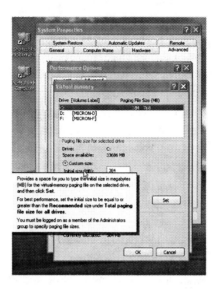

WHAT'S HAPPENING? As you can see, it is recommended that for best performance you follow Windows's suggestion and set the initial size to be equal or greater than the recommended size. You must also be an administrator to make any changes.

5   Click **Cancel**. Click **Cancel**. Click **Cancel**.

WHAT'S HAPPENING? You have, in this instance, let Windows manage the paging file.

11.22 ◦ Administrative Tools and System Information

System Information is an exceedingly useful tool. It has the ability to collect and display system configuration information for your local computer as well as remote computers. The information includes hardware configuration, computer components, and software, including driver information. You can view this information as well as access different tools by using this program. In addition, if you need technical support, the support technicians require specific information about your computer. You can use System Information to quickly find the information that these technicians need to resolve a system problem. System Information saves data files in files that have an .nfo extension.

Microsoft Management Console (MMC) is a tool used to create, save, and open collections of administrative tools, called consoles. Consoles contain items such as snap-ins, extension snap-ins, monitor controls, tasks, wizards, and documentation required to manage many of the hardware, software, and networking components of your Windows XP Professional system. MMC is a framework that hosts administrative tools. You can add items to an existing MMC console, or you can create new consoles and configure them to administer a specific system component. A full exploration of MMC is beyond the scope of this textbook. But if you look at the Administrative Tools folder found in Control Panel, you will see shortcuts to tools that you frequently use. Many of these tools require that the user have administrator privileges. Figure 11.5 displays the available tools in Control Panel. You may also add Administrative Tools to your Start menu using the Taskbar and Start Menu Properties sheet.

Figure 11.5 ◦ Administrative Tools

- Component Services allows administrators and developers to create, configure, and maintain COM (Component Object Model) applications. This is a programming tool and will rarely be used by the average user.
- Computer Management is for managing disks as well as local or remote computers. It also gives you information about your computer system.
- Data Sources (ODBC) allows you to access data from a variety of database management systems. It is a programming and administrative tool that is rarely used by the average user.
- Event Viewer allows the user to gather information about hardware, software, and system problems, as well as monitor security events.
- Local Security Policy allows a security administrator to configure security levels for local computer policies.

❉ Performance contains features for logging counter and event data and for generating performance alerts. Counter logs allow you to record data about such items as hardware usage as well as provide alerts. Thus, you can set an alert on a counter defining that a message be sent when a counter's value equals, exceeds, or falls below some specified setting.

❉ Services allows you to start, stop, pause, or resume services on remote and local computers and configure startup and recovery options. Services include such tasks as running scheduled tasks or starting a network connection.

11.23 ❉ Using System Information and Computer Management

I   Click **Start**. Point to **All Programs**. Point to **Accessories**. Point to **System Tools**. Click **System Information**.

WHAT'S **HAPPENING?** ❯ You are looking at the all the information about your computer system, such as your BIOS version and how much memory you have.

2   Expand **Hardware Resources**. Click **IRQs**.

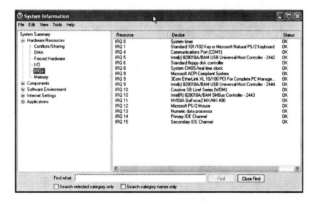

WHAT'S **HAPPENING?** ❯ Here you see what devices are claiming which IRQs.

3   Click **Tools**.

WHAT'S **HAPPENING?** Here are tools you may use. You have used System Restore. The Net Diagnostics will run different tests to check your network connections. The File Signature Verification Utility will help maintain the integrity of your system as critical files have been digitally signed. This utility can see if there have been any changes. DirectX enhances the multimedia capabilities of your computer and provides access to your display and audio cards, which allow programs to provide three-dimensional graphics and various music and audio effects. The DirectX Diagnostic tool will diagnose any problems. Dr Watson detects information about system and program failures and records the information in a log file which can be used by technical support professionals.

4   Collapse hardware resource. Close the System Information window.

5   Click **Start**. Click **Control Panel**. Double-click **Administrative Tools**. Double-click **Computer Management**.

6   Expand **Storage**, if it is not expanded. Click **Disk Management**.

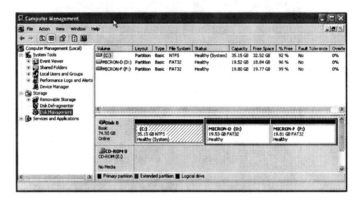

WHAT'S **HAPPENING?** Disk Management is a graphical tool for managing your disks. It provides support for partitions and logical drives. It allows the user to perform online administrative tasks without shutting down the system or interrupting other users. It also provides shortcut menus to show you which tasks you can perform on a selected object. Wizards then guide you through tasks such as creating partitions and volumes and upgrading disks. You must be an administrator to use these tools.

7   Close **Computer Management**. Close Control Panel.

WHAT'S **HAPPENING?** You have returned to the desktop.

Chapter Summary

In this chapter, you learned that errors can happen to disks and also to files. These errors include cross-linked files and lost clusters. Check Disk checks disks for logical errors in the file system and for problems that involve the physical drive. You learned that you can fill up your disk quickly with temporary files that do not get deleted and with cached files. Disk Cleanup helps you keep your disk optimized by removing these unnecessary files.

You also learned that contiguous files are those that have been written to the disk in adjacent clusters. Noncontiguous files have been written in nonadjacent clusters and thereby create a fragmented disk. Fragmentation slows your access to the disk. Disk Defragmenter repairs fragmented files.

Windows XP Professional makes it easy to maintain your disk by letting you run Check Disk, Disk Cleanup, and Disk Defragmenter on a regularly scheduled basis by using Scheduled Task Wizard to schedule the tasks. You are not limited to scheduling only those tasks. Windows XP Professional also provides a tool called Task Scheduler that allows you to schedule any program to run at any time.

Another important aspect of any computer user's routine should be the regular backing up of data. You can easily accomplish this in Windows XP Professional with the Backup program. This program allows you to complete either full or incremental backups. You can back up the whole system or just selected files. You should also create an Automated System Recovery (ASR) disk in case your system fails. In addition, System Restore will restore your system to a working state. Restore points are created automatically, but you can create your own restore points as well.

Virtual memory is space on a hard drive used to simulate an environment in which more memory is available than actually exists on the system board. Additional memory is simulated by means of a virtual paging file on the hard disk. It is advisable to let Windows manage your virtual memory paging file if you have one hard drive in your system. If you have a second, faster hard drive in your system, you may consider taking over the management of the virtual memory paging file and moving it to the faster drive.

Windows XP Professional supports Plug and Play. Plug and Play means that when you install new hardware, Windows XP Professional automatically detects it so you do not have to install any new devices manually. You may review your device settings and update drivers as well as roll back drivers in Device Manager.

System Information allows you to gather information about your system as well as run various diagnostic tools. Microsoft Management Console (MMC) is a tool used to create, save, and open collections of administrative tools, called consoles. The Administrative Tools folder found in Control Panel contains shortcuts to tools that you frequently use. Many of these tools require that the user has administrator privileges. One very useful tool is Computer Management, which lets you explore and manage your computer system.

Key Terms

archive data	disk optimization program	normal backup
backup	fragmented disk	paging file
cache	fragmented file	registration database
chain	full backup	restore point
configuration information	head crash	surge protector
cross-linked files	incremental backup	surge suppressor
defragger	initialization file	swap file
demand paging	legacy hardware	virus
differential backup	lost cluster	

Discussion Questions

1. What are three occurrences that can cause a loss of data on a hard drive?
2. What is the purpose and function of the Check Disk program that comes with Windows XP Professional?
3. What is a cache?
4. What is the purpose of Disk Cleanup? What benefits do you gain from running this program?

5. Compare and contrast contiguous and noncontiguous files.
6. How does the Disk Defragmenter utility help optimize disk performance?
7. List and explain two factors that should be considered before defragmenting your disk.
8. List and explain two ways that the Task Scheduler wizard could be used.
9. Why is it important to back up data? Programs?
10. Compare and contrast full (normal) and incremental backups.
11. What is the difference between using a differential backup or using the daily option for incremental backups?
12. Why is it wise to have more than one copy of your backup?
13. List and explain two ways that the Backup program can be used.
14. Explain how you can restore files.
15. The Automated System Recovery (ASR) is not a substitute for backing up data. Explain.
16. What is the purpose and function of the Automated System Recovery (ASR)?
17. Compare and contrast system and private initialization files found in previous versions of Windows.
18. What is the purpose and function of the Registry?
19. What is the purpose and function of System Restore?
20. What is a restore point?
21. If you use System Restore, is it still necessary to back up your data files? Why or why not?
22. What is a paging file? Explain some of the advantages and disadvantages of paging.
23. Why would you want to roll back a driver? Where would you accomplish this task?
24. What is system information? Identify two kinds of information you could locate in this tool.
25. What is the Microsoft Management Console (MMC)?

True/False Questions

For each question, circle the letter T if the statement is true or the letter F if the statement is false.

T   F   1. Check Disk cannot find or fix errors on CD-ROMs or network drives.

T   F   2. If you use System Restore, you no longer have to back up your data files.

T   F   3. You may choose to back up only your documents and settings or everyone's documents and settings when you use Backup.

T   F   4. A defragmenting program such as Disk Defragmenter compresses data.

T   F   5. Device manager is a tool that allows you to see if your devices are working properly.

Completion Questions

Write the correct answer in each blank space provided.

6. The tool that allows you to identify your BIOS version is _____.

7. If you are having problems with your system and it is in an unstable state, you may roll it back to a previous working version of your system by using _____.

8. The program included with Windows XP Professional that will eliminate cached Internet files and temporary files is _____.

9. The Registry files are kept in the _____ directory.

10. A backup that only backs up files that have changed since the last full backup and turns off the archive bit is called a(n) _____ backup.

Multiple Choice Questions

Circle the letter of the correct answer for each question.

11. The System Information window contains tools that allow you to
    a. change system information.
    b. view system information.
    c. change your monitor settings.
    d. view your monitor settings.

12. Before running the Disk Defragmenter program, be sure you have
    a. plenty of time.
    b. a backup of important files.
    c. a floppy in the drive.
    d. both a and b

13. If you wanted to update a driver for your video card, you would use the _____ tool.
    a. My Computer
    b. Performance
    c. Device Manager
    d. all of the above

14. If you wanted to know about your hard disk file systems, you would open Computer Management. Under Storage, you would select
    a. Removable Storage.
    b. Hardware Resources.
    c. Device Manager.
    d. Disk Management.

15. Which of the following statements is true?
    a. Using Backup will automatically back up the Registry.
    b. The Registry has been replaced by the .ini file.
    c. The Registry is used for configuration information about your computer system.
    d. none of the above

Application Assignments

Problem Set I—Brief Essay

For all essay questions, use Notepad or WordPad for your answer. Be sure to include your name, your class information, and which problem you are answering. Print your answer.

1. The following files can be deleted in Disk Cleanup. Briefly describe the purpose of deleting each group of files. Determine and explain which options you think are best when using Disk Cleanup.
    * downloaded program files
    * temporary Internet files
    * offline Web pages
    * Recycle Bin
    * temporary files
    * temporary Offline Files
    * Offline Files
    * catalog files for the Content Indexer

2. You are the owner of a small business. You keep your business records on a computer. Develop a plan to schedule Check Disk and Disk Defragmenter on your computer. Describe what tools you will use. Explain the reasons for your choices.

3. Define and explain the use of a paging file. When and why would you want to alter the settings?

4. *Windows XP Professional includes System Restore. This tool is a critical feature for all users.* Describe the purpose and function of System Restore. Then agree or disagree with the statement and provide the rationale for your answer.

5. *It is critical to create an ASR. It is used when* _____. Complete the fill-in portion of the question. Agree or disagree with the first statement. Give your reasons for what you filled in to complete the second statement.

Problem Set II—Scenario

You are the owner of a small business. You have an accounting program installed on the computer. The accounting program is kept in a directory called Quicken. You keep your accounting data files in a directory called Accounting. You are using a word-processing program called Word. The program files are kept in a folder called Winword. You have business letters created in Word that are kept in a folder called Letters. You also use Word to create invoices and you keep those data files in a directory called Invoices.

Develop a backup plan for your computer system. Include which files and directories you will back up and how often.

CHAPTER 12

Connectivity

In the computer world, connectivity is a reality. Connectivity can mean connecting to other computers in your home or office. It can mean sharing resources such as printers or files on your computer or accessing those resources from another computer. It can also mean connecting to resources throughout the world using the Internet. Networks provide these connections. Windows XP Professional is designed for networking; it allows you to network with others to collect information, exchange files, and share resources.

This chapter introduces the basic concepts of networking. It explains some of the terminology used in the networking world, such as client, server, peer-to-peer network, LAN, WAN, and more. If you have the appropriate hardware, it will show you how use your peer-to-peer network and then how to share resources on your network.

Networking also encompasses the Internet. You will be introduced to the basic protocols of the Internet. If you have the appropriate setup, you will learn how to connect to and navigate the Internet. You will learn how Windows XP Professional lets you automatically update any new features or fixes to Windows XP Professional. You will also learn how to customize Internet Explorer to meet your needs.

Learning Objectives

1. Explain the following terms: client, server, resources, LAN network, and WAN network.
2. Compare and contrast server-based networks and peer-to-peer networks.
3. List and explain two reasons for setting up a network.
4. Compare and contrast setting up a peer-to-peer network using bus topology and using star topology with a hub or router.
5. Explain the purposes of sharing a printer, a folder on a hard drive, and an entire hard drive.
6. Explain the purpose of file and folder permissions on an NTFS drive.
7. Explain the purpose and function of a mapped drive.
8. Explain the purpose and function of the Internet.
9. Compare and contrast the Internet and the World Wide Web.
10. Explain the following terms: Web page, home page, hyperlinks, and search engines.
11. Explain the role that TCP/IP plays in computer communication.
12. Explain how Internet Explorer can be used to move about the Web.
13. Explain how to customize Internet Explorer.

Student Outcomes

1. Use a network connection.
2. Identify a computer and its workgroup on a network.
3. Share a printer, a folder on a hard drive, and an entire hard drive.
4. Use file and folder permissions, if possible.
5. Map a drive on a network.
6. Use Internet Explorer to navigate a local area network and the World Wide Web.
7. Examine ways to customize Internet Explorer.

12.1 • Networks (LANs and WANs)

Today it is more and more common for a small business or even a home to have more than one computer. In this world of so many computers, you will probably want to connect computers together. When you connect computers together, you create what is called a *LAN (local area network)*. In networks, there are servers and clients. A *server* is a computer that provides shared resources to network users. A *client* is a computer that accesses the shared network resources provided by the server. *Resources* refers to the elements that are shared, such as a disk drive, a printer, a file, or a folder. A *server-based network* is one in which security and other network functions are provided by a *dedicated server*. A dedicated server's sole function is to provide network resources.

Server-based networks have become the standard model for networks serving more than 10 users. The key here is 10 or more users. There are many environments that have fewer than 10 users, but would still benefit from a network. Thus, there is an alternative to a server-based network. It is called a *peer-to-peer network*, or a *workgroup*. A peer-to-peer network has neither a dedicated server nor a hierarchy among the computers. All the computers are equal and therefore peers. Each computer can function as either a client or a server.

There are many advantages to setting up a network. If you have only one printer, CD-ROM drive, or Zip drive, every computer in the LAN can use that hardware. You may share an Internet connection among the computers on your network. If you and others are working on the same document, you can access the document without having to copy it to your own computer. If you have several people working on a customer list, for instance, and you can keep that information on one computer, all users can access that information and know that they are working with the most current information. You can set up local email so that you can send messages to any user on the network. If you have notebook computers (portables), you can attach or detach them from the network and update information as you need. If you are away from the office, you can dial in to your network and access the resources you need.

You may also hear the term *WAN (wide area network)*. A WAN consists of computers that use long-range telecommunication links such as modems or satellites to connect over long distances. The *Internet* is a WAN. It is a worldwide network of networks that connects millions of computers.

In order to have any kind of network, including a peer-to-peer network, you must have a *network interface card*, referred to as an *NIC*, installed into a slot in each computer so that a LAN cable connecting all the computers can be installed. One of the most common network cards is an Ethernet card. The card must fit the bus architecture slot you have available. Older desktop computers typically had an ISA (industry standard architecture). Today, most newer desktop computers have a PCI (peripheral component interconnect) slot and may not have an ISA slot at all. If you have a notebook computer, it most likely has a PCMCIA (Personal Computer Memory Card International Association) slot. You may also get an external adapter that you connect with a USB (Universal Serial Port) cable. The card must support the type of cable you will be using to connect the computers, if you choose a cabled network. If you choose a wireless network, there are no wires dedicated to carrying the network signals. Instead, each computer has a wireless network card, which allow the computers to communicate by radio waves, infrared, power wires in your walls, or even by the phone wires in your home. Furthermore, you must consider what design is the most appropriate for your network. A network design is called a *topology*. The two most common topologies for a peer-to-peer network are the *bus topology* and the *star topology*.

The bus topology uses a single coaxial cable and is commonly called Thin Ethernet, 10BASE-2, or Thinnet. If you use this method, you also need *T-connectors* and *terminator plugs*. All the computers connect to a single cable, which is why this topology is called a bus. A T-connector has one end plugged into a network interface card and two open ends (like a T) for connecting the cables that go to other computers. Once the cables are connected to the computers using the T-connectors, each end of the cable uses a terminator plug to complete the networking. Every cable end must be plugged into the network or have a terminator to complete the connection. There can be no end that is unattached. See Figure 12.1.

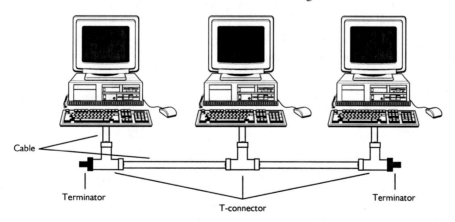

*Figure 12.1 * A Peer-to-Peer Network with a Bus Topology*

The advantages to using a bus topology are that it is easy to install and relatively inexpensive. It is also easy to expand a bus network by adding another length of cable between the terminators. A disadvantage is that if you have three or more components on the bus and one segment of the cable fails, the entire network will fail.

However, bus topology is becoming less and less common. Today, the most popular way to create a peer-to-peer network is to use a hub. This method is considered a star topology. Wireless connections are of the star type. Each connection is like a spoke of a bicycle wheel: one end connects to the hub and the other end connects to a computer or a device such as a printer. There are also two major Ethernet speeds. The original Ethernet has a speed of 10 Mbps (megabits per second). Fast Ethernet, most popular today, has a speed of 100 Mbps. See Figure 12.2.

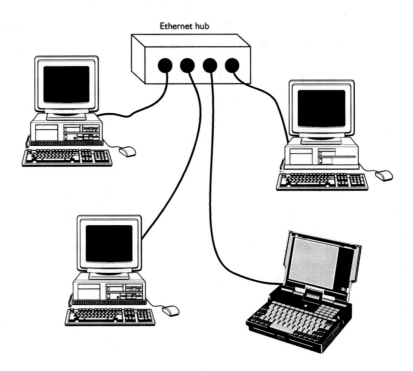

Figure 12.2 ◦ A Peer-to-Peer Network with a Star Topology

With a star topology, a single piece of defective cabling affects only the computer it connects, unless it is the hub itself. This kind of problem is known as a ***single point of failure***. Each computer would still work, but there would be no network connection to the computer on the segment of cable that failed. The disadvantages to a star topology include the following: It is more expensive than a bus topology because you must purchase additional hardware, the hub. Expansion of the network may require the purchase of an additional hub if you have used all the connections on the existing hub. Also, the wiring can become unwieldy, especially if you cannot run cable through your walls. However, if you go with a wireless network, then you obviously do not need to run wire. There is a wireless Ethernet standard called 802.11b which is becoming increasingly available and relatively inexpensive. See Figure 12.3.

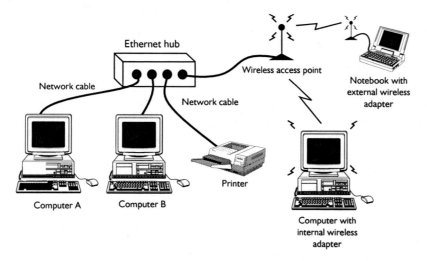

Figure 12.3 · A Wireless and Wired Network

With these topologies you can use a networkable printer, or any resource, by connecting it directly to a cable or to a hub. Only the computer that needs to use the printer must be on; no other computers on the network must be turned on. The printer must have a network interface card installed. Most laser printers can have an NIC added, but the common, inexpensive inkjet printers cannot. In that case, the printer must be connected to one of the computers on the network, and that computer must be turned on for the printer to be used by any station. Today, most users prefer a hub, which is basically a box with many connections. You will want at least as many ports as you have computers and devices that you want to connect, and you will probably want extra ports in case you add more devices or computers at a later date. Hubs are widely available with 4, 8, 16, or 24 ports. Instead of a hub, you can install a switch which distributes information faster than a hub. And you may even prefer a router, which combines a hub and a small computer that provides Internet sharing. If you use portable hard disks and video cameras, there is another standard to look at—IEEE-1394, also called FireWire.

In a server-based network you must also have software that tells the computers how to communicate with one another. The software is known as a *network operating system (NOS)*. The two most popular network operating systems are Novell NetWare and Microsoft Windows NT. Windows NT, however, is being replaced by Windows 2000 Server or Windows 2000 Advanced Server which is being replaced by Windows .NET Server. An alternative NOS is Linux, a version of an older network operating system, Unix. The server (the computer that serves the other computers on the network) uses this software. In a generic sense, a network operating system is the software you need to make your networked hardware communicate.

You have been introduced to hardware and software. There is a trilogy in networking. The third component is the *network administrator*, sometimes called the system administrator. The administrator is the person who decides how the hardware and software will be used and who will have access to what devices and resources on the network. The administrator also manages the day-to-day operation of the hardware, the network operating system, and the resources of the network.

A server-based network is beyond the scope of this textbook. However, a peer-to-peer network is not. Any computer that is running Windows has the built-in peer-to-peer software to create and administer a small network. A small network still needs the appropriate hardware, software, and administration. In a peer-to-peer network, either each computer can be administered by its user, or there can be a single administrator. The selection of the topology, network interface card, and cable or wireless model is beyond the scope of this textbook. This textbook makes the assumption that these hardware decisions have been made. Many new computers come with a built-in network card. In this chapter you will use a peer-to-peer LAN or a workgroup with the built-in networking software that comes with Windows.

12.2 ● Looking at Your Network

When Windows XP Professional is installed, it will detect your network card and install the default components. If you add your network later, you may use the New Connection wizard or the Network Setup wizard that allows you to set up your home network. You will have to name your computer. All computers must have a unique name even if they are not on a network. The setup program will provide a cryptic name for your computer. You may override this. Often, a good computer name is the name of the brand of the computer. If you had two computers with the same brand name, you could differentiate between them numerically, such as DellXPS-1 and DellXPS-2. You will also have to enter an administrator password. The administrator password is the most important password in Windows, so be sure to use a secure password as well as write it down and store it in a safe place. This password is what allows you to administer your computer. If you have more than one user on a computer, you will want each user to have a logon name. User names are commonly in the form of first initial and last name, such as Cgillay or Bpeat, or last name and first initial, such as GillayC or PeatB. If you like, you can use your entire name, such as Carolyn Z. Gillay or Bette Peat. Each logon name will have to also have a password. Passwords are case sensitive. Your password should be difficult to guess, but not so difficult that you will forget it. For this reason, you should avoid obvious passwords such as your user name, name, children's names, address, or social security number. Too often a user creates a password and then leaves it on a note taped to the computer—obviously defeating the purpose of any security.

My Network Places is your map to your network. The activities that follow are based on a specific computer configurations. These activities are meant to act as a guide to accomplishing these tasks on your system. You will have to interpret the screen examples to match your specific computer network. The steps given in the activities are related to a specific computer setup. You will not have the same setup. Thus, you will not be able to follow the steps exactly. You may have more or fewer computers or printers. Your drives may be formatted as FAT32 or as NTFS, and so on. This is meant as a guide to how a peer-to-peer network works. You may choose to only read through the steps, particularly when you do not have an equivalent computer setup. You should read through these activities, even if you cannot or choose not to follow them. This way you can see how to manipulate a network. In addition, most schools or work environments do not have the hardware, software, or support staff to allow you to do these tasks in a lab environment. In addition, most lab environments are on a server-based network and not a peer-to-peer network. If this is the case, only read the activities, do not do them. *Again, do not attempt to do these activities in a lab environment*.

12.3 ● Activity ● Looking at Your Network

Note 1: It is assumed that you have successfully installed the necessary software and hardware.
Note 2: The activity is based on a specific computer configuration. This configuration is a simple star topology that uses a hub with three computers and two printers. The three printers are part of the BOOKBIZ workgroup. The computers are identified by name. The first is identified as Micron-czg and is running Window XP Professional. The second is identified as Dell-czg and is

running Windows 2000 Professional. The third is identified as Dell 8100 (Dell-fp) and is running Windows Me. One printer is a simple inkjet printer (HP Deskjet 895 Cse) that cannot support a network card and is thus physically attached to a Dell 8100 (Dell-fp). The other printer (HP Laser Jet 4 Plus) does have a network card and is attached to the hub as well as being physically attached to the Micron-czg computer. Your network will be different and thus your display will be different.

I   Click **Start**. Right-click **My Network Places**. Click **Properties**. Right-click **Local Area Connection**. Click **Properties**.

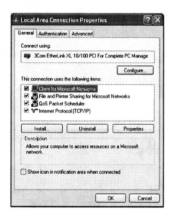

WHAT'S **HAPPENING?** > The Local Area Connection Properties sheet appears. This computer system is on a peer-to-peer network. When you are on a peer-to-peer network, you have three tabs: General, Authentication, and Advanced. The "Connect using" area shows which type of network card you have. In this example, it is a 3Com Etherlink XL 10/100 PCI. The list box cites what items the network card will use. The first item, Client for Microsoft Networks, allows you to access resources on a Microsoft Network. Its icon is a computer, █, indicating that it is your computer. The next item, File and Printer Sharing for Microsoft Network, allows other computers to access resources on your computer. The next item, QoS (Quality of Service) Packet Scheduler, provides network

traffic control. Each of the icons for these items is also a computer but with a hand underneath it, indicating that is it dealing with sharing resources, █. The last item is what protocol is being used. Its icon is representative of a protocal, █. You may also choose to display an icon in the notification area on the taskbar when you are connected to the network.

2   Select **Client for Microsoft Networks**. Click **Install**.

WHAT'S **HAPPENING?** > There are three types of network components you can install: Client, Service, and Protocol. A client allows you to access services on other computers on the network. This simply means that when you request access to another computer, you are considered a client that needs service from another computer. A *service* is work that is provided by a server. When you provide access to your devices or files, you are performing a service to others (clients) on the network. The *protocol* is a set of rules that allows computers to connect with one another and to exchange information. Computers on a network must use the same protocol in order to communicate.

3   Click **Cancel**. Click the **Authentication** tab.

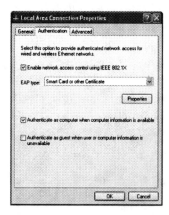

WHAT'S HAPPENING? This is the process for verifying that an entity or object is who or what it claims to be. For instance, you would want to verify the identity of a user who has access to your computer.

4   Click the **Advanced** tab.

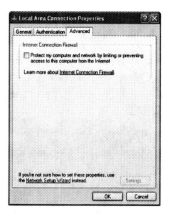

WHAT'S HAPPENING? Here you may choose to use the firewall. A *firewall* is a set of programs, located at a network gateway server, that protects the resources of a private network from users from other networks. A *gateway* is a network point that acts as an entrance to another network. Here Microsoft provides an Internet Connection Firewall (ICF), which is a specific firewall software that is used to set restrictions on what information is communicated from your home or small office network to and from the Internet. If you are using Internet Connection Sharing (ICS) to provide Internet access to multiple computers, you should enable this feature. If you are a single computer connected to the

Internet, this also protects your Internet connection. However, you may have a switch or a router that provides a firewall as well.

5   Click **Cancel**. Close the Network Connection window.

6   Click **Start**. Click **Control Panel**. Double-click **System**. Click the **Computer Name** tab.

Note: It is assumed that Control Panel is in Classic view.

WHAT'S HAPPENING? Here you see the name of your computer and the workgroup you belong to. If you clicked Network ID, Windows would bring up a wizard to help you make a network connection.

7   Click **Change**.

WHAT'S HAPPENING? Here is where you could make changes if you desired. The computer name can be any name you wish, but each computer on the network needs to have a unique name. The name can be

longer than 15 characters, but it is best to remain under 15 characters with no spaces. This is because on other network protocols names are limited to 15 characters. Again, for the name of your computer you could use the brand of the computer. But be sure to choose a name that will clearly identify which computer is which on the network. Here, this computer is identified by its brand name—micron-pc.

All computers on your network *must* use the same workgroup name. But a workgroup name cannot be the same name as the computer. The workgroup name must be identical in case and spelling on all computers. Again, you can have up to 15 characters with no spaces. Only computers with the same workgroup name can share resources.

You would need to take these same steps on every computer on your network. If the other computers were running other versions of Windows such as Windows 98 or Windows 2000 Professional, the steps would be similar but in slightly different locations. However, all of these Windows operating systems will talk XP.

8 Click **Cancel.** Click **Cancel.** Close the Control Panel window.

9 Be sure that all your computers are on. Sit at one computer, in this case the Micron-pc. Click **Start.** Click **My Network Places.** Click **View workgroup computers.** Click **View.** Click **Tiles.**

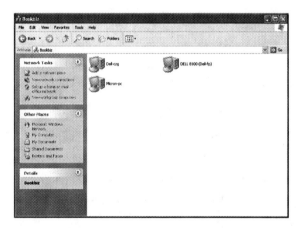

WHAT'S **HAPPENING?** You see the names for every computer on your network. You changed the view to Tiles. Be a little patient. It takes some time for the computers to see each other. Each is broadcasting its availability. (*Note:* If you do not see My Network Places or if My Network Places is empty, chances are you have a problem with your network installation, either with the hardware or with the protocols and services. Network troubleshooting is beyond the scope of this textbook. However, a simple mistake that users often make when setting up a network is that they have different workgroup names on each computer. If you are using Windows XP Professional, follow steps 6 and 7 above to make the workgroup the same name. If you are using Windows 2000 Professional or Windows Me, you can also correct this but you need to open the System icon in Control Panel, choose Networking Identification, and then choose Properties to ensure that the workgroup name is the same.)

10 (*Note:* Remember that this activity refers to a specific computer configuration. Your computer network will *not* look exactly like this example.) Double-click the **Dell 8100 (Dell-fp)** computer.

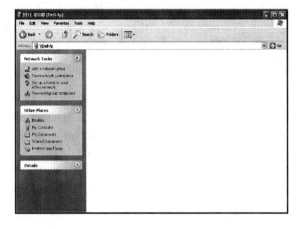

WHAT'S HAPPENING? Windows XP Professional uses a window like Internet Explorer's. Internet Explorer is a *browser* (a tool to search the Internet). However, the Dell 8100 (Dell-fp) window is empty because you have not shared any of the resources.

Note the address in the window. The Dell computer is listed as \\Dell-fp. The double backslash is the *UNC (universal naming convention)* for locating the path to a network resource. It specifies the share name of a particular computer. The computer name is limited to 15 characters, and the share name is usually limited to 15 characters. The address takes the format of *computer name\share name[\optional path]*. (Brackets are used to indicate items that are optional. They are not actually included in the name.)

11   Close all open windows.

12.4 ● Sharing Printers on a Network

There are always two parts to sharing resources—the client and the server. The server is the computer that has the resource you wish to share. The client is the computer that wishes to access the resource. The most common items to share are a printer, some other device such as a Zip drive, a folder on a hard drive, or an entire hard drive.

When you share a printer, any computer on the network can use that printer. If you do not have a hub, the printer, of course, needs to be connected physically to a computer on the network. That computer then becomes the *print server*. Often, in a large network, there will be one computer dedicated to handling printing, and it will be called the print server. In a small network, the print server is not dedicated only to printing. It can be any computer on the network that has the printer connected to it or a computer that is on the hub. Furthermore, if you have more than one printer, each can be shared. Look at Figure 12.4.

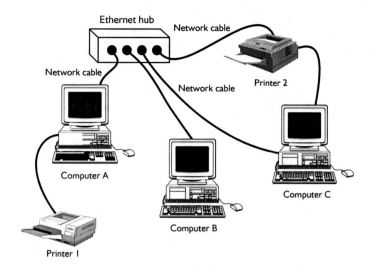

Figure 12.4 ∘ Printer Sharing on a Network

Computers A, B, and C and Printer 2 are networked with a simple hub. Computer A has Printer 1 attached to it and Computer C has Printer 2 physically attached to it. If you are sitting at Computer B and want to print, you are the client who wants to use the resource (Printer 1) of Computer A. Computer A, in this case, is the print server because Printer 1 is attached to Computer A. However, Computer A must be on in order for you to use this resource. Printer 1 is not available to you from the hub. Printer 2 is attached to the hub and is a network resource. Any computer on this network can use printer 2 at any time. Only the computer you are sitting at must be on since Printer 2 is always available as a network resource. Printer 2 must have a network card to be attached to the hub; there is special software that will set up this type of network printer connection. If you were sitting at Computer B and Computer A were not turned on, you would not be able to use the printer attached to Computer A. You also have the choice of using a printer *locally*. If you were sitting at Computer A, you could use Printer 1 locally. Locally means without using a network. You could use Printer 1 because it is physically attached to the computer. You would not need to be on the network. In this example, Printer 2 also has a local connection to Computer C. Normally, one connection is all that you would need and you would normally use the network connection. It would be unnecessary to physically attach Printer 2 to Computer C. However, if the network printer software ever failed, by having a local connection, all other computers could still use Printer 2, provided Computer C was turned on and Printer 2 was shared.

12.5 ∘ Activity ∘ Sharing Printers on a Network

Note: The following activity is based on a specific computer configuration. Your display will be different or you may not be able to do the steps if you have no network printer. If you cannot do the steps, simply read them so you can learn how to use a network printer.

1   Go to the computer that has the printer physically attached to it (the print server). In this example, it is the Dell 8100 (Dell-fp) computer. In this example, the Dell 8100 (Dell-fp) computer is running Windows Me. You can run different operating system on the different computers on your network.

2   Open My Computer. Open Control Panel. Open the Printers folder. Right-click the printer you wish to share. In this example, it is the **HP Deskjet 895Cse**.

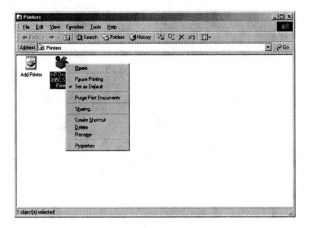

WHAT'S HAPPENING? In order for others to use this printer, you need to share it. The context menu has a choice Sharing.

3   Click **Sharing**. Click the **Shared As** button.

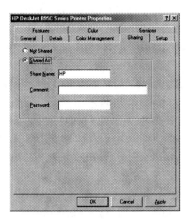

WHAT'S HAPPENING? Here you give a name to your shared printer. You again must use the same name across the network and you want the name to be descriptive.

4   In this example, key in **HPCOLOR**.

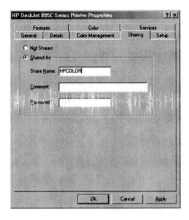

WHAT'S HAPPENING? You have named your shared printer. If you wanted, you could include a password. However, if you did that, any user who wanted to use this printer would need to know the password.

5 Click **OK**.

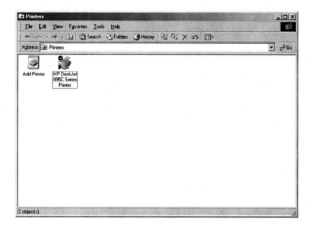

WHAT'S HAPPENING? Your printer now has a hand icon under it, indicating that the printer is shared. Now you need to go to each printer client to set up the shared printer. A printer client is any computer on your network that you want to have access to the shared printer. (*Note:* You may need your Windows CD if the printer driver is not installed on the client computer.)

6 Go to a client computer (in this example, the Micron-pc). Open My Computer. Click **Start**. Click **Printers and Faxes**.

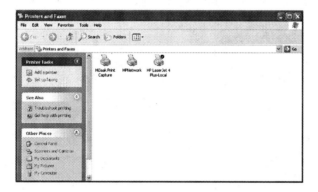

WHAT'S HAPPENING? This window has three printer icons. The first, Hijaak Print Capture, will "capture" and save as a file an image that would normally be sent to a printer. This way, if you are doing an instructional manual, for instance, and want to insert what a printed image will look like, you can use this file. This is a function of a software program, in this case, a program called HiJaak Pro. The second printer is called HPNetwork. In this example, this is the printer that is "hung" off the network. It has its own network card and special software that allows it to be attached to the hub and used by the other computers on the network. The last printer is called HP Laser Jet 4 Plus-Local. This is the same printer as the HPNetwork. However, in this case, this printer is physically attached to the Micron-pc.

7 Right-click the **HP Laser Jet 4 Plus-Local**. Click **Properties**. Click **Ports**.

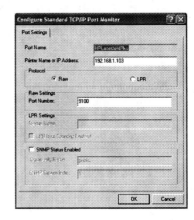

WHAT'S **HAPPENING?** Your display will not look like this. A port is a connection. The parallel port on your computer is called LPT1. Normally, if you physically connect a printer, it shows up on the port called LPT1. You can see that both the HP Laser Jet and the Hijaak Printer capture are assigned to this connection (port) as it has a check mark by it.

8   Click **Cancel**. Right-click the **HPNetwork** icon. Click **Properties**. Click **Ports**.

WHAT'S **HAPPENING?** You will not have this display. In this example, the HPLaserJet4 has been assigned a new port called HP Standard TCP/IP port with the printer name HPNetwork. This port was set up by the HP network printer software.

9   If possible, click **Configure Port**.

WHAT'S **HAPPENING?** Every device on a network has to be uniquely identified. The IP address 192.168.1.103 is a numeric assignment that is assigned to a port. When you choose to print to this printer, by virtue of the port address, it knows where to send the printer output. You are going to add the printer that is physically attached to the Dell 8100 (Dell-fp).

10   Click **Cancel**. Click **Cancel**. Double-click **Add a printer**. Click **Next**.

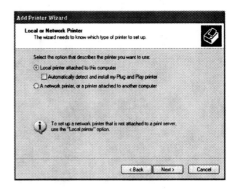

WHAT'S **HAPPENING?** You are asked whether this is a local printer or a network printer or a printer attached to another computer. The information button tells you that if you have a printer that is on hub, you choose Local printer. The reason it is considered a local printer is because of the port assignment. However, in this case, you want to select **A network printer, or a printer attached to another computer**. This HP Color printer is attached to another computer.

11 Click **A network printer or a printer attached to another computer**. Click **Next**.

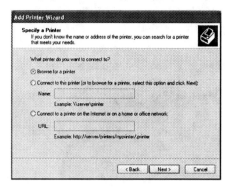

WHAT'S HAPPENING? Now you must locate your computer. If you know the name, its URL, you can key it in. Or you can browse for the printer you wish to use, and if you want to connect to a printer on the Internet or a print server, you can connect via its http:// address.

12 Be sure **Browse for a printer** is selected. Click **Next**.

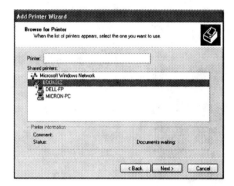

WHAT'S HAPPENING? You are looking at your network. You need to find the computer with the printer attached.

13 Double-click **DELL-FP**. This is the computer to which the printer is physically attached.

WHAT'S HAPPENING? You can see the shared resource, the HPCOLOR printer.

14 Click the printer to select it. Click **Next**.

WHAT'S HAPPENING? You may see the following dialog box (Figure 12.5). This dialog box is telling you that you do not have the printer drivers installed for this printer. If you see this dialog box, click **OK**. You will then be led through choosing the printer driver.

Figure 12.5 • The Connect to Printer Dialog Box

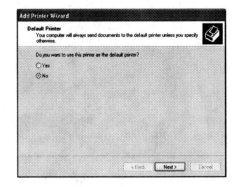

WHAT'S **HAPPENING?** You are asked if you want this to be the default printer.

15 Be sure **No** is selected. Click **Next**.

WHAT'S **HAPPENING?** You see a summary of your printer choice.

16 Click **Finish**.

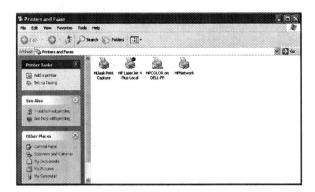

WHAT'S **HAPPENING?** You see your added printer. You know it is a network printer because the icon has the printer on a cable.

17 Right-click the **HPCOLOR on Dell-FP** printer. Click **Properties**. Click **Ports**.

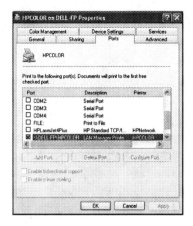

WHAT'S HAPPENING? You now see your network path. Notice the format—\\DELL-FP\HPCOLOR. The network path always begins with the double backslash (\\). It is in the format of *computer name\share name*.

18 Click **Cancel**. Close the Printers window.

WHAT'S HAPPENING? You have installed your network printer. You would have to take these steps for each client computer that you wished to access the shared printer.

12.6 ● Sharing a Hard Drive on a Network

When you share a drive, just like a printer, any computer on the network can look into that drive and use the folders and files on that drive. The computer with the drive you wish to share is taking on the role of the *file server*. Again, in a large network, often there will be one computer dedicated to being a file server. In a small network, typically there is no dedicated file server.

In a peer-to-peer network any computer on the network can share its drive, but first the drive on the server computer has to be shared in the same manner that the printer is shared. You have the choice of sharing an entire drive or selected folders. The process requires two steps. You must go to the server computer, which contains the drive you wish to share, and set up the drive so that you can share it. Then you go to the client computer and access the shared drive via My Network Places. However, when you share a drive, you are allowing any other user to have full access to your computer.

12.7 ● Permissions and Rights

If you are in a corporate or lab environment, your local computer is probably part of a domain. A domain is a group of computers that are part of a network and share a common directory database. A domain is administered by a network administrator, as a unit with common rules and procedures. Part of these common rules and procedures for a domain include access control. Access control, as its name implies, is the process of giving users, groups, and computers the ability to access objects (files, folders, and devices) on the network. This is a security measure that not only determines who can access an object, but what kinds of access that user is authorized to perform. The management of a network as well as full discussion of permission and rights is beyond the scope of this text, but there are elements of these permissions that you can use on a peer-to-peer network.

If your hard drive has been formatted with NTFS (New Technology File System), you can set permissions on files and folders that you will grant to other users. *Permissions* determine which users can access which objects (files, folders, and devices) and what kinds of access users have to those objects. These permissions include change ownership, full control, modify (read, write, and execute), read and execute, or read only. Users can be assigned to groups and you can assign permissions and rights to a group rather than on an individual user-by-user basis. The permissions that are assigned to an object depend on its type. In addition, whenever you create an object, such as a file, an owner is always assigned to it. By default, the owner is the creator of the object. No matter what permissions are set on an object, the owner of the object can always change the permissions on that object. In addition, objects inherit permissions. For instance, files within a folder inherit the permissions of the folder.

When you set up permissions, you may specify the level of access for groups and users. This means you could let one user have only read permissions to a file where another user could have read and write permissions. Read permissions mean that a user can only look at a file but not change the contents, whereas write permissions allow a user to not only look at a file but make changes to that file. You could deny some users the ability to even look at the file. These permissions can also be assigned to devices so that some users could configure the printer, whereas other users could only print from the printer or you could deny certain users the right to print at all to a specific printer.

If you are using the FAT32 file system, you can provide some security on folders when you share them on a network. You may set some permissions on folders that are shared. However, you cannot assign permissions on a file-by-file basis as you can with NTFS.

12.8 ● Activity ● Sharing Drives on a Network

Note: The following activity is based on a specific computer configuration. Your display will be different.

1   Go to the computer with a drive you wish to share. In this example, it is the Micron-PC computer.

2   Click **Start**. Click **My Network Places**. Click **View workgroup computers**. Click **View**. Click **Tiles**. Double-click the **Micron-PC**. Click **View**. Click **Tiles**.

WHAT'S **HAPPENING?** In this example, you are logged onto the Micron-PC computer. You see only the Printers and Faxes folder and the Scheduled Tasks folder. You do not see any drives available through My Network Places even though you are looking at the computer you are logged on to. The reason that you do not see any drives available is because you are looking at your own computer through the network. Nothing has been shared on the network.

3   Click the **Back** button. Double-click the Dell-czg computer icon.

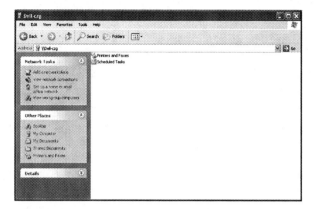

WHAT'S **HAPPENING?** If you see a flashlight icon, that indicates that Windows is looking for the network connection. Once it finds it, you will see a Printers and Faxes folder and a Scheduled Tasks icons. If you look at the Address, you see that you are looking at the \\Dell-czg computer. However, you see no drives. The Dell-czg is a computer running Windows 2000 Professional.

4   Click the **Back** button. Double-click the Dell **8100 (Dell-fp)** icon. Click **View**. Click **Tiles**.

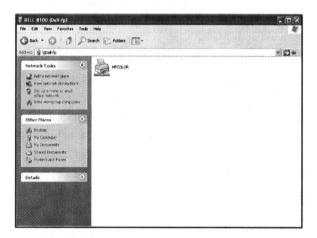

WHAT'S **HAPPENING?** You see no folders or drives, but you do see the printer you previously shared. No drives were shared on this computer either. This computer is running Windows Me. Each version of Windows will display a slightly different view.

5   Close My Network Places. Open My Computer. Click **View**. Click **Tiles**. Right-click **Drive C**. Click **Sharing and Security**.

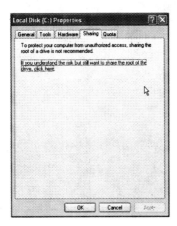

WHAT'S HAPPENING? In this example, Simple file sharing is set. This means that you are sharing everything on your hard drive. As you can see, this is not recommended since you give everyone rights to everything on your hard drive. However, you can be more specific by disabling Simple file sharing.

6   Click **Cancel**. Click **Tools**. Click **Folder Options**. Click the **View** tab. Scroll to the bottom of the window.

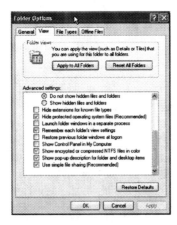

WHAT'S HAPPENING? At the bottom of the window, Use simple file sharing (Recommended) is selected. If you are using the FAT32 file system, you will not see this choice. When Simple file sharing is set, you cannot set more specific permissions on the drive.

7   Clear **Use Simple file sharing (Recommended)**. Click **OK**. Right-click **Drive C**. Click **Sharing and Security**.

WHAT'S HAPPENING? In Windows XP Professional, as in all versions of Windows after Windows 2000 Professional, all drives on your computer, such as Drive C or D, are automatically shared using the syntax of *drive letter*$, such as D$ or E$. This is known as an administrative share. This type of share allows administrators to connect the root directory of a drive over the network. These drives are not shown in either My Computer or Windows Explorer. These drives are also hidden when users connect to your computer remotely. But if any user knows your computer name, user name, and password and if that user is a member of the Administrators, Backup Operators, or Server Operators group, that user can gain access to your computer over a network or the Internet, provided that the Administrative share remains shared.

8   Click **New Share**.

WHAT'S HAPPENING? You may name the shared drive anything you like. However, simply calling it C is not a good idea. All computers have a C drive. You want to name it uniquely so that it can be identified on the network as the Micron's Drive C. You may also set how many users may be allowed to share this drive at one time. (User Limit).

9 Click **Permissions.**

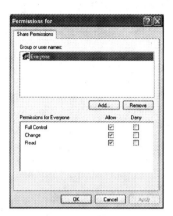

WHAT'S **HAPPENING?** As you can see, Everyone has full permission to do anything to the shared drive.

10 Click the **Add** button. Click the **Advanced** button. Click **Find Now.**

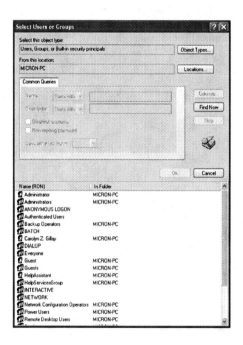

WHAT'S **HAPPENING?** Windows XP Professional provides these groups, whose membership is controlled by the administrator. There is another group called Authenticated Users, whose membership is controlled by the operating system or by the domain, if you are on a domain. Authenticated Users is the same as the Everyone group. By default

in Windows XP Professional, any authenticated user is a member of the Users group. Often, an administrator will remove the Everyone group and add specific groups who may access the information so that the environment is more secure. As you can see, as you move into the networking world, administering the system becomes more and more complex. At the moment, you will simply allow Everyone access to this drive.

11 Click **Cancel.** Click **Cancel.** Click **Cancel.** In the **Share Name** text box, key in **Micron-C.**

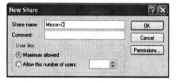

WHAT'S **HAPPENING?** In this case, you chose to name the drive by the computer brand, and you gave full access to your drive. Note that there is no space between the computer brand and the C. A hyphen was used. A space in a share name can cause problems in accessing the shared resource. To avoid problems, avoid spaces. The Micron is acting as the server computer. Remember that this is an example. Your drive names and availability will differ from the example.

12 Click **OK.** Click **OK.**

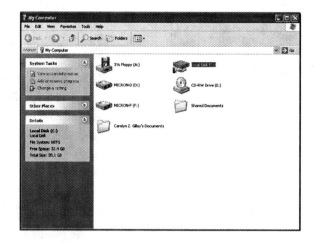

WHAT'S **HAPPENING?** Now on the Micron you have shared Drive C. You can tell by the hand under the drive icon.

13   Close My Computer. Open My Network Places. Click **View workgroup computers**. Double-click **Micron-C**.

WHAT'S **HAPPENING?** Now you see your drive represented as a folder icon. You are still the server. To test that you have made the Micron's Drive C available to others on the network, you need to go to a client computer.

14   Close My Network Places. Go to a client computer, in this case, the Dell-czg computer. The Dell-czg is using Windows 2000 Professional as its operating system. Double-click the **My Network Places** icon. Double-click **Computers Near Me**.

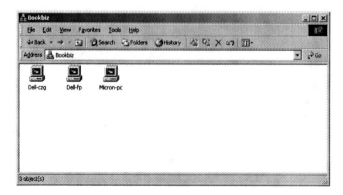

WHAT'S HAPPENING? You are now on the Dell-czg computer, the client, and wish to access the drive on the Micron computer. You should be able to because it is shared.

15 Double-click the Micron-PC icon.

WHAT'S HAPPENING? The server computer, the \\Micron-pc, wants to validate who you are. You need to connect as a user.

16 In the **Connect as:** text box, key in the following: **Everyone**. Click **OK.**

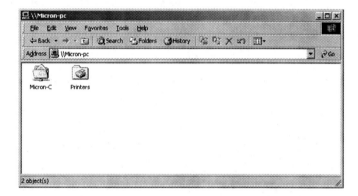

WHAT'S HAPPENING? Now you have access to Drive C on the Micron computer.

17 Double-click **Micron-C**.

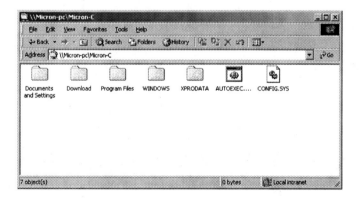

WHAT'S HAPPENING? You have full access to Drive C on the Micron. Both the title bar and the address (\\Micron-pc\Micron-C) tell you what computer you are accessing. You have been acting as the client computer, because you are logged on to the Dell-czg computer and you are able to access any shared resources (Drive C) of the Micron computer, in this case, the server. However, on a peer-to-peer network, you can switch roles and become the server and share your drives so that other users on the network can access your drives.

18 Click the **Back** button twice. Double-click the **Dell-czg** computer.

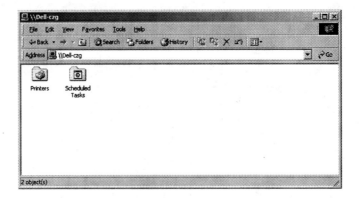

WHAT'S **HAPPENING?** Even though you are sitting at the client computer, the Dell-czg, you cannot see any of your drives because you are looking at the Dell-czg computer through My Network Places. Since no drives are shared on the Dell-czg computer, no drives on the Dell-czg computer can be seen through My Network Places.

19   Close My Network Places. Open My Computer on the Dell. Right-click **Drive C**. Click **Sharing**. Click **Share this folder**. In the **Share name** text box, key in **Dell-czg-C**. Click **OK**.

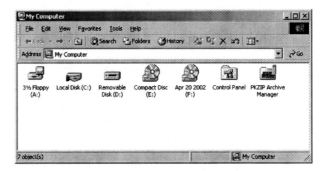

WHAT'S **HAPPENING?** You now see that on the Dell, Drive C is shared. Now anyone on another computer connected to the network can access Drive C on the Dell-czg computer. You have just acted as the server.

20   Close My Computer. Open My Network Places. Double-click **Computers Near Me**. Double-click **Dell-czg**.

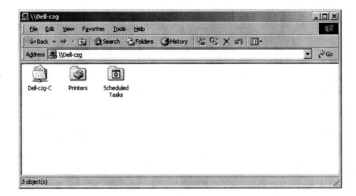

WHAT'S **HAPPENING?** As you can see, now the Dell-czg-C drive is available through My Network Places.

21   Close My Network Places.

12.9 ● Sharing Only a Folder on a Hard Drive on a Network and Setting Permissions

You do not need to share your entire hard drive. You can elect to share only a folder and limit other users on the network to accessing only that folder, not your entire hard drive. In fact, that is often what users do. They opt to share a folder or folders on their hard drive but do not want to let other users access their entire hard drive. Again, the process requires two steps. You must go to the server computer, which contains the folder you wish to share, and share it. Then you go to the client computer and access the shared drive via My Network Places or Network Neighborhood in Windows 98.

If you have NTFS as your file system, you can also set file permissions on individual files. You can allow or deny users separate permissions for a selected file. Thus, if you have a file or files that you wish to protect, you may, for instance, deny write or modify permissions. If you are on a server-based network, you will not be allowed to set permissions, except on your own files. If your system is using the FAT32 file system, you cannot set permissions on individual files and folders.

12.10 ● Activity ● Sharing a Folder on a Network

Note 1: The following activity is based on a specific computer configuration. Your display will be different.

Note 2: Use simple sharing is cleared.

1   Go to the computer that has the folder you wish to share, in this case the Micron computer.

2   Open My Computer. Right-click **Drive C**. Click the **Sharing and Security** tab. Click the **Sharing** tab. Click the down arrow in the **Share name** drop-down list box. Select **Micron-C**. Click **Do not share this folder**.

WHAT'S **HAPPENING?** Since this folder is shared, you are reminded that you are removing access to the shared drive. It states that this folder is shared more than once—the share you set up and the Administrative share. You may not see this dialog box.

3   Click **Yes**.

608 CHAPTER 12 CONNECTIVITY

WHAT'S HAPPENING? You have returned to the Sharing tab. The C$ share is displayed. If you ever removed this administrative share (C$), you could recreate it. Although you could recreate it (New Share/C$), it is not necessary, because each time you reboot, the administrative share is always recreated.

4   Click **OK**.

WHAT'S HAPPENING? You are informed that this Administrative Share will reappear the next time you boot.

5   Click **No**.

WHAT'S HAPPENING? Drive C is no longer shared.

6   Open **My Network Places**. Click **View workgroup computers**. Open the **Micron-pc** computer.

WHAT'S HAPPENING? You can see that Drive C is no longer available to the network.

7   Close the Micron-pc window. Open My Computer if it is not already open. Open Drive C. Right-click the **XPRODATA** . Click **Sharing and security**. Click **Share this folder**.

WHAT'S HAPPENING? You are going to share the XPRODATA folder. The folder name, XPRODATA, was the default for the share name. Since you did not change permissions, the default is full for everyone. You have given other users full access to that folder only.

8   Click **Apply**. Click **OK**. Close all open windows. Open **My Network Places**. Click **View workgroup computers**. Open the Micron-pc computer.

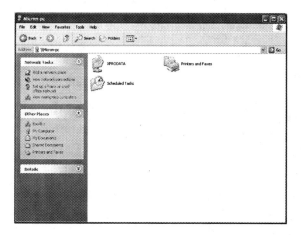

WHAT'S HAPPENING? As you can see, the XPRODATA folder is now available for other users on the network.

9   Close all open windows.

10   Open Windows Explorer. Click **Tools**. Click **Folder Options**. Click the **View** tab. Scroll to the bottom of the window. Check **Use Simple file sharing (Recommended)**. Click **OK**.

11   Open the XPRODATA folder. Right-click **ASTRO.TXT**. Click **Properties**.

WHAT'S HAPPENING? It appears that you have no way to set separate file permissions on this file. Since you returned to simple file sharing, you no longer have the options you did.

12 Click **Cancel**. Click **Tools**. Click **Folder Options**. Click the **View** tab. Scroll to the bottom of the window.

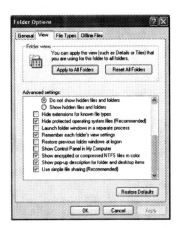

WHAT'S HAPPENING? At the bottom of the window, **Use simple file sharing (Recommended)** is selected. If you are using the FAT32 file system, you will not see this choice. When Simple file sharing is set, you cannot set individual file or folder permissions.

13 Clear **Use simple file sharing (Recommended)**. Click **OK**. Right-click **ATRO.TXT**. Click **Properties**. Click the **Security** tab. Click **Everyone**. If Everyone is not available, select **Users (MICRON-PC\Users)**.

WHAT'S HAPPENING? Everyone may Modify, Read & Execute, and Read and Write this file.

14 In the **Deny** column, click the Deny Write checkbox.

WHAT'S HAPPENING? You are denying permission to Write the file to disk.

15 Click **OK**.

WHAT'S **HAPPENING?** As the information window tells you, **Deny permissions take prece-dence over allow entries.** If you have users who are members of more than one group, setting the Deny permission will effectively bar them from writing this file to a disk.

16 Click **Yes**. Close the window.

17 Click **Start**. Click **My Network Places**. Click **View workgroup computers**. Double-click **Micron-pc**. Double-click **XPRODATA**. Double-click **ASTRO.TXT**. Go to the bottom of the file and add **JJJ**. Click **File**. Click **Save**.

WHAT'S **HAPPENING?** You have denied everyone the ability to write the file to a disk by setting the Deny permission for write.

18 Click **OK**. Click **Cancel**. Click **File**. Click **Exit**. Click **No**. Close the window.

19 Open Windows Explorer. Open XPRODATA. Right-click **ASTRO.TXT**. Click **Properties**. Click the **Security** tab. Click **Users**. Remove the Deny checkbox for Write. Click **OK**.

20 Click **Tools**. Click **Folder Options**. Click **View**. Set **Use simple file sharing (Recommended)**. Click **OK**.

21 Close all open windows.

WHAT'S **HAPPENING?** You have returned to the desktop.

12.11 • Mapping Drives

Once a drive or folder is shared, you may map a drive letter to the shared drive or folder. A *mapped drive* is a network drive or folder (one that has been shared) that you assign a local drive letter. When you map a drive or a folder, it appears as a drive on client computers in Windows Explorer and My Computer. You no longer need to browse My Network Places to have access to that shared drive or folder. You access directly from My Computer or Windows Explorer using the assigned, or *mapped*, letter. Most often you will map folders rather than entire drives.

Windows XP Professional lets you use My Network Places to map drives using the Internet Explorer–like window. In order to see the mapped drive icons, you can use the customization feature in My Computer. Windows XP Professional also allows you to map a drive by right-clicking the My Computer icon or the My Network Places icon and choosing Map Network Drive. You may also use the Tools menu in My Computer or Windows Explorer.

12.12 • Activity • Mapping Drives on a Network

Note: The following activity is based on a specific computer configuration. Your display will be different.

1   In this example, you are going to begin with the Dell-czg—the computer with a drive you wish to map.

2   Share the Dell Drive as Dell-czg-C. Return to the Micron computer.

3   Click **Start**. Right-click **My Network Places**.

WHAT'S **HAPPENING?** You see a shortcut menu listing your choices. The one you are interested in is Map Network Drive.

4   Click **Map Network Drive**.

WHAT'S **HAPPENING?** The drive listed, in this case, is Z:, the last available drive letter not assigned to any real device on this computer. The path is the UNC path to the drive that you want. If you check the Reconnect at logon box, every time you connect to the network, Drive Z on your local computer (the Micron, in this example) will actually point to Drive C on the Dell-czg computer.

5   Key in **\\Dell-czg\Dell-czg-C** and click **Finish**.

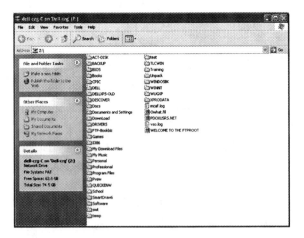

WHAT'S **HAPPENING?** You first see a message box telling you that the system is trying to connect. Then the Drive Z window opens. You see Drive Z, which is really Drive C on the Dell-czg computer.

6   Close the window. Open My Computer. Click **View**. Click **Tiles**.

WHAT'S HAPPENING? You can see that Drive Z appears in My Computer as if it were a drive on your system. You may access it in the usual way, by clicking it. You can tell it is a network drive by the icon, which looks like a regular drive icon connected to a cable. See Figure 12.6.

Figure 12.6 ∘ A Mapped Drive Icon

7   Click **Tools** on the menu bar. Click **Disconnect Network Drive**.

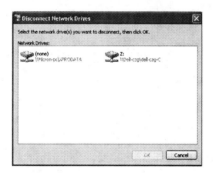

WHAT'S HAPPENING? You see a dialog box that tells you which drives are connected. In this case, you see your shared folder on the Micron and shared drive on the Dell. Every mapped drive will be listed here, and you can select what drives to disconnect.

8   Click **Drive Z**. Click **OK**.

WHAT'S HAPPENING? You see a warning that if you disconnect with open files, you could lose data. You have no open files. You may not get this dialog box.

9   Click **Yes**.

WHAT'S HAPPENING? > Your mapped drive is no longer available. The drive icon with a cable is gone.

10 Close My Computer. Open **My Network Places**. Open **View workgroup computers**. Open the Dell-czg computer. Open Dell-czg-C.

WHAT'S HAPPENING? > Since the entire drive is shared, the XPRODATA folder is available. This system also had the XPRODATA files and folders installed on it. You may map a folder as well.

11 Click the **XPRODATA** folder to select it. Click **Tools**. Click **Map Network Drive**. Click **Browse**.

WHAT'S HAPPENING? > The Bookbiz workgroup is shown as a location you can browse.

12 Expand **Bookbiz**. Expand **Dell-czg**. Expand **Dell-czg-c**. Scroll until you see **XPRODATA**. Click **Classes**.

WHAT'S **HAPPENING?** You are going to map the Class folder to Drive Z.

13 Click **OK**.

WHAT'S **HAPPENING?** You have returned to the Map Network Drive window. Drive Z is mapped to the folder Classes. Again, note that the UNC will be \\Dell-czg\Dell-czg-C \XPRODATA\Classes.

14 Click **Finish**.

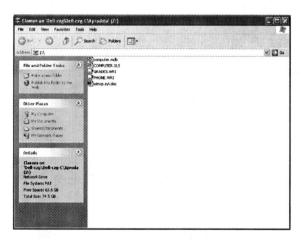

WHAT'S **HAPPENING?** Since you shared the drive, you shared all the folders on the drive and could map Drive Z (in this example) to the Classes folder in the XPRODATA folder on the Dell-czg's Drive C.

15 Close the Drive Z window. Close all open windows.

16 Open My Computer.

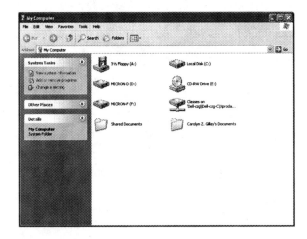

WHAT'S HAPPENING? Now Drive Z, a network drive, really refers only to the folder Classes on the Dell-czg computer. Notice that the description of the icon tells you this information.

17 Select the **Classes** folder. Right-click. Click **Disconnect**. Click **Yes**.

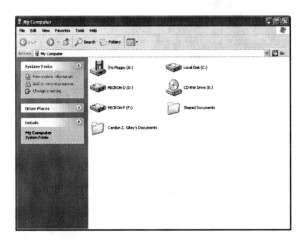

WHAT'S HAPPENING? You no longer have a mapped drive letter representing the Classes folder on the Dell-czg computer.

18 Close all open windows.

WHAT'S HAPPENING? You have returned to the desktop.

12.13 • The Internet

The Internet is an enormous, worldwide network of computers. Most simply stated, it is a network of networks. More than 500 million people and organizations are connected to the Internet (see **http://www.nua.ie/surveys/how_many_online/world.html**). By accessing this network, you can communicate with all the people who sit at those computers. You can connect to various public and private institutions in order to gather information, do research, explore new ideas, and purchase items. You can access the government, museums, companies, colleges, and universities.

The Internet is part of the *information superhighway*, a term popularized by the media. The Internet is also referred to as *cyberspace*. William Gibson, who coined the term *cyberspace* in his book *Neuromancer*, defined it as "a consensual hallucination experienced daily by billions of legitimate operators, in every nation, by children being taught mathematical concepts. A graphic representation of data abstracted from the banks of every computer in the human system. Unthinkable complexity. Lines of light ranged in the nonspace of the mind, clusters and constellations of data. Like city lights, receding . . ."

When you log on to the Internet, you are in cyberspace. You can use the Internet to communicate by email (electronic mail), chat lines, and forums, which are like bulletin boards where you leave notes or read information about a topic of interest. Email allows you to send letters and notes instantly, as you saw in an earlier chapter. Chat lines let you talk to people around the world on any subject of interest, such as computers, sewing, or Ukrainian culture. You are sure to find people who share your interests on the "Net." You may connect to the *World Wide Web (WWW)* through the Internet. You may even publish your own documents.

For most people, the best-known aspect of the Internet is the Web, an informal expression for the World Wide Web. The Web is a collection of standards and protocols used to access information on the Internet. It is an interconnected collection of millions of *Web sites* (growing at the rate of 1,000 per day). It is a virtual space accessible from the Internet that holds pages of text and graphics in a format recognizable by Web browsers. These pages are linked to one another and to individual files. Using the Web requires a browser to view and navigate through links. The most popular browsers today are Netscape Navigator and Microsoft Internet Explorer.

The World Wide Web is the graphical interface developed at the European Laboratory for Particle Physics in Geneva, Switzerland, by Tim Berners-Lee as a means for physicists to share papers and data easily. Tim Berners-Lee disseminated these tools for free, not taking any personal profit from this world-changing event. He even won a MacArthur "genius" award for the development of the WWW.

The Web and the Internet are not synonymous. The Internet is the actual network used to transport information. The Web is a graphical interface to the Internet. The Web uses three standards: *URLs (uniform resource locators)*, which tell the location of documents; *HTML (Hypertext Markup Language)*, which is the programming language used to create Web documents; and the protocols used for information transfer. Most Web traffic uses the protocol *HTTP (Hypertext Transfer Protocol)*.

URLs are a standard means for identifying locations on the Internet. URLs specify three types of information needed to retrieve a document—the protocol to be used, the server address with which to connect, and the path to the information. The URL syntax is *protocol://server name/path*; examples of URLs are **http://www.netscape.com/netcenter** and **ftp://microsoft.com**. *FTP* stands for *File Transfer Protocol*, and it is used to download or upload files. HTTP is the major protocol used to transfer information within the World Wide Web.

A Web site resides on a server. It is both the virtual and the physical location of a person's or an organization's Web pages. A *Web page* is a single screen of text and graphics that usually has links to other pages. A Web site has an address, its URL. A *home page* is the first page of a Web site. A home page can be thought of as a gateway page that starts you on your search through that Web site.

Web pages usually have hypertext links, referred to as hyperlinks or links. A hypertext link is a pointer to a Web page on the same site or on a different site anywhere in the world. When you click on a link, your browser takes you to the page indicated by the link. If you were at a site about companies that provide electronic commerce solutions for businesses and saw a link called Reference Desk, you could click it to see what references were available. From the

Reference Desk page, you could see a hypertext link to a document called "United States Government Electronic Commerce Policy." Clicking that could take you to the Web site of the Department of Commerce, where you could read the article "Surfing the Net."

A Web site's type is indicated by the "dot" part of its address. Common types include commercial sites, which end in .com (pronounced "dot com"); educational sites, which end in .edu; government sites, which end in .gov; military sites, which end in .mil; and nonprofit organizations' sites, most of which end in .org. Since addresses are being depleted due to the rapid growth of the Internet, new "dots" are being developed, even ones longer than three characters.

Since so much information exists on the Internet, a category of sites called search engines has been developed to help you find what you want. These are essentially indexes to indexes. Popular search engines include Yahoo! (**http://www.yahoo.com**), AltaVista (**http://altavista.com**), Infoseek (**http://infoseek.go.com**), Google (**http://www.google.com**), Ask Jeeves (**http://www.askjeeves.com**), Lycos (**http://www.lycos.com**), and WebCrawler (**http://www.webcrawler.com**). Many companies and organizations position themselves as *portals*. A portal is an entry to the Web. Yahoo! and Excite are now expanding beyond being just search engines and are positioning themselves as portals.

There are many ways to access information on the Internet. One common way is to have a modem, communication software, and an online provider. You set up your dial-up network in the Network Connections, found in Control Panel. You use your modem to dial out through your telephone line. In order to establish your dial-up account, you have to decide what service you are going to use. You could choose to connect to the Internet by belonging to a service such as MSN (Microsoft Network) or AOL (America Online). Each of these providers would give you detailed instructions on how to set up your dial-up account and would supply you with a local telephone number. If you used a service such as AOL or MSN, you would probably use its preferred browser, although you certainly could use any browser. Both MSN and AOL are now considered portals.

Another popular way to connect to the Internet is to use an ISP. *ISPs (Internet service providers)*, also called access providers or service providers, are companies or organizations that provide a gateway or link to the Internet for a fee. EarthLink and XO are examples of this kind of company. You would be given explicit instructions from your provider how to create your dial-up account. You may choose your browser. Most people choose either Netscape Navigator or Microsoft Internet Explorer. The ISP is simply the link to the Internet. On your browser, you can have a home page, the first page that opens when you launch your browser. With some ISPs you can have your own Web site, with a home page and one or more Web pages. Many ISPs charge a fee to create a Web site, but some provide this service at no additional cost.

There are other ways to connect to the Internet. Some cable companies provide direct cable connections. In this case, you would not use your telephone line. You would always be connected to the Internet and would not have to dial up when you wished to surf the Net. You could use Netscape Navigator or Internet Explorer as your browser, or you could use the cable company's supplied browser. The advantage of a cable connection is speed. Some people joke that when the Internet is accessed over a telephone line, WWW stands for World Wide Wait. A cable connection, on the other hand, is extremely fast.

Another choice is to use an ISDN (Integrated Services Digital Network), which is a high-speed digital phone line that transfers data at a rate five to six times faster than that of a 28.8-kilobits-per-second modem. The phone company must lay the ISDN line to your home or business, and you must have a special modem. A DSL (digital subscriber line) is yet another choice, if available. Here a user can purchase bandwidth that is potentially 10 times faster than a 28.8-kilobits-per-second modem, but still slower than cable. You may be fortunate enough to have your connection through a business or educational institution that has a T1 or T3 leased line, which provides a faster connection than any of the above choices. Another way, not that common yet, is connecting via satellites. This connection provides truly high-speed communications, but it is, at this point, not readily available. A new choice that is gaining in popularity is a wireless connection. Again, you need special types of equipment to connect in a wireless mode.

12.14 ● An Overview of TCP/IP

When discussing communication, and especially the Internet, you will hear the term TCP/IP (Transmission Control Protocol/Internet Protocol). TCP/IP is truly the protocol of the Internet. Data is transferred over the Internet through the protocol called TCP/IP.

Using the Internet is like making a telephone call. For example, you are in Los Angeles and you need to call your mother in Phoenix. You know that you do not have a direct phone line connection to your mother's home. You dial her telephone number, and the phone company decides the best way to route your call. If Los Angeles is very busy, the phone company may send your call to Phoenix through Denver if Denver is not as busy and can process the data faster. It is not important to you how the phone company manages the communication as long as you can talk to your mother.

On the Internet, data usually travels through several networks before it gets to its destination. Each network has a *router*, a device that connects networks. Data is sent in *packets*, units of information. A router transfers a packet to another network only when the packet is addressed to a station outside of its own network. The router can make intelligent decisions as to which network provides the best route for the data.

The rules for creating, addressing, and sending packets are specified by the TCP/IP protocol. TCP and IP have different jobs and are actually two different protocols. TCP is what divides the data into packets and then numbers each packet so it can be reassembled correctly at the receiving end. IP is responsible for specifying the addresses of the sending and receiving computers and sending the packets on their way. An *IP address* tells routers where to route the data. Data is divided into packets for two major reasons. The first is to ensure that sending a large file will not take up all of a network's time, and the second is to ensure that the data will be transferred correctly. Each packet is verified as having been received correctly. If a packet is corrupt, only the corrupted packet has to be re-sent, not the entire file.

A large company, college, or university will maintain a permanent open connection to the Internet (a T1 or T3 line), but this is not the case for a small office or a stand-alone PC. As mentioned previously, a single user will often access the Internet through a dial-up connection. This procedure provides a temporary connection known as a *PPP (Point-to-Point Protocol)* connection. Another older protocol that accomplishes the same task is *SLIP (Serial Line Internet Protocol)*. This connection provides full access to the Internet as long as you are online. However, if you are using a cable modem or a DSL connection, you do not need to "dial-up"; you are always connected to your provider (the cable company or phone company). The connection is more like a LAN. You are always connected to the server, which in turn is connected or is the gateway to the Internet.

Each computer connected to the Internet must have the TCP/IP protocol installed, as well as a unique IP address. The IP address identifies the computer on the Internet. If you are connected to the Internet through a permanent connection, the IP address remains a static (constant) address. If you have a dial-up account, a cable modem account, or another type of connection, you typically get a dynamic (temporary) IP address. It is a leased address and will change. The Internet Corporation for Assigned Names and Numbers (ICANN) is the nonprofit corporation that was formed to assume responsibility for IP address space allocation, protocol parameter assignment, domain name system management, and root server system management functions. This was previously performed under U.S. government contract by IANA (Internet Assigned Numbers Authority, see **http://www.iana.org**) and other entities. ICANN administers and registers IP numbers for the geographical areas previously managed by Network Solutions, Inc. When an organization applies for IP addresses, ICANN assigns a range of addresses appropriate to the number of hosts on the asking organization's network. See ICANN's Web site at **http://www.icann.org/general/abouticann.htm**.

An IP address is made up of four numbers separated by periods. An IP address is 32 bits long, making each of the four numbers 8 bits long. These 8-bit numbers are called octets. The largest possible octet is 11111111. In decimal notation, that is equal to 255. So the largest possible IP address is 255.255.255.255. This format is called dotted decimal notation, also referred to as "dotted quad." See Figure 12.7.

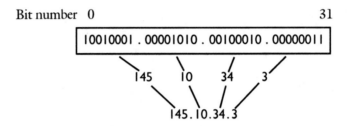

Figure 12.7 • A Dotted Quad Address

As originally designed, IP address space was divided into three different address classes: Class A, Class B, and Class C. A Class A network receives a number that is used in the first octet of the address. Class A network numbers range from 0 to 127. If an organization were assigned 95 as its network address, the hosts in the network would have IP addresses like 95.0.0.1, 95.0.0.2, 95.0.0.3, and so forth. There are no Class A network addresses remaining. Class A networks are now referred to as /8 (pronounced "slash eight") or sometimes just 8 since they have an 8-bit network prefix.

A Class B network has its network address assigned as the first two octets. The first octet can range between 128 and 191. The second octet can range between 0 and 255. If an organization were assigned 145.21, the hosts in the network would have IP addresses like 145.21.0.1, 145.21.0.2, 145.21.0.3, and so on. Class B networks are now referred to as /16 since they have a 16-bit network prefix. There are also no Class B network addresses remaining.

Today, Class C network addresses are still available. These are assigned the first three octets as their network address. The first octet can range from 192 to 254. If an organization were assigned 199.91.14, the hosts in the network would have IP addresses like 199.91.14.1, 199.91.14.2, 199.91.14.3, and so on. Class C networks are now referred to as /24 since they have a 24-bit network prefix.

There are two additional classes: Class D, which is used to support multicasting, and Class E, which is reserved for experimental use. With the explosive expansion of the Internet, IP addresses are going to be depleted. The appropriate parties are working on a solution to this problem by developing a new standard, called IP Next Generation (IPv6). In the meantime, the current system remains in place.

Even with the current system, if you had an organization with a large number of computers, you would still run out of IP addresses fairly quickly. A solution is to not assign a permanent (static) IP address to a computer, but rather assign an IP address to be used for the current work session only when the computer goes online (a dynamic—temporary—IP address). In this system, when you log off, your IP address is returned to the list of available addresses, and, since not everyone is online at the same time, not as many IP addresses are needed. The server that manages dynamic IP addresses is called a Dynamic Host Configuration Protocol (DHCP) server. Some ISPs use this method to assign IP addresses to their dial-up clients or cable clients. Others assign the address to the modem you dial into.

It would be difficult for most people to remember a numeric IP address. People remember names better than numbers. Phone numbers such as 1-800-FLOWERS or 1-800-URENTIT became popular for this very reason. Although you may not name your personal computer, computers in organizations are named so one computer can be distinguished from another. Organizations may choose names such as *pc1, pc2, mac1, mac2* or do it by department such as *sales*. Often, a computer's name will reflect its major role in the company. Thus, a computer devoted to handling electronic mail is often named *mail*, whereas a computer devoted to running the company's World Wide Web service is often called *www*. Both are easy-to-remember host names. These are in-house business names, not IP addresses for the Internet. If the computer is on the Internet, it has an IP address. An IP address can change, but typically it is not an organization's name. To give Internet addresses easy-to-remember names like this, the Internet is divided into domains. A domain is a general category that a computer on the Internet belongs to. A domain name is an easy-to-understand name given to an Internet host, as opposed to the numerical IP address. A user or organization applies for a ***domain name*** through the Internet Network Information Center (InterNIC) to ensure that each name is unique. InterNIC is now not the only organization responsible for assigning domain names. Some examples of domain names are *saddleback.cc.ca.us, solano.cc.ca.us, fbeedle.com, unl.edu, loyola.edu, bookbiz.com, dell.com*, and *microsoft.com*.

Fully qualified domain names (FQDNs) are alphabetic aliases to IP addresses. A fully qualified domain name is a host name plus a domain name. As an example, a host named *mail* with the domain name *fbeedle.com* would have the FQDN *mail.fbeedle.com*. Another host name could be *www* with a domain name of *microsoft.com;* the FQDN would be *www.microsoft.com*. A fully qualified domain name must be resolved into its numeric IP address in order to be communicated across the Internet.

The ***DNS (Domain Name System)*** provides this name resolution. It ensures that every site on the Internet has a unique address. Large domains are divided into smaller domains, with each domain responsible for maintaining unique addresses in the next lower domain (subdomain). DNS maintains a distributed database. When a new domain name is assigned, the domain name and its IP address are placed into a database on a top-level domain name server (also called a domain root server), which is a special computer that keeps information about addresses in its domain. When a remote computer tries to access a domain name and does not know the IP address, it queries its DNS server. If that DNS server does not have the IP address in its database, it contacts a domain root server for the authoritative server responsible for that domain. Then, the DNS server goes directly to the authoritative server to get the IP address and other needed information, updates its database, and informs the remote computer of the IP address of the domain name.

When you use a browser to access a site on the Internet, you key in its URL. The browser contacts the remote server for a copy of the requested page. The server on the remote system returns the page, tells the browser how to display the information, and gives a URL for each item on the page that can be clicked. Figure 12.8 describes the parts of a URL.

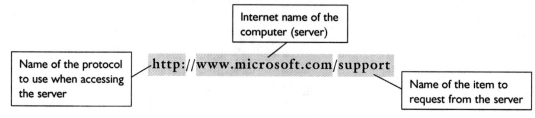

Figure 12.8 • The Parts of a URL

Figure 12.8 is the URL is for the page that gives you support for Microsoft products.

This somewhat technical discussion is not intended to confuse you but to give you some idea of Internet jargon. Terms like IP address, URL, and domain name are commonly used in conjunction with the Internet. Having some understanding and familiarity with the terms will help you navigate the Internet.

12.15 • Activity • Using Internet Explorer

Note: Since there are so many ways to access the Internet, this text assumes that your Internet connection is already established. See your instructor for details or follow your technical support person's directions for setting up your local area network connection. If you use a dial-up account, dial into your connection. You will need a user name and password supplied by the organization that provides your connection. This activity will use the example of a local area network connection.

1 Establish your Internet connection, if necessary. Click **Start**. Click **Internet**.

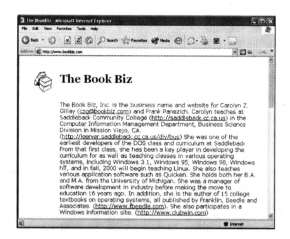

WHAT'S **HAPPENING?** While the page is loading, you see information on the status bar such as what is being downloaded. You have opened Internet Explorer, and you have connected to the Internet. Your home page will be different. In this example, the Address text box shows the address of my home page, which is **http://www.bookbiz.com**. If your window is already split, skip Step 2.

2 Click the **Search** button on the toolbar.

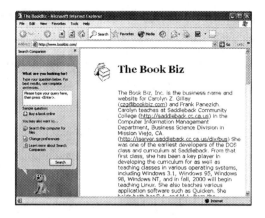

WHAT'S HAPPENING? You have opened the Search companion that you used in Chapter 5. You have four choices for the split window—Search, Favorites, Media, and History. Search allows you to search for specific information. Favorites lists any Web site that you have marked as a favorite. Media takes you to the WindowsMedia.com web site where you can look for movies, videos, music, and other media-related information and files. History shows you where you have been. Figure 12.9 shows you the parts of the Internet Explorer window. Figure 12.10 shows the Standard Toolbar buttons.

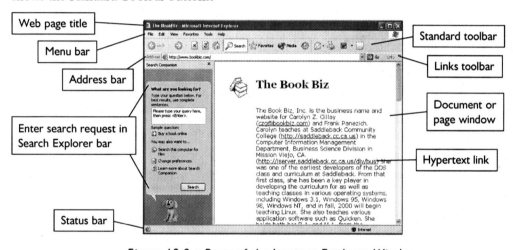

Figure 12.9 ◦ Parts of the Internet Explorer Window

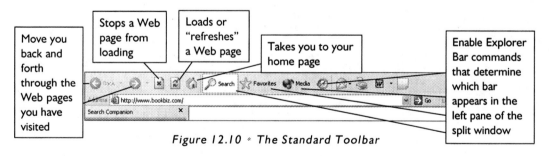

Figure 12.10 ◦ The Standard Toolbar

3 Click **Favorites**.

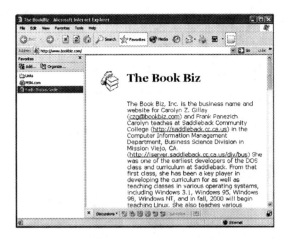

WHAT'S HAPPENING?⟩ You may have other favorites listed. The ones shown are the default favorites that Microsoft supplies.

4   Click Media.

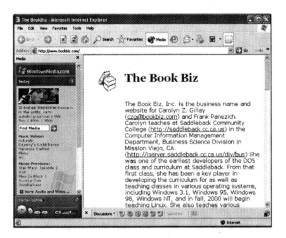

WHAT'S HAPPENING?⟩ Here is where you can search for videos, music, and media-related sites.

5   Click History.

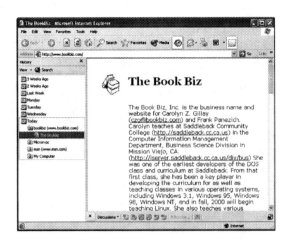

WHAT'S HAPPENING?⟩ As you can see, History is available for different lengths of time. History also shows the places you have been on your computer and on the network.

6 Click the X in the History pane, .

7 Right-click the **Go** button. Clear the Lock Toolbar if it is set.

8 In the upper-right corner of the Internet Explorer window, place your mouse pointer on the line between Links and Go until it becomes a double-headed arrow. (*Note:* If you do not have a Links toolbar, click **View**. Point to **Toolbars** and click **Links** to set it.)

WHAT'S **HAPPENING?** You can change the size and location of the toolbars.

9 Drag to the left about two inches.

WHAT'S **HAPPENING?** You have changed the size of the toolbar. You can also move the toolbars into different positions.

10 Point to **Links** and press and hold the mouse button. Your pointer will become a four-headed arrow.

11 Drag the Links toolbar down.

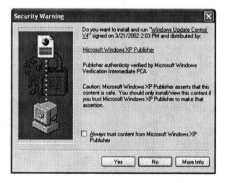

WHAT'S **HAPPENING?** You have changed the location of the Links toolbar.

12 Click **Tools**. Click **Windows Update**. Click **Yes**.

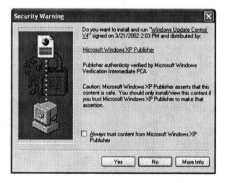

WHAT'S **HAPPENING?** Microsoft provides some security warnings. If you have a firewall, you may not be able to proceed.

13 Click **Yes**.

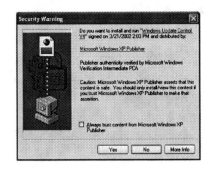

WHAT'S HAPPENING? You see another security warning. Again, if you have a firewall, you may not be able to proceed.

14 Click **Yes**.

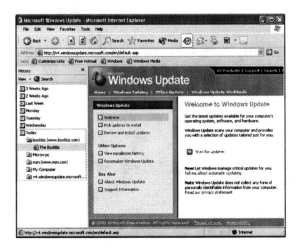

WHAT'S HAPPENING? You see the URL for Windows Update. Remember that Web pages are ever-changing, so your display may differ. Windows Update is one way to keep Windows XP Professional current. This choice is also listed on the Start menu in All Programs as Windows Update. It is an online extension of Windows XP Professional. This URL takes you to a Web site for Windows XP Professional that lets you find product enhancements, bug fixes, and specific files customized for your computer. Product enhancements include system files, device drivers, and new Windows XP Professional features. Bug fixes (also called patches) repair some part of the software that is not working correctly. Releases of software used to be numbered sequentially, such as WordPerfect 6.0, then WordPerfect 6.2. The version number would tell you the latest release of the software (which would include any fixes or enhancements). Today, software companies are releasing service packs, which are also numbered. Service packs are interim releases of software that provide enhancements, updated driver files, and patches prior to the release of a new version.

15 Press F11.

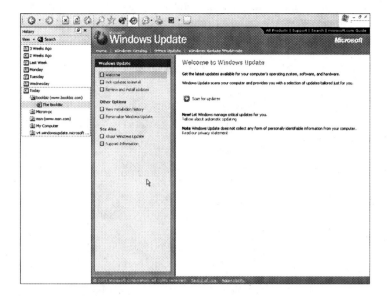

WHAT'S HAPPENING? By pressing F11 you allowed Internet Explorer to take up the entire screen so that you could better see the Web site. You can be automatically notified when there are critical releases from Microsoft.

16 Press F11 to return to a window view.

17 Click the X in Search Companion. Click the **Home** button, .

18 Close Internet Explorer. Disconnect from the Internet, if you need to. Close any open windows.

WHAT'S HAPPENING? You have returned to the desktop.

12.16 ● Navigating the World Wide Web

Internet Explorer offers you several ways to move about the Web. You may click a link to go to a specific page. Some links come with Internet Explorer. Often your computer's manufacturer will provide links such as a link to its home page for service and support. You can add your own links by dragging the icon for a Web page from the Address bar to your Links toolbar. You can key in a URL directly. You can use your Forward and Back buttons to move through pages you have visited. You can also use the History button to return to sites you have visited in past sessions. You may use Favorites, which you can add to as you find sites that are of interest. You may also use a search engine to find new Web sites.

12.17 ● Activity ● Navigating the World Wide Web

Note: This text assumes that your connection to the Internet is established.

1 Connect to the Internet, if necessary. Click **Start**. Click **Internet**.

2 Click **File** on the menu bar. Click **Open**.

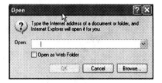

WHAT'S HAPPENING? If you know where you want to go, you can key in the address here. Open as Web Folder is for sites that allow you to act on a Web server with files and folders just as you act on your own files in Windows Explorer or My Computer.

3 If you have text that is not selected in the Open text box, select it. Then key in the following: **http://www.yahoo.com**

WHAT'S HAPPENING? You will find, as you key information in, that Internet Explorer guesses, usually correctly, what you need to type. It guesses based on what sites you have visited previously. You have keyed in a URL.

4 Click **OK**.

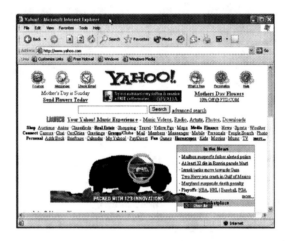

WHAT'S HAPPENING? You have gone to Yahoo!'s home page. Yahoo! is an index to sites on the Net as well as a portal. Each time you click an underlined term, called a hypertext link, you will be taken to that index of sites. Since Web sites can change frequently, your display will be different.

5 Click **Computers & Internet**. You may need to scroll down to see it.

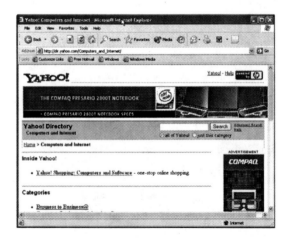

WHAT'S HAPPENING? You have gone to the page for your selected topic, Computers & Internet. (*Note:* Again, remember that Web sites are ever-changing. Your screens may look different from the examples.)

6 Scroll down until you see the category **Humor.**

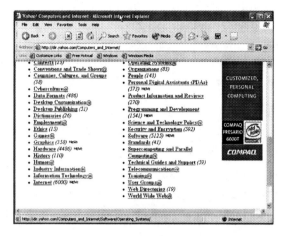

WHAT'S HAPPENING? Each one of these topics will take you to another topic. You can tell because they are underlined. The number in parentheses after a link tells you the number of entries at that site. The @ sign tells you that there are so many entries, the topic has been further subdivided.

7 Click **Humor.** Click the underlined hypertext link **Computer Cartoons.** Scroll, if necessary, to see the entries.

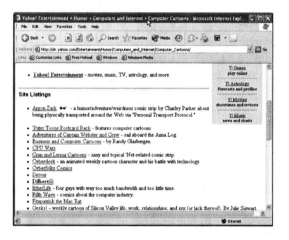

WHAT'S HAPPENING? As you can see, each click takes you to another site. Now you can see how many humor sites there are, by topic. You can also back up one page at a time. The Back toolbar button moves backward in the order in which you accessed the pages.

8 Click the **Back** button three times.

WHAT'S HAPPENING? You have returned to the first page, "Yahoo!" If you wanted to go here often, you could add it to your Favorites.

9 Click **Favorites** on the menu bar. Click **Add to Favorites.**

WHAT'S **HAPPENING?** ›› Yahoo! is being added to the Favorites menu under its name (Yahoo!), which you can use so you don't have to remember its URL. You can see the choices you have in Windows XP Professional. If you want to add a new favorite when you find a page you like, you can click Add. To delete or change your favorites, you can choose Organize from the Favorites menu. You can also return to your home page quickly.

10   Click **Cancel**. Click the Home button on the toolbar.

WHAT'S **HAPPENING?** ›› You have returned to your home page. To go to another site, you can key in the address in the Address text box.

11   Select the address in the Address text box.

WHAT'S **HAPPENING?** ›› You need to select only the part you wish to change, because typing will replace what is highlighted, leaving the unhighlighted portion as it is. However, in this case, select the entire address.

12   Key in the following: **http://www.fbeedle.com**

WHAT'S **HAPPENING?** ›› You have the URL of the home page of the publisher of this book, Franklin, Beedle & Associates.

13   Press **Enter**.

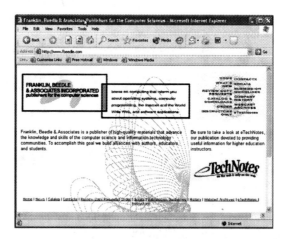

WHAT'S **HAPPENING?** ›› You can write to the publisher, see available books, and order books on the Franklin, Beedle & Associates Web site.

14   Click the Home button.

WHAT'S **HAPPENING?** ›› You have returned to your home page.

15   Click **File**. Click **Open**. Key in the following: **http://www.google.com** **Enter**.

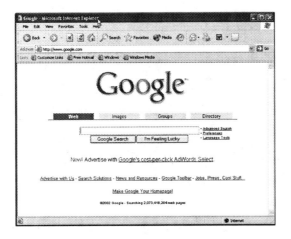

WHAT'S HAPPENING? Google is a very popular search engine. You can key in a question and it will search, looking for sites that answer your question.

16 In the Search box, key in **Computer Books**. Press ⌷Enter⌷.

WHAT'S HAPPENING? You asked for a search, which in this case took seven seconds to complete, for all the sites that list computer books. This is a search that is far too broadly stated. You got all the information—which are called hits—about computer books. In this case, there were 3,350,000 sites that deal with computer books—far too many to be useful. You need to narrow your search.

17 In the **Search** box, key in **Chrysler PT Cruiser for sale in Tustin, California** ⌷Enter⌷.

WHAT'S HAPPENING? Here you found four hits. As you can see, the more specific your question, the more appropriate your selection is and the easier it is to manage.

18 Close the browser window.

WHAT'S HAPPENING? You returned to the desktop. Depending on your setup, you may get a Disconnect dialog box. If you do not, remember that although you no longer have the browser open, your dial-up connection is still open.

19 If necessary, click **Disconnect**.

WHAT'S HAPPENING? You have returned to the desktop.

12.18 ● Customizing Internet Explorer

You may configure the settings for Internet Explorer in one location. That location can be accessed either by using the Internet Options icon in Control Panel or by right-clicking Internet from the Start menu and choosing Internet Properties. You may set up Internet Explorer to suit your own needs and style. You may customize not only cosmetic options such as colors and fonts but also more important options such as what level of security you wish to enable or what email program you wish to use.

12.19 ● Activity ● A Tour of Internet Explorer

1 Click **Start**. Right-click **Internet**. Click **Internet Properties**.

WHAT'S **HAPPENING?** There are seven tabs in the property sheet, each dealing with an aspect of customization. The General tab allows you to change your default home page. Either you may key in the URL for the page that you want or, when you are at the page that you desire as your home page, you may open the property sheet and choose Use Current. You can also customize the colors and fonts you use. You can set how many days you want visited pages kept in your history cache. You do not have to rely on Disk Cleanup to empty the cache of pages. When you use Internet Explorer, it will cache each page you visit on your computer so the next time you visit that site, the page will download faster. If you do a lot of wandering on the Web, you can fill this cache quickly. By adjusting the number of days that history will be kept and the settings for your cached pages, you can limit the amount of caching that is done.

2   Click the **Settings** command button.

WHAT'S **HAPPENING?** You have your choice as to how often your pages are cached, the location of the cached pages, as well as how much disk space you use for the cached pages.

3   Click **Cancel**. Click the **Security** tab.

WHAT'S **HAPPENING?** Set the level of security you are comfortable with. Security is a concern on the Internet. For instance, when you use the Web for shopping and fill out forms to order goods, you often use a credit card. You hardly want this information available throughout the world. Internet Explorer supports many of the security initiatives that have been developed. In addition, Internet Explorer can provide you with warnings and dialog boxes as you submit information. A secure Web site will display a lock icon on the status bar.

Internet Explorer implements security by using zones to classify Web pages. Each zone is a collection of Web pages with a common security level. The zones include the local intranet zone, which is your local hard drive and your local area network (your *intranet*). There is also a trusted sites zone into which you may add Web pages that you are sure are secure and safe. The restricted sites zone is for any Web pages that you know you do not trust. The Internet zone covers all Web pages that are not part of a previously defined zone.

4   Click the **Privacy** tab.

WHAT'S HAPPENING? A *cookie* is a block of data that a Web server stores on your hard drive. When you return to the Web site, Internet Explorer sends a copy of the cookie back to the Web server. Cookies are used to identify you as a repeat visitor to that site so that you do not have to key in information more than once. Cookies can also provide you with information. For instance, if you had purchased books at Amazon.com or Borders.com, your cookie would tell those sites what kinds of books you purchased so that the next time you visited the site, the Web server could make book recommendations based on your last purchase. As you can see, cookies raise privacy issues. How much information do you want others to have about you? It is a trade-off between privacy and convenience. Only you can decide how you feel. The default is a medium level to accept some cookies, but you can change that to refuse all cookies or to be prompted before cookies are accepted.

5   Click the **Content** tab.

WHAT'S HAPPENING? Here you can enable a content rating to set restrictions on Web sites that may have objectionable content. Only those who know the password can access these sites. Once this is enabled, you can filter out by categories such as language or violence. However, participation in the ratings system by a Web site is strictly voluntary. Only a small percentage of Web sites participate. You could also inadvertently block out content that you might be interested in. For instance, if you looked for information on breast cancer, you could be locked out of relevant sites because the word *breast* was used.

The Certificates choices provide secure communications. A certificate is an electronic statement that guarantees the identity of a person or the online security provisions of a Web site.

Personal information allows you to store information about yourself that you may want to share with Web sites that want this information. By entering the information here, you do not have to enter the same information, such as your name or address, again. Before the information is transmitted, you are notified who desires the information, how the information will be used, and if the connection is secure. Microsoft Wallet allows you to interact with merchants on the Internet that support Microsoft Wallet for online purchases.

6   Click the **Connections** tab.

WHAT'S HAPPENING? If you have not yet set up your Internet connection, you may do so here, as you may have done in the previous activity. You may make your selections by either using the connection wizard (with the Setup command button) or setting your options manually (by selecting Add for a dial-up connection or the LAN Settings command button for a network).

7   Click the **Programs** tab.

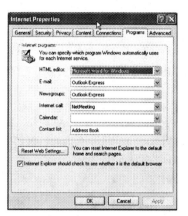

WHAT'S HAPPENING? You may choose your programs here for mail, news, and any Internet calls you make. You may also select which calendar or address book you wish to use. You may use any other compatible Internet programs you might have, such as Outlook Express. Outlook Express is the email program that comes with Windows XP Professional.

8   Click the **Advanced** tab.

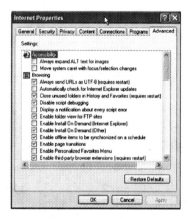

WHAT'S HAPPENING? There are many settings here that allow you to customize how Internet Explorer looks and works on your computer. Any item with a checkmark is set (enabled). The above example shows the default settings. The items are arranged by category. For instance, one way to speed up the downloading of Web pages is to go to the Multimedia section and disable all the items. Web pages will then load much more quickly because only text will be downloaded. If you wanted to see a picture or graphic, you could right-click on the icon and choose Show Picture.

9   Click **Cancel** to close Internet Properties.

Chapter Summary

In this chapter, you learned that when you connect computers together, you create what is known as a LAN (local area network). A server is a computer that provides shared resources. A client is a computer that accesses the shared resources provided by a server. Resources are the parts of the computers you share. The standard model for networks with more than 10 users is a server-based network. It is one in which network functions are provided by a computer that is a dedicated server.

For networks with fewer than 10 users, the model is a peer-to-peer network, in which all computers are equal. Each computer can function as either a client or server. A WAN (wide area network) consists of computers that use long-range telecommunication links to connect the networked computers over long distances. A network interface card (NIC) is required to set up a network. The NIC must match your bus architecture slot as well as the type of cable used to connect your network. You must have the proper networking software for your network to work. A network topology is the design of the network. Common topologies include the bus and star topologies. The bus topology connects all computers on a single line. If one computer goes down, the whole network is down. Today, most users favor a star topology using a hub or switch so that devices are independent. If one device goes down, only the device or computer that is down is affected. The rest of the network remains up and running.

A simple network has three parts: the hardware, the software, and the network administrator. Setting up a peer-to-peer network using Windows is done automatically or using the New Connections wizard or the Network Setup wizard. It sometimes requires that you have the original Windows disk. All computers on the network must use the same protocol. A protocol is a set of rules that allows computers to connect with one another and exchange information. In a peer-to-peer network, you must be sure to enable file and print sharing. In a peer-to-peer network, you must name your computer, as well as your workgroup. The workgroup name for all participants on the network must be identical.

When you share a device, any computer on the network can use that device. Common devices to share include printers, drives, and folders. The computer that has the resource must first share it so that others on the network can access it. You must name your shared resource. Others on the network will access it by its share name. My Network Places is the tool for browsing the network. If you are using the NTFS file system, you may set permissions on individual files and folders. This is considered access control since you control who accesses your information. Once a drive has been shared, you may assign a drive letter to it. This act is called mapping a drive. If you map a drive, you can access it through My Computer or Windows Explorer and need not use My Network Places.

You also learned about the Internet. You learned that TCP/IP is the protocol of the Internet. Each network has a router, a device that connects networks. A router can make intelligent decisions about which network to use to send data. TCP divides data into packets and numbers each packet. IP specifies the addresses of the sending and receiving computers and sends the packets on their way. A single user will typically access the Internet through a connection that is dial-up, is temporary, and uses PPP (Point-to-Point Protocol).

Each computer on the Internet uses TCP/IP and must have a unique IP address. An IP address is made up of four numbers separated by periods. This format is called dotted decimal notation. Each section is called an octet. IP address space is divided into three major address classes: A, B, and C. Each site attached to the Internet belongs to a domain. A user or organization applies for a domain name so that each domain name is unique. A fully qualified domain name is an alphabetic alias to an IP address. The DNS (Domain Name System) resolves the domain name into the IP address. When you connect to the Internet, you use the URL of the site you wish to visit. If you know the IP address, you may use that as well.

You learned that the Internet is a network of networks. You can use the Internet to access email, chat lines, forums, and the World Wide Web. The Web is an interconnected collection of Web sites that hold pages of text and graphics. These pages are linked to one another and to individual files. The Web is a collection of standards and protocols used to access information on the Internet. Using the Web requires a browser.

The Web uses three standards: URLs (uniform resource locators), HTML (Hypertext Markup Language), and a method of access such as HTTP (Hypertext Transfer Protocol). URLs are a standard means for identifying locations on the Internet. A Web site is both the physical and the virtual location of a person's or organization's Web pages. A Web page is a single screen of text and graphics that usually has hypertext links to other pages.

In order to access the Internet, you usually need a modem, communication software, and an online provider. Online providers include services such as AOL (America Online) and MSN (Microsoft Network). These providers now consider themselves portals. You may also use an ISP (Internet service provider). You can connect to the Internet using a phone line, a special phone line (ISDN), your cable company, a DSL, a T1 or T3 line, or a satellite.

The browser that Windows XP Professional provides is Internet Explorer. You may update Windows XP Professional through Windows Update on the Start menu so you can have the most current fixes and versions of Windows XP Professional. You may use search engines to locate information on the web. The more specific you are in your questions, the easier it is to find answers. If your question is phrased too broadly, you will have so many hits that you will find it impossible to locate what information you need. You also learned that you can customize Internet Explorer by right-clicking the Internet Explorer icon. Your customization choices include deleting cached pages, choosing your home page, setting security levels, filtering sites based on content or certification, changing your Internet connection, setting your mail and newsgroup programs, loading only text from Web pages, and denying the use of cookies.

Key Terms

browser	Internet service provider (ISP)	Serial Line Internet Protocol
bus topology	intranet	(SLIP)
client	IP address	server
cookie	local area network (LAN)	server-based network
cyberspace	locally	service
dedicated server	mapped drive	single point of failure
domain name	network administrator	star topology
Domain Name System (DNS)	network interface card (NIC)	T-connector
file server	network operating system	terminator plug
File Transfer Protocol (FTP)	(NOS)	topology
firewall	packet	uniform resource locator
gateway	peer-to-peer network	(URL)
home page	Point-to-Point Protocol (PPP)	universal naming convention
Hypertext Markup Language	permissions	(UNC)
(HTML)	portal	Web page
Hypertext Transfer Protocol	print server	Web site
(HTTP)	protocol	wide area network (WAN)
information superhighway	resource	workgroup
Internet	router	World Wide Web (WWW)

Discussion Questions

1. Define the following terms: client, server, and resources.
2. Compare and contrast a client computer and a server computer.
3. Compare and contrast a server-based network and a peer-to-peer network.
4. List and explain three reasons you might set up a network.
5. Compare and contrast a LAN and a WAN.
6. What is the purpose and function of a network interface card?
7. Compare and contrast setting up a peer-to-peer network using bus topology and using star topology.
8. Explain the purpose and function of a hub. Why would you want to use a hub?
9. Why is it important that all computers in a peer-to-peer network use the same workgroup name?
10. Explain the difference between using a printer locally and using a print server on a network.
11. List and explain the steps you need to take in order to share your drive on a peer-to-peer network.
12. When sharing your drive with another computer, why is it unwise for the share name to be C?
13. Explain the purpose and function of a mapped drive.
14. Define permissions. Define access control.
15. Compare and contrast the Internet and the World Wide Web.
16. List and explain three ways you might use the Internet.
17. List the three types of information a URL needs to retrieve a document.
18. Compare and contrast Web pages, home pages, and Web sites.
19. A Web site's type is indicated by its "dot" address. Explain.
20. What is a search engine?
21. List three ways to connect to the Internet.
22. Why is TCP/IP considered the protocol of the Internet?
23. What is a router?
24. What is the function of the TCP protocol? The IP protocol?
25. Data is divided into packets when it is transferred over the Internet. Why?
26. What is the purpose of an IP address?
27. Compare and contrast a static and a dynamic IP address.
28. Describe the format of Class A, Class B, and Class C IP addresses.
29. What is the purpose of name resolution? What is a fully qualified domain name?
30. Why can computers have both an IP address and a domain name?
31. What are service packs?
32. List and explain three ways to use Internet Explorer to move about the Web.
33. How can you tell if a Web site is secure?
34. How does Internet Explorer implement security?
35. What is a cookie? Do you think cookies are advantageous or disadvantageous? Why?
36. On the Internet, what is a certificate?
37. What could you do to download Web pages faster?

True/False Questions

For each question, circle the letter T if the statement is true or the letter F if the statement is false.

T	F	1. My Network Places allows you to browse all the resources on your network.
T	F	2. On a peer-to-peer network, anyone may access any resource, even if it has not been shared.
T	F	3. Netscape Navigator is an example of a protocol.
T	F	4. You may map both folders and drives.
T	F	5. You may set file permissions on a file located on a drive that is using the FAT32 file system.

Completion Questions

Write the correct answer in each blank space.

6. The global system of networked computers is called the _____.

7. In order to connect to a Web site on the WWW, you must key in its address, known as the _____.

8. An IP address of 121.22.34.44 is in what is called _____ notation.

9. The online extension of Windows XP Professional that provides a central location for product enhancements is called _____.

10. A network in which security and other network functions are provided by a dedicated computer is called a(n) _____ network.

Multiple Choice Questions

Circle the letter of the correct answer for each question.

11. What protocol is used to connect Windows to the Internet?
    a. PPP
    b. NetBIOS
    c. NetBEUI
    d. TCP/IP

12. If you give permission to _____, then all users may access to your shared folder.
    a. Everyone (or Users)
    b. World
    c. Power Users.
    d. Guest

13. If you wish to connect to another computer's folder, first on the server computer you must
    a. map the folder.
    b. share the folder.
    c. open My Network Places.
    d. both a and c

14. In the URL **http://www.yahoo.com/computers**, www.yahoo.com is an example of the
    a. protocol used.
    b. name of the server computer.
    c. name of the client computer.
    d. name of the item you are requesting.

15. A block of data that a Web server stores on your hard drive is called a
    a. subscription.
    b. cookie.
    c. both a and b
    d. neither a nor b

Application Assignments

Problem Set I—At the Computer

Note: To do these activities, you must have access to the Internet as well as a browser. Be sure to include your name and class information and the question you are answering.

1. Visit the site of the magazine *Scientific American* (**http://www.sciam.com**). You will be at the home page. Click **Past Issues**. Click **Issues from 1997**. Click **Dec. 1997**. Scroll until you see **Profile**. Click **Tim Berners-Lee**. Read the article and write a brief report on what you learned.

2. To know where things are going, it is helpful to know where they have been. Visit "Hobbes' Internet Timeline" (**http://www.isoc.org/guest/zakon. Click Hobbes' Internet Timeline**. Scroll through the page. Find 1993. Read the text there. Write a brief report describing one 1993 happening (from the timeline, not your memory).

3. Locate the current weather information for your city. Locate a satellite image of the weather for your area. Describe what steps you took to locate this information. Identify at least two URLs that show weather information.

4. Locate the nearest restaurant to your home that serves Chinese food. Describe what steps you took to locate this information. List the URL for this site.

5. Find out if your city has a Web site. Describe what steps you took to locate this information. Name two items that have links that are on this site. If your city does not have a Web site, locate the Web site for the city that is closest to you that does have a Web site. Describe what steps you took to locate this information. Name two items that have links that are on this site.

Problem Set II—Brief Essay

Be sure to include your name and class information and the question you are answering.

1. Briefly describe the importance and use of an IP address. Describe what it is and how it is used. Include in your discussion why a domain name must be resolved. Describe how a name is resolved.

2. *You should never allow cookies to be placed on your hard disk.* Agree or disagree with this statement. Explain your answer. Use a search engine such as Yahoo! or AltaVista and search for the keyword *cookie*. Find at least two articles that support your position. Cite the articles.

Problem Set III—Scenario

A small advertising company has three employees: Mary Brown, Jose Rodriquez, and Jin Li Yu. The office has three computers, a scanner, a laser printer, and a color printer. It has a hub. You have already set up a peer-to-peer network. The laser printer is connected to the hub. Mary's computer is also connected to the laser printer, Jose's computer is connected to the color printer, and Jin Li's computer is attached to the scanner. Mary needs access to the color printer but not the scanner. Jose needs only the color printer. Jin Li needs access to the color printer. Mary and Jose need access to a folder called Clients on Jin Li's computer. Jin Li needs access to a folder on Mary's computer called Parts. Describe what you need to do to accomplish these goals.

APPENDIX A

Installing the XPRODATA Disk Files onto Your Hard Drive

If you are working in a lab environment, you do not need to do this, since the XPRODATA directory has already been installed for you. However, if you are working on your own computer, you will need to load the XPRODATA directory onto your hard drive to do the activities and exercises beginning with Chapter 3. To install the files, take the following steps.

Note: Some virus-checking software can cause this program not to install. If this occurs, you may scan the XPRODATA disk for viruses. Then disable your virus-scanning program and proceed with step 3.

1 Boot into Windows XP Professional.

2 Place the XPRODATA disk that came with the textbook in the correct drive. Be sure it is not write-protected (move the slider on the disk so you cannot see through it).

3 Click **Start**. Point to **All Programs**. Point to **Accessories**. Click **Command Prompt**.

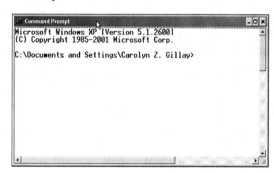

```
Microsoft Windows XP [Version 5.1.2600]
(C) Copyright 1985-2001 Microsoft Corp.

C:\Documents and Settings\Carolyn Z. Gillay>
```

WHAT'S **HAPPENING?** You have opened a Command Prompt window. Your location in the hierarchical structure in this example is C:\Documents and Settings\Carolyn Z. Gillay>. Your prompt may be in another location; it may be in the same location with your user name instead of Carolyn Z. Gillay. You key in data after the >. This is where the cursor should be flashing. You want to be at the root directory of C.

4   Key in the following:

C:\Documents and Settings\Carolyn Z. Gillay>**CD ** Enter

5   Key in the following: C:\\>**A:** Enter

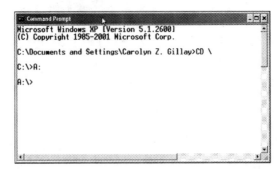

WHAT'S **HAPPENING?** You first moved to the root of C (CD C:\), then you changed your default drive to A: (A:). You are now ready to install the files to your hard drive. If you have more than one hard drive and wish to install the files on a drive other than Drive C, you may install the files by substituting your chosen drive letter for C.

6   Key in the following: A:\\>**PUT C:**

WHAT'S **HAPPENING?** You have issued the command to copy the files from the XPRODATA disk to Drive C. You must be sure to install the files onto Drive C, rather than just copy them. There are zipped (compressed) files on the XPRODATA disk that will be unzipped (uncompressed) when they are copied to your hard disk. Furthermore, not all the files on the XPRODATA disk will be copied to the hard disk.

7   Press Enter

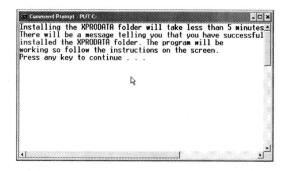

WHAT'S HAPPENING? You will see the above Command Prompt window with PUT C: in the title bar.

8   Press Enter

WHAT'S HAPPENING? As the files are being copied, you will see various messages. When the copy is complete, you will see the message below:

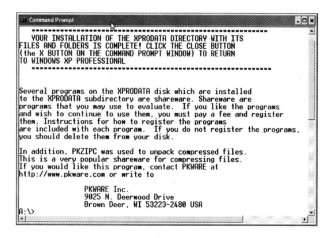

9   Click the Close button (in the upper-right corner of the title bar, ⊠).

WHAT'S HAPPENING? You have installed the files to the hard disk. If you are in a lab environment, do not delete the XPRODATA folder. If you are working on your own computer, however, you may remove the XPRODATA folder at the end of the course. To remove the XPRODATA directory from the hard drive, you may use Windows Explorer or My Computer. Select the XPRODATA folder and drag it to the Recycle Bin.

Shareware Programs Provided with the Textbook

Several programs on the XPRODATA disk that are installed to the XPRODATA directory are shareware programs. Shareware programs are for trial purposes only. If you find the programs useful and would like to keep them, you must register them and pay the registration fee.

ARGH

ARGH.EXE and ARGH.DOC are distributed as shareware. This allows you to try ARGH before you buy it, but if you continue to use it, you must register. Register by sending $10.00 to

David B. Howorth
01960 SW Palatine Hill Road
Portland, Oregon 97219

BOG2

Bog 2 is shareware. To register your copy, please send U.S. $10.00 plus postage and handling to

Pocket-Sized Software
8547 E. Arapahoe Road
Suite J-147
Greenwood Village, CO 80112 USA

Postage and Handling:
U.S. and Canada: $2.50 Overseas: $5.00 (for airmail delivery)

HANGMAN2

Hangman 2 is shareware. The registration price for Hangman 2 is U.S. $12.50. The following are accepted:

* Online registrations: http://www.personalmicrosms.com
* Checks in U.S. funds drawn on a U.S. bank
* International Postal Mail Orders
* American Express International Money Orders
* U.S. cash

Eurocheques are not accepted.

Send your registration payment to the following address:
Personal Microcosms
PMB #J 147
8547 E. Arapahoe Road
Greenwood Village, CO 80112-1430 USA

If paying by check, please make check payable to Eric Terrell.

MATCH32 Version 1.1

This game is shareware. If you like this game and play it a lot, you should register. Without registration, you can play only a limited part of this game—the first three levels out of the total 17 levels. If you register, you will receive the registration code by mail from the author. After you receive the registration code, you can do the following to activate the full version of this game:

* Under the main menu choice Tools, there is a sub-choice Register. Click on Register and you will see a dialog box.
* Type in the registration code and press the **Enter** key or click on the OK button.

To register, send a $10 check or money order to

Yuntong Kuo
P. O. Box 831
Pittsfield, MA 01202

Microlink Shareware—Shut the Box

Shut the Box is provided by

Bob Lancaster
P. O. Box 5612
Hacienda Heights, CA 91745

If you like this game, please send $5.00 to Bob Lancaster at the above address.

APPENDIX B

Hardware Overview

B.1 • An Introduction to Computers

At the most basic level, computers are calculators; but this definition is very narrow. Computers are used to handle accounting chores (spreadsheets), write books (word-processing documents), organize and retrieve information (databases), create and manipulate graphics, and communicate with the world (the Internet). In the visual arts computers have revolutionized the way films are made, games are played, and reality is perceived (virtual reality).

B.2 • Categories of Computers

Computers are categorized by a variety of factors such as size, processing speed, information storage capacity, and cost. In the ever-changing technical world, these classifications are not absolute. Technical advancements blur some categories. For instance, many microcomputers today exceed the capabilities of mainframes manufactured five years ago. In addition, the microcomputer now is the dominant computer used by most businesses. These computers are available in sizes ranging from desktop to sub-notebook. Table B.1 shows the major categories of computers.

Computer	Applications
Supercomputer: Very large computer	Sophisticated scientific applications such as nuclear physics, atomic physics, and seismology
Mainframe: Large computer	General purpose business machines. Typical applications include accounting, payroll, banking, and airline reservations
Minicomputer: Small mainframe computer	Specialized applications such as engineering and industrial research
Microcomputer: Small, general-purpose computer	General applications such as word processing, accounting for small businesses, and record keeping. Today, these computers are also known as desktops, PCs, notebooks, subcompacts, and laptops.

Table B.1 • Computer Types

B.3 • Computer Components

Although types of computers continue to grow, computers operate the same way, regardless of their category. Information is input, processed, and stored and the resulting information is output. Figure B.1 is a graphic representation of this process.

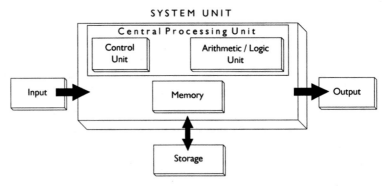

Figure B.1 • Components of a Computer System

Figure B.1 shows the process that occurs when using a computer. It represents the physical components of a computer system, referred to as *hardware*. All computer systems, from mainframes to notebooks, have the same basic hardware. Hardware by itself can do nothing—a computer system needs software. *Software* is a set of detailed instructions, called a *program*, that tells the hardware what operations to perform.

Data, in its simplest form, is related or unrelated numbers, words, or facts that, when arranged in a particular way, provide information. Software applications turn raw data into information.

B.4 • Microcomputer Hardware Components

This textbook is devoted to single-user computers—microcomputers. Microcomputers, today simply called computers, are also called micros, subcompacts, home computers, laptops, notebooks, personal computers (PCs), or desktop computers. Microcomputers are comprised of hardware components. Much like a stereo system, the basic components of a complete system, also called a system configuration, include an input device (typically a keyboard), a pointing device (a mouse or trackball), a system unit that houses the electronic circuitry for storing and processing data and programs (the central processing unit/CPU, adapter cards, power supply, and memory/

RAM and ROM), an external storage unit that stores data and programs on disks (disk drives), and an output device such as a visual display unit (a monitor). Most people also purchase a printer for producing a printed version of the results. Typically today, a system also includes speakers for multimedia activities. Figure B.2 represents a typical microcomputer system.

Figure B.2 ⁕ A Typical Microcomputer System

If you look at the back of the computer, you can see the input/output devices, called peripherals. Since they are "peripheral," or outside the case, they must communicate with what is inside the computer through cables attached to a connection that is called a *port*. Figure B.3 shows some examples of these connections.

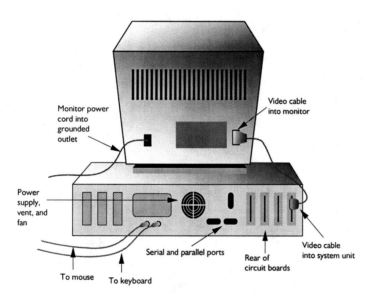

Figure B.3 ⁕ Cables Attached to a Case

B.5 ⁕ The System Unit

The system unit, as shown in Figure B.4, is the "black box" that houses the electronic and mechanical parts of the computer. It contains many printed electronic circuit boards, also called interface cards, *cards*, or *adapter cards*. One of these is a special printed circuit board called the *system board* or the *motherboard*. Attached to the system board is a microprocessor chip that is the central processing unit (CPU), random access memory (RAM), and read-only memory (ROM). The system unit is also referred to as the chassis or case. With the outer case removed, the unit looks like the diagram in Figure B.4.

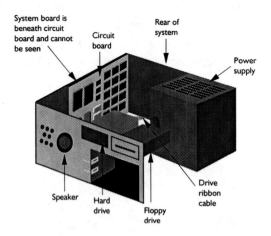

Figure B.4 * Inside the System Unit

Inside the typical system unit, you will find the following:

* A system board or motherboard that contains components such as a CPU, RAM, ROM, a chipset, and a system clock.
* Expansion slots that contain adapter cards such as a video card, a sound card, or a network interface card.
* Secondary storage units (disk drives)
* A power supply

A system unit has a power supply (to get power to every single part in the PC), disk drives (including CD-ROM drives, floppy disk drives, removable drives, and hard disk drives), and circuit boards. The motherboard, also called the system board, is the core of the system. Everything in the PC is connected to the motherboard so that it can control every part of in the system. Figure B.5 shows a system board.

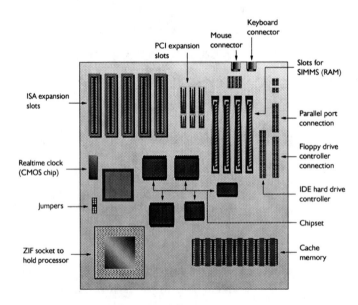

Figure B.5 * Components on a System Board

Most modern system boards have several components built in, including various sockets, slots, connectors, chips, and other components. Most system boards have the following components:

* A processor socket/slot is the place where the CPU is installed.

* A chipset is a single chip that integrates all the functions of older system chips such as the system timer, the keyboard controller, and so forth.

* A Super Input/Output chip integrates devices formerly found on separate expansion cards in older systems.

* All system boards must have a special chip containing software that is called BIOS (basic input/output system) or ***ROM-BIOS***. (***ROM*** is ***read-only memory***.) This chip contains the startup programs and drivers that are used to get your system up and running and acts as the interface to the basic hardware in your system. BIOS is a collection of programs embedded into a chip, called a flash ROM chip. It is nonvolatile, which means that, when you turn off the computer, none of the information stored in ROM is lost. ROM-BIOS has four main functions: POST (power-on self test), which tests a computer's critical hardware components such as the processor, memory, and disk controllers; the bootstrap loader, which finds the operating system and loads or boots your computer; BIOS, which is the collection of actual drivers used to act as a basic interface between the operating system and the hardware (when you run the Windows operating system in safe mode, you are running solely on BIOS drivers); and the CMOS (complementary metal-oxide semiconductor) setup, which contains the system configuration and setup programs. CMOS is usually a menu-driven program that allows you to configure the motherboard and chipset settings along with the date and time and passwords. You usually access the CMOS settings by pressing a special keystroke combination before the operating system loads. The keystroke, such as DEL or F2, depends on the computer. Most ROM is located on the system board, but some ROM is located on adapter boards.

* SIMM/DIMM (single inline memory module/dual inline memory module) slots are for the installation of memory modules. These modules are small boards that plug into special connectors on the motherboard or memory card and replace individual memory chips. If one chip goes bad, the entire module must be replaced.

* System buses are the heart of every motherboard. A ***bus*** is a path across which data can travel within a computer. A data path is the communication highway between computer elements. The main buses in a system include:

  * The processor bus, the highest-speed bus in the system, is primarily used by the processor to pass information to and from memory.

  * The AGP (accelerated graphics port) bus is a high-speed bus specifically for a video card.

  * The PCI (peripheral component interconnect) bus is a collection of slots that high-speed peripherals such as SCSI (small computer system interface) adapters, network cards, and video cards can be plugged into.

  * The ISA (Industry Standard Architecture) bus is an old bus which appeared in the first computers. Most people use it for plug-in modems, sound cards, and various other low-speed peripherals. ISA slots are gradually being replaced by PCI slots.

  * The voltage regulator is used to drop the power supply signal to the correct voltage for the processor.

  * A battery supplies power for the CMOS chip, which holds the system configuration information.

B.6 ◦ Central Processing Unit

A ***central processing unit***, most commonly referred to as a ***CPU***, is the brain of a computer and is composed of transistors on a silicon chip. It comprehends and carries out instructions sent to it by a program and directs the activity of the computer. The CPU is plugged into the motherboard.

The CPU is described in terms of its central processing chip and its model designation. Intel manufactures many of the CPU chips in Windows-based PCs. Intel processors running Windows are commonly called *Wintel* machines. These chips were, for many years, designated by a model number such as 80386 or 80486. Typically the first two numbers were dropped so people referred to a computer as a 386 or 486. With the introduction of the 80586, Intel began referring to its chips as Pentiums such as the Pentium 350. Since that time, Intel has released the Pentium II, the Pentium III, and the Pentium IV. The major competitors to Intel are AMD and Cyrix. A CPU is rated by the following items:

1. Speed. The system clock on the system board times the activities of the chips on the system board. This clock provides a beat that synchronizes all the activities. The faster the beat, the faster the CPU can execute instructions. This is measured in *megahertz (MHz)*, where one MHz is equal to 1,000,000 beats of the clock per second. The original 8088 CPU had a MHz rating of 4.77 MHz. Today, 500 is a common speed, and speeds are available up to 866 MHz or more. In fact, a 1 GHz CPU has been developed, with even faster CPUs coming.

2. Efficiency of the program code built into the CPU chip.

3. Internal data path size (word size) is the largest number of bits the CPU can process in one operation. Word sizes range from 16 bits (2 bytes) to 64 bits (8 bytes).

4. Data path, the largest number of bits that can be transported into the CPU, ranges from 8 bits to 64 bits.

5. Maximum number of memory addresses that the CPU can assign. The minimum is 1 megabyte and the maximum is 4,096 megabytes (4 gigabytes).

6. Internal cache, which is memory included in the CPU. It is also referred to as primary cache or level 1 (L1) cache.

7. Multiprocessor ability. Some chips can accomplish more than one task at a time and thus are multiprocessors.

8. Special functionality. Some chips are designed to provide special services. For example, the Pentium MMX chip is designed to handle multimedia features especially well.

B.7 • Input/Output (I/O) Buses

Adapter cards are printed circuit boards, as mentioned previously. They are installed in a system unit either when the unit is purchased or later. Adapter cards allow a user to use a special video display or use a mouse, a modem, or a fax-modem. These items are considered *peripheral devices* and are installed within a system unit in expansion slots. The number of adapter card options you can install depends on how many slots your system unit has. Inexpensive system units usually have only one or two expansion slots, but a costly system unit, especially one designed to be a network server, can have seven, eight, or more.

I/O buses allow your CPU to communicate with your peripheral devices. A peripheral device connected to your computer is controlled by the CPU. Examples of peripherals (also called peripheral device or devices) include such items as a disk drive, a printer, a mouse, or a modem. The original personal computers had nothing built into the computer except a CPU, memory, and a keyboard. Everything else such as floppy disk drivers, hard disk drives, printers, and modems were provided by add-in cards. Nowadays, computer manufacturers have found that it is less expensive to build the most common peripherals into the motherboard. Connectors to which you connect the cables for your devices are called ports. Today, most computers include a parallel port for a printer, two serial ports for devices such as an external modem or a serial mouse, two USB (Universal Serial Bus) ports and controllers for up to two floppy drives and two hard disk drives.

However, not every peripheral has a built-in connection. Data paths often stop at an expansion slot. An *expansion slot* is a slot or plug where you can add an interface card to enhance your computer system. An *interface card* is a printed circuit board that enables a personal computer to use a peripheral device such as a CD-ROM drive, modem, or joystick, for which it does not already have the necessary connections, ports, or circuit boards. Interface cards are also called cards, adapter cards, or adapter boards. The size and shape of the expansion slot is dependent on the kind of bus your computer uses.

Remember, a bus is a set of hardware lines (conductors) used for data transfer among the components of the computer system. A bus is essentially a shared information highway that connects different parts of the system—including the CPU, the disk-drive controller, and memory. Buses are characterized by the number of bits that they can transfer at one time, which is equivalent to the number of wires within a bus. A computer with a 32-bit address bus and a 16-bit data bus can transfer 16 bits of data at a time from any of 2^{32} memory locations. Buses have standards— a technical guideline that is used to establish uniformity in an area of hardware or software development.

Common bus standards include ISA (Industry Standard Architecture), PCI (peripheral component interconnect), local bus, PC Card slots—formerly known as PCMCIA (Personal Computer Memory Card International Association)—primarily used on notebook computers, and VESA (Video Electronics Standards Association) local bus.

The most recent bus standard is the *USB (Universal Serial Bus)*. It is an external bus standard that brings the plug-and-play standard capability of hardware devices outside the computer, eliminating the need to install cards into dedicated computer slots and reconfigure the system. Most computers today include a USB connection. The advantage of USB is that you may daisy chain devices. This connectivity feature means that your first device plugs into the USB connector; then the next device plugs into the first device, and so forth. You only need one USB connection, but most systems come with two. You can use each connection for many devices. In addition, USB devices can be "hot-plugged" or unplugged, which means that you can add or remove a peripheral device without needing to power down the computer. The device, however, must be USB compatible.

FireWire is a recent bus technology. This bus was derived from the FireWire bus originally developed by Apple and Texas Instruments. It is now known as IEEE 1394 rather than FireWire. This bus is extremely fast and suits the demands of today's audio and video multimedia that must move large amounts of data quickly.

B.8 ● Random Access Memory

RAM (random access memory) is the workspace of the computer. It is often referred to simply as *memory*. The growth in the size of RAM in the last few years has been phenomenal. Whereas 4 MB of memory was more than satisfactory just a few years ago, the demand based on software needs has made 128 MB of RAM commonplace, and 256 or more MB of RAM desirable. Physically, RAM is contained in many electrical circuits. However, a computer's memory is not like a person's memory. RAM is not a permanent record of anything. RAM is the place where the programs and data are placed while the computer is working. Computer memory is temporary (volatile) and useful only while the computer is on. When the computer is turned off, what is in memory is lost.

There are two types of RAM, *dynamic RAM* (*DRAM*) and *static RAM* (*SRAM*). Dynamic RAM chips hold data for a short time whereas static RAM chips can hold data until the computer is turned off. DRAM is much less expensive than SRAM; thus most memory on a motherboard consists of DRAM. Dynamic RAM chips do not hold their data long and must be refreshed about every 3.86 milliseconds. To refresh means that the computer rewrites the data to the chip. The direct memory access (DMA) takes care of refreshing RAM. The DMA controller is on the system board and is part of the chipset. It provides faster memory access because it moves data in and out of RAM without involving the CPU. Today, you also see extended data output (EDO) memory on newer computers. This RAM module works about 20 percent faster then conventional RAM, but the system board must support EDO memory. Since the speed by which you and your computer work is driven by RAM, you can expect improvements in RAM speed to continue.

B.9 ● Cache Memory

Caching is a method used to improve processing speed. It uses some of the more expensive static RAM chips to speed up data access. Basically, *cache memory* stores frequently used RAM data, thereby speeding up the process of data access. Whenever the CPU needs data from RAM, it visits the cache first to see if the data is available there. If it is, then rapid action occurs. If not, the CPU goes to RAM proper.

The cache will hold data or programming code that is often used or anticipated. This way the CPU has the instructions it needs ready and waiting without having to refresh RAM. Caches can be found in video and printer memory systems as well.

B.10 ● Controllers

A *controller* is a device on which other devices rely for access to a computer subsystem such as a disk drive. A disk controller, for example, controls access to one or more disk drives. What kind of controller interface you have will determine the number and kinds of devices you can attach to your computer. A common disk-drive controller is the Integrated Device Electronics (IDE), which resides on the drive itself, eliminating the need for a separate adapter card. Another type is the Small Computer System Interface (SCSI), pronounced "skuzzi," which is a very high-speed interface and is used to connect computers to many SCSI peripheral devices such as hard disks and printers. The original SCSI standard is now called SCSI-I, and the new enhanced SCSI standard is called SCSI-II. In addition, new developments include Fast SCSI, Fast/Wide SCSI, and UltraSCSI.

B.11 ● Connectors

Most computers have a serial port, two USB ports, and a parallel port. See Figure B.6. These connections allow devices to be plugged in. *Serial ports* communicate in series, one data bit after another, and service serial devices such as modems and mouses. *Parallel ports* communicate in parallel, eight data bits at a time, and service parallel devices such as printers. The most common configuration for a personal computer is two serial ports and one parallel port. Serial ports are referred to as COM ports, and on a standard computer they are designated as COM1 and COM2. Parallel ports are called LPT ports. The first LPT port is called LPT1. COM stands for communications and LPT stands for line printer.

A personal computer can have up to five I/O ports, usually three serial and two parallel. Although computers are limited to five ports, there can actually be more than five peripheral devices. USB ports do not figure into the five I/O ports. Today, many devices, such as Zip drives and scanners, that plug into parallel ports have a "through port" so that one LPT port can service two devices. However, today, most Zip drives and scanners are USB. If you have a SCSI interface, you may also connect a series of devices, creating a daisy chain.

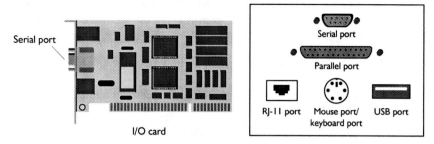

Serial port

I/O card

Serial port

Parallel port

RJ-11 port   Mouse port/   USB port
**   keyboard port**

Figure B.6 ⁕ I/O Ports

Today, many computers come with a built-in modem. If that is the case, you will have a connector called an RJ-11 telephone plug, which is identical to the plug on the back of a telephone. Having an RJ-11 connector frees up a serial port.

B.12 ⁕ Peripherals ⁕ Input Devices

How do software programs and data get into RAM? The answer is input devices. The most common input device is the keyboard, which is attached to a system unit with a cable. By keying in instructions and data, you communicate with the computer. The computer places the information into RAM. Again, most modern computers have a keyboard port to connect the keyboard. See Figure B.6.

You can also input using a pointing device, such as a *mouse*, **trackball**, track pointer, or touchpad to get to the place to enter data. (In this textbook, all such devices will be collectively referred to as a *mouse*.) Data manipulation is as easy as moving the cursor to where you want it on the screen and pressing one of the mouse buttons. Most computers today have a connector for the mouse, most commonly called the PS/2 connector. See Figure B.6.

Other input devices include modems with which data can be downloaded directly into the computer, and scanners for inserting text through optical character recognition (OCR) software and graphics. Disk drives are both input and output devices.

B.13 ⁕ Peripherals ⁕ Output Devices

In addition to getting information into the CPU, you also want to get it out. You may want to see what you keyed in on the monitor, or you might desire a printed or "hard" copy of the data. These processes are known as output. Output devices refer to where information is sent. Thus, you read information in and write information out, commonly known as I/O for input and output.

B.14 ⁕ Output Devices ⁕ Monitors

A *monitor*, also called a terminal display screen, screen, cathode-ray tube (CRT), or video display terminal (VDT), looks like a television. The common monitor size standard used to be 14 inches (measured diagonally). However, today, most users opt for at least a 15-inch monitor. The new standard is becoming the 19-inch monitor, with the 21-inch monitor gaining ground. In addition, the liquid crystal display (LCD) used on notebook computers is now becoming available as a stand-alone monitor to accompany your desktop computer. These monitors take far less space since they are completely flat. Although, these monitors were very expensive when first introduced, the prices have really dropped making this choice an affordable one.

Another important facet to a monitor is the sharpness of its image, referred to as its *resolution*. Resolution is a measure of how many pixels on the screen are addressable by software. It is measured in the number of *pixels* (dots) on the screen. A resolution of 800 by 600 means 800 pixels per line horizontally and 600 pixels vertically. Multiplying 800 by 600 will give you the total number of pixels available (480,000 pixels). The resolution must be supported by the video card controller, and the software you are using must make use of the resolution capabilities of the monitor.

In addition, to determine the sharpness of your image, you must also know the dot pitch of the pixels. *Dot pitch* is the measurement in millimeters between pixels on the screen. The smaller the dot pitch, the sharper the image. Common sizes include .25 to .31. A dot pitch of .28 or .25 will give you the best results.

Another factor in choosing a monitor is the interlace factor. An *interlaced* monitor begins at the top of the screen and redraws (refreshes) every other line of pixels, then returns to the top and refreshes the rest of the lines. A *noninterlaced* monitor refreshes all the lines at one time, eliminating the wandering horizontal line and the flickering screen. Thus, a noninterlaced monitor is the preferred choice. The refresh rate (vertical scan rate) is the time it takes for the electronic beam to fill the screen with lines from top to bottom. Video Electronics Standards Association (VESA) has set a minimum refresh rate standard of 70 Hz (70 complete vertical refreshes per second) as one requirement of Super VGA monitors. Multiscan monitors are also available. These monitors offer a variety of vertical and horizontal refresh rates but cost much more than other monitors.

Information written to the screen by the CPU needs a special kind of circuit board—a video display adapter card, commonly called a video card or a graphics adapter card—which controls the monitor. The video adapter consists of three components:

* A video chip set of some brand (ATI, Matrox, Nvidia, S3, are some of the better known brands). The video chip creates the signals, which the screen must receive to form an image.
* Some kind of RAM (EDO, SGRAM, or VRAM,). Memory is imperative, since the video card must be able to remember a complete screen image at any time. Using AGP, the video card may use the main memory of the motherboard.
* A RAMDAC, a chip converting digital/analog signals. If you have a flat-panel monitor, you do not need a the function of a RAMDAC.

In the early days of computing, the video adapters were only monochrome. The color graphics adapter (CGA) and the enhanced graphics adapter (EGA) came next, but only in 16 colors. Next was the video graphics array (VGA), which generated 256 colors. Next came the Super VGA (SVGA) format, which generated sharper resolution displayed an almost unbelievable 16 million colors. In truth, VGA was the last "real standard" working on any PC. Screen resolution has since improved relative to VGA, and the term SVGA (Super VGA) came into use. Later came XGA and other names, which each described different resolutions. Today, the terms SVGA and XGA are not used much anymore. Instead one looks at resolution, image frequency and color depth. Commonly, a video card has its own "on-board" memory, which is physically on the card. Today, 32 gigabytes of memory on a video card is common, and soon 64 megabytes will be the standard.

The standard CRT monitors will be phased out. They are being replaced by the flat and LCD (Liquid Crystal Display) monitors. The prices are dropping every day—today a 17 inch LCD costs the same as a 21 inch monitor did several years ago. In addition, you get more "viewing" with an LCD. For instance, 17.3" flat panel monitor has a visible area much bigger than that from a traditional 17" CRT monitor—it can be compared to a 19" CRT. The 17.3 inches is the visible diameter. The LCD screen is flat since it has no cathode ray tube (CRT). The screen image is generated on a flat plastic disk where millions of transistors create the pixels. In addition to the size and weight advantage, another big advantage of the LCD monitor is that it does not flicker.

B.15 ● Output Devices ● Printers

A printer is attached to a system unit with a cable, usually to a parallel port. A printer allows a user to have a hard copy (unchangeable because it is on paper) of information.

In the past, *impact printers*, such as dot-matrix printers, were used. An impact printer works like a typewriter. The element strikes some kind of ribbon, which in turn strikes the paper and leaves a mark. A dot-matrix printer forms characters by selecting dots from a grid pattern on a movable print head and permits printing in any style of letters and graphics (pictures). Dot-matrix printers are still used today for multiple-part forms that use carbon paper.

Today, *non-impact printers* are in general use. This category includes thermal printers that burn images into paper using a dot-matrix grid and *inkjet printers* that spray ionized drops of ink to shape characters. Today, inkjet printers that produce very good quality black and white as well as color images have become the most popular personal printer. The *laser printer* is more expensive, but produces fine quality black and white printing. Although laser color is available, it still remains very costly. Laser printers use a laser beam instructed by the computer to form characters with powdered toner fused to the page by heat, like a photocopying machine. Laser printers operate noiselessly at speeds up to 900 characters per second (cps), equivalent to 24 pages per minute.

B.16 ● Modems

A *modem* (*mo*dulator/*dem*odulator) translates the digital signals of the computer into the analog signals that travel over telephone lines. The speed at which the signal travels is called the baud rate—the unit of time for a signal to travel over a telephone line. The rate of transmission has increased to 56,000 baud, and will soon be even faster. The speed at which data packets travel is measured in bits per second (bps) and is usually very near the baud rate. For this transmission to occur, the party on the other end must also have a modem that translates the analog signals back into digital signals. In addition, the computer needs special instructions in the form of a software communication program.

Cable modems are also available in some areas. In this case, the cable company lays high-speed cable lines that require a special modem as well as a network interface card. This greatly increases the transmission speed. Another alternative is an integrated services digital network (ISDN) line— a high-speed telephone data line that also greatly increases speed. A digital subscriber line (DSL) is yet another choice, if available. Here users can purchase bandwidth that is potentially 10 times faster than ISDN lines but still slower than cable. *Bandwidth* can simply be described as a pipe that moves data from point A to point B. It is the data transfer capacity of a digital communications system.

Another choice for organizations such as businesses or educational institutions is a dedicated leased line that provides digital service between two locations at high speeds. A leased line is a permanent 24-hour connection to a specific location that can only be changed by the telephone company. Leased lines are used to connect local area networks to remote locations or to the Internet through a service provider. Leased lines include T-1 and T-3 connections. T-1 is a digital connection running at 1.55 megabits per second (Mbps) and costs several thousand dollars per month. A T-3 connection is equivalent to 30 T-1 lines and connections can run up to 45 Mbps. The cost limits the use to major companies or large universities. There are even satellite modems (wireless) that are incredibly fast and at this time costly but there is no question that wireless is going to be the future.

The growth of online services has made a modem or a digital connection a necessity. CompuServe, America Online, and Internet service providers—all leading to the information superhighway—make all kinds of information available. These services are the libraries of the future.

B.17 • Capacity Measurement—Bits and Bytes

A computer is made primarily of switches. All it can do is turn a switch on or off: 0 (zero) represents an off state and 1 (one) represents an on state. A *bit* (short for *binary digit*) is the smallest unit a computer can recognize. Bits are combined in meaningful groups, much as letters of the alphabet are combined to make words. A common grouping is eight bits, called a *byte*. A byte can be thought of as one character.

Computer capacities, such as RAM and ROM, are measured in bytes, originally grouped by thousands of bytes or *kilobytes* (*KB*), but now by millions of bytes or *megabytes* (*MB*, sometimes called *megs*), and *gigabytes* (*GB*, sometimes called *gigs*). A computer is binary, so it works in powers of 2. A kilobyte is 2 to the tenth power (1,024), and K or KB is the symbol for 1,024 bytes. If your computer has 64KB of memory, its actual memory size is 64 x 1,024, or 65,536 bytes. For simplification, KB is rounded off to 1,000, so that 64KB of memory means 64,000 bytes. Rapid technological growth has made megabytes the measuring factor.

You should know the capacity of your computer's memory because it determines how much data the computer can hold. For instance, if you have 32 MB of RAM on your computer and you buy a program that requires 64 MB of RAM, your computer will not have the memory capacity to use that program. Furthermore, if your computer has a hard disk capacity of 100 MB and the application program you buy requires at least 125 MB of space on the hard disk, you won't be able to install the program. Today, of course, a computer that has a hard disk of only 100 MB is very unlikely, but the principle remains the same—you have a specific amount of space on your hard disk and you can exceed the size of your hard disk if you have many large programs.

Disk capacity is also measured in bytes. A 3½-inch double-density disk holds 720KB. Because high-density and hard disks hold so much more information, they are also measured in megabytes. A 3½-inch high-density disk holds 1.44 MB. Hard disks vary in size, commonly ranging from 10 GB to over 80 GB. Today, most people consider an 20-GB hard disk a minimum requirement; it has a capacity of over twenty billion bytes. Most computer users, when referring to gigabytes, use the term gig. An 38.2 GB hard drive is referred to as an "thirty-eight point two gig" hard drive.

B.18 • Disks and Disk Drives

Since RAM is volatile and disappears when the power is turned off, *secondary storage media* or external storage media are necessary to save information permanently.

Disks and disk drives are magnetic media that store data and programs in the form of magnetic impulses. Such media include floppy disks, hard disks, compact discs (CD-ROMs), digital videodiscs (DVDs), removable drives such as Zip and Jaz drives, tapes, and tape cartridges. In the microcomputer world, the most common secondary storage media are floppy disks and hard disks, with removable drives and read/write CD-ROMs rapidly becoming a standard for most users.

Storing information on a disk is equivalent to storing information in a file cabinet. Like file cabinets, disks store information in files. When the computer needs the information, it goes to the disk, opens a file, reads the information from the disk file into RAM, and works on it. When the computer is finished working on that file, it closes the file and returns (writes) it back to the disk.

In most cases, this process does not occur automatically. The application program in use will have instructions that enable the user to save or write to the disk.

B.19 ◦ Floppy Disks

Floppy disks serve a dual purpose. First, disks provide a permanent way to hold data. When power is turned off, the disk retains what has been recorded on it. Second, floppy disks are transportable. Programs or data developed on one computer can be used by another merely by inserting the disk into the other computer. If it were not for this capability, programs such as the operating system or other application packages could not be used. Each time you wanted to do some work, you would have to write your own instructions.

Floppy disks come in two sizes: 3½ inch and 5¼ inch. The standard size used to be the 5¼ inch, but now the 3½ inch is the standard. The 5¼-inch floppy disk, technically known as a minifloppy diskette, is rarely used today. The 3½-inch diskette is a microfloppy diskette, but both are commonly referred to as floppy disks. Like a phonograph record, the 5¼-inch floppy disk has a hole (called a hub) in the center so that it can fit on the disk drive's spindle.

The disk drive spins the disk to find information on it or to write information to it. Once a disk is locked into a disk drive, it spins at about 300 revolutions per minute. The 3½-inch disk, made of a circular piece of plastic, polyurethane, or Mylar covered with magnetic oxide, is enclosed in a rigid plastic shell. The 3½-inch, 144KB diskette has a plastic shutter–covered hole in the upper-right corner. When the plastic shutter covers the opening, the disk can be written to. When it does not cover the opening, the disk is "write protected" and cannot be written or saved to. It has an opening in the upper-left corner, although this opening does not have a plastic shutter. There is a metal shutter over the area of the disk where the computer writes to the disk. The computer's disk drive opens the shutter only when it needs access. When the disk is not in the drive, the metal shutter is closed. Figure B.7 shows a 3½-inch disk.

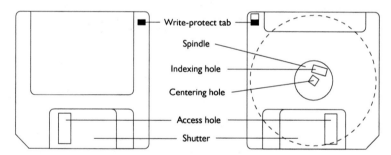

Figure B.7 ◦ A Floppy 3 ½-Inch Disk

B.20 ◦ CD-ROM

Today, a common transport device for software is a *compact disc –read -only memory (CD-ROM)*. Borrowed from the music recording business, this disc can hold up to 600 MB of data and retrieves information by laser. Although originally a read-only device, CD-ROM drives are now readily available that both read from and write to a CD (CD-RWs). CD-ROM drives are common-place, and most software companies are distributing their software via compact disc. The newest technology is *DVD*. It is an enhancement of CD-ROM technology. It provides a new generation of optical-disc storage technology. It encompasses audio, video, and computer data. DVD was designed for multimedia applications with a key goal of being able to store a full-length feature film.

B.21 ◦ Removable Disks

Recently, another type of external storage media has been developed—the removable disk. There are now hard disks that you can remove from a computer, making data portable. There are also other types of removable disk media. Two of the most common are Zip drives and Jaz drives. Zip drives come in two forms: permanent drives that are inside the computer, like a floppy drive, and portable drives that attach to the computer via a USB, serial, or SCSI port and can be moved from computer to computer easily. Zip drives use a diskette that is somewhat like a floppy disk in appearance. It can hold 100 MB of information—equivalent to more than 70 3½-inch floppy disks. Jaz drives use a cartridge rather than a disk. Currently, Jaz cartridges hold up to 2 gigabytes of data. The advent of these new disk types makes large amounts of data portable. Zip and Jaz drives read and write data more slowly than a hard disk. Zip drives in particular are becoming the popular alternative to floppy disks for storing and backing up user data.

B.22 ◦ Hard Disks

A *hard disk*, also known as a fixed disk or a hard drive, is a non-removable disk that is permanently installed in a system unit (see Figure B.8). A hard disk holds much more information than a removable floppy disk. If a floppy disk can be compared to a file cabinet that holds data and programs, a hard disk can be compared to a room full of file cabinets.

Figure B.8 ◦ A Hard Disk

A hard disk is composed of two or more rigid platters, usually made of aluminum and coated with oxide, which allow data to be encoded magnetically. Both the platters and the read/write heads are permanently sealed inside a box; the user cannot touch or see the drive or disks. These platters are affixed to a spindle that rotates at about 3,600 revolutions per minute (rpm), although newer drives rotate at 7200 rpm and even this speed can vary. A hard disk drive is much faster than a standard floppy disk drive. The rapidly spinning disks in the sealed box create air pressure that lifts the recording heads above the surface of the platters. As the platters spin, the read/write heads float on a cushion of air.

Since a hard disk rotates faster than a floppy disk and since the head floats above the surface, the hard disk can store much more data and access it much more quickly than a floppy disk. Today, a common hard disk storage capacity is at least 20 gigabytes.

B.23 ◦ Dividing a Disk

A disk's structure is essentially the same whether it is a hard disk or a floppy disk. Data is recorded on the surface of a disk in a series of numbered concentric circles known as *tracks*, similar to the grooves in a phonograph record. Each track on the disk is a separate circle divided into numbered *sectors*. The amount of data that can be stored on a disk depends on the density of the disk—the number of tracks and the size of the sectors. Since a hard disk is comprised of several platters, it has an additional measurement, a *cylinder*. Two or more platters are stacked on top of one another with the tracks aligned. If you connect any one track through all the platters, you have a cylinder (see Figure B.9).

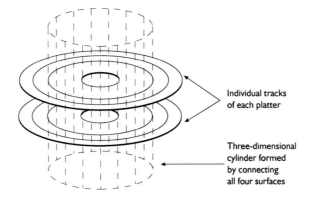

Individual tracks of each platter

Three-dimensional cylinder formed by connecting all four surfaces

Figure B.9 ∘ Hard Disk Cylinders

A *cluster* is the basic unit of disk storage. Whenever a computer reads from or writes to a disk, it always reads from and writes to a cluster, regardless of the space the data needs. Clusters are always made from adjacent sectors, from one to eight sectors or more. The location and number of sectors per cluster are determined by the software in a process known as formatting.

A disk is a random access medium, which does not mean that the data and/or programs are randomly arranged on the disk. It means that the head of the disk drive, which reads the disk, does not have to read all the information on the disk to get a specific item. The CPU instructs the head of the disk drive to go directly to the track and sector that holds the specific item of information.

B.24 ∘ Disk Drives

A *disk drive* allows information to be written to and read from a disk. All disk drives have read/ write heads, which read and write information back and forth between RAM and the disk, much like the ones on tape or video recorders.

A floppy disk drive is the device that holds a floppy disk. The user inserts a floppy disk into a disk drive (see Figure B.10). The hub of the disk fits onto the hub mechanism, which grabs the disk. When the disk drive door is shut, the disk is secured to the hub mechanism. The disk cover remains stationary while the floppy disk rotates. The disk drive head reads and writes information back and forth between RAM and the disk through the exposed head slot. Older disk drives are double-sided and can read from and write to both sides of a disk, but cannot read from or write to a high-density floppy disk. The current generation of high-density disk drives read from and write to both the old style floppy disk and the new style high-density disk.

3½-inch disk drive

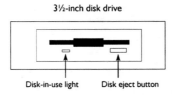

Disk-in-use light   Disk eject button

Figure B.10 ∘ A Floppy Disk Drive

B.25 • Device Names

A *device* is a place (a piece of hardware) for a computer to send information (write to) or a place from which to receive information (read from). In order for the system to know which device it is supposed to be communicating with at any given time, each device is given a specific and unique name. Device names, which are also known as reserved names, cannot be used for any other purpose. Disk drives are devices. A disk drive name is a letter followed by a colon.

Drive A: is the first floppy disk drive. Drive C: is the first hard disk drive. All other drives are lettered alphabetically from B: to Z:. You must be able to identify which disk drive you are using. Today, usually users have one floppy disk (Drive A), one hard drive (Drive C), a removable drive (Drive D), and a CD-ROM or a CD-RW drive (Drive E—although often the CD-ROM drive will have an assigned letter near the end of the alphabet such as R: to allow for the addition of more drives, both hard and removable, or for network drives). Today as well it is also common to have a CD-RW drive in addition to the CD-ROM drive. Some common examples are illustrated in Figure B.11.

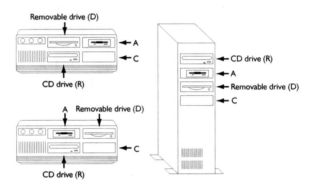

Figure B.11 • Disk Drive Configurations

B.26 • Software

Up to this point, hardware is what has been discussed. However, software is what makes a computer useful. In fact, without software, hardware has no use. You can think of hardware as a box to run software. Software is the step-by-step instructions that tell the computer what to do. These instructions are called programs. Programs need to be installed or loaded into RAM, so that the CPU can execute them. Programs usually come stored on disks. A program is read into memory from a floppy disk, CD-ROM, or hard disk. Software can also be divided into categories. The most common division is application software and system software.

Application software, as its name suggests, is a set of instructions, a complete program, that directs the computer to solve a particular problem. Application software solves problems and handles information. It is a program designed to assist the user in the performance of a specific task, such as word processing, accounting, money management, or even games. Application software may also be called software packages, off-the-shelf software, canned software, or just software. There are thousands of commercially available application packages. You may have heard of application software by brand names such as WordPerfect (word processing), Excel (spreadsheet), Quicken (money management), or Doom (game). The reason most people purchase a computer is the availability of application software.

System software is also a set of instructions or programs. These programs coordinate the operations of all the various hardware components. System software is usually supplied by the computer manufacturer because it is necessary to run application software. System software is always computer-oriented rather than user-oriented; that is, it takes care of what the computer needs so the computer can run application software.

When you purchase a computer, you usually also purchase the operating system with it, preinstalled on the hard disk. The operating system supervises the processing of application programs and all the input/output of the computer. Running a computer is somewhat analogous to producing a concert. The hardware is the musicians and their instruments. They do not change. The application software is like the score the musicians play, anything from Bach to Ricky Martin. The computer hardware can play any application software from an accounting program to a game. Like the conductor who tells the violins or trumpets when to play and how loudly, the operating system makes the computer work. It is the first and most important program on the computer and *must* be loaded into memory (RAM) before any other program.

Typically, operating systems are comprised of several important programs stored as system files. These include a program that transfers data to and from the disk and into and out of memory and that performs other disk-related tasks. Other important programs handle hardware-specific tasks. These programs check such things as whether a key has been pressed and, if it has, they encode it so that the computer can read it and then decode it so that it may be written to the screen. This program also encodes and decodes bits and bytes into letters and words.

The term *operating system* is generic. Brand names for microcomputer operating systems include System 7, Unix, Linux, MS-DOS, and UCSD-P. The most popular operating system for microcomputers has been Windows 98, which Microsoft Corporation developed and owns. It was the upgrade from Windows 95. Windows 98 is licensed to computer manufacturers, who tailor it to their specific hardware. In addition, users purchased Windows 98 commercially either as an upgrade to Windows 95 or as a complete package (if the user has purchased a computer with no operating system on it).

Microsoft also has a version of Windows called Windows NT Server designed for networked computers, with an iteration called Windows NT Workstation as a desktop interface.

In 2000, Microsoft introduced both Windows 2000 and Windows Millennium Edition (Windows Me). Windows Me was designed for the home computer user and was considered an upgrade from Windows 98. Windows 2000 is a family of operating systems that consists of Windows 2000 Server, Windows 2000 Advanced Server, Windows 2000 Datacenter Server, and Windows 2000 Professional. Windows 2000 Server replaces Windows NT 4.0. Incorporating many new features and functions, Windows 2000 Server is powerful, yet easy to manage, and is designed for the small to medium business organization with many computers that need to share data and resources. Windows 2000 Professional replaces Windows NT 4.0 Workstation, incorporating many new features and functions.

These iterations of Windows have been replaced by Windows XP Home Edition and Windows XP Professional. For the corporate network environment, Microsoft has introduced Windows .NET Server. Windows XP Home Edition is typically bundled with computer purchased for home use such as Dell, Compac or Micron PCs. It is intended for the home or a small office where security is not an issue and do not connect to a corporate network. It is compatible with any desktop or notebook computer with a single CPU and a single video display. Windows XP Professional included everything that is in Windows XP Home Edition plus all the networking and security components needed to join a Windows NT/2000/XP domain. Even if you are not a corporate user, you may still prefer to purchase Windows XP Professional for its security and networking capabilities. Also, if you have high-end hardware such as dual processors, you will need Windows XP Professional.

Most people who use a computer are interested in application software. They want programs that are easy to use. If you are going to use a computer and run application packages, you are going to need to know how to use the operating system first. No application program can be used without an operating system.

B.27 ● Operating System Fundamentals

Windows XP Professional is a program that is always working. No computer hardware can work unless it has an operating system in RAM. When you *boot the system*, you load the operating system software into RAM.

Some of the operating system (OS) software is built into the hardware. When you turn on the computer or "power up," the computer would not know what to do if there were no program directing it. The read-only memory chip called ROM-BIOS (read-only memory–basic input/ output system), abbreviated to RIOS, is built into the hardware of the microcomputer system. ROM-BIOS programs provide the interface between the hardware and the operating system.

When you turn on the computer, the power goes first to ROM-BIOS. The first set of instructions is to run a self-test to check the hardware. The program checks RAM and the equipment attached to the computer. Thus, before getting started, the user knows whether or not there is a hardware failure. Once the self-test is completed successfully, the next job or program to execute is loading the operating system.

When the operating system loads, ROM-BIOS checks to see if a disk drive is installed. In today's computers, it is possible to tell the computer where you want it to load the operating system from. It can go first to the A drive to see if there is a disk there. If it finds none, it can then go to the C drive. The OS is looking for a special program called the *boot record*. A computer can also be set up to boot from a CD-ROM or from another peripheral disk drive, such as a Zip or Jaz drive. These drives are attached to the computer by an internal interface card or a parallel port. If ROM-BIOS does not find the boot record in any of the drives it was set to look at or if there is something wrong with the boot record, you will get an error message. If the ROM-BIOS program does find the proper boot record, it reads the record from the disk into RAM and turns control over to this program. The boot record is also a program that executes; its job is to read into RAM the rest of the operating system, in essence, pulling the system up by its bootstraps. Thus, one boots the computer instead of merely turning it on.

The operating system files loaded into RAM manage the resources and primary functions of the computer, freeing application programs from worrying about how the document gets from the keyboard to RAM and from RAM to the screen. This whole process can be considered analogous to driving an automobile. Most of us use our cars to get from point A to point B. We would not like it if every time we wanted to drive we first had to open the hood and attach the proper cables to the battery and to all the other parts that are necessary to start the engine. The operating system is the engine of the computer that lets the user run the application as if driving a car.

B.29 ● Hardware Requirements for
Windows XP Professional Edition

Windows XP Professional is a powerful operating system. Although you can run most of your old programs under Windows XP Professional, you will find yourself buying the new, improved versions of your favorite application programs. These programs will be powerful and large. To run Windows XP Professional, you need at least a Pentium II Processor 233-MHz or faster processor, at least 64 MB of memory, a high-density disk drive, a CD-ROM or DVD drive, and at least a 2-GB hard disk drive with at least 650 MB available. Furthermore, you need a SVGA monitor and SVGA display adapter. You also need a pointing device such as a mouse or trackball. With this hardware, you can run Windows XP Professional and applications written for Windows XP Professional. This configuration is the absolute minimum and is really unrealistic if you want performance from your computer system.

A desirable configuration for Windows XP Professional is listed below:

Processor	Intel Pentium III 600 MHz or better
RAM	256 MB
Hard drive	20 GB with at least 2 GB free
Floppy drive	3½ inch
Removable drive	Zip drive (you may prefer a CD-RW drive instead)
Monitor	SVGA, 19 inch, high resolution, non-interlaced
Graphics	Video card with at least 32 MB of memory
CD	48X CD-ROM or better, DVD if you play many games
CD-RW	24x/10x/40x CD-RW Drive or better
Modem	56K, unless you choose to use a cable or DSL modem
Sound system	Sound card and speakers
Input devices	Keyboard and mouse
Monitor	At least a 15inch LCD or a 17 Inch CRT.

Other features that you might want to use also require other hardware:

* Microphone to record sound files
* TV Tuner card and a TV antenna or cable connection if you want to receive TV stations on your computer
* Digital camera to move graphics to your computer
* Video camera if you want to communicate via conferencing.
* Game controller to play certain video games
* Network Interface Card to set up a home network

In computers, and especially in Windows XP Professional, more is better—a faster processor, more memory, and more disk space. In addition, you must be careful if you are upgrading an existing computer to Windows XP Professional (or Home Edition). You must be sure that all of your computer's hardware components are compatible with Windows XP. This is also true with a new computer, although in general, if the new computer comes with Windows XP, its components should be compatible. However, if the hardware is not compatible with Windows XP, your computer (or certain components such as a video card) will simply not work. To find out if your computer and its components are compatible and it can be upgraded, Microsoft maintains a list called the HCL (Hardware Compatibility List). This list will let you know whether Microsoft has tested the hardware (and/or drivers) and stated whether or not the item in question is compatible with Windows XP. You can check **http://www.microsoft.com/hwtest/hcl, http://www.microsoft.com/hcl**, or **http://www.microsoft.com/windowsxp** for more information.

B.30 ⊛ Networks

Today, it is likely that you will be using a network in a work or lab environment. A *network* is two or more connected computers , and it usually has various peripheral devices such as printers. A network allows users to communicate with each other and to share information and devices.

Special operating system software and hardware are required for networking. Network software permits information exchange among users; the most common uses are electronic mail (email) and the sharing of files. With email, users can send and receive messages within the network system. Sharing files allows users to share information.

There are two kinds of networks. A *local area network (LAN)* encompasses a small area such as one office. The hardware components such as the server, the terminals, and printers are directly connected by cables. (See Figure B.12.) A *wide area network (WAN)* connects computers over a much larger area such as from building to building, state to state, or even worldwide. Hardware components of the WAN communicate over telephone lines, fiber-optic cables, or satellites. The Internet is an example of a WAN.

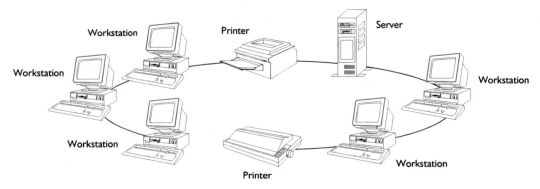

Figure B.12 * A Typical Network Configuration

APPENDIX C

Windows XP Professional at the Command Level

C.1 ● DOS Lives

Since Windows is a graphical user interface (GUI), when you boot your system, you open the desktop with icons, menus, and pictures. You run your programs and open your data files by clicking or double-clicking icons or menu choices. You accomplish a task such as copying a file by opening the Explorer window, selecting a file with your mouse, and dragging it to a different location—a procedure known as drag and drop. These are the reasons why a GUI is so popular. It is "user friendly."

In a character-based operating system (with DOS being the most common), all you see on the screen after you boot is a prompt, such as C:\>—no picture, no icons, no drag and drop. In order to accomplish any task, you need to know what command to use. For instance, to copy a file in DOS (a character-based operating system), you would need to key in **COPY** *THIS.FIL THAT.FIL*. You would need to know the command and how to use it. Hardly as easy as a drag-and-drop operation!

Why then, you may ask yourself, would you ever need to learn the "hard, archaic way" of using your computer when you can easily use the new, improved way? In fact, if you talked to many people, they would say to you, "DOS is dead; long live Windows." They would also say, "You don't need to know DOS anymore because it is all Windows." Those people are only somewhat right. They are correct in saying that DOS as a stand-alone operating system is dead. A new PC comes with Windows as its operating system, not DOS. However, they are wrong in assuming that you do not need to know DOS.

What they do not understand, and you will after completing this appendix, is that what they refer to as DOS is really the command line interface. In fact, the GUI is simply a pretty face on top of the command line interface. Windows is like the gauges on the dashboard of an automobile. When a certain red light goes on, there is trouble under the hood. The red light only alerts you to a problem. Sometimes, you may fix the problem simply by responding to the evidence given. For instance, if you see the red oil light come on, you only need to put oil in your engine. Other times, you must dig deeper to solve the problem. You must go to the engine and run diagnostic tests to identify the problem. Only then can you fix the problem.

The same is true in Windows. Windows, like the red light on the dashboard, will alert you to a problem. Sometimes you can fix it at the GUI level, and other times you must go to the command line interface to run diagnostic software to identify the problem. Once you have identified the problem, you can fix it either by running the problem-solving software you are given with Windows or by making small fixes at the system level using the command line interface.

Microsoft, even though it expects you to use the GUI for your day-to-day computer operations, still knows the importance of a character-based interface—the command line interface. That is why, with Windows 95/98, Windows XP Professional, Windows NT, Windows 2000 Server, and Windows .NET Server, one of the available choices is the command line interface. In Windows 95/98 and Windows Me, it is a menu choice called MS-DOS Prompt. In Windows NT, Windows 2000, and Windows XP Professional, it is simply called Command Prompt. You open what is called a Command Prompt window, but where you really are is right back to a character-based interface, the system level. Rather than calling it the Command Prompt window, most users simply refer to this as running DOS.

Why did Microsoft leave this option available to the user? There are many reasons. If you have any legacy devices (older devices that were designed to run on earlier versions of the operating system) such as older CD-ROM drives, modems, or sound cards, you may need to configure them using the DOS commands in the AUTOEXEC.BAT and CONFIG.SYS files. Furthermore, should your hard disk become infected with a computer virus, you can boot from a DOS boot disk and then run a DOS-based program from the command line interface to remove the computer virus. You will find that there are many tasks that still cannot be accomplished from the GUI. Windows provides utility programs that can only be run at the command line interface to help you solve problems with Windows itself. There are other tasks that, although they can be done from the GUI, are accomplished more easily and faster from the command line, and most users will use the command line in those instances. Also, you will find that even in the Windows environment, there is an assumption that the user knows DOS. For instance, you will find that error messages you receive are couched in DOS terms, such as "Path not found. Please check the location of your program and correct the path." Likewise, you will still find that there are programs, especially if you are involved in developing Web pages, that can only be run from the DOS system level (another way of saying command line interface).

Additionally, if you are a user of the Internet, which primarily runs on Unix-based computers, you often will be at the command line. Although Unix and Linux (other command line interface operating systems) do not use commands identical to DOS commands, they are in fact similar enough that, if you know one system, you can figure out the other. There are also TCP/IP command line utilities that can help you troubleshoot if you cannot, for example, connect to the Internet.

If you work with networks or plan a career in network administration, knowledge of the command line is a necessity. Network operating systems, such as Novell NetWare, rely on the command line interface. Even Windows NT, and Windows 2000 Server, and now Windows

.NET Server, Microsoft's GUI networking operating system, absolutely relies on command line interfaces. Novell, Windows NT, Windows 2000 Server, Windows .NET Server and Windows XP Professional allow you to write batch files to automate many routine tasks, but this can only be accomplished at the command line interface. In fact, Windows NT, Windows 2000 Server, and Windows .NET Server have even more powerful batch file commands available than Windows XP Professional. Almost all networking classes have as a prerequisite a working knowledge of DOS. Remember that the term DOS is used as a shorthand way of saying command line interface.

You will also find that the knowledge you gain by learning the command line interface will help you understand what is going on in the Windows environment. Let's return to the automobile analogy. Most of us are not auto mechanics and do not know how to do engine repair. Nonetheless, if you have an understanding of what is going on under the hood, you may be able to do minor repairs and preventative maintenance so you can avoid more costly, major repairs. At the very least, you will be able to explain problems to professional auto technicians in intelligent terms that will allow them to identify problems more quickly and spend their expensive time fixing, not identifying. In this chapter, you are going to work at the command line prompt (also called the system prompt), and you will learn what's under the hood of Windows. You will acquire the ability to do minor repairs and preventative maintenance as well as to explain complex problems to a software technician.

C.2 ◈ Understanding Commands

Windows operating system (OS) commands are programs, and like application programs, they perform specific tasks. OS commands are of two types: internal and external. When you boot a system, internal commands are automatically loaded and stored into memory (RAM). These internal commands are built into the command processor, CMD.EXE. This file (and, hence, these internal commands) is always placed in memory and remains in RAM the entire time the computer is on.

To use an internal command, you key in the command name at the command line or click its icon. For an internal command, Windows checks memory, finds the program, and executes it. These commands are called internal or resident because they reside in memory, inside the computer (internal). Internal commands are limited in number because they take up valuable space in memory.

External commands are stored as files on a disk. When you wish to use an external command, you call upon the operating system to load the program into RAM by keying in the program's name or clicking its icon. With an external command, Windows cannot find the program internally, so it must go to the disk, locate the file, load it into RAM, and then execute it. If Windows cannot find the file, the program cannot run. These commands are called external or transient commands because they reside in a file on a disk and must be read into RAM each time you key in the command.

You use your operating system, Windows, to load and execute programs such as Word and Quicken. When you click or double-click a program icon or choose a program from a menu, you are using a command. You are not keying in a command name, but the process is the same. For instance, the icon for Word stores the location and name of the program's executable file, such as C:\Program Files\Microsoft Office\Winword.exe. The operating system looks for the file first in memory. When it cannot find it in memory, it goes to the specified location. Windows looks on Drive C, in a folder called Program Files, and in a folder called Microsoft Office for a file called Winword.exe. When it finds it, it loads it, and you have Word available to use. You are letting the

GUI do the work. You could do the work yourself by simply keying in WINWORD at the command prompt. The end result would be the same. Windows would find and load Word for you.

If an icon stored incorrect information, such as an incorrect program location, Windows would give you an error message that it could not load Word because it could not find it. No matter how often you selected the icon, Windows would not execute the program. An icon or menu choice is only a pointer to a program. If you did not understand this process, you would not be able to use Word because you would only see the error message. If you understood the operating system process, you could either correct the pointer or run Word from the command prompt.

Although all program files are external, including all application programs, the term *external command* is actually reserved for the group of programs that perform operating system functions. These programs are files that come with Windows XP Professional and are copied to a subdirectory called C:\WINDOWS\SYSTEM32 on the hard disk when Windows is installed. These files are generically referred to as the command line utility files or system utility files.

In the Command Prompt window, unlike the Windows GUI environment, you have no icons for files. In order to use commands, you must know their file names. The DIR command, an internal command, is provided so that you may look for files on a disk from the command line. In Windows, Explorer is the equivalent of the DIR command. DIR stands for directory. When you key in DIR and press the **Enter** key, you are asking the operating system to run the directory program. The purpose or task of DIR is to display on the screen the names of all the files in a folder or directory on a disk, in other words, the table of contents of the disk. The DIR command is the first DOS internal command you will use.

C.3 • Accessing the Command Line Prompt

In order to use the command line interface, you first need to access it. You must open the Command Prompt window. You may choose to open the Command Prompt window from a menu or from the Start menu's Run command, or you may create a shortcut to it. One thing you must remember is not to turn off the computer when you are in Command Prompt window. You must exit the window and then follow the Windows XP Professional shut-down procedure.

C.4 • Activity • The Command Line Prompt

1   Boot the system.

2   Click **Start**. Point to **Programs**. Point to **Accessories**. Click **Command Prompt**.

WHAT'S **HAPPENING?** You have opened the Command Prompt window, the character-based interface. You may close this window and return to the desktop.

3   Click the X on the right corner of the title bar.

WHAT'S **HAPPENING?** ⋊ You have returned to the desktop. You can also create a shortcut to the command line. (*Note:* If you are in a lab environment, check with your administrator or lab technician to see if there are any special instructions to create shortcuts.)

4   Right-click the desktop. Point to **New**. Click **Shortcut**.

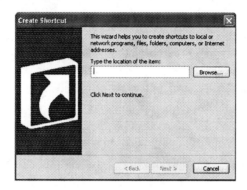

WHAT'S **HAPPENING?** ⋊ You opened the Create Shortcut wizard. A wizard can also be used to create a shortcut to the DOS command line. In order to create a shortcut, you need to know the name and location of the program of interest.

5   In the text box, key in **C:\Windows\System32\cmd.exe**. Click **Next**.

WHAT'S **HAPPENING?** ⋊ You may use any name you wish for your shortcut. However, in this example, Windows XP Professional automatically gives the shortcut the name of the cmd.exe program file.

6   Key in **Command Prompt**. Click **Finish**.

WHAT'S **HAPPENING?** ⋊ You have created a shortcut on the desktop. By double-clicking it, you can go to the command line interface, referred to as Command Prompt.

C.5 ◦ Controlling the Appearance of the Command Prompt Window

Since you are using Windows XP Professional, everything initially appears in a window with a title bar. The command line interface appears in the Command Prompt window. When in this window, you can use the Minimize button, the Maximize button, and the Restore button as you have been doing throughout this textbook.

When you are in the window view, you may alter the size and color of the text in the window; the background color, size, and location of the Command Prompt window, and the size of the cursor. You may also dispense with the window altogether and view the command line in full-screen mode. To toggle (switch) between the window and full-screen modes, you may press the **Alt** + **Enter** keys.

The default values of the Command Prompt window can be modified prior to opening the window or once you are in the window. For example, you can change the window's properties prior to opening the Command Prompt window by right-clicking the Command Prompt shortcut you just created and clicking Properties. You can also right-click the Command Prompt shortcut located on the Start/Programs/Accessories menu and click Properties. You alter the properties while in the Command Prompt window by accessing the Control menu.

C.6 ◦ Activity ◦ Altering the Command Prompt Window

I   Right-click the Command Prompt shortcut on your desktop. Click **Properties**.

WHAT'S HAPPENING? The Command Prompt Properties dialog box appears. Seven tabbed pages contain a variety of properties that you can change. The Shortcut page above shows C:\Windows\System32\cmd.exe as the target file for this shortcut. The Start in text box indicates the C:\Windows\System32 folder is the default directory when you open the program.

2   Press the **Tab** key to move to and highlight the text in the Start in text box. Key in the following:
     C:

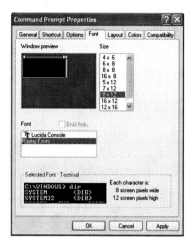

WHAT'S **HAPPENING?** You want the root directory of Drive C to be the default directory when you open the Command Prompt window.

3 Click the **Options** tab.

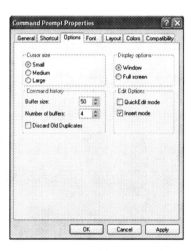

WHAT'S **HAPPENING?** You can change the cursor size, the number of buffers used to store command history, display options, and edit options.

4 Click the **Large** Cursor size option button. Click the **Font** tab.

WHAT'S **HAPPENING?** You may choose a font size. Your choice is either the TrueType Lucinda Console font or Raster Fonts. Typically a raster font is clearer and sharper in a Command Prompt window, which is why it is the default. TrueType fonts are better for use in applications such as Word and Excel.

5 Click the **Layout** tab.

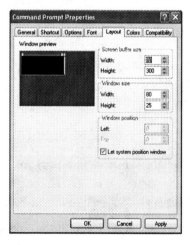

WHAT'S **HAPPENING?** You can specify the number of characters stored in a line in a buffer (Screen buffer size), and the window's size and position onscreen.

6 Click the **Colors** tab.

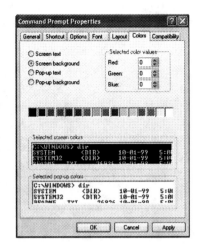

WHAT'S HAPPENING? The four option buttons and the color bar allow you to quickly select colors for the screen text, the screen background, the pop-up text (in pop-up windows), and the background in pop-up windows.

7   The **Screen Background** option button should be selected. Click the color black.

8   Click the **Screen Text** option button. Click the color white.

9   Click **Apply**. Click **OK.**

10   Double-click the Command Prompt shortcut.

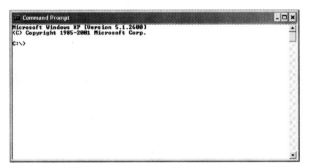

WHAT'S HAPPENING? The Command Prompt window appears onscreen displaying the property changes you just made. The default directory is the root of Drive C (C:\), and the large rectangular flashing cursor is easily visible. The background color is white and the text is black.

11   Click the Control menu button in the upper-left corner of the title bar. Click **Properties**. You can also access this menu by right-clicking the title bar.

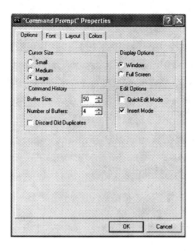

WHAT'S HAPPENING? The four pages containing options to change the window's properties are available while you are in the window. However, the General, Shortcut, and Compatibility pages are not available.

12   Click the **Small** Cursor Size option button. Click **OK**.

WHAT'S HAPPENING? You have a choice of applying the changes only to the current window or of modifying the shortcut that started this window.

13   Click the **Modify shortcut that started this window** option button. Click **OK**.

14   Press the Alt + Enter keys.

WHAT'S HAPPENING? Now DOS is no longer in a window and is in full-screen mode. Toggling back and forth between the two views is easy—press the Alt + Enter keys.

15   Press the Alt + Enter keys.

16   Key in the following: C : \ >**EXIT** Enter

WHAT'S HAPPENING? You have closed the Command Prompt window and returned to the desktop.

C.7 • Command Syntax

Using DOS commands is very different from using Windows XP Professional. Windows XP Professional is a graphical user interface; DOS is a character-based operating system. You must know the *command syntax* of DOS in order to be able to use it. All languages have rules or conventions for the characters used in writing. *Syntax*, or the order of a language, is important. For example, in a statement in English the noun (the person, place, or thing) is followed by the verb (the action). In another language, however, the syntax or order might be different; first comes the verb, then the noun.

Computers also communicate with languages. You must speak a computer's language and follow its command syntax exactly because the computer has a limited understanding of language. You cannot key in any word and expect the computer to understand. You can only key in words that the computer recognizes. Windows XP Professional hides the details of the commands and instead presents you with icons and menus. When you are using DOS or the Run command on the Start menu, you are not assisted in this way. You must use the computer's vocabulary with the proper syntax. The computer cannot guess what you mean. For example, if I said, "Going I store," people would probably understand. However, if I keyed in an incorrect word or put correct words in the wrong order, the computer would respond with the message "Bad command or file name." This statement would be the computer equivalent of "I do not understand."

In a computer language, a command can be compared with a verb, the action you wish to take. In Windows XP Professional, you use Windows Explorer or My Computer to list the files on your disk. In DOS, you use the command DIR to list your files. You must key in DIR at the command prompt. In doing so, you are asking DOS to run the program called DIR, which lets you see the table of contents or the directory of a disk.

C.8 • Parameters

In Windows XP Professional, to list your files alphabetically by name, you open Windows Explorer and then choose View/Arrange Icons by/Name from the menu. With DOS commands, you can do the same thing, but you need to know the parameters. A *parameter* is information that you want a command to have. Some commands require parameters, while other commands let you add them only when you need to.

Some parameters are variable. A *variable parameter* is one to which you supply the value. This process is similar to a math formula. For instance, x + y = z is a simple formula. You can plug in whatever values you wish for x, y, and z. If x = 1 and y = 2, you know z = 3. These values are variable; x can equal 5 and y can equal 3, which makes z equal to 8. These variables can have any numerical value you wish. You can also have z = 10 and x = 5, and mathematically establish the value of y. No matter what x, y, and z equal, you can establish the value of each. Other parameters are *fixed parameters*. For instance, if a formula reads x + 5 = z, then x is a variable parameter and 5 is a fixed parameter. You can change the value of x but not the value of 5.

When you are working with some DOS commands, you can add one or more qualifiers or modifiers to the command to make it more specific. These qualifiers are the parameters. This process is the same in English. If I give my son my credit card and tell him, "Go buy," I have given him an open-ended statement—he can buy anything (making him one happy guy). However, if I add a qualifier, "Go buy shoes," I have limited what he can do. Limiting is precisely what parameters do to a command.

C.9 • Reading a Syntax Diagram

DOS is like a foreign language. How do you know what the commands are, what the syntax is, and what the parameters are? The syntax information is provided through online help. You access it by entering the name of the command followed by /?.

A *syntax diagram* tells you how to enter a command with its optional or mandatory parameters. However, you need to be able to interpret syntax diagrams. They can also be found in other software applications. As a matter of fact, if you get into the nuts and bolts of Windows XP Professional, you will find that it, also, has commands with syntax diagrams that can be run from Start/Run.

An example of a DOS command is DIR. When you key in DIR, you get a list of files. If you key in DIR /?, you will see a syntax diagram. Here is a brief example of a formal command syntax diagram:

```
DIR [drive:][path][file name] [/P] [/W]
```

The first entry is the command name. You may only use DIR. You cannot substitute another word, such as DIRECTORY or INDEX. Then you have items that follow the command. In this case, everything is in brackets (except DIR), indicating that these parameters (the items in brackets) are optional. Whenever you see brackets, you can choose whether or not to include those parameters; they are the *optional parameters*.

C.10 ● Using Fixed Parameters with the DIR Command

As the previous syntax diagram showed, DIR is one of the commands with optional parameters. Two of the optional parameters are fixed. They allow you to control the way the operating system displays the table of contents for the disk: /W for wide display and /P for pause display. In the DIR command syntax diagram, the /W and the /P are in brackets. You never key in the brackets, only / (forward slash or slash), also known as a *switch*, and W or P. You must be careful to use the forward slash (/). The \ is a backslash and is always referred to as such. The word *slash* by itself always refers to the forward slash.

When you key in DIR, the list of files scrolls by so quickly that you cannot read it. There is an efficient way to solve this problem—using the /P parameter. The /P parameter will display one screen of information at a time. It will also give you a prompt to which you must respond before it will display another screenful of information.

C.11 ● Activity ● Using DIR

Note: You may choose to be in a Command Prompt window or go to full screen.

1　Double-click the Command Prompt shortcut icon on the desktop. Click the Maximize button or press ⎡Alt⎤ + ⎡Enter⎤ if you want to be in full-screen mode.

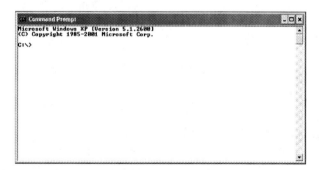

WHAT'S HAPPENING? ⯈ If you look at the screen, you may see C:\WINDOWS\SYSTEM32> instead of C:\>, with a blinking cursor following it and the color selection may be a black background with white text. If you did not use the shortcut to the Command Prompt, you will probably be at C:\Windows\SYSTEM32. In this example, you are looking at C:\>, known as the *prompt* because it is prompting you to do something. Being in a character-based operating system does not mean that the rules of an operating system have changed. You are on a default drive (C) in a default directory (the root of Drive C). If you want to see the files in this directory, you need to issue a command. You must key in information and press ⎡Enter⎤. There is nothing to click. The screen displays that follow will be in full screen mode. You may work in the Command Prompt window if you wish. The only difference is that in full screen mode, you do not see the title bar nor do you have menu choices.

2   Key in the following: C:\>**CD** [Enter]

3   Key in the following: C:\>**DIR** [Enter]

```
Command Prompt                                                    _ □ ✕

C:\>DIR
 Volume in drive C has no label.
 Volume Serial Number is 3C92-007C

 Directory of C:\

03/22/2002  10:57 AM                      0 AUTOEXEC.BAT
03/22/2002  10:57 AM                      0 CONFIG.SYS
05/02/2002  11:08 AM    <DIR>               Documents and Settings
03/29/2002  12:44 PM    <DIR>               Download
05/02/2002  09:43 AM    <DIR>               Program Files
05/17/2002  09:07 AM    <DIR>               WINDOWS
04/03/2002  10:50 AM    <DIR>               XPRODATA
                 2 File(s)              0 bytes
                 5 Dir(s)   34,875,613,184 bytes free

C:\>
```

WHAT'S HAPPENING? You are looking at the files and folders (directories) in the default directory. Your display will be different because you will have different files and folders on your computer.

4   Key in the following: C:\>**DIR /X** [Enter]

```
Command Prompt                                                    _ □ ✕

C:\>DIR /X
 Volume in drive C has no label.
 Volume Serial Number is 3C92-007C

 Directory of C:\

03/22/2002  10:57 AM               0              AUTOEXEC.BAT
03/22/2002  10:57 AM               0              CONFIG.SYS
05/02/2002  11:08 AM    <DIR>      DOCUME~1       Documents and Settings
03/29/2002  12:44 PM    <DIR>                     Download
05/02/2002  09:43 AM    <DIR>      PROGRA~1       Program Files
05/17/2002  09:07 AM    <DIR>                     WINDOWS
04/03/2002  10:50 AM    <DIR>                     XPRODATA
                 2 File(s)            0 bytes
                 5 Dir(s)   34,875,592,704 bytes free

C:\>
```

WHAT'S HAPPENING? As you remember, in Windows XP Professional, all files receive a DOS file name that follows rigid rules—there should be a file name of no more than eight characters, followed by a period, followed by a file extension (file type) with no more than three characters. There must be no spaces in the file name. If you have a file with a long file name, the long file name is in the column on the far right and the short DOS name is to the left of it. Remember, when Windows XP Professional creates a DOS file name, the long file name is truncated.

In this example, the long file name Program Files, which refers to a directory, has the DOS alias of PROGRA ˜ 1. Essentially, Windows XP Professional truncates the file name to the first six characters. It uses designations like ˜ 1 to indicate similar files. The numbers increase so that each file has a unique name. Thus, if you had a file called WINDOWS Help32.BMK and a file called

WINDOWS Sysfile.BMK, the DOS file names would be WINDOW ~ 2.BMK and
WINDOW ~ 3.BMK. As you can see, DOS file names can be exceedingly cryptic. See Figure C.1
for a description of the parts of the screen.

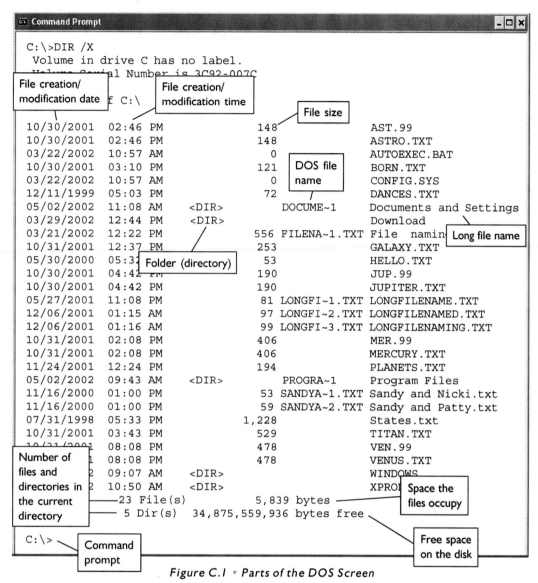

Figure C.1 ⬦ Parts of the DOS Screen

5   Key in the following: C : \ >**DIR /W** `Enter`

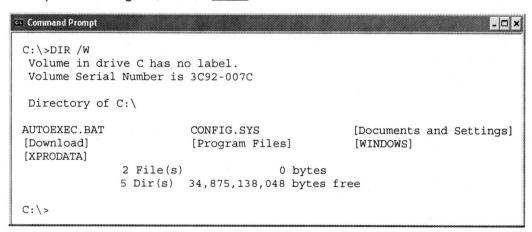

WHAT'S **HAPPENING?** By using the /W parameter, you have displayed only the folder and file names. Another useful parameter is /P. The /P parameter stops the screen display from scrolling.

6   Key in the following: C:\>**DIR/?** Enter

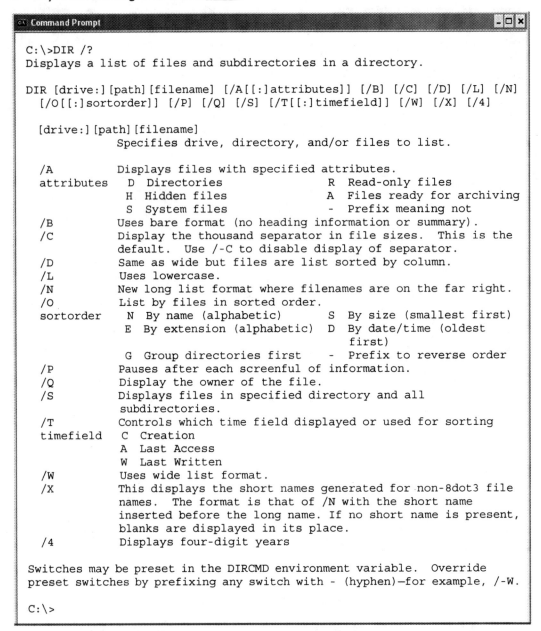

```
C:\>DIR /?
Displays a list of files and subdirectories in a directory.

DIR [drive:] [path] [filename] [/A[[:]attributes]] [/B] [/C] [/D] [/L] [/N]
  [/O[[:]sortorder]] [/P] [/Q] [/S] [/T[[:]timefield]] [/W] [/X] [/4]

  [drive:] [path] [filename]
                Specifies drive, directory, and/or files to list.

  /A          Displays files with specified attributes.
  attributes  D  Directories              R  Read-only files
              H  Hidden files             A  Files ready for archiving
              S  System files             -  Prefix meaning not
  /B          Uses bare format (no heading information or summary).
  /C          Display the thousand separator in file sizes.  This is the
              default.  Use /-C to disable display of separator.
  /D          Same as wide but files are list sorted by column.
  /L          Uses lowercase.
  /N          New long list format where filenames are on the far right.
  /O          List by files in sorted order.
  sortorder   N  By name (alphabetic)     S  By size (smallest first)
              E  By extension (alphabetic) D  By date/time (oldest
                                              first)
              G  Group directories first  -  Prefix to reverse order
  /P          Pauses after each screenful of information.
  /Q          Display the owner of the file.
  /S          Displays files in specified directory and all
              subdirectories.
  /T          Controls which time field displayed or used for sorting
  timefield   C  Creation
              A  Last Access
              W  Last Written
  /W          Uses wide list format.
  /X          This displays the short names generated for non-8dot3 file
              names.  The format is that of /N with the short name
              inserted before the long name. If no short name is present,
              blanks are displayed in its place.
  /4          Displays four-digit years

Switches may be preset in the DIRCMD environment variable.  Override
preset switches by prefixing any switch with - (hyphen)—for example, /-W.

C:\>
```

WHAT'S **HAPPENING?** This is an example of DOS online help. It is neither as user friendly nor as helpful as Windows online help. However, it does provide a syntax diagram along with list of available parameters for the DIR command. A brief explanation appears next to each parameter.

7   Place the MYDATADISK disk in Drive A. Key in the following: C:\>**DIR A:/X** Enter

```
C:\>DIR A:/X
 Volume in drive A is MYDATADISK
 Volume Serial Number is 2CF2-7020
```

```
    Directory of A:\

04/22/2002  06:02 PM    <DIR>                       LEVEL-1
04/22/2002  06:27 PM    <DIR>                       DATA2
04/23/2002  09:15 AM    <DIR>                       MEDIA
04/23/2002  09:15 AM    <DIR>                       SPORTS
04/23/2002  10:48 PM    <DIR>                       GAMES
04/23/2002  10:58 PM    <DIR>          ASTRON~1     ASTRONOMY
04/23/2002  11:08 PM    <DIR>                       BIZ
04/24/2002  10:04 PM    <DIR>                       PEOPLE
07/31/1999  12:53 PM                46              STEVEN.FIL
05/04/2002  11:07 AM            16,384              ASTRO.bkf
               2 File(s)        16,430 bytes
               8 Dir(s)        855,040 bytes free

C:\>
```

WHAT'S HAPPENING? The default drive and directory is still the root of C (C:\>), but you are looking at the files and folders on Drive A. Your directory list may differ slightly from the one shown above, depending on the work you completed in previous chapters. If you want to look inside a folder, you must key in the path name.

8   Key in the following: C : \ >**DIR A:\ASTRON ~ I** [Enter]

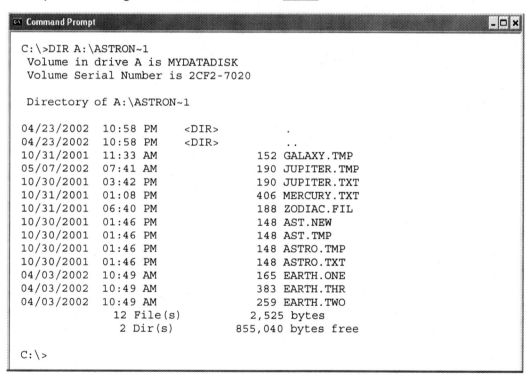

```
C:\>DIR A:\ASTRON~1
 Volume in drive A is MYDATADISK
 Volume Serial Number is 2CF2-7020

 Directory of A:\ASTRON~1

04/23/2002  10:58 PM    <DIR>              .
04/23/2002  10:58 PM    <DIR>              ..
10/31/2001  11:33 AM              152 GALAXY.TMP
05/07/2002  07:41 AM              190 JUPITER.TMP
10/30/2001  03:42 PM              190 JUPITER.TXT
10/31/2001  01:08 PM              406 MERCURY.TXT
10/31/2001  06:40 PM              188 ZODIAC.FIL
10/30/2001  01:46 PM              148 AST.NEW
10/30/2001  01:46 PM              148 AST.TMP
10/30/2001  01:46 PM              148 ASTRO.TMP
10/30/2001  01:46 PM              148 ASTRO.TXT
04/03/2002  10:49 AM              165 EARTH.ONE
04/03/2002  10:49 AM              383 EARTH.THR
04/03/2002  10:49 AM              259 EARTH.TWO
              12 File(s)        2,525 bytes
               2 Dir(s)       855,040 bytes free

C:\>
```

WHAT'S HAPPENING? You substituted A:\ASTRON ~ 1 for [*drive*:][*path*] in the syntax diagram. This directory has a long file name. The long file name is ASTRONOMY.

9   Key in the following: C : \ >**DIR A:\ASTRONOMY** [Enter]

```
C:\>DIR A:\ASTRONOMY
 Volume in drive A is MYDATADISK
 Volume Serial Number is 2CF2-7020
```

```
Directory of A:\ASTRONOMY

04/23/2002  10:58 PM    <DIR>          .
04/23/2002  10:58 PM    <DIR>          ..
10/31/2001  11:33 AM              152 GALAXY.TMP
05/07/2002  07:41 AM              190 JUPITER.TMP
10/30/2001  03:42 PM              190 JUPITER.TXT
10/31/2001  01:08 PM              406 MERCURY.TXT
10/31/2001  06:40 PM              188 ZODIAC.FIL
10/30/2001  01:46 PM              148 AST.NEW
10/30/2001  01:46 PM              148 AST.TMP
10/30/2001  01:46 PM              148 ASTRO.TMP
10/30/2001  01:46 PM              148 ASTRO.TXT
04/03/2002  10:49 AM              165 EARTH.ONE
04/03/2002  10:49 AM              383 EARTH.THR
04/03/2002  10:49 AM              259 EARTH.TWO
              12 File(s)          2,525 bytes
               2 Dir(s)       855,040 bytes free

C:\>
```

WHAT'S **HAPPENING?** You can use the long file name, provided that it does not have spaces. If it has spaces, you must enclose the name with double quotation marks. If you want to change default drives, you key in the drive letter followed by a colon.

10 Key in the following: C:\>**A:** Enter

WHAT'S **HAPPENING?** Now Drive A is the default drive and its root directory is the default directory. You can tell this by looking at the command prompt (A:\>). If you wanted to look in the directory ASTRONOMY, you would not have to include the drive letter since you are already in Drive A. DOS will always assume the default drive and directory unless you specify otherwise.

11 Key in the following: A:\>**C:** Enter

WHAT'S **HAPPENING?** You have returned to the root of C. You may also change directories. The command is **CD** [*path*].

Note: Remember, if XPRODATA is on a drive other than C: you will need to include the drive letter.

12 Key in the following: C:\>**CD \XPRODATA\LEVEL-1\LEVEL-2\LEVEL-3** Enter

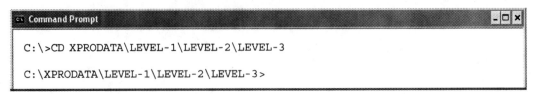

WHAT'S **HAPPENING?** You changed the default directory to LEVEL-3, which is under LEVEL-2, which is under LEVEL-1, which is under XPRODATA, which is under the root of C.

13 Key in the following: `C:\XPRODATA\LEVEL-1\LEVEL-2\LEVEL-3>`**A:** Enter

```
C:\XPRODATA\LEVEL-1\LEVEL-2\LEVEL-3>A:

A:\>
```

WHAT'S **HAPPENING?** You have changed drives so that the default drive is the root of A.

14 Key in the following: `A:\>`**C:** Enter

```
A:\>C:

C:\XPRODATA\LEVEL-1\LEVEL-2\LEVEL-3>
```

WHAT'S **HAPPENING?** DOS remembers the last directory you were in before you changed drives. If you want to move down the directory tree, you must key in the entire path name. However, if you want to move up the tree, you may take a shortcut. If you key in **CD ..** you will move up one level.

15 Key in the following: `C:\XPRODATA\LEVEL-1\LEVEL-2\LEVEL-3>`**CD ..** Enter

```
C:\XPRODATA\LEVEL-1\LEVEL-2\LEVEL-3>CD ..

C:\XPRODATA\LEVEL-1\LEVEL-2>
```

WHAT'S **HAPPENING?** You have moved up one level and the default directory is now XPRODATA\Level-1\Level-2.

16 Key in the following: `C:\XPRODATA\LEVEL-1\LEVEL-2>`**EXIT** Enter

WHAT'S **HAPPENING?** The command prompt window (DOS) is a program. You must exit it to return to Windows XP Professional desktop.

C.12 • Global File Specifications and Wildcards

Using the DIR command and a file specification, you can find one specific file that matches what you key in. Every time you wish to locate a file, you can key in the entire file specification. Often, however, you wish to work with a group of files that have similar names or a group of files whose names you do not know. DOS has a shorthand system that allows you to operate on a group of files rather than a single file. This system is formally called *global file specifications;* informally, it is called using wildcards. These are the same wildcards that can be used in Windows XP Professional when using Search. Conceptually, wildcards come from card games where the joker can stand for any card of your choice. In DOS, the question mark (?) and the asterisk (*) are the wildcards. These symbols stand for unknowns. The * represents or substitutes a group of characters; the ? represents or substitutes a single character. Many commands allow you to use global file specifications. You will use the DIR command to explore the use of wildcards.

C.13 ● Activity ● DIR and Wildcards

1   Open the Command Prompt window.

2   Key in the following: C : \ >**CD \XPRODATA** Enter

```
Command Prompt                                                    _ □ ×

C:\>CD XPRODATA

C:\XPRODATA>
```

WHAT'S **HAPPENING?** You are at the command line interface. You made the default directory C:\XPRODATA.

3   Key in the following: C : \XPRODATA>**DIR *.TXT** Enter

```
Command Prompt                                                    _ □ ×

C:\XPRODATA>DIR *.TXT
 Volume in drive C has no label.
 Volume Serial Number is 3C92-007C

 Directory of C:\XPRODATA

10/30/2001  02:46 PM               148 ASTRO.TXT
10/30/2001  03:10 PM               121 BORN.TXT
12/11/1999  05:03 PM                72 DANCES.TXT
03/21/2002  12:22 PM               556 File  naming rules.txt
10/31/2001  12:37 PM               253 GALAXY.TXT
05/30/2000  05:32 PM                53 HELLO.TXT
10/30/2001  04:42 PM               190 JUPITER.TXT
05/27/2001  11:08 PM                81 LONGFILENAME.TXT
12/06/2001  01:15 AM                97 LONGFILENAMED.TXT
12/06/2001  01:16 AM                99 LONGFILENAMING.TXT
10/31/2001  02:08 PM               406 MERCURY.TXT
11/24/2001  12:24 PM               194 PLANETS.TXT
11/16/2000  01:00 PM                53 Sandy and Nicki.txt
11/16/2000  01:00 PM                59 Sandy and Patty.txt
07/31/1998  05:33 PM             1,228 States.txt
10/31/2001  03:43 PM               529 TITAN.TXT
10/31/2001  08:08 PM               478 VENUS.TXT
              17 File(s)          4,617 bytes
               0 Dir(s)  34,873,389,056 bytes free

C:\XPRODATA>
```

WHAT'S **HAPPENING?** You asked DOS what files have an extension of .TXT and are located in the XPRODATA directory. You did not know anything about the file names, only the file extension. The DIR command searched the table of contents of C:\XPRODATA. Since you did not include a drive or a path, the command assumed the default drive and directory. The command found 17 files that matched *.TXT. Now, how does the question mark differ from the asterisk?

4   Key in the following: C : \XPRODATA>**DIR ?????.TXT** Enter

```
Command Prompt                                                    _ □ ×

C:\XPRODATA>DIR ?????.TXT
 Volume in drive C has no label.
 Volume Serial Number is 3C92-007C
```

```
     Directory of C:\XPRODATA

10/30/2001  02:46 PM              148 ASTRO.TXT
10/30/2001  03:10 PM              121 BORN.TXT
05/30/2000  05:32 PM               53 HELLO.TXT
10/31/2001  03:43 PM              529 TITAN.TXT
10/31/2001  08:08 PM              478 VENUS.TXT
               5 File(s)         1,329 bytes
               0 Dir(s)  34,873,389,056 bytes free

C:\XPRODATA>
```

WHAT'S HAPPENING? This time you asked your question differently. You still asked for files that had the file extension of .TXT in the XPRODATA directory. However, you used ? five times. The DIR command responds to these by looking for file names that start with any letter and are no more than five characters in length. The ????? represented five characters. This time, only five files matched your request. Note how the above screen display differs from the screen display in step 3. This time you do not see any file name longer than five characters. Although the ? is helpful in specific cases, the * is used more often. In fact, ????????.??? is the same as *.*.

5   Key in the following: C:\XPRODATA>**DIR EXP*.*** Enter

```
⌨ Command Prompt                                                    _ □ ✕

C:\XPRODATA>DIR EXP*.*
 Volume in drive C has no label.
 Volume Serial Number is 3C92-007C

 Directory of C:\XPRODATA

04/03/2002  10:50 AM           13,824 EXP01FEB.xls
04/03/2002  10:50 AM           13,824 EXP01JAN.xls
04/03/2002  10:50 AM           13,824 EXP01MAR.xls
04/03/2002  10:50 AM           13,824 EXP02FEB.xls
04/03/2002  10:50 AM           13,824 EXP02JAN.xls
04/03/2002  10:50 AM           13,824 EXP02MAR.xls
04/03/2002  10:50 AM           13,824 EXP03FEB.xls
04/03/2002  10:50 AM           13,824 EXP03JAN.xls
04/03/2002  10:50 AM           13,824 EXP03MAR.xls
               9 File(s)        124,416 bytes
               0 Dir(s)  34,873,389,056 bytes free

C:\XPRODATA>
```

WHAT'S HAPPENING? You asked the DIR command to show you all the files located in the XPRODATA directory that start with the letters EXP. The *.* following the EXP represents the rest of the file name and the file extension. Some budget files appeared. The letters EXP mean expenses, followed by the year (01,02, or 03) and the month (JANuary, FEBruary, or MARch). The file extension is .XLS, meaning data is in these files; they are not program files. Since these files have the XLS file extension, they were created with Excel. You may not be interested in all the files. In this case, you want to know what expense files you have in your directory for 2001.

6   Key in the following: C:\XPRODATA>**DIR EXP01*.*** Enter

```
⌨ Command Prompt                                                    _ □ ✕

C:\XPRODATA>DIR EXP01*.*
 Volume in drive C has no label.
 Volume Serial Number is 3C92-007C
```

```
 Directory of C:\XPRODATA

04/03/2002  10:50 AM             13,824 EXP01FEB.xls
04/03/2002  10:50 AM             13,824 EXP01JAN.xls
04/03/2002  10:50 AM             13,824 EXP01MAR.xls
              3 File(s)          41,472 bytes
              0 Dir(s)  34,873,389,056 bytes free

C:\XPRODATA>
```

WHAT'S HAPPENING? You asked for all the files (DIR) in the XPRODATA folder that were expense files for 2001. The rest of the information in the file names was represented by `*.*`. On your screen, you got the 2001 files. Suppose you are interested in all the files with data about January. You include JAN in the file name to indicate the kind of data in the files. You no longer care about the year, only the month.

7   Key in the following: C:\XPRODATA>**DIR EXP*JAN.*** [Enter]

```
C:\XPRODATA>DIR EXP*JAN.*
 Volume in drive C has no label.
 Volume Serial Number is 3C92-007C

 Directory of C:\XPRODATA

04/03/2002  10:50 AM             13,824 EXP01JAN.xls
04/03/2002  10:50 AM             13,824 EXP02JAN.xls
04/03/2002  10:50 AM             13,824 EXP03JAN.xls
              3 File(s)          41,472 bytes
              0 Dir(s)  34,873,356,288 bytes free

C:\XPRODATA>
```

WHAT'S HAPPENING? You asked for file names that specifically start with EXP and end with JAN. The middle characters, represented by the first *, could be any number of characters between EXP and JAN. The second * acts as a place holder. You could use the question mark and key in the command as **DIR EXP??JAN.***. That request would be asking for files with only two characters between EXP and JAN.

8   Key in the following: C:\XPRODATA>**CD ** [Enter]

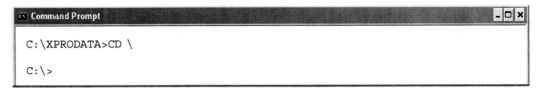

```
C:\XPRODATA>CD \

C:\>
```

WHAT'S HAPPENING? You returned to the root directory of C.

9   Key in the following: C:\>**EXIT** [Enter]

WHAT'S HAPPENING? You are back at the Windows XP Professional desktop.

C.14 ● Creating Directories and Copying, Renaming, and Deleting Files

In Windows XP Professional, although you can copy and rename files and folders in Windows Explorer or in My Computer, there are certain limitations. For instance, when you copy a file, you cannot give it a new name. If you are in the same folder, the default file name is *Copy of the-original's-file-name*. You must copy the file and then rename it, which is a two-step process. If you want to copy a group of files and give them new names, you cannot do it in one step. Although you can easily copy a group of files, the files keep the same names. You must rename each file individually. You also cannot give a whole group of files new names in Windows XP Professional.

For instance, if you were in Windows XP Professional and wished to copy a group of files with the extension .TXT to a floppy disk for archival purposes, but wanted to give them the extension .OLD, you could select the files, click Send To, and choose Drive A. On the floppy disk, the files would all have the extension .TXT. You would have to change each file individually from .txt to .old. When you have tasks like this to perform, it is easier to do them at the Command Prompt.

With the COPY command, you retain the original file and make a copy. You start with one file and end with two. If you do not give a new name to the copy, the COPY command will assume the default and keep the old file name. With the REN command, you start with one file and end up with the same file under a new name. The rename command, REN, does not let you specify a new drive or path. Remember, you are not making a copy of a file, but using the same file. The file does not move in the process of renaming. You use the DEL command to delete files. If a file is an ASCII file (text file), you may display its contents with the TYPE command.

You may also create directories at the command line. The syntax is:

```
MD [drive:][path]
```

The COPY syntax in DOS is:

```
COPY [drive:][path]file name [drive:][path]file name
```

or conceptually:

```
COPY source destination
```

The REN command has a similar syntax:

```
REN [drive:][path]file name1 file name2
```

The syntax for the DEL command is:

```
DEL [drive:][path]file name
```

The syntax for the TYPE command is:

```
TYPE [drive:][path]file name
```

C.15 ● Activity ● Using COPY, REN, and DEL

Note: You may use either upper- or lowercase letters when you key in your commands and file names. In the examples, what you key in will be in uppercase.

1   Open the Command Prompt window.

2   Key in the following: C:\>**A:** Enter

3   Key in the following: A:\>**MD APXC** Enter

4   Key in the following: A:\>**DIR APXC** Enter

```
Command Prompt                                                    _ □ ✕

C:\>A:

A:\>MD APXC

A:\>DIR APXC
 Volume in drive A is MYDATADISK
 Volume Serial Number is 2CF2-7020

 Directory of A:\APXC

05/17/2002  05:10 PM    <DIR>          .
05/17/2002  05:10 PM    <DIR>          ..
              0 File(s)              0 bytes
              2 Dir(s)         854,528 bytes free

A:\>
```

WHAT'S HAPPENING? You accomplished several things. You first changed the default drive to A. You then created a directory called APXC and then you looked to see what was inside the directory (DIR APXC). Now you are going to copy some files to that directory.

5   Key in the following: A:\>**COPY C:\XPRODATA*.TXT APXC** Enter

```
Command Prompt                                                    _ □ ✕

A:\>COPY C:\XPRODATA\*.TXT APXC
C:\XPRODATA\ASTRO.TXT
C:\XPRODATA\BORN.TXT
C:\XPRODATA\DANCES.TXT
C:\XPRODATA\File naming rules.txt
C:\XPRODATA\GALAXY.TXT
C:\XPRODATA\HELLO.TXT
C:\XPRODATA\JUPITER.TXT
C:\XPRODATA\LONGFILENAME.TXT
C:\XPRODATA\LONGFILENAMED.TXT
C:\XPRODATA\LONGFILENAMING.TXT
C:\XPRODATA\MERCURY.TXT
C:\XPRODATA\PLANETS.TXT
C:\XPRODATA\Sandy and Nicki.txt
C:\XPRODATA\Sandy and Patty.txt
C:\XPRODATA\States.txt
C:\XPRODATA\TITAN.TXT
C:\XPRODATA\VENUS.TXT
       17 file(s) copied.

A:\>
```

WHAT'S HAPPENING? You used a wildcard to copy all the files that had any file name but had the .TXT extension. As each file was copied, the name was displayed. You asked to copy (COPY) all the files that had .TXT as an extension from the XPRODATA folder on Drive C (C:\XPRODATA*.TXT) to the APXC folder (APXC) on Drive A. You did not need to specify A:\ since your default was the root of A. You knew that by the prompt (A:\>). You did have to specify the directory (APXC); otherwise the files would have been copied to the default drive and directory, the root of A. Since you did not specify any destination file names, the default was to keep the same file names.

6   Key in the following: A:\>**DIR APXC** Enter

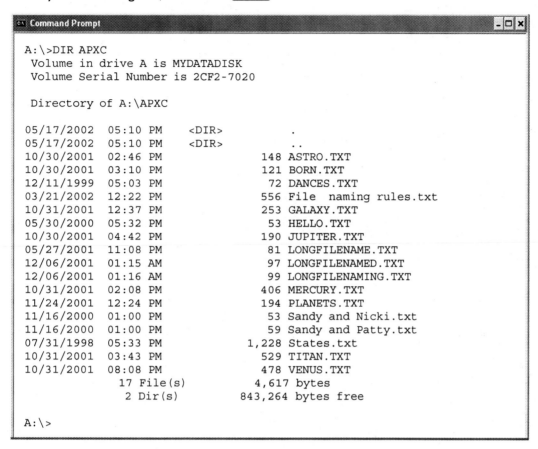

```
A:\>DIR APXC
 Volume in drive A is MYDATADISK
 Volume Serial Number is 2CF2-7020

 Directory of A:\APXC

05/17/2002  05:10 PM    <DIR>          .
05/17/2002  05:10 PM    <DIR>          ..
10/30/2001  02:46 PM               148 ASTRO.TXT
10/30/2001  03:10 PM               121 BORN.TXT
12/11/1999  05:03 PM                72 DANCES.TXT
03/21/2002  12:22 PM               556 File  naming rules.txt
10/31/2001  12:37 PM               253 GALAXY.TXT
05/30/2000  05:32 PM                53 HELLO.TXT
10/30/2001  04:42 PM               190 JUPITER.TXT
05/27/2001  11:08 PM                81 LONGFILENAME.TXT
12/06/2001  01:15 AM                97 LONGFILENAMED.TXT
12/06/2001  01:16 AM                99 LONGFILENAMING.TXT
10/31/2001  02:08 PM               406 MERCURY.TXT
11/24/2001  12:24 PM               194 PLANETS.TXT
11/16/2000  01:00 PM                53 Sandy and Nicki.txt
11/16/2000  01:00 PM                59 Sandy and Patty.txt
07/31/1998  05:33 PM             1,228 States.txt
10/31/2001  03:43 PM               529 TITAN.TXT
10/31/2001  08:08 PM               478 VENUS.TXT
              17 File(s)          4,617 bytes
               2 Dir(s)         843,264 bytes free

A:\>
```

WHAT'S **HAPPENING?** All the files that you copied are in the APXC folder with the same file names.

7   Key in the following: A:\>**CD APXC** Enter

```
A:\>CD APXC

A:\APXC>
```

WHAT'S **HAPPENING?** You made APXC the default directory. When you issued the command, you could have keyed in CD A:\APXC. That command uses the absolute path. The *absolute path* is the entire path name. Instead, you used the relative path name, APXC. The *relative path* is the path that is "relative" to where you are. Since the default was the root of A (A:\), you only needed to key in APXC because it was relative to where you were. Using an absolute path is like giving someone directions from Los Angeles to New York. If the person were in Los Angeles, you could give them detailed instructions on how to get to New York (absolute). However, if the person were already in St. Louis, you would give them directions relative to the fact that they were already in St. Louis; they would not need to return to Los Angeles to go to New York. It would not be incorrect to give them absolute directions (from Los Angeles to New York), but it would be unnecessary (they are already in St. Louis).

8   Key in the following: A:\APXC>**COPY HELLO.TXT HELLO.TXT** [Enter]

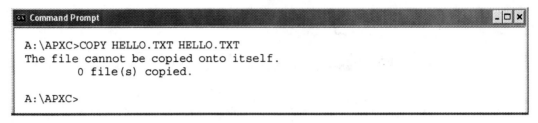

```
A:\APXC>COPY HELLO.TXT HELLO.TXT
The file cannot be copied onto itself.
        0 file(s) copied.

A:\APXC>
```

WHAT'S HAPPENING? A file name must be unique in a directory on a drive. You may copy the file, but you must give it a new name.

9   Key in the following: A:\APXC>**COPY HELLO.TXT HI.FIL** [Enter]

10   Key in the following: A:\APXC>**TYPE HELLO.TXT** [Enter]

11   Key in the following: A:\APXC>**TYPE HI.FIL** [Enter]

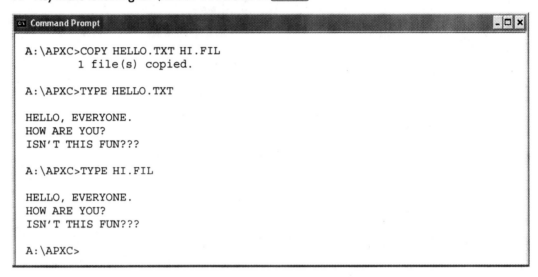

```
A:\APXC>COPY HELLO.TXT HI.FIL
        1 file(s) copied.

A:\APXC>TYPE HELLO.TXT

HELLO, EVERYONE.
HOW ARE YOU?
ISN'T THIS FUN???

A:\APXC>TYPE HI.FIL

HELLO, EVERYONE.
HOW ARE YOU?
ISN'T THIS FUN???

A:\APXC>
```

WHAT'S HAPPENING? You issued several commands. First you copied the file HELLO.TXT to a new file called HI.TXT in the APXC folder. Then, using the TYPE command, you displayed the contents of each text file. As you see, even though the names are different, the contents are the same.

12   Key in the following: A:\APXC>**COPY SANDY AND NICKI.TXT SANDY.TXT** [Enter]

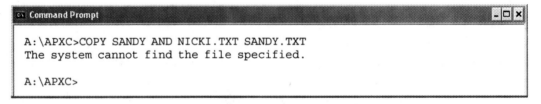

```
A:\APXC>COPY SANDY AND NICKI.TXT SANDY.TXT
The system cannot find the file specified.

A:\APXC>
```

WHAT'S HAPPENING? When you are at the command line, spaces are a problem. The file SANDY AND NICKI.TXT is a long file name with spaces in it. The COPY command read each space as a delimiter. A delimiter is a special character that sets off, or separates, individual items in a set of data. There are different delimiters, such as the period that separates a file name from a file extension or the / that is used to indicate a switch. You may use spaces, but you must use quotation marks around the file name so that the command line can treat everything within the quotation marks as one unit. However, in general, avoid using spaces in file names. If you feel you must separate items in a file name, use a hyphen or underscore.

13 Key in the following: A:\APXC>**COPY "SANDY AND NICKI.TXT" SANDY.FIL** Enter

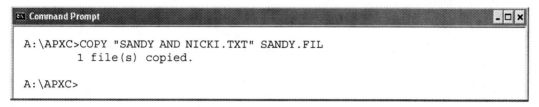

```
A:\APXC>COPY "SANDY AND NICKI.TXT" SANDY.FIL
        1 file(s) copied.

A:\APXC>
```

WHAT'S **HAPPENING?** The use of quotation marks allowed you to use a long file name with spaces at the command line. Renaming files is just as easy. If you only need to rename one file, it is just as easy to do it in Windows XP Professional GUI. However, if you want to rename a group of files, there is no way to do this in Windows XP Professional GUI. In this situation the command line interface becomes very handy.

14 Key in the following: A:\APXC>**COPY C:\XPRODATA*.99** Enter

15 Key in the following: A:\APXC>**DIR *.99** Enter

16 Key in the following: A:\APXC>**REN *.99 *.OLD** Enter

17 Key in the following: A:\APXC>**DIR *.99** Enter

18 Key in the following: A:\APXC>**DIR *.OLD** Enter

```
A:\APXC>COPY C:\XPRODATA\*.99
C:\XPRODATA\AST.99
C:\XPRODATA\JUP.99
C:\XPRODATA\MER.99
C:\XPRODATA\VEN.99
        4 file(s) copied.

A:\APXC>DIR *.99
 Volume in drive A is MYDATADISK
 Volume Serial Number is 2CF2-7020

 Directory of A:\APXC

10/30/2001  02:46 PM                148 AST.99
10/30/2001  04:42 PM                190 JUP.99
10/31/2001  02:08 PM                406 MER.99
10/31/2001  08:08 PM                478 VEN.99
               4 File(s)          1,222 bytes
               0 Dir(s)         839,680 bytes free

A:\APXC>REN *.99 *.OLD

A:\APXC>DIR *.99
 Volume in drive A is MYDATADISK
 Volume Serial Number is 2CF2-7020

 Directory of A:\APXC

File Not Found

A:\APXC>DIR *.OLD
 Volume in drive A is MYDATADISK
 Volume Serial Number is 2CF2-7020
```

```
Directory of A:\APXC

10/30/2001  02:46 PM                148 AST.OLD
10/30/2001  04:42 PM                190 JUP.OLD
10/31/2001  02:08 PM                406 MER.OLD
10/31/2001  08:08 PM                478 VEN.OLD
               4 File(s)          1,222 bytes
               0 Dir(s)       839,680 bytes free

A:\APXC>
```

WHAT'S HAPPENING? You copied the .99 files from the C:\XPRODATA directory. You then saw that they were in the APXC directory. You then renamed all the files with the .99 file extension to the same file names, but gave them a new extension of .OLD. You then used the DIR command to see that there are no more files with the .99 file extension, only those with the .OLD file extension. You can also delete files easily.

19 Key in the following: A:\APXC>**DEL *.OLD** Enter

20 Key in the following: A:\APXC>**DIR *.OLD** Enter

```
█▓ Command Prompt                                          _ □ x

A:\APXC>DEL *.OLD

A:\APXC>DIR *.OLD
 Volume in drive A is MYDATADISK
 Volume Serial Number is 2CF2-7020

 Directory of A:\APXC

File Not Found

A:\APXC>
```

WHAT'S HAPPENING? You have deleted any file that had the .OLD extension. These files were deleted without going to the Recycle Bin. They are gone and irretrievable—good if you are certain you want to delete the files, bad if you accidentally deleted the wrong files. When you delete files at the command line, they are removed.

21 Key in the following: A:\APXC>**CD ** Enter

22 Key in the following: A:\>**EXIT** Enter

WHAT'S HAPPENING? You moved to the root directory of A and then closed the command line window and returned to the desktop.

C.16 ● Windows Explorer Parameters

Windows Explorer is also a command that can be executed either in the Command Prompt window or by using Run from the Start menu. Its syntax is:

```
EXPLORER.EXE [/N],[/E],[options],[folder]
```

The parameters have the following meanings:

- /N will open a new copy of Windows Explorer.
- /E will expand a folder to display its contents

When you use [options], you may use either of the following:

* /ROOT selects a folder as the root of a folder tree
* /SELECT highlights a folder's parent and displays the parent's contents

The [*folder*] can be any folder name or path, such as C:\XPRODATA or C:\Windows. The commas are required between the switches. These parameters allow you to customize where and how Windows Explorer will display a window. You can also create shortcuts that will reflect an often-used Windows Explorer view.

C.17 • Activity • Using Windows Explorer Parameters

Note: If Run does not appear when you click the Start button, then right-click the taskbar. Click Properties. Click the Start Menu tab. Click Start Menu. Click Customize. Click the Advanced tab. In the Start Menu items list box, scroll until you locate Run. Click to set it. Click OK. Click OK.

1 Click **Start**. Click **Run**. Clear the command line text box. Then key in the following:
Explorer /n,/e,/root,C:\XPRODATA

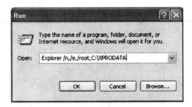

WHAT'S **HAPPENING?** You are asking to open Windows Explorer with C:\XPRODATA as the default directory in Explorer window. The commas are required. To ensure the correct path, you could have also keyed in the absolute path: **C:\Windows\Explorer.exe /n,/e,/root,C:\XPRODATA**

2 Click **OK**.

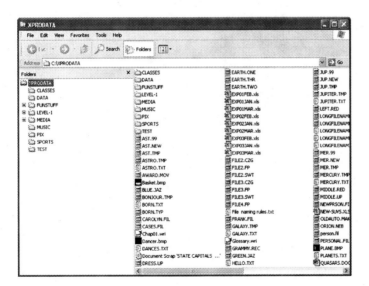

WHAT'S **HAPPENING?** As you can see, your Windows Explorer window opened and not only made the XPRODATA folder the default folder but also expanded the XPRODATA folder. The view will vary depending on what view you last left it in.

3 Close Windows Explorer.

4   Click **Start**. Click **Run**. Clear the command line text box, then key in the following: **Explorer /n,/e,/select, C:\XPRODATA\level-1\level-2** Enter

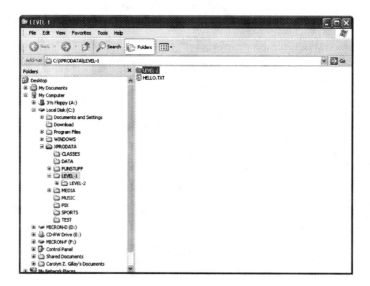

WHAT'S **HAPPENING?** Now Windows Explorer opened Level-1, with the Level-2 folder high-lighted in the contents pane. You can use this feature to your advantage. For instance, you have a folder that you would like to access quickly at any time. You can create a shortcut to that folder and place it on the Start menu.

5   Close Windows Explorer.

6   Right-click the desktop. Point to **New**. Click **Shortcut**.

WHAT'S **HAPPENING?** You opened the Create Shortcut dialog box. It requires a command line.

7   In the text box, key in the following: **Explorer /n,/e,/root,C:\XPRODATA**

8   Click **Next**.

9   In the Select name for the shortcut text box, key in the following: **XPRODATA Folder**

10   Click **Finish**.

WHAT'S **HAPPENING?** You now have a shortcut to the XPRODATA folder on the desktop.

11   Drag the shortcut to the XPRODATA folder to the Start menu button and drop it.

12 Click the Start menu.

WHAT'S HAPPENING? ⊳ You have a shortcut to the XPRODATA folder on the Start menu.

13 Open WordPad. Maximize it.

14 Click the Start menu. Click **XPRODATA Folder**.

WHAT'S HAPPENING? ⊳ You now can open the XPRODATA folder from wherever you are. You can change the view to whatever you prefer.

15 Close Windows Explorer. Restore WordPad. Close WordPad.

16 Remove the XPRODATA Folder shortcut from the desktop and from the Start menu. (*Hint:* Right-click **XPRODATA** on the Start menu. Click **Remove from the taskbar**. Click **Properties**. Click the **Advanced** tab. Click **Remove from This List**.)

WHAT'S HAPPENING? ⊳ You have returned to the desktop.

C.18 ● TCP/IP Utilities ● Using the Command Line Interface with the Internet

Although you will normally use a browser such as Netscape Navigator or Internet Explorer to surf the Net, Windows provides a series of commands, also called utility programs, that run at the command line interface. These commands are a set of tools that can help you troubleshoot problems as well as offer you connections to computers not connected to the Web, such as Unix system computers. These utilities are automatically installed when the TCP/IP network protocol is installed. These tools are:

Command	Purpose
Arp	Displays and modifies the IP to Ethernet translation tables.
Hostname	Displays the host name portion of the full computer name of the computer.
Ipconfig	Displays the IP address and other configuration information (Windows XP Professional only).
FTP	Transfers files to and from a node running FTP services.
lpq	Displays the status of a print queue on a computer running Line Printer Daemon (LPD).
lpr	Sends a file to a computer running Line Printer Daemon (LPD) in preparation for printing.
Nbtstat	Displays protocol statistics and current TCP/IP connections using NetBIOS over TCP/IP.
Netstat	Displays protocol statistics and current TCP/IP connections.
Nslookup	Displays information that you can use to diagnose Domain Name System (DNS) infrastructure.
Ping	Verifies connections to a remote host or hosts.
Rexec	Runs commands on remote computers running the Rexec service (daemon).
Route	Manually controls network-routing tables.
Rsh	Runs commands on remote computers running the RSH service or daemon. Windows XP and Windows 2000 do not provide an RSH service.
Telnet	Starts terminal emulation with a remote system running a Telnet service. Windows XP Professional provides a graphical version of this utility, as well as the MS-DOS-based service.
Tracert	Determines the route taken to a destination.

Table C.1 ● Internet Utilities

If you want help on any of these commands, at the command line key in the command name, a space, and then -?, such as **ping -?**. In the next activities, you will look at some of these utilities.

C.19 ● Ping

If you are using your browser and cannot connect to a site, ping is an easy diagnostic tool for checking to see if the computer you are trying to reach is up and running. You can use ping (Packet InterNet Groper) to check out your connection to your service provider or to another computer. Ping sends out a request to see if a computer at an address you specify is there. It affirms whether that computer is up and running. You can ping either the IP address or the host name of the computer you are trying to reach. Ping sends four packets of data to the specified computer. If your ping is successful, you see four replies on the screen display. If any of the packets did not successfully reach their destination or were returned to your computer, you will see a "Request timed out" message. If the IP address is verified but the host name is not, there is some kind of name resolution problem. You can also ping yourself using the special loopback address (127.0.0.1). A loopback allows you to test network functions without having a network card successfully installed. However, you should be aware that pings are not always reliable. Some Internet sites do not allow their hosts to be pinged, because the servers would then be wasting their time responding to pings. Not responding to pings is a means of providing security as well.

C.20 ● Activity ● Using Ping

1   If necessary, log onto the Internet.

2   Click **Start**. Point to **All Programs**. Point to **Accessories**. Click **Command Prompt**.

3   In the Command Prompt window, key in the following:
     C:\>**PING WWW.FBEEDLE.COM** Enter

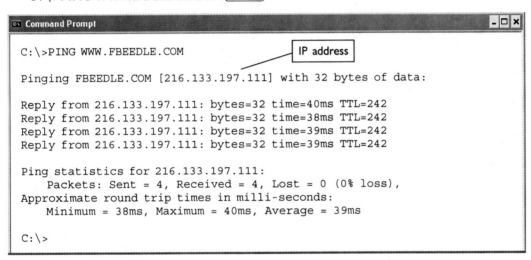

```
Command Prompt                                                  _ □ ×

C:\>PING WWW.FBEEDLE.COM                          IP address

Pinging FBEEDLE.COM [216.133.197.111] with 32 bytes of data:

Reply from 216.133.197.111: bytes=32 time=40ms TTL=242
Reply from 216.133.197.111: bytes=32 time=38ms TTL=242
Reply from 216.133.197.111: bytes=32 time=39ms TTL=242
Reply from 216.133.197.111: bytes=32 time=39ms TTL=242

Ping statistics for 216.133.197.111:
    Packets: Sent = 4, Received = 4, Lost = 0 (0% loss),
Approximate round trip times in milli-seconds:
    Minimum = 38ms, Maximum = 40ms, Average = 39ms

C:\>
```

WHAT'S **HAPPENING?** You have successfully pinged the publisher of this book. Note the IP address - 216.133.197.111. It may not be the same as the example so be sure and use what IP address appears on your screen.

4   Key in the following: C:\>**PING 216.133.197.111** Enter

```
Command Prompt                                                  _ □ ×

C:\>PING 216.133.197.111

Pinging 216.133.197.111 with 32 bytes of data:

Reply from 216.133.197.111: bytes=32 time=46ms TTL=242
Reply from 216.133.197.111: bytes=32 time=40ms TTL=242
Reply from 216.133.197.111: bytes=32 time=46ms TTL=242
Reply from 216.133.197.111: bytes=32 time=39ms TTL=242
```

```
Ping statistics for 216.133.197.111:
    Packets: Sent = 4, Received = 4, Lost = 0 (0% loss),
Approximate round trip times in milli-seconds:
    Minimum = 39ms, Maximum = 46ms, Average = 42ms

C:\>
```

WHAT'S **HAPPENING?** You have pinged both the IP address and the host name. You now know this site is up and running.

5   Key in the following: C:\>**PING 127.0.0.1** [Enter]

```
Command Prompt                                                      _ □ ×

C:\>PING 127.0.0.1

Pinging 127.0.0.1 with 32 bytes of data:

Reply from 127.0.0.1: bytes=32 time<1ms TTL=128
Reply from 127.0.0.1: bytes=32 time<1ms TTL=128
Reply from 127.0.0.1: bytes=32 time<1ms TTL=128
Reply from 127.0.0.1: bytes=32 time<1ms TTL=128

Ping statistics for 127.0.0.1:
    Packets: Sent = 4, Received = 4, Lost = 0 (0% loss),
Approximate round trip times in milli-seconds:
    Minimum = 0ms, Maximum = 0ms, Average = 0ms

C:\>
```

WHAT'S **HAPPENING?** You have just pinged yourself. Remember that 127.0.0.1 is the loopback address and is the IP address of your computer.

6   Close the Command Prompt window.

GLOSSARY

absolute path   The direct route from the root directory through the hierarchical structure of a directory tree to the subdirectory of interest.

active desktop object   A piece of Web content placed on the desktop that needs to be updated on a regular basis, such as stock market prices or a weather map.

active window   The window that is currently in use when multiple windows are open.

ActiveX   A set of technologies that enables software components to interact with one another in a networked environment, regardless of the language in which the components were created. ActiveX is used primarily to develop interactive content for the World Wide Web, although it can be used in other kinds of programs.

adapter card   A printed circuit board that is installed in a computer to allow the installation and control of some type of device, such as a monitor.

adapter segment   The area between the end of conventional memory and the beginning of extended memory. See also *upper memory area*.

add-on   An accessory or utility program designed to work with, extend, and increase the capabilities of an original product.

allocation unit   See *cluster*.

alphanumeric keys   The keys on a keyboard that are letters (A–Z), numbers (0–9), and other characters such as punctuation marks.

ANSI   An acronym for American National Standards Institute. A coding scheme used for transmitting data between a computer and peripherals. Each character has a numerical equivalent in ANSI.

app   See *application package*.

application package   A computer program that is user-oriented and is usually for a specific job, such as word processing. Application packages are also called *packages, off-the-shelf software, canned software,* or *apps*.

application program   See *application package*.

application software   See *application package*.

application window   The window of the application that is currently open and on the desktop. An application window may also contain a document window.

archival backup   A backup procedure in which all the files on a hard disk are backed up by being copied to floppy disks or some other backup medium.

archival data   Information that is stored in archive files.

archive attribute   See *archive bit*.

archive bit   A file attribute that gives the backup history of a file (whether or not a file has been backed up). Archiving to save a file usually refers to long-term storage.

archiving a file   Removing a file from a hard disk and storing it on another medium for historical purposes.

arithmetic/logic unit   The circuitry that a computer uses for mathematical and logical functions and is an integral part of a microprocessor chip.

ASCII   An acronym for American Standard Code for Information Interchange. A coding scheme used for transmitting data between a computer and peripherals. Each character has a numerical equivalent in ASCII.

ASCII editor   A program that is similar to a word-processing program but is unable to perform any special editing. No embedded codes are inserted into documents. ASCII editors can only edit ASCII text files, also called text files or unformatted text files. ASCII editors are also called *text editors*.

asynchronous   Not synchronized; not happening at regular time intervals.

asynchronous communication   A form of data transmission that uses only two wires for communication between computers (generally for communicating via modems). Data is transmitted by the sending of one character at a time with variable time intervals between characters and a start bit and a stop bit to mark the beginning and end of the data.

attachment   An external document included as part of an email message.

AUTOEXEC.BAT   A batch file (a set of specific commands) that automatically executes every time the system is booted. Although it is not necessary in Windows 98, if there is an autoexec.bat file Windows will follow the instructions in it.

automatic link   In object linking and embedding, this feature will update a linked object automatically whenever the original file is modified.

AutoPlay   The feature that causes an audio CD placed in a CD-ROM drive to play automatically. To bypass this, hold the Shift key down when inserting the disc.

AutoRun   The feature that causes a program CD placed in a CD-ROM drive to execute automatically. To bypass this, hold the Shift key down when inserting the disc.

background color   The color that is in the background in Paint. It is not the current drawing color.

background printing   Printing a document in the background while another program is being worked on in the foreground.

background program   In Windows 98, which has multitasking capabilities, background program refers to a program that is being executed in the background at the same time that the user is working with another program in the foreground. For example, printing one document (background program) while at the same time editing another document (foreground program).

backup   The process in which the user makes a copy of an original file or files for safekeeping.

bandwidth The data transfer capacity of a digital communications system.

bank switching Method of expanding an operating system's memory by switching rapidly between two banks of memory chips.

batch file A text file of DOS commands. When its name is keyed in at the DOS system level, the commands in the batch file are executed sequentially.

batch processing A manner of running programs without interruption. Programs to be executed are collected and placed into prioritized batches, and then the programs are processed one after another without user interaction or intervention.

baud rate Measure of how fast a modem can transmit data. Named after the French telegrapher and engineer J.M.E. Baudot.

beta test A formal process of pretesting hardware and software that is still under development with selected "typical" users to see whether any operational or utilization errors (bugs) still exist in the program before the product is released to the general public.

binary value A binary value is a variable-length set of hexadecimal digits.

BIOS An acronym for basic input/output system. A program that controls input/output devices.

BIOS bootstrap A process that occurs before booting. The program that controls this process is in the BIOS chip and the CMOS setup of the computer. A POST (power-on self test) is performed, wherein the computer checks its physical health. Plug-and-play devices are identified and configured, and a bootable partition is executed.

bit The smallest unit of information, expressed in binary numbers 0 and 1, that a computer can measure. Eight bits make a byte.

bitmap font A font that a printer creates dot by dot. When displayed on the monitor, bitmap fonts are created pixel by pixel.

bootable disk A disk containing the operating system files.

booting the system The process of powering on a computer. When first turned on (a cold boot) or reset (a warm boot), a computer executes the software that loads and starts the computer's operating system. The computer can be said to pull itself up by its own bootstrap.

boot record If a disk is a system disk, the boot record contains the bootstrap routine used for loading. Otherwise, the disk will present a message that the disk is a nonsystem disk. Every disk has a boot record. The boot record also contains such information as the type of media, the number of tracks and sectors, and so forth.

boot sector The first sector on every logical drive.

boot sector virus A virus that replaces a disk's original boot sector with its own and then loads itself into memory. Once in memory, it infects other disks.

bootstrap The process a computer uses to get itself ready for loading the operating system into memory. It pulls itself up by its bootstraps.

browser An application software package that allows you to easily explore the Internet and the World Wide Web.

buffer A temporary holding area for data in memory.

bug An error in software that causes the program to malfunction or to produce incorrect results.

built-in font A resident font that comes with a printer.

bulletin board service (BBS)   A service that users link to using their modems. Some BBSs allow users to read and post messages, download program fixes or other programs, and much more.

bundled   Describes programs included with a larger program to make the larger program more attractive or functional. It is also used to describe a purchase of hardware that includes all devices as well as installed software.

bus   A set of hardware lines (wires) that are used for data transfer among the elements of a computer system.

bus topology   A topology (network design) for a local area network in which all computers or peripherals (nodes) are connected to a main communications line (bus). On a bus network, each node monitors activity on the line.

byte   A unit of measurement that represents one character (a letter, number, or punctuation mark). A byte is comprised of eight bits. Computer storage and memory are measured in bytes.

cache   A place in memory where data can be stored for quick access.

cache memory   A place in memory where data can be stored for quick access.

caching   A process where Windows sets up a reserved area in RAM where it can quickly read and write frequently used data without having to read from or write to the disk.

card   A short name for an adapter card.

cascaded   Windows layered on top of one another.

cascading menu   A menu that opens another menu. A secondary menu will open as a result of a command issued on the first or primary menu. A right-pointing arrow next to the primary menu indicates that a cascade menu is available. Also called a hierarchical menu.

case sensitive   Describes a program that distinguishes between upper- and lowercase characters.

CD-ROM   An acronym for compact disc–read-only memory. It usually refers to a disc that plays in a CD-ROM device.

central processing unit (CPU)   The central processing unit (CPU) is the brain of the computer. It carries out the instructions or commands given to it by a program.

chain   When referring to the file allocation table, a pointer that links clusters together.

channel   A Web site that has been expressly designed for push technology so that content can be delivered to your computer system.

character set   A grouping of alphabetic, numeric, and other characters that have some relationship in common. A font file has character definitions.

character string   A set of letters, symbols, and control characters that are treated as a unit.

checkbox   A box that is clicked to either set or unset a feature.

child directory   An analogous title given to offshoots (subdirectories) of any root or subdirectory.

child menu   A menu in a hierarchical menu structure that is under the parent menu above it. Each subsequent child menu becomes a parent to the next menu in the hierarchy.

child window   A window that belongs to a parent window. A child window can have only one parent but one or more child windows of its own.

clean boot   A booting process that bypasses the CONFIG.SYS and AUTOEXEC.BAT files.

clicking   Pressing and releasing the left mouse button once.

client   In networking, a client is a computer that accesses the shared network resources provided by the server.

client application   An application program that is receiving an object from the server application.

clip art   A collection of proprietary or public-domain photographs, maps, drawings, and other graphics that can be "clipped" from the collection and incorporated into other documents.

Clipboard   A special memory area used by Windows that stores a copy of the last information that was copied or cut. A paste operation passes data from the Clipboard to the current program. The Clipboard allows information to be transferred from one program to another, provided the second program can read data generated by the first.

Close button   A button that shuts down a window and closes an application package or dialog box.

cluster   The smallest unit of disk space that DOS or Windows 95/98 can write to or read from. It is comprised of one or more sectors. A cluster can also be called an *allocation unit*.

cluster overhang   Since clusters are made up of one or more 512-byte sectors and Windows 95/98 reads to or writes from only one cluster at a time, a file will occupy more space than it needs for its data, causing cluster overhang.

CMOS   An acronym for complementary metal-oxide semiconductor. CMOS, maintained by a battery pack, is memory that is used to store parameter values, such as the size and type of the hard disk and the number and type of floppy drives, the keyboard, and display type, that are used to boot PCs.

coaxial cable   A type of cable used in connecting network components.

cold link   See *manual link*.

Color box   In Paint, the box that displays the foreground and background colors you may use in your drawing.

combo box   A combination text box and list box.

command   An instruction that is a program that the user keys in at the command line prompt. This instruction executes the selected program.

command button   A button that, when selected by the user, performs the desired action.

COMMAND.COM   That part of the operating system that the user actually communicates and interacts with. It processes and interprets what has been keyed in. It is also known as the command processor or the command interpreter.

command interpreter   See *command processor*.

command processor   That portion of an operating system that interprets what the user keys in.

command syntax   The vocabulary, order, and punctuation necessary to execute a command properly.

communication protocol   A set of communication rules that enable computers to exchange information.

compact disc–read-only memory   See *CD-ROM*.

Component Object Model (COM)   A specification developed by Microsoft for building software components that can be assembled into programs or add functionality to existing programs running on Microsoft Windows platforms. COM is the foundation for OLE and ActiveX.

compound document   A document that contains information, data, or other objects created from more than one application program.

compressed file   A file written (utilizing a file compression utility) to a special disk format that minimizes the storage space needed.

compressed volume file (CVF)   A single file that contains all the compressed data for a drive compressed by DriveSpace.

computer virus   A computer program designed as a prank or sabotage that can replicate itself by attaching to other programs and spreading unwanted and often damaging operations. A virus can be spread to other computers by floppy disk and/or through electronic bulletin boards.

conditional processing   A comparison of two items that yields a true or false value. Once the value is determined, a program can be directed to take some action based on the results of the test.

configuration information   Information about your system such as the hardware applications and user preferences.

container   In object linking and embedding, the receiving document keeps the information about where the object came from. The receiving document is the container.

container application   In object linking and embedding, the program used to contain or receive data from the server application. It is also called the client application.

container object   Also called a nested object, is an object that can contain other objects.

context menu   A menu that opens with a right-click of the mouse. It is also referred to as a pop-up menu or a shortcut menu.

contiguous   Describes elements that are next to each other. Contiguous files are those files that are written to adjacent clusters on a disk.

control   Provides a way the user can interact (provide input) with available choices. Usually a control is a way to initiate an action, display information, or set the values that you are interested in. Example of controls include command buttons, options buttons, drop-down list boxes, and text boxes.

Control key   The key labeled **Ctrl** on the keyboard that, when held down with another key, causes the other key to have another meaning.

controller   A board that goes into the computer and is needed to operate a peripheral device.

control menu   Has an icon, located in the upper-left corner of a window, that can be opened to provide commands to manipulate the window. These commands are usually keyboard oriented rather than mouse oriented. The icon is referred to as the control-menu icon.

control-menu icon   In Windows, the icon that can be clicked to provide a drop-down menu with additional commands. It is also called the control-menu box.

conventional memory   The first 640KB of memory, where programs and data are located while the user is working.

cookie   On the World Wide Web, a block of data that a Web server stores on your computer system. When you return to the same Web site, your browser sends a copy of the cookie back to the server. Cookies are used to identify users, instruct the server to send a customized version of the requested Web page, or submit account information for the user.

CPU   See *central processing unit (CPU)*.

cross application dragging and dropping In OLE, when selecting an object, dragging it out of the server application and dropping it into a client document.

cross-linked files Two files that claim the same sectors in the file allocation table (FAT).

current directory The default directory.

cursor The location where the user can key in information.

cutout When using Paint, an area selected with a selection tool.

cyberspace A term used when referring to the Internet; a virtual place where computers can connect and individuals or organizations can communicate.

cylinder The vertical measurement of two or more disk platters that have the track aligned. It is used when referring to hard disks.

data Information, in the widest possible sense. Usually it refers to the numbers and text used by a computer to do the work requested by the user.

database A collection of related information (data) stored on a computer, organized, and structured so that the information can be easily manipulated.

database management program An application program that allows for manipulation of information in a database.

data bits A group of bits used to represent a single character for transmission over a modem. A start bit and stop bit must be used in transmitting a group of data.

data file A file that is usually composed of related data created by the user with an application program. They are organized in a specific manner and usually can be used only by this program.

debugging Finding and correcting problems in a program. Debug is also a program usable at the command line interface.

dedicated server A computer in a server-based network that is devoted to providing network resources.

default What the computer system or computer program "falls back to" if no other specific instructions are given.

default drive The disk drive that the OS looks on to locate commands or files if no other instructions are given.

default folder The folder data will be read to or written from unless you change it.

default subdirectory The subdirectory that the computer "falls back to" when no other specific instructions are given.

defragger A means to optimize performance on a disk. Running the Disk Defragmenter program rearranges the storage of files on a disk so that they are contiguous.

delimiter A special character that is used to separate information so that an operating system such as Windows 98 can recognize where one part of a parameter ends and the next one begins.

designated drive See *default drive*.

desktop The on-screen work area that emulates the top of a desk.

destination document In OLE, a document or program in which an object is embedded or linked.

destination file The desired file that data is to be sent to.

device A piece of computer equipment, such as a disk drive or a printer, that performs a specific job.

device driver   Software necessary for the use of a hardware device. The program controls the specific peripheral device.

device icon   A small graphic that represents a device such as a printer or a disk drive.

device-independent bitmap (DIB)   A format that eliminates some but not all of the device specificity by including information about the color palette and resolution of the originating device. The intent of the DIB format is that no matter what video mode you are using, you can display the file.

device name   A reserved name that the operating system assigns to a device, such as PRN for printer.

dialog box   In a graphical user interface, a box that either conveys information to or requests information from the user.

differential backup   A differential backup backs up all the selected files that have changed since the last time an All selected files backup was used.

directional keys   Keys used to move the cursor in various directions.

directory   The location or container where documents, program files, devices, and other folders are stored on your disk. The terms *folders* and *directories* are synonymous.

directory tree   The structure of the current disk drive.

disk   A magnetically coated disk that allows permanent storage of computer data.

disk buffer   Acts as the go-between for a disk and RAM.

disk cache   An area in memory where Windows 98 looks for information prior to reading from or writing to the disk for the purpose of optimizing performance.

disk compression program   A means to increase disk space by fooling the operating system into thinking that there is more space on the disk.

disk drive   A device that rotates a disk so that the computer can read information from and write information to the disk.

disk file   A file that is stored on a disk.

disk optimization program   A means to optimize performance on a disk. Usually the user runs the Disk Defragmenter program that rearranges the storage of files on a disk so that they are contiguous. It is also called a *disk defragger*.

docucentric   Describes a paradigm or model that designs a computer system or program around the fact that what is most important to the user is the data (the document), not the program that created it.

document   A self-contained piece of work created with an application program and, if saved on a disk, given a unique file name by which it can be retrieved.

documentation   Written instructions that inform the user how to use hardware and/or software.

document file   A data file whose information was created in an application file and saved to a disk.

documenting   Writing the purpose of and instructions for a computer program.

document window   A window that belongs to a program window and is always contained within a program window.

domain name   An alphabetic alias to the IP address. Some examples of domain names are saddleback.cc.ca.us and daedal.net.

Domain Name System (DNS)   The system by which domain names are translated into their IP numeric addresses.

DOS   An acronym for disk operating system, the character-based operating system commonly used on microcomputers. It is also a shorthand way of referring to the command line interface.

dot   A subdirectory marker; a shorthand name; the . for the specific subdirectory name.

dot-matrix printer   A printer that produces text characters and graphics by creating them with a series of closely spaced dots. It uses a print head, platen, and ribbon to form the characters.

dot pitch   In printers, the distance between dots in a dot matrix. In video displays, a measure of image clarity. In a video display, the dot pitch is the vertical distance, expressed in millimeters, between like-colored pixels. A smaller dot pitch generally means a sharper image.

double-clicking   Pressing and releasing the left mouse button twice in rapid succession.

downloading   Receiving a file from a remote computer while connected by a modem, another outside connection, or a network.

downward compatible   Describes software/hardware that can be used on older computer systems.

dragging   Placing the pointer over an object, holding down the left mouse button, and moving the object to another location.

dragging and dropping   Moving or manipulating an object or document across the desktop and dropping it in another location.

drawing area   In Paint, the area where you create your drawing.

drive letter   A letter of the alphabet that identifies a specific disk drive.

driver   A piece of software that tells a piece of hardware how to work.

drop-down list box   A box that contains a default selection. However, if the user clicks on the down arrow, a list box drops down and displays further choices.

drop-down menu   A menu that presents choices that drop down from the menu bar when requested and remain open on the screen until the user chooses a menu item or closes the menu.

DVD   An enhancement to CD-ROM technology. It provides the next generation of optical disc storage technology. It encompasses audio, video, and computer data. DVD is not an acronym but a trademark.

DWORD   In the Registry, DWORD values are data that are represented by numbers four bytes long.

dynamic data exchange (DDE)   A set of standards that supports data exchange among application programs.

dynamic link library (DLL)   A feature that allows executable routines to be stored separately as files with DLL extensions and to be loaded only when needed by a program. A DLL file does not consume any memory until it is used. Since a DLL file is separate, a programmer can make corrections or improvements to only that module without affecting other programs or other DLLs. Also, the same dynamic link library can be used with other programs.

dynamic RAM (DRAM)   Memory chips that hold data for a short time. DRAM is less expensive than SRAM and thus, most memory is DRAM. See also *static RAM*.

ellipsis   Three dots that can appear after a menu item or on a command button. If you choose the item, a dialog box will open.

email   Short for electronic mail. Email is a note or message that is sent between different computers that use telecommunications services or are on a network.

embedding   Taking data (an object) from one document from an application and placing it in another document from another application.

Emergency Repair Disk   A bootable disk that has critical system files on it.

end-of-file (EOF) marker   A symbol that alerts the operating system when a file has no more data.

enhancement   Increases the capabilities of a computer by adding or updating hardware or software.

event   An action performed by you or by your program that your computer can notify you of. Usually the notification is a sound, such as a beep if you press an incorrect key.

executable   Refers to programs that place instructions in memory. The instructions are followed by the computer.

executing a program   A process where instructions are placed in memory and then followed by the computer.

expanded memory   Additional hardware added to the computer that makes more memory available. Only programs that are designed to use expanded memory can take advantage of it.

expanded memory emulator   A memory manager that uses extended memory to emulate expanded memory.

expanded memory manager (EMM)   A software program that must be installed in order to use expanded memory.

expansion slot   An empty slot or space inside a system unit that can be used for adding new boards or devices to expand the computer's capabilities.

exporting   Using an existing file or data in the file and sending it to another file.

extended memory   Memory above 1 MB.

extended memory manager   A software program that must be installed in order to use or install extended memory.

extension   See *file extension*.

external command   A program that resides on a disk and must be read into RAM before it can be used.

external storage media   Storage devices that are outside the computer system. Floppy, CD-ROM, and removable drives are the most common external storage media.

FAT   See *file allocation table (FAT)*.

FAT file system   The system originally used by MS-DOS to organize and manage files. The FAT (file allocation table) is a data structure is created on a disk when the disk is formatted. When a file is stored on a formatted disk, the operating system places information about the stored file in the FAT so that the operating system (DOS) can retrieve the file later. Windows 98 can use the FAT file system.

file   A program or a collection of related information stored on a disk.

file allocation table (FAT)   A map of the disk that keeps track of all the clusters on a disk. It is used in conjunction with the directory table.

file attributes   Attributes are stored as part of a file's directory entry and describe and give other information about the file.

file extension   The last portion of a file name following the last period. Usually file extensions describe the type of data in the file. See also *file type*.

file format   A special format used to construct a file so an application program can read the data. It consists of special codes that only the creating application program understands.

file infector virus   Adds programming instructions to files that run programs. The virus then becomes active when you run the program.

file name   A label used to identify a file. When most users refer to the file name, they are referring to the file specification.

file server   On a network, a file storage device that stores files. On a large network, a file server is a sophisticated device that no only stores files but also manages them and maintains order as network users request files and make changes to the files.

file specification   The complete name of a file, including the file name and the file extension (file type).

file type   The last portion of a file name following the last period in a file name. Usually file types describe the type of data in the file. See also *file extension*.

Fill   The Paint tool that is used to fill a closed image with the selected foreground color.

fill style   In Paint, ways of displaying objects such as outline in foreground color and no fill color.

firewall   A security system intended to protect an organization's network against external threats, such as hackers. A firewall prevents computers in the organization's network from communicating directly with computers external to the network and vice versa.

firmware   Software and hardware that is designed for a specific task and has been permanently stored in ROM (read-only memory) rather than on a disk. Firmware cannot usually be modified by the user.

fixed disk   See *hard disk*.

fixed parameter   A parameter whose values are specific and limited.

flag   A marker of some type used to process information. File attributes are commonly called flags because they indicate a particular condition of a file.

flaming   Sending or posting an abusive or personally insulting email message or newsgroup posting.

floating   Describes a toolbar or taskbar that can be positioned anywhere on the screen and does not have to be anchored to a window.

floppy disk   A magnetically coated disk that allows permanent storage of data.

floppy disk drive   See *disk drive*.

flushing the buffer   A process where the operating system writes information to a disk after a buffer has been filled.

folder   The location or container where documents, program files, devices, and other folders are stored on your disk. The terms *folders* and *directories* are synonymous.

folder icon   The graphic representation of a folder that will open when you double-click it.

Folders pane   The left pane of the Explorer window.

font   A typeface (set of characters) that consists of several parts, such as the type size and weight (i.e., bold or italic).

footer   One or more identifying lines printed at the bottom of a page.

foreground   Describes the application or window that the user is currently working on.

foreground application   An application or window that the user is currently working on. It is also referred to as the foreground window or active window.

foreground color   The current drawing color in Paint.

foreground window   An application or window in which the user is currently working. It is also referred to as the foreground window or active window.

formatting   Preparing a disk for use. It can also refer to the way data looks in a document.

form feed   An operation that advances the hard copy on the printer to the next page.

fragmented   See *fragmented disk*.

fragmented disk   A disk that has many noncontiguous files on it.

fragmented file   A file that is written to a disk in noncontiguous clusters. See also *noncontiguous*.

free system resources   System resources are used with such actions as drawing the screen and keeping track of what memory is available. Free system resources are what is not being used. It is not to be confused with available memory.

freeware   A computer program given away free of charge and often made available on the Internet or through newsgroups.

FTP (File Transfer Protocol)   A protocol that allows files to be transferred to and from a node running FTP services.

full backup   A backup procedure that backs up every file on a disk, regardless of whether a file has changed or not.

full system backup   A backup procedure that backs up every file on a disk, including special system files, regardless of whether a file has changed or not.

function keys   Programmable keys on a keyboard. F1 and F2 are examples of function keys. Function keys are program dependent.

gig   A colloquial term for gigabyte.

gigabyte (GB)   A unit of measurement equal to approximately one billion bytes.

glide pad   An input device that is a small, smooth object on which you move your finger to control the action of the pointer.

global file specifications   The symbols * and ?, also called wildcards, that are used to represent a single character (?) or a group of characters (*) in a file name.

graphic file   Pictures and drawings that can be produced on the screen or printer and are saved in a file.

grid of cells   Two sets of lines or linear elements at right angles to each other. A spreadsheet is a grid of rows and columns; a graphics screen is a grid of horizontal and vertical lines of pixels. In optical character recognition, a grid is used for measuring or specifying characters.

GUI (graphical user interface)   A display format that allows the user to interact with the computer by using pictorial representations and menu choices to manage the computer resources and work with application programs.

hard copy   A printed paper copy of information that is created when using the computer. It can also be referred to as a printout.

hard disk   A disk that is permanently installed in a computer system and has a larger capacity to store files than a floppy disk. Hard disks are measured in megabytes or gigabytes.

hard disk drive   See *hard disk*.

hard return   Generated when **Enter** is pressed. The system will not move a hard return, but will move a soft return.

hardware   Physical computer components.

hardware interrupt   A request for service or a signal from peripherals to the CPU for attention so the device may be serviced.

head crash   A hard disk failure in which a read/write head, normally supported on a cushion of air, comes into contact with the platter, damaging the magnetic coating in which data is recorded.

header   In word processing or printing, text that is to appear at the top of pages.

head slot   Exposes the disk surface to the read/write heads via an opening in the jacket of a floppy disk.

heaps   Thirty-two-bit regions of memory that are used by Windows to manage system resources.

hexadecimal   A numbering system that uses a base of 16 consisting of the digits 0–9 and the letters A–F.

hidden file   A file that is not displayed in Explorer or My Computer or when the DIR command is used in the DOS window.

hierarchical menu   A menu that opens another menu. A secondary menu will open as a result of a command issued on the first or primary menu. A right-pointing arrow next to the primary menu indicates that a cascade menu is available. It is also called a cascading menu.

hierarchical structure   The logical grouping of files and programs based on pathways between root directories and their subsequent directories. It is also called a tree-structured directory.

hierarchy   A group of things that are ordered by rank. In a disk's structure, it is a dependent relationship where one folder is dependent on the folder above it. Every disk begins with the root directory (folder), with subsequent folders branching from the root.

high-capacity disk   See *high-density disk*.

high-density disk   A floppy disk that can store up to 1.2 MB on a 5¼-inch disk or 1.44 MB on a 3½-inch disk.

high-level formatting   Also known as logical formatting. The process that Windows 98 uses to structure a disk so that files can be stored or retrieved.

highlighting   The process of selecting an object, text, or an icon. Objects must be selected before they can be acted upon. Highlighting is indicated by reverse video.

high memory area (HMA)   High memory is the first 64KB of extended memory.

HKEY   In the Registry, HKEY is short for Handle to a KEY.

HKEY_Classes_Root   In the Registry, this is an alias for HKEY_Local_Machine. It contains settings for shortcuts, drag and drop, and file associations.

HKEY_Current_Config   In the Registry, this is also an alias for HKEY_Local_Machine, which contains the current configuration for your computer.

HKEY_Current_User   In the Registry, this is an alias for the branch in HKEY_Users, which applies to the user who is currently logged on.

HKEY_Dyn_Data   In the Registry, this is also an alias for HKEY_Local_Machine, which contains information that is changing such as the status of a plug-and-play device.

HKEY_Local_Machine   In the Registry, this contains configuration data that is specific to your computer such as what hardware you have installed as well as your program settings. The information in this key applies to every user who uses this computer.

HKEY_Users   In the Registry, this is the other major key that contains the configuration information for any user who logs onto the computer. In addition to maintaining information that applies to all users on that machine, it also contains information that is specific to each user. There will be a subkey for each user who has a profile.

home page   On a server, the first screen that appears when you select a Web site.

hot link   In OLE, a connection between two programs that share a data file. An update in one file will automatically update the object in the other file or any other file using the object.

housekeeping task   Any number of routines to keep the environment where programs run in good working order.

hovering   A mouse technique that highlights objects with an underline as you drag your mouse, which indicates that you have selected an object.

HTML (Hypertext Markup Language)   The programming language with which Web documents are created.

HTTP (Hypertext Transfer Protocol)   A common protocol used to access sites on the Internet.

hypertext   A means to easily jump from one logically related topic to the next.

IAP   Internet access provider.

icon   A symbol that represents a more simple access to a program file, a data file, or a task.

impact printer   A type of printer that transfers images onto paper through a mechanism that strikes a ribbon and transfers the images to paper. It is similar to a typewriter.

importing   Bringing information from one program into another. You can import an entire file or part of a file.

incremental backup   A backup process that only backs up files that have changed since the last full or incremental backup.

information superhighway   Refers to the Internet. A worldwide network of networks that provides the ability to gather information, do research, explore ideas, purchase items, send email, and chat with people around the world. See also *cyberspace*.

.INI files   See *initialization files*.

initialization files   Files that initialize a program or process. In earlier versions of Windows, the operating system and most application programs stored information about the users, environmental parameters, and necessary drivers in .INI files. The .INI extension is derived from initialization files.

initializing   Getting a medium (a disk or a file) ready for use.

initializing a disk   Getting a disk ready for use. It is another term for formatting a disk.

inkjet printer   A nonimpact printer that prints by spraying a matrix of dots onto the paper.

in-place editing   Editing an object created in another document without having to open the other document. The menus and toolbars of the current program will be temporarily replaced with the menus and toolbars of the program that created the edited object. It is also called visual editing.

input   Refers to data or information entered into the computer.

input buffer The portion of computer memory that has been set aside to store keyed in data arriving for processing.

input device A means to get information into RAM by communicating with the computer. Typical input devices include the keyboard and the mouse.

input/output The process of data and program instructions going into and out of the CPU (central processing unit). It is also referred to as I/O.

insert A mode that allows the user to enter data in which new text is inserted at the cursor, pushing all text that follows to the right.

install Copying files (programs) from a CD or floppy disk onto the hard disk.

integrated circuit An electronic device that combines thousands of transistors on a small wafer of silicon (chip). Such devices are the building blocks of computers.

integrated pointing device An input device that is an eraser-like object on the keyboard that you can manipulate to control the cursor.

interactive Describes the ability to update data within the computer system instantaneously.

interactive booting When you choose to interactively boot, you will be asked by the operating system if you want each line in the CONFIG.SYS file and the AUTOEXEC.BAT to execute.

interactive processing Sometimes called online or real-time mode, interactive means interacting directly with the computer.

interface Hardware and/or software needed to connect computer components. Also used as a synonym for interacting with a computer.

interface card The circuit board that is needed to connect computer components.

interlaced A technique used in some monitors in which the electron beam refreshes (updates) all odd-numbered scan lines in one vertical sweep of the screen and all even-numbered scan lines in the next sweep. The picture on these monitors tends to flicker. See also *noninterlaced*.

Internet A network of networks that connects computer users around the world.

intranet A network designed for information processing within a company or organization.

I/O See *input/output*.

IP address A unique numeric address that identifies a computer on the Internet.

ISP (Internet service provider) A company or organization that provides a gateway or connection to the Internet, usually for a fee. It is also called an access provider or a service provider.

keyboard A major device used for entering data into a computer consisting of a typewriter-like collection of labeled keys.

keyboard buffer See *input buffer*.

keys The Registry is a hierarchical structure. Keys and subkeys are similar in concept to folders and subfolders like Explorer. At the top of the hierarchy are the Registry keys. Registry keys can also have several keys or subkeys. This is known as *nesting*.

kilobyte (KB) A unit of measurement equal to 1,024 bytes.

LAN See *local area network (LAN)*.

landscape A printing orientation that prints horizontally (sideways) on the paper.

laser printer   A high-resolution nonimpact printer that provides letter-quality output of text and graphics. Laser printers are based on a technology in which characters are formed by a laser and made visible by the same technology used by photocopy machines.

lasso   A means to select objects by using the mouse to draw an imaginary line around the objects.

last known good   Shorthand for saying that USER.DAT and SYSTEM.DAT were saved the last time you successfully booted.

legacy hardware   Hardware that is not plug-and-play compatible.

legacy software   Older versions of software that were designed to run on earlier versions of operating system, such as DOS.

light pen   A pointing device (connected to the computer by a cable and resembling a pen) that is used to provide input to the computer by writing, sketching, or selecting commands on a special monitor designed to respond to the light pen.

line feed   An operation that advances the hard copy to the next line of text whether or not the line is full.

link   In object linking and embedding, establishes a connection between two applications and their data. Link, when used with the Internet, refers to an element that allows the user to "jump" to another related topic.

linked object   In object linking and embedding, an object that is created by the source program. As a result of this link, any changes to the source document are automatically updated in the destination document.

list box   A box that presents the user with a list of options. It is used in menus and dialog boxes.

loading   Placing information (data or programs) from storage into memory.

local area network (LAN)   A network of computer equipment located in one room or building and connected by a communication link that enables any device to interact with any other in the network, making it possible for users to exchange information, share peripherals, and draw on common resources.

local bus   See *bus*.

locally   In a networked environment, this means that you are not using the network, but only your own local computer.

local printer   A printer physically attached to your computer.

logical device   A device named by the logic of a software system regardless of its physical relationship to the system.

logical disk drive   A drive named by the logic of the software (operating) system. It is an "imaginary drive" that acts exactly like a real disk drive.

logical formatting   See *high-level formatting*.

logical view   A view of items that are represented by icons rather then by their physical presence.

logo   A distinctive signature or trademark that usually functions as a graphical representation of a company.

long file name (LFN)   The term used in Windows 98 to indicate that file names are no longer limited to the 8.3 character file names. In Windows 95 and in Windows 98, file names cannot exceed 255 characters.

loop back   The address 127.0.0.1, which is used to send data to your own computer without using the network card. The data "loops back."

lost cluster   Clusters that have no directory entry in the directory table and do not belong to any file. They are debris that results from incomplete data, and they should be cleaned up periodically with Check Disk.

low-level formatting   Also known as physical formatting. The process of numbering the tracks and sectors of a disk sequentially so that each can be identified. On a hard disk, this process is done by the manufacturer of the hard disk.

macro   A short key code command which stands for a sequence of saved instructions that when retrieved will execute the commands to accomplish a given task.

main memory   See *random access memory (RAM)*.

mandatory parameter   A parameter that must be used with a command.

manual link   In object linking and embedding, a link that is not updated automatically when changes are made in the destination document. The user must choose to update the object. It is also called a *cold link*.

mapped drive   A network drive or folder (one that has been shared) that you may assign a local drive letter.

master boot record (MBR)   Used before booting. It determines the location of the bootable partition of the hard disk and gives control over to it.

Maximize button   A button that makes the current window fill the entire screen.

meg   A colloquial term for *megabyte*.

megabyte (MB)   A unit of measurement that is roughly equal to one million bytes.

megahertz (MHz)   A unit of measurement used to compare clock speeds of computers.

memory   The temporary workspace of the computer where data and programs are kept while they are worked on. It is also referred to as *RAM (random access memory)*. Information in RAM is lost when the computer is turned off, which is why memory is considered volatile.

menu   A list of choices (selections) displayed on the screen from which the user chooses a course of action.

menu bar   A rectangular bar, usually in a program, in which the names of the available, additional menus are shown. The user chooses one of these menus and a list of choices for that menu is shown.

message box   A type of dialog box that informs you of a condition.

microcomputer   A personal computer that is usually used by one person. It is also referred to as a desktop computer or a stand-alone computer.

microfloppy disk   A 3½-inch floppy disk encased in a hard plastic shell.

MIDI (Musical Instrument Digital Interface)   A way to get input from your musical instruments into a computer and then modify and store the sounds you recorded.

minicomputer   A mid-level computer larger than a microcomputer but smaller than a mainframe computer. It is usually used to meet the needs of a small company or department.

minifloppy disk   A 5¼-inch floppy disk.

Minimize button   A button that reduces the current window to a button on the taskbar.

modem   Short for modulator/demodulator. A device that provides communication capability between computers using phone lines. Modems are typically used to access online services, such as AOL (America Online) or an ISP.

monitor   A device similar to a television screen that displays the input and output of the computer. It is also called a *screen*, *display screen*, *cathode-ray terminal*, or *VDT (video display terminal)*.

monospaced typeface   A typeface that gives all characters in the set the same width.

motherboard   The main computer board that holds the memory and CPU, as well as slots for adapter cards. The power supply plugs directly into the motherboard. It is also called a *system board*.

mouse   A small, hand-held device that is equipped with one or more control buttons and is housed in a palm-sized case. It is used to control cursor movement.

mouse pointer   An onscreen pointer that is controlled by the movement of the mouse.

mouse trail   A "ghost" of the mouse pointer that follows the movement of the mouse around the screen. It is used to improve the visibility of the cursor.

MS-DOS   An abbreviation for *Microsoft disk operating system*, a character-based operating system for computers that use the 8086 or above microprocessor.

multitasking   Describes the ability to work on more than one task or application program at a time.

multithreading   Describes the ability to work on more than one thread (small task) at a time.

naming convention   A logical naming scheme for files and folders for facilitating the saving and retrieving of files and folders.

nested object   Also called a *container object*, an object that can contain other objects.

nesting   In the Registry, when registry keys have several keys or subkeys.

Net   A colloquial name for the *Internet*.

netiquette   A combination of the words *network* and *etiquette*. It is a set of principles of courtesy that should be observed when sending electronic messages such as email and newsgroup postings.

network   A group of computers connected by a communication facility called a server, which permits the sharing and transmission of data. In addition, it allows the sharing of resources, such as a hard drive or a printer.

network administrator   The person who decides how the hardware and software will be used on a network.

network interface card (NIC)   An expansion card used to connect a computer to a local area network.

network operating system (NOS)   An operating system installed on a server in a local area network that coordinates the activities of providing services to the computers and other devices attached to the network.

newsgroup   A forum, usually on the Internet, for threaded discussions on a specified range of subjects. A newsgroup consists of articles and follow-up posts from users.

newsreader   A program that allows you to read newsgroup postings and to post your own messages.

NIC   See *network interface card*.

nonbootable disk   A disk that does not contain the operating system files. The computer cannot boot from it.

noncontiguous   Describes files that are written to a disk in nonadjacent clusters or clusters that are not next to one another.

nonimpact printer   A type of printer that transfers images onto paper by means of ink-jet sprayers, melting ink, or lasers.

noninterlaced   A display method on monitors in which the electron beam scans each line of the screen once during each refresh cycle. Monitors that are noninterlaced generally have clearer images and do not flicker. See also *interlaced*.

NOS   See *network operating system*.

null value   A test for nothing (no data).

numeric keypad   A separate set of keys next to the main keyboard that contains the digits 0 through 9. It also includes an alternate set of commands that can be toggled such as **PgUp** and the arrow keys. These functions are program dependent.

object   Most items in Windows are considered objects. Objects can be opened, have properties, and be manipulated. Objects can also have settings and parameters.

object conversion   Lets users edit an object if they have some program that will convert the data.

object linking and embedding (OLE)   A method of allowing application programs to share information without needing to copy the physical data into each application.

octet   Refers to one of the four sections of the dotted-decimal notation address.

offline   Describes a printer that may be attached to the computer but is not activated and ready to print. It also refers to not being connected to a network or the Internet.

offline compression   A program that reads data in from an uncompressed file and outputs it to a new file that is compressed.

OLE automation   In OLE, the ability to create scripts or macros that move data between two or more programs by using a programming language such as Visual Basic.

OLE-aware   Describes Windows-based application programs that support and recognize OLE.

OLE-compliant   See *OLE-aware*.

online   Describes a printer that is not only attached to the computer but also activated and ready for operation. When referring to communication, it refers to being attached to another computer, a network, or the Internet.

online help   On-screen assistance consisting of advice or instructions on utilizing the program's features. It can be accessed without interrupting the work in progress.

on-the-fly compression   See *real-time compression*.

opaque   Cannot be seen through. When dragging an object in Paint, the opaque option will keep the background of the new location from being visible.

open scroll area   An area on a scroll bar to the right or left of the scroll box that will move you in large increments through a document.

operating system (OS)   A master control program or set of programs that manages the operation of all the parts of a computer. An operating system, known as *system software*, is loaded into memory when the computer is booted. It must be loaded prior to any application software.

optional parameter   A parameter that may be used with a command but is not mandatory.

option button   Part of a list of choices presented to the user. Only one option can be selected at a time. Option buttons provide mutually exclusive choices.

orphan   In word processing, the first line of a paragraph that is at the bottom of the page that precedes it.

overhead   Information that provides support to a computing process but often adds processing time that causes the performance of a program or peripheral to be slower than usual.

overtype   See *typeover*.

overwrite mode   The mode in which newly typed characters replace existing characters to the right of the cursor.

overwriting   Replacing data by writing over old data with new data. Usually when you copy a file from one location to another, the file that is copied overwrites the file that was there.

packet   A unit of information transferred between computers via a network or a modem.

pane   A division in a window.

PANOSE file   A file that is created for a particular font and stores information about the font's size, attributes, and design.

parallel   In data transmission, it refers to sending one byte (eight bits) at a time.

parallel port   An input/output connector for parallel interface devices.

parameter   A qualifier or modifier that can be added to a command and will specify the action to be taken.

parent directory   The subdirectory above the current subdirectory. The parent directory is always one step closer to the root than the child.

parent menu   A menu in a hierarchical menu structure that is at the top of the menu system. A parent menu may have a child menu; a child menu may become a parent and have child windows of its own.

parent window   A window that is the owner of any objects in it. If there is a folder in the window, it is a child to that parent. A child window can have only one parent, but it can have one or more child windows of its own.

parity   Parity bit is a simple method used to check for transmission errors. An extra bit is added to be sure that there is always either an even or an odd number of bits.

partitioning   Physically dividing a section of the hard disk from other sections of the disk and then having the operating system treat that section as if it were a separate unit.

password   A unique set of text or numbers that identifies the user. Passwords are used when logging onto networks and when Windows 98 has user profiles set up.

path   Tells Windows where to look for programs and files on a disk that has more than one directory.

path name   Information that tells the operating system where to look for program files on a disk that has more than one folder (directory).

peer-to-peer network   A network that has no dedicated servers or a hierarchy among the computers. All the computers are equal, and therefore peers. Each computer can function as either client or server.

pel   See *pixel*.

peripheral device Any device, such as a keyboard, monitor, or printer, that is connected to and controlled by the CPU.

physical formatting See *low-level formatting*.

physical memory The actual memory chips in a computer.

physical view A view of folders that shows the hierarchy of a file system, indicating drives and where they are located.

pixel The smallest element on the display screen grid that can be stored or displayed. Pixels are used to create or print letters, numbers, or graphics. The more pixels, the higher the resolution.

plotter A special kind of printer used to draw charts, diagrams, and other line-based graphics. Typically plotters use pens to draw on paper or transparencies.

Plug and Play A feature of Windows that automatically detects and configures a new hardware device when it is added to a computer system.

point Fonts are measured in points. The more points, the larger the font. A point is $\frac{1}{72}$ of an inch.

pointer An arrow or other indicator on the screen which represents the current cursor (mouse) location.

pointing Placing the mouse pointer over an object.

Point-to-Point Protocol (PPP) A temporary dial-up connection that uses this protocol provides full access to the Internet as long as you are online.

pop-up menu A menu that opens with a right-click of the mouse. It is also referred to as a *shortcut* or *context menu*.

port A location or place on a CPU to connect other devices to a computer. It allows the computer to send information to and from the device.

portal An entry point to the World Wide Web (WWW). It is sometimes called a gateway. Search engines such as Yahoo! and service providers such as MSN are positioning themselves as portals.

portrait The most common printing mode for letters and other documents. This mode prints with the narrower side of the page across the top.

posting Submitting an article in a newsgroup or other online conference. The term is derived from the posting of a notice on a physical bulletin board.

power cycle Physically turning the computer off, waiting at least five seconds, and turning the computer back on.

PPP See *Point-to-Point Protocol*.

primary mouse button The mouse button used for most operatins, usually configured as the left mouse button.

printer A computer peripheral that produces a hard copy of text or graphics on paper.

printer driver Software used to send correct codes to the printer. It is also called *driver software* since it drives the printer.

printer font A font that a printer is capable of printing.

print job A print job usually consists of a single document, which can be one page or hundreds of pages long.

print queue A list of files that have been sent to the printer by various applications. The print manager sends the files to the printer as the printer becomes available.

print server   On a network, a computer that is dedicated only to printing.

print spooler   A program that compensates for differences in rates of the flow of data by temporarily storing data in memory and then doling it out to the printer at the proper speed.

process   An executable program or part of a program that is a coherent set of steps. The process consists of the program itself, the memory address space it uses, the system resources it uses, and at least one thread.

program   A set of step-by-step instructions that tells the computer what to do.

program approach   A paradigm of treating programs as central. In order to use data, you must first open your program and then open your file. See also *docucentric*.

program file   A file containing an executable computer program. See also *application software* and *application program*.

progress bar control   See *progress bar indicator*.

progress bar indicator   A control that is a visual representation of the progress of a task.

prompt   A symbol on the screen that tells the user that the computer is ready for the next command. In the DOS window, the prompt usually consists of the letter of the current drive followed by a greater-than sign (e.g. A>, B>, C>).

property sheet   A special kind of dialog box that allows the user to view or change the properties (characteristics) of an object.

proportional typeface   A typeface that varies the space given to each character. For instance, the *M* will take more space than the *I*.

protected mode   An operating mode in which different parts of memory are allocated to different programs so that when programs are running simultaneously they cannot invade each other's memory space and can access only their own memory space.

protocol   A set of rules or standards designed to enable computers to connect with one another and to exchange information.

push technology   A method of distributing information over the Web by automatically sending updates from Web sites.

queue   A line up of items waiting for processing.

RAM drive   Creates a disk drive in memory to emulate a disk drive.

random access memory (RAM)   See *memory*.

read-cache   Intercepts, makes a copy of, and places into memory the file that has been read. When a program makes a request, Windows checks to see if the data is already in the read-cache. Read-cache is used to optimize performance.

read-only attribute   Prevents a file from being changed or deleted.

read-only memory (ROM)   Memory that contains programs written on ROM chips, retained when the computer is turned off. ROM often controls the startup routines of the computer.

real mode   A single-task working environment. DOS runs in real mode.

real time   The actual amount of time the computer uses to complete an operation.

real-time compression   A background program that compresses and uncompresses files as they are used.

rebooting   Reloading the operating system from a disk.

redirection   A process in which a character-based operating system or the command line in Windows takes standard input or output from devices and sends it to a nonstandard input or output device. The redirection symbol is >.

registration database   In older versions of Windows, a file called REG.DAT. This file was the registration database. It contained information about how various applications would open, how some of them would print, file extensions, how OLE (object linking and embedding) objects were handled, and so forth.

Registry   A mechanism in Windows that stores user information, application program information, and information about the specific computer. The Registry centralizes and tracks all this information. It is critical to the running of Windows. It is comprised of two files: USER.DAT and SYSTEM.DAT.

Registry keys   In the Registry, keys can contain one or more other keys and values. Each key and value must have a unique name within a key or subkey.

relative path   The path from where you are to where you want to go in relation to the directory tree hierarchical structure.

required parameter   See *mandatory parameter*.

reserved memory   See *upper memory area*.

resident font   A font stored in a printer.

resolution   The sharpness and clarity of detail attained by a printer or a monitor in producing an image.

resource pool   The pool used by Windows to manage Windows itself. There are three pools: the system pool, the user pool, and the GDI pool.

resources   In a network environment, resources are what are provided by the server. Resources are the parts of the computer you share, such as a device or file.

Restore button   A button on a window's title bar that returns the window to its previous size.

restoring   Copying some or all of your files to your original disk, another disk, or another directory from your backup media.

Rich Text Format (RTF)   A file format that allows different applications to use formatted text documents.

right-clicking   Pressing the secondary mouse button, usually the right mouse button.

right-dragging   Dragging while holding the secondary mouse button, usually the right mouse button.

ROM   See *read-only memory (ROM)*.

ROM-BIOS (read-only memory–basic input/output system)   A chip built into the hardware of a system. Its functions include running self-diagnostics, loading the boot record, and handling low-level system tasks.

root directory   The directory that Windows creates on each disk when the disk is formatted. The backslash symbol (\) is used to represent the root directory.

router   A device that connects networks. A router can make intelligent decisions about which network to use to send data.

RTF   See *Rich Text Format (RTF)*.

sample box   In a dialog box, an area where a preview of your selections can be seen.

sans serif font   A typeface with no serifs.

scale   Various sizes a font can be made to print in.

scanner   A device that enables a computer to read a handwritten or printed page.

scrap   A file created when you drag part of a document to the desktop or to a folder. It must originate in a program that supports OLE.

screen capture   A picture of a screen. To capture the screen to the Clipboard, you press the [Print Screen] key. To capture the active window, you press [Alt] + [Print Screen]. See also *screen dump*.

screen dump   A transfer of the data on the monitor to a printer or another hard-copy device. See also *screen capture*.

screen font   A font that is used to display text and graphics on the monitor.

screen saver   An image that prevents screen burn-in and provides a modicum of security if passwords are used.

scroll bar   A feature used to move through a window when the entire contents will not fit.

scroll box   The box in a scroll bar that shows you your relative position in a window or document. It can be dragged with the mouse to move rapidly through the window or document.

scrolling   Vertical movement through text.

search criteria   The instructions or limitations for a search for files or folders.

search path   The set path for searching for program files.

secondary storage media   Data storage media other than RAM. Typically disks, tapes, or removable drives such as ZIP drives.

sector   Data is stored on a disk in concentric circles (tracks) that are divided into sectors. A sector is a portion of a track. A sector is 512 bytes long, based on industry standards.

selection bar   In WordPad, an imaginary area just outside and to the left of the text in a document. When you are in the selection bar, you can use shortcuts with the mouse to select text.

Serial Line Internet Protocol (SLIP)   An older protocol that provides a temporary dial-up connection for full access to the Internet as long as you are online.

serial port   A communications port to which a device, such as a modem or a serial printer, can be attached. Data is transmitted and received one bit at a time.

serif font   A font with thin lines (serifs) at the ends of each letter.

server   On a network, a computer that provides shared resources to network users. It is also used to refer to an application that provides data or an object in object linking and embedding.

server application   An application program that provides data (an object) in object linking and embedding. It is also known as the source application.

server-based network   A network model in which security and other network functions are provided by a dedicated server.

services   A way to allow you to share files and devices on a network. There are other services such as being able to remotely administer a network.

shareware   Software that is free on a trial basis with the option to either purchase it or remove it from your hard disk.

shortcut   An icon that is created to represent commonly used objects. The icon is placed on the desktop or another location for easy access. A shortcut provides a pointer to the actual object, and it can usually be recognized by a right-bent arrow on top of the object's normal icon or by the word *shortcut*.

shortcut menu A menu that opens with a right-click of the mouse. It is also referred to as a *pop-up* or *context menu*.

single point of failure Desribes how, if the hub in a star topology fails, the entire network goes down.

sizing buttons Allow the user to minimize or maximize a window.

slider A control that allows you to adjust or set values when there is a range of values. You move the slider with the mouse.

SLIP See *Serial Line Internet Protocol (SLIP)*.

soft return A code that is automatically inserted when the end of a line is reached in a document. Unlike a hard return, if text is inserted or removed, software will automatically adjust the text to fit within the margins.

software Programs that tell the computer what to do.

software package See *application package*.

source application The application program that provides data (the object) in object linking and embedding. It is also known as the server application.

source document In object linking and embedding, the document in which a linked object was created.

spin box A control that allows you to either key in a number or click on the up or down arrow to increase or decrease a quantity. Usually a control that has numeric quantities to choose will be a spin box.

spinner A synonym for a *spin box*. See also *spin box*.

splash screen The first screen that appears when you boot the system or load a program. It is often a decorative screen to look at while the program or system is loading.

split bar In Explorer, a bar that divides the window to enable the user to see the structure of a disk on the left and the contents on the right.

spool file Stores a data document in a queue while it waits to be printed. The Windows print manager intercepts a print job on its way to the printer and sends it to disk or memory instead, where the print job is held until the printer is ready for it. The term *spool* comes from "simultaneous peripheral operations online."

spreadsheet program A program for budget management and financial projections.

standard A set of detailed technical guidelines used to establish conformity in software or hardware development.

standard error A process in which a character-based operating system or the command line in Windows writes error messages to the screen.

standard input A process in which a character-based operating system or the command line in Windows expects to receive information, usually from the keyboard.

standard output A process in which a character-based operating system or the command line in Windows expects to send information, usually to the screen.

star topology A local area network (LAN) design in which each device (node) is connected to a central point.

Start button   The first button on the taskbar. Clicking the Start button opens the Start menu, which opens further menus for the user to access programs and data.

static exchange   Data that is created in one application and can be copied or moved to a different document created with a different application program. This data cannot be edited or changed in the new document.

static RAM (SRAM)   Memory chips that can hold data until the computer is turned off. See also *dynamic RAM*.

status area   An area located at the right side of the taskbar that is used by Windows and other programs to place information or notification of events. If you were printing, for example, an icon of a printer would appear in the status area.

status bar   A bar that supplies information about the current window.

stop bit   Indicates the end of an asynchronous serial transmission.

string   A string of data is a variable-length set of characters. String values are always enclosed in quotation marks.

stroke weight   The thickness of a font.

subdirectory   The location or container where documents, program files, devices, and other folders are stored on a disk. The terms *subfolders*, *folders*, *directories*, and *subdirectories* are used interchangeably.

subfolder   A folder beneath a folder. The terms *subfolders*, *folders*, *directories*, and *subdirectories* are used interchangeably.

subkeys   In the Registry, a key can have a key beneath it, known as a *subkey*.

subscription   Sets up a Web browser to check a Web page for new content. The program can then either notify the user about the new content or automatically download it to the user's computer.

supporting   Describes a program's ability to read from and write to a specific file format.

surfing the Net   Exploring the Internet by moving from topic to topic.

surge protector   A device that prevents surges from reaching a computer or other kinds of electronic equipment. It is also called a *surge suppressor*.

surge suppressor   See *surge protector*.

swap file   When you are running several programs and running out of memory, Windows moves programs or data from memory to a swap file, which is space on the hard disk. When memory is freed up, Windows moves back to memory what was in the swap file.

switch   A modifier that controls the execution of a command. Typically the forward slash (/) is used to indicate a switch. See also *parameter*.

synchronizing files   Updating files and folders that are duplicated. It is used with My Briefcase.

syntax   The proper order or sequence of a computer's language and commands.

syntax diagram   A graphic representation of a command and its syntax.

sysing a disk   Placing the operating system files on a disk without removing the data that is there. The command is SYS.

system board   Also known as a *motherboard*, it is the main circuit board controlling the major components of a computer system.

system configuration   The components that make up a specific computer system.

system date   The current date kept by the computer system.

system disk   See *bootable disk*.

system policies   System policies are designed to override to any settings contained in SYSTEM.DAT and USER.DAT. System policies often contain additional information that is specific to a company and is established by the system administrator. These policies are contained in a file called POLICY.POL and are created with the Policy Editor.

system prompt   A symbol on the screen that tells the user that the computer is ready for the next command. It is used in the command line interface and usually consists of the current drive letter followed by the greater-than sign, as in C:\>.

system resources   An area in memory that Windows uses for critical operating system tasks, such as drawing windows on the screen, using fonts, or running applications.

system software   A set of programs that coordinates the operations of the hardware components.

system time   The current time kept by the computer.

taskbar   The bar on the screen that lets you move between any open programs, files, folders, or windows by displaying a button for each open item. The taskbar includes the Start button as well as the status area where Windows and other programs can place notification of events.

taskbar button   The button on the taskbar that indicates an open program, file, or window. Clicking the specific button on the taskbar will activate that choice.

T-connector   A device used in a network which has one end plugged into the network card and two open ends (like a T) for connecting the cables that go to the computers.

terminator plug   A device used with T-connectors so that there is no unplugged end in a network.

text box   A place where the user can key in information.

text editor   A program that is similar to a word-processing program but is unable to perform any special editing. No embedded codes are inserted into documents. ASCII editors can only edit ASCII text files, also called *text files* or *unformatted text files*. Text editors are also called *ASCII editors*.

text file   A file that contains text. It consists of data that can be read, such as letters and numbers, with an ASCII editor such as Notepad or in the DOS window.

Thinnet   A single coaxial cable.

thread   A small part of a program with a very narrow focus. A thread is a subset of a process. It is a set of commands that does a specific task within a process. It runs in the process's allocated space using the process's allocated system resources.

tiled   A display mode that divides the screen equally among the open windows.

title bar   A bar located at the top of a window that contains the name of the program.

toggle switch   A switch that turns a function on or off like a light switch.

token   A binary shorthand for repetitive words or phrases. When a file is decompressed, the tokens are read and the original characters are restored.

toolbar   A toolbar appears in a window or on the desktop and provides shortcuts for entering menu commands. Rather than access the menu, you click a button on the toolbar.

Tool Box   In Paint, the collection of tools that are used to create graphic images.

Tool Options box   When a specific tool is selected in Paint, it provides options for that tool. For instance, if you selected the Line tool, the Tool Options box would show what line thicknesses were available.

ToolTip   A brief description of a button. The user activates a ToolTip by pausing the mouse pointer over a button on a toolbar or the taskbar.

topology   A design or configuration formed by the connections between devices on a local area network (LAN).

track   A concentric circle on a disk where data is stored. Each track is further divided into sectors. All tracks and sectors are numbered so that the operating system can quickly locate information.

trackball   A device used to move the cursor on the monitor. It usually consists of a stationary box that holds a ball that the user rotates to move the cursor.

tracking speed   The rate at which the mouse pointer moves across the screen.

transparent   A feature in Paint that, when copying or moving an object, allows you to see through the object to the background.

transparent to the user   Describes a program or process that works so smoothly and easily that it is invisible to the user.

tree structure   The organizational properties of a tree that relate to the structure of a disk from the root directory down.

Trojan horse virus   A virus proffered as a legitimate program that, when run, begins a destructive process that unequivocally destroys data and programs on a disk.

troubleshooter   A step-by-step guide to assist you in analyzing and solving a problem.

TrueType font   A font that is provided with Windows and is capable of printing on any printer. The font usually looks on the screen like it will when it is printed. See *WYSIWYG*.

tweaking a system   Making final changes and fine-tuning a system to improve performance.

twisted-pair cable   A type of cable also known as 10BASET, 10BT, Ethernet, TPE, or RJ-45.

typeface   The design of a group of letters, numbers, and punctuation, such as Arial or Times New Roman.

typeover   The process of deleting existing characters as you key in new ones.

typing replaces selection   The process of deleting existing characters by selecting them and keying in data. What you key in replaces your selection.

UNC   See *universal naming convention (UNC)*.

unformatted text file   See *text file*.

Unicode   A 16-bit character set intended to accommodate all the commonly used characters in all languages.

uniform resource locator (URL)   A standard format for identifying locations on the Internet. URLs specify three types of information needed to retrieve a document: the protocol to be used, the server address with which to connect, and the path to the information. The URL syntax is *protocol/servername/path;* an example of a URL address is **http://www.netscape.com**.

uninterruptible power supply (UPS)   A device that ensures electrical flow to the computer is not interrupted because of a blackout and that protects the computer against potentially damaging events, such as power surges and brownouts. All UPS units are equipped with a battery and a loss-of-power sensor; if the sensor detects a loss of power, it switches over to the battery so that the user has time to save his or her work and shut off the computer.

universal naming convention (UNC)   A convention used to locate the path to a network resource. It specifies the share name on a particular computer. The computer name is limited to 15 characters, and the share name is usually limited to 15 characters. It takes the format of *computername\sharename*[*optional path*].

universal serial bus (USB)   The latest bus standard. It is an external bus standard for the computer that brings plug-and-play capability. It eliminates the need to install cards into dedicated computer slots and to reconfigure the system.

Unzip   A shareware utility program that uncompresses files compressed by the PKZIP or WinZip shareware utility program.

upgrading   Purchasing the latest version of software and replacing your existing version with it.

uploading   Sending a file to another computer while connected by a modem, another outside connection, or a network.

upper memory area   The area reserved for running a system's hardware. Programs cannot store information in this area. It is also called *adapter segment* and *reserved area*.

upper memory block (UMB)   The unused part of the upper memory area. It can be used for device drivers if the computer is a 386 and you have DOS 5.0 or above.

UPS   See *uninterruptible power supply*.

URL   See *uniform resource locator*.

user profiles   In Windows, enabling profiles allows more than one user to use the same computer and retain his or her own personal settings on the desktop.

utility   A program for carrying out specific, vital functions that assist in the operation of a computer or software.

utility program   See *utility*.

values   In the Registry, keys and subkeys contain at least one value with a special name (default). If the default value has no data, it is read as value not set. Values have three parts: the data type, the name, and the value itself. Values are like the files under folders in Explorer. A value has data like a file has data. There are three types of data: binary, strings, and DWORD values.

variable parameter   Value/information provided by the user.

vector font   A font in which the characters are drawn using arrangements of line segments rather than arrangements of bits.

verbs   In the Registry, the Shell subkey defines the actions that are possible for a specific file type. It contains a number of subkeys under it that define verbs. Each verb contains a subkey whose default entry value defines the command.

version   A numbering scheme that indicates the progressive enhancements and improvement of software.

VFAT (virtual file allocation table) file system   An extension of the file allocation table, with which it is compatible. It provides the ability to handle long file names. See also *file allocation table (FAT)*.

video card   A circuit board that controls the capabilities of the video display.

virtual   Describes a device, service, or sensory input that is perceived but is not real.

virtual disk drive   See *RAM drive*.

virtual machine (VM)   An environment in memory that, from the application's point of view, looks like a separate computer, complete with all the resources available on the physical computer.

virtual memory   Memory that does not actually exist. The user can extend the size of a computer's memory by using a disk to simulate memory space.

virus   A program that has damaging side effects. Sometimes the side effects are intentionally damaging, other times not.

visual editing   Editing an object created in another document without opening the other document. The menus and toolbars of the current program will be temporarily replaced with the menus and toolbars of the program that created the object. It is also called in-place editing.

volume label   An electronic label for a disk that the user can assign when it is formatted.

volume serial number   A number randomly assigned to a disk when it is formatted.

wallpaper   A graphic image file that serves as a background on the desktop, behind all open windows.

WAN   See *wide area network (WAN)*.

Web   A colloquial expression for the World Wide Web (WWW).

Web browser   A software program for navigating the Internet. Two popular programs are Netscape Navigator and Microsoft Internet Explorer.

Web page   On the Internet, a single screen of text and graphics that usually has hypertext links to other pages.

Web site   Both the physical and virtual location of a person's or an organization's Web page.

What's This?   A feature that allows the user to right-click an item to obtain a brief description of it.

wide area network (WAN)   A network that consists of computers using long-range telecommunication links.

widow   In word processing, the last line of a paragraph that appears at the top of the next page rather than staying with the rest of the paragraph.

wildcards   The symbols * and ?, also called global file specifications, that are used to represent a character (?) or a group of characters (*) in a file name.

window   A defined work area (rectangular frame) on the screen that is moveable and sizeable; information with which the user can interact is displayed in it.

window border   The outline of a window that separates it from other windows or objects on the screen.

Wintel   A computer that uses the Microsoft Windows operating system and an Intel central processing unit (CPU).

wizard   A program that uses step-by-step instructions to lead the user through the execution and completion of a Windows task.

word-processing program   Software that allows the user to write, edit, and print any type of text.

word wrap   A feature in software that automatically moves text to the next line when the current line is full.

workgroup   Another name for a peer-to-peer network.

World Wide Web (WWW)   A virtual space accessible from the Internet that holds pages of text and graphics in a recognizable format. These pages are linked to one another and to individual files. The Web is a collection of standards and protocols used to access information on the Internet.

wrapping   Continuing a movement, with the cursor or a search operation, to the beginning or to a new starting point rather than stopping when the end of a series is reached. In a window, a title or an icon label would have additional lines created for the text to be displayed, if necessary.

write-cache   A write-cache intercepts, makes a copy of, and places into memory what a program has tried to write to a disk. At a specified time or when the system is less busy, it writes what is in memory to disk. Write-caching is more dangerous than read-caching. It is used to optimize performance.

write-protected disk   A floppy disk that can be only read from, not written to.

WWW   See *World Wide Web (WWW)*.

WYSIWYG   An acronym for *what you see is what you get*. It is displayed on the screen in the manner in which it will be printed.

zip   A type of file. Its contents have been compressed by a special utility program, usually PKZIP or WinZip, so that it occupies less space on a disk or other storage device.

INDEX

OTHER TITLES

from Franklin, Beedle & Associates, Inc.

To order these books and find out more about Franklin, Beedle & Associates, visit us online at www.fbeedle.com

Operating Systems

Linux User's Guide: Using the Command Line and Gnome Red Hat Linux (isbn 1-887902-50-3)
Understanding Practical Unix (isbn 1-887902-53-8)
Windows Millennium Edition: Concepts & Examples (isbn 1-887902-49-X)
Windows 98: Concepts & Examples (isbn 1-887902-37-6)
Windows 95: Concepts & Examples (isbn 1-887902-00-7)
Windows 2000 Professional Command Line (isbn 1-887902-79-1)
Windows 2000 Professional: Concepts & Examples (isbn 1-887902-51-1)
Windows User's Guide to DOS: Using the Command Line in Windows 2000 Professional
    (isbn 1-887902-72-4)
Windows User's Guide to DOS: Using the Command Line in Windows Millennium Edition
    (isbn 1-887902-64-3)
Windows User's Guide to DOS: Using the Command Line in Windows 95/98 (isbn 1-887902-42-2)
Windows XP Command Line (isbn 1-887902-82-1)

Software Applications

Access 97 for Windows: Concepts & Examples (isbn 1-887902-29-5)
Excel 97 for Windows: Concepts & Examples (isbn 1-887902-25-2)
Microsoft Office 97 Professional: A Mastery Approach (isbn 1-887902-24-4)

The Internet & the World Wide Web

Internet & Web Essentials: What You Need to Know (isbn 1-887902-40-6)
Learning to Use the Internet & the World Wide Web (isbn 1-887902-78-3)
Searching & Researching on the Internet & the World Wide Web: Second Edition (isbn 1-887902-56-2)
Searching & Researching on the Internet & the World Wide Web: Third Edition
    (isbn 1-887902-71-6)
Web Design & Development Using XHTML (isbn 1-887902-57-0)
The Web Page Workbook: Second Edition (isbn 1-887902-45-7)
Upcoming: JavaScript Concepts & Techniques (isbn 1-887902-69-4)

Computer Science

ASP: Learning by Example (isbn 1-887902-68-6)
Basic Java Programming: A Laboratory Approach (isbn 1-887902-67-8)
Data Structures with Java: A Laboratory Approach (isbn 1-887902-70-8)
Computing Fundamentals with C++: Object-Oriented Programming & Design—Second Edition
    (isbn 1-887902-36-8)
Computing Fundamentals with Java (isbn 1-887902-47-3)
Upcoming: Fundamentals of Secure Computing Systems (isbn 1-887902-66-X)
Guide to Persuasive Programming (isbn 1-887902-65-1)
Upcoming: Modern Programming Languages: A Practical Introduction (isbn 1-887902-76-7)
Prelude to Patterns in Computer Science Using Java—Beta Edition (isbn 1-887902-55-4)
XML: Learning by Example (isbn 1-887902-80-5)

Professional Reference & Technology in Education

The Dictionary of Computing & Digital Media Terms & Acronyms (isbn 1-887902-38-4)
The Dictionary of Multimedia (isbn 1-887902-14-7)
Technology Tools in the Social Studies Curriculum (isbn 1-887902-06-6)